Sept 97
Company Sec
nct

COMPANY STRUCTURES

Australia
The Law Book Company
Brisbane, Sydney, Melbourne, Perth

Canada
Carswell
Ottawa, Toronto, Calgary, Montreal, Vancouver

AGENTS

India
N.M. Tripathi (Private) Ltd
Bombay

Eastern Law House (Private) Ltd
Calcutta

M.P.P. House
Bangalore

Universal Book Traders
Delhi

Aditya Books
Delhi

Israel
Steimatzky's Agency Ltd
Tel Aviv

Pakistan
Pakistan Law House
Karachi, Lahore

COMPANY STRUCTURES

*Law, tax and accounting for companies
and groups growing and evolving*

by

David Wainman

London
Sweet & Maxwell
1995

Published in 1995 by
Sweet & Maxwell Limited of
South Quay Plaza, 183 Marsh Wall, London E14 9FT
Typeset by Midlands Typesetting Limited of Loughborough
and printed in Great Britain by Short Run Press, Exeter

No natural forests were destroyed to make this product;
only farmed timber was used and re-planted.

A CIP catalogue record
for this book is available
from the British Library

ISBN 0–421–50730 6

©
David Wainman
1995

All rights reserved.
UK statutory material in this publication
is acknowledged as Crown copyright.
No part of this publication may be
reproduced or transmitted in any form or
by any means, or stored in any retrieval system
of any nature without prior written permission,
except for permitted fair dealing under the
Copyright, Designs and Patents Act 1988, or
in accordance with the terms of a licence issued
by the Copyright Licensing Agency in respect of
photocopying and/or reprographic reproduction.
Application for permission for other use of
copyright material including permission to
reproduce extracts in other published works shall
be made to the publishers. Full acknowledgement
of author, publisher and source must be given.

PREFACE

Every business is different, and every business leader is unique

Two platitudes – clichés – neither more than half true. In relation to leaders there was some research carried out a few years ago which concluded that their skills and personalities were enormously varied, but that they did share two qualities essential for their jobs. First, they had to be able to see just a little bit further into the future than other people, and second, they had to know how they and their subordinates would perform under pressure.

The researchers said that those leaders could buy-in the first, by surrounding themselves with seers – those who have *understanding*; it is a gift to the extent derived from intuition, but the more vital part comes from experience and from the hard thought that experience should engender.

Which brings us to the first of our platitudes; while different businesses have distinguishing features, they share frameworks, have patterns of operations whose similarities are remarkable. Frameworks and patterns are capable of being understood.

They are set partly by company law and accounting thought, partly by tax constraints, and to a large extent by the economic relationships between the directors of businesses, their customers and their suppliers – those who supply the necessary capital and labour among them. Knowledge of all the separate rules will get us some part of the way, knowledge of company law, of accounting, and of tax; but if we seek understanding, to be able to see what the future may be – can be – we need to be able to put all that knowledge together, to weave its strands into the right patterns.

Roget's Thesaurus offers some alternatives for platitude; twaddle, claptrap, bunkum, rubbish, balderdash, moonshine, fiddlestick, flummery, inanity, rot, tosh, bosh, havers, blethers, tripe, bilge, bull, hooey, hokum, boloney. But I do not think he was describing the attempt to understand the framework of business.

David Wainman
23 August 1994

TABLE OF CONTENTS

	Page
Preface	v
Table of Cases	xxi
Table of Statutes	xxix
Table of Statutory Instruments	xxxiv
Table of EC Legislation	xxxv

1 INTRODUCTION

1.1	**Companies** – Their purposes	1
1.2	Relationships with shareholders, directors, employees, financiers, customers, suppliers	1
1.3	Public and private companies	2
1.4	**Limited liability** – Changing to and from that status	3
1.5	Losing more than the company's capital	3
1.6	Banks and their charges	4
1.7	Shareholders' loans to the company	4
1.8	Subordination	5
1.9	Lease guarantees	6
1.10	**The shareholder's relationship with the company** – Memorandum and Articles, remuneration of directors, dividends	7
1.11	**Shareholders' loss of their investment** – Or loss of more than that; where limited liability does not work	8
1.12	The company approaching insolvency	8
1.13	Implication of the figures	9
1.14	The event which tips the company into insolvency	10
1.15	What possibility is there of recovering the situation?	11
1.16	**Wider relationships** – Creditors and employees as well as shareholders	11
1.17	Liabilities which flow from the decision to stop trading	12
1.18	Ranking of creditors – secured, preferred, guaranteed	13
1.19	Ordinary creditors	14
1.20	The deficit borne by the ordinary creditors, including those who are also shareholders	15
1.21	**The company and its owners set apart**	16
1.22	**corporate governance**	17
1.23	Divergence of interests of the company and its directors	18

1.24	**The auditors' role**	19
1.25	Auditors' client relationships	20
1.26	**The accounts** – The requirement to display equity and veracity	21
1.27	Auditors' sanction for the only-slightly-imprudent company	22
1.28	Auditors' persuasive powers	23
1.29	Auditors' judgment, and generally accepted accounting principles	23
1.30	**What the owners, and others, get out of the company**	24
1.31	Tax assumptions	24
1.32	Pre-tax cost to company of individual's net benefit of £10,000	26
1.33	**Dividends**	27
1.34	ACT; effects of imputing part of company's tax so that it is treated as shareholder tax	28
1.35	Offset of ACT against the company's mainstream tax	28

2 VALUE

2.1	**Values at three levels**	30
2.2	Values within the company	30
2.3	Carrying values and historic costs	31
2.4	Historic costs included in accounts, and the different concept of accounts prepared on historic cost principles	31
2.5	Revaluations: to a value to the business, or to a realisable value	32
2.6	**Current costs**	33
2.7	The pool of unexpired costs	34
2.8	**Maintainable profits**	35
2.9	**Retained earnings**	36
2.10	**Shareholder values**	36
2.11	Increasing dividends	37
2.12	**The investor's yield**	38
2.13	**Dividend growth and company growth**	39
2.14	The present value of the stream of increasing dividends	40
2.15	Arithmetic; changing the figures	41
2.16	More changes in the figures	42
2.17	**How valid is arithmetic as a basis for valuing shareholdings?**	43
2.18	The present value is the same whether we hold forever, hold for a time and then exit, or exit immediately	43
2.19	**The first qualification – company and dividend growth rates**	44

2.20	The second qualification – entrepreneurs are unable to set a target yield in the build-up	45
2.21	The third qualification – dividend growth arising from factors other than retentions, and dividends taken as an alternative to remuneration	46
2.22	Realised profits under GAAP – are they a sound guide to the retentions from which growth is actually financed?	47
2.23	**Borrowings by the company**	48
2.24	Receipts in the hands of the lender	49
2.25	**The relationship between shareholder values and the values of the loan creditors' rights**	50
2.26	The company which repays its borrowings	50
2.27	Dividends and retentions after the service of the debt	51
2.28	Putting a present value on those dividends	52
2.29	Putting a value on the company as a whole	53
2.30	**The company which keeps its borrowings intact rather than repaying**	53
2.31	A less difficult way of arriving at a present value of the stream of dividends	54
2.32	Explanation why the company which keeps its borrowings outstanding appears more valuable than the one which repays	55
2.33	**Risk that aimed-at earnings yields can fall while borrowing costs do not do so**	56
2.34	What is the validity of the gearing ratio?	57

3 INCORPORATION

3.1	**Why incorporate?**	58
3.2	The absence of limited liability	59
3.3	The company as a water tank	59
3.4	Tax outflows, and the water left in the tank thereafter	60
3.5	Distributions in the ordinary (Companies Acts) sense and in the tax sense; the absence of any relationship of either to the company's taxable income less tax on it	60
3.6	The potentially high tax cost of distributions	60
3.7	The question whether distributions are desirable	62
3.8	The unincorporated business's figures	62
3.9	The company's figures	63
3.10	If the business is incorporated, are there different approaches possible to its financing?	65
3.11	Saving future taxes without tax cost today	66
3.12	**Non-tax aspects of the separation of the business from its owner by incorporation**	67
3.13	Single member companies	67

CONTENTS

3.14	The procedure for the formation of a company	68
3.15	The shelf company	69
3.16	**The issue of shares for cash**	70
3.17	**Conversion of debt into equity**	72
3.18	Connected parties' conversion of debt into equity	72
3.19	Reverse Nairn Williamson	73
3.20	**The issue of shares for non-cash consideration by private companies**	74
3.21	Spargo's case	75
3.22	Zevo Finance	76
3.23	The shares issued are themselves the consideration given by the company for the non-cash assets acquired, but the value to be attributed to that consideration must be related to the non-cash assets	77
3.24	The Steel Barrel case	77
3.25	Stanton v Drayton	78
3.26	**Valuing the assets acquired for the issue of shares**	79
3.27	Accounting for the assets, and the premium on the shares	80
3.28	Difficulties over attributing any value at all	81
3.29	Difficulties in valuation of non-cash consideration (continued)	82
3.30	More difficulties over the valuation of assets	83
3.31	There are circumstances in which there is no need – or only a limited need – for a share premium; and assets do not therefore need to be revalued	84
3.32	**Incorporating the sole trader's business**	84
3.33	VAT: the transfer of the business as a going concern	85
3.34	The individual's income tax cessation when he incorporates	86
3.35	Transferring the business, together with all its assets, into a company	87
3.36	The hold-over of the individual's capital gain on incorporation	88
3.37	Stamp duty in the straightforward incorporation	89
3.38	Can stamp duty be avoided?	90
3.39	The implications of the full capitalisation that results from section 162	91
3.40	Transfer values of capital allowance assets, and of stocks, on incorporation of an individual's business	92
3.41	**The alternative method of incorporation of the individual's business**	93
3.42	Gifts of business assets, the ability to retain other assets, and stamp duty implications	93

CONTENTS

3.43	Operation of the hold-over for capital gains tax	94
3.44	Advantages and disadvantages of the gift of business assets route compared to the section 162 route	95

4 RESERVES

4.1	**Capital and reserves**	97
4.2	**Accounting theory**	98
4.3	Enterprises and the objectives of accounts	99
4.4	Recognition	100
4.5	Change	101
4.6	Prudence and the recognition of profits	102
4.7	Realisation of profits (first instalment)	103
4.8	Measurement	104
4.9	Realisation of profits (second instalment)	105
4.10	Realisation of profits (continued)	106
4.11	Realisation of profits (continued)	107
4.12	**Capital – Fixed and circulating**	107
4.13	Fixed and circulating capital (continued)	108
4.14	**Capital maintenance**	109
4.15	Capital maintenance (continued)	111
4.16	**Starting to draw the threads together**	112
4.17	Matching and prudence	113
4.18	The balance-sheet approach	114
4.19	Measurement and re-measurement	115
4.20	The statement of recognised gains	116
4.21	The ongoing problem of goodwill	116
4.22	**You cannot draw the threads any tighter together**	117

5 COMPANY TAX

5.1	**Taxes on incorporation of the company**	119
5.2	Tax on forming, and changing the shape of, groups of companies	119
5.3	**Tax liabilities, not rules of computation**	120
5.4	**Computation of trading income under tax rules**	122
5.5	Tax liabilities in groups	124
5.6	**Pay and file** – The first part of the process is paying; how do the Revenue set about encouraging and enforcing payment?	126
5.7	Filing – the second part of the process	128
5.8	**Advance corporation tax**	129
5.9	The cash implications of ACT	131
5.10	Setting off the ACT against corporation tax	131
5.11	Setting off the ACT against corporation tax (continued)	132
5.12	Illustration of ACT off-set in an analysed profit and loss account	133

5.13	Irrecoverable ACT	134
5.14	**Restriction on the off-set of ACT**	135
5.15	Restriction on the off-set of ACT (continued)	136
5.16	**Tax costs of the ill-advised transaction**	138
5.17	The ill-advised transaction (continued)	139
5.18	**Deferred tax**	140
5.19	Deferred tax (continued)	141
5.20	Deferred tax (continued)	141
5.21	**The deduction of income tax at source**	142
5.22	**Loans to participators**	143
5.23	**Group relief**	145
5.24	Group relief (continued)	145
5.25	Rationale of, and payments for, group relief	146
5.26	**Group income**	148
5.27	**The company and its owner or owners**	149
5.28	The company and its owner or owners (continued)	150
5.29	**Capital gains tax – the tiering or cascading effect**	150
5.30	Capital gains tax – the tiering or cascading effect (continued)	151
5.31	Capital gains tax – the tiering or cascading effect (continued)	152
5.32	**Beneficial ownership**	152
5.33	Beneficial ownership as the basis of tax legislation	153
5.34	Changes in beneficial ownership	154
5.35	**The Wood Preservation line of cases**	155
5.36	**The Sainsbury case**	156
5.37	Marginalising Wood Preservation	157
5.38	**Groups and arrangements**	158
5.39	Double jeopardy	161
5.40	Beginnings and endings	162
5.41	Is it possible to define the word 'arrangements'?	163
5.42	Options: the change in the law	163

6 GROUPS OF COMPANIES

6.1	**Companies in a group** – Legal requirements, and relationships between the group companies	165
6.2	The rules for joiners and leavers	166
6.3	Cash	166
6.4	**Creation of the group**	167
6.5	Companies Act definitions of holding companies and subsidiaries (and related terminology)	168
6.6	**Transactions off-balance-sheet**	169
6.7	Further off-balance-sheet possibilities	170
6.8	**Single member companies in a group context**	171

CONTENTS

6.9	What the Statutory Instrument could have said	172
6.10	The so-called informal decision	174
6.11	**Directors' insurance**	175
6.12	**Share premium accounts** – The reliefs available from these requirements in the case of mergers and group reconstructions	176
6.13	Shearer v Bercain	177
6.14	The 1947 Cohen Committee	178
6.15	The law that resulted from Cohen	179
6.16	But could that law really mean what it said?	180
6.17	Relief in respect of group reconstructions	180
6.18	Subsequent move of s-subsidiary from transferor to recipient	181
6.19	**The statutory reliefs from share premium requirements** – Section 132 Companies Act 1985	182
6.20	Merger relief under section 131 Companies Act 1985	184
6.21	Requirements for, and effects of, merger relief	185
6.22	**Stamp duty on the acquisition of target's shares**	186
6.23	**Acquisition accounting and merger accounting**	188
6.24	The consolidation process	189
6.25	Bringing the targets assets into the predator's consolidation	190
6.26	Balancing the predator's account – what the differences are called and what they mean	191
6.27	Criticisms possible of each accounting method	192
6.28	**Goodwill**	193
6.29	The nature and disposition of goodwill: the debate continues	194
6.30	**The requirements for merger accounting**	195
6.31	**Groups in the tax legislation**	196
6.32	**VAT group registration** – remember also the transfers of going concerns	197
6.33	**Stamp duty relief on transfers between associated companies**	198
6.34	Stamp duty reduction on a predator company's acquisition of the undertaking of a target – section 76 of the Finance Act 1986	199
6.35	Further analysis of section 76 of the Finance Act 1986	200
6.36	**Other taxes** – implications for other taxes of transactions within section 76	201
6.37	**Connected parties**	202
6.38	Connected parties' definitions – some illustrations	204
6.39	**Distributions** – some of the concepts	204
6.40	Common control of distributor and recipient of distribution	205

CONTENTS

6.41	Common control of distributor and recipient (continued)	206
6.42	**The capital gains tax group**	206
6.43	Group transfer price is retrospectively replaced by an open market price (on a deemed sale and repurchase by transferee) if that transferee ceases within six years to be a member of transferor's group	208
6.44	Definition of the capital gains tax group	208
6.45	The asset pregnant with gain; value, and transfer price	209
6.46	Movement of the asset for shares – capital gains effects	210
6.47	The issue of shares – meaning of the phrase in this context	211
6.48	Capital gains tax implications of the issue of shares	212
6.49	The acquisition cost of the tranches of shares issued	213
6.50	**Distributions** – Why the transfer of the asset to the subsidiary, either for cash earlier put into that subsidiary, or for the issue of the subsidiary's shares, is not a distribution	214
6.51	A different definition of distribution, and the different route by which it can be avoided – why none of this is relevant to the transactions in paragraphs 6.45 to 6.49	215
6.52	The relief given by section 209(5) achieves what it was meant to achieve, but cannot be taken as exempting more transactions than it was ever drafted to cover	216
6.53	The holding company with subsidiaries which are respectively transferor and recipient of the asset	217
6.54	Why the asset-transfer from one subsidiary to another of the holding company is not a distribution	219
6.55	The transfer of a shareholding from one group company to another, for the issue of shares by the recipient	220
6.56	**Capital gains tax (again)** – The recipient's capital gains position resulting from the transfer to it of the shareholding	221
6.57	The up-rating of the recipient's capital gains base cost	222
6.58	Can paper for paper be excluded?	223
6.59	**Reculer pour mieux sauter**	224
6.62	**A scheme of reconstruction or amalgamation**	226
6.63	Arrangements and reconstructions	227
6.64	Devising a more radical scheme	228

6.65	Schemes without the courts' sanction	229
6.66	The definitions of reconstructions and amalgamations	230
6.67	Interpretation of stamp duty legislation and other tax statutes	231
6.68	Playing down the importance of the scheme	231
6.69	Further definitions	232
6.70	**Capital gains tax on reconstructions and amalgamations**	234
6.71	The transfer of the undertaking, and the shareholding changes, in the course of a reconstruction or amalgamation	235
6.72	The changes in shareholdings associated with the reconstruction or amalgamation	236

7 CONSORTIA

7.1	**The meaning of consortium** – Its purpose and how it is managed	237
7.2	Leasing as a sales-aid	237
7.3	The lease terms	238
7.4	Further assumptions: the absence of profit and of equity	239
7.5	The tax advantages of leasing	240
7.6	Group relief by way of a consortium claim	241
7.7	**The shareholders' agreement**	242
7.8	Extending the shareholders' agreement to cover items which are difficult or impossible to forecast	243
7.9	**The autonomous, jointly-owned, company**	244
7.10	The financing of the autonomous company, in part, with equity	245
7.11	The autonomous company needs to earn a reward on its equity	245
7.12	Management of the jointly owned company	247
7.13	One example; the summit meeting	248

8 DIRECTORS – THE COMPANY'S PUBLIC FACE

8.1	**The duties of directors** – Relationship with shareholders, creditors, employees and the public generally	249
8.2	**The company's constitution**	249
8.3	**Shareholders' ultimate control**	251
8.4	The four main areas in which shareholders exert their control	252
8.5	Appointment and removal of directors	253
8.6	Preventing directors' removal, and requiring it	254
8.7	**Shareholders' control over directors' remuneration**	255

8.8	Disclosure of directors' emoluments and other benefits	257
8.9	**Directors' tax**	258
8.10	**Directors' responsibility to the company, and to others**	264

9 MAINTENANCE OF CAPITAL

9.1	**Payments out of capital**	266
9.2	Capacity and constitution	266
9.3	**The facts in the Rolled Steel Products case**	267
9.4	The directors' authority	268
9.5	The knowledge of the third party	269
9.6	The directors' misuse of their authority	269
9.7	Shareholders' ratification in *RSP*	270
9.8	The company's objects clause	271
9.9	Separate and ancillary objects	272
9.10	What is in the mind of the directors	273
9.11	Binding transactions, those which are void or voidable and those which are capable of rectification	274
9.12	The facts in the Ridge Securities and Halt Garage cases	275
9.13	**Aveling Barford v Perion**	276
9.14	Aveling Barford v Perion (continued)	277
9.15	Perion's argument in defence	277
9.16	Mr Justice Hoffmann's limits on ratification	278
9.17	Mr Justice Hoffmann's limits on ratification (continued)	279
9.18	Making the adjustments	280
9.19	**Financial assistance for the purchase of a company's shares** – Set against the background theory of capital maintenance	281
9.20	Financial assistance under sections 151 to 158 Companies Act 1985	282
9.21	Definition of financial assistance in section 152(1)(a)	283
9.22	Definition of financial assistance (continued)	284
9.23	Practical implications	285
9.24	The whitewash procedure under sections 155 to 158	286
9.25	**The predator's distributable profits after the acquisition**	287
9.26	The target's pre-acquisition profits	289
9.27	**The 1947 Cohen Committee**	290
9.28	Applying Cohen's thinking to the predator's payment	291
9.29	**What happens if the former predator contemplates selling the target?**	291

CONTENTS

9.30	Profit in the consolidated accounts on the sale of the target	292
9.31	Profit in the consolidation (continued)	293
9.32	Profit in the predator's solus accounts	294
9.33	Is that distributable profit in the predator's solus accounts?	295
9.34	Further quirks of parent companies' distributable profits	296

10 SHARE OPTION AND INCENTIVE SCHEMES

10.1	Identifying the benefit	297
10.2	The executive share option scheme	299
10.3	Identifying the benefit – how great is it, and at whose expense is it provided? (continued)	300
10.4	Identifying the benefit – what are the tax liabilities, and what is the after-tax cash (or asset) left available?	300
10.5	Identifying the benefit – perceptions of the public, and of the option holder	302
10.6	The rise in the share price is the real benefit	303
10.7	Design features	304
10.8	Design features (continued)	305
10.9	Design features otherwise known as general conditions	306
10.10	Tempus fugit	308
10.11	Share trusts	309
10.12	The requirement for sales of shareholdings by those leaving employment	310
10.13	The ESOT, Employee Share Ownership Trust approved under the Finance Act 1989	311
10.14	The approved profit-sharing scheme	313
10.15	The approved profit-sharing scheme – release date and retention period	314
10.16	The approved profit-sharing scheme – events before the release date which result in a tax penalty	315
10.17	The approved profit-sharing scheme – the penalties	315
10.18	Are tax privileges worthwhile?	316

11 DISPOSALS

11.1	Introduction	318
11.2	The common features of disposals and acquisitions	318
11.3	Setting the scene	319
11.4	Group asset companies	320
11.5	Group asset companies (continued)	322
11.6	Stamp duty	323

11.7	Unbundling a company before sale	325
11.8	Working through the thought processes of unbundling	326
11.9	Working through the thought processes of unbundling (continued)	327
11.10	**Trade and asset transfers – cessations and clawbacks of reliefs for the disponor**	328
11.11	Hive-downs, viewed as an alternative to the sale of a trade and assets	329
11.12	**Trade and asset transfers – the values used, and the possibilities of carry forward of losses and other reliefs**	331
11.13	Trade and asset transfers – the values used (continued)	332
11.14	Trade and asset transfers – the carry forward of losses, and so on	333
11.15	**Pre-disposal dividends**	334
11.16	Pre-disposal dividends (continued)	335
11.17	**Pre-disposal reorganisations of companies – the possibility of splitting a company**	336
11.18	The possibility of splitting a company (continued)	337
11.19	The effects of previous reorganisations	340
11.20	The effects of previous reorganisations (continued)	340
11.21	**Transactions in securities**	341
11.22	Transactions in securities (continued)	342
11.23	Paragraph D companies	342
11.24	The distribution of profits	343
11.25	The exemptions and procedure for applying for clearance	344
11.26	**Share exchanges (paper-for-paper transactions) including earn-outs**	346
11.27	Clearance for paper-for-paper transactions	348
11.28	**The loss of beneficial ownership**	349
11.29	**Directors' compensation for loss of office**	350
11.30	Directors' compensation for loss of office (continued)	351
11.31	The tax position on directors' compensation for loss of office	352
11.32	**Asset disposals and VAT**	353
11.33	**Transfer of a going concern**	354
11.34	Sales of let buildings as TOGCs	356
11.35	Sales of let buildings as TOGCs (continued)	357
11.36	**The Transfer of Undertakings (Protection of Employment) Regulations 1981**	358
11.37	It is not possible to opt out of the TUPE regulations where the necessary conditions are present	358

11.38	The economic entity which must be transferred	359
11.39	Must the economic entity be a commercial venture?	360
11.40	Dismissals and redundancies because of the transfer	360
11.41	The contracting out of governmental and local government services	362

12 ACQUISITIONS

12.1	Introduction	364
12.2	The Financial Services Act 1986	365
12.3	The Financial Services Act 1986 – investment business	365
12.4	The Financial Services Act 1986 – investment advertisements	366
12.5	Heads of agreement	367
12.6	Heads of agreement (continued)	368
12.7	The purchase contract	369
12.8	The purchase contract (continued)	370
12.9	Date of completion	371
12.10	The Warranted Accounts	371
12.11	The Warranted Accounts (continued)	372
12.12	The implications of warranties	373
12.13	The implications of warranties (continued)	374
12.14	Disclosures against warranties, and the disclosure letter	375
12.15	Indemnities contrasted with warranties	376
12.16	Profits and pricing	377
12.17	Identifying tax liabilities for indemnification	377
12.18	Identifying tax liabilities for indemnification (continued)	378
12.19	Identifying tax liabilities for indemnification (continued)	379
12.20	Devising the formula which defines the liabilities to be indemnified	380
12.21	Devising the formula which defines the liabilities to be indemnified (continued)	381
12.22	The predator's objective – including the special case of the predator which is a company owned by a management buy-out team	382
12.23	Hive-downs	383
12.24	Hive-downs, identifying what the predator is acquiring	386
12.25	Hive-downs, identifying what the predator is acquiring (continued)	387
12.26	Hive-downs; verification, and the business's records	387

12.27	Hive-downs; verification, and the business's records (continued)	388
12.28	**Due diligence**	389
12.29	Due diligence (continued)	390
12.30	**Completion** – The last chance for altering or aborting the acquisition	391
12.31	Completion – also the start of a different era for vendors, target and predator	392
12.32	Conduct of claims	394

13 COMPANY PURCHASES OF OWN SHARES

13.1	**Introduction – Part 1:- The law in 1980**	395
13.2	**Introduction – Part 2:- The Companies Act 1981 and the Finance Act 1982**	396
13.3	**The capital redemption reserve**	397
13.4	Illustrative balance sheet for the simple transaction	398
13.5	Purchase partly out of proceeds of a new issue	399
13.6	Purchase partly out of capital	400
13.7	Purchase out of capital which exceeds the nominal amount of the shares purchased	401
13.8	Procedures for the purchase of shares out of capital	402
13.9	Procedures for the purchase of shares out of capital (continued)	403
13.10	**Stamp duty**	404
13.11	**Schemes and arrangements** – The purchase by a party other than the company itself	405
13.12	Schemes and arrangements outlawed by the tax legislation	405
13.13	Benefiting a trade without there being a scheme	406
13.14	Benefiting a trade without there being a scheme (continued)	407
13.15	**Other requirements of the tax legislation**	408

14 DEMERGERS

14.1	**Introduction**	410
14.2	Re-examination of those potential tax liabilities	410
14.3	**The three possible forms of demerger**	412
14.4	The third fundamental	414
14.5	**Practical possibilities**	415
14.6	Practical possibilities (continued)	416
14.7	**The back door to demergers**	417

Index	421

TABLE OF CASES

Abbott v Philbin [1961] A.C. 352; [1960] 3 W.L.R. 255; 104 S.J. 563; [1960] 2 All E.R. 763; [1960] T.R. 171; 53 R.&I.T 487; 39 T.C. 82; 39 A.T.C. 221; [104 S.J. 518; 230 L.T. 107; 53 R.&I.T. 508; 67 Tax. 276], H.C.; reversing [1960] Ch. 27; [1959] 3 W.L.R. 739; 103 S.J. 898; [1959] 3 All E.R. 590; 38 A.T.C. 284; *sub nom.* Philbin v Abbot [1959] T.R. 277; [76 L.Q.R. 182; 53 R.&I.T. 4; 110 L.J. 70; 104 S.J. 221]; [1959] 1 W.L.R. 667; 103 S.J. 451; [1959] 2 All E.R. 270; [1959] T.R. 103; 52 R.&I.T. 423; 38 A.T.C. 92; [[1969] B.T.R. 24] 10.4
Associated Portland Cement Manufacturers Ltd v Price Commission, The [1975] I.C.R. 27; (1974) 119 S.J. 63, C.A. 4.7
Atherton v British Insulated and Helsby Cable Ltd [1925] *See* British Insulated & Helsby Cables Ltd v Atherton
Aveling Barford Ltd v Perion Ltd [1989] BCLC 626; [1989] P C C 370; *Financial Times*, April 28, 1989 .... 1.8, 6.45, 9.2, 9.13, 9.14, 9.15, 9.17, 9.18, 11.8, 14.5
Ayerst v C.&K. (Construction) [1976] A.C. 167; [1975] 3 W.L.R. 16; 119 S.J. 424 [1975] S.T.C. 345; [1975] T.R. 117, H.L.; affirming [1975] 1 W.L.R. 191; (1974) 119 S.J. 100; [1975] 1 All E.R. 162; [1975] S.T.C. 1; [1974] T.R. 269, C.A.; affirming [1974] 1 All E.R. 676; [1974] S.T.E. 98; [1973] T.R. 303 .... 5.32, 5.34, 12.23

Bassett Enterprise Ltd v Petty [1938] 21 T.C. 730 .... 11.31
Baytrust Holdings v I.R.C.; Firth (Thos.) & Brown (John) (Investments) v I.R.C. [1971] 1 W.L.R. 1333; [1971] 3 All E.R. 76; [1971] T.R. 111; 50 A.T.C. 136; *sub nom.* Baytrust Holdings v I.R.C., 115 S.J. 624 .... 6.34, 6.66
Belmont Finance Corp. v Williams Furniture Ltd (No. 2) [1980] 1 All E.R. 393, C.A. 9.12
Booth (EV) (Holdings) Ltd v Buckwell (1980) 53 T.C. 425; [1980] S.T.C. 578; [1980] T.R. 249 .... 11.12, 11.13
Bork (P.) International A/S v Foreningen of Arbejdsledere i Danmark; Olsen v Junckers Industreiv A/S; Hansen v Junckers Industriev A/S; Handels-og kontorfunktionaerernes Forbund i Danmark v Junckers Industriev A/S [1989] 1 RLR 41, European Ct. 11.40
Bridge v Deacons [1984] A.C. 705; [1984] 2 W.L.R. 837; (1984) 128 S.J. 263; [1984] 2 All E.R. 19; (1984) 81 L.S.Gaz. 1291; (1984) 134 New L.J. 723, P.C. 12.31
British Insulated & Helsby Cables Ltd v Atherton [1926] A.C. 205; [1925] All E.R. Rep. 623; 95 L.J.K.B. 336; 14 L.T. 289; 42 T.L.R. 187; *sub nom.* Atherton v British Insulated & Helsby Cables Ltd 10 T.C. 188, H.L.; affirming S.C. *sub nom.* Atherton v British Insulated & Helsby Cables Ltd [1925] 1 K.B. 421; 10 T.C. 177, C.A. 5.4
Brookland Selangor Holdings v I.R.C.; Kuala Pertang Syndicate v I.R.C. [1970] 1 W.L.R. 429; (1969) 114 S.J. 170; [1970] 2 All E.R. 76; [1969] T.R. 485; [34 Conv. 298] 5.35, 6.69
Burman v Hedges & Butler Ltd [1979] 1 W.L.R. 160; (1978) 122 S.J. 792; [1979] S.T.C. 136; [1978] T.R. 409; [1981] T.C. 50 .... 6.9

TABLE OF CASES

Bushell v Faith [1970] A.C. 1099; [1970] 2 W.L.R. 272; 114 S.J. 54; [1970] 1 All E.R. 53, H.L.; affirming [1969] 2 Ch. 438; [1969] 2 W.L.R. 1067; 113 S.J. 262; [1969] 1 All E.R. 1002, C.A. [86 L.Q.R. 155] 8.6

Campbell Connelly & Co. Ltd v Barnett [1992] BTC 164; [1992] EGCS 44 .... 6.42, 6.52, 11.4
Cane v Jones [1980] 1 W.L.R. 1451; (1979) 124 S.J. 542; [1981] 1 All E.R. 533 .... 6.10
Clark v Follett [1973] T.R. 43; sub nom. Clark v Follett; Follett v Clark [1973] S.T.C. 240; 48 T.C. 677 .... 6.37
Cleary v I.R.C. [1968] A.C. 766; [1967] 2 W.L.R. 1271; 111 S.J. 277; [1967] 2 All E.R. 48; [1967] T.R. 57; 46 A.T.C. 51, H.L.; affirming sub nom. I.R.C. v Cleary; I.R.C. v Perren [1966] Ch. 365 [1966] 2 W.L.R. 790; 110 S.J. 190; [1966] 2 All E.R. 19; 44 T.C. 399; [1966] T.R. 39; 45 A.T.C. 36; [1966] C.L.Y. 6178; [30 Conv. 329], C.A; reversing [1965 Ch. 1098; [1965] 3 W.L.R 219; 109 S.J. 357; [1965] 2 All E.R. 603; [1965] T.R. 149; 44 A.T.C. 142; T.C. leaflet No. 2147; [1965] C.L.Y. 1962; [29 Conv. 326; 75 Tax 57] 5.27, 11.23, 11.24, 14.4
Commissioner of Taxes v Nchanga Consolidated Copper Mines [1964] A.C. 948; [1964] 2 W.L.R. 339; 108 S.J. 73; [1964] 1 All E.R. 208; [1964] T.R. 25; 43 A.T.C. 20, P.C. 5.4
Cotman v Brougham [1918] A.C. 514; [1918–19] All E.R. Rep. 265; 87 L.J. Ch. 379; 119 L.T. 162; 62 S.J. 534; sub nom. Anglo-Cuban Oil, Bitumen & Asphalt Co. Ltd, Re; Cotman v Brougham 34 T.L.R. 410, H.L. 9.9
Cowcher v Mills (Richard) & Co. Ltd [1926] 10 T.C. 216 .... 5.4
Crane-Fruehauf Ltd v I.R.C. [1975] 1 All E.R. 429; [1975] S.T.C. 51; [1974] T.R. 389, C.A.; affirming [1974] 1 All E.R. 811; [1974] S.T.C 110; [1973] T.C. 309 .... 6.69
Craddock (HM Inspector of Taxes) v Zevo Finance Co. Ltd [1944] 1 All E.R. 566; 27 T.C. 274, C.A. affirmed [1946] 1 All E.R. 523n; 174 L.T. 385; 27 T.C. 284, H.L. 3.22, 6.48, 6.57, 11.5

De Beers Consolidated Mines v Howe [1906] A.C. 455 .... 6.8
Drown v Gaumont-British Picture Corporation Ltd [1937] Ch. 402 .... 6.13
Dunstan v Young, Austen Young Ltd [1989] S.T.C. 69; 62 T.C. 448; [1989] L.S.Gaz. February 15, 41, C.A. 3.17
Duomatic Re [1969] 2 Ch. 365; [1969] 2 W.L.R. 114; (1968) 112 S.J. 922; [1969] 1 All E.R. 161 .... 8.9

Ebrahimi v Westbourne Galleries [1973] A.C. 360; [1972] 2 W.L.R. 1289; 116 S.J. 412; [1972] 2 All E.R. 492, H.L.; reversing sub nom. Westbourne Galleries, Re [1971] Ch. 799; [1971] 2 W.L.R 618 [1970] 115 S.J. 74; [1971] 1 All E.R. 56, C.A.; reversing [1970] 1 W.L.R. 1378; 114 S.J 785; [1970] 3 All E.R. 374 .... 8.5
Escoigne Properties Ltd v I.R.C. [1958] A.C. 549; [1958] 2 W.L.R. 336; 102 S.J. 159; [1959] 1 All E.R. 406; [1958] T.R. 37; 37 A.T.C. 41; [108 L.J. 422; 25 Sol. affirming [1957] 1 All E.R. 291; 50 R.&I.T. 199; sub nom. I.R.C. v Escoigne Properties [1956] T.R. 453; 35 A.T.C. 438; [223 L.T. 101; [1957] B.T.R. 179; 21 Conv. 1723; [1957] C.L.Y. 3394, C.A.; reversing [1956] 1 W.L.R. 980; 100 S.J. 568; [1956] 3 All E.R. 33; [1956] T.R. 263; 4 R.&I.T. 653; 35 A.T.C. 281; [[1956] B.T.R. 184; 20 Conv. 510]; [1956] C.L.Y 8487 .... 6.33, 11.6

TABLE OF CASES

Express Engineering Works Ltd, Re [1920] 1 Ch. 466; [1920] All E.R. Rep. Ext. 850; 89 L.J. Ch. 379; 122 L.T. 790; 36 T.L.R. 275, C.A. 610

Furniss v Dawson [1984] A.C. 474; [1984] 2 W.L.R. 226; (1984) 128 S.J. 132; [1984] 1 All E.R. 530; (1984) 55 T.C. 324; [1984] S.T.C. 153; (1984) 81 L.S.Gaz. 739; (1984) 134 New L.J. 341; [1985] S.L.T. 93; (1985) 82 L.S.Gaz. 2782; 104 *Law Notes* 292, H.L.; reversing [1983] 3 W.L.R. 635; (1983) 127 S.J. 619; [1983] S.T.C. 549, C.A.; (1982) 126 S.J. 83; [1982] S.T.C. 267 .... 11.25

Gardner v Iredale [1912] 1 Ch. 700; 81 L.J. Ch. 531; 106 L.T. 860; 19 Mans. 245 .... 3.29
Godden v Wilson (A.)'s Stores (Holdings) Ltd [1962] T.R. 19; 40 T.C. 161; 40 A.T.C. 25, C.A.; affirming [1961] T.R. 205; 40 A.T.C. 213; [1961] C.L.Y. 4204 .... 5.4, 11.31
Golden Horseshoe (New) Ltd v Thurgood [1934] 1 K.B. 548; [1933] All E.R. Rep. 402; 103 L.J.K.B. 619; 150 L.T. 427; 18 T.C. 294, C.A. 4.12

Halt Garage, Re (1964) Ltd [1982] 3 All E.R. 1016 .... 9.12, 9.16, 9.17, 9.18
Harmony and Montague Tin & Copper Mining Co., Re (Spargo's Case) (1873) 8 Ch. App. 407; [1861–73] All E.R. Rep. 261; 42 L.J. Ch. 488; 28 L.T. 153; 21 W.R. 306, L.J.J. 3.21, 3.22
Harrison v Nairn Williamson Ltd; [1978] 1 WLR 145; [1978] 1 All E.R. 608; [1978] S.T.C. 67; 121 S.J. 776, C.A. affirming [1976] 1 WLR 1161; [1976] 3 All E.R. 367; [1976] S.T.C. 500; 120 S.J. 783 .... 3.19
Harrods (Buenos Aires) Ltd v Taylor-Gooby, 108 S.J. 117; 41 T.C. 450; *sub nom.* Taylor-Gooby v Harrods (Buenos Aires) Ltd [1964] T.R. 9; 43 A.T.C. 6, C.A.; affirming [1963] T.R. 137; 42 A.T.C. 143; [1963] C.L.Y. 1728 .... 5.4
Henriksen v Grafton Hotel Ltd [1942] 1 All E.R. 678; [1942] 2 K.B. 184; 111 L.J.K.B. 497; 167 L.T. 39; 58 T.L.R. 271; 86 S.J. 310; 24 T.C. 456, C.A. 11.4, 11.21
Heydons Case (1584) 3 Co. Rep. 7a; 76 E.R. 637 .... 6.33
Hooper v Western Counties and South Wales Telephone Co. [1892] 68 L.T. 78; 41 W.R. 84. 9 T.L.R. 17; 37 S.J. 10; 3 R. 58 .... 6.66
Horsley & Weight Ltd, Re [1982] Ch. 442; [1982] 3 W.L.R. 431; [1982] 3 All E.R. 1045; (1982) 79 L.S.Gaz. 919, C.A. 8.10, 9.4, 9.6, 9.11, 9.12, 9.17

I.R.C. v Cleary; I.R.C. v Perren. *See* Cleary v I.R.C.
— v Parker [1766] A.C. 141; [1966] 2 W.L.R. 486; 110 S.J. 91; [1966] 1 All E.R. 399; [1986] T.R. 1; 43 T.C. 396; 45 A.T.C. 1; [30 Conv. 146], H.L; reversing [1965] Ch. 1032; [1965] 2 W.L.R. 1141; 109 S.J. 177; [1965 1 All E.R. 796; T.C. leaflet No. 2136; *sub nom.* Parker v I.R.C.; Tomlinson v I.R.C. [1965] T.R. 23; 44 A.T.C. 17 [1965] C.L.Y. 1964, C.A.; reversing [1965] Ch. 510; [1964] T.R. 293; 43 A.T.C. 294; T.C. leaflet No. 2115; [1964] C.L.Y. 1853....... 11.21
— v Thomson (Patrick) Ltd (In Liquidation); I.R.C. v Allan (J&R) (In Liquidation); I.R.C. v Pettigrew & Stephens [1956] T.R. 471; 50 R.&I.T. 95; 37 T.C. 145; 35 A.T.C. 487; 1957 S.L.T. 235; [958] B.T.R. 89] 11.31
— v Ufitec Group Ltd [1977] 3 All E.R. 924; [1977] S.T.C. 363, D.C. 5.35
— v Wiggins [1979] 1 W.L.R. 323; (1978) 122 S.J. 863; [1979] 2 All E.R. 245; (1983) 53 T.C. 639; [1979] S.T.C. 244; [1978] T.R. 393 .... 11.24, 11.25

TABLE OF CASES

Introductions Ltd, Re.; Introductions *v* National Provincial Bank [1970] Ch. 199; [1069] 2 W.L.R. 791; 113 S.J. 122; [1969] 1 Lloyd's Rep. 229; *sub nom.* Introductions Re; Introductions *v* National Provincial Bank [1969] 1 All E.R. 887; [32 W.L.R. 565], C.A.; affirming [1968] 2 All E.R. 1221 .... 9.9

Jacgilden (Weston Hall) *v* Castle; Jacgilden (Weston Hall) *v* I.R.C. [1971] Ch. 408; [1969] 3 W.L.R. 839; [1969] 3 All E.R. 1110; 45 T.C. 685; *sub nom.* Jacgilden (Weston Hall) *v* Castle; Same *v* I.R.C. (Weston Hall) *v* Castle [1969] T.R. 317 .... 5.28
Jamieson (Liquidators of the City of Glasgow Bank) *v* Mackinnon [1882] Court of Sessions, 4th Series, Vol. IX, 536 .... 4.9

Kingston Cotton Mill Co. (No. 2) [1896] 2 Ch. 279; 65 L.J. Ch. 673; 74 L.T. 568; 12 T.L.R. 430; 3 Mans. 171; 40 S.J. 531, C.A.; affirming [1896] 2 Ch. 331; 65 L.J. Ch. 290; 73 L.T. 745; 44 W.R. 363; 12 T.L.R. 123; 40 S.J. 144; 3 Mans. 75 .... 1.25
Kirby *v* Thorn EMI plc [1987] 1 W.L.R. 445; (1987) 131 S.J. 1456; [1988] 2 All E.R. 947; [1987] S.T.C. 621; [1987] 2 FTLR 403; (1987) 84 L.S.Gaz. 2693, C.A.; reversing [1986] 1 W.L.R. 851; (1986) 130 S.J. 485; [1986] S.T.C. 200; (1985) 83 L.S.Gaz. 1063 ... 12.3
— *v* Wilkins [1929] 2 Ch. 444; 142 L.T. 16 .... 13.1

Lever Bros Ltd *v* I.R.C. [1938] 2 All E.R. 808; [1938] 2 K.B 518; 107 L.J.K.B. 669; 159 L.T. 136; 54 T.L.R. 892; 82 S.J. 452, C.A. 6.66
Litster *v* Forth Dry Dock & Engineering Co. Ltd [1989] 1 A.C. 546; [1989] 2 W.L.R. 634; [1989] I.C.R. 341; (1989) 133 S.J. 455; [1989] 1 All E.R. 1134; [1989] IRLR 161; [1989] 2 C.M.L.R. 194, H.L. 11.40

Mairs *v* Haughey [1993] BTC 339 .... 11.31
Mallalieu *v* Drummond [1983] 2 A.C. 861; [1983] 3 W.L.R. 409; (1983) 127 S.J. 538; [1983] 2 All E.R. 1095; [1983] S.T.C. 665; (1983) 133 New L.J. 869; (1983) 80 L.S.Gaz. 2368, H.L.; reversing [1983] 1 W.L.R. 252; (1983) 127 S.J. 37; [1983] 1 All E.R. 801; [1983] S.T.C. 124, C.A.; affirming [1981] 1 W.L.R. 908; (1981) 125 S.J. 205; [1981] S.T.C. 391; [1981] T.R. 105 .... 13.13
Melon *v* Powe (Hector) [1981] I.C.R. 43; [1981] 1 All E.R. 313; [1980] IRLR 477, H.L.; affirming [1980] IRLR 80, C.A. 18.38
Minister of National Revenue *v* Anaconda American Brass [1956] A.C. 85 [1956] 2 W.L.R. 31; 100 S.J. 10; [1956] 1 All E.R. 20; [1955] T.R. 339; 49 R.&I.T. 333; 34 A.T.C 330; [72 L.Q.R. 175; 134 Acct. 80], P.C. reversing *sub nom.* Anaconda American Brass *v* Minister of National Revenue [1952] 3 D.L.R. 580; [1952] C.L.Y. 1620 .... 2.7
Moore *v* Mackenzie & Sons; I.R.C. *v* Same [1972] 1 W.L.R. 359; [1972] 2 All E.R. 549; *sub nom.* Moore *v* Mackenzie & Sons, 116 S.J. 198; [1971] T.R. 457; 48 T.C. 196 .... 11.13
Morris *v* Kanssen [1946] A.C. 459; [1946] 1 All E.R. 586; 115 L.J. Ch. 177; 174 L.T. 353; 62 T.L.R. 306, H.L.; affirming *sub nom.* Kanssen *v* Rialto (West End) Ltd [1944] Ch. 346; [1944] 1 All E.R. 751; 113 L.J. Ch. 264; 171 L.T. 3; 60 T.L.R. 471; 88 S.J. 471, C.A. 9.5
Morris (Herbert) Ltd *v* Saxelby [1916] 1 A.C. 688; [1916–17] All E.R. Rep. 305; 85 L.J. Ch. 210; 114 L.T. 618; 32 T.L.R. 297; 60 S.J. 305, H.L.; affirming [1915] 2 Ch. 57, C.A. 12.31

TABLE OF CASES

Nairn Williamson. *See* Harrison v Nairn Williamson Ltd (1977) 3.19
National Westminster Bank plc *v* I.R.C. [1993] T.L.R. 10 January 1994, [1994] 3 WLR159 C.A. 3.16, 6.47
Nordenfelt *v* Maxim Nordenfelt Guns and Ammunition Co. Ltd [1984] A.C. 535; [1981–4] All E.R. Rep. 1; 63 L.J. Ch. 908; 71 L.T. 489; 10 T.L.R. 636; 11 R. 1, H.L.; affirming *sub nom.* Maxim Nordenfelt Guns and Ammunition Co. *v* Nordenfelt [1893] 1 Ch. 630, C.A. 12.31

Odhams Press Ltd *v* Cook [1940] 3 All E.R. 15 .... 7.8
O'Keeffe *v* Southport Printers Ltd (1984) 58 T.C. 88; [1984] S.T.C. 443; (1984) 81 L.S.Gaz. 1685 .... 5.4; 11.31
Ormond Investments Co. *v* Betts [1928] A.C. 143; [1928] All E.R. Rep. 709, 97 L.J.K.B. 342; 138 L.T. 600; 13 T.C. 400, H.L. 6.67
Osborne *v* Steel Barrel Co. Ltd [1942] 1 All E.R. 634; 24 T.C. 303, C.A. 3.24, 6.14, 6.15, 6.71
Overy *v* Ashford Dunn & Co. Ltd [1933] 17 T.C. 497; 49 T.L.R. 230... 11.31
Owen *v* Southern Railway of Peru. *See* Southern Railway of Peru *v* Owen
Oxford Benefit Building & Investment Society, Re (1886) 35 Ch. 502; 55 L.T. 598; 35 W.R. 116; 3 T.L.R. 46; *sub nom.* Oxford Building Society, Re; exp. Smith 56 L.J. Ch. 98 .... 4.11

Parway Estates Ltd *v* I.R.C. (1957) 45 T.C. 135; [1958] T.R. 193; 37 A.T.C. 164, C.A.; affirming [1957] T.R. 329; 36 A.T.C. 310 .... 5.32
Payne (David) & Co. Ltd, Re; Young *v* Payne (David) & Co. Ltd [1904] 2 Ch. 604; [1904–7] All E.R. Rep. Ext. 1051; 73 L.J. Ch. 849; 91 L.T. 77; 20 T.L.R. 590; 48 S.J. 572; 11 Mans. 437, C.A. 9.9
Pepper *v* Hart [1993] 1 All E.R. 42 .... 11.23
Peters (George) & Co. Ltd *v* Smith; Williams *v* Young (J.J.) & Son [1963] T.R. 329; 41 T.C. 264; 42 A.T.C. 389 .... 11.31

Rask and Christensen *v* ISS Kantloneservice A/S, November 12, 1992, E.C.J. 11.41
Regent Oil Co. *v* Strick; Regent Oil Co. *v* I.R.C. [1966] A.C. 295; [1965] 3 W.L.R. 696; 109 S.J. 633; [1965] 3 All E.R. 174; [1965] T.R. 277; 44 A.T.C. 264; 43 T.C. 1, H.L.; affirming *sub nom.* Strick *v* Regent Oil Co. [1964] 1 W.L.R. 1166; 108 S.J. 500; *sub nom.* Strick *v* Regent Oil Co.; I.R.C. *v* Regent Oil Co. [1964] 3 All E.R. 23; 43 T.C. 1; T.C. leaflet No. 2103; *sub nom.* Regent Oil Co. *v* Strick [1964] T.R. 2.7; 43 A.T.C 198; [28 Conv. 321]; [1964] C.L.Y. 1830; C.A.; affirming [1964] 1 W.L.R. 309; 108 S.J. 54; [1964] 1 All E.R. 585; [1963] T.R. 471; 42 A.T.C. 530; T.C. leaflet No. 2089, [28 Conv. 84]; [1963] C.L.Y. 1737 .... 5.4
Rendell *v* Went [1964] 1 W.L.R. 650; 108 S.J. 401; [1964] 2 All E.R. 464; [1964] T.R. 133; 43 A.T.C. 123; 41 T.C. 641; [28 Conv. 321; 73 Tax. 221; 114 L.J. 451], H.L.; affirming All E.R. 325; *sub nom.* Went *v* Rendell [1963] T.R. 261; 42 A.T.C. 255, C.A.; reversing 107 S.J. 253; 42 A.T.C. 122; *sub nom.* Rendell *v* West [1963] T.R. 111; [1963] C.L.Y. 1752 .... 6.11
Ridge Securities Ltd *v* I.R.C. [1964] 1 W.L.R. 479; 108 S.J. 377; [1964] 1 All E.R. 275; 44 T.C. 373; [1963] T.R. 449; 42 A.T.C. 487; T.C. leaflet No. 2086; [235 L.T. 217; 1964] BTR 168] 9.12, 9.16, 9.17, 9.18
Rolled Steel Products (Holdings) *v* British Steel Corp. [1986] Ch. 246; [1985] 2 W.L.R. 908; (1984) 128 S.J. 629; [1985] 3 All E.R. 1; (1984) 81 L.S.Gaz. 2357, C.A.; affirming [1982] Ch. 478; [1982]

TABLE OF CASES

3 W.L.R. 715; [1982] 3 All E.R. 1057; (1982) 79 L.S.Gaz. 129 ....   8.2, 9.2, 9.3, 9.4, 9.5, 9.6, 9.7, 9.8, 9.9, 9.10, 9.11, 9.15

Sainsbury (J.) plc v O'Connor (HMIT) [1991] 1 W.L.R. 963; [1991] S.T.C. 318; (1991) 135 S.J. (L.B.) 46, C.A.; affirming [1990] S.T.C. 516 .... 5.36, 5.40, 5.41, 5.42, 6.7, 7.13, 12.8
Saloman v Saloman & Co. Ltd; Saloman & Co. Ltd v Saloman [1987] A.C. 22; [1985–9] All E.R. Rep. 33; 66 L.J. Ch. 35; 75 L.T. 426; 45 W.R. 193; 13 T.L.R. 46; 41 S.J 63; 4 Mans. 89, H.L.; reversing sub nom. Broderip v Saloman [1985] 2 Ch. 323; 64 L.J. Ch. 689; 72 L.T. 755; 43 W.R. 612; 11 T.L.R. 439; 39 S.J. 522; 2 Mans. 449, 12 R. 395, C.A. 9.12
Secretary of State for Employment v Spence [1986] Q.B. 179; [1986] 3 W.L.R. 380; [1986] I.C.R. 651; [1986] 3 All E.R. 616; (1986) 130 S.J. 407; [1986] 3 C.M.L.R. 647; [1986] I.R.L.R. 248; (1986) 83 L.S.Gaz. 2084, C.A.; affirming [1986] I.C.R. 181, E.A.T. 11.40
Schmidt v Spar- Und Leihkasse Der Fruheren Amter Bordesholm, Kiel Und Cronshagen; Case No C-392/92; [1994] IRLR 302 .... 11.38
Shearer v Bercain [1980] 3 All E.R. 295; 124 S.J. 292; [1980] T.R. 93; (1983) T.C. 698; [1980] S.T.C. 359 .... 3.24, 3.26, 6.13, 6.14, 6.16, 11.24, 13.8
Shepherd v Law Land plc [1990] S.T.C. 795; *Financial Times*, November 30, 1990 .... 5.24, 5.40
Slaney v Kean [1970] Ch. 2443; [1969] 3 W.L.R. 240; 113 S.J. 587; [1970] 1 All E.R. 434; [1969] T.R. 159; 45 T.C. 415 .... 12.32
Smith (George J.) & Co. Ltd v Furlong [1968] T.R. 437; 113 S.J. 56; sub nom. Smith (George J.) & Co. v I.R.C. [1969] [45 T.C. 384] 11.31
South African Supply and Cold Storage Co. Ltd, Re [1904] 2 Ch. 268... 6.66, 6.72
Southern Railway of Peru v Owen [1957] A.C. 334; [1956] 3 W.L.R. 389; 100 S.J. 527; [1956] 2 All E.R. 728; [1956] T.R. 197; 32 A.T.C. 147; 49 R.&I.T. 468; sub nom. Owen v Southern Railway of Peru, 36 T.C. 634; [72 L.Q.R. 486; [1956] B.T.R. 6], H.L.; affirming sub nom. Owen v Southern Railway of Peru (1955) 48 R.&I.T. 319; 36 T.C. 616; sub nom. Southern Railway of Peru v Owen [1955] T.R. 87; 34 A.T.C. 80 [72 L.Q.R. 25]; [1955] C.L.Y. 1291, C.A.; affirming [1954] T.R. 335; 47 R.&I.T. 782; 33 A.T.C. 344; 36 T.C. 602; [1954] C.L.Y. 1563 .... 5.4
Spijkers v Gebroeders Benedik Abattoir cv (c-231/82) [1986] 2 C.M.L.R. 296; [1986] 3 E.C.R. 1119, European Ct. 11.38
Stanton v Drayton Commercial Investment Co. [1983] A.C. 501; [1982] 3 W.L.R. 214; [1982] 2 All E.R. 942; [1984] T.C. 286; [1982] S.T.C. 585; [1982] C.L.R. 198; (1982) 79 L.S.Gaz. 1176, H.L.; affirming [1981] 1 W.L.R. 1425; (1981) 125 S.J. 498; [1982] 1 All E.R. 121 [1982] T.R. 263; [1981] S.T.C. 525, C.A.; reversing [1980] 1 W.L.R. 1162; (1980) 124 S.J. 361 [1980] 3 All E.R. 221; [1980] T.R. 117; [1980] S.T.C. 386 .... 3.25, 6.48, 6.55, 6.57, 6.59, 11.5
Stichting (Dr Sophie Redmond) v Bartol (c-29/91) [1992] IRLR 366, European Ct. J. 11.39
Strick v Regent Oil Co. See Regent Oil Co. v Strick; Regent Oil Co. v Strick v I.R.C.
Strong & Co. of Romsey Ltd v Woodifield [1906] 5 T.C. 215 .... 5.4
Swithland Investments Ltd v I.R.C. [1990] S.T.C. 448 .... 6.69
Symons v Weeks (1982) 565 T.C. 630; [1983] S.T.C. 195, D.C. 5.4

Tal y Drws Slate Co., Re; Mackley's Case [1875] 1 Ch. D. 247; 45 L.J. Ch. 158; 33 L.T. 460; 24 W.R. 92 .... 6.22

TABLE OF CASES

Trevor v Whitworth [1887] 12 A.C. 409; [1886–90] All E.R. Rep. 46; L.J. Ch. 28; 57 L.T. 457; 36 W.R. 145; 3 T.L.R. 745; 32 S.J. 201, H.L. 13.1
Trinidad Leaseholds v I.R.C. *See* Union Corp. v I.R.C.
Turquand, Royal British Bank v Turquand (1856) 6 E.&B. 327 .... 9.5, 9.6

Union Corp. v I.R.C.; Johannesburg Consolidated Investments Co. v Same; Trinidad Leaseholds v Same [1953] A.C. 482; [1953] 2 W.L.R. 615; 97 S.J. 206; [1953] 1 All E.R. 729; [1953] T.R. 61; 34 T.C. 207; 46 R.&I.T. 190; 32 A.T.C. 73, H.L.; affirming [1952] W.N. 119 [1952] 1 T.L.R. 651; 96 S.J. 150; [1952] 1 All E.R. 646; [1952] T.R. 69; 45 R.&I.T. 189; 31 A.T.C. 99; [126 Acct. 508; 49 Tax. 146; 19 sol. 207; 68 L.Q.R. 308; 16 Conv. 235]; [1952] C.L.Y. 2816, C.A.; affirming [1951] W.N. 448; [1951] 2 T.L.R. 582; 95 S.J. 484; [1951] T.R. 271; 44 R.&I.T. 560; [67 L.Q.R. 446; 15 Conv. 371]; 1 C.L.C. 807 .... 6.8

Vestey v I.R.C.; Lord Vestey v I.R.C.; Baddeley v I.R.C.; Payne v I.R.C. [1980] A.C. 1148; [1979] 3 W.L.R. 915; (1979) 123 S.J. 826; [1979] 3 All E.R. 976; [1979] T.R. 381; 54 T.C. 503; [1980] S.T.C. 10, H.L.; affirming [1979] Ch. 198; [1978] 3 W.L.R. 693; (1978) 122 S.J. 746; [1979] 2 All E.R. 225; [1978] T.R. 155; [1978] S.T.C. 567, D.C.; reversing [1978] 2 W.L.R. 136; (1977) 121 S.J. 730; [1977] T.R. 221; [1977] S.T.C. 414; 130 New L.J. 2525; [1980] Acct. 469, 647; [1980] B.T.R. 4; 131 New L.J. 121 .... 6.42

Walker's Settlement, Re [1935] Ch. 567; [1935] All E.R. Rep. 790; 104 L.J. Ch. 274; 153 L.T. 66; 51 T.L.R. 389; 79 S.J. 362, C.A. 6.66
Westcott v Woolcombers Ltd [1987] S.T.C. 600; [1987] 2 FTLR 429; (1987) 84 L.S.Gaz. 2537, C.A.; affirming [1986] S.T.C. 182; (1986) 83 L.S.Gaz 1319 .... 6.56, 11.19
Wigan Coal & Iron Co. Ltd v I.R.C. [1945] 1 All E.R. 392; 173 L.T. 79; 61 T.L.R. 231 .... 11.9
Wood Preservation v Prior [1969] 1 W.L.R. 1077; (1968) 1125 S.J. 927; [1969] All E.R. 364; [1968] T.R. 353; 45 T.C. 112, C.A.; affirming (1968) 1125 S.J. 275; [1968] 2 All E.R. 849; [1968] T.R. 37 ..5.35, 5.36, 5.37, 12.8

TABLE OF STATUTES

1862	Joint Stock Companies Act (25 & 26 Vict., c. 9)	1.5	1980	Companies Act (c. 22) 13.1
1891	Stamp Act (54 & 55 Vict., c. 39)		1980	Finance Act (c. 48) .... 14.1 Sched. 18, para. 12 ...... 14.2
	s. 14(4)	3.21	1981	Finance Act (c. 35) 11.31
1927	Finance Act (17 & 18 Geo. 5, c. 10)	6.69		Companies Act (c. 62) 6.16, 13.2
	s. 55 .... 5.32,	6.62		s. 52 .... 13.10
1930	Finance Act (20 & 21 Geo. 5, c. 28)		1982	Finance Act (c. 39) 13.2
	s. 42 .... 5.38, 6.33, 6.47, 11.6		1983	Value Added Tax Act (c. 55) s. 29 ....5.38, 6.32
1947	Companies Act (10 & 11 Geo. 6, c. 47)	6.14		s. 29A .... 6.32 s. 33 .... 5.38, 11.33
1948	Companies Act (11 & 12 Geo. 6, c. 38)			Sched. 1, para. 1(5) 11.32 Sched. 6, Item 6, Group
	s. 56(1)	6.15		5 .... 11.3
	s. 222(f)	8	1985	Companies Act (c. 6) .. 2.4,
	Sched. 8, para. 15(5) ...	6.14		3.5, 5.17,
1960	Finance Act (8 & 9 Eliz. 2, c. 44)			5.22, 6.5, 6.6, 6.46, 8.9, 14.1
	ss. 28 et seq. 11.21			Part V 4.12
1967	Finance Act (c. 54)			Part VII 6.5
	s. 27	5.38		Part X 8.10
	(3) 6.33,	11.6		Part XIII 6.63
	(a)	6.33		ss. 1–3 .... 3.14
	(c)	11.6		s. 1 .... 1.10
1970	Taxes Management Act (c. 9)			s. 2(5)(c) .... 6.47 s. 5 .... 13.1
	s. 41A	5.6		ss. 7, 8 .... 3.15
	s. 41B	5.6		s. 7 .... 1.10
1970	Income and Corporation Taxes Act (c. 10)	6.43		(1) .... 8.2 s. 8(2) 8.2
	s. 233	6.52		s. 10 ....1.10, 3.14
	(2)(b)	6.52		s. 13 .... 3.14
	(3)	6.52		s. 14 .... 3.14
	s. 278 .... 11.18			(2) 6.47
	Sched. 8, para. 13 ..... 11.31			s. 22(1) 6.47
1972	European Court Act (c. 68)			s. 35 ....9.5, 9.10 s. 35A 9.5, 9.10
	s. 9	9.5		s. 35B 9.5, 9.10
1973	Finance Act (c. 51)			s. 80 .... 3.16
	Sched. 19, para. 13 ...	3.21		s. 88(2)(a) 3.21
1977	Finance Act (c. 36)			(b) 3.21
	s. 41	6.68		(i) 3.21, 3.37
1978	Employment Protection (Consolidation) Act (c. 44)			(3), (4) .... 3.21 s. 89 .... 3.16 s. 91 .... 3.16
	s. 57(3) 11.40			s. 95 .... 3.16
				s. 99(1) 3.16, 3.21
				(2) 3.28

TABLE OF STATUTES

1985 Companies Act—cont.		1985 Companies Act—cont.	
(4)	3.16	(4)	6.5
s. 100	3.16	s. 259(1)	6.5
s. 101	3.14	s. 262(3)	4.7, 4.20
s. 103	3.26	s. 263	6.71
(5)	6.71	(1)	5.18
s. 106	3.14, 6.49	(3)	2.22, 4.1
ss. 108–111	3.26	s. 276	11.9
ss. 117–197	4.12	s. 291(3)	8.5
ss. 117, 118	3.14	s. 293	8.5
s. 130	3.26	ss. 303, 304	8.5
(1)	6.15	s. 303	6.10, 8.6
ss. 131–134	3.26	s. 309	8.10
ss. 131, 132	6.16	s. 310	6.11
s. 131	6.20, 6.21, 9.25, 9.33, 11.15, 12.1, 13.8	(3)(a)	6.11
		(b)	6.11
s. 132	6.17, 6.19, 6.20, 14.6	ss. 311–347	8.10
(8)	6.21	s. 311(1)	8.9
s. 143(1)	13.1	s. 312	8.7
(3)	13.1	s. 314	11.30
ss. 144 et seq.	13.1	s. 315(1)(b)	11.30
s. 145(3)(a)	13.9	s. 316(3)	8.7, 11.30
ss. 151 et seq.	3.11	s. 319	8.6
ss. 151–158	8.4, 9.20	s. 330	5.22
s. 152(1)(a)	9.21, 9.23	(2)(a)	8.8
(iv)	9.24	s. 344	5.22
(3)(a)	11.16	ss. 381A et seq.	13.9
(b)	9.23	s. 381A-381C	8.3
ss. 155–158	9.20, 9.24	s. 381A	6.9
s. 155	13.8	s. 382B	3.13, 6.10
ss. 159–181	13.2	s. 425	6.36, 6.60, 6.63, 12.23, 14.5
(3)	13.3, 13.15	s. 427	6.64
s. 160(1)	13.5	(2)(a)	6.62, 6.64
s. 162(2)	13.3, 13.5, 13.15	(3)(a)	6.64
s. 164(2)	13.9	(b)	6.64
(6)	13.9	s. 428	11.26
s. 170(1)	13.4	ss. 459 et seq.	8.5
(2)	13.5	s. 459	6.65
s. 171(4)	13.6	s. 461	13.1
(5)	13.7	s. 592	8.8
s. 173(3)	13.9	s. 596(1)	8.8
s. 225(1)	6.24	s. 736	6.32, 8.8
(3)	6.24	(1)	6.5
(4)(a)	6.24	(2)	6.5
s. 226	1.23	s. 738(2)	3.21
(1)	9.34	s. 743	9.20
(2)	1.17	s. 744	6.21
s. 227	6.5	Sched. 4	1.24, 4.1
s. 233	1.23	paras. 10–13	5.4
ss. 235–237	1.24	para. 12(a)	4.7, 4.10, 5.4, 6.64
s. 246	1.23, 1.25	para. 13	4.17
s. 247	8.8	paras. 16–28	2.4
s. 251	1.23	para. 19(2)	9.26
s. 252	1.23	paras. 29–34	2.4, 4.15
s. 256	4.7		
(1)	1.25		
s. 258	6.5	para. 36A	1.25
(2)(c)	6.5		

1985	Companies Act—*cont.*		1986	Finance Act—*cont.*	
	para. 54	5.2		Chap. III	12.3
	(2)	5.3		s. 3	12.3
	para. 89	5.4		s. 44(9)	12.4
	Pt. I, s. B	4.1		s. 57(2)	12.4
	s. C	2.6		(3)(*c*)	12.4
	Sched. 41A	6.22, 6.30		Sched. 1, para. 21	12.3
	para. 6(2)	4.5, 6.25		Pt. I	12.3
	paras. 8–11	6.22		Pt. II	12.3
	para. 8	6.30	1988	Income and Corporation	
	para. 9(5)	6.28		Taxes Act (c. 1)	6.39, 8.9
	para. 10	6.30		s. 6(4)(*a*)	5.3
	Sched. 5, para. 29(3)			s. 14(2)	5.8
	(*a*)(i)	9.33		s. 18	5.42
	Sched. 6	8.8, 11.30		(1)(*a*)	5.3, 5.4
	para. 1(2)(*b*)(ii)	8.8		s. 20	5.8
	(4)(*c*)	11.30		s. 33A	11.4
	para. 8	11.31		s. 33B	11.4
	para. 13(3)(*c*)	8.8, 11.30		s. 74(*f*)	5.4
				(*j*)	5.4
	Pt. I	8.8		s. 85	10.14
	Pt. II	8.8		s. 90	11.31
	Sched. 8	1.23, 1.24		s. 100(1)(*a*), (*b*)	12.23
	para. 3(3)	8.8		(*a*)	3.40, 5.38, 11.12
	para. 8(2), (3)	1.23		s. 131(1)	8.9
	para. 10(2)	1.23		s. 135	3.29, 10.1, 10.4, 10.5
	Sched. 10A	6.5			
	para. 4	6.5		s. 148	11.31
1985	Company Securities (Insider Dealing) Act (c. 8)	8.10		ss. 153–168	8.9
				s. 154	8.9
				(2)	8.9
1985	Finance Act (c. 54)			s. 156	8.9
	s. 55	6.69		(2)	8.9
1986	Finance Act (c. 41)			(5), (6)	8.9
	s. 7	6.36		(8)	8.9
	s. 66	13.10		s. 157	8.9
	s. 73(4)	14.2		s. 162	3.29
	ss. 75–77	6.47, 6.62, 6.69		s. 164	8.9
				s. 166	8.9
	s. 75	6.22, 6.61, 6.62, 6.64		s. 185	10.1, 10.5
				(5)	10.2, 10.10
	s. 76	6.22, 6.31, 6.34, 6.35, 6.59, 6.61, 6.70, 11.18, 14.7		s. 186	10.1
				(2)	10.14
				(3)	10.17
	s. 77	6.22		(4)	10.15, 10.17
	(*e*)-(*h*)	13.10		(11)	10.14
1986	Insolvency Act (c. 45)			(12)	10.17
	s. 107	1.19		s. 187(2)	10.17
	s. 110	14.5, 14.7, 12.23		(10)	10.12
	s. 214	1.5		s. 198	8.9
1986	Company Directors Disqualification Act (c. 46)	8.5		s. 202A	3.29, 8.9
				s. 202B	3.29, 8.9
				s. 203(2)	8.9
	s. 11	8.5		s. 203A	8.9
1986	Financial Services Act (c. 60)	1.2, 12.1, 12.2, 12.3, 12.4, 12.5, 12.28		s. 208	5.8
				s. 209	6.51, 13.2
				(1)	6.39, 6.61, 11.18

1988	Income and Corporation Taxes Act—cont.		1988	Income and Corporation Taxes Act—cont.	
	(2)(a)	6.52		s. 395(1)	11.14
	(b)	6.39, 6.50, 6.52, 6.54, 13.2, 14.7		ss. 402–413	7.6
				s. 402(6)	7.6
				s. 403(2)	5.25
	(4)	6.51, 6.52		s. 405(1)	5.39
	(5)	6.51, 6.52		s. 410	7.6
	(6)	6.39, 11.10		(1)(b)	5.40
ss. 213–218		14.1		(2)(b)	5.40
s. 213		14.2		s. 412(1)(b)	7.6
	(2)	14.2		(c)	7.6
	(3)(a)	14.3		(2)	7.6
	(b)(i)	14.3		s. 413(3)(a)	5.39
	(ii)	14.3		(6)(a)	5.39
	(4)	14.3		s. 414	5.22
	(8)(a), (b)	14.3		s. 416	6.37, 6.39, 6.40
	(c)	14.3		(2)	5.33
	(d)	14.4		s. 419	5.22
	(11)	14.4		s. 574	3.17
s. 214		14.4		s. 579(1)	11.31
s. 215		14.6		s. 580(3)	11.31
ss. 219–229		13.2		s. 592(4)	5.3
s. 219(1)(a)		13.13, 13.14		s. 703	11.25, 13.9
	(b)	13.14		s. 703C(1)	11.23
s. 220(1)-(3)		13.3		s. 704D(2)	11.23
	(5)-(9)	13.15		s. 707	11.25
s. 221		13.15		s. 709(1)	11.22
s. 223(1)		13.15		s. 765(1)(d)	6.7
s. 227		13.12		s. 768	12.23
s. 228		13.12		s. 790	5.13
s. 233(2)		5.8		s. 793	5.13
s. 239(2)		5.15		s. 797	5.13
s. 240		5.26, 5.38		s. 832(1)	10.9
	(11)(a)	5.40		(3)	13.13
s. 247		5.38, 9.20		s. 833(1)	5.3, 11.22
	(1)(a)	5.39		s. 839	6.39
	(b)	5.39, 7.11		Sched. 6	8.9
	(1A)(a)	5.39		Scheds. 9, 10	10.1
	(b)	5.40		Sched. 9, para. 2(1)	10.8
	(9)(c)	5.39		(3)	10.8
s. 248(2)		5.26		para. 27(3)	10.10
	(4)	11.28		Pt. II	10.9
s. 249		5.8		Sched. 12, para. 5(3)(a)	5.41
s. 254		6.54		Sched. 13	5.15
	(2), (3)	6.54		Sched. 16	5.21
	(4)	6.54		Sched. 18	5.24, 7.6
	(6), (7)	13.2		para. 5B(1)	5.24
s. 338(5)(a)		5.4		Sched. D	5.4
s. 343		5.38, 6.61, 11.11, 11.14, 12.23		Sched. E	8.9
			1988	Finance Act (c. 39)	
	(4)	12.23		ss. 77–80	10.1
s. 349(2)(a)		1.32	1989	Finance Act (c. 26)	8.9
s. 360(1)		12.22		ss. 39–41	8.9
s. 361(3)		12.22		s. 136	11.16
s. 386		3.34, 11.14	1989	Companies Act (c. 40)	6.5, 9.5
s. 393A(3)(b)		5.25			

TABLE OF STATUTES

1990	Capital Allowances Act (c. 1) 5.7
	s. 24(6) 11.12
	s. 77 .... 5.38
	(3) 3.40
	s. 158 .... 3.40, 5.38
1992	Taxation of Chargeable Gains Act (c. 12) 6.39, 12.23
	s. 17 .... 3.42, 6.37, 6.57, 11.5
	(1) 3.18, 3.19, 6.37, 6.56
	(a) 3.29, 12.23
	(b) 10.13, 10.14
	(2) 3.19
	s. 18(1) 6.37
	(2) 3.29, 6.37
	(4) 3.29
	s. 28(2) 5.34
	ss. 30–34 .... 5.30
	s. 30(1) 11.16
	(a) 6.53
	(5) 6.53, 11.16
	s. 31 .... 9.20, 11.16
	(1) 9.20, 11.16
	s. 32(2) 6.53
	(a) 3.25
	(b) 6.49
	s. 60 .... 5.33
	(2) 3.38
	s. 104(1) 6.49
	s. 117 .... 11.26
	s. 122 .... 13.2
	(5)(b) 5.8
	s. 126(2)(a) 3.17
	s. 127 .... 6.55
	s. 128(2) 3.17
	s. 135 .... 11.26, 11.27, 13.11
	(3) 6.55
	s. 136 ...... 6.53, 6.72, 11.18, 11.19, 14.2, 14.7
	(2) 6.62
	ss. 137, 138 .... 6.55
	s. 137(1) 13.9
	s. 138 .... 11.27
	s. 139 ..... 5.38, 6.71, 11.18, 12.23, 14.2
	(1) 6.67
	(5) 6.68
	(9) 6.62

1992	Taxation of Chargeable Gains Act—cont.
	s. 141 .... 5.8
	s. 145 .... 10.4
	s. 152 .... 3.36, 3.44
	s. 162 .... 3.35, 3.36, 3.37, 3.41, 3.44, 6.42, 11.11
	s. 165 .... 3.42
	s. 170 .... 5.38, 6.31, 6.44
	(8) 5.42
	(10) 6.44
	(11) 12.23
	s. 171 .... 11.5, 12.23
	(1) ... 6.37, 6.42, 6.45, 6.53, 6.56
	(3) 6.56
	s. 175 .... 5.38
	s. 176 .... 11.16
	s. 177A 6.42
	ss. 178, 179 .... 6.43, 6.44, 6.45
	s. 179 .... 11.5, 11.6, 11.7, 11.8, 11.11, 11.17, 11.18, 11.28, 12.18, 12.21, 12.23, 12.24, 14.2, 14.6, 14.7
	s. 192 .... 14.2
	(2)(a) 14.6
	(b) 14.6
	(3) 14.6
	ss. 227–229 .... 10.13
	s. 238(2)(d) 10.14
	s. 253 .... 3.17
	s. 278 .... 6.43
	s. 286 .... 3.42, 5.38, 6.39
	(5), (6) 6.37
	(5) 6.56
	(6), (7) 3.18
	(7) 3.29
	s. 288(5) 6.47
	s. 402 .... 5.38
	Sched. 7A 6.42
1992	Finance Act (No. 2) (c. 48) 11.4
	s. 24 .... 5.42
	s. 25(1) 11.18
1993	Trade Union Reform and Employment Rights Act (c. 19) 11.39

TABLE OF STATUTORY INSTRUMENTS

1981 Transfer of Undertakings (Protection of Employment) Regulations) (S.I. 1981 No. 1794) 3.32, 11.3, 11.36, 11.37, 11.38, 11.39, 11.41, 12.24
    reg. 5(1) 11.40
    (3) 11.40
    reg. 8(1) 11.40
    (2) 11.40

1985 Companies (Tables A to F) Regulations (S.I. 1985 No. 805) 8.5
    Table A ... 8.2, 8.3, 8.4, 8.5
    r. 36 .... 8.3
    r. 37 .... 8.3
    r. 38 .... 8.3
    r. 40 .... 8.3
    r. 42 .... 8.3
    rr. 46, 47 .... 8.3
    r. 70 .... 8.4
    r. 72 .... 8.4
    rr. 73, 74 .... 8.4, 8.5
    r. 75 .... 8.5
    r. 79 .... 8.5
    r. 81(b) 8.5
    (c) 8.5
    (e) 8.5
    r. 82 .... 8.4, 8.7
    r. 83 .... 8.7
    r. 85(a) 8.10

1985 Value Added Tax (General) Regulations (S.I. 1985 No. 886)
    regs. 29, 30 .... 6.32

    reg. 33(1)(e) 11.32
    (2) 11.32
    Part VA 11.35

1987 Stamp Duty (Exempt Instruments) Regulations (S.I. 1987 No. 516) 11.9

1988 Financial Services Act 1986 (Investment Advertisements) (Exemptions) Order (S.I. 1988 No. 316)
    art. 9 .... 12.4
Financial Services Act 1986 (Investment Advertisements) (Exemptions) Order (S.I. 1988 No. 716)
    art. 4 .... 12.4
    art. 5 .... 12.4

1990 Accounting Standards (Prescribed Body) Regulations (S.I. 1990 No. 1667) ...11.25

1992 Companies (Single Member Private Limited Companies) (S.I. 1992 No. 1699) ... 6.8, 3.13

1992 Value Added Tax (Special Provisions) Order (S.I. 1992 No. 3129) 3.33, 5.38, 11.33

1993 Income Tax (Employment) Regulations (S.I. 1993 No. 744) 8.9

EC LEGISLATION

1977 Acquired Rights Directive Council Directive 77/187 of February 14, 1977 (O.J. 1977, L61/26)................ 11.36, 11.39, 11.40, 11.41

EC Seventh Company Law Directive 83/349 of June 13, 1983, based on Article 54(3)(g) of the treaty on consolidated accounts (O.J. 1983 L193/1)......... 6.5, 6.30, 6.34

EC Twelfth Company Law Directive of December 21, 1989 on single-member private limited-liability companies (O.J. 1989 L395/40)....... 6.8

CHAPTER 1

INTRODUCTION

Companies

1.1 Their purposes

This is a book about companies, and its primary focus is on the ways in which companies are organised to do business.

That last word reminds us that there are companies formed for other purposes: charities, research institutes, learned societies, housing associations, trade associations and some members' clubs, for instance, may be incorporated as companies. Many of these are limited by guarantee rather than the more familiar structure of having a share capital divided into shares. But the feature which most clearly differentiates them from the others is that they can be described as *not-for-profit* companies, prevented by their constitutions from aiming to generate profit, and from distributing to their members either any surplus they might produce by chance or the assets they come to own.

Those are not the companies we will be looking at. We will concentrate on the companies whose objectives are profit and growth. We can leave *not-for-profit* companies with only one word of warning to the reader. Their activities are almost entirely covered by the same legislation which governs the profit-making companies we will be examining – but it is frequently necessary to read these rules from an entirely different perspective when dealing with the two very different types of organisation.

1.2 Relationships with shareholders, directors, employees, financiers, customers, suppliers

However, focusing our entire attention onto companies would be of only limited utility. The companies' owners, and their relationships with those companies, must be as important a part of our studies; and we need also to widen our consideration to embrace the effects on our companies of their dealings with the bankers and others who supply loan finance, the companies' directors, managers and employees, the customers who buy the companies' products and the suppliers of their raw materials and other inputs. And since the profits and growth that our companies are seeking will not always be internally generated, we will also need to focus on those other surrounding companies who might be predators or targets in acquisitions and mergers, or might take part with our own in business combinations.

INTRODUCTION

Widening our view still further, we will observe the effects on our companies, their owners and directors, of the control framework operated for the general public by those organisations put in place to watch and care for the public interest; the regulation of companies lies within the responsibilities of the Department of Trade, of which the Registrar of Companies is a division.

That regulation has an extra depth if the companies concerned are financial service companies, or insurance companies. If they are banks, a considerable part but not all of the regulation of their business and capital adequacy lies with the Bank of England. Companies whose shares are listed on the stock exchange must comply with that exchange's listing requirements (the yellow book) and with the rules of the takeover panel, and their directors must not overstep the line drawn by the Department of Trade in relation to insider dealing. Where companies' market shares may be too large, they will attract the attention of the Office of Fair Trading, or of one of the regulators of special industries (the Office of Gas Supply, for instance). Each of these could be the subject of an entire book; we will limit ourselves to a brief look, in chapter 12, at the Financial Services Act implications of a private company acquisition, and will do little more than mention in that same chapter takeovers of and by listed companies, and their stock exchange implications.

1.3 *Public and private companies*

We will thus not be looking at the special regulation in that last paragraph as much as the general company law aspects in the paragraph before it. But there is one aspect of company law which we will need to watch carefully throughout, namely the differences between public and private companies. The prime distinguishing feature is that the first can offer their shares for allotment to the public, which the second may not. The world at large sees which companies are privileged and which not, in that the public company includes plc in its name (public limited company) while private companies describe themselves only as limited or ltd. What may be less apparent to the world is the tighter degrees of regulation and accountability required from the plc in comparison with the less formal rules under which private companies can operate. See paragraph 8.2 and in particular Note 3 thereon for an explanation of how the differentiation of private and public companies is written into the Companies Acts.

And there is another emanation of Government to whose concerns we will find ourselves needing to devote the greatest care. One is tempted to say that if their businesses and the earning of their profits are the main objectives of our companies, of their owners and their directors, then the task of ensuring that their *tax* burdens are neither capricious, excessive nor accelerated should not distract these businessmen from their gainful activity. Unfortunately that does not seem to be the way the world works – *getting the tax right* requires totally disproportionate skills and effort.

Limited liability

1.4 *Changing to and from that status*

It is entirely possible to do business otherwise than through a company. As we will see in paragraph 3.8 below, it will generally be advantageous for a new business to be started by an individual trading as such (a sole trader), or by two or more such individuals trading in partnership. Changing from one to the other is not difficult or laborious, and should cost little or nothing.

Changing from either a sole trader or a partnership to a company may involve some modest level of cost as explained in paragraphs 3.29 to 3.34, but again it should be a straightforward process and in particular there should be very little in the way of a tax *toll-charge* payable on this change. (It is worth noting that the reverse is not true; to move from a company structure to sole trading or to a partnership will almost always be an expensive exercise, and in particular the tax penalties that are involved will usually rule it out. This is a matter to which we will give some consideration in the final chapters of this book. It is sufficient at this stage to say that one must be sure that a company is necessary, and that it will continue to be the preferred method of operation, before one takes this one-way step of moving from sole trader or partnership to a company.)

It is often said that the limited liability enjoyed by the shareholders of a company is a privilege, and that it is rational for them to *pay* by their acceptance that the company must operate only within the companies' legislation – that law itself being primarily designed for the public's protection. That may have been a reasonable view in 1862 when limited liability was reintroduced for participants in joint stock companies and these incorporations seemed to have emerged at last from the shadow cast 142 years earlier by the South Sea Bubble. The trouble is that nearly another 142 years have passed since 1862, and the underlying concept requires re-examination, particularly in the way in which some of its operations have become distorted, as we will see.

1.5 *Losing more than the company's capital*

First, what is meant by limited liability? Using an example constructed in the simplest terms, we can assume that a company's operations had been commenced with a sum of capital subscribed by its shareholders. If the company were to spend more than that (if for instance it spent the original capital on the purchase of an oil concession which turned out to be *dry*, but it had meanwhile borrowed from a bank the wages of its workers for the period they were drilling fruitlessly) then it seems clear that the company will be unable to repay the bank, in the absence of any prospect of income. We say that, being unable to meet its liabilities when they fall due, the company has become insolvent; and, for reasons that we indicate below (but whose real implication we will illustrate in paragraph 1.15), that liquidation is indicated. The liquidator will realise what assets he can, meaning that he may be able to find someone willing to give him something for the drilling equipment, but is unlikely to be able to sell the *dry* concession. Therefore, if he is able to pay anything back to the bank, it will probably be only a fraction of the company's total borrowing. The limited liability of the company's shareholders means that they cannot be called on to pay any more in to the company (or to its liquidator); their loss is limited to the amount they paid on the shares they originally took up.

But 130 years on from the 1862 Joint Stock Companies Act, life is never as simple as that. First, the company's directors become personally liable for its debts if they permit it to *trade wrongfully*.[1] This term is not statutorily defined, but it is generally accepted that it covers more than fraudulent trading by such directors. Once a company has reached the point at which its directors could not rationally expect it to trade out of its insolvency (to generate income to a sufficient extent that the company's assets once again enabled it to meet its liabilities as they fell due), it becomes *wrongful* for them to obtain further credit for the company. In the example above, the bank would be interested to know whether those directors might, for instance, have received some months earlier, but chosen to ignore, geologists' reports that further drilling was not justified; if so, increasing the company's overdraft for the further wages paid against professional advice might be a cost for the directors personally.

1.6 *Banks and their charges*

Second, banks do not lend today, at least not to owner/managed businesses, without both security over property or investments, and personal guarantees from the owner/managers themselves. Only in exceptional circumstances would the bank be satisfied with a charge over an owner-managed business's own property and investments; normally it would envisage taking security also over the owners' personal assets.

Carrying this into the simple example above, with a change in the terminology to reflect with greater precision the fact that our oil exploration activity is in a company controlled by shareholder/directors, we would see the bank enforcing its security over those shareholders' houses; and those shareholders left to step into the bank's shoes – taking over its claim against the liquidator for anything he might realise from the company's assets. If the shareholders did not wish to lose their homes, but could offer the bank cash from alternative sources under their personal guarantees, this would no doubt be accepted; the shareholders' claims against the liquidator would be the same.

1.7 *Shareholders' loans to the company*

However, that picture is still over-simplified to the extent of being misleading. Shareholder/directors who incorporate their business into a company today might or might not cause that company to issue

---

[1] Section 214 Insolvency Act 1986.

shares for the full amount of their investment; it is straightforward to provide any balance by loan, and certainly one could expect that if the company needed further finance from the shareholders after its initial formation, this might (also) be put in as a loan. There are many occasions on which such shareholder/directors would prefer to be able to draw money from their company by having it repay borrowings, rather than having it pay salary or dividends. The loan may be interest-free, but if it is not, the lender's right to a flow of interest is another variant on his methods of drawing cash from the company. (By contrast, the complexities surrounding the possibility of the company's reducing its share capital would tend to rule this out.)

But one of the results of such loans is that if the company were thereafter to hit a rough patch and to start losing money, it could tip over into insolvency that much quicker; its liabilities now include shareholder loans as well as its external liabilities, and the margin between its total liabilities and its total assets is correspondingly narrower. (That margin is of course the same figure as the company's capital, or to be more precise its shareholders' funds. The balance sheet numbers, as shown in Table 1, show the precise significance of the shareholders' decision to lend money to their company as opposed to subscribing further capital into it.)

Table 1: The Company's Balance Sheet (1)

		Shares & loans		Shares only
Fixed assets		200		200
Current assets		1,030		1,030
Liabilities – owners	(300)		–	
– other	(900)	(1,200)	(900)	(900)
Total net assets		30		330
Share capital		100		400
Profit & loss (deficit)		(70)		(70)
		30		330

1.8 *Subordination*

However, there are two ways in which the shareholder in this situation can assist the company. He can convert his loan into shares, that is to say, he can cause the company to issue further shares to him in satisfaction of his loan.[2] Such a satisfaction of the loan is a reduction

---

[2] The question of how many shares can be issued will be discussed in paragraph 3.24 below. The relevant question is this: if the loan is (say) £1,000 but because of the company's financial situation the lender could not expect that company to be able to repay the full £1,000, would the company be issuing shares at a discount if it issued 1,000 shares of £1? For present purposes, we can continue our discussions without resolving this point.

in the company's liabilities – shifting it away from its insolvency by £1 for each £1 of loan satisfied.

But we have already noted in paragraph 1.07 that the shareholder might prefer to remain a loan creditor than to become a holder of more shares – and that once such shares have been issued, it is difficult to revert to the former position. So, in line with the shareholder's belief that the company's problems are only temporary, he would normally wish to preserve his loan as a loan, but nevertheless give the company the comfort of being able to say to its other creditors that its ability to meet its obligations to them when due could not be jeopardised by the shareholder's also requiring repayment of the amount of his loan.

There is a straightforward way of reconciling these seemingly conflicting requirements. Our shareholder retains his loan as a loan, but declares it to be *subordinated* to the entitlements of the company's other creditors, that is to say that he will not call for its repayment if or to the extent that that could lessen those other creditors' ability to obtain full repayment. Such a subordination has the effect of allowing the company to leave the debt out of account in its assessment of its solvency.[3] However, it is obvious if one thinks about it that if subordination is achieved by agreement between the lender and the company that the former will not call for repayment, that agreement could at any time be cancelled or varied by the parties; this would remove the protection that the company's other creditors thought they had, and might also mean that the company's directors found themselves *trading wrongfully*, as explained in paragraph 1.5 above. If subordination is to be effective it needs to be achieved by something less easy to reverse than an agreement between lender and company – the most common method is a deed of trust executed by the lender in favour of a trustee for the company's other creditors.

1.9 Lease guarantees

The heading over paragraph 1.4 was *Limited liability*. We have noticed the ease with which this concept can be subverted, in the case of companies controlled by shareholder/directors, by the banks' requirements for security and personal guarantees from those individuals.

There is likely to be a second subversion for any such company which holds any type of property on lease. Lessors customarily require personal guarantees from the shareholder/directors of the company's obligations under any lease.

In the case of land and buildings, a shareholder can expect to be required to take an assignment of the lease into his own name from that of the company, thus making him liable for future instalments of rent for the remaining term of the lease.[4] It is scarcely necessary to stress

---

[3] *Aveling Barford Ltd v Perion Ltd* [1989] BCLC 626, a case we will need to examine in depth in paragraph 9.13.

[4] Although true in substance, this may be an oversimplification of the procedure, for the reasons explained in paragraph 1.17 and Note 10.

the burden that this can place on a guarantor's shoulders – particularly if the lease concerned forbids him from subletting at a rent lower than that he himself is required to pay, and the landlord declines to waive this clause.

If a company breaches a lease of machinery or plant, the penalty that is most likely to be written as a part of the lease terms is a requirement for immediate payment of all future rentals due had the lease run its full term (with immediate payment also of any unpaid arrears). Although the lessor can also be expected to repossess his asset, the lease will probably not require him to account to the lessee for any sale proceeds he may achieve – any such reduction of the immediate debt from the company being a matter for negotiation. Once again, a shareholder who personally guarantees the company's liability under such a lease must understand what he is doing.

The shareholder's relationship with the company

1.10 *Memorandum and Articles, remuneration of directors, dividends*

Conventionally, it is said that a shareholder's relationship with the company is governed by its Articles of Association. A company is formed by its prospective original shareholders registering, with the Registrar of Companies, a *Memorandum of Association*, accompanied by *Articles of Association*.[5] The first of these is a declaration by those prospective shareholders (who *subscribe* to this declaration and are usually referred to as the subscribers) that they wish to be formed into a company having the objects and the capital stated.

The second document, the Articles, is essentially a contract between the company and those who are its shareholders at any given time, setting out the rights and obligations of those shareholders. One would look to the Articles, for instance, for the rules covering the shareholders' appointment of directors to run the company for them, the way in which those directors should account to shareholders for their actions, and for the company's state of affairs and results; also the way in which those directors should be remunerated, including who should fix the level of that remuneration. One would also find in the Articles the provisions dealing with the payment of dividends by the company to its shareholders, and their ability to *exit*, either by sale of their shares or by their agreeing to liquidate the company.

But what we have seen in this chapter so far is that in a company controlled by shareholder/directors one needs to look beyond the terms of the Articles to see the full scope of the relationships. Those who fix the directors' remuneration will be an overlapping, if not identical, body to those to whom it is paid. Those entitled to dividends will also be the

---

[5] Sections 1, 7 and 10 Companies Act 1985. The registration of Articles of Association is not mandatory; see paragraph 8.2 and Note 3 thereon for the position in the (unusual) event of a company not registering Articles.

same, although they will take dividends in shareholding proportions – which may be quite different from the way in which they take directors' remuneration.

Shareholders' loss of their investment

1.11 *Or loss of more than that; where limited liability does not work*

As we have also seen, the shareholders may have made funds available to the company on loan alongside those put into it for shares. And some or all of the shareholders may be guarantors, or providers of security, supporting the company's borrowings and other commitments.

Provided that they have not, in their capacity of directors, been trading wrongfully (and provided that they hold shares which have been fully paid up)[6] shareholders can still say *of their investment in the company's shares and their loans to it* that they enjoy limited liability. That is not to deny that they may lose their employment and employment income, as well as their investment, if the company fails; but anyone is deluding himself who still believes that a company's owners can lose no more than that.

It is usually said that what was in the minds of successive legislators from 1862 onwards, when they permitted the formation of limited liability companies, was that business, and the earning of profit, are of benefit to the community generally; but that business, and the earning of profit, can never be free from risk. In order to encourage businessmen to take those risks, it was reasonable for the community in general (which chiefly means the community in the persons of bankers, landlords, suppliers and employees, but can also include disappointed customers) to offer them this relatively small safety net.

If that analysis is fair, it is clearly also true that the existence of that safety net is now regarded as of less significance by the holders of shares in major listed companies than it is by those holding shares in, or contemplating forming, small companies. Neither group is of course free from risk, but the first may perceive their greater risk as being that their investment might be diminished by a fall in profits in one line of business or one geographical sector, rather than by the company itself going into an insolvent liquidation. There has however been a small number of spectacular exceptions to show that this perception is not an absolute truth.

1.12 *The company approaching insolvency*

If the general analysis is fair, it is not obvious why legislators who claim to be strongly in favour of the small business have seen no need in recent

---

[6] The shareholders' liability on partly paid shares will be dealt with in paragraph 3.21 below.

years for the owners of small companies to be enabled to rebalance a relationship with banks and landlords which today makes a mockery of the concept that such owners can enjoy limited liability.

What is however vital is that we work through in some detail the implications of this fact – that bankers and landlords are able to protect their interests outside the company while others look only to it. This necessitates an illustration of what is likely to result from a company collapse. We start with an expanded version of the balance sheet from Table 1, shown in Table 2 in the left hand column. (We can assume that it was derived from the management accounts prepared to a very recent date, and therefore shows the company's position immediately before the events presaged in the succeeding columns – whose significance is explained below).

Table 2: The Company's Balance Sheet (2)

	Starting balance sheet		Adjust 1	Adjust 2	Adjust 3	Final statement
Fixed assets						
Leasehold improvements		25		(25)		nil
Owned plant		75		(50)	(25)	nil
Leased plant		100		(50)	(50)	nil
		200				
Current assets						
Debtors	730		(400)	(100)		230
Stock & wip	300			(200)		100
	1,030					
Current liabilities						
Lease creditor	(75)			(25)	100	nil
Bank	(350)				25	(325)
Suppliers	(325)					(325)
Taxes	(150)					(150)
Unpaid wages				(50)		(50)
Redundancy				(500)		(500)
Owners	(300)		(170)		(50)	(350)
			30			(1,370)
Share capital			(100)			(100)
Profit & loss deficit			70	400	1,000	1,470
			30			(1,370)

1.13 *Implication of the figures*

The left hand column in Table 2 shows the balance sheet of a company which appears, from a financial point of view, to be somewhat stretched. The bare figures do not give us all the background information, but we can be confident that the following are reasonable deductions. First, the amount of £150 owing for taxes is a clear danger signal; this is unlikely to be taxes on profits, if the company is making losses. It is much more likely to be arrears building up of VAT, PAYE and NIC. Where is the company to find the money to pay this off when the authorities find out (as they inevitably will) that the company has got into arrears to this extent?

The bank has already allowed the company's overdraft to build up to £350; we will see in a moment that the company's owned plant has been charged as security, but its balance sheet value is only £75. It may be that the bank[7] also holds a charge over the work in progress and debtors of the company; but since banks do not set great store by such charges, that suggests that the bank holds additionally some security and a personal guarantee from the company's owner. And it also suggests that what the bank will be chasing for is a plan for the reduction of the overdraft, not its increase to meet arrears of tax. Reducing the overdraft does not look as if it will be all that easy, given that the company is not generating profit; and its suppliers cannot be all that happy over continuing to supply it with goods at all, let alone doing so on increasing levels of credit.

The one obvious source of cash to put the company back onto a more even keel is its debtors – the customers to whom it has been selling on credit terms. But if it were an easy matter to extract cash from them, why has the company not done so before now? A reasonable deduction would be that those customers are just as financially stretched as is this company.

1.14 *The event which tips the company into insolvency*

The company may be in a difficult situation, but it is not necessarily one that is yet terminal. The balance sheet in Table 2 seems to show that the company has an overall excess of assets over liabilities, even if the £300 lent to it by its owners (out of the total of £400 they have put in) were to be treated as repayable.

If that £300 were subordinated to the entitlements of other creditors, the company would have an excess of current assets over current liabilities; its directors could reasonably say that it could be expected to meet its liabilities as they fell due, even if they had to admit that this would be at best a difficult course and that it could be only too easy for the company to be blown off that course.

But that off-course deflection is precisely what we see happening in the first of the adjustment columns in paragraph 1.13. The company's most significant debtor goes into liquidation, leaving the company no prospect of recovery of any of the £400 owed to it.

---

[7] In England, and only with relatively recent effect in Scotland; in Scottish law floating charges were until 1985 of only doubtful validity. It is also worth saying that the ability to grant a floating charge over its assets is one of the advantages that a company has over any unincorporated form of business.

When one slots that adjustment into the balance sheet, it is immediately obvious just how disastrous it is. The profit and loss deficit rises from £70 to £470, and what had been an overall excess of total assets over liabilities turns into a deficit of £370. Its current assets now fall short of its current liabilities by £270, even on the basis of treating the shareholder/directors' loan as not repayable. The combination of these two factors render it no longer possible for the directors to continue trading – unless they can find an immediate injection of cash. It is vital that those directors appreciate that, with the company currently insolvent, their only possible defence to a charge of wrongful trading would be their ability to show that it could, and would, be restored to solvency in the very near future. It is also important that the directors appreciate that creditors will tend to be unimpressed by directors who claim to have been unaware of the state of their company's finances, when hindsight shows them to have been continuing to take on debt although insolvent.

1.15 *What possibility is there of recovering the situation?*

How much cash would really be needed to achieve viability is of course a matter of judgment. One way of looking at this would be to say that if the shareholder/directors were to put in an additional £400, not only would the company's ratios of assets to liabilities be reinstated, but it would actually be in a better position; it would have £400 of cash with which to reduce its arrears of tax, its overdraft and the amounts owed to suppliers. Before its customer failed, it had merely the prospect of obtaining that £400 from its sales ledger balances over a period.

But that coin has another side. The company's ratios have merely been held, not improved. And its prospect of squeezing a steady flow of cash out of the remaining balances in its sales ledger, to keep the operation going in the next few months, must be less – given that the balances have been slimmed from £730 to £330. One would have to warn the shareholders that if they wished to keep the company trading, they should face the fact that it would need more than £400 injected, on top of the £400 that they had invested in the past.

Some people find it helpful, in analysing these problems, to differentiate *liquidity*, the availability of cash in the near future after taking into account financial commitments over this period, and *solvency*, referring to the availability of cash over the longer term to meet financial commitments as they fall due. These definitions come from the Accounting Standards Board's draft *Statement of Principles*.

Wider relationships

1.16 *Creditors and employees as well as shareholders*

How realistic a course it might be to put more than £400 more into the company is a matter of the shareholders' views of two sides of another coin; first, what profits can the operation be expected to generate, and how soon can it be returned to the making of profits? and second, how sure is it that the operation has a long-term future – that putting more money into it at this stage is not simply throwing good money after bad?

One way of assisting the owners to arrive at the decision they must make is to try to show them how a liquidation might proceed – what, if anything, they and the other parties having claims on the company might expect would result from a liquidation. For our current purposes in this book, this is also probably the best way there is of gaining the insight we need into the relationships between our company and all of those other parties – a matter which we said in paragraph 1.2 must be central to the whole process of our consideration of the various changes we will be thinking about through any illustrative company's life. At every point its owners and directors (and their advisers) must remain aware of the effects any proposal might have on those around the company, suppliers, customers and employees, as well as its effect on the company itself.

For these purposes we can avoid spending much time on the procedures. We can outline one straightforward way of doing things, without also mentioning alternative courses. It is sufficient to say that it is already obvious, and will become more so as we proceed, that this will be an insolvent liquidation.[8] The directors will therefore need to call in a licensed insolvency practitioner, and his immediate task will be to ensure that the company stops incurring further debt, that he obtains control of its assets to preserve them for the creditors, and that the necessary steps are taken for those creditors to be notified of the proposed liquidation of the company. Usually, and we will assume that this is the case here, this will involve his making the staff redundant.

1.17 *Liabilities which flow from the decision to stop trading*

The two immediate implications of all of this are shown in the second of the two adjustment columns in Table 2:

- certain liabilities are brought into existence by the company's decision to stop trading. The workforce become entitled to their pay for the broken period from the last pay day to the date of their dismissal and for pay in lieu of notice. They also become entitled to claims for redundancy. The plant leasing company will say that the company's ceasing to trade is an event of default under the lease, requiring that the company immediately pay the total of all future rentals; since the company's balance sheet would have shown as a creditor only the discounted present value of a stream of future payments, this represents an immediate increase in the sum owed to the leasing company.

---

[8] This paragraph contains only the briefest summary of rules to which we will need to refer at a number of points in this book.

- second, the company needs to recognise that its assets can only be regarded as worth what they will realise if the liquidator sells them for what he can get;[9] in the case of his realisation of sales ledger balances, he would acknowledge that he will not have the advantage of a continuing trading relationship to help him extract full payment from all debtors.

The effect of these shows up in the second adjustment column; the combination of further liabilities of £575, and a fall in the value of assets by £425, would shift the profit and loss account to a total debit balance of £1,470 – if the liquidator actually thought in terms of a company in liquidation still having such an account on the face of a balance sheet. The shortfall on the company's liquidation is shown as coming out at £1,370.

There is a third implication, although the balance sheet does not disclose it. The company's liquidation will be an event of default under its lease of its real property. The landlord is able to require the guarantor (on our assumed facts this is the company's owner) to take the lease into his own name.[10]

1.18 Ranking of creditors – secured, preferred, guaranteed

It is the question of who loses that £1,370 that must particularly interest us. Before we can answer that, however, there are certain adjustments between the specific creditors, which we explain below:

(a) The only true *secured creditor* is the bank, and its security over the owned plant is only expected to realise £25. That means that the balance of £325 owed to the bank will be recovered by it from

---

[9] An accountant would describe the balance sheet figures in the left hand column in Table 2 as being the *going concern* basis; he would describe their being written down as envisaged in this paragraph as an adjustment onto a *realisation* basis. The first of these is one of the fundamental accounting concepts set out in *Statement of Standard Accounting Practice No. 2*, (SSAP 2); what this means is that the assumption that the company will continue to operate as a going concern will underlie its preparation of its accounts, and that these accordingly show the true and fair view of its position required by section 226(2) Companies Act 1985. If the assumption that the company will continue as a *going concern* ceases to be tenable, then the fact that its accounts are prepared on a *realisation* basis must be made clear.

[10] For technical reasons this is usually phrased as a requirement that the guarantor take a new lease on identical terms rather than that he take an assignment of the existing lease. Insolvency law gives the liquidator the right either to take on, or alternatively to disclaim, any contract which the company had before its liquidation, but he would only want to take on the lease if he could realise cash from an assignment of it. The landlord would be content with this if the liquidator had an assignee lined up, and the latter was strong enough financially to be an acceptable tenant. If the landlord has written the lease in terms allowing him to forfeit it on the company's liquidation, and then to require the guarantor to take a new lease, that is a threat which will spur the liquidator to find an assignee (if the lease does have a value); without that spur, the liquidator might leave the landlord in limbo for an extended period.

the owner, out of the security[11] (and guarantee) given by him; and that in turn enables him to claim against the company, standing in the bank's shoes.

(b) The plant lessor does not hold security – the plant concerned has throughout remained its own asset;[12] the lessor *repossesses* his asset, and the fact that his doing so enables him to realise £50 by selling it does not of itself reduce his ability to claim that the company owes him £100, being the total of all future rentals. But his most likely action will be to sell the asset in order to mitigate his *loss* and then to claim the balance from the company's owner under the latter's guarantee. The figures in the third adjustment column assume that the owner pays £50 under that guarantee, and once again claims against the company standing in the lessor's shoes.

(c) The assets which will remain for the liquidator to realise will therefore be the debtors and work-in-progress, together estimated to produce £330.

(d) The liquidator will meet his own fees out of that, let us assume £25.

(e) The next group in the queue are creditors who have *preferential* status, namely the Government in respect of £150 of taxes, and of £50 of unpaid wages and pay in lieu of notice. The Department of Employment itself pays out both those unpaid wages, and the redundancy payments, in the case of insolvent liquidations; and then claims against the company in the liquidation. But it only has a preference for the wages, its claim for the redundancy being as an ordinary creditor. The department's taking responsibility for making the payments not only gives employees who have lost their jobs considerably quicker access to the cash than they might otherwise have, but also enables the Department of Social Security to deal more rationally than would otherwise be the case with those employees' other claims for assistance.

1.19 *Ordinary creditors*

Thereafter, the company's *ordinary* creditors rank in the liquidation, *pari passu*.

On our assumptions, the assets available to meet their claims will be £105, (£330 less £25 for the liquidator and £200 for the preferred creditors). The ordinary creditors concerned are shown in Table 3.

---

[11] It might have been expected that as well as having a charge over the company's fixed asset, the bank would have taken the floating charge over its work-in-progress and debtors referred to in paragraph 1.13 and Note 7. We have not assumed that it has done so in this case.

[12] It is an accounting convention that leased assets are shown on the lessee's balance sheet and the lessee simultaneously shows itself as owing the lessor a sum equal to the present value of future rentals payable. The requirement for this is in SSAP 21, but it fails to represent the legal relationships which come to the fore when the lease is terminated.

Table 3: The Company's Ordinary Creditors

The suppliers		325
The Government, claiming in respect of the redundancy payments it has made to employees		500
The company's owners, claiming in respect of		
guarantee payment to plant lessor	50	
guarantee payment to bank	325	
previous loan to company[13]	300	675
		1,500
Assets available to meet these claims		105
Dividend payable 7p in the £		

The company's deficit has increased to £1,395, in place of £1,370, because of the liquidator's entitlement to be paid his fee before all others.

The bank has achieved full repayment of its £350; the lessor of the plant has received the full amount of future rents rather sooner than he would otherwise have had them; the employees have had their unpaid wages and redundancy; the Government has got its taxes, and a full refund of the wages it had disbursed (but only 7p in the pound of the redundancy payments).

1.20 *The deficit borne by the ordinary creditors, including those who are also shareholders*

The ordinary creditors shown above have borne the whole deficit; the suppliers have lost £302 of their £325. But the largest of the ordinary creditors, and the largest losers, were the owners. They have had to find additional cash of £50 and £325 with which to pay off the plant lessor and the bank, and thereafter they recover from the liquidator 7p in the pound on £675, namely £47. In their capacity as shareholders (in respect of the £100 they originally put into the company for the issue of shares) there is nothing at all available for them. And in their capacity as guarantors of the company's real property lease, they have had to take on what would have been the company's obligations for future rentals payable to the landlord.

One could perhaps safely draw the following conclusion from the figures that we have been examining in the last nine paragraphs. Even if it is some fairly modest disaster that brings a company down, it will be true

---

[13] In paragraph 1.8 above we explained that an owner lending money to his company could *subordinate* his debt to those of the other creditors, so that he would not be paid out until and unless they had received their own full entitlements. However the liquidator can recognise only one class of ordinary creditors, all ranking *pari passu*, (section 107 Insolvency Act 1986). It is possible to preserve the effect of subordination of debt into liquidation, one of the ways of doing so being that the lenders vest their rights in a trustee who is instructed not to make any claim unless it is clear that all other creditors will be fully repaid.

that (given that company is already financially stretched) its suppliers and those shareholders who have lent it money or guaranteed its debts are unlikely to get much out of its demise, if anything. Shareholders who have charged their own assets, and/or guaranteed borrowings or leases have, indeed, a very real downside risk – demonstrating that the words 'limited liability' have little relevance for small businesses today.

If there are no shareholder guarantees, the other creditors will lose even more. (Had the bank and the plant lessor not been able to call on the company's owners for £325 and £50, it would have been they who claimed as ordinary creditors for these sums, and they who lost 93p in the pound on those amounts.)

Those are the fundamental premises that ought to inform all our considerations of the relationships between companies, their shareholders and their creditors. Whenever we come across proposed transactions that could reduce the security (using that word in a non-banking sense) of any creditor's rights against a company, we need to appreciate how much those creditors may lose; and what rights they may have to object to or prevent a transaction which would disadvantage them.

1.21 The company and its owners set apart

What we have seen demonstrated in paragraphs 1.18 and 1.19 has been the distribution of a company's assets in its liquidation.

Except in a liquidation,[14] however, the company's assets and liabilities need to be recognised as being separate from those of its owners. In the shareholder/director controlled company it would be ridiculous to say that those owners were *separated* from their company; but it is vital that we, and they, understand that there is a clear, indisputable line which sets the company's assets and liabilities, and its activities, apart from those of the owners. If the latter treat the company as no more than their incorporated pocket-book, nothing but trouble can result.

And recognition of the dividing line affects more than just financial aspects. A company's objectives, and those of its owners, will not necessarily always totally coincide; what is good for General Motors may be good for America, but it is not hard to think of examples in which either or both of the General Motors shareholders and those who run the company could find themselves perceiving that its good was not necessarily their own.

The author makes no apology, here, for a line of analysis treating the company anthropomorphically – imputing motives and objectives to it as if it were an individual, with a life and intelligence of its own. There is no dispute that a company is a separate *persona*, distinct from its owners and its directors. It makes use of those directors' decision-making skills and power. But its *corporate* actions are its own; it is neither possible

---

[14] There are other ways than liquidation in which the assets of a company can be extracted into the hands of its shareholders. We will look at these in chapters 13 and 14 below.

nor correct to regard it as if it were transparent – as if what it did was no more than the actions taken in common by a body of separate owners, taking advice from an overlapping body of individuals giving that advice as directors, but again merely advising in common. A bee in a swarm achieves individual and collective action with that kind of unanimity of purpose and result with all her sisters; but humans need to strip the individual of specific rights and obligations, and *invest* (in both senses) them in a separate entity if that entity is thereafter to operate as effectively as the new colony of bees.

1.22 Corporate governance

Those who run General Motors, or any other US company, tend to be referred to as its *officers* rather than it directors. Although some of those officers may have seats on the board, the majority of the directors tend to be non-executives whose role is broadly that of shareholder representatives.

In recent years there have been many cases in which officers' actions (this is not directed at General Motors) were clearly detrimental to the interests of the company. A straightforward illustration would be the officers who, faced with an unwanted (and job-threatening) take-over bid for their company, arranged for it:

- to borrow money in order to buy its own shares in the market, in part to try to deter the bidder by keeping the shares' price high, and in part to prevent those shares falling into his hands;

- and then by borrowing still more funds, those officers agreed in response to the bidder's *greenmail* to buy back from the bidder those shares that he had managed to acquire;

and they did all this merely to keep the control of their company out of that bidder's hands. At the end of such a battle, those officers would preside over a company:

- whose shareholders' funds had been decimated by the purchases of its own shares, but saddled instead with very large levels of debt taken on for those purposes;

- whose share price had declined dramatically, in part because of the bidder's withdrawal, but also in recognition of the company's parlous financial state, as described above;

- were it not for that fall in share price, it might be possible to envisage that the company could turn back the clock, by a rights issue of shares the proceeds of which could be used to repay borrowings. In the harsh, real world such an issue is unlikely to be feasible in a collapsed market – which could only respond by collapsing still further.

There will of course be more factors than this that need to be weighed in the balance, but at the most basic level the officers' job-preservation would appear to have imperilled both the company's health and the shareholders' wealth.

1.23 *Divergence of interests of the company and its directors*

In the UK, the ways in which the interests of directors can diverge from those of the company and/or those of its owners may be less dramatically apparent and less likely to jeopardise the company's very existence; but that does not mean that there are no such divergences.

It has certainly been said, for instance, that dubious (creative) accounting techniques have been employed by a number of boards; and the suspicion must be that some part of the motivation may have been either or both of

- job-protection by directors who needed *success* to be written across the face of the company's profit and loss account, to make the directors' own high earnings less unpalatable to shareholders, and to keep the share price up to deter bidders;

- a high share price is an overall motivation for management, particularly so in those companies with share option or incentive schemes for employees; this makes the directors' task of running the company less onerous than it might be with a less encouraged management team. All of this enables one to assume that the directors may have had other factors in mind than merely the values of their own options.

Choice of such inappropriate accounting techniques was laid, in that preceding paragraph, at the door of the directors, without criticism also being made of the auditors. That does reflect the prime legal position in sections 226 and 233 Companies Act 1985. It is the directors who have responsibility for preparation of the accounts, for signing them, and presenting them to the members of the company at the annual meeting.[15] The auditors' responsibility for reporting whether they show

---

[15] The general rule stated above relates to what might be called the accounts for members. Directors can avoid the full requirements set out in two cases: a listed plc is permitted to send only summary financial statements rather than full accounts to those shareholders who choose to have only the former (section 251 Companies Act 1985); and a private company can dispense with the need for laying accounts at a general meeting, but not with the requirement to send them to members (section 252 Companies Act 1985).

Note the exemptions in section 246 and schedule 8 to Companies Act 1985 permit small and medium sized companies to file 'abbreviated' accounts with the Companies' Registrar, but do not exempt the companies concerned from preparing 'full' accounts for their members. Both forms are 'statutory accounts' (paragraph 10(2) of schedule 8) and the auditors' report on the abbreviated accounts is required both to confirm the company's entitlement to file such accounts and to repeat the full wording of their report on the full accounts (paragraphs 8(2) and (3) of schedule 8). Please see the comments in Note 18 below with regard to the compliance of small and medium companies' accounts with *Accounting Standards*.

continued

THE AUDITOR'S ROLE

'a true and fair view' obviously should enable those auditors to require the figures and the presentation to be changed if the directors' view is unsatisfactory.

1.24 The auditors' role

The Companies Act requires auditors to report to the members of a company whether its accounts show a true and fair view of its position at the date of those accounts, and of the profit or loss for the period to that date.[16] They must also form a view on various other specified matters, but are only required to report on any shortcomings, and can remain silent if matters are acceptable:

- whether they have been given all the information and explanations necessary for the purposes of their audit;

- whether proper books and accounts have been kept, and the accounts are in agreement with those books;

- whether the information in the directors' report is consistent with the accounts;

- whether the disclosures of earnings and benefits of directors are correct (if they are not, the auditors should supply the information required by the Act).

It is easiest to comment on those requirements, and on what can and cannot be expected of auditors, by starting from a quite different direction. The uncovering of fraud does not figure directly in that explanation of responsibilities; however an auditor would say it was an integral part of his duties to examine the company's *internal controls*, these being the checks and balances in its system of accounting for its operations designed to ensure that what the books show is complete and accurate. One part of such internal controls could be the supervision by managers of the parts of the work done by each of their subordinates, including the methods available (and used) by them to *prove* one person's work by reference to another's figures, and to satisfy themselves about any unexpected answers the system may throw up. Well designed and implemented internal controls are the best deterrent against fraud; if fraud does neverthless occur, it must almost by definition involve collusion between members of staff (and probably at least one manager)

---

continued
   This book does not attempt to cover the Companies Act provisions (mainly in schedule 4 to the Act) which prescribe what *full* accounts should contain, nor the permitted abbreviations referred to (in schedule 8 to the Act), for which the reader is referred to those provisions or the standard texts on the subject. However, what the exemptions in schedule 8 do clearly indicate is how fallacious it is to assume that full availability to the public of all financial information is still a part of the *price* payable by all companies for the privilege of their owners' limited liability.

[16] Sections 235 to 237 Companies Act 1985.

to subvert these controls. Although direct investigation does not always, at least immediately, uncover determined, sophisticated fraud of this kind, it is frequently uncovered by indirect methods, such as changing the individuals doing particular jobs, or even ensuring that they take holidays. The other indirect method is to insist that management investigate in depth those business areas achieving results consistently below expectations.

1.25 *Auditors' client relationships*

The fact that it has never been realistic to imagine an auditor's prime function as uncovering fraud has been expressed by describing auditors as the watchdogs of commerce, not the bloodhounds.[17] After acting as watchdogs they can have no difficulty over the question whether they have been given all the information and explanations they needed; they are of course also well placed to report to the company's members on the accuracy and completeness of the books, and of the accounts prepared from them. They will also know how consistent is the directors' report, and how accurate the disclosure of their earnings. But all these are ancillary to the question whether the accounts show a true and fair view.

Auditors admit that there are two weaknesses in their position, which can all too easily give rise to weaknesses in the way they discharge their central function:

- they are appointed and their fees are fixed by the company's membership only in theory; in practice it is the company's management which does this. The main value seen by management in the audit function is having the auditor, as an independent professional, examine the working of the company's internal controls, and probably also interpret some aspects of the business's results which management itself may not previously have appreciated;

- there is no direct guidance in the Companies Act on the meaning of the 'true and fair view'. Although accounting standards now have statutory force,[18] the Act does not require in so many words that a

---

[17] Per Lopes J, in *Re Kingston Cotton Mill Co. (No. 2)* [1896] 2 Ch. 279 (CA) at 288.

[18] By SI 1990 No. 1667 made under section 256(1) Companies Act 1985, the Accounting Standards Board was prescribed as a standard issuing body. Its immediate action, on 24 August 1990, was to issue under the Act all 22 extant *Statements of Standard Accounting Practice* (SSAPs) which had previously been issued, on a non-statutory basis, by the six accountancy bodies. Since then the Accounting Standards Board has issued further *Financial Reporting Standards* (FRSs) under the Act. Its foreword to these standards, under the heading 'Scope', says that 'accounting standards are applicable to financial statements ... that are intended to give a true and fair view ...', which appears to indicate their applicability to all accounts of all companies. The general thrust seems to be that wherever standards lay down rules for profit recognition, and for accounting measurement, these shoud be observed by all companies. Disclosure requirements, on the other hand, have in at least some instances
continued

company's accounts must comply with them, nor does it say that non-compliance will be one and the same as an untrue and unfair view. There is merely a very strong view[19] that that is how the Act would be interpreted were a case to come before the courts. The Act does specifically require disclosure in the accounts where a company has not complied with applicable standards, the reasons for non-compliance, and what the figures would have been had it done so.[20]

It is not hard to see that the first of these points will encourage an auditor trying to maintain and enhance his client relationship and fees to think that his client is management – rather than the company's membership to whom he owes his prime legal duty. And it is this *closeness* of management and auditors which can too easily exacerbate the second point, as an example can illustrate.

The accounts

1.26 *The requirement to display equity and veracity*

A hire purchase company's business can be described as essentially that of providing money for its customers' purchases (let us assume entirely cars), that money being repaid by the customers in instalments with interest through the term of each deal. That is a simplification of the *substance* of the business, and does not pretend to explain the legal *form*; there is no true loan of money, but there is a car which belongs to the hire purchase company until each transaction is completed (although at some point in the course of the hiring the company largely loses its right to repossess that car).

But there are two factors clearly visible to the hire purchase company's management. In each deal, most of its own work is done at the start and

---

continued
   been treated as less essential, so that small companies are exempted from preparing the cashflow statement in FRS 1, and companies up to ten times that size have exemption from some of the disclosures of research and development and segmental results in SSAPs 13 and 25.
[19] Leonard Hoffmann QC and Miss Mary Arden (as they then were) said in a joint opinion in 1983:
   'the value of a SSAP to a court which has to decide whether accounts are true and fair is two-fold. First, it represents an important statement of professional opinion about the standards which readers may reasonably expect in accounts which are intended to be true and fair ... Secondly, because accountants are professionally obliged to comply with a SSAP, it creates in the readers an expectation that the accounts will be in conformity with the prescribed standards. This is in itself a reason why accounts which depart from the standard without adequate justification or explanation may be held not to be true and fair.'
[20] Paragraph 36A of schedule 4 to Companies Act 1985. The small and medium sized companies referred to in section 246 Companies Act 1985 (see Note 14) are exempted from this disclosure, but that does not mean that they are exempted from compliance with the standards.

little through the rest of the period; and the finance provided at the start reduces progressively as the hiring proceeds. Let us suppose, therefore, that the company's directors take the view that 90 per cent of the expected profit from each deal should be recognised in the company's accounts for the period in which the deal concerned was signed up. No legislation forbids them from taking this stance, and although there is an accounting standard which most people would read as deprecating it, it does not actually prevent it.

It does not take any very great accounting skills or knowledge to see that the outcome of the directors' view in a period of increasing volumes of business written by the company concerned is that its profit figures for each successive year will increase even faster than that volume. But as soon as the economy turns down, with fewer people buying new cars, and some of those with existing deals failing to keep up their payments, it is not hard to see that a hire purchase company with its own high levels of borrowing from its own bank is likely to show significant losses in its accounts within a very short time.

The auditors may well have believed throughout that the directors' accounting method was unwise, perhaps even undesirable; but the directors had fully accepted the necessity that the accounts spell out exactly how profits were being recognised – that is what they had put into the accounting policy note in the accounts.

1.27 *Auditors' sanction for the only-slightly-imprudent company*

So the question remains, was the view shown in the accounts *untrue and unfair*, or was it acceptable on the basis of the accounting policies spelled out? One could, slightly unfairly, put an analogous question as follows: if you see *Hamlet* from the gods, your viewpoint will be less ideal (and less expensive) compared with the person who is sitting in the middle of the stalls or the front of the circle. But is *Hamlet* any less true? Is it impossible to obtain a *fair* view from anywhere other than the best seats? And is the off-centre, distorted, view from the gods the same thing as an *untrue and unfair view*? If the accounting policy note tells the user of the accounts where you were sitting, should he not be able to make allowances when you tell him that the ghost was audible but not visible – he would appreciate that a ghost on the battlements, and any other player at the back of the stage, would be hidden from the gods by the proscenium arch.

To come back to the direct question of the truth and fairness of the hire purchase company's accounts, one could give an indirect answer as follows: the accounting standard SSAP 2 requires that *prudence* be one of the policies used in preparing accounts. If the directors were being *imprudent* in choosing their policy, they should have admitted that fact in the accounting policy note, because they were failing to comply with an applicable accounting standard. But being prudent or not is a matter of degree; the directors would say that they were not imprudent, or if they were, they were only very slightly imprudent. The auditors' sanction of putting a qualification in their report or withholding any report is generally seen by the public as meaning that the directors must have been so imprudent that the company will fail tomorrow – even though tomorrow is still in a period of boom and expansion, and there is no reason for expecting over-borrowing to be instantly lethal unless the company persists in that course, and in foolhardy trading generally, into a slump.

1.28 *Auditors' persuasive powers*

What auditors ought to be able to do is the two-fold task of always making sound decisions about what is exactly true and fair (erring neither towards over-prudence nor imprudence) and, second, always being able to persuade the directors of their client companies of the virtue of the auditors' judgments, and how unsafe those directors' judgments are in comparison. In the real world, some auditors are not supermen; some judge it wrongly, and some may get that right but fail to be persuasive enough with the clients' directors.

The illustration on which we have been focusing has concentrated on one judgment area in which there might be a reasonably broad consensus that the directors might have taken an unrealistically optimistic view.

1.29 *Auditors' judgment, and generally accepted accounting principles*

It has to be borne in mind, however, that there are other areas about which there is little dispute among accountants and directors, but where the end result might seem odd to the visitor from Mars. If, for instance, a company incurs a considerable amount of expense on market research and marketing, it would normally write it off as it incurred it. We might picture the expenditure being both incurred and written off in 1993. That means that it is the profits being earned from the goods being sold in 1993 that are reduced.

Picture, however, the normal pattern of events in which the company's 1993 research related to a new product which would not start to be produced and sold until 1994 at the earliest; and that the research did in fact show encouraging prospects, so that the marketing expenditure was also laid out in the course of 1993, and was designed to develop a space in the marketplace from which the company's sales would benefit for at least the years 1994 to 1996. It is undeniably *prudent* to write off the expenditure in 1993; but does it show *a true and fair view* of the profits made in 1994 to 1996 from the sale of this new product? Or does it over-state those profits at the expense of those derived in 1993 from a quite different product?

In a steady-state company, incurring similar levels of expenditure of this type each year and bringing a similar number of new products to market each year, there is obviously no overall distortion. But the fast expanding company could be deferring the recognition of its profits, and the contracting company accelerating it. How true and fair is this? A company which stops all market research and marketing will report an increase in its profits in the short term, compared with what would otherwise have been the case; does this make any sense?

The one thing that can always be said to be true is that accounts and accounting are always judgmental, and equally that they are always complex. One has to work hard at the task of understanding what a company's accounts can tell one about it and its results – and it is seldom that one can get all the information one needs out of a single year's accounts.

1.30 What the owners, and others, get out of the company

We headed paragraph 1.21 *The company and its owners set apart*, and in that and subsequent paragraphs we have been looking at the company as such a separate entity, carrying on its own business and making its own profits from doing so.

We can perhaps liken this company to a tank whose contents are fed, and whose water level is increased, by the profits flowing in; but at the same time, we know perfectly well that the tank has various pipes coming out of it, through which what would otherwise have been the company's retentions are drained off to its owners and others. Each of these outlets has its different implications for the company and for the recipient, and we need to have some understanding what these are:

- repayment by the company of loans previously advanced to it by its owner is a method of extracting cash from the company without tax effects on repayer or recipient;

- the company can return to shareholders amounts previously subscribed as share capital in one of three ways. Redeemable shares can be redeemed; shares can in certain cases be purchased from a particular shareholder by the company; and the company can be put into liquidation, the final stage of which for a solvent company would comprise the distribution of its surplus assets among its shareholders. Each of these has different tax implications for company and shareholder, and each is a complex procedure, only permitted to a company under strict conditions. That complexity suggests that it is inappropriate to do more here than mention the possibilities. Examining what is involved in share redemptions and in company purchases of own shares must be held over to chapter 13, and we do not deal in any depth, in this book, with liquidation procedures;

- payment by the company of interest on borrowings;

- payment of dividends;

- payment of salaries, commissions and bonuses, and/or directors' fees.

1.31 *Tax assumptions*

We can briefly compare the effect on the company of the last three of those types of payment if we show how much the company needs to pay out, pre- and post-tax, in order to put £10,000 into the hands of a recipient individual. We assume he is entitled to the single person's allowance of £3,445, and pays tax on the next £3,000 of his income at the lower rate of 20 per cent, before reaching the 25 per cent basic rate.

When the company pays earnings we assume that they are fully deductible in its corporation tax computation;[21] we also assume in this case that it is the individual who is paying his own pension contribution into a personal pension scheme;[22] finally, in the calculations relating to earnings, we assume that the employer and the individual pay full national insurance contributions.[23]

Table 4 in the next paragraph summarises the results.

---

[21] The *abnormal* cases in which a deduction may not be allowed to the company for earnings include excessive earnings paid by an owner-managed investment company; earnings paid to family members whose contribution to the company's activities, and responsibility level, cannot justify the amounts paid; and remuneration, including compensation for loss of office, paid to a company's owners at the time at which they sell the company, see paragraphs 11.29 to 11.31.

[22] There are three regimes under which a pension could be provided. So far as the company's corporation tax is concerned, each of the three types of payment it could make would be fully deductible (although in exceptional cases of large *catch-up* contributions there may be a need to spread the deduction over a number of years). If the company contributed to an occupational scheme, the funds it paid in would not be regarded as the employee's pay for any purpose, that is to say, he would not be taxed on them as if they were earnings, neither he nor the employer would pay NIC on them, and if his pension were calculated on his final salary, the employer's contributions would not be counted into that. The second regime is the occupational scheme which is *contributory*, that is to say, the employee is required to make contributions alongside those of the employer. So far as tax is concerned the position is the same, but for NIC purposes amounts paid to the employee as earnings which he pays into the scheme *are* treated as his earnings, and therefore cost him and the employer extra NIC; they are also counted into his salary, and this may be relevant not only for calculating pension, but for calculating the maximum contributions he is allowed to pay. The third regime is the one assumed here, namely the personal pensions route, under which whatever the employer pays is treated in the first instance as earnings in the employee's hands, and fully subject to tax and NIC accordingly. However, if *he* pays an amount into a personal pension scheme, he is allowed to pay that contribution *net*, and the scheme recovers the tax from the authorities. Effectively therefore he gets tax relief for his contribution (and can get further relief if he is taxed at the higher rate rather than the basic rate) but there is no relief from NIC. In the example in paragraph 1.32 the employee's gross earnings are £12,634; the gross pension contribution allowable at 17½ per cent of that is £2,211, and the net amount the employee hands over to his personal pension scheme is £1,659.

[23] He is not *contracted out* of the state earnings related pension scheme (SERPS); there are two possible ways in which he could have been contracted out. The first is through an occupational pension scheme of his employer's, in which case the amounts paid by both employer and himself as NIC are reduced, but the employer's scheme undertakes to pay an enlarged pension to replace the lost SERPS, and therefore needs to be fed with enlarged contributions in order to do so. The second form of contracting out is by the individual himself, through a (separate) personal pension scheme; he and his employer continue to pay full NIC, but a part of those contributions (together with a tax relief element and a premium) are refunded direct by the Department of Social Security to the personal pension scheme, and this again undertakes to pay a pension to replace the individual's SERPS.

1.32 Table 4: Pre-tax Cost to Company of Individual's Net Benefit of £10,000

	Earnings	Interest	Dividend
Pre-tax cost to company		11,985	12,415
individual's earnings	12,634		
employer's NIC	1,314		
	13,948		
less tax at *small companies* 25%	3,487	2,996	3,104
Post-tax	10,461	8,989	9,311
Cash rec'd by individual from company			
under deduction of basic rate[24]		8,989	
with tax credit at 20%			9,311
net salary paid in cash	9,447		
Add repayment of personal allowance			
£3,445 at 25%		861	
£3,445 at 20%			689
£3,000 at 25 less 20%		150	
	9,447	10,000	10,000
Deduct net amount paid to personal			
pension scheme	1,658		
	7,789		
Add amount received into pension			
scheme as above	1,658		
Tax refund made to it by			
Inland Revenue	553	2,211	
	10,000	10,000	10,000
Tax and other amounts paid and not recoverable:			
individual's personal tax		1,985	1,639
individual's PAYE	2,148		
less refunded to pension			
scheme as above	553	1,595	
individual's NIC		1,039	
employer's NIC		1,314	
corporation tax not imputed to			
shareholder			776
Pre-tax cost to the company	13,948	11,985	12,415

[24] A company making a payment of *annual interest* is required to deduct and account for basic rate tax (section 349(2)(a) ICTA 1988). The *pre-tax cost* to the company of £11,985 is the aggregate of the net cash it pays to the lender of £8,989 and the basic rate tax on that sum, £2,996, which it pays over to the Inland Revenue. It is only the coincidence that the small companies' rate of corporation tax is equal to the basic rate of income tax which results in the company's corporation tax relief on its gross interest being equal to the income tax it has paid on the lender's behalf. The individual recipient claims tax repayments (in this case) so that the first £3,445 of this income suffers no tax, and the next £3,000 pays tax at 20 per cent.

1.33 Dividends

Conventional wisdom, and conventional accounting, say that a dividend is an appropriation of profits once earned, not an expense incurred in the earning of those profits. Therefore a company which made a pre-tax profit of £12,415 would show its tax liability on that as being corporation tax at the 25 per cent rate amounting to £3,104. That would leave it with £9,311 of post-tax profits, and it could, if its directors so wished, pay the whole of that out to its shareholders as a (net) dividend. That is precisely how the accounts do show a dividend, as a net amount taken out of post-tax profits.

The imputation system (in the form in which it has operated since the March 1993 Budget changes) treats an amount equal to 20/80ths of the dividend – being part of the tax burden of the company – as *imputed* to the shareholder; his dividend receipt carries with it a *tax credit*, available to satisfy his own tax liability on that dividend. And his liability on dividends, unless his income exceeds £23,700, is only 20 per cent, not the basic rate of 25 per cent.

Therefore, if we draw up a profit and loss account for the company which shifts the *imputed* tax away from the company, and onto the shoulders of the shareholder, the result would be as shown in Table 5.[25]

Table 5: Profit and Loss Account

	Small company	Full rate
Pre-tax profits	12,415	1,241,500
Corporation tax which cannot be imputed to shareholder		
6.25%	776	
16.25%		201,744
Gross dividend	11,639	1,039,756
Net dividend	9,311	831,805
Tax credit, being corporate tax[26] imputed to shareholder	2,328	207,951
Total tax, 25% of 12,415	3,104	
33% of 1,241,500	—	409,695

---

[25] See the explanation in paragraph 1.34 below why there are advantages, in the context of the explanations in this book, for treating dividends as not simply taxable in the shareholders' hands, but as deductible in the company's computation.

[26] Setting out the figures in a profit and loss account format, whether in the normal pattern or in our variant shown here, does not make it obvious how, and when, the tax is paid. The *advance corporation tax* on the dividend (the same figure as is imputed as tax credit to the shareholder, respectively £2,328 and £207,951) is paid after the end of the calendar quarter in which the dividend is paid. Corporation tax of respectively £3,104 and £409,695, (25 per cent and 33 per cent of profits) would be payable on the due date for the company's liabilities; but it is only the balance of these figures, £776 and £201,744 which remain to be paid at that time.

1.34 ACT; *effects of imputing part of company's tax so that it is treated as shareholder tax*

Looking first at the small companies' column in Table 5, one can see that the aggregate of the company's tax, £3,104, has been reallocated so as to be regarded as

```
  6.25 %  of pre-tax £12,415 =     776
 18.75 %  of pre-tax £12,415 =   2,328 = 20/80ths of net div £9,311
 25.00 %                         3,104
```

However, we have explained without yet having justified our approach of regarding tax imputed to the shareholder as *his* tax, and not as being any part of the company's liability or burden. It is not the way the company reflects its results in its profit and loss account — but one can easily see why it chooses to do things differently. What it, and those who analyse its accounts in order to compare its figures with those of other companies, want to see is a pre-tax figure which is comparable between companies and between years in each company, and also tax charges which are similarly comparable. This would not be possible if the tax charge were an amalgam of 25 per cent of part of the profits and 6.25 per cent of the remainder.

The reason why we need a different approach is that we are looking at our companies as machines generating shareholder returns. The only effective way of comparing (across all shareholders exempt and taxable, across all companies, and all years) the total of the returns in distributed form (dividends) and those not distributed (increases in the company's earning power from retentions and other causes) is to look at shareholders' entitlements in gross terms.

In the next chapter, we will show the relationships (in theory and also in practice) between

- dividends, which the small company is able on our basis to distribute after having paid only 6.25 per cent *company tax*;

- retentions, which are retained only after suffering 25 per cent company tax; and

- the increase in the level of dividends, stemming from those retentions. Although the *capital* retained in this way has itself suffered 25 per cent tax, those earnings from it which form the increase in dividend levels suffer only 6.25 per cent.

1.35 *Offset of ACT against the company's mainstream tax*

The tabulation in paragraph 1.33 and our explanation why it is rational and necessary for our purposes in this book do nothing to help us to see two particular features of the imputation system. (The profit and loss account format also obscures these points.)

First, whenever one is considering the off-setting of advance corporation tax (ACT), one must be clear which ACT one is setting against which mainstream tax. If we assume that the profit and loss figures set out above are those for 1994, it is probable that the whole (or at least some) of the dividend shown as payable out of that year's profits will actually be *paid* in 1995; its ACT will be off-settable against mainstream tax to be charged on the 1995 profits. Where this is relevant, one would expect to find a corresponding overlap at the beginning of the year – some or all of the dividend shown as payable out of the 1993 profits will actually have been paid during 1994; it is the ACT on the 1994 dividend payments that one sets off against the 1994 corporation tax figure shown above of £409,695 (£201,744 plus £207,951).

The second sidelight on the figures comes from the 1993 Budget changes. If the company is liable only at the small companies' rate, that means retentions are taxed at 25 per cent while distributed profits pay only 6.25 per cent in the company's hands; the shareholder receives a dividend which has a tax credit of 20 per cent of gross (20/80ths of the net dividend). But one needs to follow this through – those shareholders liable to tax at the higher rate must pay a further 20 per cent in order to make up their full 40 per cent tax liability. Those who are exempt from tax, primarily the pension funds, are able to recover only 20 per cent – the 6.25 per cent (or 16.25 per cent) sticks to the Chancellor's fingers.

But there are two further aspects which we will examine in chapter 5, at paragraphs 5.8 to 5.13 and in the related Notes, namely the workings of the rules under which ACT can be set against corporation tax liabilities, and the restrictions built into these rules. Also the ways in which the figures can be fitted together if the distributable profits in the company's accounts differ from the post-tax amount of those profits on which it has paid corporation tax.

CHAPTER 2

VALUE

2.1 Values at three levels

Value is a deceptively simple word, but one which seems to have as many meanings as there are people pontificating. What renders the discussions in this chapter more complex than would otherwise be the case is that we must recognise that there are three separate levels at which values need to be considered:

- the values to the company of its assets;
- the value of the company as a company;
- the value to the shareholders (and other providers of finance) of their interests in the company.

If there is a single shareholder, owning the company in its entirety, the second and third values may be closely related, if not identical. In all other cases, we will see that values at the different levels are almost totally unrelated.

What we need to understand are the principles which determine these different values, and to understand why their relationships are so tenuous. Fitting all the factors together is undoubtedly an art, but many of the individual principles are economic, and can be expressed as theorems which have an application for all companies.

2.2 *Values within the company*

Let us begin on the company's balance sheet. It shows, among other things, some of the company's fixed assets – its plant and its buildings, for instance. It is unlikely to show one very real asset, the goodwill the company has built up among its customers; it is equally unlikely to put a value on a number of other intangibles, such as know-how, patents, or the values of *brands*. We can bring out the relevant points about asset values, however, by concentrating on buildings.

If buildings were acquired or constructed some considerable time ago, the *carrying value* at which they are shown on the balance sheet may be low, because *historical costs* were low by comparison with costs expressed in present day, inflated, money. Buildings acquired more recently, at the top of a property boom which has since painfully collapsed, may have a *cost* greater than could now be realised from their sale. And there is a third possibility, namely that the company's buildings may have been recently *revalued*.

2.3 Carrying values and historic costs

Each of those emphasised words and phrases has a particular meaning for accountants who prepare balance sheets; accountants would hope that the words would be understood in those same senses by the users of those balance sheets. Carrying value, for instance, is designed to convey only a neutral message – that the balance-sheet figure is specifically not claimed to represent any of the *real* values that could be attributed to the asset. The more significant two among the such *real* figures would be value to the business, and realisable value. One could illustrate the difference between these, perhaps, by considering the premises of a retailer who sells saddlery, clothing and other requisites to the equestrian fraternity, and also sells fodder for horses. His premises have always been close to the town centre, and what has happened recently is that that centre has been enclosed by a ring road, and pedestrianised. Because space is at a premium within the ring, and his shop with its yard behind it could be redeveloped for a considerably larger shop (perhaps with offices or a hotel above it), its market or realisable value has increased. On the other hand, the existing premises' value to the saddlery business is, if anything, reduced since few of the former customers find it convenient to park outside the ring road and therefore to have to carry sacks of oats and bran a considerable distance back to their Range Rovers.

Our retail saddler is carrying on a business which is a going concern.[1] Ideally his accounts should reflect a figure for the premises' value in the context of the business for which he is using them, that is to say, a value in line with what another retail saddler would think it appropriate to pay for premises from which to carry on a similar business. That suggests that a fifty-year-old *historical cost* would not have much merit; and nor would the price that a developer would be willing to pay to turn those premises into something completely different. It is the value in his own business which must be of greater significance if our particular retailer is intending to stay in business in the same place.

2.4 Historic costs included in accounts, and the different concept of accounts prepared on historic cost principles

However, there are three specific points (and a much broader general implication in the next paragraph), all of which follow from the discussion above:

- one of the meanings of historical cost is the one we have so far used, that is to say, the cost of acquisition of a particular asset at some date in history. A second meaning is that used in paragraphs 16 to 28 of

---

[1] The going concern concept, the first of the four fundamental accounting concepts in *Statement of Standard Accounting Practice No. 2*, was referred to in paragraph 1.17 and Note 9 thereto.

schedule 4 to the Companies Act 1985. Those paragraphs describe a method of accounting based on all assets being carried in the accounts at original costs (with the exception that any permanent *diminution* in value must be reflected by a provision reducing that original cost). This is in contrast to the *alternative accounting rules* in paragraphs 29 to 34 of the same schedule, which envisage revaluations to market value or current cost;[2]

• although that previous point would appear to indicate that any company's accounts must be framed either wholly on historical costs, or wholly using revaluations, this does not happen in practice. Many companies use historical costs for most assets, but periodically revalue their properties. The accounting policy notes in their accounts make it clear that those accounts are prepared on an historical cost basis, subject to certain assets being shown at revalued amounts;

• that point leads to the third, which is that whether to revalue, what to revalue, and how often to revalue should all be questions on which a business has a policy which users of its accounts can ascertain. If that policy is to revalue only when and to the extent that the result will prove flattering, it cannot be said that this is particularly meritorious.

2.5 Revaluations: to a value to the business, or to a realisable value

The last word in that last point brings us face to face with the most important point about asset valuations. We have noted that it would be unusual for the revaluations to be an attempt by the business to show

---

[2] The Companies Act 1985 does not define the terms market value and current cost. Neither is governed by any operative SSAP or FRS. (The proposed standard relating to market value has not yet progressed beyond the stage of an exposure draft, ED51; the standard on current costing, SSAP 16, was withdrawn for lack of support.) It is possible to give some explanation in the following general terms.

There is guidance on methods of arriving at market value in *Statements of Asset Valuation Practice* issued by the Royal Institution of Chartered Surveyors. Within the general concept of an open market value, it is recognised that the valuation may be on the basis of existing use, an alternative use, or a forced sale. No particular comment is called for on the existing use value of a saddlery business, but there are certain other types of business, hotels and licensed premises being the principal examples, where the premises' value normally includes *trading potential*. It is not always easy to separate the potential of the premises from the goodwill built up by a particular occupant. The RICS notes that the alternative use value would not normally be a satisfactory basis to include in the accounts of a going concern whose value in existing use was lower, but where the business had no intention of selling the premises. The forced sale value seems only likely to be appropriate in those cases where premises must be sold without an opportunity to hold on to them long enough to ensure the best price is obtained.

Current cost was (rather than is) an entire concept of accounting, under which assets were to be valued at the lower of net current replacement cost and their *recoverable amount*, the latter being the higher of net realisable value and an extremely subjective concept described as *value in use*. We return to this concept in paragraph 4.19.

what its assets would produce on a total break-up (that is, we do not believe they are the open market values for any available alternative uses); the implication is therefore that the business does regard its accounts and the revaluations they contain as having some other merit, as having another use; and the context for this would appear to be the view of the business as a going concern. The kinds of questions users of accounts prepared on this basis expect to be able to answer are: do the trading results provide an adequate return on the capital employed? How does this business's answer to that question compare with the answer which its competitor gets to the same question?

The answers to comparative questions are only valid when one is comparing like with like; in this example, when the accounts avoid the distortions which would arise if this, or the competitor's, business were to compare current trading results with asset values which came from an entirely different era and framework of costs.

In each of this and the previous two paragraphs, there is an implication that revaluation to a *value to the business* is, like 1066, *a good thing*, while any other approach is not (this might facetiously be described as a value judgment). Where revaluations which reflect the values of assets to the businesses have some merit is solely that internally consistent figures within a set of accounts allow a greater degree of reliance to be placed on ratios; and consistency across different businesses allows comparisons to be made.[3] If all you are trying to do is to count pounds and pence, then asset values are irrelevant.

That makes it obvious that a sensible revaluation policy will help investors, parent companies, predators, analysts and any others looking at the company from the outside; the company and its own management may not see such a policy as quite so necessary.

2.6 Current costs

It would be inappropriate to spend too much time on a system of accounting which has ceased to be required or recommended, but there is one particular aspect of it which is worthy of examination.

Assume that a company's activities involve it carrying a reasonably high level of stocks. An oil company which buys oil from fields in the Middle East would probably sell that oil only two months later if all its sales were in Europe. On an historical cost basis of accounting, the profits it makes on its April sales are calculated by deducting the costs

---

[3] The comparisons we are discussing here are comparisons of asset values, and asset-based ratios. It is noteworthy that the Accounting Standards Board, in its statement FRS 3 (paragraph 26), requires companies to disclose by way of note the amount of their profits on an 'unmodified historical cost basis' if this is materially different from the profit shown in their accounts – and explains the primary purpose of this as being 'to present the profits of entities that have revalued their assets on a more comparable basis with those that have not'. This is a matter which we will have to discuss and analyse in chapter 4.

it incurred in February in acquiring the oil concerned[4] (together with the costs incurred between February and April in shipping and refining it, but for simplicity let us leave those out of account).

However, if the cost price of oil in the Middle East has doubled between February and April, this company's *historical cost* profits in its April accounts can be strongly argued to be misleading. Unless the company puts up its April selling price, its cash realised in that month will only enable it to buy a lesser volume of the higher-cost April oil in the Middle East; and unless it widens its margins again when it sells those April acquisitions in Europe in June, it will only be able to buy still smaller volumes of the oil whose cost has again gone up in the Middle East between April and June.

Current costing was designed to overcome this problem, by ensuring that it would, in these circumstances, have been the replacement cost price of oil in April which was deducted from the April sales proceeds in arriving at the April profits; that the historical cost of oil in February did not enter into the equation.

There is a good deal more to current costing[5] than that, but we might say that this particular feature of the system could be dealt with (without any other adjustment to the accounts) simply by treating stocks on a last-in, first-out basis. Each month's purchases through to April are debited into a stock account, but when a figure has to be taken out of that account to be matched in the profit and loss account with the April sales, it is the *April* costs which are taken out, not the February costs.

2.7 *The pool of unexpired costs*

If this were the method used to deal with the *cost of stock consumed* in the profit and loss account, the *number* which remains in the stock

---

[4] In the course of the 1973 and 1977 oil shocks, the extra profits shown by the oil companies on an historic cost basis were referred to as 'stock profits'. (The companies' historic cost accounts deducted the lower-level, actual, costs of oil from the later, increased-level, sales prices of the same oil, since the companies had increased their selling prices in order to be able to finance their unchanged volumes at the higher costs prevailing after the shocks.) The terminology now favoured by the Accounting Standards Board, and illustrated by it in reference to oil companies during the Gulf War, is 'holding gains (or losses)', which the Board differentiates from 'trading margins'.

[5] There are two distinct accounting methods for *capital maintenance*, that is to say, for excluding the effects of changing prices when measuring a business's capital and its ability to earn profits. Current cost accounting was the approach which the Government required the accounting profession to develop in the 1970s, and it is this approach which is still enshrined in the phraseology of section C of schedule 4 to the Companies Act 1985. As can be seen from the example, it seeks to maintain the business's *physical capital*, defined here as its ability to continue a particular volume of turnover. The other method, current purchasing power accounting, seeks to maintain a *financial capital* by excluding general inflation. Our illustrative oil company can be seen to have used a CCA approach to take out the (sterling) difference in the cost of oil between February and April. Under CPP the adjustment would have been a (sterling) inflation measurement for that period, regardless of the fact that movements in oil prices and in inflation were quite different.

account in the balance sheet is no more than a residue of costs; it is not necessarily related in any direct way to any one or more month's acquisitions – and particularly not to any recent month's acquisitions. For the reasons which we have made clear in the course of this explanation, there are valid arguments that the profit and loss figures are more informative when arrived at on this basis; the argument is overwhelming if one believes that there should be a direct relationship between cash generation and profit; profits *must* in that case be calculated on a *current cost basis* in a period of substantial changes in cost levels.

But at the same time, the *pool of unexpired costs* which is all that the stock-in-trade number would be in the balance sheet can be criticised[6] as having no significance – even of being untrue and unfair.

There are arguments in either direction. What we need is to understand what those arguments are, and what significance (or lack of it) the accounting figures may have if derived on any of the different principles we have looked at in this and the previous two paragraphs. We commenced this discussion of *values within* the company by thinking about the premises on its balance sheet; we have rapidly progressed to the *values within* the company of the stocks on its balance sheet – and we have been considering at the same time the way in which reported profits will be different if the company uses different approaches to its accounting for stocks.

2.8 Maintainable profits

It is those profits that are the more important key to the next levels of values to which we need to turn; it is the company's ability to earn profits that underpins its value as a company, and the values of the shares in it which its shareholders own.

The asset and liability figures which it shows on its balance sheet may have a degree of consistency with its profits; or, despite their all being denominated in pounds and pence, they may in fact be as different as apples and oranges. Even if there is a degree of consistency (the pounds are all today's pounds, and each asset is looked at in its present context rather than in some quite different one) ratios and comparisons still need to be handled with extreme care. The return on capital employed, for instance, will be very different between capital-intensive manufacturing businesses and businesses relying largely on human capital (for example advertising agencies and accounting firms). Rates of return are also

---

[6] It is said, for instance, that neither this calculation of profit, nor this valuation method for stocks, is acceptable in arriving at profits for tax purposes. In a Canadian excess profits tax case which reached the Privy Council in 1955, Lord Simonds said: 'there is no room for theories as to flow of costs, nor is it legitimate to regard the closing inventory as an unabsorbed residue of cost rather than as a concrete stock of metals awaiting the day of process' (*Minister of National Revenue v Anaconda American Brass Ltd*, [1956] AC 85 at page 102).

inextricably linked to risk, and to the extent to which businesses are cyclical.

These are not only the reasons for the lack of a clear relationship between the company's assets and its value. They are also a large part of the reason why estimating the company's value is even more of an art than is the process of valuing its assets. We have obtained insights into asset values, rather than reaching any single conclusion or solution. There is no such unique answer.

But it is time to move on to think about the company's value.

2.9 Retained earnings

Let us envisage two identical companies, each of which is to be broken up a year hence. Let us then go on to envisage that one makes a post-tax profit of £1,000 during that year, reflected in its balance sheet at the break-up date by an increased cash balance; but that the other enjoys neither profit nor an increase in its cash balance.

It is rational to say that each £1 of retained earnings increases the value of the first company by £1, in comparison with the second. But that phraseology indicates the extreme narrowness of the proposition:

- it is only true when comparing the two companies. It is not true that the first company will produce £1,000 more then than it would today, or that the second will produce an unchanged amount. There are other factors which can and will change the values of each of those companies between today and the day a year hence when they are broken up. The size of the petty cash box on which the first is sitting at that time is only one of those factors;

- it is only true if the companies are to be broken up. If they continue to operate their values are wholly determined by the level of the rewards they can generate for their shareholders – a concept that we will develop through the remainder of this chapter.

But from that second point it is immediately obvious that the reward-generation capacity of the first company is greater than that of the second *only* by reference to the £1,000 the first is sitting on, and the second is not. It is the benefit that the shareholder derives thereafter from that cash, not the cash itself, that is relevant; both the shareholder's value and the company's value flow from the use of the asset, its earning power, not that asset's existence or intrinsic value.

2.10 Shareholder values

We therefore need to pick up the concepts of value for the shareholder, to evolve a method enabling us to put a present value on the company's earning power, including what it pays out by way of dividends.

The easiest way to do that is through an illustration, into which we will introduce assumptions about earnings, dividends and retentions (see Table 6). We start with dividends, and an assumption that they increase at the rate of 3.75 per cent per annum in real terms. Since we are totally accustomed to a world where inflation is as certain as death and taxes, we assume that inflation will continue to run at 3 per cent per annum. The way we will fit these figures together is to set this year's (gross) dividend at £10,000; this is not due to be paid until a year from now. The dividend in respect of the second year, payable in two years' time is:

$$£10,000 \times 1.0375 \times 1.03 = £10,686$$

These dividends are the *gross* figures, based on the assumption spelled out in paragraph 1.34 (and for the reasons there given) that that part of the tax originally paid by the company which can be imputed to the shareholder has been so imputed – and can therefore be treated for our purposes as shareholder tax.

Table 6: Shareholder Values

	Year 1	Year 2
Pre-tax profits	10,667	11,398
less corporation tax not capable of being imputed, 6.25%	667	712
	10,000	10,686
Net cash received by shareholder	8,000	8,549
Tax credit for shareholder	2,000	2,137
	10,000	10,686

When we describe a dividend as producing a specific percentage yield on an amount invested, it is the gross figure which we use for purposes of this calculation; we do not thus need to use different yield structures for taxable and tax-exempt shareholders.

2.11 *Increasing dividends*

The previous paragraph's pattern of dividends increasing in real terms may in fact be partly based on the company's growth in size and efficiency – the economies of scale, and the tighter and more effective management which the larger organisation should be able to move towards.

But the other component in the company's ability to grow on which we will focus more tightly is its retention of profit for investment in the business (see Table 7). The assumption we make here is that the the company's pre-tax profits exceed its (gross) dividend, throughout,

Table 7: Increasing Dividends

First year	Total profits	Retained profits	Dividend
Pre-tax profits	24,000	13,333	10,667
Tax at 25% and 6.25%	4,000	3,333	667
	20,000	10,000	10,000
Net dividend	8,000		8,000
Tax credit	2,000		2,000
Retention	10,000	10,000	

Second year	Total profits	Retained profits	Dividend
Pre-tax profits	25,646	14,248	11,398
Tax at 25% and 6.25%	4,274	3,562	712
	21,372	10,686	10,686
Net dividend	8,549		8,549
Tax credit	2,137		2,137
Retention	10,686	10,686	

by a factor of 2.4 times; or to put that into investment jargon, its dividend is 2.4 times covered. (In fact, this calculation is more often made on the face of the profit and loss account, where the dividend is of course shown net. An analyst would be more likely to say that the (net) dividend was covered three times.)

We will demonstrate in a moment that dividend growth at an assumed 3.75 per cent per annum is totally consistent with all our other assumptions.

2.12 The investor's yield

We need one final assumption to build into this example before we can pull all the strands together and demonstrate that they fit and make sense.

We assume that an investor in these shares would be looking for a rate of return (in real terms) of 7.5 per cent (again in real terms); since we know that the company's pre-tax profits are one fifth larger than its post-tax profits (£24,000 compared to £20,000 in the year 1 figures in Table 7) this could be translated into a pre-tax return of 9 per cent. *Rates of return* in this sense are emphatically not a single year's dividend expressed as a percentage of the sum invested by the shareholder. They are a combination of dividend yield with growth in value. The reasons why these shareholder returns equate to the company's pre- and post-tax

DIVIDEND GROWTH AND COMPANY GROWTH

profits (given the basis on which we are predicating this illustration) are more subtle; but they will become apparent as we work, and discuss, the figures.

At this point all we need to do is to apply these percentages at the pre- and post-tax levels in Table 7. This produces total values which we will show in Table 8 to be appropriate for the shareholders' interest in the company one year hence and two years hence (when the dividends of £10,000 and £10,686 are paid, and when like amounts are retained by the company).

Table 8: The Investor's Yield

Value at start	258,900		
Value at end year 1		266,667	
Yield thereon			
at 9% equals pre-tax profits			24,000
at 7.5% equals post-tax profits			20,000
Value at start year 2	276,667		
Value at end year 2		284,967	
Yield thereon			
at 9% equals pre-tax profits			25,646
at 7.5% equals post-tax profits			21,372

The yields, we said, are real rates. What we have done is to *inflate* the values at the beginning of each year by 3 per cent (from £258,900 to £266,667 for instance) and then apply the yield percentages to those *end-year* figures.

2.13 Dividend growth and company growth

We are now in a position to demonstrate how the figures in our example do *work* (see Table 9 and the following explanation).

The first column shows capital invested in the company at the beginning of each relevant year (that is, each of the first ten) and the second column shows the amount to which 3 per cent inflation has carried it by the end of the year. The assumption here is that the company's assets and earning power are maintained despite the effects of inflation.

In the third column is shown the pre-tax profit, worked out at 9 per cent of the second column amount. In the fourth column the proportion of that pre-tax profit that is retained is shown (arrived at by dividing the pre-tax profit by 2.4 or five twelfths).

That retention is then added to the second column figure in order to arrive at the capital invested figure for the start of the next year (for instance, on the first year's line, £266,667 plus £10,000 make the starting figure on the second year's line of £276,667).

VALUE

Table 9: Dividend Growth and Company Growth

Year's start	Infl'n add 3%	Pre-tax 9% yield	Post-tax retention	3% disc.	Pres't money	7.5% disc.	Disc'd pres. value
258,900	266,667	24,000	10,000	.9709	9,709	.9302	9,032
276,667	284,967	25,646	10,686	.9426	10,073	.8653	8,716
295,653	304,523	27,407	11,420	.9151	10,451	.8050	8,412
315,943	325,421	29,288	12,203	.8885	10,842	.7488	8,119
337,624	347,752	31,298	13,041	.8626	11,249	.6966	7,835
360,793	371,617	33,446	13,936	.8375	11,671	.6480	7,562
385,553	397,120	35,741	14,892	.8131	12,108	.6028	7,298
412,012	424,372	38,193	15,914	.7894	12,562	.5607	7,044
440,286	453,495	40,815	17,006	.7664	13,003	.5216	6,798
470,501	484,616	43,615	18,173	.7441	13,522	.4852	6,561
							77,377

The figures in the fourth column are the retentions, but the reader will remember that the company's (gross) dividends are exactly the same. A dividend of £10,000 on a capital invested which has grown by the time of payment to £266,667 is a yield of 3.75 per cent. A retention of a further £10,000 post-tax can be seen as a doubling of that post-tax yield to the aimed at 7.5 per cent.

2.14 *The present value of the stream of increasing dividends*

But what Table 9 also makes clear is that each year's retention of 3.75 per cent of the company's *value* is what makes possible the dividend growth of 3.75 per cent. Adding the first year's retention of £10,000 to the end of year 1 value of £266,667, and inflating the answer by 3 per cent through year 2, produces a value at the end of year 2 of £284,967; that in turn gives rise to a year 2 dividend of £10,686 which shows a (real) increase of 3.75 per cent over the year 1 dividend.

That dividend growth can be seen if one reads down the sixth column in Table 9, where the figures of £9,709, £10,073, £10,451 and so on show in each case an increase of 3.75 per cent over the previous year's figure.

The sixth column, as indicated, shows the dividends expressed in terms of present money. The present value of that stream of dividends can be calculated by discounting back to the present the figures in that sixth column — which is what is done in the eighth column (using a 7.5 per cent discount rate, since that is the real return we are looking for). Thereafter it is straightforward to extend that final, eighth, column forward into the future to the point at which, although the dividends themselves are growing ever larger, their discounted present values are negligible:

DIVIDEND GROWTH AND COMPANY GROWTH

First ten years, per Table 9	77,377
Next ten years	54,249
Third ten years	38,034
Fourth ten years	26,667
Fifth ten years	18,696
Sixth ten years	13,108
Seventh ten years	9,190
	and so on
	258,900

2.15 Arithmetic; changing the figures

All that we are looking at is arithmetic. One can change the figures and still produce sensible, internally consistent answers. For instance, if we left the first year's earnings where they were before, but assumed that the investor demanded a higher yield (10.8 per cent pre-tax, 9 per cent post-tax); and assumed that the company could respond by generating commensurately higher growth from its retentions, we could rewrite Table 9 as in Table 10.

Table 10: Changing the Figures (1)

year's start	infl'n add 3%	pre-tax 10.8%	post-tax retention	3% disc.	pres't money	9.0% disc.	disc'd pres. value
215,750	222,222	24,000	10,000	.9709	9,709	.9174	8,907
232,222	239,189	25,831	10,763	.9426	10,145	.8417	8,539
249,952	257,451	27,804	11,585	.9151	10,601	.7722	8,186
269,036	277,127	29,928	12,470	.8885	11,080	.7084	7,849
289,577	298,264	32,213	13,422	.8626	11,578	.6499	7,525
							41,006

The starting investment figure of £215,750 is arrived at by working out that a pre-tax yield of 10.8 per cent on £222,222 produces the assumed earnings of £24,000; then discounting the £222,222 back 12 months to eliminate the first year's inflation.

The retention of £10,000 of post-tax profits at the end of the first year, along with £222,222 then invested, enables the company to generate pre-tax earnings of £25,831 in the second year, representing a yield of 10.8 per cent (both a higher yield and a higher rate of growth as we have noted than achieved in Table 9).

The original rate of dividend (in real terms) £9,709 on an investment of £215,700, is 4.5 per cent, which is what we would expect. And that is also as we would expect the real rate of growth in the dividends;

the sixth column figures, £9,709, £10,145, £10,601 and so on are each 4.5 per cent greater than the year before.

And if we were to calculate the present value not just of the first five years' dividends (£41,006 as in Table 10) but of the whole stream of dividends out to infinity, that present value would be £215,750.

2.16 *More changes in the figures*

And in the same way that we can alter the yields without destroying the theory, we can also change the ratio of retentions to dividends. We can assume the position as shown in Table 11.

Table 11: Changing the Figures (2)

	Total profits	Retained profits	Dividend
Pre-tax profits	24,000	17,143	6,857
Tax at 25% and 6.25%	4,715	4,286	429
Post-tax profits	19,285	12,857	6,428
Net dividend	5,142		5,142
Tax credit	1,286		1,286
Retention	12,857	12,857	

In Table 11, assuming that the pre-tax earnings yield is still 10.8 per cent, tax has increased to 2.122 per cent and the post-tax yield becomes 8.678 per cent; within the latter, retentions are 5.785 per cent, and dividends at exactly half of the retention rate, namely 2.893 per cent.

We can accordingly rewrite our table a third time, as shown in Table 12 (in a slightly changed format, since both retentions and dividends need to be shown; the 3 per cent inflation discounts are omitted for reasons of space).

All of the figures in Table 12 fit together in just the same way as the slightly different ones in earlier tables, and it would be tedious to repeat

Table 12: Changing the Figures (3)

Year's start	Infl'n add 3%	Pre-tax 10.8%	Post-tax retention 5.785%	Div'nd 2.893%	Pres't money	8.678% disc.	Disc'd pres. value
215,750	222,222	24,000	12,857	6,428	6,241	.9201	5,742
235,079	242,131	26,150	14,009	7,004	6,602	.8467	5,590
256,140	263,824	28,493	15,264	7,632	6,984	.7791	5,441
279,088	287,461	31,046	16,631	8,316	7,389	.7169	5,297
304,092	313,215	33,827	18,121	9,061	7,816	.6596	5,155
							27,225

the explanations already given. However it is worth spelling out that the present value of the stream of dividends in the final column can still be calculated as being £215,750. At first glance this might not seem to be arithmetically probable; the present value of the first five years' dividends in Table 12 is £27,225, whereas the equivalent value in Table 10 was £41,006. The *shape* of the two columns of figures is however significantly different, and the total of each does come to the same amount.

2.17 How valid is arithmetic as a basis for valuing shareholdings?

The question that we must now answer is whether a present value of an expected flow of dividends is a valid method of putting a value on the shareholders' interest in the company?

What we have seen so far is a selection of sets of assumed data, each of them internally consistent, and each taken to be realistic:

- when we worked on a 9 per cent pre-tax yield, we came up with a value of £258,900 for the shareholding, and since the company was retaining half of its post-tax profits, its total growth was a function of that retention and the yield it squeezed out of both its existing assets and the additional assets acquired with the retentions;

- when we changed to a 10.8 per cent pre-tax yield, we concluded that the shareholding must be worth less, £215,750. But that was merely because the fixed point of departure was a first year earnings level of £24,000;

- still at 10.8 per cent pre-tax, we saw two different patterns of growth in the company's activities, and two patterns for the graph showing dividend increases. Between these patterns there was one external factor which obviously affected the company's growth and dividends. When it retained a greater proportion of its profits, its tax burden increased – from 1.8 per cent out of the 10.8 per cent, to 2.765 per cent;

- the implication of that last point, of course, is that the post-tax shareholders' yield fell from 9 per cent to 8.035 per cent. We managed to persuade ourselves that that did not decrease the *value* in the shareholders' hands – by using a discount factor to get back to present value of 8.035 per cent in place of 9 per cent. (Or to put it differently, by assuming that it was the pre-tax yield rather than the post-tax one which was the determinant of the shareholdings' value.)

2.18 *The present value is the same whether we hold forever, hold for a time and then exit, or exit immediately*

We do not deny for a moment that the values we have arrived at would need to be revised:

- if the entire framework of world (including UK) interest rates were to move upwards; or

- if this company's business were to be seen to be more risky than was first thought;

so that a 9 per cent, or 10.8 per cent, pre-tax yield for the shareholders might no longer be regarded as sufficient.

But on the basis of our alternative assumptions, there is one thing we can say about the values of £258,900 or £215,750 at which we have arrived. Each can be seen as either:

(1) the present value, as we have shown in the previous paragraph, of the dividend flow out to infinity – that is to say, a value consistent with the shareholders continuing to hold those shares indefinitely; or

(2) the present value of the first (say) five years' dividends, plus the present value of the sale proceeds receivable in five years' time for the shares – on the footing that a purchaser at that time would be willing to pay a price for the shares which recognised his expectation of dividends increasing on the appropriate basis through succeeding years from the year 6 figure.

Or to encapsulate that into a single proposition, assuming a purchaser requiring the same return as we have ourselves achieved, the present value is the same whether we hold for ever, hold for a time and then sell, or sell immediately.

But there are three very important qualifications to be made to that proposition.

2.19 The first qualification – company and dividend growth rates

All of our figures have been based on the assumption that the increase in the dividends reflected the company's own growth through retentions. If there had been growth in dividends and in pre-tax profits, but the two rates of growth had not been *related* in the way we have illustrated, then one would have had to recognise that our calculations would not have produced a satisfactory answer.

The easiest way of arriving at something that might be logically defended would be to assume that at some point in the future the company would change from its under-distributing policy onto our *related* policy; that is to say, it would start paying in line with earnings on investment plus retentions. Thus the dividend flow would be deflated for a period of years, but would then step up to a level higher than our tables have produced (because the deflated dividends would have been compensated by higher retentions). Thereafter dividends and retentions would increase at the same real rates we have demonstrated.

If we were able to construct such tables, we would find that the present values of the dividend flows to infinity would be the same as the £258,900, or alternatively the £215,750, at which we arrived.

However, that itself needs to be qualified. At any point before step-up to the full dividend policy (based on previous retentions and growing in line with the company's growth) the timing of that step-up is unknown. An incoming investor would be unlikely to pay as much for shares on the basis of *hope* that they might shortly give him a proper yield, as he would pay for shares which were already providing such a yield. This is the factor which can result in shares having very little value:

- if they represent only a small percentage holding, that is, the holder has little opportunity to change dividend policy;

- if the company is not listed, so that the performance of its shares is not subjected to the demands of the investing public;

- if there is no eager purchaser willing at any time to acquire shares from a small shareholder.

2.20 The second qualification – entrepreneurs are unable to set a target yield in the build-up

What actually happens to our company may of course be rather different from the continuous progression that we have envisaged. For instance, it might be more likely that the shareholders would be able to sell their expanded company to a predator; and that the £258,900 value would therefore come from the combination of the present values of the deflated dividends up to that sale, plus an exit price based on the predator's views of the pre-tax profits his target could generate thereafter.

It is more or less axiomatic that the original owners would think during their build-up period of profits, investment and expansion, not a rate of return. If they drew dividends at all, these would start at deflated levels; the *step up* would, so far as they were concerned, then be to an exit price of whatever they thought they could obtain from a predator – not a price pre-planned when they started. The return the predator thought he could squeeze out of the company would not be related to any previous return it had generated. In this situation of entrepreneurs building up a company with a view to its possible sale, their tax position is always very relevant to the aims they set for their company, as we will see throughout this book. But tax is only one of the factors. Probably just as significant is the underlying economic truth: when the company is small, the risks for its investors are high, and the shares' value correspondingly low. As it grows, and risks can be expected to decrease, the shares' value can be expected to grow faster than the pre-tax profits of the company. We must always be willing to change our assumptions to reflect the changing circumstances of the company itself.

The heading to paragraph 2.17 asked how valid was arithmetic as a method of valuing shareholdings. So long as we do not ignore the qualifications in these last few paragraphs (and the one further qualification in the next one) we can answer that question by saying that arithmetic is fundamental, not only for putting a value on shareholdings, but on the companies themselves in which those shares are held. The art lies in estimating future figures – earnings, yields, risks, the *capital invested* in the company and the economic background against which it is operating.

2.21 The third qualification – dividend growth arising from factors other than retentions, and dividends taken as an alternative to remuneration

There is more than one aspect to this.

First, we have been treating our company as if its only payments to its shareholders, the only reward they obtained from their ownership of the company, was a stream of dividends. We know that that will not normally be true, and that in an owner-managed business dividends and earnings are alternatives. We further know that there is no warrant for assuming that dividends are purely the reward paid to suppliers of capital, while earnings are full recompense for work performed by hand and brain.

If we were trying to put a figure on what a different owner of the company could derive from owning it, while at the same time he retained its existing owners to continue running it, then we would almost certainly have to make adjustments to those managers' earnings in order to gain a fairer picture of the company's maintainable profits.

Next, it will have been becoming increasingly obvious to the reader through these last few paragraphs that the linkage between accounting retentions, and the increase in the company's size, may be less direct than we have implied. One needs the saving phrase 'all things being equal' between the statement that the retention increases the company's *operating capacity*,[7] and that this in turn should be reflected in a proportionate increase in pre-tax profits.

That is not the only source from which profit increases can be derived. Efficiency and economies of scale are possibilities; so is innovation; so are reputation, customer-relationships, the goodwill built up by the business which can be seen to be succeeding – all the intangibles which differentiate businesses on the way up from those which are no longer climbing.

The trouble with writing about profits and values, and introducing words such as efficiency and economies of scale (not only introducing them but having the gall to describe them as intangibles) is that hard-nosed businessmen will ask whether the author has any idea what he is talking about. Surely profits are made from transactions? It is the difference between what I sell my goods for, and what they cost me to make or to purchase, that produces my profit; the capital I have invested is essential, but it does not determine my profit.

The businessman is right, of course; but so is the author, and it is only the latter's failure to explain his terms of reference fully enough that gives rise to the failure in communication. Let us go back to the phrase *operating capacity* which we used a few lines back. We pictured in paragraph 2.6 an oil company shipping oil from the Middle East

---

[7] See paragraph 2.6 and Note 5 thereon. *Operating capacity* was the non-financial measure of the company's capital which current cost accounting sought to maintain through periods of changing prices. That phraseology itself reminds us that *capital* in an economic sense defines a company's size, its ability to handle a particular volume of business, and thus to generate profits commensurate with that volume.

THE THIRD QUALIFICATION

for sale in Europe. If it were true that the logistics of production and shipping meant that oil produced in February was invariably sold in April (could not be sold earlier and was never sold later) then it is clear that one feature of the oil company's operating capacity would be its ability to *turn over its stocks* six times a year. If one thinks through what that phrase means, the only inference that can be drawn is that there is some factor limiting the business's operating speed. It is unlikely, but assume for illustration that the only factor which does limit this is tanker capacity and speed. Then assume that tanker speeds can be increased so that what had been a two month trip can be accomplished in six weeks. The oil company can now either increase production, or purchase more Middle Eastern crude, because what had been its volume of stocks (in the holds of tankers) can now be turned over eight times a year rather than six. It has potentially increased its profits from their previous level by one third – and the extra cash investment the business needs for this expansion, that is, to be able to pay suppliers for the increase in throughput, is at most the cost of one cycle's increased volume (if the producers are paid cash at the date of lifting; if they do not get their money until cash is received from European customers, no extra *investment* is needed).

Sailing your tankers faster is *efficiency*. So is making suppliers wait for their cash until you have been paid yourself. If sailing faster uses more fuel, the degree of efficiency is reduced; so is it also if the producers insist on earlier payment, and you have to pay overdraft interest to your bank to manage this. All of this extends, rather than invalidates, the concept that there is a relationship between capital invested (loosely *capacity*) and maintainable profits.

2.22 Realised profits under generally accepted accounting principles – are they a sound guide to the retentions from which growth is actually financed?

A third aspect was made as a particular point much earlier in this book. Profits, in an ideal world, would be the difference between the income earned in a year, and the costs of generating that income – whether those costs were incurred in that same year or another.[8] But

---

[8] That income and costs should be matched, that a profit and loss account is not the same thing as a receipts and payments account, is one element of the fundamental accounting concept of *accruals* in SSAP 2. Matching involves bringing into the profit and loss account for a year the revenue and profits to be dealt with in that year, and then 'including in the same account the costs incurred in earning them (so far as these are material and identifiable)'. Thus one might expect costs incurred in an earlier year might often need to be carried forward, to be written off in the profit and loss account of some later year when revenue resulted. But there is a qualification to this, in that if there is a conflict between this suggestion that costs can be carried forward, without being written off, and the other fundamental concept of *prudence*, the latter prevails. Prudence would prevent the carrying forward of any cost unless it was *reasonably certain* that it would be possible to absorb it against later, and related, revenues. For further discussion of the relationship of prudence and matching, see paragraph 4.17.

in paragraph 1.29 we spent time considering the incidence of costs of market research and marketing. We assumed that those costs were all incurred in 1993, and all designed to boost the sales of a new product whose sales were expected to start in 1994 and continue through to 1996. The uncertainty, looked at from an end of 1993 viewpoint, of the 1994 to 1996 sales meant that the 1993 costs needed to be written off in the year they were incurred; what we said in paragraph 1.29 was that it could be argued that the 1994 to 1996 profits would accordingly be overstated when sales for those years were measured against an amount of related costs which omitted some material 1993 expenditure which had already been written off.

That is only a part of the story. If at the end of 1993, we believed that that year's profits should not be reduced, but that the expenditure concerned should be carried forward to be written off in 1994 and later, then the company's *retentions* would have been larger at the end of 1993 by that same amount. Our arithmetic has implicitly assumed that profits were ideally measured, and that so also were retentions – but more than that, that the retentions themselves generated an increase in profits. The 1993 profits which the company should have reported would have shown it *increasing its capacity*, and the 1994 to 1996 profits would have represented the proper return from that increased capacity.

And there is a third aspect of this question of writing off, or not writing off, expenditure at the end of 1993. A profit and loss account can only have *realised profits*[9] credited to it, and only from them can dividends be declared. Both company law and accounting practice mean that those realised profits are quantified *conventionally*, prudently, which can mean with *lags* that are difficult to identify. All our measurements use an elastic measuring rod. Theory is simple; it is only application which is difficult. But there is no other way in which one can arrive at a value.

2.23 Borrowings by the company

We have spent considerable time on the question of shareholder value, and will need to return to it; but now we need a short digression.

Let us assume that our company borrows £100,000, which it undertakes to repay in ten annual instalments, the first of these being at the end of one year after drawdown. We are still as accustomed as we were in paragraph 2.10 to a world in which inflation is continuing, and we therefore assume the same 3 per cent per annum. We also assume that the lender, having calculated what he believes will be the *real* rate of interest (excluding the inflation element) during the ten years, and having also assessed what premium over that he needs for the risks of lending to this particular company, is prepared to lend at a real 5.5 per cent.

---

[9] Section 263(3) Companies Act 1985.

BORROWINGS BY THE COMPANY

The total rate to be paid by the company is a compounding of those figures:

1.03 × 1.055 = 1.08665, that is, an interest rate of 8.665 per cent.

Applying that rate to £100,000 outstanding for the first year (the interest is paid annually in arrear at the same time as the principal instalment is repaid) to £90,000 for the second year, and so on, gives a schedule of repayments as shown in Table 13.

Table 13: Schedule of Repayments

	Principal	Interest	Total
End year 1	10,000	8,665	18,665
2	10,000	7,799	17,799
3	10,000	6,932	16,932
4	10,000	6,066	16,066
5	10,000	5,199	15,199
6	10,000	4,333	14,333
7	10,000	3,466	13,466
8	10,000	2,600	12,600
9	10,000	1,733	11,733
10	10,000	867	10,867

2.24 *Receipts in the hands of the lender*

If we take an actuarial look at the receipts in the hands of the lender (rather than thinking only of what he should be putting in his tax return as taxable income), the picture can be seen in Table 14.

Table 14: Receipts in the Hands of the Lender

	Receipt in cash	Discount to allow for 3% inflation	Present money value	Discount for 5.5% yield	Principal value
End year 1	18,665	0.9709	18,121	0.9479	17,175
2	17,799	0.9426	16,777	0.8985	15,072
3	16,932	0.9151	15,495	0.8516	13,195
4	16,066	0.8885	14,274	0.8072	11,522
5	15,199	0.8626	13,111	0.7651	10,032
6	14,333	0.8375	12,004	0.7253	8,706
7	13,466	0.8131	10,949	0.6874	7,527
8	12,600	0.7894	9,947	0.6516	6,481
9	11,733	0.7664	8,992	0.6176	5,554
10	10,867	0.7441	8,090	0.5854	4,736
					100,000

The right hand column in Table 14 confirms what we knew to be the basis on which the lender was prepared to lend, namely that he wanted to be able to earn 5.5 per cent on his money in real terms, after allowing for 3 per cent inflation. If one discounts his actual receipts, first by 3 per cent to eliminate inflation and to arrive at present purchasing power figures, and second by 5.5 per cent representing his aimed-at return, it is obvious that one will arrive back at the £100,000 present day value that the lender has advanced.

2.25 The relationship between shareholder values and the values of the loan creditors' rights

What was explained in the last paragraph was, however, the lender's perspective on the loan. The company's perspective is subtly different. What the company does is devote a certain amount of its pre-tax profits in each of the ten years concerned to paying off the loan. As this burden on its profits is reduced, the levels of profits attributable to the shareholders increase.

We must now examine the position of the company which has both equity and loan finance. What we need to quantify is the additional value the company derives from its borrowing; and what effect that borrowing has on the shareholders' interest in the company. We go back, for purposes of these explanations, to the assumptions:

- in paragraph 2.12, that the company could generate a pre-tax yield of 9 per cent from its use of funds;

- in paragraph 2.23, that the company's borrowing costs would be 8.665 per cent (made up of the lender's wish to generate a real 5.5 per cent return, and his estimate that inflation would continue to run at 3 per cent);

and pause only momentarily to point out that were the company not confident that it could generate more from its use of these borrowed funds than it had to pay to borrow them, it obviously would not borrow in the first place. (This is one of those areas in which using pre-tax rates of return does make the analysis much easier.)

2.26 *The company which repays its borrowings*

The first case we consider is that of the company which raised £258,900 of equity finance from shareholders, and borrowed £100,000 on top, that borrowing to be repaid as indicated in paragraph 2.23 (Table 13) by ten annual instalments of principal.

The easiest way to demonstrate the effects of this is to think of the company in two separate divisions:

- first (although this can only make sense after we have explained the shape of the company's remaining activities) we assume that the company has the use of the borrowed funds indefinitely, and can generate its target 9 per cent pre-tax from such use;

- next, in its second, separate, division the company also generates that target 9 per cent from the use of its £258,900 of equity, but out of that it pays interest and repays principal of its loan, so that its shareholders only have the benefit of the balance left after such repayments.

When we think how best we could set about quantifying the value to the company of its use of £100,000 in the first of its divisions, it is clear that we could construct a table along the same lines as Table 9 in paragraph 2.13. It would show the £100,000 funds growing in line with inflation, and growing also through retention of half the post-tax earnings of 7.5 per cent while paying out dividends in each year equal to the amounts of its retentions. Every figure in such a table would be the same as in Table 9, except that each would be reduced by a factor of 100,000 over 258,900. It would therefore be no surprise to anyone to hear that the present value of the expected stream of dividends generated from the company's use of these funds would not be the starting investment figure of £258,900 in Table 9, but rather the amount of £100,000.

2.27 Dividends and retentions after the service of the debt

Table 15, showing the results of the company's second division, is rather more laborious; it shows the shareholder value, starting with the £258,900 of equity funds which are the source for the servicing and repayment of the borrowing, and for retentions and dividends to the extent the company's funds will stretch further:

Table 15: Results of the Company's Second Division (1)

Start of year	Add 1.03%	9% yield	Principal repayment	Interest	Balance	Tax	Retention
258,900	266,667	24,000	13,333	8,665	2,002	334	834
267,501	275,526	24,797	13,333	7,799	3,665	611	1,527
277,053	285,365	25,683	13,333	6,932	5,418	903	2,258
287,623	296,252	26,663	13,333	6,066	7,264	1,211	3,027
299,279	308,257	27,743	13,333	5,199	9,211	1,535	3,838
312,095	321,458	28,931	13,333	4,333	11,265	1,878	4,694
326,152	335,937	30,234	13,333	3,466	13,435	2,239	5,598
341,535	351,781	31,660	13,333	2,600	15,727	2,621	6,553
358,334	369,084	33,218	13,333	1,733	18,152	3,025	7,563
376,647	387,946	34,915	13,333	867	20,715	3,453	8,631
396,557	408,474	36,762	–	–	36,762	6,127	15,318

Although the arrangement of columns is slightly different, the general approach in Table 15 is similar to that in Table 9. The second column shows capital invested at the beginning of the year having increased in line with inflation by the end of the year; and the third column shows the

9 per cent pre-tax return calculated from the inflated figure in column 2. Repaying £10,000 of loan, which is not a tax deductible transaction, utilises in column 4 £13,333 of pre-tax profits, but the payment of interest in column 5 is tax deductible, and accordingly utilises only an amount of pre-tax profits equal to the (gross) interest charge (taken from paragraph 2.23).

At that point, therefore, the company is left with a balance of pre-tax profits shown in the seventh column. The assumption is that post-tax retentions, and dividends, are equal; that is to say, the tax charge absorbs 1.5 per cent out of the pre-tax yield, leaving 7.5 per cent as the post-tax yield, equally split between the retention and the dividend. This is of course the same ratio as shown in Table 7, £4,000 to £10,000 to £10,000. As one works through the table, each year's starting investment is the aggregate of the figures in columns 2 and 8 from the previous year.

2.28 *Putting a present value on those dividends*

There are two valuations one can draw out of the figures in Table 15.

First, the present value of the dividend stream (identical to the amounts retained) for the first ten years can be arrived at by discounting the figures back using factors representing the 3 per cent inflation and the 7.5 per cent post-tax yield required on the dividends. This is shown in Table 16.

Table 16: Present Value of Dividends

834	.9709	.9302	753
1,527	.9426	.8653	1,245
2,258	.9151	.8050	1,663
3,027	.8885	.7488	2,014
3,838	.8626	.6966	2,306
4,694	.8375	.6480	2,547
5,598	.8131	.6028	2,744
6,553	.7894	.5607	2,753
7,563	.7664	.5216	3,023
8,631	.7441	.4852	3,116
			22,164

Second, in year 11 the dividend the company could be expected to pay will be £15,318; and from then on the increase in the dividends will be the same nominal 6.8625 per cent as we saw in Table 9 (being the compounding of 3 per cent inflation and a real 3.75 per cent).

From paragraph 2.14 we could deduce that the present value (start of year 1) of a dividend stream from year 11 onwards was £181,523 when the level of that year 11 dividend was £19,420 (1.0686 times the year 10 dividend of £18,173 in paragraph 2.14 is £19,420). Based on the smaller dividend of £15,318 now envisaged for year 11, we can say that the present value of the dividend stream from year 11 onwards has decreased to £143,181.

Therefore, putting those two figures together, we get:

Present value of first ten years' dividends	22,164
Present value of remainder of dividends	143,181
	165,345

2.29 *Putting a value on the company as a whole*

What that in turn tells us about the value of the company as a whole is:

Present value of what we have treated as the first separate division of the company, that is to say the earning power of the borrowed funds, available indefinitely	100,000
Present value of the second separate part of the company, namely the earning power of the £258,900 of equity, after allowing for the repayment out of this source of the borrowings, as in paragraph 2.28	165,345
	265,345

That figure shows an answer which should not surprise us. The shareholders' value is greater, but not all that much greater, than the £258,900 figure of the company which was financed only with equity.

The greater amount of funds available in this most recent example, in the form of the borrowings, has earned slightly more (at 9 per cent pre-tax on *capital* which was inflating at 3 per cent) than those funds cost to borrow (8.667 per cent pre-tax). And the period during which those additional funds were available to the company was relatively brief; that follows from our assumption that the repayment of the loan takes place within ten years by annual instalments.

2.30 **The company which keeps its borrowings intact rather than repaying**

As an alternative to the assumption that the company repays its borrowings through a period of ten years, we need to ask what would be the position if it succeeded in persuading its financier to allow it to keep the loan intact.

We again split the company into two divisions, but they are different from those demonstrated before:

VALUE

- first, the equity investment of £258,900, which is used, as was the case in paragraph 2.17, wholly for dividends and retentions, without regard to any other activities of the company;

- second, those other activities consist of borrowings, with their interest cost being met out of the pre-tax yield, and the balance of that yield being used for retentions and dividends.

It is important that we maintain the overall position that retentions and dividends proceed in line, because any other assumption will result in a tax burden on the company which absorbs a different proportion of its pre-tax earnings, and therefore will give a non-comparable picture of its post-tax earnings and therefore its value.

Our table for the second of the company's divisions (Table 15) can be rewritten in the form of Table 17:

Table 17: Results of the Company's Second Division (2)

Start of year	Add 1.03%	9% return	Principal repayment	Interest	Balance	Tax	Retention
100,000	103,000	9,270	–	8,665	605	101	252
103,252	106,348	9,571	–	8,665	906	151	378
106,726	109,928	9,894	–	8,665	1,229	205	512
110,440	113,753	10,238	–	8,665	1,573	262	656
114,409	117,841 and so on	10,606	–	8,665	1,941	323	809

2.31 *A less difficult way of arriving at a present value of the stream of dividends*

But the trouble with Table 17 is that the retentions in the final column (and the dividend stream which is identical) do not form a *regular* progression of numbers, and it is not therefore at all easy to calculate what is its present value.

What makes life easier is to separate the table into its two components; first, a *positive* table (Table 18) starting with £100,000 of capital, showing the pre-tax earnings derived by the company from its use, and the dividends and retentions that it will provide. (We only need to show a couple of lines.)

Table 18: Positive Table Showing Present Value

Start of year	Add 1.03%	9% yield	Principal repayment	Interest	Balance	Tax	Retention
100,000	103,000	9,270	–	–	9,270	1,545	3,863
106,863	110,069	9,906	–	–	9,906	1,651	4,128

We can then move on to construct the *negative* table (Table 19), which shows interest costs, and shows also the reductions in dividends and in retentions which result therefrom.

Table 19: Negative Table Showing Present Value

Start of year	Add 1.03%	9% yield	Principal repayment	Interest	Balance	Tax	Retention
–	–	–	–	8,665	8,665	1,444	3,611
3,611	3,719	335	–	8,665	9,000	1,500	3,750
7,469	7,693	692	–	8,665	9,357	1,560	3,899
11,592	11,940	1,075	–	8,665	9,740	1,623	4,058
15,998	16,478	1,483	–	8,665	10,148	1,691	4,229

We can see without difficulty that the figures in Table 17 are simply the difference between the *positives* and the *negatives* in Tables 18 and 19.

The advantage of the *negative* table is that it is rather easier to put a present value on that final column of figures (or strictly to put a present value on the identical column of *negative* dividends). That present value is approximately £56,400.

2.32 *Explanation why the company which keeps its borrowings outstanding appears more valuable than the one which repays*

Therefore, to arrive at the present value of the company we have been envisaging from paragraph 2.30 onwards, with its maintained borrowings we need to aggregate:

- the value of the straightforward equity investment into the company   258,900

- the value of the use of its borrowed funds, without regard to their interest cost, per the uncompleted Table 18   100,000

        358,900

- less the *negative* present value representing the interest costs of the borrowed funds, expressed in terms of reductions in dividends and retentions in Table 19   56,400

        302,500

That figure of £302,500 is quite considerably greater than the £265,345 which we calculated in paragraph 2.29 was the present value of a company which was committed to repaying its borrowings over a ten year period. And that should not be any surprise.

The company which can maintain its borrowings, if it can both:

- earn more pre-tax on the borrowed funds than they cost to borrow; and

- accumulate that excess year by year keeping up with inflation even before earning the pre-tax return referred to above, while that same inflation wastes away the interest costs of the borrowing;

must be better off if it can maintain its borrowings than it would be if it repays them.

2.33 Risk that aimed-at earnings yields can fall while borrowing costs do not do so

That in turn means of course that the shareholders are better off holding shares in a company which borrows than in one which does not do so.[10] But every silver lining has a cloud. If the company should get into financial difficulties, the fact that the lenders have a priority in front of the ordinary shareholders means that the very fact of the company's borrowing has added to the risk the ordinary shareholders face.

This is not simply a question what funds would be available to the shareholders if the company were to go into liquidation – with the loan creditors entitled to full repayment of their loans before the shareholders were entitled to any repayment on their shares.

If the company were to continue operating profitably, but could not continue generating a return on its funds of our assumed 9 per cent pre-tax, it would be the ordinary shareholders who would see their value fall. And that fall would not be the shortfall in the return applied to the equity funds of £258,900, but applied to £358,900, the whole of the funds at the company's disposal.

Borrowings can therefore be said to result in increased risk for the ordinary shareholders, as well as providing them with the opportunity for increased profits and value. Many shareholders believe that there is a target relationship between borrowings and equity (referred to in the jargon as the *gearing ratio*); they are therefore happy to see a company increase its total borrowings in line with its own growth, but would prefer that the increased level of borrowings was kept within the same percentage of equity – £100,000 of borrowings in our case is approximately 40 per cent of the equity funds of £258,900. Those who believe in the sanctity of gearing ratios move from boom times into recession with a warm, comfortable feeling that their companies are safe, and will be able to keep out of trouble.

---

[10] This has always been the classic argument for investment through investment trust companies which are permitted to borrow, rather than through unit trusts which may not.

2.34 What is the validity of the gearing ratio?

The reason for the author's somewhat more jaundiced view is merely his inability to accept that it is as simple as that makes it seem.

First, a gearing ratio calculated from the capital and retained earnings number on the balance sheet has little relationship to the *equity* which the shareholders really have locked into their company. We have already seen enough examples in this and the previous chapter of the ways in which balance sheets fail to present an adequate picture of asset *values* to be somewhat leery of the balancing shareholders' funds figure on the other side of the balance sheet; no accountant would seriously claim that *shareholders funds* reflected the real equity of the company.

But even if that number did have the meaning that is ascribed to it, the risks associated with borrowings do not arise mainly from the amounts on the balance sheet. It is at the figures in the profit and loss account, and in the cashflow forecasts, that one needs to look. What puts the company in jeopardy is the volatility of the yield it can earn on the total funds it employs, in relation to the volatility or otherwise of the outflows that result from its borrowings. And the circumlocution in that last phrase, 'outflows that result from borrowings', is a reminder that lenders can demand repayment of principal as well as payment of interest, and habitually do so at the most inconvenient of times.

So we can end this chapter where we began. We all think we know the meaning of the word *value*. What we must strenuously avoid, in a company context, is any temptation to see simple shortcuts – any assumptions that figures in accounts can be accepted without enquiry as having meanings that experienced users of accounts know they do not have. But above all, we need to understand the relationships between earning power and value; companies are not the same as Rembrandts.

CHAPTER 3

INCORPORATION

3.1 Why incorporate?

Circumstances vary. Businesses differ.

It is certainly appropriate to balance the arguments for and against trading through a company; but the next few paragraphs will show that it is not sensible to try to lay down a universal rule determining when to incorporate – as opposed to operating as an individual *sole trader* or through a partnership. First, there are many factors which may incline, or impel, the decision in one direction or the other; second, neither those factors, nor the trading operations themselves, remain static. What might have been the optimum choice yesterday does not necessarily remain desirable tomorrow. But the third point is that incorporation is for all practical purposes an irreversible step. It is not at all difficult to move an unincorporated business and its assets into a company, but considerable problems arise when one attempts to disincorporate.

At least that is the irreversibility situation at the time of writing. There are always committees within the professional bodies beavering away on schemes to ease disincorporation, and urging change on the Department of Trade and the Inland Revenue. From time to time, those latter bodies even appear encouraging and receptive to such ideas, but no official action has been forthcoming – as yet.

3.2 *The absence of limited liability*

Therefore one does need to see clearly what one stands to gain and what one loses by operating through a company.

Limited liability was never intended to prevent a company from losing its all; but the architects designing limitation saw it as protecting shareholders from losses beyond the amounts they had paid (or had a commitment to pay) for their shares. The illustration in paragraph 1.20, however, showed very clearly that in the owner-managed company the owners are likely to find themselves paying, from their own assets, considerably more than that amount to the banks and other financiers if the company should fail. Even if the company's owners do succeed in operating behind the shield of limited liability, those involved in its management lose any protection if they allow the company to continue obtaining credit when it should have been clear to them that it had no possible way forward, other than an insolvent liquidation.[1]

---

[1] Paragraphs 1.4 to 1.6 above. We will also notice some aspects, in chapters 6 and 9 below, of the question whether it is realistic to assume that liabilities can be limited through the establishment of separate subsidiaries.

It is no serious oversimplification to say that the entrepreneur commencing business should work on the assumption that the company's financiers will require security and/or guarantees which circumvent his limiting liability. Employees and suppliers may also lose, alongside the entrepreneur, if his company fails; but he is more or less certain in these circumstances to lose more than his company.

3.3 *The company as a water tank*

The other main area we need to consider is tax. The usual way in which this explanation is started is by describing a company as a two-level operation; profits made by the company are taxable in its hands, and the net-after-tax amounts are subject to tax a second time in the hands of the company's owners. That second level tax may either be capital gains tax paid by the shareholder if he sells at a price which reflects those net-after-tax amounts retained within the company; or it may be income tax payable by the shareholder if the company distributes its profit to him.

That may be true in the most general of terms, but it is subject to so many major qualifications and exceptions that it cannot be regarded as the best way of drawing the picture.

Better by far to envisage the company as a water tank, with a number of pipes through which water can pour into it to fill it up, and a number of pipes out of the bottom through which that water can be made to flow out – either to shareholders, or to employees, or to suppliers of goods and services, or to providers of finance; these are only examples, and not meant to be a comprehensive list.

3.4 *Tax outflows, and the water left in the tank thereafter*

The picture we need of this water tank is one which brings home to us the five specific points in this and the next paragraph, and from which we can draw out a much more fundamental implication in paragraph 3.6.

One of the outflow pipes from the company is its tax liability. That tax liability arises on a figure, calculated period by period within the tank, as the aggregate of some inflows after deducting some outflows. Sales receipts are counted in, funds borrowed from financiers are not; staff costs are deductible, purchases of office buildings not. The purpose of this description is however not to produce either a list of all possible inflows and outflows, or a comprehensive definition of taxable profits, but merely to indicate that there are many reasons why flows of funds and taxable profits differ.

After the company has paid its tax there will remain in the tank an amount of water. There are some but not many possibilities that some of this can flow out to shareholders without a tax cost to them or the company; one example is the case of shareholders who are also lenders able to demand repayment of the principal of loans they have made to the company. There are other outflow pipes which create a straightforward tax liability for those shareholders while at the same time saving tax for the company; wages or salaries paid to them are one example.

3.5 *Distributions in the ordinary (Companies Acts) sense and in the tax sense; the absence of any relationship of either to the company's taxable income less tax on it*

There will then still be in the tank a volume of water which can, potentially, flow out to shareholders through the residual outflow pipe which we can call 'distributions' while we are using that word in its ordinary English sense and not as a term of art from tax legislation. A further ordinary English point here is that some only of this volume of water will be 'distributable' under the Companies Acts rules, and some will not. If it is desired to get that last amount into shareholders' hands some other, less obvious, route than dividends (even perhaps the ultimate step of liquidation) may be the only way.

The third ordinary English point is that the the volume of water remaining in the tank for those distributions has very little direct relationship with what is left of the company's taxable profits after that tax has been paid on them. But if we move from ordinary English to tax terminology, there are two specific matters to consider. Most (but not quite all) of these funds, if they are allowed to flow from the company to shareholders along the residual outflow pipe, will need to be treated in the special tax sense as *distributions*.

The other tax aspect is that most (but not quite all) distributions involve the paying company handing over tax to the Revenue at the time of payment, and involve an individual recipient counting them into his income. Nevertheless the effective burden of these requirements will be quite different where a company is making such a distribution within the level of its own taxed profits – as against doing so out of amounts not so taxed. When we were examining the impact of the imputation system on dividends in paragraphs 1.33 and 1.34, we were able to conclude that the company's final tax burden was 6.25 per cent on distributed profits, and the shareholder's was 20 per cent of the gross dividend (equating 18.75 per cent of the pre-tax profits from which that dividend was derived). We will see as we proceed that it is by no means always the case that the company's liabilities are reduced from 25 per cent to 6.25 per cent – although the shareholder may still be taxed on an income basis.

3.6 *The potentially high tax cost of distributions*

That last sentence calls for an illustration. Let us assume that a company has £1,000 of profits which are subject to corporation tax, and £400 of exempt profits – perhaps the part of a capital gain covered by indexation relief. Table 20 shows how its tax liabilities would change on three assumptions.

Between (a) and (b) the Inland Revenue obtain no more tax, because the higher shareholder tax on the increased distribution is wholly matched by the reduction in the company tax. Between (b) and (c) this

Table 20: Tax Liabilities

			Taxable distributed		Taxable retained	Exempt retained	Total
(a)	*that £600 net was distributed*						
	pre-tax			800		200	400	1,400
	net distribution			600				600
	shareholder tax			150				
	corporation tax	200				50		250
	less ACT	150		50				
	retention			nil		150	400	550
								1,400
						no longer retained		
(b)	*that £750 net was distributed*							
	pre-tax			800		200	400	1,400
	net distribution			600		150		750
	shareholder tax			150		37½		
	corporation tax	200			50			250
	less ACT	150		50	37½	12½		
	retention			nil		nil	400	400
								1,400
							no longer retained	
(c)	*that £1,070 net was distributed*							
	pre-tax			800		200	400	1,400
	net distribution			600		150	320	1,070
	shareholder tax			150		37½	80	
	corporation tax	200			50		nil	330
	less ACT	150		50	37½	12½		
	retention			nil		nil	nil	nil
								1,400

is not the case. What we are illustrating is one form of the phenomenon referred to as *unrelieved ACT*.

But there is a further aspect. If the shareholders are liable not at 20 per cent, but at the higher rates, the water meter on that residual (distribution) outflow pipe from the company to the shareholders can create extremely high tax liabilities. (Part of this will be the unrelieved ACT already mentioned, and the remainder will simply be the shareholders' higher rate liabilities which they would not suffer if the company retained, rather than distributing, its funds.)

3.7 The question whether distributions are desirable

The obvious conclusion from the figures in Table 20 is that the tax authorities will never take less than £250; one appears not to be saving tax by distributing less than the net £750 shown. But that is only true if the shareholder is liable only at 20 per cent – if he is liable at higher rates, then every pound of distribution increases the overall tax cost. And even if the shareholder is liable only at 20 per cent, any distribution in excess of the £750 shown will increase the tax cost.

We must therefore always question whether we should allow any flow through the pipe; or whether there is some other transaction which can achieve a similar result without so high a cost. 'Similar' may mean trying to put the shareholder into the position he would have been in had a distribution been made, but without necessarily reflecting that in the company's mirror-image position.

It is hardly an exaggeration to say that the most important single subject in this book is distribution. But there is still the earlier question in paragraph 3.1, *Why incorporate?* We have not yet identified whether there is an obvious tax advantage in operating a business through a company, or in not doing so.

We need to be careful that we compare like with like. This is easiest if we envisage a business able to generate a specified level of annual profits, needing to pay interest and make principal repayments on its borrowings, and needing to provide a level of net income to its owner. We can look at this business both outside and inside a company. The advantage of incorporation would be the extent to which a company ended up with larger retentions than the unincorporated business was able to achieve – or the disadvantage would be smaller retentions for the company.

For this business, in Table 21 we scale up, *pro rata*, the figures of the company we were looking at in paragraph 2.26.

Table 21: The Relationship between Equity, Borrowings and Profits

Equity	258,900	420,213
Borrowings	100,000	162,327
	358,900	582,540
Pretax profits at 9 per cent	33,270	54,000
Interest	8,665	14,064
Principal repayment	10,000	16,233

3.8 The unincorporated business's figures

There are two further points we need to assume. First, the owner of this business wants to be able to draw £10,000 of spendable income; second, and additionally, he wants a contribution of £1,500 paid into a pension scheme.

WHY INCORPORATE?

Table 22: The Unincorporated Business

Profits, pre-interest and pre-tax		54,000
Deduct outgoings allowable for tax purposes		
interest	14,064	
pension contribution	1,500	
half of NIC class 4 (7.3% of profits between £6,340 and £21,840)	566	16,130
		37,870
Taxable income is £34,425, being that £37,870 less the personal deduction of £3,445, tax on that being		
3,000 at 20 per cent	600	
20,700 at 25 per cent	5,175	
10,725 at 40 per cent	4,290	10,065
34,425		27,805
Deduct outgoings not allowable for tax		
NIC class 2 (£5.55 per week)	289	
other half of NIC class 4	566	
principal repayment	16,233	
drawings	10,000	27,088
Retainable earnings		717

In the unincorporated business, the figures work out as shown in Table 22.

The whole of the business profits (calculated in Table 22 at £37,870 after those deductions that are allowable) are taxed as if they were the individual trader's own income. On the face of it, that appears to leave him able to draw £26,950 (£27,805 less the NIC of £289 and £566); the fact that he does in fact draw only £10,000 does not affect his tax liability, or any of the other figures set out in the table.

3.9 The company's figures

If we assume that the business is incorporated, then we need to assume that the indiviudual's drawings are made by way of salary, and the first calculation we need is that of the tax and NIC (in this case employer's and employee's class 1) on that salary. Because the bands to which the various tax and NIC percentage rates apply are different, Table 23 looks more complex than it actually is.

The table indicates that there is an advantage in operating in incorporated form, at this level of earnings. And the reason can be quite easily

Table 23: The Incorporated Business

Gross		Tax	Employee's NIC		Net	Employer's NIC	
2,808	–	–	2.0%	56	2,752	10.4%	292
637	–	–	10.0%	64	573	10.4%	66
3,000	20%	600	10.0%	300	2,100	10.4%	312
7,038	25%	1,759	10.0%	704	4,575	10.4%	732
13,483		2,359		1,124	10,000		1,402

The company's figures then proceed as follows:

Profits, pre-interest and pre-tax		£54,000
Deduct outgoings allowable for tax purposes		
interest	14,064	
pension contribution	1,500	
salary as above	13,483	
employer's NIC as above	1,402	30,449
		23,551
Deduct corporation tax at 25%		5,888
		17,663
Deduct outgoings not allowable for tax		
principal repayment		16,233
Retainable earnings		1,430

seen if it is compared with Table 22; the self-employed pay less NIC,[2] but this is more than out-weighed by the fact that the self-employed individual's earnings took him into the 40 per cent income tax band on the top £10,725 of his income, while in this paragraph neither the salary earner, nor the company itself, paid tax at any rate higher than 25 per cent. However, the advantage appears to be only around £700 (£1,430 retention compared to £717 in the previous paragraph). It would be surprising if that were not swallowed up by the costs of operating a company. At income levels lower than those illustrated,

---

[2] The self-employed obtain fewer benefits from these lower NIC contributions. They do not qualify for any SERPS (state earnings-related pension scheme) for instance; nor are they entitled to any earnings-related supplements to unemployment benefit should they become entitled to draw such benefit. It is always dangerous to treat as if it were merely a tax what is in part at least a payment by employed earners into contributory schemes.

it is unlikely there would be any tax advantage in incorporating a business.[3]

3.10 If the business is incorporated, are there different approaches possible to its financing?

At the end of that first year, the company's balance sheet would show the position as in Table 24 (the opening, comparative, figures being shown in the right hand column).

Table 24: Balance Sheet End of First Year

		Comparatives
Total assets (as acquired with original equity and borrowings, and increased with retention of £1,430)	583,970	582,540
Less borrowings (after repayment)	146,094	162,327
	437,876	420,213
Share capital	420,213	420,213
Retained earnings (this is the profit and loss figure; the repayment of borrowings is not a reduction here)	17,663	
	437,876	

But there is an alternative, hinted at in paragraph 1.37 above. The owner of this company has so far drawn a salary, the gross amount being £13,483. Since he would not reach a 40 per cent tax rate until he had income of £27,145 (that is to say, he moves beyond the £3,445 personal deduction plus the basic rate band of £23,700) it would cost no more tax if he were to draw a further dividend of £13,662 gross, £10,930 net. This would accelerate the company's tax (ACT) on this

---

[3] It is a straightforward arithmetical calculation that if one were to leave the interest expense and the individual's drawings unchanged, but reduce the business's earnings by £4,753 to £49,247, this would:

(a) in the case of the unincorporated business reduce after tax profits by 60 per cent of £4,753, thus eliminating the retention and reducing the amount of principal that could be repaid to £14,098,

(b) in the case of the company reduce the after tax profits by 75 per cent of £4,753, thus eliminating the retention and reducing the amount of principal that could be repaid to £14,098.

Any greater reduction in earnings would, on the data shown, push the unincorporated business into a better position than the company.

dividend, but would not change the overall level of the tax burden.[4] And provided the owner promptly lent the amount of the net dividend back to the company, it would not be prevented from making its principal repayment to the bank, and still having £1,274 of extra assets on its balance sheet. The figures would then be as shown in Table 25.

Table 25: Balance Sheet if Dividend Paid and Lent Back to Company

		Comparatives
Total assets (as acquired with original equity and borrowings, and increased with retention of £1,430)	583,970	582,540
less bank borrowings after repayment	146,094	162,327
Shareholder loan	10,930	
	426,946	420,213
Share capital	420,213	420,213
Retained earnings (this is the profit and loss figure after the dividend of £10,930 net; the repayment of borrowings is not a reduction here)	6,733	
	426,946	

3.11 Saving future taxes without tax cost today

If the owner of this company envisages selling it in a few years time, this does save some tax. Whatever he would have received as vendor in the form of sale proceeds will be reduced by £10,930 with a consequent saving of capital gains tax on those smaller proceeds; but he will still receive the same overall figure, because the purchaser will undertake to procure that the company repays £10,930. That repayment has no tax effects either for the vendor or for the company.[5] The saving may not appear large, but that is simply because this one year's figures are not large.

If the owner envisages retaining the company, and envisages that his own salary and dividends from it will put him into a higher tax bracket within a few years, it clearly makes sense for him to draw this dividend

---

[4] ACT at 20/80ths of the net dividend is equivalent to 18.75 per cent of the profits out of which it is paid. That is the liability which is accelerated. The remaining 6.25 per cent of the profits out of which the dividend is paid is still due at the same date as would have been the 25 per cent on the profits if a dividend had not been paid.

[5] The subject of financial assistance by a company for the purchase of its own shares, generally prohibited by sections 151 and onward Companies Act 1985, is more fully dealt with in paragraphs 9.19 and onward below. This transaction is unobjectionable (despite the company's assets being paid to a vendor and the purchaser therefore paying less for its shares) provided that the company's *net* assets are not reduced. Equal reductions in its assets and its liabilities do not contravene the provisions.

today, and thus put himself in a position to be able to enjoy the cash by way of repayment from the company at any time he wants it in the future. To be able to save future taxes without tax cost today is always a worthwhile course.

3.12 Non-tax aspects of the separation of the business from its owner by incorporation

The heading to paragraph 3.1 was *Why incorporate?* and what we have been attempting to do in the intervening paragraphs is to look at some of the factors which may suggest incorporation, or incline the decision the other way. By far the most important of those factors are these, which can be seen to be interrelated:

- incorporation separates the business and its assets from the owner, the first being enclosed within and the second outside what we have characterised as a watertight tank. That of itself imposes a degree of discipline on the owner, and on anyone else involved, discipline that would not otherwise have been there. One might draw an analogy with the difference between the man who owns and occupies his own house, and the man who has put his house in trust for his children, retaining only the right to occupy it for his own lifetime. Its condition at his death, and their subsequent ability to enjoy occupation, may not previously have much concerned him; but the aspects of continuity, and the dual position in which he himself stands as occupant but at the same time as guardian of the property for future occupants are ever present reminders of the difference the trust has made;

- there are pipes between the company and its owners, along which water may flow out of, or into, the tank. But those flows will frequently cost money, which further trammels the owners' activities and enjoyment;

- the company is a separate entity which has its own dealings with third parties. Its owners need to consider carefully how their own dealings with it may affect its own position *vis-à-vis* the outside world. Is it, for instance, so good an idea to strip it of distributable profits, and lend them back to it, if those who read its balance sheet might see this as leaving it over-borrowed, and not properly placed to cope with some downturn in its business or in the economy as a whole? Perception is as important as truth in questions such as this.

The decision to incorporate is never simple; but we must continue our examination on the assumption that that is the chosen course.

3.13 Single member companies

The possibility of forming companies with only one member (or of allowing the membership of existing companies to be changed so that only a single member remains) was opened up from 15 July 1992 by Statutory Instrument No. 1699 of 1992. But, even limiting our comments here to the company whose single member is the individual who owns it and is its sole director, it has to be said that the *separation* of the company and that individual is made more, rather than less, uncertain:

- The general public are supposed to be put on notice that the company has only one member by that being stated in its register of members, but it need not specifically notify the Registrar of Companies.

- Contracts between member and company must be written, or recorded in memorandum form, or in the director's minutes. But the public, including the company's creditors, would have no access to this information unless the company went into liquidation. Another problem arises from the exemption allowed for contracts entered into in the *ordinary course of the company's business*, which is nowhere defined.

- But it is the member's decision-making process which generates the greatest uncertainties. He can hold formal, one-person, meetings if he goes through the required procedures for calling members' meetings. Alternatively he can use the written resolution procedure, avoiding the formalities for meetings, but substituting others in their place (for instance the need to send resolutions to the auditors and to give them seven days to decide whether the resolution affects them and whether they should be allowed a meeting so as to be able to speak, but not vote, against it). Without their acceptance the resolution would be ineffective.

- That leaves the possibility of the *informal decision* procedure, arising from the preservation into the Companies Act 1989 of the principle that all of the members of a company acting together can do things in a way which does not comply with the provisions of the Act (subject of course to the qualification that the things done must be within the company's powers). However the statutory instrument fails to confirm the principle's existence or to indicate an acceptable way of making decisions, confining itself simply to a necessity for them to be recorded in writing and notified to the company.[6]

3.14 The procedure for the formation of a company

The procedure for the formation of a company involves the *subscription of its Memorandum* by its original shareholder or shareholders, who by subscribing apply also to have the company issue to it or them

---

[6] The Companies Registry regards the provision (in the new section 382B CA 1985) requiring written records of decisions notified to the company as merely a sweeping-up provision, dealing with 'recording of decisions by the sole member'; indeed that is its heading. We will examine the uncertainties left by the Statutory Instrument's drafting in paragraphs 6.8 to 6.10 below, the last of these addressing in particular the informal decision problems. It can perhaps be said that the level of uncertainty *may* be less in a case where the sole member/director is an individual, than is the subsidiary company whose sole member is the parent company.

its original (or founders') share or shares. In a public company those subscribers must pay cash for their shares, and the company may not start business or borrow funds until its allotted share capital is at least £50,000, and at least one quarter of the nominal value (plus the whole of the premium if any) has been paid up on every share allotted, although in the case of shares other than the subscribers' shares this *payment* may be in money or money's worth. The second stage of the procedure is that that Memorandum, and the company's Articles of Association are filed with the Registrar of Companies. It is his issue of a certificate of incorporation which brings the company into existence.[7]

3.15 *The shelf company*

Where a ready-formed company (usually referred to as a shelf company) is acquired from solicitors it is normal for there to have been two subscribers to its Memorandum, for those subscribers to take one share each on which no amount of cash has been paid, but the price of which becomes a debt due to the company on incorporation; for them also to be directors (and one of them to be secretary). That makes it clear that, at least partly because of the uncertainties referred to in paragraph 3.13 and Note 6, it is more usual for companies to continue to be formed with two members; if it is thereafter desired that such a company should drop to having a single member, there is no technical problem over registering both of its shares into his name. But we will assume unless otherwise stated that we are dealing throughout this book with what it is convenient to call multi-member companies. Taking the company down from the shelf and activating it thus involves:

- its new shareholders applying for the transfer and registration of the subscribers shares into their names, using for that purpose share transfer forms signed by the subscribers;

- those subscribers, in their continuing capacity (at least pro tem) as directors assenting to the changes in the share register;

- the new shareholders, or those nominated by them being appointed directors to replace the original directors, and a new secretary being appointed in place of the original.

---

[7] Sections 1, 2 and 3 CA 1985 deal with the company's Memorandum, and sections 7 and 8 with its Articles of Association. They are to be filed in accordance with section 10, the effects of the company's registration are set out in section 13, and thereafter the effect of the Memorandum and Articles are spelled out in section 14, all in CA 1985. Sections 101, 106, 117 and 118 CA 1985 deal with the minimum capitalisation of a public company. The Memorandum can be viewed as the company's notice to the public (through the Registrar) of the company's existence, initial capitalisation, purposes, and the identity of its founders. The Articles can be thought of as the contract between the company and its shareholders, present and future. It is possible, although unusual, for a company to have no Articles, in which case the need to register them clearly does not apply. A discussion of how the company would then operate – what replaces the Articles – fits better into paragraph 8.2 but the whole of chapters 8 and 9 can be seen as a wide-ranging examination of the powers and responsibilities of shareholders and directors.

INCORPORATION

At that point a private company is operational, and if its new owner is a company we will see in chapter 6 that it is a subsidiary of that parent and able to engage in certain transactions with its parent without tax costs. Usually at the end of the board meeting at which the foregoing has taken place the solicitor/subscribers resign as directors. Where, in the chapters which follow, it is necessary to achieve the incorporation of companies, we will assume that this is the procedure followed (unless otherwise specified);[8] and therefore any new company can be assumed to commence with two shares subscribed, nil paid, but with ownership in the desired hands and directors appointed by those owners. Where a company is purchased from formation agents, pre-prepared, blank, share transfer forms, written resolutions by the original directors assenting in blank to those share transfers, and undated resignation forms from original directors and secretary are needed because of the non-attendance at the initial board meeting of the subscribers/initial directors.

3.16 The issue of shares for cash

In the private companies we have been looking at in the last three paragraphs, the only shares we have so far *issued* have been the subscribers' share or shares.

The issuing of shares has been used here as a non-technical term, which seems to square reasonably well with its use (for instance in tax legislation)[9] to cover the whole process by which the company raises money by *issuing* shares. In fact it is the directors who allot shares, other than the subscribers' shares, and they do so under authority granted by members.[10] The allotment may be for cash or non-cash consideration, or alternatively shares may be allotted as paid up in part or whole (including the premium element if any) if the company has available

---

[8] There are difficulties with this procedure in the case of some reconstructions. See Note 35 on paragraph 6.22 for a discussion of the problem, and its possible solutions.

[9] The courts have interpreted 'issued' in different ways, depending on the context in which the word was used. But in a recent application to the court in a tax matter it was necessary to fix a precise point at which shares could be said to have been issued (*National Westminster Bank plc and Another v IRC* [1993] *Times Law Reports* 10 January 1994); the Court of Appeal, reversing the High Court decision, held that this was the time when the parties were entered in the share register, and not the earlier time at which they became bound, the company to register the shareholder, and the prospective shareholder to take the shares and give consideration for them. The House of Lords, [1994] 3 WLR 159, has upheld that Court of Appeal decision, albeit only by a narrow majority, confirming that the actual dates of registration, not the earlier *binding contract* or the later issue of the share certificates, were appropriate for the purposes of the Business Expansion Scheme legislation the courts had all been considering. This lined up with the decision that the issue of a renounceable (or for that matter non-renounceable) allotment letter gave a mere right to have shares issued, and did not itself constitute the issue. See also paragraph 6.47 and Note 86 thereon for further implications of the word 'issued'.

[10] Section 80 CA 1985. The paying up of shares in cash or non-cash is in section 99(1) and the issue of bonus shares, fully or partly paid, in section 99(4). The ban on the allotment of shares at a discount is in section 100.

profits or appropriate reserves for this. But shares may not be allotted at a discount.

The Companies Act also contains provisions referred to as the *pre-emption rights*, designed to preserve each shareholder's right to preserve his own percentage holding in the company, and not to have this diluted by the directors' allotment of further shares to other shareholders or others.[11] The company's members can deny themselves this protection if they want to do so, either by agreeing in the Memorandum or Articles that they should not have these rights; or by overriding them to a limited extent (and for a period which does not normally exceed five years) by authorising the directors to allot up to a specified number of shares in order to make acquisitions.

3.17 Conversion of debt into equity capital

The conversion of debt into capital is regarded as an allotment of shares for cash; if £100 of debt is to be *paid off* by the issue of shares having a nominal value of £100, that must imply that the debt is really *worth* its face value.

Any other assumption would imply that the company was issuing shares at a discount. If there is any likelihood that a creditor might claim that a company's capitalisation of debt contravened this, it would be preferable that cash actually be injected into the company for the shares issued, and thereafter that that cash be used to repay the borrowings.[12][13]

---

[11] The pre-emption rights are in section 89 CA 1985. The possibility of excluding them in the company's Memorandum or Articles is in section 91, and section 95 enunciates the principle that the company's having given the directors specific or general authority to allot up to a specified number of shares, for instance for acquisition purposes, is itself a legitimate overriding of the pre-emption rights of existing shareholders.

[12] If the debt has been subordinated (paragraph 1.8), neither the straightforward capitalisation of it into shares nor its repayment in cash out of the proceeds of a share issue would be permissible – unless the terms of the subordination were to allow for these transactions. When one thinks this through, it seems obvious that creditors would not be being prejudiced by either transaction, in fact their position would be if anything improved. Corporate lawyers might be accused of dancing on the point of a pin in a case such as this.

[13] There is however a quite different matter, which can be equally significant. Bearing in mind that a loss on shares is likely to be allowable under the capital gains tax legislation, whereas it is less likely that a lender will obtain relief for a loss if a loan is not repaid in full, what is the capital gains tax acquisition value, in the hands of the shareholder, of the new shares issued to him as capitalisation of his debt? The general principle is that that cost must be the amount called up, since this is to be regarded for the reasons explained in the text as having been paid in cash. But that general principle is then made subject to the two statutory exceptions also mentioned in the text and referenced in Notes 16 and 17, which override the general principle in those particular circumstances but only those. It is worth noting, however, that section 574 TA 1988 permits what would otherwise be a capital gains tax loss on shares to be treated in certain circumstances as a loss deductible from income. And section 253 TCGA 1992 allows some losses on loans to be treated as effective for capital gains tax purposes.

There are three possible cases needing consideration: first, if there is only one shareholder (or if there is more than one but the amounts of loan each is capitalising is in proportion to their shareholdings). The question is whether any issue of new shares falls within the capital gains *reorganisation* provisions, being 'in respect of and in proportion to ... (his or their) holding of shares in the company'.[14] It is vital that we appreciate, in answering that question, that there really are two transactions, the allotment of shares by the directors comes first, and the calling up of the unpaid liability, in fact settled out of the debt, follows. Particularly in the light of the pre-emption rights referred to in the previous paragraph, it is difficult to argue that the allotment is not both 'in respect of, and proportionate to ... '.[15] One is almost inevitably dragged into those reorganisation provisions and, as they now stand, they also now include a further requirement that the acquisition cost of the new shares shall for capital gains tax purposes be arrived at on open market principles. That means that one will be limited to an acquisition cost no greater than the amount by which the shareholding increases in value as a result of the reorganisation.[16]

3.18 *Connected parties' conversion of debt into equity*

The second case is the one in which the shareholdings and the loan capitalisations are not proportionate, but the shareholders involved are regarded as *connected with* the company. The basic capital gains tax rule in this case is that whatever might otherwise have been regarded as the asset's (the additional shares') acquisition cost is to be ignored, and their market value is to be substituted.[17] Once again, one is driven to the same conclusion as follows from the different route decreed in the previous paragraph; it is not possible to turn a fall in value that has

---

[14] Section 126(2)(a) TCGA 1992.

[15] The Court of Appeal decided in *Dunstan v Young Austen Young Ltd* [1989] STC 69 that an allotment of shares to the 99.9 per cent shareholder (the 0.1 per cent legal holder being only a nominee for that first beneficial holder) did fit within the phrase. The changes in the wording of the legislation since the events the court was considering make the case for the applicability of these provisions, if anything, more persuasive. In paragraph 3.19 there is a reference to an arrangement which was based on an issue of shares not being made in the form of a rights issue (that is straightforward), but also made so as to fall outside the words quoted 'in respect of and in proportion to ...'. It follows from what has been said here that this is now less easy to achieve than it was at the time of the events outlined in paragraph 3.19.

[16] Section 128(2) TCGA 1992: '... any consideration shall be disregarded to the extent it exceeds ... the amount by which the market value of the new holding ... exceeds the market value of the original shares'. Note that meaning of the original shares is self-evident, but that throughout the reorganisation provisions the phrase 'new holding' is defined to mean not the shares which are new, but the total number of shares after the reorganisation.

[17] The definition of persons connected with a company is to be found in the combined application of section 286(6) and (7) TCGA 1992. There is a multiplicity of forms of connection, but any of them brings in section 17(1) TCGA 1992, requiring in this case that the additional shares be deemed to have been acquired at their open market value. All these provisions, and the way in which they operate, are looked at in some depth in paragraph 6.37 and the Notes on that paragraph.

already occurred on the loan into an allowable capital gains tax loss on the shares.

If there is a case which does not fall within either of the above, then the *prima facie* assumption is that the shareholder concerned, any other shareholders, and the company must each have been operating *at arm's length*; therefore whatever figures they agreed between themselves should be acceptable to the tax authorities. Substituting any other assumption could be argued to involve either the shareholder we have been looking at, the others, or the company, giving up value to one or more other party.

3.19 *Reverse Nairn Williamson*

Some ancient tax avoidance devices, and the legislative provisions enacted to prevent them, become such dim memories that tax advisers live in fear of re-inventing them without realising or remembering. Nairn Williamson, the taxpayer in a celebrated 1977 case, was essentially in the position described as the second illustration in the preceding paragraph. Both tax and companies' legislation was differently drafted at that time, and the company was able to put forward a tenable argument that its transaction was not one in which it was required (in the manner indicated) to substitute a £72,000 market value as the acquisition cost of loan stock for which it had subscribed £210,000. Nairn Williamson did however lose that argument in the Court of Appeal. The case itself is of no continuing significance, because all of the legislative provisions on which it was fought have since changed, including even the fact that the loan stock involved would today not be an asset within the scope of capital gains tax.

But on the back of the court's decision (that market value must be substituted) a different device was invented which came to be known as reverse *Nairn Williamson*. If an entrepreneur had built up a very successful company from small beginnings, he might find himself with shares which had a £100 original cost, and a value of (say) £100,000. He could arrange that the company made an issue of a very large number of shares for which the cash to be subscribed was considerably less than their full value, but issued them in such a way that they did not fall within the *reorganisation* provisions referred to in paragraph 3.17 and Notes 14 and 15 thereon. Thus if he subscribed £80,000 for a further £80,000 shares, the market value of these new shares he came to own would be:

$$\frac{80{,}000}{80{,}100} \times (100{,}000 + 80{,}000)$$

that is to say, the proportion of the enlarged share capital they represented, applied to the company's existing value increased by the new capital injected into it[18]

---

[18] This valuation formula is of course extremely crude, and must only be regarded as providing an illustration of the relative scales of the numbers.

That produces a *cost* for the new shares of £179,775, and if this is added to the £100 cost of the shares he already held, and the entrepreneur sells the company for the £180,000 we have assumed to be its increased worth, his capital gain would be almost nothing – or at least it would have been, until the enactment of the legislation which now prevents this interesting transaction.[19]

3.20 The issue of shares for non-cash consideration by private companies

What the law could, or could not, allow was originally developed by judicial exposition of various problems brought into the courts, but has lately been codified in statutory form. It is therefore tempting to assume that it is now all cut and dried, that there are no loose ends, or any particular room for manoeuvre; but we will see that this is not as true as might be presumed.

We need to deal first, as indicated by the heading to this series of paragraphs, with the private companies' issues of shares for non-cash consideration. Different criteria apply in public companies, so that it is sensible to deal with them separately in paragraph 3.26 and Note 33 thereon.

Next, throughout what follows, it is worth remembering that we have to consider three separate aspects. First and most obvious, there are the company and contract law provisions governing the company's ability to issue shares as consideration for its receipt of the assets, or anything else, we will be looking at; provisions which reflect through into the effects on other shareholders and on creditors.

Second, there are tax implications, one of the most important being the effects on the previous owner of assets, since he might be expected to have a capital gains tax disposal when he makes the relevant transfer to the company, and he could also be expected to have a cessation of trade if he incorporates his business. We will need to analyse what reliefs may be available for the transferor, and how these affect the company and those who become its owners.

But the third matter we will also need to bear in mind is stamp duty. Asset transfers will usually involve documents, and those documents will usually be conveyances. Once again, there are some reliefs, but we need to understand whether, and how, duty can be avoided.

There is a fourth matter, namely the accounting implications for the acquiring company. We will start our examination of this in paragraphs 3.26 to 3.29, but thereafter we will be returning, repeatedly, throughout this book to this same subject.

---

[19] Section 17(2) TCGA 1992. This overrides the requirement in subsection (1) that market value be substituted, and therefore leaves him with the actual £80,000 as the cost of the shares acquired. It overrides that market value rule because the two conditions in subsection (2) are met, namely that the company did not *dispose* of shares when it issued them to him, and he paid less than their market value.

3.21 Spargo's case

The story probably starts with *Spargo's case*.[20] Mr Spargo transferred some mining licences to a company for shares, while his fellow promoters put in cash for their shares. He managed the company, and when it failed its creditors claimed that since he had not paid for his shares he had an uncalled liability, and the liquidator could demand payment.

The foregoing is actually a collapsing into a single stage of the two-stage transaction he had undertaken. The law[21] did not then permit the company to issue shares for mining licences. What he did was to sell the mining licences to the company under an oral contract for a cash sum left owing to him. Then, when the company issued shares to him, he released the debt as payment for them.[22] The court had no difficulty in accepting that Mr Spargo's shares were fully paid, and that he had no further liability on them.

The case is also useful in pointing a way in which it may be possible to avoid stamp duty.[23] The first requirement is that the assets are of a kind that can be transferred without the necessity for a written contract (they might for instance comprise the assets of a business to be transferred as a going concern, or shares in a non-UK company being acquired whose domestic laws allowed transfer without a document to effect it). The assets are accordingly transferred to the company under an oral contract; and the second requirement is that the consideration must be expressed as a cash sum left outstanding. It then follows that (as explained above) the company's allotment of shares is treated as

---

[20] *Re Harmony and Montague Tin & Copper Mining Co. (Spargo's case)* (1873) 8 Ch. App. 407. There is an apocryphal story about a very senior advocate who always quoted *Spargo's case* as the authority for any proposition he was advancing, when he could not remember what the real authority was. It was said that senior judges would invariably remember the name from their days at law school, but would have forgotten long since what the case actually decided; even if a judge were later to try to look it up he would be foiled by the fact that it is listed only under H for Harmony rather than S for Spargo. The advocate therefore relied (and it never failed) on the judge merely nodding sagely, and allowing him to proceed.

[21] That part of what is now section 99(1) CA 1985 allowing for shares to be paid up in *money's worth* did not then exist.

[22] The release would now fall squarely within the definition in section 738(2) CA 1985 of what constitutes payment in cash which includes cases in which 'the consideration . . . is a release of a liability of the company for a liquidated sum'.

[23] Stamp duty is payable on a document by which assets are *conveyed or transferred on sale* to a company. If the document expresses the consideration for the conveyance as being the issue by the company of its shares, then the latter are treated as issued for non-cash consideration, and the (stamped) conveyance must be filed with the return of allotments at Companies House (section 88(2)(b)(i) CA 1985). In the case of allotments of shares for non-cash consideration where there is *no* document conveying the assets, it is necessary that *particulars* of the assets transferred be filed in the same way, and those particulars need to be stamped (section 88(3) and (4) CA 1985). Until 1988, there was an exemption from duty on these conveyances and deemed conveyances (paragraph 13 of schedule 19 to FA 1973), where the consideration for the transfer was the issue of shares on which capital duty was payable, but this exemption was withdrawn when capital duty was abolished.

for cash. The only document brought into existence[24] is the return of allotments for cash. There is thus no return for non-cash allotments[25] (with a conveyance or particulars attached) and nor is there a document (here or left abroad) transferring assets for cash consideration; there is nothing which needs a stamp affixed.

3.22 *Zevo Finance*

After *Spargo's case* we can move forward to *Zevo Finance*.[26] Here again the judiciary, in this case the House of Lords, were developing law which was not spelled out in any statute.

Sir Otto Beit and his family owned all the shares in a private investment company, Zevo Syndicate Ltd. Following his death, his executors decided on a reconstruction, dividing the investments between two new companies; Zevo Trust Ltd took what were described as the sounder investments, and the more speculative investments were put into Zevo Finance Ltd. The latter transfer was described as being a transfer of a part of the undertaking of Zevo Syndicate, as outlined in a schedule to the agreement, the consideration being that Zevo Finance agreed to take over specified obligations of Zevo Syndicate, and as to the balance to issue fully paid ordinary shares. The balance sheet of Zevo Finance resulting from this agreement showed:

Share capital	620,030	Investments	1,029,959
Debentures with accrued interest	409,929		
	1,029,959		1,029,959

Zevo Finance was a company whose trade was dealing in shares (this was before the days of capital gains tax, so gains and losses on the disposal of its investments would either have been outside the scope of tax, or trading profits and losses, depending upon the status of

---

[24] The procedures explained in this paragraph 3.21 however apply where the return is of allotments for cash and there is *no* written contract. That raises the question what happens if, in the case of a cash allotment, there *is* a written contract (for instance for the transfer of shares in a non-UK company) which is executed and left abroad (because in the cash allotment case it is not necesary to file it with the return of allotments). The normal stamp duty rule for a document which would need stamping if it were executed in the UK, but which is in fact executed abroad, is that duty only becomes payable if and when the document is brought into the UK. This normal rule would therefore seem to allow duty to be deferred, perhaps indefinitely, without penalty for late stamping. But in this particular case the exercise would be fruitless because the *cash* allotments return would need to be treated under section 14(4) Stamp Act 1891 as being the 'instrument ... relating to ... any matter or thing done ... in the UK'; although it primarily relates to the issue of the company's shares, it also relates to the conveyance. Therefore it requires stamping by virtue of section 14(4).
[25] The return is under section 88(2)(a) CA 1985 for cash allotments, and section 88(2)(b) for non-cash consideration.
[26] *Craddock (HM Inspector of Taxes) v Zevo Finance Co. Ltd* [1946] 1 All ER 523, 27 TC 267.

the company). In the year following the reorganisation, Zevo Finance sold some of the investments, showing a loss of £80,503 by reference to those investments' *costs* included within the £1,029,959. The Inland Revenue argued that the value at which the investments should have been transferred between the companies totalled only £363,173 (using stock exchange prices) and that on that footing Zevo Finance had actually made profits of £31,729 on the investments sold.

Zevo Syndicate had previously been taxed as a dealer in shares. In its final accounts to the date of reorganisation, if it had been treated as having *disposed* of the shares in question for £363,173 rather than £1,029,959, it would have made a loss for tax purposes, and would not (as the law stood, and with its trade having ceased) have been able to obtain any relief for some £700,000 of that loss.

3.23 The shares issued are themselves the consideration given by the company for the non-cash assets acquired, but the value to be attributed to that consideration must be related to the non-cash assets

It was no part of the taxpayer's argument that it would have been inequitable to have left the original company with unusable losses, and taxed the successor on profits, both stemming from the £363,173 stock exchange prices. Rather, the taxpayer argued that the actual purchase price it had paid was £1,029,959.

It is worth quoting from Lord Greene MR in the Court of Appeal, since this analysis was unanimously approved by the House of Lords:

> The terms on which the Syndicate and its liquidator agreed to part with these investments were (1) that the Respondents should take over the liability on the debentures; (2) that the Respondents should issue fully paid shares to the holders of the Syndicate ... By no possible means can this arrangement be varied so as to leave the shareholders with shares on which only part of the nominal amount (or indeed nothing) is to be treated as having been paid. The fallacy, if I may respectfully so call it, which underlies the argument is to be found in the assertion that where a company issues its own shares as consideration for the acquisition of property, these shares are to be treated as money's worth as though they were shares in another company altogether, transferred by way of consideration for the acquisition. This proposition amounts to saying that consideration in the form of fully paid shares issued by a company must be treated as being the *value* of the shares, no more and no less. Such a contention will not bear a moment's examination where the transaction is a straightforward one and not a mere device for issuing shares at a discount. In the everyday case of reconstruction, the shares in the new company allotted to the shareholders of the old company as fully paid will often, if not in most cases, fetch substantially less than their nominal amount if sold in the market. But this does not mean that they are to be treated as issued at a discount, or that the price paid by the new company for the assets which it acquires from the old company ought to be treated as something less than nominal value of the fully paid shares.

3.24 *The Steel Barrel case*

The result at which Lord Greene thus arrived was that the Inland Revenue were not entitled to displace the £1,029,959 *cost* of the investments, because they could not displace the fully paid par value of the shares issued. This is the same result which Lord Greene had previously reached in the earlier *Steel Barrel* case,[27] although his *ratio decidendi* in that case adds a different slant:

> The primary liability of an allottee of shares is to pay for them in cash; but when shares are allotted credited as fully paid, this primary liability is satisfied by a consideration other than cash passing from the allottee. A company, therefore, when in pursuance of such a transaction it agrees to credit the shares as fully paid, is giving up what it would otherwise have had, namely, the right to call on the allottee for payment of the par value in cash. A company cannot issue £1,000 nominal worth of shares for stock of the market value of £500, since shares cannot be issued at a discount. Accordingly, when fully paid shares are properly issued for a consideration other than cash, the consideration moving from[28] the company must be at the least equal in value to the par value of the shares and must be based on an honest estimate by the directors of the value of the assets acquired.

We will come back to the honesty of estimations in paragraph 3.26.

3.25 Stanton v Drayton

There is, however, one more final case in which the House of Lords rejected another of the Inland Revenue's suggestions of a different valuation process. *Stanton v Drayton*[29] took place after the introduction of capital gains tax, and against the framework of that tax's legislation.

Drayton bought a portfolio of investments from Eagle Star. It later sold some of them, and the question was what had been their acquisition cost under the capital gains tax rules. The total price agreed between Drayton and Eagle Star had been £3,937,962. This had been agreed to be satisfied by the issue by Drayton of its own shares, but the deal itself (and therefore the issue of the shares) was conditional on Drayton's shareholders approval and the Stock Exchange granting a listing to the new shares. The second condition was satisfied three weeks after the agreement was signed, and at the time that agreement thus became final and binding, the shares which Drayton had agreed to issue had a market value of only £3,076,532.

---

[27] *Osborne v Steel Barrel Co. Ltd* [1942] 1 All ER 634, 24 TC 293.

[28] In *Shearer v Bercain*, referred to in paragraph 3.26 below but examined in greater depth in paragraphs 6.13 onwards, Walton J said:

> 'when Mr Bromley first read me that passage I assumed that the words "consideration moving from the company" must be meant to read "consideration moving to the company", but on rereading and reflection I now see that this is erroneous. What Lord Greene M.R. is saying in that passage is that, because shares cannot be issued at a discount, if the company issues shares in exchange for stock, the minimum value which the directors must have placed upon that stock, fairly and honestly, is the nominal value of the shares.'

The author has to admit, respectfully, having on a first reading fallen into exactly the same error as Mr Justice Walton.

[29] *Stanton (HM Inspector of Taxes) v Drayton Commercial Investment Co. Ltd* [1983] AC 501, 55 TC 286.

What is to be treated as the portfolio's acquisition cost for capital gains[30] is 'the amount or value of the consideration, in money or money's worth, given by' the acquiring party, namely Drayton. Elsewhere in the capital gains tax legislation one is frequently directed to substitute an open market value for an agreed figure, but the Lords were unanimous in saying that there was no call to do so in this case. But Lord Roskill sounded the note of warning:

> For myself I would not go so far as to say that in every case of this kind the value of the consideration in money's worth must always be determined by reference to the price at which the shares credited as fully paid were issued, for it is possible that there might be a very long delay between the conclusion of the conditional agreement and the agreement becoming unconditional, during which period some catastrophic event might occur gravely affecting the value on the latter date. I would wish to reserve for future consideration whether in such a case it might not be legitimate to adduce evidence, if the evidence were available, pointing to the conclusion that the value of the consideration in money's worth was less than the price previously agreed between the parties. But on the facts of the instant case I can see no basis on which it could be legitimate to go behind the figure of 160p per share.

3.26 Valuing the assets acquired for the issue of shares

What Lord Greene said in the *Steel Barrel* case (paragraph 3.24) was that the allottee's obligation was to give consideration (in that case in non-cash form) for the shares he was to be allotted, and the value of that consideration must be at the least equal to the par value of the shares 'and must be based on an honest estimate' by the directors of the value of the assets acquired.

The statement is quite clear; it does not prevent shares being issued for a consideration that is greater than their par value – that is to say, the issue of shares at a premium; and it does not allow for such a premium to be treated as non-existent where the honest estimate shows that it does exist.

We will see when we come to examine the saga of *Shearer v Bercain*[31] following paragraph 6.13, when and why the concept was written into company law that a premium achieved, whether on shares issued for money or for money's worth, must be treated as a non-distributable reserve, as quasi-capital; why it took so long for accountants (and many company lawyers) to grasp the implications of this change in the law; and the ways in which this particular area of law has needed to be relaxed.[32] That discussion fits more neatly into the part of this book which deals specifically with a company's allotment of shares to acquire the specific form of money's worth that is the share capital of

---

[30] Now re-enacted in section 38(1)(a) TCGA 1992.
[31] *Shearer (HM Inspector of Taxes) v Bercain Ltd* [1980] 3 All ER 295, 53 TC 698.
[32] The full rigour of the share premium rules is in section 130 CA 1985, and the relaxations in sections 131 to 134 of that Act.

a *target* company, rather than fitting into these paragraphs dealing with the acquisition of assets generally.

What it is appropriate to note here is merely the skeleton; flesh can be added to the bones as we proceed. The directors of private companies have a duty to make an honest estimate of the value of non-cash assets acquired for shares; and the formalities are considerably greater in the case of public companies, in that the valuation must be obtained from an independent expert.[33]

3.27 *Accounting for the assets, and the premium on the shares*

The company's accounting figures follow from the mandatory terms of section 130, Companies Act 1985, requiring that:

> If a company issues shares at a premium, whether for cash or otherwise, a sum equal to the aggregate amount or value of the premiums on those shares shall be transferred to an account called *the share premium account*.

If we assume that the directors of a private company make an honest estimate that the asset they are acquiring has a value of £1,000, and the nominal value of the shares issued on the company's incorporation, when it acquires the asset, is £200, then the commencing balance sheet will show:

Share capital	200	Asset	1,000
Share premium account	800		
	1,000		1,000

Those figures draw attention not just to the asset's carrying value, but to the effect that has on the company's subsequent profits. If the asset is one which does not have an unlimited future useful life, if for instance it is machinery or plant which will wear out or become obsolescent, the depreciation that it is necessary to provide out of the company's future profits will be the figure needed to write down £1,000 to its eventual sale or scrap value. If the asset were stock in trade, and the fall in its value derived from changes in prices in the market place, it would be necessary to write it down. The same would apply to any permanent diminution in the value of a fixed asset. Only exceptionally can a company take any such write-down otherwise than through its profit and loss account.

All this gives rise to two sets of questions. First, there is the network of questions over the basis of the directors' honest estimation of the

---

[33] The main valuation requirement is in section 103 CA 1985, and the ancillary provisions about arrangements, filing and so on, in sections 108 to 111 of that Act. There are exceptions from the requirement for valuation when, *inter alia*, an offer is made to the shareholders of a target company that the predator company we are looking at will allot shares as consideration for the acquisition of their shares in that target; and where the predator makes a similar offer to the target's shareholders to acquire not the target's shares but its assets and liabilities.

value of the assets acquired; everything we saw in the previous chapter indicated that the value of a business as a going concern (we were looking there at this value reflected in the shares of a company carrying on such a business) may bear little relationship to the value in that target company's accounts of the assets it reflects in those accounts – whether or not revalued at the time of the company's acquisition. Second, there are accounting rules regarding the writing down of any asset whose value the acquiring company should not, it is argued, continue indefinitely to carry in its balance sheet.

3.28 Difficulties over attributing any value at all

We will come back repeatedly in the course of this book to the subject of valuation of non-cash *assets* for which a company may issue its shares. The whole question of valuation is questionable and debatable not only for the reasons set out in the last paragraph, but because there are many instances in which there can be real difficulties in attributing any values at all.

One example of a difficult valuation is the company which contracts to have work done for it; a public company cannot issue shares for money's worth taking the form of an undertaking to do work or to perform services,[34] but there is no statutory prohibition on such a transaction by a private company.

Just how difficult are the problems, however, is best explained by looking at an example. An inventor owns 99 of the shares in a £100 company which holds the rights to an idea which needs development, and particularly needs marketing. He brings together an investor willing to put £30,000 into the venture, and a salesman willing to put in his skills, on the footing that they will each have (at the end of, say, two years) equal stakes in the company. The plan is that the salesman's efforts will have resulted in contracts for sales in line with the company's initial production capacity, and he and they agree that his shareholding should be conditional on his achieving these *targets*.

The mechanical aspects of the plan are that the inventor subscribes at par for another 384 shares, and the investor subscribes £30,000 for 483 shares (£29,517 being credited to share premium account). The company then contracts that it will issue the salesman 33 shares in two years time, conditional on his having achieved contracts for a target level of sales, and each of the investor and the inventor grant him a call option, entitling him to purchase at a purely nominal price 150 shares from each of them, at the end of the same two years, this option again being conditional upon his having achieved the target sales. Until and unless the salesman is issued his 33 shares (and exercises his call options), the company will have share capital of £966, split equally between inventor and investor. When and if the salesman comes in, each of the three will have 333 shares.

---

[34] Section 99(2) CA 1985.

3.29 Difficulties in valuation of non-cash consideration (continued)

An old case[35] suggests that the company and the salesman need to contract for the *work* he is to do, putting a monetary price on it. It is his release of the company's (monetary) indebtedness which is the proper consideration for its issue of the shares. If that were not the case, and if after the company had made the issue the salesman's *work* turned out to be non-existent or deficient, the company's only right against him would be for damages for breach of contract; this, the judge suggested, could not be a proper basis for the company's issuing shares credited as fully paid.

But that has not answered the question what should be the amount of the contracted sum? £33 has the merit only of showing that the shares have not been issued at a discount; it is difficult to believe that the value to the company of the business brought in by this salesman is not more than £33, especially given the whole background of the other two shareholders being prepared to let him into their joint venture. That would suggest a much higher contract sum than £33 – and a credit to share premium account on the issue.

It is however tax considerations which are paramount in these valuation questions. First, what we envisage is a contract under which the salesman is to work for £33 (if we stick with that figure). Under ordinary schedule E principles, that becomes taxable income when he is entitled to the cash.[36] Probably the simplest way of allowing him to turn £33 owing by the company into 33 shares issued to him by the company is to give him an option, exercisable contingently on the targets' being achieved. If so, the *gain realised on the exercise* is taxable at that point, this gain being defined as the difference between the then value of the shares, and the amounts he has paid on grant and exercise.[37] (If the contract is not structured as an option, there is a different tax provision which produces much the same result.)[38] Thus the salesman will need to

---

[35] In *Gardner v Iredale* [1912] 1 Ch. 700, Parker J said that if a company were to allot shares in this way the rights the company had against the shareholder to demand payment for his shares would be displaced; the company's rights would instead become those for damages for breach of contract. Although his remarks were *obiter*, he suggested that this would not be a transaction the courts could accept. However, if the company made a contract to pay a stipulated price for the services, and the prospective shareholder released that debt as *payment* for his shares, Parker J indicated that he would be less concerned. That does seem to imply that the company must be able to envisage its being, at the time of the transaction, already indebted for services which had yet to be performed.

[36] Sections 202A and 202B ICTA 1988.

[37] Section 135 ICTA 1988. Except in the case of those options granted and exercised in approved share option schemes, this section taxes gains deemed to be made on 'the exercise ... of a right to acquire shares ... obtained by that person as a director or employee'. It seems extremely hard to resist the suggestion that the salesman's option was granted to him precisely because of his being a director or employee.

[38] Section 162 ICTA 1988. Under this exceptionally difficult provision, it seems that the measure of the amount assessable is the same as that under section 135, namely the difference between the value of the shares at the date of their issue, and any

continued

agree with the Inland Revenue the value of 33 shares (out of 999 in issue) in order to calculate what tax he has to pay on the issue; and structuring this part of the transaction to involve only a small percentage holding could help to keep the value low.

Tax problems also arise over the other shareholders' disposals, and his acquisitions from them – valuations which all interact.[39]

3.30 *More difficulties over the valuation of assets*

If the asset is a shareholding acquired in another company, one of the possible reasons why the value of that holding might fall is that the company concerned might pay up as a dividend some or all of the profits it had retained prior to its acquisition. The way in which such a fall in value is accounted for is, as we will see in paragraph 6.14, more a matter of accounting convention than precision in valuation theory – and in any event it does not directly affect the figure which was put on the shares issued to acquire the other company shareholding.

Another aspect is goodwill, a subject which we will look at in greater depth in paragraphs 6.26, 6.28 and 6.29 below. At this point, all that we need to say is:

---

continued

sums paid for them; the condition for the section's applicability is worded slightly differently, namely that 'the shares are acquired at an under-value in pursuance of a right or opportunity available by reason of his employment'; but the year in which this income is treated as being taxable is the subject of complex and capricious rules.

[39] At all times after the investor, the inventor and the salesman start working together it is hard to resist the conclusion that they are 'two or more persons acting together to ... exercise control of a company', albeit the salesman does not become a shareholder for two years. All three of them are therefore connected parties, under section 286(7) TCGA 1992, 'in relation to the company'. The significance of parties being connected for capital gains tax purposes is that transactions between them are defined as not being at arms' length (section 18(2) TCGA 1992), and the Inland Revenue are generally able to substitute an open market value for whatever price the parties themselves may have used (section 17(1)(a) TCGA 1992). If in accordance with his option the salesman acquires 150 shares in the company from the investor for a nominal price, this means that that nominal price has to be struck out for capital gains tax, and a proper price substituted in its place – provided that the phrase last quoted 'in relation to the company' means (or includes) 'in relation to transfers between those connected parties of shares in the company'. But it is extraordinarily difficult to think what it does mean if not that. Therefore, it would seem that the inventor, with his low acquisition cost for shares, will be treated as making a gain on his sale of 150 shares to the salesman; the investor has a much higher cost for his shares, and may well appear to make a loss on his sale, but it will be one of those losses which is available only against a subsequent gain made on a disposal to the same connected party (section 18(4) TCGA 1992).

The valuation of the shares in the hands of the salesman who acquires them would be the same as that deemed to be the others' disposal values – if it were the capital gains tax rules that one was concentrating on.

But there must be a strong likelihood that the Inland Revenue would argue that these options to acquire shares from other shareholders are also within the scope of section 135 TA 1988 (as in Note 37), being gains realised by the exercise of rights to acquire shares 'obtained by that person as a director or employee'. If that is the case, the difference between what the salesman pays and the value of the shares at the time of the options' exercise will be taxed as earnings.

- if the company we are looking at acquires a business as a going concern, the *value* attributed to it may be greater that the aggregate of the values put on its individual tangible assets – the difference being the business's goodwill;

- alternatively, if our company acquires another, the *value* attributed to the shares acquired may be greater than the aggregate *in the target's own balance sheet* of its own assets, even if those assets are realistically revalued at the date of acquisition.

The first of these forms of goodwill has to be reflected as a separate asset in the individual accounts of our company. The second will not appear in those accounts (because the only asset they disclose is a shareholding in the target, at an attributed *cost*). But when the target company's accounts are consolidated into those of our company, a goodwill figure will appear in the consolidation.

There are differing views on how goodwill should be quantified – it is the difference between a value put on the consideration given for the acquisition, and the value put on the assets of the acquired business, each of which is, to put it mildly, debatable. And there are differing views whether goodwill can be retained indefinitely in the acquirer's balance sheet, or how it should be written off.

3.31 *There are circumstances in which there is no need – or only a limited need – for a share premium; and assets do not therefore need to be revalued*

There is also a wider question that requires to be thought through before any of those in the previous paragraph, namely the circumstances in which it is legitimate to use an entirely different approach – what we described in paragraph 3.26 above and Note 28 thereto as the way in which the full rigours of the share premium rules have in fact been relaxed, and the reasons why this has been necessary.

As already indicated, these questions will engage us repeatedly throughout, but the principal discussion fits most appropriately into chapter 6, from paragraph 6.12 onwards.

3.32 Incorporating the sole trader's business

After considering the main effects of incorporation in the first twelve paragraphs of this chapter, looking at the mechanics of the issue of shares for cash and for non-cash consideration in the next ten, and then commenting briefly in the last four on the accounting implications of share premium accounts, we now need to focus on the detail; to see just how an individual might approach the incorporation of his business.

The procedures we will look at have the threefold purpose of first avoiding the individual's paying unnecessary tax and other amounts on his ceasing as an individual to carry on his business, second, avoiding unnecessary tax liabilities arising by reference to its transfer to the company, and third, setting up both the individual as shareholder, and the company as trading vehicle, in the best shape for their ongoing operations.

There are various matters which need mentioning, but no more at this stage. If the individual, either for himself or for his employees, had a pension scheme operating, he will need to consider how best to continue its operations from the company. The transfer of his business as a going concern will come within the scope of the TUPE regulations.[40] Unless the people who were employed by him before the change are offered continuing employment by the company on the same or similar terms thereafter, they will have a right to redundancy payments from the company, and probably will also have a claim for unfair dismissal.

3.33 VAT: *the transfer of a business as a going concern*

If we assume that the individual's business has been a going concern it is rational to assume also that it has been registered for VAT purposes. Its cessation will therefore be an event necessitating de-registration; but more importantly, it would be an event on which the business would be regarded as disposing of all of its assets (making supplies of all of its goods) and thus needing to charge VAT on all of those supplies. However, there is a relief from the requirement that VAT be charged in this way – the *supplies* of assets are treated as outside the scope of VAT – if the individual's business is transferred as a going conern to another person (the company) who uses those assets in carrying on the same kind of business, and who is already or immediately becomes registered for VAT purposes.[41] Note that this is a mandatory provision; if the transfer fits within the rules, the *supplies* are outside the scope of VAT, and if the transfer does not, then VAT must be charged. There is no question of the parties needing to elect, or being able to fail to elect for the treatment. Note also that the provisions override both taxability and exemption; the fact that some (or even all) of the assets to be transferred would, had they been within the scope of the tax, have been exempt is irrelevant (for instance commercial buildings dating from prior to 1989 on which 'exemption has not been waived'). When the transfers are made as part of a TOGC, they are outside the scope of tax.[42]

---

[40] The Transfer of Undertakings (Protection of Employment) Regulations 1981, SI 1981 No. 1794. The operation of these regulations is examined in paragraphs 11.36 to 11.41.

[41] The Value Added Tax (Special Provisions) Order 1992, SI 1992 No. 3129. The transfers of going concerns under the VAT legislation is dealt with in more detail in paragraphs 11.32 to 11.35.

[42] There is a useful corollary for this last item; if the individual incurs costs in transferring his exempt asset, any VAT on those costs (VAT on lawyers' fees for instance) would normally be irrecoverable, because it would be attributed to the making of an exempt supply. However input tax is fully deductible if he makes no exempt supplies – and that is exactly the situation we are envisaging. His only supplies are outside the scope of tax. They are accordingly not exempt, and the individual cannot be treated as part exempt by reason of the non-supply made in the course of the of his transfer of his business.

3.34 *The individual's income tax cessation, when he incorporates*

When the individual transfers his business to the company, this constitutes for income tax purposes a cessation of his trade, so that his assessments are made under the cessation provisions, subject to what is said below:

1. at the time of writing income tax is charged on trading profits of the self employed on the *preceding year* basis. What most people understand by this phrase is that the accounts profits of the year to (say) June 1993 are taken as the measure of the assessment for the year 1994/95. What most people fail to appreciate is that if the business had started at (say) the beginning of the fiscal year 1990/91, there would have been five full years' assessments, (1990/91 to 1994/95 inclusive), but the profits going into the measure of those assessments would have been those earned over three and a quarter years only, (from April 1990 to June 1993);

2. if the individual continues to trade until end-March 1996, but then stops, (for instance because his business is transferred to a company), his final assessment (1995/96) will be based on profits earned during those twelve months, April 1995 to March 1996;

3. therefore, on that cessation, it would appear that twenty one months' profits from July 1993 to March 1995 will *fall out of assessment*; logic would say that that compensated for the fact apparent in the first head above that at commencement some twenty one months' profits have been assessed twice. (There are provisions which allow the taxpayer and the Inland Revenue, at commencement and cessation respectively, some discretion over the precise twenty one months which are counted twice/omitted, but this is not a book which needs to become bogged down in the detail);

4. however the 1994 Finance Act contains the first tranche of the legislation to move the assessment of the self employed onto an *actual* basis;

5. if this basis had been fully operational before 1994/95, the assessment for that year would have been based not on profits to 30 June 1993 but on those to 30 June 1994;

6. the final year's assessment for 1995/96 would (subject to what is said in 9 below) have been based on the profits earned during the whole period after the end of the basis period for 1994/95, start-July 1994 to end-March 1996, that is to say twenty one months;

7. therefore, the concept of *profits falling out of assessment* appears on that basis to have been abolished, what has actually happened is that it has been transmuted, as explained below;

8. in the changeover year, (let us assume that the changeover took place in 1993/94, purely in order to illustrate the theory), the profits assessed would have been a twelve months proportion of the twenty four months profits to 30 June 1993. In effect half of these twenty four months profits have fallen out;

9. and on the occasion of the changeover a calculation is made of a figure of *overlap profits*, a further sum which can be deducted on the occasion of the individual's cessation. In the case we are considering of an individual continuing to trade beyond the end of the changeover year, (March 1994 on our assumptions), the definition of *overlap profits* requires that one look for the fiscal year after the changeover year, (1994/95); identify its basis period (accounts to June 1994); the overlap profits are those earned in the part of that basis period falling before the end of the changeover year (the period of nine months July 1993 to March 1994). The effect can thus be seen as analogous to the falling out of assessment of profits for nine months to March 1994;

Those rules are simply the straightforward, normal case, rules for assessments of an individual trader. No attempt has been made to introduce the anti-avoidance provisions dealing with changes in the accounting dates, and in the constitution of firms, around the actual changeover year which is to be 1996/97.

The individual contemplating incorporation needs to be aware that the choice of date for doing so will have some effect on his assessments, but that against the complexity of the rules and the variety of possible circumstances it is possible to say no more than that this can be advantageous or penal.

The individual also needs to be aware of another implication of his proposed *cessation*, which is that the normal rules for the calculation of profit in the period up to its date are rather different from those applying at each year-end in a continuing business. For instance, work in progress and stock in trade must generally be brought into the final account at their realisable value, and not at cost if the latter is lower. As another instance, assets on which capital allowances have been claimed must generally be treated as if they had been sold, so allowances are clawed back if the deemed sale figure exceeds their tax written down value. Lastly, losses generally disappear when a business ceases.[43] Under those three *general* rules (work in progress, stock in trade, and capital allowances), the individual might expect to incur extra income tax in his final trading period, or increased tax thereafter if losses are forfeit. We will see that the first two effects can be avoided on his incorporation of his business into a company, although losses are more of a problem.

3.35 *Transferring the business, together with all its assets, into a company*

We next need to explain the procedures for the transfer of the business into the company. Section 162 TCGA 1992 is headed 'Transfer of

---

[43] There is a little known provision, section 386 TA 1988, which allows an individual (or a partnership) who incorporates his business into a company to treat income which he subsequently derives from that company as if it were income from the previous trade. This enables him to carry forward a loss at the date of incorporation against that subsequent income whether he receives it in the form of dividends 'or otherwise', a phrase thought to include salary. The author admits to never having seen this provision in operation, but it is interesting that it was one of those accepted as being relevant to the incorporation of Lloyd's Names in January 1994.

business to a company' and is sidelined 'Rollover relief on transfer of business'. That makes it sound appropriate, but we will see when we come to paragraph 3.41 that it is not the only available route.

What section 162 envisages is the individual transferring to the company his business as a going concern, together with all of its assets. He can if he wishes retain in his own hands what might have been the business's cash balances; and there will possibly be other assets which are not strictly a part of the business, such as investments acquired out of its earlier profits, or property which has become surplus to its requirements and is let. But all other assets are to be transferred. Although the legislation is silent, it would normally be advantageous (and the Inland Revenue accept although they do not require it) that the transferee company assumes some or all of the liabilities. The Inland Revenue people responsible for income tax and capital gains tax say that when the company assumes obligations of the individual in this way, their *assumption* is not to be regarded as any part of the consideration given by the company for the assets[44] – or to put it in different words, it is the business's *net assets* which are transferred, for a consideration only in the form of shares attributable to their *net* value. No lawyer finds such a concept easy to accept. Like such lawyers, the Stamp Office, also a part of the Inland Revenue, takes the opposite view from its colleagues. Any *conveyance* of the assets of the business needs to be stamped by reference to the consideration, and liabilities assumed (along with the shares issued and any other consideration given) are all counted. The value for stamp duty is thus the *gross assets*.

Reverting to income tax and capital gains tax, the Inland Revenue accept that their view of the transfer makes it possible for the parties to meet the further requirement of section 162, namely that 'the business is so transferred wholly . . . in exchange for shares issued by the company to the person transferring the business'.

3.36 *The hold-over of the individual's capital gain on incorporation*

The words omitted from the quotation at the end of that last paragraph were 'or partly'; but let us ignore that for the moment, and assume that the company issues only shares, and does not make any further payment or become indebted to the tranferor individual.

What section 162 achieves is a hold-over of any capital gain that individual would otherwise have realised on his disposal of his business and its assets to the company. Land and buildings spring to mind as the assets on which such gains may arise, but that overlooks the fact that goodwill may also be a very real feature of the business, using the word goodwill in the economists' sense – the value attributable to the business's ability to generate profits which exceed the sum of a normal return on the net assets and a normal reward to the individual for his labour.

---

[44] Extra Statutory Concession D 32.

The individual comes to hold shares in the company, and their capital gains tax acquisition value is reduced by the *held-over gains* on his disposal to it of goodwill and any other assets within the scope of capital gains tax. Only a disposal of his shares triggers that held-over gain; this is not one of those instances in which disposals by the company of any of the assets it has received can create a liability in the individual's hands. The company does of course own the assets, and *its* capital gains tax acquisition cost for them is their full market value at the time of their transfer.[45]

If we change the assumption with which we started this paragraph, and envisage the transferee company issuing shares for only, say, three quarters of the value of the net assets transferred, and paying the balance in cash by borrowing from a bank, section 162 would allow three-quarters of the individual's gain to be held over, and would require that he paid tax on the remaining quarter.

3.37 Stamp duty in the straightforward incorporation

Clearly the procedures used in allotment of shares must be permissible under the Companies Acts, but at the same time we should aim not to pay unnecessary stamp duty and make sure that we do not disqualify ourselves from section 162 (or from the other reliefs which we have still to look at).

There are methods explained in the next paragraph for avoiding stamp duty. But if these are thought to create problems disproportionate to the amount of that duty, then the individual would be likely to choose to have a document evidencing his transfer of the business and its assets to the company; and the company would allot shares for that non-cash consideration. The document would spell out the total assets being transferred, would spell out also that the company was assuming specified liabilities of the transferor, and that there was to be an allotment of shares treated as fully paid up for a non-cash consideration.

---

[45] It has been suggested that if there is an unincorporated business which owns, but is intending to sell, an asset on which a very considerable capital gains tax liability would arise, and if that liability cannot be deferred through the replacement of business assets rollover relief in section 152 TCGA 1992, then incorporating the business provides another method of deferring the gain. The author would hesitate to recommend this course unless the individual fully understood and accepted that the actual disposal proceeds of the asset would then be realised within the company, and that extracting them into the shareholder's hands could be an expensive process. Also that if that shareholder were to dispose of his shares, the capital gains tax liability would seem likely to represent a disproportionately large share of the proceeds, partly because of the held-over gain, and partly because of the reduced indexation relief caused by that hold-over. The capital gains tax liability on a disposal of the shares by their owner might suggest that he should retain them until death, and the inheritance tax implications could suggest the same. If the company was to be liquidated thereafter, the uprated capital gains tax *cost* of its shares might enable the asset's disposal proceeds to be extracted into the hands of the company's then owners without too great a tax liability. But all this indicates just how rigidly the initial decision locks the company and its owners onto a particular long-term course, from which any deviation is likely to be very expensive.

The document would need to be adjudicated for stamp duty purposes,[46] and the amount of that duty would (as already indicated) be payable on *consideration* representing the value of the total assets.

There are cases (not incorporation by an *individual*) where stamp duty can be reduced through the transferor retaining certain assets, debtors being the obvious example; this has the double advantage of saving duty by reducing the value transferred, and also providing such a transferor some cash from realisation of those debtors. We know that the company's paying cash to an individual as part of the total consideration would create a capital gains tax liability, and if such an individual were subsequently to extract cash from the company by other means there could be a tax cost. Just those same principles apply in the other transfers referred to. However, that alternative possibility of trying to save stamp duty and capital gains tax by leaving the debtors untransferred is not available for the individual using this section 162 route for incorporating his business; the section states its requirement unambiguously, it is the business together with *all* of its assets, or all of those assets other than cash, that must be transferred.

3.38 *Can stamp duty be avoided?*

If it is thought feasible to save stamp duty, then the transfer procedure, and that for the allotment of shares, needs to be rather different:

- the allotment of the shares must be for cash (rather than for a non-cash consideration). It would be normal for there to be a share premium account created, the cash being greater than the nominal value of the shares, but there is no right and wrong, nor any requirement of law, about this. The cash is not called up, but left as a debt due to the company from the individual;

- the company will also assume the individual's obligations for his business's liabilities. Again, the amount he should pay the company for doing so will be left as a debt due to the company from him;

- the transfer of the business (and of its assets, but we will deal further with these below) must be accomplished by an oral, rather than a written contract.[47,48] The sum for which the business and its assets are thus transferred is of course equal to the aggregate of the two debts in the previous heads, thus making the shares fully paid, and eliminating the outstanding for the assumption of liabilities;

---

[46] The document would need to be filed, along with the return of allotments for non-cash consideration, with the Registrar of Companies, section 88(2)(b)(i) CA 1985.

[47] Remember that avoiding stamp duty requires not only the absence of any written contract, but also the procedure of allotting shares for a cash consideration to be paid through the extinction of a liquidated debt. See Note 23 on paragraph 3.21 for the procedure requiring filing and stamping of *particulars* if the mistake is made of allotting shares for a non-cash consideration.

[48] It is not within the compass of this book to discuss the extent to which the transfer of the business by an oral contract may weaken the company's ability to complete contracts originally undertaken by the individual, and to collect money originally due to that individual.

- if the business assets include land or buildings, it is possible to transfer the beneficial interest[49] to the company while leaving the legal interest in the hands of the individual. An *agreement for sale* achieves this, the individual agreeing that he *will* convey the property to the company or to another party at its direction, but only when called on to do so by the company. (The company, with the equitable interest that such an agreement gives it, would not normally call for the conveyance of the legal title until it wished to sell, and could then have it conveyed direct to the purchaser, the stamp duty on that conveyance being the responsibility of the purchaser. But it has to be said that if the company wishes to borrow on the security of the property, a bank is unlikely to look favourably on such an equitable title.)

3.39 *The implications of the full capitalisation that results from section 162*

It is appropriate here to point out that the share premium rules will have resulted in the company commencing its life with all of its assets including goodwill fully valued in its accounts, and mirrored by share capital (and share premium). It is not possible, except to the limited extent explained below, to establish the company with indebtedness to its owner alongside its share capital and premium. We are not achieving the setting up of a company whose owner will be able to extract cash from it tax free, in the guise of repayment of loans, at a point after the company itself has generated cash resources in excess of its then needs.[50]

There can be an exception to this, but the extent of this is likely only to be marginal. If the individual retains what were the cash resources of his business when incorporating its remaining assets, then it would probably be true that the company would need to replace at least some of those funds by borrowing (either from the individual or externally) in order to be able to operate. Not alternatively but additionally, if he is prepared to contemplate some immediate tax liability it is also true that the individual can extract cash as part payment for the transfer of his business,[51] once again the company presumably needing to borrow externally in order to make such a payment.

We looked, in paragraphs 3.27 and 3.28, at the accounting implications of the company starting life with all of its assets fully valued in its accounts in relation to quantifying the company's future profits (for instance the need to provide depreciation on revalued costs rather than original costs, and the questions about recognising diminution in the values of assets, especially goodwill). But there are two particular kinds of asset which the individual will have transferred to his company, along with his business; in each case we need to think rather more

---

[49] The whole of the capital gains tax legislation focuses on acquisitions and disposals of the beneficial interest in land and other assets, not the legal ownership, section 60(2) TCGA 1992.
[50] See paragraphs 1.30 and 3.4.
[51] See final sentences of paragraph 3.36.

carefully about the tax and accounting implications than simply to say that everything is transferred at market value.

3.40 *Transfer values of capital allowance assets, and of stocks, on incorporation of an individual's business*

The first type of asset is plant and machinery, and other items, on which capital allowances can be claimed. It will generally be true that the open market value of these assets will be greater than the figure which we can conveniently describe as their *tax written down value* (although tax legislation has used other phraseology for many years). We noted the implication in paragraph 3.34 – if the individual were simply to dispose of these assets on the *cessation* of his trading at their full value, he would face a tax liability on the difference, the liability which is variously described as a *balancing charge* or as a *clawback of allowances.*

He and the company can comply with the share premium requirements that the transfer is made, and accounted for, at full value while avoiding a balancing charge if they make an election that *for tax purposes* the transfer be treated as made at tax written down value.[52] Notice that this will mean that the company's tax allowances on these assets will thereafter always be smaller than the depreciation in the accounts, and taxable profits correspondingly inflated by comparison with accounting profits.[53]

The second asset is work in progress and stock in trade, also noted in paragraph 3.32 as needing to be brought into the final profit and loss account on a cessation at market value; once again one might generally expect this value to be higher than cost, and thus to give the individual a tax liability for which he would see no logical basis. In this case, if transferor and transferee do in fact use the higher market value as the basis of their contract and their accounting (to comply with the share premium concepts) there is no election available to them under which they can displace this with some lower figure for tax purposes. All that the tax law allows is that they can each calculate their profits by

---

[52] The election is under section 77(3) CAA 1990 in respect of plant and machinery, and under section 158 of the same Act in respect of all other types of assets qualifying for capital allowances.

[53] If the differences between tax figures and accounts figures are material, and if those differences will reverse in later years, accountants are required by SSAP 15 to provide for *deferred taxation*. This is a little-understood concept which we will need to look at in slightly more detail in chapter 5, paragraphs 5.18 to 5.20. For present purposes it can be simplifed by saying that if capital allowances in the early years of an asset's life are greater than depreciation in the accounts, and this will reverse in the later years, accountants do not believe it assists an understanding of the accounts to show a tax charge in the profit and loss account in those early years calculated on a profit lower than the profit shown in the accounts, and to show tax charges in later years on correspondingly higher figures than accounting profits. The *equalisation* between the years is the purpose of *deferred tax*.

However, what we are looking at here is not a *timing difference* which will *reverse*; capital allowances will in the circumstances we are envisaging be lower overall than depreciation.

reference to the *contractual* figure.[54] What is in fact always done is that cost (not market value if it is higher) is used in the contract and in the accounts of each party; also, despite the clear share premium rules mentioned in paragraph 3.39 and despite tax and stamp duty being calculated on a basis that is similar, many companies' directors frequently prepare its accounts without reflecting a value for its acquisition of goodwill; and everyone lives thereafter on tenterhooks lest Lord Greene might rise from his grave to point out that this is less than an honest estimate.

3.41 The alternative method of incorporation of the individual's business

We said in paragraph 3.33 that there was an alternative method for incorporating a business, different from the method heavily signposted in the capital gains tax legislation as giving *rollover relief on the transfer of a business*; we have been looking at that signposted route, which we could recapitulate as involving:

- the business, together with *all* its assets (or all of its assets other than cash) needing to be transferred into the company;

- the shareholder(s) receiving shares whose capital gains tax acquisition value is reduced by the gains *rolled* against their value from the assets transferred in. It is the deferral of the capital gain on the individual(s) transfers of those assets which lies at the heart of this section 162 procedure;

- *cessation* of the individual(s) business for income tax purposes, resulting under present rules in changes in the basis periods for the final assessments, but probably not causing any increases in profits, (clawback of allowances, revaluation of stock in trade, and so on);

- the company commencing business with all of its assets fully valued, and with share capital (and premium), but with no distributable reserves. It will certainly need to provide depreciation on those full values of depreciable assets, and will need also to consider whether goodwill may also need to be amortised.

Some at least of those points may be regarded as mixed blessings. In particular, the requirement that all of the assets be transferred may be a restriction which some taxpayers might wish to avoid – and which they might also find unnecessarily expensive in those cases where avoiding stamp duty may not be as simple as it may have been made to sound in paragraph 3.36.

3.42 *Gifts of business assets, the ability to retain other assets, and stamp duty implications*

The alternative route seeks the same deferral of capital gains on the individual(s) disposal to the company of the assets transferred to it, but

---

[54] Section 100(1)(a) ICTA 1988.

does so using section 165 of the Taxation of Chargeable Gains Act 1992, whose side heading is 'Relief for gifts of business assets'. The company is incorporated, allotting a small number of shares to the individual for cash, as a separate, preliminary, event. Thereafter:

- only those assets which he wishes to transfer to the company need to be transferred. He could, for instance, retain and collect the debtors, which could have the dual advantage of saving stamp duty on a transfer, and of enabling him to put the cash (or some of it) collected into the company as a loan rather than as share capital;

- in the case of assets which *are* transferred, the price for which they move from the individual to the company will be less than their market value (as will be explained below). For stamp duty purposes there is no longer any concept that a transfer at an undervalue needs to be stamped by reference to a full market price; the so called *voluntary dispositions* charge was repealed many years ago. If there is a stamp duty charge, it is on the consideration specified in the document, and not on any sum substituted in its place.

3.43 Operation of the hold-over for capital gains tax

How that transfer price might be arrived at, and what are its surrounding implications, needs to be discussed against the background of some illustrative figures. Let us look at two specific assets which are to be transferred:

	Original cost	Indexation to date	Present value
Factory building	£15,000	£9,000	£50,000
Goodwill	nil	nil	10,000

The first principle under capital gains tax law is that this transferor and transferee are connected parties, and therefore the transfer price will be the full present value[55] – subject to the adjustments to be made below. Next, that would obviously mean that the individual realised gains of £26,000 and £10,000 on the factory and the goodwill respectively – but again these are subject to adjustment. Thirdly, section 165 permits the receipt of 'actual consideration', despite the presence of the word 'gift' in its side heading; what the section says is that if that actual consideration exceeds the sums allowable as a deduction (respectively £24,000 and nil in our figures) then there will be a restriction of the relief. We will assume that the factory is transferred at £24,000 and the goodwill at £100.[56]

---

[55] Sections 286 and 17 TCGA 1992.

[56] The figure put on the goodwill transfer is a purely nominal one, while there are obvious reasons for transferring the factory building at what might be regarded as its *base cost* for CGT purposes.

However, the first point to bear in mind is that the individual as transferor, and the company as transferee, are clearly connected parties; there are some who suggest that the Inland Revenue could if they wanted argue that in the circumstances the individual

continued

The relief the section provides is a hold-over of the gain otherwise realised by the individual – subject to any restriction required by reference to the actual consideration. In the case of the factory, the individual's gain of £26,000 is fully held over, because no part of that hold-over needs to be cut back. In the case of the goodwill, his total gain was £10,000, and £100 of that is immediately chargeable in his hands because his actual consideration exceeded his deductible expenditure by that amount. £9,900 is held over.

The company's capital gains tax acquisition costs for the assets concerned are their full values reduced by the held-over gains, that is to say, a net £24,000 in the case of the factory, and a net £100 for goodwill. If the company were to dispose of these assets for more than those figures, *it*, not the individual, would be taxed on the gain. (This is different from the section 162 position, where the company's acquisition costs are the assets' full values, and it is the individual who would have his held-over gain taxed if he sold his shares in the company.)

3.44 Advantages and disadvantages of the gift of business assets route compared to the section 162 route

It needs to be pointed out that if that factory had been transferred by the individual to the company for £23,000 rather than £24,000 all of those capital gains tax figures would have been the same. What would have been different would have been the company's balance-sheet carrying value for the asset, and the capital or loan which it showed opposite it. And the stamp duty would have been less.

---

continued

does receive *actual consideration* for the transfers not only in the form of the agreed prices of the assets, but (presumably) in the form of additional value attributable to his shareholding. The author is not one of those who believes this argument to be correct; and it is not one that the Inland Revenue are currently taking. But if it could be justified, the result would be that the individual would have gains with no ability to hold over any part of them.

The different question is whether there is any essential reason for having a transfer of the goodwill (at the purely nominal figure illustrated) – and if there is, whether there is a need for it to be documented. It could be said that there is unlikely to be any dispute between the individual and the company, and that many of the others who have an interest are going to be more impressed by the facts than by documentation. If the VAT authorities see a company registered and complying with the VAT requirements, and an individual de-registered, this should satisfy them about the transfer of a trade as a going concern, and if the Inland Revenue see closing stocks in the individual's final profit and loss account at the same figure as it is brought into the company's first account, they also should be content. But there will be others interested in the continuity of their relationships with the business; its suppliers, for instance, need to agree to the company's assumption of the individual's obligations to them, and can also be expected to be concerned whether the company will thereafter have the substance, and activity, to warrant their continuing to extend credit to it. This document is needed not in isolation, but as an integral part of a much larger network of agreements. Because the consideration is nominal the stamp duty will be nominal.

We have thus identified three advantages, and one disadvantage, of this method of incorporation through the *gifts of business assets* route, compared with the method in paragraphs 3.33 and onward:

- it is not necessary to transfer all the assets;

- the prices at which they are transferred can produce a much more flexible set of figures in the recipient company's accounts, both because asset valuation is not constrained by the rules for allotment of shares for non-cash consideration, and because it is possible to set the company up with debt not just with shares and a share premium;

- stamp duty is less of a problem; but

- the company has considerably lower acquisition values for its assets, should it subsequently realise them.[57]

There is however one significant question we have failed to look at closely enough. Let us assume that when the individual incorporated this company, prior to the transfers we have been looking at, he subscribed £24,100 for 24,100 shares. (Later, when the company acquired the factory and the goodwill from him, it paid that cash back to him.) His acquisition value of his shares is thus £24,100.

When he sells assets to the company at undervalues, in effect *giving* the company a further £35,900, this does *not* increase the acquisition cost of his shares. It does increase the value of the company, and reflects through, obviously, into the value of his shares – but not their capital gains tax cost. His gift does not alter the number of shares he owns, nor their rights, only the assets of the company which is the subject matter of those rights.[58]

A gift doubles up the company's and its shareholders' capital gains.

---

[57] This would not be a problem if one were certain that the company's disposals would always give rise to gains which it could roll over under the rules for replacement of business assets in sections 152 and onward TCGA 1992.

[58] In August 1988 the accountancy bodies in the course of their normal dialogue on tax difficulties and anomalies asked the Inland Revenue for the following confirmation:

'in the US it is normal commercial practice to inject capital into a company by way of a capital contribution without going through the formalities of a share issue. We should appreciate confirmation that such contributions can rank as part of the basic cost of the shares for capital gains purposes.'

The Inland Revenue's response was:

'confirmation cannot be given. In order to qualify expenditure has to be on an asset. Capital contributions may be allowed when they were paid at the same time as the acquisition of the shares themselves when they may be treated as being in the nature of a share premium. In other circumstances it is difficult to see how they could be treated as money expended on shares. The contributions do not affect the rights attaching to the shares and – although there may be an indirect effect – are not, therefore, directly reflected in their value.'

CHAPTER 4

RESERVES

4.1 Capital and reserves

We have already come across, in a number of places in this book, a figure which we have called, colloquially, *shareholders' funds*: the aggregate of share capital, amounts already set aside into various reserve accounts, and the profits retained in the profit and loss account. As an example, we commented in paragraphs 2.33 and 2.34 on the relationship between it and the company's borrowings – the so-called gearing ratio. One part of that comment consisted in pointing out the obvious fact that the balance sheet figure of shareholders' funds will seldom if ever bear any relationship to the shareholders' values invested in the company.

But the balance sheet is nevertheless a significant document, probably the most significant of the primary accounting statements a company must produce. It is in that context that we need to look first at the legal position,[1] and then go on to think hard and carefully about the figures a company can and must show. In these thought processes, what is sometimes seen as little more than the *balancing figure*, namely the aggregate of capital and reserves, is the appropriate starting point.

Schedule 4 to the Companies Act 1985 is headed 'Form and content of company accounts'. Section B of Part I of that schedule sets out the prescribed formats with one or other of which the balance sheet must comply, (and also four profit and loss formats). In each of the balance sheet formats, the main and subsidiary captions are:

I   Called up share capital
II Share premium account
III Revaluation reserve
IV Other reserves

    1   Capital redemption reserve
    2   Reserve for own shares
    3   Reserves provided for by the articles of association
    4   Other reserves

V   Profit and loss account

---

[1] Perhaps the most vital legal implication, for the purposes not only of this book but for companies' operations generally, is the requirement in section 263(3) CA 1985 that dividends can be paid only out of 'accumulated, realised profits so far as not previously utilised by distribution or capitalisation, less its accumulated, realised losses, so far as not previously written off in a reduction or reorganisation of capital duly made'. We will see when we look in chapter 9, at some *ultra vires* transactions that an absence of distributable profits can, as explained in paragraph 9.15, render impossible some transactions, some aspects of proposed reorganisations, which might otherwise have been legitimate.

There is one detail which we can rapidly dispose of. The first head is *called up* share capital, which does not necessarily mean *paid up*; calls made may not have been paid. Unpaid calls must be reflected on the assets side of the balance sheet formats – the capital figure is not *netted*.

4.2 Accounting theory

The Accounting Standards Board (ASB, to use its TLA[2]) has identified as primary financial statements:

- The balance sheet;
- The profit and loss account;
- The statement of recognised gains;
- The cashflow statement.

The first and second are of course called for by the Companies Acts, while the third is required by FRS 3, and the fourth is the subject matter of FRS 1.

In parallel with its programme of producing *Financial Reporting Standards*, the ASB is also developing a *Statement of Principles*, defining those principles that underlie accounting and financial reporting. From the discussion drafts and exposure drafts of chapters of this work that have so far appeared, the radical direction and extent of the ASB's intended work is clear. And it is equally clear that the ASB is responding to requests made (to it and its predecessor body) by a wide range of organisations in industry and commerce as well as the accounting profession for such a review of the fundamental concepts of accounting. Thus the CBI, in a comment addressed to the ASB although in response to an ASC exposure draft[3] said:

> The CBI urges ... the Accounting Standards Board to conduct a review of the fundamental concepts of accounting with a view to developing an approach which places greater emphasis on the value of assets, particularly where present accounting conventions are at variance with business realities.

The *balance-sheet approach* to accounting that is suggested there is clearly visible throughout the ASB's work to date, both in the FRS's so far produced and in the statement of principles.

In the light of the ASB's authority and persuasiveness, it is at the same time inevitable and desirable that some of the accounting theory

---

[2] Three letter acronym.
[3] This comment was made in a response to ED 47, the exposure draft on goodwill issued shortly before the ASC ceased operations; this was the exposure draft proposing that predators should no longer have a choice between immediately writing off goodwill against reserves, or alternatively amortising it over a period through profit and loss account, but that the latter should be the mandatory treatment. As indicated in Note 44 on paragraph 6.28, this proposal has been overtaken by the ASB's announcing that goodwill is an element in its current programme for review.

and concepts in the next paragraphs are explained in the ASB's own terminology – what gives an added pleasure to this from the author's point of view is his respectful and (almost) total agreement with the Board's views.

4.3 *Enterprises and the objectives of accounts*

Hieratic language is a tongue spoken only by High Priests. Its disadvantage is that it is understood only by other High Priests. One of the great dangers of accounting is that its language can only too easily be inaccessible to non-accountants, and that even accountants themselves can confuse and be confused. What we will therefore try to do in the paragraphs which follow is to explain the meaning of accounting terminology when we first introduce the words and phrases – even in those cases in which we may already have used these words earlier, without explanation.

Enterprise: The ASB makes clear that its accounting principles, and requirements regarding accounts and disclosures, apply not only to companies but to all commercial or industrial reporting enterprises, whether in the public or the private sector (and although certain changes of emphasis would be needed in their application, the principles apply equally to profit-oriented and not-for-profit organisations).[4]

The word enterprise can be used to apply to a single company (which may of course be the parent of a group) or it can be applied to the parent company in relation to the consolidated financial statements which it prepares to show the position of the companies constituting that group looked at together.

Position, performance, cashflows and financial adaptability: these are the objectives of financial statements – the information that a user would hope to be able to discover about the entity reported on. The first three are familiar, although there are probably few users who derive all the information they should from reading the accounts.[5] The last also seems obvious when one has once spotted the point, but the ASB's insight is illuminating. Having defined financial adaptability as the entity's ability to take effective action to alter the amounts and timing of cashflows to respond to unexpected needs or opportunities (and having given as

---

[4] Introduction paragraph 1.1.

[5] *Articulate*: The ASB says that the four primary financial statements identified at the beginning of the previous paragraph articulate (or interrelate) because they reflect different aspects of the same transactions or events affecting the enterprise. The fact, however, that 'the different primary statements are in general founded on the same judgments and methods of calculation for the differing aspects of related items' means that one can gain further insights by, for instance, analysis of ratios of debtors (balance sheet) to sales (profit and loss account). It is easy to see why the ASB needed to include those words 'in general' in that quotation, and why the analysis may not be as well founded as one could wish; were sales translated from a foreign currency into sterling at average monthly exchange rates through the year while debtors were translated for balance sheet purposes at the closing rate at the year end? (*Statement of Principles* chapter 6 paragraph 9).

a specific example the ability of an enterprise to obtain cash by selling assets without disrupting current operations), the ASB points out that financial adaptability generally involves making sacrifices as well as gaining an advantage – sacrificing what might have been a higher rate of return on other forms of asset to hold those readily marketable assets.[6]

4.4 *Recognition*

Recognition: The title of the new financial statement which the ASB has called for, the *Statement of Recognised Gains*, suggests quite correctly that there could be gains which were not recognised; and that *recognition* is an event which gives the particular gains concerned a different quality – that implication is also quite correct. But we need to understand the word 'recognised' in a wider context than that; recognition is not limited to gains, or losses.

Recognition of any item for the purposes of the financial statements is the basic start-point of book-keeping. The company's incorporation involves recognising the interrelated facts that the founder members have agreed to subscribe (say) £100 for their shares and the company has agreed to issue and allot those shares to the founder members. The company's cash in hand changes from zero to £100; cash is an asset, and one which can validly be recognised in the financial statements, unlike such items as the value of a company's own brands, or the goodwill it has created for itself through its operations. The two facts that there is an item which is an *element*[7] of financial statements, and that there has been a change in an asset or liability inherent in that item, are necessary parts of the recognition process; but there is a third factor, that the item must be capable of being measured in monetary terms with sufficient reliability for that monetary figure to be put into the accounts. There is obviously no difficulty over the £100 which we have assumed the company's founders have agreed to subscribe. But we will need to look at some of the implications of the measurement process in paragraph 4.9 below. As one example of a problem area, we saw in paragraphs 3.28 and 3.29 the difficulties inherent in a company's agreeing to issue shares to an incoming shareholder (we assumed in that case he had an option to subscribe for them) if the consideration he was to give was not cash but *work*. Although we were primarily considering the difficulties of valuing (measuring) this for purposes of Company Law (and for tax),

---

[6] *Ibid.*, chapter 6 paragraph 33.
[7] The elements of financial statements are assets, liabilities, equity, gains, losses, contributions from owners, and distributions to owners. In the main these are self-explanatory, but we will need to spend a little time in later paragraphs on the significance of 'equity', and on the meaning of 'gains' and 'losses'.

However, it is worth pointing out that equity is defined as the excess of assets over liabilities; each of gains, losses, contributions from owners and distributions to owners is defined as either an increase or decrease in assets or liabilities. It therefore follows that it is possible to say that the second of the requirements we noted in the text for *recognition*, namely a change in assets or liabilities must always be involved, there is no possible change in any of the elements listed in this footnote which would not be, or be reflected in, an asset or liability change.

we could equally have pointed out that the same measurement problem occurs in the process of *recognition* for the financial statements.

4.5 Change

Thus, what we *recognise* in the accounting process are measurable changes in assets or liabilities. These may be matched by changes in other assets or liabilities; when a customer pays the amount he owes to the company, the balance shown in his account (debtor, among current assets) goes down, and the matching increase is in cash. Or the change in assets or liabilities may be matched by a change in one of the other types of element in the financial statements; if a creditor waives the amount owed to him by the company, the decrease in current liabilities is matched by an increase in profits.

Change: The question we have so far not answered is what we mean by the word 'change'. Accounting theory says that there needs to be clear evidence of any such change before it can be recognised, and that it must have taken place before the date of the balance sheet (or of the accounts generally). The following are forms of evidenced change:

- transactions – that is to say, transfers of assets or liabilities to or from an external[8] party. It was a transaction that we saw happening when the customer paid the amount he owed to the company;

- contracts – what a lawyer would call executory contracts, enforceable but as yet unperformed promises given to or by an external party to transfer assets or liabilities in the future. If the company's contractual arrangements with the suppliers of its raw materials are such that a firm order placed by the company gives the supplier an enforceable right to deliver, and to be paid, then the company should recognise the purchase when that order is placed, not at the later point when the goods are delivered. In fact, many businesses use delivery as the recognition point – because (as the ASB points out) their contractual arrangements can properly be regarded as not giving either purchaser or supplier enforceable rights earlier;[9]

---

[8] Both in this head and in the next one there is an emphasis laid on the transaction or the contract involving an external party. This means external to the entity being reported upon. If that entity is a parent company, but it is its solus accounts that are under consideration, then its subsidiary is external, and the parent could recognise a profit on a sale of stock to that subsidiary. However if one were preparing accounts which consolidated the parent's and the subsidiary's figures, the principles of consolidation are such that not only would the intra-group profit not be recognised, and the subsidiary's holding of stock would be brought in at the parent's cost not the subsidiary's (paragraph 6(2) of schedule 4A to CA 1985) but the sale/purchase, and the debtor/creditor, in the respective companies' accounts would also be washed out. The end result is thus a complete absence of any transaction when the counter-party (subsidiary) cannot be regarded as external.

[9] This is the analysis set out in chapter 4, paragraph 32, of the *Statement of Principles*. It is reinforced by the ASB's observation that 'in most routine sale and purchase orders there will not be a firm commitment ... *inter alia* ... the entity could cancel the contract without incurring a severe penalty'.

- events – these are limited to those characterised as involving a change in the benefits associated[10] with an asset or a liability, rather than events which merely involve a revaluation of the flow of benefits so associated but not a change in the benefits themselves. The passage of time can in certain cases be a relevant event – an interest payment date turns interest accruing into interest payable or receivable; and the expiry of a lease results in the property's reversion to the landlord.

4.6 Prudence and the recognition of profits

Transactions, contracts and other events[11] are thus what provide the necessary evidence of changes in assets or liabilities which can then be *recognised* in the financial statements.

There is one fundamental point that has to be made here. If the change involves recognition of a profit or gain, more persuasive evidence is needed than is called for if it is a loss, or a reduction in value which is being reflected. That is known as the *concept of prudence*.[12]

What we have been considering in the last few paragraphs has been the recognition of gains for the purposes of the statement of recognised gains. We will come back to that statement below, but at this point it is sensible to make a diversion, to move onto the more tightly drawn rules for recognising profits[13] in the profit and loss account. Identifying the processes involved in this latter area will give us a clearer idea of the differences between these two parts of the financial statements, and their distinct purposes.

Profits must be earned: That is a reference to the fact that the transaction, contract or other event by reference to which recognition takes

---

[10] 'The benefits associated with an asset' may at first seem an unhandy circumlocution; but it is a helpful phrase for the very good reason that it reminds us of the basic objective of a company's accounts, namely to represent its assets and liabilities financially. The figure in the fixed assets heading is not the factory building, but a sum of money taken as being the value to the business of that factory, which might be the present value of a stream of rental receipts if the company's business is the letting of factories, or could possibly be the related to the expected sale price if the factory is surplus to requirements, but will usually be the much more difficult to quantify value of the business's own occupation. However, if the factory burns down, there is still a figure in the same heading in the balance sheet representing the claim against the insurance company for cash with which to provide temporary accommodation, and in due course a permanent replacement – these two being still represented at their respective values to the business. The change from a standing factory to a burnt one could of course justify the recognition of loss on underinsurance, or gain on overinsurance.

[11] The previous paragraph only gave some examples of *events* rather than a comprehensive list or explanation; but for our purposes in this book, we only need an indication of this word's significance.

[12] The concept of prudence is the fourth of the fundamental accounting concepts in SSAP 2. The other three are the going concern concept, the accruals concept, and consistency.

[13] If it is a *gain* which is recognised in a statement of recognised gains, then it seems logical that the item that would be shown in a profit and loss account would be a *profit*. However, there is no magic in the terms – and the ASB refers to both as gains.

place must have happened. The legal arrangements differ from business to business, but the commonest method of fixing a date for the sale of goods may be their delivery to the customer. However, in the case of the supply of services, and particularly those which are supplied continuously (for instance tax advice supplied by an accounting firm to a major corporate group), what would constitute the *sale* enabling the firm to recognise profit (and to change work in progress into a sum owed by the client) would today not just be the firm's issue of a feenote, but its obtaining of the client's agreement to that fee.

4.7 *Realisation of profits (first instalment)*

Profits must be realised: This second requirement for profit recognition comes from the Companies Acts.[14] The interpretation of the word 'realised' is partly a matter of accounting principles, but there are more prescriptive legal aspects as well. We will look first at the principles and thereafter at the prescriptions.

The ASB's *Statement of Principles* indicates three possible sets of conditions, the second and third of which are narrowly defined, and relatively easy to identify. It is convenient to deal with them first, and then to come back to the wider, and more problematical, first set of circumstances:

(2) *A change in an asset or liability not held for continuing use in the business, but which is readily convertible into money*

- what this heading refers to is the bank, financial institution, or dealer in commodities which accounts for its liquid, dealing, portfolio by *marking to market*, that is to say, by valuing each asset or liability at realisable value, rather than carrying them (in the more traditional way of accounting for *stocks*) at the lower of cost and net realisable value;

---

[14] Paragraph 12(a) in schedule 4 to CA 1985. The definition of the phrase 'realised profits' is in section 262(3) of the Act, which requires that this be achieved 'in accordance with principles generally accepted, at the time when the accounts are prepared, with respect to the determination for acounting purposes of realised profits'. *Financial Reporting Standards* (and *Statements of Standard Accounting Practice*) must undoubtedly be a part of generally accepted accounting principles since they, and the ASB who has *issued* them, have statutory recognition under section 256 of the Act. However, it is obvious that FRSs and SSAPs do not constitute the whole of generally accepted accounting principles; the ASB's *Statement of Principles*, as discussed in these paragraphs, must also be a highly persuasive part. Some years before the ASB commenced its work on these principles, the Industrial Relations Court, and on appeal the Court of Appeal, considered the meaning of the phrase 'generally accepted accounting principles' in *Associated Portland Cement Manufacturers Ltd v The Price Commission* [1975] ICR 27. By a happy coincidence the auditor of APCM who gave expert evidence to the courts was also the Chairman of the then Accounting Standards Committee, Sir William Slimmings. His evidence was clearly persuasive enough that the courts held unanimously that generally accepted accounting practice meant practices which were generally accepted by *accountants*, and that the courts' role was neither to try to make its own judgment about those practices, nor to evolve legal definitions, but merely to discover as a fact whether a particular practice was accepted at a particular time.

- marking to market is only appropriate where the company's business can and does involve not infrequent realisations of the assets concerned rather than their being held for substantial periods, and there is an available and liquid market place in which they can be realised, and by reference to which appropriate market prices can be determined;

(3) *The gain results from a liability expiring, being cancelled or otherwise ceasing to exist*

- little needs to be said here other than that discharging a liability by paying it off would be a *transaction* which would need to be considered under the next category, below. However there could be previously recognised liabilities in the accounts, liabilities under guarantees for instance, or deferred income carried in the accounts as if it were a liability in cases where an insurer had received premiums in advance in respect of risks which had an unexpired future term; in such circumstances, the expiry of the guarantee exposure or of the insurance term would allow the release into profit and loss account of the *profit* thus realised. And that expiry could not be fitted within the definitions in either the previous, or the next, heads.

4.8 *Measurement*

The principal circumstance which permits the crediting to profit and loss account of amounts characterised as realised profits is:

(1) *A transaction whose value is measurable with sufficient reliability has occurred.*

That brings us straight up against the next bit of hieratic language, the concept of *measurement*. To an accountant, measurement means putting a monetary figure on an asset or liability. Surely, the reader might say, that should have referred only to assets – are not all liabilities, by definition, amounts of money which the company owes to others? Most, yes, but not all. The company might have an obligation to deliver 50 tons of copper in three months' time; or to find tenants by a target date for the building it has just constructed, with the penalty if the whole is not let, of itself taking the vacant space until it does achieve a letting; the risks carried by an insurance company are liabilities which are not easy to define in monetary terms until claims are lodged and agreed; but at a much simpler level a liability which does not need to be paid off for some months has a present monetary value lower than its face value – even the Merchant of Venice appreciated that as he discounted his bills of exchange. And pension fund trustees understand the problem even more clearly as they attempt to quantify, today, the cost of providing a deferred annuity for an early leaver. They know the level of the annuity because it is based on service to the date he left and salary at that date; they know the date at which the annuity is due to commence, which is what would have been his retirement date had he not left; what they do not know is the rate at which their funds will grow (by reinvested income and capital appreciation, what actuaries call *the valuation rate of interest*) during the time before the annuity starts, and while it continues; and they do not know how long the annuitant will live (or whether he may die before any annuity ever starts).

The pension trustees do not need to know the eventual outcome in order to be able to measure their liability. But they do need a stated basis (which in their case would be an assumed valuation rate of interest, and some mortality tables). They need to state that basis in their accounts, as well as the *measurement* they derive from it. And they must believe their basis would be widely (if not universally) accepted in their business and circumstances.

4.9 Realisation of profits (second instalment)

There is a parallel set of questions raised by our thinking in the previous paragraph about measurement of liabilities. We assumed that the liabilities existed – but did not directly face or answer the question what was the transaction, contract or other event which had called for their recognition. For the early leaver, it was obviously his leaving; but the *trigger* is less clear in the case of the insurance company, drawing up its financial statements to a date somewhere in the middle of the year for which it has provided cover for a policy holder, and where that policy holder has not yet notified a claim but an event may already have taken place which would justify such a claim.

The significance is that the trigger date chosen for the recognition of, and measurement of, the liability does itself affect the basis on which that measurement is made. And the second point is the one made in paragraph 4.7 above, that the *prudence concept* decrees that one recognises losses more readily than one does profits.[15]

Let us get back to the main subject we have been discussing since paragraph 4.7, namely the recognition of profits in the profit and loss account. We saw in that paragraph that they must be *earned*. We started considering in paragraph 4.8 the necessity for them to be *realised*, and we have so far thought about that word in the context of the conceptual framework of accounting set out in the ASB's *Statement of Principles*, the transactions and so on which permit the recognition process to start, and the measurements which it may involve.

Realised has a further, rather different, implication. Between 1858 and 1870 the City of Glasgow Bank lent a total of £905,000 to an American railroad company for the construction of its line. Those advances were fully secured by mortgage bonds issued by the railroad; the initial loan had been only £107,000 but the total figure had built up by means of further advances through the years, and in particular the bank had permitted the railroad to borrow, rather than pay, the interest due on the loan. (But in its books this increase in the amount owed by the

---

[15] We are discussing accounting principles in this chapter. When we get to the principles under which losses and provisions for losses can be deducted for tax purposes, in paragraph 5.4 and Note 10 thereon, we will see that the rules are somewhat tighter.

railroad was matched by interest credited to profit and loss account.) In 1878 the bank failed, and it was alleged that Mr Mackinnon, a director from 1858 to 1870 (but not in the final eight years to its failure) had improperly paid dividends for the 12 years.[16]

4.10 *Realisation of profits (continued)*

The Companies Acts did not of course contain the word 'realised' at that time; the allegation was that if the interest had not been received, and profits were thus smaller, then the dividends must have been paid out of capital.

What makes this case fascinating is that it was not all that *sinful* – by the time it finally came to court it was clear that the bank's depositors had lost none of their money, and the shareholders lost only a proportion. Secondly, the judgments rehearse all the arguments that continue to this day, and are still just as far from being finally resolved.

How we have tried in the last 20 years, half-heartedly, to reach a resolution is by doing no more than begging the question in the Companies Acts (parroting the words 'only profits realised at the balance sheet date shall be included in the profit and loss account');[17] but going somewhat further in SSAP 2, which says:

> profits are not (to be) anticipated, but are recognised by inclusion in the profit and loss account only when realised in the form either of cash or of other assets the ultimate cash realisation of which can be assessed with reasonable certainty.

Even in relation to cash, that takes us little further; would the bank and its American railroad have been in any different position if interest had been remitted in cash, and that same cash had been remitted back as further advances – in place of this being achieved by straightforward book-keeping entries?

But it is the assessing of ultimate cash realisation over which the mind boggles most. In the Court of Session, Lord Mure said that the interest was 'paid in money's worth in the shape of these mortgage bonds'. Lord Shand said that although he believed that the bank did *substantially* receive the interest regularly, the real question should have been 'at the time of balancing each year, was there on a sound valuation a profit to carry to profit and loss account?' Lord Deas inclined to a different answer, saying that 'the adventurous appropriation of unpaid interest to the payment of dividends ... must be seen to have been so sufficiently perilous as to make it rather a danger to be avoided than an example to be imitated'.

---

[16] *Jamieson & Others (Liquidators of the City of Glasgow Bank) v Mackinnon* [1882] Court of Session, 4th Series Vol IX, at 536.
[17] Schedule 4, paragraph 12(a) CA 1985.

4.11 Realisation of profits (continued)

Lord Glencorse, Lord President of the Court of Session[18] summed the position up as follows, and the author does not believe that a single word needs altering 112 years later:[19]

> But if no dividend could be paid except out of cash in hand or in bank, representing profits or interest actually received, it is obvious that the business of such a company could not be practically carried on; and the existing shareholders of the company would have good reason to complain that they were deprived of their just share of the profits of the concern actually earned and well earned, because these profits could not be converted into cash before the balance sheet of the year was struck.
>
> When profits have been earned and not paid, but invested on undoubted security, and these profits have been carried to the credit of the profit and loss account, and a dividend paid out of the balance of the profits thus obtained, it is no doubt true, in a literal sense, that the dividend is to the extent of these unpaid profits paid out of capital; because the company not having cash to represent these earned and secured profits, must find the money to pay the dividend elsewhere; and they can find it nowhere except by applying to the purpose cash which forms part of the floating balance of capital. But if the unpaid profits are fully secured, they become a part of the capital of the company, as a *surrogatum* for the cash of equal amount taken from the floating capital and paid as dividend; and thus the capital is not diminished, but a certain part of the floating balance of capital becomes invested in the securities which the company holds for the earned but unpaid profits in question.

Capital

4.12 Fixed and circulating

That quotation from Lord Glencorse might remind us that the capital he was considering was not the same matter dealt with in Part V of the Companies Act 1985 (sections 117 to 197), which principally deals with *share* capital, its increase, maintenance and reduction.

Investors invest their capital in shares issued by the company; the proceeds of those share issues are thereafter employed by it for the

---

[18] How Professor David Walker describes Lord Glencorse demands quotation in full:

> 'On the bench he was dignified, patient and courteous. As a judge (he) was unquestionably the best of the century and laid down law in classic fashion in what have, ever since, been deemed leading cases. He had great reverence for Scots Law as a national institution. His contributions to the formulation of the law have been immense and his judgments are of the highest authority.' (*The Oxford Companion to Law*, Clarendon Press, 1980).

[19] There have been later cases on the meaning of the phrase 'realised profits'. The Chancery Division of the High Court decided in 1886, for instance, that nothing short of realisation in cash could ever do (*The Oxford Benefit Building Society* case). In the author's view, Lord Glencorse's view is to be preferred.

purposes of its business — and it is that employment which is the true essence of the company's *capital*. Double entry book-keeping is all done with mirrors, and it is easy to look at the reflection of the real thing, that reflection being in a share capital account (and possibly a share premium account) and to assume that that is what is meant by capital. It is not.

Adam Smith, another Scot, saw it equally clearly in the second book of his *Wealth of Nations*:

> Fixed capital is what the owner turns to profit by keeping it in his own possession, and circulating capital is what he makes profit of by parting with it and letting it change masters.

If we imagine a newspaper business, its fixed capital would be its premises, printing machinery and all the typesetting and word-processing equipment that is nowadays connected into it. The circulating capital would be stocks of newsprint and ink, balances of money owed to the newspaper by its wholesale distributors and by those who have bought advertising space in it, less balances of money owed by it to its own suppliers, and some balance of cash in hand and in the bank.

The picture we have so far drawn of the business's realising profits in its profit and loss account (as opposed to recognising gains elsewhere) would have it ignoring any changes that there might be in the value of its premises; but in relation to its circulating capital doing just what Lord Justice Romer envisaged in 1933:[20]

> The profits or losses in a year of trading cannot be ascertained unless a comparison be made of the circulating capital as it existed at the beginning of the year with the circulating capital as it exists at the end of the year. It is indeed by causing floating capital to change in value that a loss or a profit is made.

4.13 Fixed and circulating capital (continued)

However Lord Romer immediately went on to point out that the problem inherent in his accounting system was that of

> ... determin(ing) whether a particular asset belongs to the one category or the other. It depends in no way upon what may be the nature of the asset in fact or in law. Land may in certain circumstances be circulating capital. A chattel or a chose in action may be fixed capital. The determining factor must be the nature of the trade in which the asset is employed.

What he failed to spell out was that the exercise is more difficult still when one recognises that liabilities as well as assets have to be analysed; and that it is not actually possible to ignore changes in the value of fixed capital assets, because there is a little item called depreciation.

But the difficulties in his start/finish comparison of circulating capital (and the fact that we do now have an easier way of arriving at

---

[20] *Golden Horseshoe (New) Ltd v Thurgood* [1934] 1 KB 548 at 563. It was in the course of his judgment in this case that Lord Justice Romer quoted Adam Smith as above.

the identical profits he had in mind) should not prevent us from acknowledging that the great bulk of most companies' resources are *employed as capital* in their businesses. The author prefers to draw a picture along the same kind of lines as the assets side of a bank's balance sheet (the most liquid assets at the top, and fixed assets at the bottom) as shown in Table 26.

Table 26: Fixed and Circulating Capital

Profit awaiting distribution	represented by cash
Amounts held within the company which are not employed in its business	represented probably by investments, land held as an investment, or *hobby* assets
Circulating capital	represented by stocks, debtors, working cash balances less creditors and circulating borrowings
Fixed capital	represented by investment in subsidiaries, premises, plant, less borrowings of a capital nature

The lines which separate these categories are not only fuzzy and difficult to define, but are also permeable; they do not prevent assets and liabilities from changing category. In particular, they do not prevent the charging of depreciation which has to be seen in terms of this table as a decrease in profit arising from a mandatory transfer out of that line onto the fixed capital line to make good what would otherwise have been a diminution in the fixed capital.

4.14 Capital maintenance

Table 26 is so generalised and unspecific that we would be unwise to use it as a lighthouse for navigating through rock-begirt waters. But there are four points which it does bring out:

• assets can change from category to category, and so can liabilities. But even if a particular asset and liability are, and remain, in the same category there is no necessary sense in which they remain connected. A company may borrow specifically for the purchase of a building, but a few years later it may well repay the borrowing without selling the building, or sell the building without repaying the borrowing (if the lender accepts alternative security). What the Inland Revenue refers to as the 'hypothecation'[20a] of liabilities and assets may sometimes exist, but can never be regarded as permanent and unchanging;

• most businesses' hunger for *capital* is such that if a positive decision is not taken to distribute, any available cash will swiftly be transposed into circulating capital. This need not, of course, be a permanent transformation, because the company is free to distribute the amount at a later time;[21]

• but although it is true in formal, legal, terms that a company can later pay out to shareholders amounts which although shown as distributable in its profit and loss account have *de facto* been transformed into circulating (or even fixed) capital – it is likely

---

[20a] In the real world, it is not assets that are hypothecated to liabilities, but cashflows. The best way to illustrate the concept is in a foreign currency, and using a transaction in which we can try to separate risk from assets and liabilities, (one would probably try to do things differently in practice but that does not invalidate the points brought out by a slightly artificial example). A UK company borrows Brazilian reals in order to purchase and expand a Brazilian subsidiary. The UK company's liability is not hypothecated against its *shareholding*, in the sense that anyone would expect the borrowing to be repaid out of a sale of the subsidiary; the plan is that the borrowing will be repaid out of a *flow of Brazilian dividends*. If the Brazilian real depreciates by 10 per cent (a) against sterling, it is not this change itself that matters – it is the question whether the depreciation reduces the earning power of the subsidiary. We will assume that the Brazilian real earning power remains the same, i.e. that sterling earnings fall by one tenth. But suppose some further one-off event occurs in Brazil which cuts by a further one third (b) the earning power of the subsidiary for the foreseeable future, (imposition by the Brazilian authorities of swingeing price reductions on its products). This diminishes the value of the UK company's investment; and this time it does also diminish the reals flowing back to the UK as dividends from which the borrowing can be serviced and repaid. Therefore the balance of the repayment reals the lender needs, must be provided by purchase in the market – and the UK company is at a continuing exchange risk until the borrowing is fully repaid.

If we think about the sterling figures the UK company reflects in its accounts, the initial depreciation of the real at (a) above does not affect the UK company's profits – the liability and the asset of Rs1,000 each, which originally stood at £100 are each reduced to £90. In accounting terms that gives a loss, permanent diminution in asset value, washing out against a gain on the reduction in the liability; of course the dividend flows which the UK company had expected to be worth £100 over the next three years will be worth only £90, so that the profit and loss account looks less healthy than it might have done; but the UK company would not be making at that stage any *loss* when it repaid its borrowings out of these dividends. But when one adds in the effect of the price controls, the subsidiary's value falls by a third, from £90 to £60, and the UK company must show as a loss that permanent diminution of £30.

Second, the dividend flow in the next three years can be expected to be Rs667, (£60), the implication being that the remaining Rs333 to service the debt will need to be purchased. So long as the real remains steady against sterling, those Rs333 can be bought for £30, which will mean that the repayment of the loan will not create any further loss, or profit, to be recognised in the UK company's accounts. But if the UK company wants to hedge its currency exposure, (although the total amount may be visible on its balance sheet as a difference between asset of Rs667 and liability of Rs1,000), the actual cover needed and dates at which it is needed, involves forecasting both exchange rates and cashflows.

[21] Provided its distributable profits have not by that later time been eroded or eliminated by subsequent losses, and nor have they been *capitalised* under the provisions of Article 110 of Table A (or equivalent provisions in a company's Articles).

that the company's creditors would look askance at any excessive action of this kind. The significance of this point is that bankers and bondholders are types of creditors who are likely to try to impose restrictions on the company's actions in this area; the distributability of profits does need to be considered not only in relation to their legal availability in the profit and loss account, but also in relation to banking covenants and undertakings of a similar nature;

- the fourth point brings us to a different, and more specific, meaning of the phrase 'capital maintenance'.

4.15 *Capital maintenance (continued)*

In paragraphs 2.6 and 2.7 we referred to the accounting systems which the Companies Act defines as 'Alternative accounting rules', that is to say, as alternative to the historic cost system.[22] The driving force which prompted the development of these systems is described as 'capital maintenance'.

In a period of inflation, a company needs to maintain its fixed and circulating capital in real terms, not merely in nominal money terms; if it keeps its capital standing still in terms of a depreciating currency, it will in reality be shrinking. The accounting system which would have maintained a company's capital in real monetary terms (against general price inflation) is known as the *current purchasing power* system. The government determined in the early 1980s that this should not be the route taken in the UK, and the alternative system developed by the UK accounting bodies in line with this government directive was *current cost accounting*.

This does not set purely financial benchmarks for the measurement of maintenance of capital, but instead seeks to maintain a company's *operating capacity*. Clearly this is more difficult to measure; and the processes of measurement necessarily involve not only more complex, but more subjective, judgments. If the costs of different raw materials (and the costs of labour) are subject to differing rates of inflation, then assessing the company's need for circulating capital with which to finance its continuing levels of production will be difficult. The amount the business needs to set aside out of what would (on historic cost principles) have been reported as profit will be the subject of intense debate among the few people in any company in a position to contribute to this debate; but so far as concerns those outside the company, the figures which eventually result from that debate will be even more difficult to understand – and in particular will be even more difficult to compare with those of other businesses.[23]

---

[22] Section C (paragraphs 29 to 34) of schedule 4 CA 1985.
[23] We saw some of the concepts and the problems of current cost accounting in paragraph 2.6 and particularly Note 5 thereon. But it is sensible, at this point, to give one more example of the conceptual problems. Assume a business is financed half by borrowings, and half by shareholders' equity. The lenders know very well that their principal is being eroded by inflation, and the interest rate they demand is designed to protect their capital against this. But unless they *lend* to the company each year the
continued

4.16 Starting to draw the threads together

We have covered a considerable amount of ground in this chapter but have purposely not yet drawn the various threads together. It is this we now need to do.

An appropriate starting point is the CBI's request to the ASB, quoted already in paragraph 4.2 above:

> The CBI urges ... the Accounting Standards Board to conduct a review of the fundamental concepts of accounting with a view to developing an approach which places greater emphasis on the value of assets, particularly where present accounting conventions are at variance with business realities.

As we said in that paragraph, the *balance-sheet approach* to accounting chimed well with the ASB's own thinking, as we can see in the current work emerging from the ASB:

● the main change to the way in which profits are arrived at in the profit and loss account has been the differentiation of profits on continuing operations, and those from operations which are being or have been discontinued.[24] The profit and loss account is not a forecast of what the future may hold, but this information makes it considerably more transparent than it was before;

● alongside that, there is the requirement that profits from acquired businesses should also be separately disclosed where the amounts are material;[25]

● and there is now a more or less total ban on describing anything mildly embarrassing as an *extraordinary item* so as to avoid its having an effect on earnings per share.[26]

---

continued

extra interest (not the nominal interest they would have asked for in a non-inflationary environment, but the excess over that, which they require in the actual inflationary circumstances), then their contribution to the company's financing will be decreasing; and the shareholders' contribution will have to expand to fill the gap. Does this mean that the shareholders' *profit* is what the company has earned, reduced not only by the amount the shareholders need to set aside to maintain 'their' 50 per cent of the company's operating capacity but by what the shareholders would need to set aside if it were they and they alone who had to maintain the whole of the operating capacity? (the second assumes that the company cannot and does not borrow more, either from the existing lenders or from other providers of finance). This question is known technically as the *gearing adjustment*; those who believe that the company can borrow (and if it does not do so that is its choice) say that profits should not be reduced by what is in effect its decision to increase the shareholders' proportionate commitment. But those who do think this are matched by equal numbers who think the opposite. When the Inland Revenue faced this conundrum (in paragraphs 9.14 to 9.17, 13.6 to 13.19, and 13.39 to 13.78 of the 1982 Corporation Tax green paper (Cmnd 8456)), the difficulties they saw formed a large part of the reasons why they were never able to contemplate taxing companies on CCA profits.

[24] FRS 3 paragraphs 14 and 17 to 18.
[25] *Ibid.*, paragraph 16.
[26] *Ibid.*, paragraphs 19 to 22.

4.17 Matching and prudence

Although work on this has been less high-profile than the three items mentioned above, ASB has continued to refine its guidance on the subject of *matching*.[27] What we discussed in paragraph 1.29 was the company which incurred costs in 1993 on a marketing campaign which was produce sales of a new product in the years 1994 to 1996. That was an example of a cost which it would have been quite inappropriate to match with the revenues and profits which it was hoped would flow from it, because 1994 to 1996 revenues and profits were, at the end of 1993, insufficiently certain to materialise at all so that no 'relationship' could be 'established or justifiably assumed', to quote SSAP 2. What we could have derived from those thoughts about matching that we have discussed in this chapter is that the incurring of the costs in 1993 was undoubtedly a transaction which needed to be recognised in that year – but there are two possible forms in which it could have been recognised. It would theoretically have been possible to recognise it as an asset (expenditure which could have been reflected in the balance sheet at least for a period), but only if the value of that asset had been *measurable*. Everything that we have said here is a clear indication that it could not meet those criteria. Therefore the only recognition available is as a *loss*, an amount to be immediately written off under the prudence concept.

Matching and *prudence* are frequently at odds, as SSAP 2 itself admits and as we noticed in paragraph 2.22 when we were thinking about the pattern of a growing company's profits and retentions. When the requirement to write off expenditure supersedes the possibility of carrying it forward to be matched against related income, the accounts are always capable of being criticised for a failure to that extent to make sense. This is not a matter that ASB can put right.

The areas in which ASB is active are some of those in which matching principles have been purposely distorted by some companies in recent years. We will see when we come to paragraph 6.27 that if a predator company acquires a target, and at the time of that acquisition makes a substantial provision for expenditure to be incurred on the target's *reorganisation*, the effect is that the amount provided can be treated as

---

[27] Matching is the second part of the 'accruals concept' in SSAP 2. The accruals concept calls for:

'revenue and costs (to be) accrued, that is recognised as they are earned or incurred, not as money is received or paid, matched with one another so far as their relationship can be established or justifiably assumed, and dealt with in the profit and loss account of the period to which they relate ... Revenue and profits dealt with in the profit and loss account are matched with associated costs and expenses by including in the same account the costs incurred in earning them, so far as these are material and identifiable.'

The Companies Act reflects this requirement in very much less specific wording:

'All income and charges relating to the financial year to which the accounts relate shall be taken into account, without regard to the date of receipt or payment' (paragraph 13 of schedule 4 CA 1985).

an additional element of the purchase price of the target, and as such does not appear in the predator's profit and loss account in the period in which the reorganisation actually occurs. The accounts thus appear to show that it is more profitable to reorganise newly acquired businesses than to do the same for your existing businesses – an accounting concept which is open to some criticism.

4.18 *The balance-sheet approach*

The primary aim of the Accounting Standards promulgated by the original Accounting Standards Committee used to be to narrow the areas of difference and variety in the accounting treatment of matters with which they deal.[28] There has been a subtle widening of that objective in the ASB's statement which now supersedes the original foreword to the *Standards*:

> Accounting Standards are authoritative statements of how particular types of transaction and other events should be reflected in financial statements and accordingly compliance with accounting standards will normally be necessary for financial statements to give a true and fair view.[29]

But the word 'standards' also has another connotation, visible in ASB's statement of its aims:

> The aims of the Accounting Standards Board are to establish and improve standards of financial accounting and reporting, for the benefit of users, preparers, and auditors of financial information.[30]

Each entity's accounts are to be more informative, which means more comprehensive and comprehensible. And different entities' accounts need to be more comparable. All of these are better achieved by a greater emphasis being placed on the balance sheet than has been given to that document in the last 20 or so years. It has been no accident that we have been devoting time and attention to the company's fixed and circulating capital (paragraphs 4.12 and 4.13), and to capital maintenance (paragraphs 4.14 and 4.15).

What we need, and what the ASB recognises that we need, are balance sheets which account for these net assets in a way which makes it possible to understand better

- how the company is positioned, and performing;

- the extent to which it is financially adaptable;

- whether the cashflows it reports (not in the balance sheet) are what might be expected from the shape and size of its operations;

- these balance sheets do not pretend to show the company's economic wealth[31] (because goodwill is not fully reflected, and there

---

[28] ASC's explanatory foreword to *Statements of Standard Accounting Practice*, issued May 1975, revised August 1986. This document was superseded by the document referred to in Note 29 below, and withdrawn.
[29] ASB's foreword to *Accounting Standards*, paragraph 16, 1993.
[30] ASB's *Statement of Aims*, 1991.
[31] *The Statement of Principles*, chapter 5 paragraph 3.

are difficulties we will discuss in the next paragraph over showing all assets at current economic value), but they do show net assets; and the other primary financial statements supplement them by explaining the changes to net assets.

4.19 *Measurement and re-measurement*

One aspect of the more intelligible balance sheet is a more enlightened use of measurement. When the company acquired its premises 50 years ago the sum it paid was not only an objective, but a meaningful, measure of value to put into the balance sheet. Today's user of the balance sheet might prefer information that was more up to date, even if this involved some degree of subjective judgment of values. The information that today's user would always reject as precisely accurate and utterly useless is the aggregation into a single figure of costs of different premises acquired over the whole period of 50 years.

The attempt to put some meaning into the fixed capital figures is best achieved if a *value to the business* can be identified:

The lower of	REPLACEMENT VALUE	*If replacement value is lower,*
and	RECOVERABLE AMOUNT	*that shows that the asset is worth replacing*
recoverable amount is the		
higher of	VALUE IN USE	*Use the higher, more profitable*
and	REALISABLE VALUE	*of the alternatives*

An asset's net realisable value will usually be within the directors' knowledge. Replacement value would be close to it, if a buyer's price and a vendor's proceeds were similar; but one might need to consider another dimension – whether one would choose an identical asset to replace the one being considered. The code words here are *modern equivalent asset.* If you are thinking about the replacement value of a 50-year-old printing press, the kind of thing built like a Rolls Royce and which purrs along at a sedate rotation rate, applying only one ink-colour at a time, with plenty of down time for washing out the rollers and for general greasing and polishing, the real question is whether that is the type of press one would buy as a replacement today? Even if realisable value is known, replacement value can clearly be a more complex, and subjective question.

And *value in use* may be even more subjective – arriving at a value from an estimate of the revenue streams that your Rolls Royce press will be able to continue generating in a market place which is becoming daily more heavily dominated by printers who have switched to more modern presses; those newer machines' initial cost may be high, but their throughput is vastly greater, so that their owners are hungry for work at almost any price to keep the presses turning.

4.20 *The statement of recognised gains*

The profit and loss account is a primary financial statement required by law. The statement of recognised gains is a primary financial statement called for by FRS 3, and standards have a legal basis.[32]

The profit and loss account stands separate, but the profits recognised in it are also shown in the statement of recognised gains, usually as one of the lines, or columns, in which the latter is customarily drawn up.

Gains which can go into the profit and loss account *must* do so; all others go through the statement of recognised gains. Those others, excluded from the profit and loss account, are of two kinds. We have seen that gains which are not *realised* cannot by law be credited to the profit and loss account. The surplus arising on the revaluation of a property is thus one example of a gain excluded from the profit and loss account. The second kind of excluded gain can most clearly be illustrated through an extension of the first. That property cost £100 and was revalued at the first year end to £120, and then sold in the next accounting period for £150. The first year's accounts showed an unrealised £20 surplus being credited through the statement of recognised gains into a revaluation reserve. But the gain that was *realised* in the second year must surely have been £50? That may or may not be the case, says the ASB, but the amount that can be credited to profit and loss account in the second year is only £30;[33] the grounds for this are that the first year's exclusion (whether required or permitted by an accounting standard or, as here, required by law) is not a reversible exclusion in the presentation[34] of the profit and loss account. Earnings per share in the second year, calculated from what is shown as that year's profit in the profit and loss account, will include only the £30, not £50.

4.21 *The ongoing problem of goodwill*

We briefly introduced the concept of goodwill in paragraph 3.30, and will look in greater detail at its meaning and significance in paragraphs 6.26, 6.28 and 6.29. The relevant aspects for the purposes of a consideration of a company's reserves are:

- a predator which buys a target company for a price greater than the value of the target's net assets,[35] and then consolidates the net

---

[32] See paragraph 1.25 and Note 18 thereon.
[33] FRS 3, paragraph 21.
[34] But this is a presentational point. The £20 as well as the £30 does qualify as a realised, and therefore distributable, profit in the second year under section 262(3) CA 1985. The transfer from a non-distributable, revaluation reserve into the carried forward balance of profit and loss account is normally made in the *Reserves note* to the financial statements.
[35] The target's net assets should be revalued at the time of acquisition. The general approach to this revaluation exercise is that explained in paragraph 4.19, but ASB's thinking (at the time of writing) goes rather further than that, as we will see in paragraph 6.26. This is outlined, and the thinking explained, in *Financial Reporting Exposure Draft 7*, a draft which has yet to be converted into a *Standard*.

assets into its own balance sheet, will thereby create a *difference*, the figure needed to make the balance sheet balance which is what an accountant calls goodwill. Those who acquire companies which make high profits without very much in the way of balance sheet assets (advertising agencies, for instance, when consumer spending and advertising are booming) are likely to find large goodwill figures emerging;

• most, but not all, accountants agree that goodwill should be written off, rather than carried indefinitely in the balance sheet. One possibility is to write it off through profit and loss account, by which is generally meant amortising it over 20 years. The disadvantage of that is, of course, that the resulting deflation of profits, and capacity to pay dividends, during a 20-year period is likely to make any *high-goodwill* predator unduly vulnerable himself to a takeover bid;

• so a second possibility is simply charging the goodwill against reserves.[36] That is not regarded by ASB as recognising a loss, and it must not be accomplished through the statement of recognised gains (and losses), but it does obviously affect the aggregate reserve balances of the predator.

ASB believes meaningful comparisons should be possible between the accounts of companies which have adopted the different approaches above, if they later sell their target companies. If the first sells for more than his then carrying value, he can and should not only credit to the profit and loss account that excess, but also credit back the amortisation he has previously (and with hindsight unnecessarily) debited to profit and loss. The other predator which had charged the whole of goodwill against reserves must write it back into his accounts[37] (again not a recognition of a gain in the statement of recognised gains), because otherwise he could claim to have *realised* a manifestly untrue and unfair profit on his disposal.

4.22 You cannot draw the threads any tighter together

The aggregate of share capital and reserves does *not* represent the economic value of the company. When we made that statement in paragraph 4.18 the reasons we gave were those quoted by the ASB, that goodwill is not fully reflected in the balance sheet and assets are

---

[36] The merger reserve, explained in paragraph 6.25 and Note 41a thereto, is one of the most widely used reserves. Predators who themselves have insufficient reserves (perhaps because their reserves have been depleted on earlier acquisitions) have been known to charge off goodwill in a *reserve* which had no existing credit balance, so that the result of the book-keeping transaction is the figure known in the trade as the *dangling debit*.

[37] ASB's *Urgent Issues Task Force* Abstract No. 3, of December 1991. But as in Note 34, this is a presentational point. What the company is entitled to treat as distributable profit (within the profit and loss account balance) may be rather different, as we will see when we analyse this in paragraphs 9.32 to 9.33.

not shown at current economic value. We could expand on those by saying that the processes of *accounting recognition* are such that whole areas of a company's profit-making capacity cannot be treated as assets: a marketing campaign for a new product; or the time, money and effort invested by its advertising agency in establishing and building its client relationships, and its own image, in order to be able to turn its asset into continuing future business and profits. Notice that that last sentence used the words 'invested' and 'asset' without doing any violence to the English language – but that accounting is unable to *recognise* this in its figures.

The first question flowing from that is what meaning is there in the reserves figures in the balance sheet? The author's response is that it is the movements in reserves, rather than their actual size at any moment, which can tell us more. That in turn means that we almost certainly need to look at the financial statements for a number of past years, alongside those for the most recent one, if we are to make much sense of the figures. And the company which wants to help users of its accounts to make sense of its figures will make sure that each material movement in reserves can be individually identified – that figures are not aggregated and netted-off in such a way that it is impossible to see what has really happened.

A different question is whether there is any possibility that accounting could be *improved* so that balance sheets could be made to reflect economic wealth? This reminds the author of welding shops. One can do precision welding under controlled conditions so that even though the process involves heating small parts of the metal to exceptionally high temperatures there are no stresses in the joint which might lead eventually to fatigue and collapse; or one can do it rather more roughly and readily, if cost does not allow anything else. But what one cannot do is both types of welding in one shop. It is that same difficulty which makes it difficult for accountants to mix in the same financial statements quite precise figures for current assets and income, with much more subjective estimates of the values of the company's goodwill, *brands*,[38] wealth, health, and the sum of human happiness.

---

[38] Intangible assets clearly can have considerable value. But one of the necessary conditions for that value is to be reflected in a balance sheet was said in SSAP 22, the original *Standard* dealing with goodwill, was that the asset must be *separable*. The ASC explained that what they meant by this was that the asset 'could be identified and sold separately without disposing of the business as a whole'. Goodwill could not meet that requirement. A *title* could almost certainly not meet it in a newspaper business, but clearly an individual *title* could do so in a book publishing business; the problem would be how many individual titles could be regarded as separable, and whether there is any logic in putting a value on them, while continuing to put no value on the remainder. In a 1989 research study on the subject of *brands* the London Business School said that continuing the present position, in which it is permissible to include values for brands, whether purchased or home-grown, 'would be highly unwise'. The ASB has not yet turned its attention to this question, except that in its *Statement of Principles*, (chapter 4 paragraph 6), it has said that separability should not be a criterion necessary for recognition of an item in financial statements.

Chapter 5

COMPANY TAX

5.1 Taxes on incorporation of the company

We succeeded, in chapter 3, in saying very little about the taxation of companies as ongoing entities. More or less the only matters on which we did comment were the so-called *toll charges* which constitute the tax costs of incorporating a company – or can in some instances be deferred, or be reduced or avoided, if it is possible to handle the incorporation in a way which makes available the various reliefs:

- the capital gains tax position of the owner, when he disposes of his business's assets, including goodwill, to the company, and receives as consideration for that transfer the shares issued by the company (we noted the different arrangement, with different results, where the owner made a gift of his business to a company whose shares he already owned);

- stamp duty on the owner's transfer of those assets to the company;

- the provisions which allow the owner, and the company, to continue operating for VAT purposes as if there had been no change – as if the individual's business had not made *supplies* of all of its assets to the company (if there had been such supplies made by the owner to the company, it would be necessary for VAT to be charged on them, and accounted for to Customs and Excise);

- the sole trader's computation of profits on his cessation, and the company's profit for its first trading period, in the light of the normal rules for valuing (on cessation) stock in trade, and assets on which tax depreciation has been claimed. But we noted that there are conventions which should enable the individual to avoid any extreme tax penalty for the period to the date of his cessation.

In the context that chapter 3 was addressing the subject of the incorporation of a company, that was clearly the explanation that was necessary of the tax implications of that process.

5.2 Tax on forming, and changing the shape of, groups of companies

In the next chapter (chapter 6) we will move on to the processes of forming, and of changing the shape of, groups of companies. It makes sense, and is the course we will adopt, that we should explain as we step through the group-formation processes, and the possible kinds of changes of shape, what are *their* tax implications.

But those explanations will be less difficult – the general reader must find the subject more accessible – if we interpose at this point some general comments on the taxation of companies. What is needed is a brief explanation how (that is to say, when and for what reasons) a company normally becomes liable to pay tax.

A payment of tax implies a reduction of the company's net assets; which in turn implies a reduction in the company's profits (that is what the *tax charge*[1] is, the line in the profit and loss account which reduces pre-tax profits to a post-tax figure). But the greater part of the tax charge in almost every profit and loss account precedes the payment of tax; we describe the tax charged in the profit and loss account as *provided*, meaning that at the end of the accounting period concerned it is reflected as a liability in the balance sheet. In those circumstances, the subsequent period's payment of the tax has no effect on the company's net assets, nor its profit and loss account. But we will also see that there are opposite possibilities, where the payment of tax precedes the provision; where accountants think it appropriate to treat the payment as creating a matching *asset* in the balance sheet (a recoverable, or a debtor), and it is only at a later point that that recoverable is itself eliminated by being written off as part of the profit and loss tax charge. It is vital that as well as knowing the cashflow effects of tax, we understand its profit and loss, and balance-sheet, effects.

We can extend all of those discussions to deal not just with individual companies but also companies in groups – although at this stage we will look only at the *steady-state* company, or group; we are not discussing in this chapter tax on the reorganisations and other changes which we have yet to reach in chapter 6, those arising when we start forming groups, and then changing their shapes.

5.3 Tax liabilities, not rules of computation

The obvious place to start is the company's liability to tax on its *profits*.[2] In the next paragraph we set out the principal reasons why a company's

---

[1] 'The tax charge' is the phrase used in SSAP 8, and also in general use colloquially, to describe the single line in the profit and loss account on which is shown, as one figure,

    (1) UK corporation tax on profits;

    (2) tax attributable to dividends received;

    (3) irrecoverable ACT; less

    (4) relief for overseas taxation; but including also a profit reduction for

    (5) overseas taxation.

How that single figure is made up between those categories must be shown under the requirements of SSAP 8.

The Companies Act caption in the profit and loss account is 'tax on profit or loss on ordinary activities' and its make-up is required to be shown along the same lines, except that irrecoverable ACT does not need to be separately shown (paragraph 54 of schedule 4 to CA 1985).

[2] 'Profits' is used throughout the legislation on company tax to mean income plus capital gains, section 6(4)(a) TA 1988; but paradoxically the phrase used in tax

continued

trading income may be differently quantified[3] in its accounts and in its tax computations.

However, for the purposes we have set ourselves in this book, we need not investigate such detailed rules as the one preventing a company from deducting expenses incurred on entertaining UK-based customers but permitting such deductions for the entertaining of overseas customers (its taxable profits are calculated after treating the second as an expense in arriving at those profits, but without the first being similarly deducted).

What is relevant for our purposes is the fact, rather than the reasons for that fact, that taxable profits are almost always either greater or less than accounting profits, with the result that the effective rate of tax can be seen to be greater or less than the *statutory rate*. The deviation mentioned above is unlikely to be large enough to be of any concern, but there can be more significant differences. In those cases there are rules, and underlying truths, which we must keep in view. In part, the rules are Companies Act requirements on disclosure;[4] in part they are in *Statements of Standard Accounting Practice*.[5]

In paragraph 3.38, and Note 49 thereon, we introduced the concept of *deferred tax*. If a company can for instance claim a much greater amount of tax depreciation allowances than the amount shown as depreciation in its accounts for the year concerned, but that position will reverse

---

continued
  legislation to describe the income derived from a trade is 'annual profits or gains' (section 18(1)(a) TA 1988), and that specifically excludes capital gains (section 833(1) TA 1988. Viscount Addington introduced an income tax on 'annual profits or gains' in 1803, and over the following two centuries, the Revenue has never found it possible to change that phrase).

[3] The UK system is described as *schedular*, meaning that income is quantified under a number of separate schedules related to its source (for example, income from a trade, rental income, income from UK securities and from foreign securities). Total income is the aggregate of the figures from these schedules, and from that total income certain amounts can be deducted in order to arrive at taxable income; these deductions include, for instance, relief for trading losses (which can include relief brought forward, and brought back as well as for losses of the year) and the so-called *charges on income* of which the most significant example is interest paid (even here one has to say that some interest is a trading expense, but some is a charge).

  This explanation is not meant to clarify all of these rules – but merely to indicate that when we discuss the levels of different classes of income (for ACT set-off purposes for instance in paragraph 5.12), or the surrender of certain types of loss (under group relief in paragraph 5.21), the rules we are referring to are dealing specifically with income and losses quantified under the rules of one or more schedules, not with a single figure representing the end result of the whole of the company's operations.

[4] Company law requires disclosure, that is to say that an explanation be given, where the tax charge in the profit and loss account differs by any material amount from the figure that might be expected, namely the rate of tax applied to the accounting profits. Disclosure is customarily made by way of a note to the company's statutory accounts, rather that a figure or description in the body of those accounts. This particular disclosure is called for by paragraph 54(2) in schedule 4 to CA 1985, necessitating that 'particulars be given of any special circumstances which affect liability in respect of taxation of profits'.

[5] SSAP 8 spells out the standard 'Treatment of Tax under the Imputation System', and we will illustrate the principles in paragraphs 5.7 to 5.15 below. SSAP 15 deals with the subject of deferred tax.

thereafter, then its first year tax depreciation entitlement could be expected to produce abnormally low tax; and correspondingly the years of reversal would show higher effective tax rates. It is indisputable that that is the cash position. But accountants say it gives a truer and fairer picture of profits through the years if those profits are not boosted by the low tax charge in the first year, and then deflated by the high charges in later years.[6] We will look at the theory, and the accounts presentation, of deferred tax in paragraphs 5.18 to 5.20.

5.4 Computation of trading income under tax rules

A discussion limited to a single paragraph can obviously do no more than record some of the main principles giving rise to differences between the accounting and tax calculations of trading income:

- the timing of tax depreciation allowances, compared to that of accounts depreciation, has already been mentioned — but it is also relevant that there are some classes of capital expenditure which do not qualify for tax depreciation;

- the Companies Act accounting principles[7] including the one dealing with the timing of recognition of profits (realisation) are accepted by the Inland Revenue.[8] If two qualifications may be needed of that statement, they would be first that the Revenue argue that the deductibility of provisions for bad debts is fixed by the tax statute's wording, not an accountant's application of the Companies Act provision.[9] Second, a provision for *any kind* of loss can only be allowable for tax purposes if it is possible to form a reasonably clear view what should be the size of the loss concerned;[10]

---

[6] Even clearer as a distortion between accounting and taxable profits which is self-cancelling over the years is the rule that a company cannot deduct a provision made for a pension fund contribution; it is only the actual cash payment to the trustees which gives a deduction (section 592(4) ICTA 1988).

[7] Paragraphs 10 to 13 and 89 of schedule 4 to CA 1985 mirror the fundamental accounting concepts of the going concern, accruals, consistency and prudence in SSAP 2. Under paragraph 12(a) it is provided that 'only profits realised at the balance sheet date shall be included in the profit and loss account'.

[8] The wording of section 18(1)(a) ICTA 1988 refers to the schedule D charge being on annual profits or gains 'arising or accruing', but it is clear in practice (and from many cases, of which *Symons v Weeks* [1982] 56 TC 630 is probably the clearest authority) that the Revenue do not claim they can tax income as it *accrues*, but only when it has been *realised* under ordinary principles of commercial accounting.

[9] Section 74(j) ICTA 1988 prohibits any deduction for doubtful debts except 'to the extent they are respectively estimated to be bad'. This is interpreted by the Inland Revenue to prevent any *statistical* approach to the making of provisions for doubtful debts, such as saying that experience shows that 3 per cent of a portfolio of consumer credit loans will be uncollectable; but it is also said to be require a stricter examination of individual debts than the Companies Act formula in paragraph 89 of schedule 4, which requires provision to be made for 'any ... loss which is either likely to be incurred, or certain to be incurred but uncertain as to the amount or as to the date on which it will arise'.

[10] This is the conclusion of *Owen v Southern Railway of Peru Ltd* [1956] 36 TC 602. It can perhaps best be illustrated in the area of pure risk. A Ltd borrows deutsche

continued

- the trading expenditure deductible for tax purposes has been described as that incurred, wholly and exclusively, in carrying on the trade in order that profits may be earned[11] (this being a less restrictive formula than saying that only expenditure incurred in earning profits could be deducted). One category of expense which this is likely to prohibit from being deducted is what might be described as *close down* costs, and those continuing to be incurred after the cessation of a trade or part of it;[12]

- *capital* items can cause differences between accounting and taxable profits in two distinct ways. First there are items on which the profit or loss is calculated for tax purposes under capital gains rules while the accounting result is merely part of trading income. The calculation of a capital gain includes indexation, and may also involve valuation

---

continued

marks for five years at 8 per cent and lends them to B Ltd at 10 per cent. The reason for the interest differential is that A Ltd undertakes to accept back, in full satisfaction of the loan, either deutsche marks, or an amount of sterling equivalent to the deutsche marks not at the rate ruling at the end of the five years, but at the rate ruling at the start of that period. If the deutsche mark strengthens, B Ltd will repay in deutsche marks, and A Ltd's profit will have been five year's interest differential. If it weakens, B Ltd will repay in sterling, and A Ltd's profit will have been reduced by the exchange loss. The point, however, is that although there are ways of forecasting what the sterling/deutsche mark exchange rate may be in five years time, and therefore what may be the reduction in profit, there is only the flimsiest logical, or statistical, reason for suggesting that A Ltd's profit for year 1 of the deal is one year's interest differential reduced by a provision equal to one fifth of (or perhaps the whole of) the forecast exchange loss. That is not a *hard* enough calculation of a provision to meet the criteria in the *Southern Railway* case.

[11] The original formulation was by Lord Davey in *Strong & Co. of Romsey Ltd v Woodifield* [1906] 5 TC 215 at 220:

'These words ... appear to me to mean for the purpose of enabling a person to carry on and earn profits in the trade etc. I think the disbursements permitted are such as are made for that purpose. It is not enough that the disbursement is made in the course of, or arises out of, or is connected with the trade, or is made out of the profits of the trade. It must be made for the purpose of earning the profits.'

The last sentence of that quotation appears to narrow the wider implication in the first; but Lord Davey's meaning has been clarified in a number of subsequent cases, perhaps most succinctly by Lord Willmer in *Harrods (Buenos Aires) Ltd v Taylor-Gooby* [1964] 41 TC 450 at 467:

'The (disbursement in) any given year is a payment necessarily made in order to ensure that trading will be allowed to continue during the next and succeeding years. In this respect the (disbursement) is clearly made for the purpose of earning profits from the continuance of trading.'

[12] For instance the payments made by the trader to his landlord as compensation to the latter for the trader's having brought his lease to a premature end, see *Cowcher v Richard Mills & Co. Ltd* [1926] 13 TC 216. It should be added that there is a fine line between on the one hand expenditure on closing down a trade or on a closed down trade, and on the other hand ensuring the orderly conduct of a trade until it can be closed down, see *Godden v Wilsons Stores (Holdings) Ltd* [1962] 40 TC 161, in which a company sold its business and gave its manager six months pay in lieu of notice, which was not deductible; compared with *O'Keefe v Southport Printers Ltd*, [1984] 58 TC 88, in which payments to employees in almost exactly similar circumstances were deducted, under the orderly conduct formula.

at some *base date*, and the reliefs for *rollover* and/or for transfer of assets within groups;

• the second aspect is the tax statute's ban on the deduction of *capital* expenditure.[13] What many taxpayers see as manifestly unfair is that disallowance is not matched by any relief depreciating the *asset* through the period of its *lasting value*.

5.5 Tax liabilities in groups

Each of those deviations between theoretically expected, and actual, tax liabilities in the two previous paragraphs can be described as either *permanent* or as *reversing*. Over the whole life of the asset which qualified for generous front-end tax depreciation, the aggregate tax depreciation and the aggregate accounts depreciation will be equal; the difference in the first year reverses[14] in later years. No such effect

---

[13] Section 74(f) ICTA 1988. In this much litigated area, the courts have repeatedly asserted their right to decide what is capital, as distinct from revenue, expenditure – and have not accepted that the principles used by accountants (as part of ordinary commercial accounting) are conclusive. When the courts have decided their answer in one case, and expressed it in 'phrases (that) are essentially descriptive rather than definitive', it is exceptionally dangerous to apply those words unthinkingly in different circumstances; 'a Court's primary duty is to inquire how far a description that was both relevant and significant in one set of circumstances is either relevant or significant in those which are presently before it'. Both those quotations come from Lord Radcliffe in *Nchanga Consolidated Copper Mines* [1964] 1 All ER 208 at 212. With that warning, one can identify some principles the courts appear to have used in determining that the following are the two main classes of expenditure that are capital:

– first, once and for all expenditure, with a view to bringing into existence an asset or an advantage for the enduring benefit of the trade, per Viscount Cave in *Atherton v British Insulated and Helsby Cables Ltd* [1925] 10 TC 155 at 192 and 193.

– second, where the *advantage* takes the form of *rights*, although those rights might be no different from those that could be acquired by means of deductible expenditure, the actual manner of their acquisition was capital. The payment of a premium for the grant of a lease gives the leaseholder the same rights that a different landlord might have granted him for the payment of rent, but that does not make the premium deductible, per Lord Reid in *Strick v Regent Oil Co. Ltd* [1965] 43 TC 1 at 31.

On the other hand, section 74(f) ICTA 1988 makes it clear that interest paid can be deducted, even if the borrowings are for a capital purpose. In the case of the interest which is not deductible in arriving at trading income, but instead is relieved as a charge on income (see Note 3 above) a modest amount of care (section 338(5)(a) ICTA 1988) will ensure that relief is available even where it might similarly be possible to suggest the interest had capital characteristics.

[14] The explanation in the text makes the difference between permanent and reversing differences sound much more clear-cut than it ever is in practice. One problem can be illustrated by reference to the start-up company which buys one new machine each year for four years, but thereafter expects merely to replace one machine every year. In that *steady-state*, fourth year onwards, position, its accounts depreciation and its capital allowances for each year will have stabilised, and will be equal; should one therefore say that any difference which accumulates in the first four years is a permanent difference? A different problem arises where accountants would say that

continued

flows from the disallowance of entertaining expenses, nor from the differences in the last three heads in the previous paragraph. However those reversing examples in the two previous paragraphs affected only an individual company's position. The position becomes quite considerably more complex in a group.

The company whose tax depreciation allowances so considerably exceeded its accounts depreciation could, for instance, have produced a tax loss from that distortion. It could have surrendered that loss to another group company under the *group relief* arrangements to which we will come in paragraph 5.23 below. That would produce distortions spanning the accounts of both companies, that is to say, an abnormally low tax charge in the other company in the year of surrender, and correspondingly higher tax charges in the first company's accounts in the future.

But a moment's thought would show that unlike the problem in the previous paragraph, which distorted only the profit and loss accounts between years, this *group* arrangement distorts also the cash position between the companies. The beneficiary of the surrendered losses also enjoys a cash saving, whereas the company which gave up those losses gives up also the cash saving that would otherwise have flowed from a loss carry forward to a later year.

This may be desirable. But it would be possible, as an alternative:

- to obtain for the group, but not within what we described above as the beneficiary company, those same cashflow advantages out of the immediate surrender of the tax loss; and
- to maintain at the same time the integrity[15] of the companies;

---

continued

a debit tax deferral is needed, that is to say, where in the initial years' accounting profits are lower than tax profits, but this is expected to reverse. The classic example of this is the bank's general provision for bad debts. The Revenue do not give tax relief when the provision is charged against profits, but do give that relief when specific bad debts are charged against the provision. The accountant's problem is one of *prudence*; can he allow the bank to show a lower tax charge in the first year, when he does not know whether there will actually be a tax saving in the later year? There would be no such saving if the bank made an overall loss in that later year. There is a third problem where it simply is not possible to know whether certain items will reverse; the rules for capital allowances on industrial buildings, and commercial buildings in enterprise zones, are such that the capital allowances given on their cost can be *clawed back* if they are sold within 25 years, but otherwise these allowances become permanent. Whether the owner depreciates the building for accounts purposes or does not, how he should account for the tax reliefs is a problematical area.

[15] In the pre-1984 tax regime, particularly with the generosity of the tax depreciation allowances then available, the leasing subsidiaries in many financial groups assumed that there was little likelihood of tax liabilities crystallising in later years, because a constant stream of new business could be relied on to make the early years' allowances (losses) a permanent feature rather than one which would reverse. The change in the regime, and the dramatic reduction in the rates of tax depreciation allowances, in 1984 put many of these companies in danger of insolvency.

by getting the *benefit* into the company which is *entitled* to it – by having the loss-claimant compensate its fellow group member.[16]

Pay and file

5.6 The first part of the process is paying; how do the Revenue set about encouraging and enforcing payment?

Corporation tax on the company's profits is due nine months and one day after the end of its accounting period.[17] It is the company's responsibility to calculate, and pay, its own liability. The encouragement of prompt and full payment takes the form of interest charged on amounts paid late. That encouragement is strengthened by two tiers of penalties:

- penalties fixed in monetary terms for the late filing of returns. We will glance at the required contents of the return in the next paragraph, although they are not part of this book's objectives. But the penalties for late filing are part of the Revenue's attempts to obtain tax on the due dates;

- penalties at a percentage of unpaid tax in cases where not only is the return late, but tax is underpaid as well.

---

[16] *Payments for group relief* are legislated as part of the rules, as we will explain in paragraph 5.25 below. The need to keep constantly in mind the preservation of companies' integrity goes beyond group situations. We will see in chapter 7, paragraph 7.6, that it is just as necessary to make equivalent arrangements in the case of a company owed by a consortium.

[17] There are two points. An accounting period of a company for corporation commences when the company first has a source of income. It ends (and except where asterisked the succeeding accounting period begins) at the earliest of a list of specified dates, which can be seen to be more comprehensive than really relevant to the normal company:

– each accounting date of the company (and if there is a gap between periods for which a company makes up accounts, the end of that gap);
– the end of 12 months from the beginning of an accounting period (relevant if there is an accounting period longer than a year, in which case this is always split into the first 12 months and the remainder);
– the company beginning to trade, or ceasing* to trade (or to be subject* to UK corporation tax on (all of) its trade(s) – this being relevant to the non-resident company which closes its UK branch but does not stop all of its trading elsewhere);
– the company becoming or ceasing* to be UK resident;
– the company ceasing* to be within the scope of corporation tax, which means either ceasing to have any source of income, or being finally wound up

The second point is that until 1965, every company paid tax on 1 January in the fiscal year after that in which its accounting year ended. The company whose accounting year had ended on 31 December 1964 paid tax on 1 January 1966, and so also did the company whose accounting year had ended on 30 April 1964. For new companies after 1965 the interval was set at nine months. The intervals (12 months, 20 months and nine months for the companies mentioned) were harmonised at the present nine months level in the three years from March 1988 (*old* companies paid more frequently than once a year during this process).

Interest and penalties are, however, only encouragements. If the company fails to pay tax which the Inland Revenue believes to be due, the age-old collection and enforcement arrangements remain in place, unchanged by pay and file having been superimposed.

What the Inland Revenue need, in the circumstances we are envisaging, is to establish a debt due from the company to the Crown, which they can then pursue by legal means. The steps are as follows. The Inspector of Taxes can make an estimated assessment.[18] Although the company can appeal, the tax charged by that assessment is due 30 days after the assessment's issue (this will in these cases always be later than the normal due date for the tax concerned). There are procedures under which a taxpayer can agree with the Inspector that some part of the tax charged in an estimated assessment should be *postponed* pending the agreement of the correct liability, but once again it is unlikely here that an Inspector would be sympathetic to an application for postponement.[19]

The Revenue have been creaking and groaning for years under administrative procedures which have required assessments (almost invariably estimated) in advance of every payment date for every company. They clearly look forward with pleasure to having to continue estimating only where companies' non-compliance with pay and file forces them to do so.[20]

---

[18] The procedure of estimating the amount of a taxpayer's income is centuries older than corporation tax. Both parts of the phrase 'estimated assessment' have been severely degraded by the procedures the Inland Revenue have used since 1964. Before 1964, an assessment started as an estimate, made by local Commissioners on the recommendation of a Surveyor of Taxes (later renamed an Inspector), of the subject's taxable *income*. Income tax (which was what companies as well as individuals then paid) was in many cases charged not on income received in a monetary form but on annual values, for instance the income-producing capacity of land in its owner's hands, whether or not he let it and, if he did, regardless of the fact that his rents might be more or less than the *estimated* figure. Once the Commissioners had issued the estimate, the taxpayer had 30 days within which to appeal – that appeal being at that time an investigative process conducted by the Commissioners themselves (not a judicial process fought by taxpayer and Revenue on an adversarial basis before Commissioners acting judicially). Their investigation could result in an increase in the assessment, its confirmation at the original level, a reduction, or its discharge. If there was no appeal, the original estimate became final and binding at the end of the 30 days from issue.

That last sentence remains true today, but almost the only other part of the original structure still visible is the Inspector's duty to 'estimate' (although that word itself has disappeared from the statute) 'to the best of his judgment' what is the taxpayer's income, in those cases where the taxpayer has not made a return which the Inspector regards as satisfactory.

[19] A refusal of a postponement application can itself be the subject of an appeal but once again one would have to expect the the Inspector to fight any such appeal, and that if the company did take it to a hearing it would lose.

[20] See the Inland Revenue's booklet *A First Guide to Corporation Tax Pay and File*, paragraph 5.2. The Inland Revenue's promise under pay and file is that they will no longer issue estimated assessments designed to establish a collectible debt, except in two circumstances: first, after the company's return has been filed, it is possible for it to be judged by the Inspector to be unsatisfactory; alternatively, when the date for filing it has passed without its being filed. Final assessments, the Inland Revenue say, will only be issued when the figures have been agreed.

continued

5.7 Filing – the second part of the process

If we followed through the thought processes underlying that last paragraph, we would say that the main purpose of a company's corporation tax return was to supply to the Inspector, in a standard format, a computation of the company's taxable profit (backed up with information which will enable him to verify it, principally the company's statutory accounts[21]). That is certainly one of its purposes.

But there are other purposes of the return, although only the last two we list need detailed discussion in subsequent paragraphs:

- should the computation rules produce what it is convenient to call an income loss,[22] the Inland Revenue need a *claim* from the

---

continued

If the result of a company's operations for a year is a loss, the Revenue's formal agreement of its amount is a *determination* (section 41A TMA 1970), and their promise is that these will be forthcoming as soon as they have agreed the figures. Should a taxpayer not agree with the Revenue's determination, an appeals procedure exists which almost exactly mirrors that for appeals against assessments which the taxpayer wishes to dispute. This appeals procedure may be particularly appropriate in cases where the Revenue re-determine *downwards* an earlier determination, this being the equivalent of their making an additional assessment (section 41B TMA 1970).

(Where a company has claimed the benefit of another's loss under the group relief arrangements explained in paragraph 5.23, or has surrendered its loss to another, the assessment or determination will reflect the company's figures after the claim or surrender.)

[21] The statutory accounts must accompany the return, and what the Inland Revenue want is the *full* shareholders' accounts. They do not want the summary financial statements which a public company is permitted to send to those shareholders who ask not to be sent full accounts; these are not in any event statutory accounts. Nor do they want the abbreviated accounts which small and medium sized companies can file with the Companies' Registrar (see paragraph 1.23 and Note 15 thereon).

The directors' report and the auditors' report have as a matter of Companies law to be annexed to a company's accounts, so they must clearly also be sent to the Revenue. But the latter have indicated that they will also wish to see any other *reports*. What they have in mind may become clearer with the passage of time, but if a company believes that it is appropriate that shareholders receive, to assist their understanding of the accounts, a statement by the Chairman, then it is difficult to believe that the Inland Revenue would not think it necessary for their own better understanding. Similarly, if the accounting profession believes that companies should publish an Operating and Financial Review, then any company which does so should expect that the Revenue would want to see it. The Accounting Standards Board's statement of July 1993 made it clear that the production of an Operating and Financial Review was voluntary, and that its precise form and content was a matter for companies who wished to produce such statements. The ASB did however make very clear its own view that this was to be regarded as *best practice*, and that this view was supported by the Financial Reporting Council, the Hundred Group of Finance Directors, and the London Stock Exchange. The OFR is described as a report on the year under review, including a discussion and interpretation of the business, the main factors, features and uncertainties that underlie it and the structure of its financing. Although it is not a forecast of future results, it should nevertheless draw out those features of the year under review which are relevant to an assessment of future prospects.

[22] A loss calculated under the capital gains regime is only available to set against capital gains in the same year or subsequent years in the same company. But a company which sustains a trading loss, or has certain other types of expense which exceed related income (and the amount of the loss exceeds its net capital gains) has various options how that excess is to be used.

ADVANCE CORPORATION TAX

company how it wishes to take advantage of it, because there are frequently different routes available. A trading loss can, for instance, be carried forward to be set against subsequent trading income – or it can be set against other profits (income and gains) of the same year or of specified earlier years, and that does not exhaust all of the possibilities. The detail of the rules is less important for our purposes than that there are choices, and that the Revenue wants the return to show what the company has chosen;

• outside the field of losses there are other areas in which the company has some choice how its figures are to be calculated. The clearest examples are in the capital allowances field. A company is not allowed a deduction for what we have called accounts depreciation, but tax depreciation allowances (or to use the legislative term 'capital allowances') can be deducted, computed under detailed rules.[23] The relevant point is again that there are different choices available – plant claimed as having only a *short life* produces a different profile of allowances from plant for which such a claim is not made. The company's tax return shows what *claim* it is making;

• thirdly, the company must notify the Revenue of any *group relief* claim that affects its liabilities. We will look at this in paragraph 5.23 below;

• and last, there are Advance Corporation Tax and Income Tax, to which we need to turn our immediate attention.

5.8 Advance corporation tax

Advance corporation tax is payable 14 days after the end of each quarter, in respect of the dividends (or other distributions) paid in that quarter.
That statement needs immediate qualification:

• ACT does not apply to dividends paid within groups of companies where a group income election applies;[24]

• ACT does not apply to *scrip dividends*, that is to say, bonus shares issued in lieu of a cash dividend;[25]

---

[23] These rules are to be found in the Capital Allowances Act 1990. These allowances are defined by reference to the company's capital expenditure, and that expenditure is further defined by reference to classes of assets. Buildings in enterprise zones; other industrial buildings and qualifying hotels; machinery or plant; houses let on assured tenancies; mineral extraction; agricultural buildings; dredging; and scientific research, are the main categories, but there are myriad sub-categories and detailed rules for each. Short-life assets are a sub-category of machinery or plant, their tax allowances distinguished from those for other plant in that every disposal of any such asset produces an individually calculated *balancing allowance or charge* rather than merely an adjustment of the *pool* value on which future allowances are calculated.

[24] Group income is examined in paragraph 5.26 below.

[25] Scrip dividends, referred to in the tax legislation as 'stock' dividends, are defined in section 249 ICTA 1988. They include bonus shares issued to a shareholder who has

continued

- ACT does not apply to an exempt purchase by a company of its own shares or an exempt distribution in a demerger;[26]
- ACT does not apply to so-called non-qualifying distributions.[27]

In principle, ACT does apply to all other dividends and distributions. The word 'dividend' has no special meaning in tax legislation. The distributions which are treated as analogous to dividends (having the ancillary result that they are not deductible in arriving at corporation taxable profits) are defined in detailed and wide ranging provisions. Many of these we can ignore, for the very simple reason that we will avoid suggesting the transactions they are designed to catch, for instance the payment of excessive rates of interest, non-deductible, and costing ACT.

Those definitions of distributions which are central to the purposes of this book will be discussed in chapter 6, at paragraphs 6.39 to 6.41, and 6.50 to 6.55. We will see that there are some transactions between companies which would be caught within the basic definitions, but are specifically relieved from being regarded as distributions, and from being subject to ACT.

Additionally, to put the words in context, we need to be aware that income tax is to be assessed on all dividends and distributions by UK companies.[28] If we were to re-express this rule to say that all dividends and distributions were income of the recipients, this would be only an

---

continued
an option by which he can choose shares in place of a cash dividend, and bonus shares issued on a class of capital which carries the right to such bonus issues in place of cash dividends. A shareholder who is liable to the higher rate of income tax will be assessed on a *gross equivalent* figure to collect that higher rate tax. Any individual holder, including an executor or trustee, and whether or not liable at the higher rate, is allowed to treat an amount equal to the cash dividend as being the capital gains tax cost of the shares received, section 141 TCGA 1992.

[26] Demergers are the subject of chapter 14 below, and company purchases of own shares are dealt with in chapter 13.

[27] Non-qualifying distributions are defined in sections 14(2) and 233(2) ICTA 1988. In brief they can be explained as provisions dealing with the issue by a company of redeemable bonus shares, that is to say, shares which can be expected to turn into cash in the shareholders' hands, to the extent that the cash concerned does not represent a refund to him of cash originally subscribed for the shares concerned. Thus, as well as assessing the nominal value of the shares when originally issued, the Revenue also assess cash which reaches the shareholder's hands when the shares are redeemed, to the extent that cash exceeds the nominal value already assessed at the time of the shares' issue.

[28] Section 20 ICTA 1988. This requires that any distribution 'not specifically exempted from income tax' be assessed, and be treated as income 'regardless how it may fall to be treated in the hands of the recipient'. The first of the quoted phrases relates primarily to capital dividends, treated in principle as proceeds of disposals or part disposals under capital gains tax rules; they are defined in section 122(5)(b) TCGA 1992 in an almost perfectly circular manner as any distribution except one which in the hands of the recipient constitutes income for income tax purposes. The second quoted phrase seems to be a reference to such items as the dividend apportioned to capital in a trust account (to benefit the remainderman not the lifetenant), where the amount is not exempted from assessment, and for tax purposes is treated as income of the trust, although not part of the lifetenant's entitlement under its terms.

approximation to the truth (in part because of cases such as those referred to in Note 28) but also because there would be one major exception: dividends received by a UK company are *not* its income for *corporation* tax purposes.[29] This is the transparency point explained at the end of paragraph 5.9.

5.9 *The cash implications of ACT*

The first sentence of the previous paragraph said that ACT was payable 14 days after the end of each quarter in respect of the dividends and distributions in the quarter.

That is only one part of the rules regarding the cash impact of ACT; gaining a picture of the remainder of the cash implications, and more particularly of the balance-sheet and profit and loss account presentation, is easiest if we look in the first instance at the simplest possible example, and then discuss some complications which could alter the basic picture.

The company pays a dividend on 30 September, year 1, of £300. It had received a £100 dividend (with a tax credit of £25) earlier in the same month from a subsidiary. The company's year end is 31 December, and we assume that its trading profits (equal to its taxable profits) to 31 December, year 1, will be £1,000:

- the company records the receipt of the dividend from its subsidiary by crediting £125 as income and including £25 in its tax charge, both of these being profit and loss account entries (one can describe this procedure as crediting the dividend received at a figure grossed up by the ACT rate, which is taken as 20/80ths);

- the company's payment of its own dividend shows in its profit and loss account as a payment out of post-tax income of £300;

- on 14 October, year 1, the ACT which the company pays over to the Inland Revenue is £50. That figure is arrived at by deducting from the ACT on the company's own dividend (20/80ths of £300 = £75) the ACT on the subsidiary's dividend received, £25. One way of rationalising these figures is to say that the payment of a dividend through a second company *should* be wholly transparent – and that is what we see. The Inland Revenue is receiving £50 from this company, and will simultaneously be receiving £25 from the subsidiary in respect of its dividend payment. The shareholders receive a dividend which they regard as a *gross* £375, with a credit for tax already paid in respect of it of £75 (satisfaction of their lower and/or basic rate liabilities in cases where they are not liable beyond those).

5.10 *Setting off the ACT against corporation tax*

As indicated, the company pays £50 to the Revenue on 14 October, year 1. That payment is *not* reflected within the tax charge in the profit and

---

[29] Section 208 ICTA 1988.

loss account – it is a balance sheet item, an asset; although we will see in the next couple of sentences that by the time the balance sheet comes to be prepared two and a half months later that has become only a half truth.

At 31 December, the company provides for the corporation tax payable on its trading profits:

$$\text{£1,000 at 25 per cent} \qquad \text{£250}$$

that £250 is shown as part of the tax charge in the profit and loss account; and the other side of the double-entry is that it appears as a current liability, due in less than 12 months, on the face of the balance sheet. It is here, however, that we see the half truth mentioned at the beginning of this paragraph. The amount that will actually be *paid* to the Inland Revenue on 1 October year 2 is £200, that is to say, the corporation tax on profits *of* the year, after off-setting the ACT already paid over in respect of dividends paid *in* the year. The balance sheet presentation is therefore to net off the *asset* of £50 mentioned at the start of this paragraph against the liability of £250 we are now looking at, in order to show a net liability of £200.

The position would be slightly more complicated if the company's accounts to 31 December, year 1, also showed a recommendation for a final dividend for that year, payable (if agreed by the annual meeting) in April, year 2. Let us assume that that recommended dividend is £400. That figure is shown in the profit and loss account as a further decrease in the retained profit. The ACT which will need to be accounted for in respect of it (on 14 July year 2) will be £100. If that ACT will simply reduce a corporation tax liability, then the *asset* created on the cash payment in July year 2 will simply be set against a *liability* arising from a profit and loss account charge; since the dividend is to be paid in year 2, it will be the corporation tax payment for year 2 against which we will be making the off-set (the liability provided at the end of year 2 on those profits).

5.11 *Setting off the ACT against corporation tax (continued)*

What we need to do is think about those *assets*. At the beginning of paragraph 5.8 we created an asset of £50 by paying ACT of that amount to the Revenue on 14 October, year 1. At 31 December, year 1, we netted off that £50 against the liability for £250 of corporation tax. There are no problems up to that point.

Proposing the final dividend of £400, however, implies proposing a payment of ACT on 14 July of year 2 of £100. If we are confident that when that cash is paid away, we can create a further £100 asset, there is again no problem. But creating that asset is only legitimate if we are confident that it will be off-settable against a corporation tax liability (which in the normal event would be that payable on 1 October, year 3, by reference to profits of year 2). If £100 of ACT will not be off-settable, it must be written off through profit and loss account – we would otherwise be understating the cost of that dividend; the writing off of ACT is something we must look at in greater detail in paragraph 5.15.

In other words, *irrecoverable ACT* would, on the basis we are envisaging, arise as a result of our paying that final dividend. This is not the normal way in which irrecoverable ACT actually arises in practice, but subject to what is said below it is a perfectly possible way for it to arise. If for instance the company made no profits in year 2, there could be no off-set on the basis we have been assuming.

Are we allowed, at 31 December year 1, to assume that there will be sufficient profits in year 2 – that there will be a corporation tax provision made in the profit and loss account in 12 months' time at a sufficient level, to permit the off-set to be made or would we be *anticipating* profits[30] if we did, now, assume such an off-set?

Fortunately, we can escape answering the question. If we were to assume that there were no profits in year 2, and ask 'what then?' the answer we would get is that if ACT on a year 2 dividend cannot be set against year tax on 2 profits, it can be carried back for off-set against tax on year 1's profits (and in fact those of the previous five years). There are sufficient profits of year 1, and tax on them, to absorb the ACT on this proposed final dividend.

5.12 Illustration of ACT off-set in an analysed profit and loss account

It may help the reader to see the mechanics if we set out the profit and loss figures as in Table 27, showing first the totals, and then showing separate columns for that part of the interim dividend *franked* by the dividend received, the balance of the interim dividend, the proposed final dividend, and the profits retained.

Table 27: ACT Offset

	Total	Div rec'd	Bal of interim	Final	Ret'd profit
Pre-tax profits	1,000		267	533	200
Dividend received	125	125			
	1,125				
Tax charge	275	25	67	133	50
	850	100	200	400	150
Dividends paid & proposed	700	100	200	400	–
Retention	150				150

---

[30] The 'concept of prudence' in SSAP 2 does not permit revenue or profits to be anticipated, but allows them to be recognised by inclusion in the profit and loss account only when realised in the form either of cash or of other assets the ultimate cash realisation of which can be assessed with reasonable certainty. This prohibition on anticipating profits extends not just to the profits themselves, but to their further implications, such as their availability or otherwise for ACT set-off.

The column headed 'Div rec'd' makes clear the meaning of the expression 'franking'. ACT is not paid by this company on the dividend it receives (it was paid by the subsidiary from which the dividend came). But the fact that £100 had been received enables £100 to be paid. What is described as *franked income* is the *gross* of £125.

The next two columns show that part of the company's profits used[31] to pay the balance of the interim dividend, and the proposed final. In each case, the 25 per cent corporation tax charge is sufficient to allow for the off-set of ACT at 20/80ths of the dividend (this is less than the limit of 20 per cent of profits examined in paragraph 5.14 below).

Using the perspective explained in paragraph 1.34, saying that the tax credit attached to the dividend is shareholder tax rather than company tax, we would say that in the third column in Table 27 profits of £267 have been subjected to company tax at 6.25 per cent, that is, £17, and that the (gross) dividend of £250 has then suffered shareholder tax at 20 per cent, namely £50. That is not, however, the profit and loss account presentation.

The final column of Table 27 makes it clear that the company's tax burden on the proportion of pre-tax profits which it retains is 25 per cent; that is not only our paragraph 1.34 perspective, but that of the profit and loss account.

5.13 Irrecoverable ACT

We now change the data, by assuming this company had income arising abroad, which had suffered foreign tax.

If the foreign gross were £200, and the foreign tax suffered on it £50, then those would have been the figures included in the profit and loss account, at the pre-tax level and in the tax charge. The fact that profits of a UK company are subject to foreign tax does not *exempt* them from UK tax, our system of giving relief for foreign taxes is not one of the exemption systems found in many other EC states. Our system gives *credit*[32] against corporation tax for the foreign tax concerned.

---

[31] The word 'used' has to be understood as referring to the accounting thought-processes reflected in the final sentences of paragraph 5.9 above. In cashflow terms, the ACT will, to the extent of £50, be paid on 14 October year 1, and £100 will be paid on 14 July year 2. The £50 will reduce a corporation tax liability otherwise payable 1 October year 2, and the £100 will in the normal course reduce one payable 1 October year 3; because, however, we are *not* able to demonstrate before the start of year 2 that profits will materialise, and are not able to show that there will be a liability for tax on 1 October year 3, we have adopted a different basis for showing that ACT is fully off-settable. We will also see when we follow through the statutory limitations on the off-set of ACT in paragraph 5.14 that taxable profits of £750 (a tax charge at 25 per cent of £187.50) would be sufficient to provide the off-set of £150 ACT on net dividends of £600; but paying such a dividend does of course require that there are other distributable profits available in addition to the post-tax £562.50 which a pre-tax profit of £750 would imply.

[32] The basic relief-by-credit is in section 793 ICTA 1988, but this is worded to give that credit only if it is 'allowable under any arrangements'. There are two kinds of arrangement, one being the so-called double tax conventions which are in fact treaties negotiated between the UK and other states which determine

continued

We therefore assume that a credit of £50 will be given, reducing the UK corporation tax liability by that amount. In the tax charge is now included the UK liability of £50, a reduction of £50 in the form of the credit given against that, and a further charge of £50 in respect of the foreign tax suffered.

At that stage no change is needed to our analysis of the profit and loss account in Table 27. The company is entitled to say that it is those foreign profits that it has retained. What follows from that is that the company is claiming:

- the off-set of ACT against column 3 and 4 UK corporation tax which would otherwise be genuinely, and fully, payable; and

- tax credit relief for foreign tax against column 5 UK corporation tax, again otherwise genuinely, and fully, payable.

5.14 Restriction on the off-set of ACT

If there are insufficient profits to cover both ACT off-set and tax credit relief for foreign taxes, it is the off-set that is reduced.

Therefore if we were to change the assumptions yet again, to say that the foreign profits were £300 gross, with £75 of foreign tax suffered (but still adopt for illustration purposes the basis of looking only to year 1's profits for cover for off-set and credit) we would find ourselves short, as shown in Table 28.

Table 28 is not prepared in a 'standard' form, and therefore calls for some explanation. The three analysis columns (dividend received, profits charged to UK corporation tax, and profits charged to foreign tax) start straightforwardly by showing what would appear to be the profits from which the company could pay its own dividends, and the profits it could retain. The first of those columns does demonstrate, as explained in paragraph 5.09, that £100 of the dividends paid are *franked* by the dividend received. In the column for profits charged to UK corporation tax we will explain in the next paragraph that the corporation tax charge of £175 permits an off-set of ACT of £140, and what we therefore show is a permitted payment of £560 out of the total dividends paid

---

continued

- which of those states has the right to tax profits of companies (and other taxpayers) whose activities could attract tax in both territories;

- in cases in which either state does have such rights, the extent to which each will give credit (or some other form of relief) against its own taxes for tax paid to the other state.

However in the case of states with which the UK does not have any treaty, UK tax law allows broadly similar relief by the other *arrangement* allowing credit for foreign taxes suffered, referred to as unilateral relief and legislated in section 790 ICTA 1988.

For both treaty relief and unilateral relief there are limits on the quantum of credit (section 797 ICTA 1988) which can be explained in simplified terms by saying that if the overseas tax rate is higher than the UK tax rate, credit will only be given at the UK rate.

COMPANY TAX

Table 28: ACT Offset Restricted

	Total	Div rec'd	Charged profits	Foreign profits
Pre-tax profits	1,000		700	300
Div received	125	125		
	1,125			
Tax charge at 20%	25	25		
UK CT at 25%	175		175	
foreign at 25%	75			75
	850	100	525	225
'reallocate'			35	(35)
			560	190
Dividends paid and proposed	700	100	560	40
ACT thereon not off-settable	10			10
	140			140

and proposed. Since a net dividend of £560 cannot come out of post-corporation-tax profits of £525, it is clear that the difference comes from the final column's profits (the balance which in earlier workings we had assumed would be retained); that is the significance of the *reallocation* of £35 out of that column. The last £40 of the dividends paid and proposed involve a payment of £10 of ACT (20/80ths) which, again as explained below, is not off-settable.

5.15 *Restriction on the offset of ACT (continued)*

The restriction on the level of ACT which can be off-set is in section 239(2) TA 1988: 'the amount of ACT to be set against a company's (corporation tax) liability for any period . . . shall not exceed the amount of ACT that would have been payable . . . in respect of a distribution made at the end of that period of an amount which, together with the ACT so payable in respect of it, is equal to the company's profits charged to corporation tax for the period'.[33] In Table 28, the company's profits charged (as interpreted for these purposes) to corporation tax are £700,

---

[33] For completeness it should be said that the ACT which we are looking at, to determine whether it can or cannot be fully off-set against the company's corporation tax liability, is the ACT which that company has actually *paid*. The rules which allow a company *not* to pay ACT on a dividend in circumstances in which it has *franked income* (a dividend received from a company which has itself paid ACT) are in schedule 13 to TA 1988.

RESTRICTION ON THE OFF-SET OF ACT

so the off-settable ACT is £140. That last figure fixes the dividend of £560 on which full off-set is available.[34]

But although that is the statutory wording, what we have shown in the table is not the years' income which will in the ordinary course be brought into the set-off calculations. That brings us back to the question in paragraph 5.11. Can we assume that the company will in year 2 make profits of £50, fully subject to UK taxes, and above and beyond those needed to provide the off-set of year 2's dividends? If the answer is yes, then we can assume that those profits *will* enable an offset to be achieved for the £10 of ACT which we were treating as irrecoverable in the accounts presentation being considered in the last paragraph.

Alternatively, must we write off that £10? Writing off irrecoverable ACT is best understood as the recognition that paying the last £40 of the final dividend costs not £40, the cash going to shareholders, but is envisaged as costing that £40 plus a further payment of £10 to the Inland Revenue beyond what will be *recovered* from the Revenue by the set-off procedure we have been discussing.[35]

---

[34] What we now see is rather different from the simplistic figures of our paragraphs 1.33 to 1.34 perspective on the levels of company tax and shareholder tax. That gave us the left hand column below, but what we now see is the right hand column position:

	Non-optimal Paragraph 1.34		Optimal Paragraph 5.12	
Pre-tax profits, taxable		12,415		12,415
non taxable				621
				13,036
Company tax	at 6.25%	776	at 5%	621
Gross dividend		11,639		12,415
Shareholder tax at 20% of gross dividend		2,328		2,483
Maximum net dividend on which company obtains off-set		9,311		9,932

First, observe that the total tax is still £3,104 (this being the 25 per cent corporation tax rate applied to unchanged taxable profits of £12,415). But, second, if the non-shareholder proportion of this can be met from a *non-taxable* source, then the law allows a larger proportion of the £3,104 total to be regarded as ACT off-settable, what we have called shareholder tax; and a smaller proportion can therefore be regarded as company tax; or the company tax can be said to be a lower percentage of taxable profits. We said in paragraph 5.3 that 'where accounting and taxable profits differ there are rules, and underlying truths, which we must keep in view'. It was this implication for the effective burdens of tax that we had in mind as perhaps the most important of those truths. Remember that the profits which are distributable in the company's accounts can differ from the profits *taxable* for the specific year in which the dividend is paid for a multitude of reasons; one which we have not mentioned in these paragraphs is that the company may have distributable balances brought forward available from earlier years.

[35] That cost of £10 on the last £40 of a £400 final dividend is of course the ultimate cost. Soon after the dividend is paid, an ACT payment of £100 will be made (and

And the word 'envisaged' brings out the second implication: ACT whose off-set cannot be assumed in the preparation of one set of accounts (because there is insufficient present and past income, and future income is not to be anticipated) may in fact turn out to be off-settable when and if income is received in a later period, in excess of that needed for that later period's ACT. In technical terms one says unrelieved ACT can be carried forward. The amount written off in this year's tax charge can potentially then be written back.

5.16 Tax costs of the ill-advised transaction

What we said in paragraph 1.21 was that 'there is a clear, indisputable line which sets the company's assets and liabilities, and its activities, apart from those of the owners. If the latter treat the company as no more than their incorporated pocket-book, nothing but trouble can result'. Let's look for some trouble.

A company has been making steady profits of around £20,000 per annum and has been distributing these to its proprietor by way of dividend. It thus has only a minimal balance of retained profits brought forward in its profit and loss account; we can also assume that the ACT paid on recent years' dividends has been off-set against the company's past years' corporation tax liabilities, but that there is no further capacity for the absorption against those liabilities of any further ACT – should the company now incur more than can be off-set against its current tax liability.

The company has a property carried in its balance sheet at an original cost figure of £10,000, and its proprietor wishes to have the company give him that property, as a dividend *in specie*, in lieu of paying him a cash dividend for the current year. Can this be done and, if it can, what would be its effects?

The property's open market value is estimated to be £100,000; that is the figure which will have to be used in calculating the tax liabilities arising out of a transaction between connected parties (the company and its owner; we will look at the definitions, and the effects, of connected party transactions in greater depth in paragraphs 6.37 and onward, but for present purposes all we need to understand is that the asset's open market value must be used for tax purposes). The first implication is that the company will be disposing of an asset, the deemed proceeds to be brought into a capital gains computation being £100,000. We assume a 1982 valuation, indexed to date, to be £30,000, thus producing a gain of £70,000 and a corporation tax liability at 25 per cent of £17,500.

Second, the company has trading income for the year of its normal £20,000, and a corporation tax liability on that of £5,000.

---

continued
with a dividend proposed for payment in April year 2, the ACT payment date will be 14 July year 2.) If only £90 were the aggregate of the ACT that could be set off against corporation tax due at 1 October year 3, and at any of the earlier and later payment dates against which a set-off is technically permissible, then the write-off and the ultimate cost would coincide.

TAX COSTS OF THE ILL-ADVISED TRANSACTION

5.17 *The ill-advised transaction (continued)*

If all that the company were doing with its property were revaluing it from £10,000 to £100,000, that would not produce a profit which could be treated under the Companies Act 1985 as realised. But if the company were proposing to dispose of the property to its shareholder as a dividend *in specie*, not only would that gain be *recognised*, it would also be treated as *realised*, and the dividend would be shown at the full value of the property, £100,000.[36] The profit and loss account would therefore be as shown in Table 29.

Table 29: Profit and Loss Account – Company giving Property to Shareholder

Profit on ordinary activities		20,000
Profit on disposal of property		90,000
		110,000
Corporation tax on		
ordinary activities	5,000	
capital gain on property disposal	17,500	
	22,500	
irrecoverable ACT	7,000	29,500
		80,500
Dividend		100,000
		(19,500)

The total ACT on a dividend of £100,000 is £25,000. Of that, an amount of £18,000 would be capable of off-set against the corporation tax shown in Table 29 of £22,500.[37] Therefore the balance of ACT (£25,000 – £18,000) would have to be treated as irrecoverable, and written off.

What one can clearly see from the above is that the profit on ordinary activities could support a dividend of £15,000; but that the further accounting profit of £90,000 is insufficient to meet all three of the corporation tax (on capital gains) arising on it, the distribution of £85,000 out of it, and the irrecoverable ACT arising from it. In other words that the dividend would be unlawful, as shown in Table 30.[38]

---

[36] The ASB's *Statement of Principles*, chapter 4 paragraph 17.
[37] The taxable profits total £90,000. The maximum ACT offsettable against corporation tax (at 25 per cent of that, £22,500) is the ACT appropriate to a notional dividend of £90,000 gross, namely £18,000. The actual ACT on a dividend of £100,000 (that being the *net* received by the shareholder) is £25,000.
[38] Section 263(1) CA 1985. When we examine dividends *in specie* in greater depth in paragraph 11.9 and Note 16 we will make the point that it is necessary for the payer of such a dividend to have (before the revaluation of the asset) distributable profits at least equal to the asset's carrying value in his books. 'Distributable' can only mean after-tax, and that is manifestly not the case here.

Table 30: Analysis of the Ill-advised Transaction

		Ordinary		Other
Profits		20,000		90,000
Corp. tax (incl. on C. Gain)	5,000		17,500	
Dividend (total 100,000)	15,000		85,000	
Irrecoverable ACT	nil	20,000	7,000	109,500
				(19,500)

5.18 Deferred tax

Let us go back to the circumstances we were considering at the end of paragraph 5.3. The company's taxable profits for the year we are looking at are £600, while its accounting profits (at the pre-tax level) are £1,000; the reason is that capital allowances exceed depreciation by £400, but our calculation is that next year capital allowances will be less than depreciation by £100, and in the year after by £300, so that the whole difference will have *reversed* by the end of those two years.

The first part of the theory of deferred tax is easiest to explain if we assume that pre-tax profits in the accounts for all three years will be £1,000, as shown in Table 31.

The line described in Table 31 as the *current tax charge* has been calculated on the taxable profit; but it is not thought rational, still less true and fair, to suggest that the subtotal line below it adequately shows the company's pattern of profits; truer and fairer is to segregate into a different *reserve* the amount by which year 1's cashflow has been boosted (but year 2's and 3's cashflows will be reduced) by accelerated capital allowances. If the pre-tax profit is level through the three years, and the tax rate is constant, accounting theory suggests that *distributable* profits should also be shown to be level; and accounting presentation normally combines into a single figure on the tax charge line in the profit and loss account what we have shown as separate current tax charges and transfers to and from deferred tax. The figure is only analysed in the notes to the accounts.

Table 31: Deferred Tax

	Year 1	Year 2	Year 3	Total
Pre-tax profit	1,000	1,000	1,000	3,000
Current tax charge	(150)	(275)	(325)	(750)
Subtotal	850	725	675	2,250
Transfer to deferred tax	(100)			(100)
Transfer from deferred tax		25	75	100
Post-tax, distributable, profit	750	750	750	2,250

5.19 *Deferred tax (continued)*

A second, interrelated part of deferred tax theory relates to the balance sheet treatment of the item. We described it in the previous paragraph as a *reserve*.

It is clear that if the rate of tax increased from 25 to 30 per cent for each of years 2 and 3, the current tax charges for those years would increase from £275 and £325 to £330 and £390. The amounts by which it would be logical to reduce those last two, by transfers from deferred tax, would be £30 and £90. But if there is only £100 in the deferred tax account, it is difficult to transfer £120 out of it. What that appears to suggest is that if the tax rate does increase, a company's immediate response should be to make an immediate transfer to deferred tax to up-rate the balance of the account:

End year 1 – capital allowance acceleration £400 at 25% £100
– needed £400 at 30% 120

– further transfer into deferred tax account £ 20

That is of course the underlying truth. If a taxpayer has been *enjoying* an acceleration of tax reliefs, and tax rates then go up, what he suffers is not merely higher rates on what he and his accountant may think of as future profits, but also on the *acceleration*.

The thought processes in the last two sentences would be wholly persuasive, indeed inescapable, if the deferred tax account were a balance sheet liability. If at the end of year 1, the company were statutorily compelled not just to provide for the tax actually payable nine months later on £600, but also the tax payable in 21 and 33 months on £100 and £300 respectively, then it would show its aggregate tax liability at £250. But the theory of deferred taxation is less rigorous than that. The balance in the deferred tax account is shown in the balance sheet under the caption 'provision for liabilities and charges', a heading which places the account in a category somewhere between liabilities and shareholders' funds – and which does not share all the characteristics either of a liability or of a non-distributable reserve. Rationalisation and analysis cannot be pursued too far; all that one can say is that from some standpoints it is part of shareholders' funds, but from others it is not.

5.20 *Deferred tax (continued)*

The ambivalences of deferred tax theory and the problems over deciding what is a reversing difference and what a permanent one, (see Note 14 on paragraph 5.5), have however not discouraged accountants from building a superstructure onto the top of the simple concepts explained in paragraph 5.18. Let us go back to the data we were using for year 1, and consider what the profit and loss account would need to show if the company paid a dividend of £700.

The profits chargeable to tax were £600, the corporation tax thereon £150, and the maximum ACT that could be set against that corporation tax would be £120. A dividend of £700 involves ACT of £175, so it seems that £55 of that ACT would be irrecoverable, and would need to be written off. That would produce the left hand column below:

Table 32: Deferred Tax Charge Eliminating the Need to Write off ACT

Pre-tax profits		1,000		1,000
Current tax charge (£150 + 55)	205		150	
Transfer to deferred tax	100	305	100	250
		695		750
Dividend		700		700
Retention (deficit)		(5)		50

No, says the accounting profession; that is not correct. The figures in the right hand column are the correct answer. The implication which underlies that transfer of £100 to a deferred tax account is that the company's taxable profits are to be treated *for accounting purposes* as being £1,000, although £400 will not be taxed immediately, and the Inspector of Taxes will only be told of £600. If the profits are £1,000, then the company could pay a dividend of up to £800 before it ran into any restriction on its ACT set-off, and therefore there is no need to treat any of the ACT as irrecoverable.[39]

5.21 The deduction of income tax at source

It was a fundamental principle of Addington's income tax of 1803 that the Inland Revenue looked in preference to payers rather than to recipients for the tax on those classes of income derived from capital. It was, and still is, easier to ask ICI to pay over to the Revenue the income tax on the debenture interest it pays to many thousands of debenture holders than it would be assess all those separate recipients for the tax concerned. Until 1965, companies were themselves liable to income tax, and the ultimate efficiency was achieved by the Revenue's assessing ICI not simply on its profits but on a composite figure – what its profits would have been had it not been entitled to deduct its debenture interest in ariving at those profits; and allowing ICI to retain what it had withheld.

---

[39] If one tried to rationalise that answer, one could say that the aggregate figure on the tax charge line, £250, should be regarded as a 25 per cent current tax provision on £600 profits for this year, a deferred tax provision on £100 for next year, and a deferred tax provision on £300 for the year after. Which would be a valid point of view if it were true that tax was being *provided* (as a *liability*) for the future years, rather than being *reserved*. One cannot pursue analysis and rationalisation too far.

THE DEDUCTION OF INCOME TAX AT SOURCE

During the years since 1965 the classes of income which are subject to *deduction of tax at source* have been reduced (the single largest reduction resulting from the imputation system in 1972; dividends are no longer treated as having had income tax deducted at source, because the ACT/tax credit system is distinct). Second, it is now necessary for the Revenue to use separate mechanisms to collect from companies the income tax which they have withheld; that is to say, they collect this tax separately from assessing corporation tax on profits. We do not need to look at the detail of the rules,[40] but merely to say that:

- if a company withholds tax at source from a payment, it must account for that tax to the Revenue 14 days after the end of the calendar quarter in which the payment is made;

- amounts received by a company, where the payer has withheld income tax, have nevertheless to be included in the recipient's corporation taxable income (at the gross amount);[41] but the income tax withheld can be set against income tax otherwise assessable under the previous head, or if tax on receipts exceeds that on payments (or if there are no payments) the excess tax thus suffered by the company can be used as an off-set against its corporation tax liability for the year – and if there is an excess here as well, can be repaid.

That last point means, of course, that ACT's restrictions on off-set are not paralleled here; tax withheld by the company will always be a balance sheet liability, and tax suffered will always be an asset.

5.22 Loans to participators

When we were considering in paragraphs 1.30 to 1.32 the payment by a company of earnings, interest and dividends to its shareholders (or to those of them who were directors as well as shareholders) we naturally assumed that the recipients would themselves be taxed on the receipts as income.

It is in general contrary to the provisions of the Companies Act for a company to lend money to its directors;[42] despite that, the Inland

---

[40] Schedule 16 to TA 1988.
[41] A company's receipts under deduction of income tax are assessable to corporation tax, and the income tax already deducted at source is available as a credit against the recipient's income tax or corporation tax. If the amount creditable exceeds the liability, the excess is repaid. In every one of these respects the position is thus different from that of a company's receipts of franked investment income, the treatment of which was explained at the end of paragraph 5.8, and in Note 29. This is only one among a number of instances where the tax treatments of two items of income or expense are diametrically different, although seen through the windows of the Clapham omnibus the items concerned appear indistinguishable.
[42] Section 330 CA 1985. The provisions in that and succeeding sections through to section 344 relating to loans, guarantees and *credit transactions* for directors and their associates are exceedingly complex and detailed, and it would not be appropriate to analyse them in detail in this book. It can be said that their broad thrust is to prohibit a wider series of transactions in the case of public companies (including

continued

Revenue have always assumed that anti-avoidance legislation is needed to treat as *income* in the hands of shareholders and shareholder/directors of *close companies*[43] any amounts lent to them by their companies. Section 419 of the Income and Corporation Taxes Act 1988 provides that such loans, outstanding at the end of any accounting period of the company, are to be the subject of a corporation tax charge on the company; the corporation tax concerned is not, however, due for payment nine months after the end of the accounting period, but a mere 14 days after that period end.

If the loan is subsequently repaid (which includes cases in which an amount of remuneration is voted to a director, and treated as satisfied out of the earlier advance), the corporation tax is repayable. But as might be expected, given the Revenue's predilection for what is sometimes called *left-handed legislation*, the repayment can only be made on a claim, which readers will remember is made in the return filed 12 months after the end of the year in which the event (loan repayment) takes place. If the loan is outstanding at the end of year 1, the company pays corporation tax 14 days into year 2. Let us assume the director pays income tax under PAYE a month later when his remuneration is voted, this being one of the company's actions in year 2. Some 24 months after that, the company's corporation tax is refunded (without interest because the refund was not due until the date for the filing of the year 2 claim).

---

continued
    private companies which are members of a group which includes a public company) than is the case for other private companies. But to provide exemptions for what might be seen as straightforward commercial transactions, such as the company which gives a director an advance before a business trip on the understanding that he will account for his expenditure on his return, and hand back any unspent part of that advance. The Companies Act disclosure requirements for directors' loans are referred to in paragraph 8.8 and Note 17.

[43] The definition of a close company is in section 414 TA 1988. Once again it is an exceptionally complex and detailed provision. Its flavour is insufficiently caught by the normal two line summary, that a company is close if it is under the control of:

- five or fewer participators; or
- participators who are directors;

even when one understands that the word 'participator' is wider than shareholder, since it includes loan creditors, and those who have the right to become shareholders or loan creditors, and when one understands also that 'control' is defined in the widest possible terms.

    What is straightforward is that listed companies are *not* close provided that 35 per cent of their shares are in the hands of the public, and companies controlled by such listed companies are not close.

    With those exceptions, it is probably fairer to say that there are very few other companies which are *not* close – this being the result of the provisions under which the rights of any participator can be treated as belonging to any *associate* of his, so that one shareholder can for instance be treated as owning not only his own shares but those of his wife, parents, partners, children, brothers and sisters, treated as owning also all the shares held in any trust set up by him or by any of those relatives, and *all* the shares held in any trust in which he is or could be a beneficiary. Once one has identified a few *central* family members along those lines, it is extremely unusual to find any company with less than 50 per cent of the shares under the *control* of five or fewer such individuals.

5.23 Group relief

Where one company has a corporation taxable profit, while an associate has a loss, there are provisions enabling the second to agree to surrender its loss and the first to claim the benefit of that loss, so that the profits, and corporation tax liability, of the first are correspondingly reduced.

That general statement needs immediate clarification:

- there are two forms of group relief, the second of which is sometimes referred to as consortium relief. In relation to the latter all that we need to say in this chapter is that a consortium is the group of companies who jointly own another company – the word does not refer to that jointly-owned company itself; losses can be surrendered (in either direction) between a company and a member or members of the consortium (who between them own 75 per cent or more of its shares, none of them owning less than 5 per cent nor 75 per cent or more). The amounts to be surrendered to or by any member of that consortium must be proportionate to its holding in the jointly held company. We will look at an example of consortium relief in paragraph 7.6;

- what we can concentrate on here is what is more correctly described as group relief, which requires a 75 per cent or more ownership relationship between claimant and surrendering company, but then permits 100 per cent of a loss to be surrendered against 100 per cent of a profit.

Group relief, as we noted in paragraph 5.6, must be dealt with in the corporation tax filings of claimant and surrendering companies, that is to say, the amounts and the parties involved in each surrender must be shown.

5.24 *Group relief (continued)*

There are a number of other principles which apply to group relief, and of course also to consortium group relief:

- each only applies within an accounting period, or the overlapping parts of periods if the companies have different year-ends. It is not possible to surrender in year 2 a loss brought forward from year 1, or to carry back from year 3 a loss of that year so as to be able to surrender it in year 2;

- trading losses can be surrendered[44] (capital allowances which exceed trading losses being treated for this purpose as trading losses),

---

[44] There is a what might be seen as a curious imbalance in the legislation. A claimant company can only claim the benefit of a loss from another to the level of the claimants's total profits; and in quantifying those profits it must make every reduction available to it by claiming losses and allowances for the year, and brought forward (but not carried back from any subsequent year). Thus the amounts that it can claim (should be surrendered to it) by way of losses will be reduced so that the result of the surrender can never give the claimant an overall loss for the year.

continued

and so also can an excess of interest paid over income, but a *capital gains* loss cannot be surrendered;

• *ownership* (of claimant by surrendering company, or vice versa, or common ownership) is the necessary precondition for group relief; the legislative rule was, until 1990, interpreted by the Inland Revenue to mean that that ownership must exist throughout the period for which the relief is claimed. However, a recent case[45] has shown that if there is a break in ownership during the course of an accounting period, group relief can still operate, on the basis of apportionment of the figures, for the part of the period up to that break;

• that explanation does not indicate just what may be regarded as breaking the ownership link, and how one may determine the date of the break. These are complex problems which we will look at in paragraphs 5.40 to 5.42 below; they have very real relevance to the acquisitions and disposals at which we will be looking in chapters 12 and 11. We can mention the existence of, but for the purposes of this book need not spend time examining, extremely detailed rules applicable in those cases where substance may not coincide totally with form, for the purpose of fixing whether an ownership link does or does not exist.[46]

5.25 Rationale of, and payments for, group relief

If one assumes that each company in a group aims to make profits, a specific company which sustains a loss in its trade in one specific year

---

continued
   The surrendering company on the other hand is permitted to calculate its losses available to be surrendered in such a way that it *can* be left with income, and a tax liability, after making the permitted surrender. (It can for instance surrender the amount of a trading loss for the year, without having first claimed to set any part of that loss against other income for the year, or of earlier years. Perhaps this is not all that odd, if the Revenue's objective is to prevent groups from creating overall losses in any particular claimant, without worrying whether residual income and liabilities may be left in the claimant or in the surrendering company.)

[45] *Shepherd v Law Land plc* [1990] BTC 561. In that case, the accounting periods of claimant and surrendering company each ran for 12 months to 31 March 1983. For a period of five weeks, from 6 January 1983 to 11 February 1983, a potential outside purchaser had the option to acquire the share capital of Law Land's subsidiary, and it was agreed by the parties that the granting of the option concerned on 6 January broke the link between Law Land and its subsidiary.
   The legislation would now be section 410(1)(b)(i), read together with paragraph 5B(1) of schedule 18 to ICTA 1988. However, the court decided that Law Land was entitled to group relief for the period from 1 April 1982 to 5 January 1983 – and when the option lapsed without having been exercised, Law Land became entitled once again to group relief for the period from 12 February to 31 March 1983. Until that case was decided, it was normal for a company which was *about to leave a group* to bring its accounting period to an end shortly before doing so, in order to have a (shortened) accounting period throughout which it had been a member of the group, and for which it was therefore entitled to claim or surrender group relief. Needless to say most such companies, and their purchasers, regarded the effort and expense of preparing an extra set of accounts to the changed accounting date as a burden they could have done without.

[46] Schedule 18 to TA 1988.

should always be able, itself, to obtain tax relief for that loss. Depending on the level of the loss concerned, and the levels of the company's:

- income from other sources in the year concerned;
- total income in the preceding three years; and
- income from the same trade in subsequent years;

the benefit of that tax relief might be obtainable with little delay in the first two cases, or with some greater delay in the third case. There is also the question whether setting the loss back in the second case might fail to achieve repayment of the 25 per cent corporation tax charge (what we have been assuming to be the rate applicable for all of the companies with which this book is primarily concerned); if ACT had been off-set against the profits of the earlier year concerned, setting back a loss against those profits would only achieve a repayment of the excess of corporation tax over that ACT.

A delay in obtaining relief, or a restriction on the amount of that relief, are two of the reasons why group relief is a valuable facility. The third reason is that there can be companies whose activities can be expected to generate tax losses in most if not all years. The leasing company whose figures we look at in paragraphs 7.8 and onward would be an example if it were to expand the volume of its leasing activity year by year. But there are other group member companies which may be in a similar tax position.[47]

The factor common to all of those examples of companies which sustain losses is that those losses *should* generate tax reliefs, the final deterioration in the companies' position should be the post-tax-relief amount. If these losses are surrendered, and it is the claimant which therefore obtains the tax relief, it is common (if not universal) practice for that claimant to pay to the surrendering company a sum equal to the tax relief – and the timing selected for this payment is commonly the date on which the surrendering company would itself have been able to obtain tax relief had it retained the benefit of its own loss.

---

[47] A company which does not trade 'on a commercial basis and with a view to the realisation of gain' is prevented from claiming to set its trading loss against other income of the same period, and from setting it back against income of previous years, section 393A(3)(b) TA 1988. It is similarly prevented from surrendering the offending loss under the group relief procedures, section 403(2) TA 1988. But the quoted words are incomplete; it is the 'realisation of gain in the trade or in any larger undertaking of which the trade forms a part' on which the company is enjoined to set its mind. Clearly this allows some latitude over timing – a start-up operation may not be expected to generate profit in (say) its first three years. Second, the interpretation of the phrase 'larger undertaking' is the same as that discussed in paragraphs 6.34 and 6.35 below, namely all the trades carried on not only by the company but by its parent, fellow-subsidiaries, and subsidiaries.

Leasing companies for instance expanding the volume of their businesses, particularly if doing so at a time when generous capital allowances are available for their capital expenditure, may well produce continuous tax losses – but the services they supply to their customers are part of a total package offered by the banks or financial institutions of which they are (generally) subsidiaries, and those parents undoubtedly aim for overall profits from their *undertakings*.

5.26 Group income

When we started looking at ACT in paragraph 5.8, the first of the exceptions we noted was that it did not apply to dividends paid within groups of companies in which there was a *group income* election in force. (There is an entirely parallel set of rules relating to dividends paid by a jointly owned company to the members of a consortium which own it, but we will concentrate here on the group position.)

The level of ownership by parent of subsidiaries needed for such elections is 51 per cent or more. Once an election has been accepted by the Inland Revenue:[48]

- it is permissible for a subsidiary to pay a dividend to its parent without accounting for ACT. That is not however mandatory – a dividend, or a part of a dividend, can still be paid with ACT (in which case the recipient is able to treat it as franked investment income). If the subsidiary is not wholly owned, the part of its dividend payable to shareholders other than the parent is of course subject to ACT in the ususal way;

- it is also permissible for interest to be paid between any group companies without the need for income tax to be withheld at source (as paragraph 5.21 above makes clear would otherwise have been required). Whereas the dividends mentioned in the previous head necessarily move *up* a group, the interest we are considering here may be paid in ether direction between parent and subsidiary, or between fellow-subsidiaries.

If one were to imagine a group comprising only trading subsidiaries owned by a parent whose only activity was the holding of their shares, it would obviously be possible for them to pay *dividends gross* (to use the normal colloquialism); but it would not seem at first glance to be very tax efficient, since the parent would need to account for ACT when it in turn paid dividends to its shareholders, and since the parent has no income subject to corporation tax it would not be immediately self-evident how the parent could set off that ACT. There is however a provision[49] enabling the parent to set off its ACT against its subsidiaries'

---

[48] Section 248(2) TA 1988 allows the Inspector a period of three months after the companies in the group send him their joint election to be treated as a *group* before he must give effect to it. In practice the Revenue are able to agree elections very much more rapidly than this. There have been numerous cases in which the formality of making an election has been overlooked, and dividends have been paid without the payer accounting for ACT. The legislation gives no indication that the Revenue have any alternative but to demand the ACT concerned from the payer, and experience shows that whenever ACT is paid late an interest charge is invariably levied. If the omission to elect was a simple error, the company's immediate course must be confession and abject apology – and experience has shown that the Revenue are not as averse to accepting retrospective elections as is sometimes thought (at least on the first occasion; it is inadvisable to make a habit of it).

[49] Section 240 TA 1988. The thrust of this section is that the subsidiary to whom the ACT is surrendered is deemed to have itself paid the dividend or dividends (or proportions of them) to which the surrenders relate, and to have done so on the

continued

corporation tax liabilities (and permitting the subsidiaries to pay the parent for the benefit they thus receive).

5.27 The company and its owner or owners

This chapter on the taxation of companies would be incomplete unless we highlighted the fact that there are three matters we need to keep under review whenever there is a transaction between a company and its owners:

- first, there is the transaction's tax effect within the company. This may be absolutely simple and straightforward in the case, for instance, of the company's payment of a normal dividend out of profits. Or may be more complex in the case of the *ill-advised* dividend we looked at in paragraph 5.16;

- second, there is the transaction's effect in the hands of the owner. For instance, the normal basis for incorporation in paragraph 3.35, and the alternative method in paragraph 3.41, leave the owner with differing tax results;

- but third, there are transactions which, because of the relationship between owner and company, can be penally treated – including being treated as if they had been completely different transactions from what was actually done. The clearest example of the latter was the family who owned all the share capital of two companies, each of which had considerable retained profits and cash balances. Rather than pay dividends at a time when the top rates of income tax were very high, the family extracted cash from one of the companies by selling to it their shares in the other company. This cash receipt was however recharacterised for tax purposes as a dividend.[50]

We need to think about all of these transactions between companies and owners against the general background of companies legislation:

- which might be perceived as encouraging the parties to deal with each other on an arm's length basis; but

- as not preventing a company from making certain types of gifts (or transfers at undervalue) to its owners; the most commonly occurring ones are called dividends or distributions, but we will look in due course at rather more specialised forms: companies buying back their own shares, and demerging some of their activities. The general limitation on all of these is that they can only be done out of distributable profits;

---

continued
 date(s) on which the parent actually paid the dividend(s). This enables the subsidiary to set the ACT off against its corporation tax for the year, or for the six years before that, or to carry it forward, under exactly the same rules as we looked at in the final lines of paragraphs 5.11 and 5.15.
[50] *CIR v Cleary* [1968] AC 766. See paragraph 11.23 below.

- owners can also make gifts to companies; that was a part of the alternative incorporation process referred to above, but such gifts generally carry certain tax disadvantages.

5.28 *The company and its owner or owners (continued)*

There is in tax legislation more than a general encouragement for owners to deal with their companies at arm's length, there is a requirement as we noted in paragraph 5.16 that enables[51] the Inland Revenue to substitute open market prices in place of any others that the parties have used if the owners and the company are *connected parties*. The definition of that phrase is something we will examine in paragraphs 6.37 and 6.38 (and Note 64 on those paragraphs). For the purposes of the bird's eye view we are trying to achieve in the previous paragraph, this one and the next three, all that we need is to be aware of the point.

5.29 **Capital gains tax – the tiering or cascading effect**

Companies pay corporation tax on capital gains. What we must see very clearly is what effect that tax has on the translation of value locked inside a company into cash in the owner's hands.

Consider the owner whose company has a subsidiary which a third party wishes to buy. The owner wishes to retain the parent company, but does not see any particular use, inside that company, to which he could put the proceeds of the subsidiary's sale. That implies that he wants to extract into his own hands the relevant cash.

If we start by thinking just about the flow of cash, we might see:

• sales proceeds received by parent		5,000
• deduct corporation tax on capital gains at what we will assume in order to add point to the illustration to be the full rate of 33 per cent of gain of £3,000 (using 1982 base value of subsidiary and indexation)		990
		4,010
• ACT in excess of the £600 which can be off-set against the £990 corporation tax above	322	
• dividend	3,688	4,010

---

[51] But this is a one way option. It is open to the Revenue to require the substitution of a different price where the law gives them this right. It is not open to the taxpayer to ask the Revenue to ignore what he actually did, and tax him by reference to a price he later realises he would have liked to have used; see *Jacgilden (Weston Hall) Ltd v Castle* [1969] 3 All ER 1110.

The shorthand calculation of the irrecoverable ACT, in a case such as this where the limitation on the dividend is the cash available, is to say that the off-settable ACT is £600 if the chargeable profits are £3,000. Therefore the *gross* dividend would be the aggregate of that £600 and the available profit and loss balance of £4,010. If the *gross* is £4,610, the total ACT is £922, £600 off-settable and £322 irrecoverable. When the net dividend of £3,688 is received by an individual owner who is subject to the higher rate of income tax, he pays another 20 per cent (of the gross equivalent £4,610) leaving him with £2,766 in his pocket.

The other way of looking at this is to say that 13 per cent of £3,000 capital gain is the company tax, and that on the £4,610 balance in the company 40 per cent goes as shareholder tax, leaving £2,766 to the individual. Either viewpoint leads to the conclusion that the total tax take is 44.7 per cent.

5.30 Capital gains tax – the tiering or cascading effect (continued)

If, before selling the subsidiary, it were possible to arrange for it to pay a *group* dividend of £1,000 to its parent, then it would be logical to assume that the disposal proceeds would be £1,000 less, and that the capital gain would be reduced by the same £1,000.

That would produce a slight improvement

• dividend received by parent		£1,000
• sales proceeds received by parent		4,000
		5,000
• deduct corporation tax on capital gains at 33 per cent of gain of £2,000, (using 1982 base value of subsidiary and indexation)		660
		4,340
• ACT in excess of the £400 which can be off-set against the £660 corporation tax above	548	
• dividend	3,792	4,340

That net dividend of £3,792 costs another £948 of higher rate tax, leaving the individual with £2,844 – overall tax being 43.1 per cent.

Stripping out a group dividend must always be sensible, if it is possible. And that leads on to the thought that if it were possible to strip out the whole of the target subsidiary's increase in value (so that there was no corporation tax charge in the parent which sold it), then the overall liability would be minimised at 40 per cent. But our discussions in earlier chapters have demonstrated that it never is possible to strip out the whole of that value increase.[52] There is for instance at the simplest level the factor we have identified as the accounting mismatch; the expenditure of £1,000 on a marketing campaign in 1993 can be expected to generate sales in 1994 to 1996, the present value at end 1993 of the profits on these future sales being estimated to be £1,500 (see discussion in paragraphs 1.29 and 2.22). The £500 excess that the expenditure generates would be reflected in a purchaser's offered price. But the spending of the £1,000 *reduces* the company's distributable profits by that sum, rather than creating an asset of £1,000 which could be carried forward, still less an asset of £1,500 and distributable profits of £500.

5.31 *Capital gains tax – the tiering or cascading effect (continued)*

What we call the accounting mismatch may be related as above to expenditure which is sufficiently intangible not to create an asset capable of being reflected in the accounts. But there may be increases in the value of the business which are unrelated to any specific expenditure; the company which builds up its good name, its reputation for a good product or service, and its reputation as a group of people who are pleasant to deal with, is likely to be putting effort rather than identifiable money into this activity.

Those who try to rationalise taxation say that it is reasonable, when all of these intangibles are reflected in the price at which the business changes hands, to tax the vendor on the gain he has realised – that that is the purpose of capital gains tax. But since the purchaser will have all of the fruits of these intangibles reflected in *his* trading income in the period immediately after his purchase, those rationalisers have to go on to argue that, actually, the purchaser does not see them reflected because they are masked by his own continuing incurring of expenditure and so on, which will only turn into realised profits in years even further ahead. The author's rather more cynical view may be clear: trying to rationalise taxation is not the most useful way to spend one's days.

Understanding is what we need, rather than rationalisation. Understanding of companies, and of their owners. Understanding of the way in which taxation works, and therefore of its effects on them. And understanding of the ways that those companies and their owners can most effectively achieve their aims and desires.

5.32 Beneficial ownership

There is one specific tax concept which it is essential to understand. A very large part, if not quite the whole, of UK tax legislation is based on

---

[52] A number of ways of creating, artificially, greater levels of realised profits have been developed over the years, so as to make it possible to strip out larger dividends before sales of subsidiaries. The Inland Revenue moved to make these ineffective for tax purposes in sections 30 to 34 TCGA 1992.

the concept of beneficial ownership, as opposed to legal ownership. It is therefore necessary to spend some time on disentangling these two.

English law recognises that legal title can be, and frequently is, held by a person different from the owner of the equitable interest or interests in property. The equitable interest, as is well known, was a concept of English law developed by the Court of Chancery as an expansion of the strict law of trusts. Lord Diplock explained it thus:

> The archetype is the trust. The *legal ownership* of the trust property is in the trustee, but he holds it not for his own benefit but for the benefit of the *cestui que trust*, or beneficiaries. Upon the creation of a trust in the strict sense as it was developed by equity the full ownership in the trust property was split into two constituent elements, which became vested in different persons: the *legal ownership* in the trustee, what came to be called the *beneficial ownership* in the *cestui que trust*.[53]

Lord Diplock equates equitable ownership which in 1976, the time he was speaking, was a term well understood by lawyers, with beneficial ownership, a phrase which was less well understood, as will appear below.

The phrase 'beneficial ownership' had first appeared in a taxing statute in section 55 of the Finance Act 1927, the stamp duty section on which have been fought a large number of cases, and at which we will need to look in paragraphs 6.66 and 6.69. It made a second appearance in a broadly similar context in the still operative *associated companies* stamp duty provision, section 42 of the Finance Act 1930, to which we will come in paragraph 6.33.

A suggestion in 1957 that it should be interpreted 'in its ordinary or popular sense' was rejected in the Court of Appeal by Lord Jenkins, who demanded instead the 'legal meaning' of the phrase, saying that he could derive no assistance from consideration of what the ordinary person would mean by the words 'beneficial owner' in their ordinary sense.[54] How we can best proceed, in seeking that legal meaning, is first to identify why this is necessary.

5.33 Beneficial ownership as the basis of tax legislation

The whole of capital gains tax is built on the idea that the acquisition and disposals of chargeable assets to which the tax applies are those of the assets' beneficial owners,[55] and that a change which only affects the legal ownership of an asset will not normally be relevant. Thus there is no disposal, or liability, when there is a change in the individuals who are trustees at a particular time in a continuing trust.

Similarly, where for income or corporation tax purposes it is necessary to identify ownership or control, it is the same beneficial ownership

---

[53] Lord Diplock in *Ayerst (HMIT) v C & K (Construction) Ltd* [1976] AC 167. See paragraph 12.23, and in particular Note 27 thereon, for a fuller analysis of the concepts of beneficial ownership in liquidation, which was what Lord Diplock was considering in that case.
[54] *Parway Estates Ltd v IRC* (1957) 45 TC 135.
[55] Section 60 TCGA 1992.

basis that needs to be applied. For instance, we will see in paragraphs 6.37 and 6.38 that his or their *control* of a company may lead to a person or group of persons being treated as 'connected with' the company, a phrase which has a particular significance for capital gains tax purposes; but that same concept of *connection* may also convert into *distributions* for advance corporation tax purposes payments which would not otherwise have been within the scope of ACT.

The control referred to is defined[56] in terms of the person 'exercising, or being able to exercise or being entitled to acquire, direct or indirect control over the company's affairs, and in particular but without prejudice to the generality of the preceding words, if he possesses or is entitled to acquire – (a) the greater part of the share capital ... or of the voting power'. All this makes it obvious that one needs to look for the substance rather than the mere legal form.

If the shareholder is a nominee, one looks for the holder standing behind that mask. If the shareholder has, by contract (including by the granting of options), restricted his ability to enjoy the fruits of something he previously owned in a fuller way, and/or has circumscribed his right to dispose of it (or to deal with any disposal proceeds from it), then one looks for the person who has stepped (or will be able to step) into the ownership and control out of which the first person has contracted.

5.34 Changes in beneficial ownership

There is little dispute where straightforward sale and purchase contracts are concerned.

If there is an executory contract, that is to say, a contract which each party had undertaken to perform but had not yet performed (A agrees to sell the property, and B agrees to buy it and pay for it), that is sufficient to move the beneficial ownership from A to B at the date of the contract. The legal ownership follows at completion. If the contract were subject to a condition precedent (the sale is conditional upon the vendor obtaining planning consent for development for housing), then beneficial ownership would not pass until the condition was fulfilled.[57]

---

[56] Section 416(2) TA 1988.

[57] The example in the text is clearly a condition precedent, the legal effect of which can be stated in general terms to be that until and unless the condition is fulfilled, there is no contract. That is precisely the basis adopted in the capital gains tax legislation, which provides that 'if the contract is conditional ... the time at which the disposal and acquisition is made is the time when the condition is satisfied' (section 28(2) TCGA 1992). A condition subsequent appears to be different: 'I agree to buy your company, and you agree to sell it to me, effective the end of this month. Once the sale has been effected you and I will both do what we can to persuade the company's major customer to continue doing business with it despite the change in its ownership. But if we fail to persuade him, I reserve the right to demand that you take the company back from me, and refund my purchase price, at any time in the six months after you sold it to me'. There is, in that case a binding contract, and there is a possibility that it could later be reversed. Beneficial ownership is moved by the original contract, and may be moved back by its reversal. The original contract appears to be the effective date for capital gains tax purposes. But there is a major qualification

continued

The test could be expressed in the question 'would the courts grant specific performance as a remedy for one party if the other defaulted?'

In the context of those simple contracts, it is also clear that the beneficial ownership's being lost by the vendor is not only synonymous, but also synchronous, with its being acquired by the other party.

There are certain other instances in which one party could lose its beneficial interest without it being clear for a period who would become the next owner of that beneficial interest. One such was the matter Lord Diplock was considering in paragraph 5.32 in the *Ayerst* case; when a company passes a resolution to go into liquidation, the legal ownership of its assets remains with it, although it is the liquidator (in place of the directors) who thereafter has power to deal with those assets. However, although the company ceases to have any control over its assets, ceases to be able to dispose of them – still less to dispose of any proceeds of sale, and in that sense could be argued to have lost any beneficial ownership; nevertheless for capital gains tax purposes it is not treated as having made any disposals by passing that resolution to liquidate; beneficial ownership can best be regarded as having gone into suspense until the point at which the liquidator sells or otherwise transfers the asset to a new owner in whose hands the beneficial ownership can be seen to have re-emerged. The same would apply for property in the hands of a trustee in bankruptcy, or of an executor in the course of administering an estate.

5.35 The Wood Preservation line of cases

In contrast to the position explained in the previous paragraph, that on a sale and purchase beneficial interest moves at contract from vendor to purchaser, there was a line of cases developing in the late 1960s through to the 1990s which seemed to show a different pattern. *Wood Preservation*[58] was decided in 1968. Two years later some of its thought processes were followed in *Brooklands Selangor*.[59] And in 1977 there was the *Ufitec* decision.[60]

All three cases related to arrangements for the disposal by their shareholders of companies, and in all three the contracts were subject

---

continued
 needed to that last statement. English conveyancing law and procedures operate on the basis that *completion* (the process by which legal title is moved) does not take place until a contract has become *unconditional*, and the meaning of that last word is taken for this purpose to be until it is clear that conditions precedent have been fulfilled and that no condition subsequent can operate to reverse what had become a binding contract. One could therefore say that the effect of this conveyancing rule is effectively to turn conditions subsequent into conditions precedent, and to mean that no contract can be binding until all have been *fulfilled*, including in the sense of that last word that there is no possibility of the contract being reversed.

[58] *Wood Preservation Ltd v Prior (HMIT)* [1968] 45 TC 112.
[59] *Brooklands Selangor Holdings Ltd v IRC* [1970] 2 All ER 76.
[60] *IRC v Ufitec Group Ltd* [1977] STC 363.

to conditions.[61] However, the point that was seen as crucial by the courts in all three cases was that the vendors had lost anything that could be thought of as *ownership* of the shares. In *Wood Preservation*, the condition was entirely in the purchaser's favour (that the purchaser could withdraw unless the target company could produce evidence that one of its long-term sales contracts would survive its change of ownership without being cancelled). One of the arguments was that Wood Preservation's agreement to sell was effectively not conditional but binding, because the purchaser could have waived that condition (and in fact did so), so that at any time he could have obtained specific performance. But that was not the only point that weighed with Lord Donovan:

> (The vendor) could not have disposed of the shares to anybody else; had it tried to do so it could have been restrained by injunction. Second, it could not declare or pay any bonus or dividend on its shares; it had specifically precluded itself from doing so. Third it would have been bound at any time actually to transfer the target's shares if (the purchaser) waived the condition . . . (the vendor) though still the legal owner of the shares, is bereft of the rights of selling or disposing or enjoying the fruits of these shares.

With some hesitation the Court of Appeal concluded in *Wood Preservation*, 'not deciding this case in the least upon the merits', that beneficial interest had left the vendor without having yet reached the purchaser.

5.36 The Sainsbury case

This case came to the Court of Appeal in May 1991.[62] When Sainsbury and a Belgian company (GB) set up Homebase as a jointly owned company, it was intended to be owned 70 per cent by Sainsbury and 30 per cent by GB. But in order to allow Sainsbury the advantage of group relief for Homebase's losses in the early years, Sainsbury actually took 75 per cent, retaining an option to *put* 5 per cent to GB, and allowing GB a *call* option over the same 5 per cent.

There were two questions, the second of them being whether those options constituted *arrangements* whose existence would prevent surrenders under the group relief mechanism. We have already looked at the group relief rules earlier in this chapter, and will come back, in paragraphs 5.40 to 5.42, to the subject of the cut-off of the relief

---

[61] The statement that the contracts contained conditions is inexplicit and therefore not as helpful as one could wish. Note 57 above has discussed the distinction between conditions precedent and subsequent. What we are looking at here is different. The existence of a condition precedent means that, until and unless it is fulfilled there is no contract at all – I agree to buy this land, and you agree to sell, conditional on planning permission being granted. What we are differentiating here is a condition in a quite different sense, one which results in a binding contract, but with an agreement within it that completion will be held in abeyance until the fulfilment of the *condition* – I agree to buy your house conditional on your repairing the roof. By neglecting to repair the roof, you cannot escape your obligations to transfer the house to me, and I cannot escape my obligation to acquire and pay for it.

[62] *J. Sainsbury Plc v O'Connor (HMIT)* [1991] BTC 181.

when there are arrangements which *will* lead to the surrendering and claimant companies ceasing to be associated.

But the first question was more basic: while the options remained unexercised, did Sainsbury have beneficial ownership of 75 per cent of the Homebase shares or only of the 70 per cent of them to which its holding would fall on exercise?

Neither Sainsbury nor GB could sell their shares during the option period without the permission of the other, and the payment of dividends was only possible with the same unanimous agreement. But those conditions each applied to the parties' entire holdings. They could not have any bearing on each of their beneficial ownerships. All that the Inland Revenue was able to argue against Sainsbury's ownership of the 5 per cent was that, if a dividend *had* been paid on these shares to Sainsbury, the option price would have been adjusted by a like amount so as to pass the benefit of that dividend to GB. The Court of Appeal held that this did not mean that Sainsbury had no beneficial entitlement to the dividend, as a dividend.[63]

Therefore Sainsbury's ownership was more than the 'mere legal shell' identified in *Wood Preservation*. Therefore Sainsbury was the beneficial owner of its 75 per cent.[64]

5.37 *Marginalising Wood Preservation*

What is more important, however, than the decision itself is the way in which the Court of Appeal managed to distance itself from its earlier decision in *Wood Preservation*, and to marginalise what might be described as the temporary disappearance of beneficial ownership which had been developed by that case. (The Court of Appeal is bound by its own precedents, and overruling *Wood Preservation* would not have been permissible.)

> Nor in the absence of authority to the contrary would I be able to grasp the concept of the beneficial ownership being suspended somewhere between the vendor and the purchaser. I would think that it must be vested in the one or in the other and, if it has not passed to the purchaser, that it must remain in the vendor. That is not in any way to cast doubt on the well known examples of suspension of beneficial ownership to which Lloyd LJ

---

[63] The court did not spell this out, but there are several senses in which one can say that Sainsbury was entitled to the dividend. Even if one took the view that there was a logical compulsion in the argument that one or other option must be exercised (the options did in fact expire, unexercised by either party), if a dividend had been declared Sainsbury would have the use of the cash. And Sainsbury would be irreversibly entitled to the dividend as *income*, because even if the *benefit* were passed to GB, that company would receive it as a price adjustment, not as income (and nor would such a price adjustment reduce Sainsbury's income).

[64] But the conclusion of the Court of Appeal, that Sainsbury was the owner of 75 per cent for group relief purposes, has been overruled by a change in the law, see paragraph 5.42. That change, where options exist, has the same effect for two other *grouping* purposes, namely the ability of a company to pay group dividends without ACT, and its ability to surrender ACT to a subsidiary. Each of these is also dealt with in paragraph 5.42.

has referred. They are far removed from contracts for the sale of land or of shares. (Nourse LJ)

> ... that being so, the ground (the fact that the vendors rights were no more than a mere legal shell) on which the Court of Appeal held that the vendors in *Wood Preservation* were not the beneficial owners of the shares in question does not apply ... I would not for my part be willing to extend the decision ... beyond what was actually decided. How otherwise could one ever draw the line? (Lloyd LJ)

Under any normal contract, beneficial ownership passes from vendor, and simultaneously arrives with the purchaser, when the contract is made, or if later, when it becomes unconditional. We can of course recognise that there will be many contracts which are non-binding for other reasons than that they contain a condition precedent on the face of the document.[65]

5.38 Groups and arrangements

Those paragraphs introducing the concepts of beneficial ownership have been an unavoidable prelude. We need to understand what it is all about if we are to make sense of capital gains tax. We need it if we are to come to grips with the other *group* situations in tax legislation, and the ways in which these are affected by changes in the ownership of companies, and by plans for such changes.

It is appropriate to set out a list of the principal areas which we have already looked at, or which we will need to examine, in which beneficial ownership has an effect on tax liabilities:

- the grouping of companies for VAT, section 29 of the Value Added Tax Act 1983, which we will come to in paragraph 6.32;

- the relief from stamp duty on transfers between associated companies, section 42 of the Finance Act 1930 (as amended by section 27 of the Finance Act 1967), which we will look at in paragraph 6.33;

- the connected parties rules, section 286 of the Taxation of Chargeable Gains Act 1992 and the parallel provisions of section 839 of the Income and Corporation Taxes Act 1988, which we will look at in paragraph 6.37. Each of those can reasonably be thought of as anti-avoidance legislation, empowering the Inland Revenue to substitute an arms' length price where the parties have contracted for some other price which might have resulted in reduced tax liabilities;

---

[65] If for instance the owners of a Lloyd's Agency company contract to sell the company to other prospective shareholders, the sale agreement will be ineffective (the Articles of the company concerned have to make a change in the ownership of 33 per cent or more of the shares impossible) without the consent of the Council of Lloyd's. If the company were to register such a transfer without consent, it would be prevented from carrying on business at Lloyd's. In such a case it would be consent from the Council of Lloyd's which makes the contract binding, and it is that that transfers beneficial ownership.

- but mention also needs to be made of the rules which deal with the transfer between connected parties of assets on which capital allowances are available. Those parties can elect for a transfer price which does not give rise to adjustments of allowances previously claimed, sections 77 and 158 of the Capital Allowance Act 1990, the first of these dealing with machinery or plant, and the second with other assets. We have mentioned this only in one specific application, that of the individual incorporating his business (paragraph 3.38), but it extends to all transfers between connected persons;

- in contrast to that, the transfer of stock in trade from a business that is ceasing has generally to be done at market value – and the exception to that rule does not depend on any relationship between transferor and transferee. They are allowed to use for tax purposes some other price in those instances where that other price will be brought in to the transferee's accounts as his opening value as well as the transferor's accounts as his disposal value, section 100(1)(a) Income and Corporation Taxes Act 1988. Again we looked only at the specific application of his rule in an individual's incorporation of his business (paragraph 3.38);

- we will look at the group of companies recognised for capital gains tax purposes, section 170 of the Taxation of Chargeable Gains Act 1992, paragraph 6.42;

*- we have looked in paragraph 5.26 at the *group income elections* which permit companies covered by an election to pay dividends up through a group without the payer accounting for advance corporation tax; and to pay interest between any companies (upwards, downwards or sideways within the group) without the payer deducting or accounting for income tax, section 247 of the Income and Corporation Taxes Act 1988.

- we will try strenuously in paragraphs 6.50 and onward to clear away the confusions surrounding those asset transfers (including transfers of cash) which fall within the definition of *distributions*, but which may be taken out of that category by some relieving provision. The relieving provisions we will look at include:

   (1) section 209(1) of the Income and Corporation Taxes Act 1992, distributions in liquidation, paragraph 6.61,

   (2) section 209(5), distributions by a company to a *member* which controls the payer or is under common control with it, paragraphs 6.51 and 6.52,

   (3) section 209(6), distributions by one company to another where there is no control or common control, paragraph 6.39;

   (4) section 254(4) in the way in which the Inland Revenue interpret it, distributions within 90 per cent groups, paragraph 6.54; and

   (5) generally, transactions which are not distributions because full value is received by the payer, paragraph 6.50;

* See additionally section 5.40 and Note 70.

* ● we have noted in paragraph 5.26 that a parent company's advance corporation tax can be set off against the corporation tax liability of its subsidiary, section 240 of the Income and Corporation Taxes Act 1988;

* ● we have looked in paragraphs 5.23 to 5.25 at the rules for *group relief*, permitting a member of a group which has sustained a loss (as computed for corporation tax purposes) to surrender the benefit of that loss to another group member with a profit in the same period, so as to enable that recipient to pay tax only on the excess of its profit over the loss surrendered, section 402 of the Income and Corporation Taxes Act 1992. The cut-off rules, bringing the availability of group relief to an end when the *group* relationship between companies is to be severed is something we are leading up to in paragraphs 5.40 to 5.42, and which underlies all our discussions in the chapters on acquisitions and disposals;

● when a reconstruction (using that word in its widest sense, not in the rather more restricted definition used in paragraphs 6.66 to 6.69) results in a trade previously carried on in a predecessor company being carried on thereafter in a successor (and provided certain conditions are met concerning continuity of ownership, and the continuity of the trading operations), there is a carry forward of losses and a continuity of capital allowance claims between the companies, section 343 of the Income and Corporation Taxes Act 1988. Unusually, this is not a provision whose benefits need to be claimed by the parties – it was, when it was originally enacted, anti-avoidance legislation and is still mandatory. This fits into paragraph 6.61;

● never under any circumstances forget that Value Added Tax needs to be considered when a trade and its assets are moved (unless of course the movement is within a VAT group), and that the parties cannot choose their VAT treatment – the transfer of going concern provisions either apply or do not, section 33 of the Value Added Tax Act 1983 and SI 1992 No. 3129 (see paragraph 3.31 but see also the rather fuller discussion in paragraphs 11.32 onwards);

● there is a multiplicity of capital gains tax provisions which can allow transfers of assets (including the goodwill of trades) between companies without an immediate tax charge for the disponor. (This is in addition to the *group* provisions already mentioned.) Those we will come to in chapter 6 are:

(1) section 139 of the Taxation of Chargeable Gains Act 1992, the reconstruction involving the transfer of a business (paragraph 6.67),

(2) section 175, deferring the tax charge in a rather different way after disposal of an asset by a group company if there is a reinvestment of proceeds by another group company (paragraph 6.42).

If we were to look at overseas matters, we would see that businesses, including assets and goodwill, can now be transferred in many

GROUPS AND ARRANGEMENTS

instances from UK companies to non-resident companies, and from UK branches of such non-residents to UK companies (in each case subject to conditions), without a tax toll-charge on the movement.

That does not pretend to be a full list of all of the ways in which transactions between companies can have tax effects which are different by reason of the companies' own relationships; and in the next paragraph we need to explain the asterisks against three items.

5.39 *Double jeopardy*

There are areas of what we have over-simply called *group* relationships which require extreme care, the first being what we might describe as the possibility of double relief. This is easiest to explain by reference to a single company owned between them by a parent and a company holding a minority of its shares. A group income election allows dividends to be paid by the subsidiary to its *parent* (51 per cent)[66] without ACT and allows either to pay interest to the other without deducting income tax at source. Similarly, the group relief provisions allow the surrender of losses by *parent* (75 per cent)[67] to subsidiary, or vice versa.

Those are the *group* arrangements; but there are also *consortium* provisions for both reliefs. The simplest definition of a consortium is that a company is owned by a consortium if 75 per cent or more of its ordinary share capital is owned by companies, none of which own less than 5 per cent.[68] It is therefore obvious that a company may be simultaneously a subsidiary under the *group* rules, and within the definition of a company owned by a consortium under those latter rules – for instance if A Ltd owns 76 per cent of it and B Ltd owns 24 per cent.

When one puts together the facts that the *group* relief provisions allow a 75 per cent subsidiary to surrender the whole of its losses to its parent, while the *consortium* relief (to coin a phrase) provisions allow that same jointly owned company to surrender 24 per cent of its loss to the minority shareholder, it is obvious that rules will be thought necessary to prevent it from being able to surrender more losses than it has actually sustained.

Using a somewhat broad brush approach, the Inland Revenue have decreed that any company within the *75 per cent* definition is automatically debarred from simultaneously being within the *consortium* rules.[69] This may be necessary for the Revenue's protection to prevent

---

[66] Section 247(1)(a) TA 1988.
[67] Section 413(3)(a) TA 1988.
[68] Section 247(9)(c) TA 1988 in relation to group income, and section 413(6)(a) in relation to group relief.
[69] Section 405(1) TA 1988 in relation to group relief – the somewhat nebulous wording of this being needed to cover cases in which the group relationship does not continue throughout the relevant accounting period; if the surrendering company is a group member throughout, the *potential* relief attributable to group claims will always be the whole of its surrenderable loss. In the case of group income, the debarring of

continued

124 per cent of the jointly owned company's loss being surrendered between A Ltd and B Ltd. It is harder to see why the jointly owned company can be allowed to pay 76 per cent of its dividends without ACT, but must be forced to account for ACT on the other 24 per cent.

5.40 Beginnings and endings

The starting date for the availability of what we have loosely described as *group* situations is generally the date at which one company acquires beneficial ownership or control of the necessary percentage of the other, or both come within the ownership or control of another person. One would logically assume that their end-dates could be identified equally straightforwardly, as the points at which beneficial ownership or control was lost.

Matters are not quite as simple as that, as we will see. There are wider provisions common to each of the three asterisked headings in paragraph 5.38; in each of the relevant sections in the legislation,[70] there is reference to the entitlement to these reliefs ceasing to be available when 'arrangements are in existence' for the companies concerned to cease to be associated.

That phrase could of course mean more or less anything. The Revenue have done two things. They have amended the law so as to overrule the effect of the *Sainsbury* decision, as we will see in paragraph 5.42. Second, they have outlined the interpretation they would generally put on *arrangements* in a *Statement of Practice* and an *Extra Statutory Concession*.[71]

One preliminary point needs mention. The Inland Revenue's original interpretation had been that if, in a 12-month accounting period, there were arrangements in existence for only a few days or weeks, this prevented any surrender of, or claim for, group relief for the whole 12 months. This was shown in the case referred to in paragraph 5.24 (and Note 45)[72] to be wrong. That decision has not been overruled, and nor has the law been changed. Law Land Plc *arranged* to sell a

---

continued
the consortium claim for those within the group definition is the exclusion from section 247(1)(b) of companies within section 247(1A)(a). It is often said that there is no logic in tax, but it could also be said that many rules seem designed for no purpose other than to trap the unwary.

[70] Section 247(1A)(b) TA 1988 deals with the cut-off of the jointly owned company's right to pay dividends gross when arrangements are in existence for it to become a 75 per cent subsidiary; section 240(11)(a) deals with arrangements for a subsidiary to cease to be sufficiently owned for its parent to be able to surrender ACT to it; section 410(1)(b) and (2)(b) deals with arrangements for companies to cease to be sufficiently connected for the surrender of losses in a group or a consortium.

[71] SP 3/93, and ESC C 10, the latter as revised on 13 January 1993.

[72] It is perhaps worth pointing out that on the wording of the group relief rules as interpreted in *Shepherd v Law Land plc* [1990] BTC 561, the existence of the *arrangements* disqualified only five weeks' proportion of the claim. But the wording of the rules dealing with surrenders of ACT is different. For that, it is necessary that there be a parent/subsidiary relationship *throughout* the accounting period, so that a five-week break would prevent surrenders at any time in the period.

subsidiary, and five weeks later the arrangements were aborted. It lost only five weeks' proportion of the year's group relief claim.

What the Extra Statutory Concession allows to be disregarded are the arrangements normally found in consortia under which other members have rights (or obligations) to buy out a member who defaults, or wishes to leave; similarly it allows to be disregarded a lender's rights by way of security over holdings of shares. Only when and if the shareholdings did change hands would entitlements to relief change – in line with those changes, not any earlier *arrangements*.

5.41 Is it possible to define the word 'arrangements'?

It is more difficult to encapsulate the Inland Revenue's *Statement of Practice*. Its basic intent is to identify the earliest point at which it could be said that a vendor and purchaser had not only reached agreement concerning the sale of a shareholding, but can be reasonably regarded as committed.

Thus, if the parties are free to contract with each other, the Inland Revenue does not believe that beneficial ownership of the target passes only when a legally enforceable contract exists, but rather when an offer has been made and accepted – albeit that acceptance is made *subject to contract*. Needless to say it will be relatively easy to fix this point in the context of some negotiations, but extremely hard in others. One fixed point in this otherwise difficult navigation is that no *arrangements* exist until shareholders have given approval (or indicated to the directors that they will give approval), in those cases in which such approval may be needed; the Inland Revenue accept that these cases include not only ones in which the Stock Exchange requires that shareholder approval is obtained, but also reconstructions for which such approval may be a Companies Act requirement.

The author believes that another useful approach was signposted by Millett J in the High Court in the *Sainsbury* case. He pointed out that an arrangement may not be legally binding, and therefore may never be put into effect. He was looking at a specific anti-avoidance provision which calls for an assumption to be made that 'effect would be given to those arrangements'.[73] His insight was that such a provision 'requires the arrangement to be identified'. The implication is that if what is under discussion between the parties (at that particular time not legally binding) has not reached a sufficiently precise state of agreement so that the parties would know what their positions would be if it were *assumed to be given effect*, then it cannot at that time be an arrangement.

5.42 Options – the change in the law

Options were central to the *Sainsbury* case. Neither the High Court nor the Court of Appeal accepted the Revenue's view that the GB's call option under which it was entitled to demand that Sainsbury transfer

---

[73] Paragraph 5(3)(a) of schedule 12 TA 1988.

to it 5 per cent of the Homebase shares (which would seemingly have reduced Sainsbury's holding from 75 per cent to 70 per cent) was an *arrangement* which prevented Sainsbury's beneficial ownership of 75 per cent – as the law then stood.

The Court of Appeal decision in May 1991 was followed in November of that year by the Revenue's announcement of legislation[74] to overrule the decision. The law which they needed to amend was itself extremely complex anti-avoidance legislation, so once the Inland Revenue discovered that it did not say what they meant it to say, it is unsurprising that the amendments they introduced are even more complex. For present purposes it is sufficient to say that their thrust is to declare that in any case in which any party's beneficial ownership of a company's shares is affected by the existence of *arrangements*, or options, then it is necessary to calculate what percentage he owns without regard to them, and to re-calculate a second time on the assumption that effect is given to the arrangements (or that the options are exercised) and the lower of the two percentages is then the one to be taken.

This new rule operates in determining entitlement to group relief and consortium group relief. It also applies for the other two reliefs asterisked in paragraph 6.74, namely the group income election to pay dividends without ACT and interest without withholding, and the entitlement of a parent to surrender ACT.

However it only applies in part for capital gains tax. The procedure here[75] is that one determines first whether there is the necessary 75 per cent relationship at each tier in the group, asking what is the beneficial ownership of shares, and whether there are *arrangements* of the type outlined in paragraphs 5.40 and 5.41 which could affect this. The second step is to determine whether there is an effective 51 per cent relationship between the two companies in the group at which one is looking; at this second step one is specifically permitted to ignore the 1992 amendments which would deem options to have been exercised.

---

[74] The amending legislation was in section 24 F(No. 2)A 1992, introducing amendments to schedule 18 TA 1988.

[75] See paragraph 6.44 for the explanation of the rules for determining membership of a capital gains tax group. The provision allowing one to ignore the 1992 amendments has been written into section 170(8) TCGA 1992.

CHAPTER 6

GROUPS OF COMPANIES

Companies in a group

6.1 *Legal requirements, and relationships between the group companies*

As a subject, *groups of companies* is huge, and must necessarily be split between several chapters. In chapter 3 we saw something of the way in which individual companies are formed, and operate. Chapter 5 gave us an insight into the taxation of those companies, on their ongoing operations; and looked also at the concessions that are made where such companies are members of a group, how far their legal *separateness* is overridden by rules which allow *group* treatment.

In this chapter we start looking at the formation of groups, and at ways in which their shapes can be changed; but we will try to concentrate on their *internal relationships:*

- how, and perhaps some of the reasons why, a company might form a subsidiary. Or a company might interpose another company between itself and its shareholders. In each case the result is the creation of a group of parent and subsidiary;

- company law imposes a number of requirements on the group, for instance in relation to the preparation of consolidated accounts. But these accounting rules for groups have to be set into the wider context of the framework of rules dealing with accounting on the formation or acquisition of subsidiaries, and so on. And all these accounting aspects have themselves to be fitted into the all-encompassing background of company law;

- one salient feature of that company law background is a recognition that companies still remain separate legal entities, even if one owns the share capital of another, or some third person owns the capital of them both (separation which is in no way lessened by any need for an accounting *picture* which displays certain aggregate figures for two or more companies taken together). But there is a tension between this legal separateness, and the concepts inherent in some parts of the tax legislation which envisage, for instance, some flexibility in the movements of shareholdings, of cash and of other assets between companies, and as another instance the matter looked at in the last chapter, the setting off of losses of one company against profits of another; none of these reflects quite the same degree of separation and independence.

In all of these areas we will be looking primarily at the relationships between the companies that form our group; and we will be thinking rather less about the population around and outside the group, vendors for instance from whom subsidiaries might be acquired, or the predators who might be eyeing our group or some of its members.

6.2 *The rules for joiners and leavers*

However, still in this chapter, we need to widen our perspectives to encompass:

- the various ways in which a group can expand by the addition of companies from outside – phraseology purposely chosen so as to allow us to examine the differences in theory (and in practice) when expansion is by acquisition, and by merger;

- we need to have some grasp of some of the transactions possible under other corporate legal systems, but not in the United Kingdom, such as the US merger which does not result in a parent/subsidiary group but in a single corporation, combining the attributes and shareholders of the two predecessors (and that last word is itself a misnomer since neither does in fact decease);

- and we need to know also what are the implications of the splitting up of groups, either simple division into separate groups, or single companies leaving a group (and although this may not be seen as quite the same subject, by the transfer of businesses or other significant assets, out of groups).

What we can appropriately leave to be dealt with in later chapters is the battleground in which a company (already in a group or in the process of changing into one) interacts with the target which it is seeking to acquire, and both sets of shareholders also tend to become more or less involved in the interplay. If what is to be acquired is not a target company but a trade and its related assets, then the questions have some similarities but there are also significant differences.

Acquisitions can be made for cash, or for the issue of shares or debentures – or any combination. There are acquisitions which necessitate a restructuring of the predator's group, or of the target and the group from which it is to be acquired – or restructuring of everything in sight. We will see as our discussion of these matters develops in chapters 11 and 12 that there are parts of the exercise which can be satisfactorily examined solely from the predator's viewpoint, others which we can look at from the standpoint of the vendor – but there is a middle ground which we will find makes better sense if our discussions look simultaneously at the implications for all those involved; dealing in distinct sections with the predator's, target's, and vendor's positions would make the overall picture harder to comprehend.

6.3 *Cash*

The other thread that we will see running through the whole of chapters

11 and 12, through all our discussions on acquisitions, restructurings and disposals, is a focus on cash.

Shareholders' values are a function of their expected dividend flow, and their expected exit price. Where the company continues (or where its business and assets remain within a company even if it is a different one) any exit price received by a departing shareholder will itself reflect the new owner's expectations of his future dividend flows and exit price.

In the most straightforward world in which all companies always continue, a world in which the original draftsmen of company law and tax law might be suspected of having lived out their lives, there appeared to be only two possibilities:

- exit prices were received in cash, that cash being derived from new investors until then outside the corporate sector; or

- exit prices were received in non-cash form, in shares issued by a predator.

But as soon as one sets that out in those terms, one sees that there is every possibility of deriving an exit price in cash from a predator – which will reflect through (by affecting the level of its assets and earning power) into the dividend expectations and exit price expectations of its own shareholders. And only a little bit of ingenuity might be needed in order to derive a cash exit price not from the predator but from the target itself.

With such possibilities opened up it is clear that the principles underlying both company law and taxation are only too easy to subvert; it is no longer enough to say, simply, that income can be paid out and is to be fully subjected to tax, while capital must be maintained and only its growth is to be taxed. Both company law and tax law must try rather harder to define what is meant by income, and when some flow of cash dressed up as *capital* must be treated as income. So also must accounting rules attempt the same differentiation.

How the authorities have sought to keep control of these Hydra's heads will engage us to some extent in this chapter, but we will need to return to the subject in chapters 9, 11 and 12.

6.4 Creation of the group

What we need to bear in mind is that a group of companies can be established in many different ways, just as there can be different reasons why it is thought appropriate to take this course:

- a company can form one or more subsidiaries, causing them to allot shares to the parent, the consideration being either cash, or non-cash such as the hive-down of businesses and assets;

- a company (which we will sometimes describe as the prospective parent but in some circumstances is better described as an intermediate holding company) can be formed with a view to its allotting shares to those who already hold shares in one or more other companies (the prospective subsidiaries) in consideration for those shareholders transferring to the prospective parent their holdings of subsidiary shares;[1]

- a company can buy another or others, for cash or by the allotment of shares, from those who are the existing shareholders of these prospective subsidiaries.

Each of those is expressed in terms of *ownership* of the subsidiary by the parent, and we will see in the next three paragraphs (and have already seen in paragraphs 5.32 onwards in relation to tax) that that word needs to be treated with some care.

6.5 Companies Act definitions of holding companies and subsidiaries (and related terminology)

The basic Companies Act definitions are, however, framed in terms of the parent being a *member* of its subsidiary, and having *control*. There are two separate relationships, defined slightly differently:

- the general relationship is that of a *holding company* and its *subsidiary*, the former either holding a majority of the voting rights, or having rights either to control the constitution of the board or to control a majority of the voting rights.[2] If the holding company has a subsidiary which is in turn a holding company with its own subsidiary, that last is also a subsidiary of the first. For convenience we will refer to such second-tier subsidiaries as sub-subsidiaries;

- within that general relationship there is also defined a wholly owned subsidiary, namely the subsidiary which has no members other than the holding company, its subsidiaries, or nominees for either;[3]

- besides the foregoing relationships which apply generally throughout the Companies Acts, there is a distinct relationship which is relevant for Part VII of the Companies Act 1985 which contains the provisions dealing with accounts and audit. Each separate company has its individual obligations under this legislation, but in addition a *parent company* is required under section 227 to prepare group

---

[1] When the two brewers, Bass and Charrington, merged in the late 1960s they did so by forming a new holding company (Bass-Charrington) which acquired the entire share capitals of both existing companies.

[2] Section 736(1) CA 1985 reads:

'A company is a *subsidiary* of another company, its *holding company*, if that other company

(a) holds a majority of the voting rights in it, or
(b) is a member of it and has the right to appoint or remove a majority of its board of directors, or
(c) is a member of it and controls alone, pursuant to an agreement with other shareholders or members, a majority of the voting rights in it,

or, if it is a subsidiary of a company which is itself a subsidiary of that other company.'

[3] Section 736(2) CA 1985.

accounts, consolidating with its own figures those of its *subsidiary undertakings*. That last word is important, in that partnerships and unincorporated associations carrying on trade or business (whether for profit or otherwise) are all within the definition of undertaking.[4]

The necessity for building groups, for accounts consolidation purposes, which include entities other than companies arose under the EC Seventh Company Law Directive, and is understood to reflect the German position, where non-corporate entities occur more frequently in group structures than is the case in the UK or other EC states. Since defining a subsidiary undertaking[5] meant defining its relationship with a parent, it was necessary to introduce the concept of a parent undertaking – but as stated in the second sentence of the third head above, only a parent undertaking which is itself a *company* has an obligation under section 227 to prepare and file group accounts.

6.6 Transactions off-balance-sheet

There are two types of transactions, related perhaps but distinct, which are referred to as being capable of being dealt with off-balance-sheet. The concept is simply that of avoiding the necessity under the Companies Act to show the figures concerned in the consolidation.

An example of the first type relates to leasing. Prior to the change in the structure of capital allowances in 1984, establishing a leasing subsidiary was a recognised way of sheltering the profits of its parent from tax. This shelter resulted from the subsidiary's tax reliefs for capital expenditure and interest on borrowings preceding its receipt of equivalent levels of taxable rental income, thus generating *losses* which it could surrender to its parent. If we picture a profitable industrial company

---

[4] Section 259(1) CA 1985.

[5] The definition of parent undertaking in relation to subsidiary undertaking, in section 258 CA 1985, is in identical terms to that of holding company and subsidiary company (see Note 2, but substitute the former phrases in place of the latter), except that there are two further circumstances in which an undertaking is to be regarded as a parent undertaking:

'(a) it has the right to exercise a dominant influence over the (subsidiary) undertaking
  (i) by virtue of provisions contained in the undertaking's memorandum or articles, or
  (ii) by virtue of a control contract (section 258(2)(c) CA 1985);
(b) an undertaking is also a parent undertaking in relation to another undertaking, a subsidiary undertaking, if it has a participating interest in the undertaking, and
  (i) it actually exercises a dominant influence over it, or
  (ii) it and the subsidiary organisation are managed on a unified basis'
(section 258(4) CA 1985).

It is necessary to read with these section 258 definitions the further provisions in schedule 10A to the Companies Act 1985. Paragraph 4 of that schedule, for instance, gives definitions of the phrases 'dominant influence' and 'control contract', which are not concepts with which many UK corporate lawyers had any great familiarity until they were introduced into UK companies' legislation in 1989.

aiming to generate sufficient losses in a leasing subsidiary to shelter the company's profits, then even a rudimentary knowledge of the leasing business would enable us to see that within a few years the large volume of assets on the subsidiary's balance sheet and the correspondingly large borrowings made by it to finance them, would overshadow its parent's own figures in the consolidated balance sheet. This could only too easily restrict the parent's ability to borrow for its own business. In such circumstances, there is an obvious incentive for the *parent* to seek a way of *owning* its *subsidiary* which avoids the necessity for including the subsidiary's balance sheet numbers in the consolidated balance sheet. That is to say, the parent would want to account only for the subsidiary's earnings or dividends, not its assets and liabilities, in the parent's consolidation; but at the same time the parent would want to retain the tax advantage of being able to accept surrender of tax losses from the subsidiary.

The second area which it could be desirable to keep off-balance-sheet is the disclosure of risk; for instance a subsidiary may perhaps have built up and then sold a portfolio of residential mortgages, but sold on the basis that the subsidiary will repurchase any mortgage on which the mortgagor defaults. If the risk is material enough to need to be shown in the subsidiary's own accounts, the questions at its parent level are whether it is material for the purposes of the consolidation – if so whether there is a way of omitting the subsidiary from the consolidation.

6.7 *Further off-balance-sheet possibilities*

So far we have described all this as no more than a disclosure question, dependent only on the rules for including, or excluding, items from consolidated accounts. But there are wider implications. If they had taken place, the hypothetical events described below might have occurred some years ago, at a time when the UK and other Governments were encouraging a boycott of South Africa, and trades unions and others around the world were simultaneously pressing companies in their own countries to exert any leverage they could on South African businesses to improve the pay and conditions of black workers.

The management of our imaginary UK parent company, not wanting adverse publicity concerning a small subsidiary in South Africa but at the same time not particularly wanting to dispose of it at a fire-sale price, came up with the following scheme. They would sell their entire shareholding in the subsidiary to a friendly but secretive foreign bank; the proceeds of the sale would be left on deposit with the bank concerned; and the interest it paid on that deposit would be related, not too clearly but nevertheless related, to the dividends which the bank was able to extract from what had technically become its subsidiary.[6] What

---

[6] What the UK parent might have overlooked was what is now section 765(1)(d) TA 1988, which makes it a criminal offence for a UK resident, unless he has Treasury

continued

all that illustrates is just how difficult it can be to decide what is true and fair. On the face of it, the UK company does appear to have shed its *ownership*; but do we know the whole story? Did the bank have an option to *put* the shares back to the company, or the company an option to *call* for them?[7] How closely was the deposit interest related to the expected dividends? And what would have happened if the South African subsidiary had made losses for some years and then gone into liquidation? Perhaps just as important as those financial aspects is the question of control – who (in fact, not just in theory) appoints the board of directors of the South African company?

What those questions illustrate is just how difficult it is to produce legislation which would be watertight; even asking companies and their managements to observe the spirit rather than the letter of rules is likely to be problematical. It is not, however, a problem which is central to this book; we will give a view where it is necessary to do so, but not prescribe for every possibility.

6.8 Single member companies in a group context

In a group context, a single member company[8] could be the holding company if it, and the entire group below it, were owned and controlled by a single individual. But it is perhaps more likely that the single member company would be seen as an appropriate vehicle to use as a wholly owned subsidiary. There are overseas legal systems under which the English idea of a wholly owned subsidiary having on its register any shareholder other than its holding company is not only incomprehensible, but illegal.

Our earlier discussion (paragraph 3.13) showed that the statutory instrument's draftsman had been less than helpful. Looking at the problems again, in a group context, we can see that administration of wholly owned subsidiaries raises the following ambiguities:

---

continued
consent, to sell shares in a non-resident subsidiary to another non-resident; the bank was needless to say one of those. When one invents illustrations it does no harm to have them demonstrate the number of angles one must have in mind all the time if one is considering some unusual transaction. Treasury consent is less difficult to obtain now than was the case when exchange control was in operation, but it is vital not to overlook the need to obtain it in appropriate circumstances.

[7] If there are *cross-options*, that is to say, one party has a put and the other a call, common sense indicates that one or other *must* be exercised, because a price movement in either direction will make the exercise worthwhile for one or other party. But common sense is a bad guide to the legal position, as we could have seen in the *Sainsbury* case in paragraph 5.36. In that case neither of the cross-options was in fact exercised; and in relation to the narrow point at issue in that case, the Revenue have found it necessary to disallow the relief that was at issue by enacting a provision that *deems* one or other to have been exercised. The law would not normally assume that either would be.

[8] See the discussion in paragraph 3.13. The rules are in Statutory Instrument 1992 No. 1699, The Companies (Single Member Private Limited Companies) Regulations 1992, which implement the EC 12th Company Law Directive.

- the subsidiary and its parent are legally separate entities, and each must always recognise this in their dealings not only with outsiders (particularly their creditors) but also in their dealings with each other. Dealings is a carefully chosen word, because we are not talking only about trading transactions – what we are considering spills over into the next heading;

- there are some matters outside the subsidiary's competence, which require the attention of its shareholders – which means the attention of corporate representatives nominated to act on the parent's behalf in that role. Changing the subsidiary's *objects* in its memorandum is a clear example, and changing its name would be another. Less obvious, but nevertheless also a matter for shareholders rather than directors, is the entire auditor-relationship, appointment, receipt of the audit report, and fixing remuneration.[9] It should also be pointed out that the appointment of the subsidiary's directors is a matter for its shareholders. In each of the areas mentioned in this head, the parent's corporate representatives are likely to be appointed by its management, but must take their decisions as shareholders not as managers;

- third, there is the fact that the subsidiary's directors, once appointed, have responsibility for a number of disparate matters. In the management of the subsidiary's day-to-day activities they answer in practice to the parent's *management*, but the Companies Act makes them accountable (in the true sense of the word) to their own company's shareholders. In their *direction*[10] (as distinct from management) of their subsidiary, they are answerable to shareholders (which seems to mean ultimately, although perhaps indirectly, answerable to the shareholders of the parent).

6.9 What the Statutory Instrument could have said

Against that confused background, what one could have hoped to find in a Statutory Instrument aimed at the effective use, in groups, of single member companies would have included:

---

[9] See paragraphs 1.24 to 1.28.

[10] What in tax law is referred to slightly confusingly as the 'central mind and management' of the company, the function exercised by the directors at their meetings of deciding such matters as whether the company should expand, or should diversify into a new area. In UK tax law it is the country where the directors exercise this function that the company is regarded as *really doing business*, and therefore as being resident. See *De Beers Consolidated Mines v Howe* [1906] AC 455, 5 TC 198, but see also the judgment of Sir Raymond Evershed MR in *Trinidad Leaseholds Ltd v IRC* [1952] 1 All ER 646, 34 TC 207: 'The company may be properly found to reside in a country where it really does business, that is to say, where the controlling power and authority which, according to the ordinary constitution of a limited company, is vested in its board of directors, and the exercise of that power and authority, is to some substantial degree to be found. In our judgment, the formula where the central power and authority abides does not demand that the Court should look, and look only, to the place where is found the final and supreme authority.'

- first, but perhaps of the least real importance, some simplification and speeding up of the procedures for calling, holding, and recording the decisions of 'meetings' (that word has to be put into quotation marks) of the sole shareholder of the subsidiary. Notices calling the meeting, appointment of representatives by the corporate shareholder, consents to short notice, and all the usual mindless documentation could have been simplified for the 21st century;

- there is perhaps some hope that the alternative procedure, *written resolutions*[11] in place of meetings, could be speeded if the Department of Trade and Industry were to feel able to enact one of the suggestions in a consultation paper put out on 5 August 1993, that the law should do away with the need for auditors' consent to any such resolution. At present the law gives auditors the right to attend and speak at shareholders' meetings, and the requirement that they be given notice of matters proposed to be decided by written resolution is designed to protect their rights (by enabling them to insist that a meeting be called so that they can voice their objections);

- third, clarification on the question who, and in what capacity, is empowered to make the decisions in the various areas indicated in the previous paragraph.[12] If it is considered that the roles of

---

[11] Sections 381A to 381C CA 1985.

[12] There is a much wider point here than it would be reasonable to expect the Statutory Instrument to have been able to clarify; it has implications which are not limited to the case of single-member companies, although they might be even more clearly apparent in those cases than elsewhere. Consider the following statement: 'It is of course of the essence of any subsidiary company that, broadly speaking, it should conform to the wishes of its parent company. The parent company, of necessity, appoints its directors, directly or at a remove; the parent company is often its main, frequently its sole, source of finance; its directors are often directors of the parent company, who thus carry the policy of the parent company directly into the boardroom of the subsidiary. All these factors may, and indeed sometimes do, lead to the board of the subsidiary company pursuing policies which commend themselves to the parent company but which, viewed objectively, ought not to commend themselves to an independent board of directors.' Walton J was contemplating (in *Burman v Hedges & Butler Ltd* [1978] 52 TC 501) an extreme case of subsidiary conformity to its parent's wishes. Zagal Ltd had borrowed £4 million on instructions from its parent Joseph E Seagram & Sons Inc. in order to pay £1.7 million to acquire the share capital of The Old Bushmills Distillery Ltd from Hedges & Butler, and to lend £2.3 million to Bushmills so that the latter could pay off its indebtedness to companies in Hedges & Butler's group. And it was said to be *inconceivable* that Zagal would thereafter do anything with its new subsidiary, or the borrowing it had undertaken in connection with its acquisition, until after completion of all the moves in the tax scheme that the court had in front of it. At that time, Seagram would tell Zagal what to do next.

It was urged on Walton J that the part Zagal played, as outlined above, showed that at no stage could it have been a company acting as principal – that it could only have been acting as an agent for a principal standing behind it, namely Seagram.

The judge refused to agree. The first leg of his reasoning was his description, quoted above, of the parent/subsidiary relationship; he pointed out that all the events which the Inland Revenue argued must prove the existence of an agency relationship were actually entirely consistent with a subsidiary relationship (in the light of the

continued

shareholder and of management must be kept clearly separate at the subsidiary level (so as to mirror the parent's shareholders' and directors' separation), then it would have been logical to ensure that the subsidiary's *shareholder* function would not be performed by a representative appointed by the parent's *management*;

• finally, those who promulgated the Statutory Instrument might have indicated whether they had considered, or had rejected, the possibility of simplification and rationalisation based on seeking not just accountability but transparency (glasnost). If the latter were possible, it could be described as a recognition of the reality – that in a group owned and controlled by a single individual, both the shareholder, and the management, decisions stop at his desk. Pretending that there are separate tiers of decision makers at each step up the group's corporate structure must be an excursion into never-never land.

Whether the draftsman of the Statutory Instrument gave any thought to any of the foregoing is not at all clear.

6.10 *The so-called informal decision*

There is one other matter which the single-member company legislation does not touch. It is a general principle of law that the members of a company, acting together and unanimously, can make decisions in ways other than those envisaged in the Companies Acts.[13] The provisions referred to in the previous paragraph, allowing the use of written

---

continued
subsidiary's willingness to *conform*). But the judge's second leg was conclusive for a tax case – the Commissioners had found as a fact that the relationship went no further than parent/subsidiary, and it was not possible for the courts to disturb that finding.

What we are left with is a clear indication that it is possible for a subsidiary (or any group company) to act as principal, or to act as agent for another. Whether it *is* acting in the one capacity or the other is simply a question of fact. However, that does not make it any easier for outsiders to dicover what those facts may be. These are layers of ambiguity which the Companies Acts do not touch.

[13] See, for instance, *Re Express Engineering Works Ltd* [1920] 1 Ch. 466, and *Cane v Jones* [1980] 1 WLR 1451. Notice particularly that it would be an incorrect formulation to say that 'the shareholders acting unanimously can override the provisions of the Companies Acts'; the correct formulation is to be found in *Cane v Jones*, at 1459: 'all the corporators acting together can do anything which is *intra vires* the company'. If the act lays down a procedure but the shareholders unanimously adopt a different one, the courts will not deny them that right to run their affairs in their own way. But if what the act lays down is more than a procedure, it is a requirement of law, then the company would be acting *ultra vires* if it ignored that requirement, and the shareholders would not be able to ratify its action (see the explanation in paragraphs 9.15 and 9.16). The line between when it is permissible to override a procedure and when a requirement may not be overridden is a fine one; for instance in paragraph 8.6 and Note 12 the requirement in section 303 CA 1985 is that shareholders can remove a director by ordinary resolution. A company which attempted to override that by providing in its Articles that only a special resolution would suffice failed in this attempt.

resolutions for purposes for which meetings would be the normal procedure, are an illustration of the principle that members have been recognised over the years to have a degree of flexibility that the original draftsman of the legislation failed to admit.

This flexibility seems to be further extended by the Statutory Instrument's wording, writing as it does into the Companies Act 1985 a new section 382B. This section makes reference to the the company's single member taking a decision which could have been (but was not) made at a general meeting, and could have been (but was not) made in a written resolution. The decision concerned is declared to be valid, and the section merely requires that the member's decision be recorded, and provided to the company.

There is thus a reference to the possibility of decisions being made, but without any indication of a method of making them. Certainly, the colloquial description 'informal decisions' takes one no further. Faced with that degree of uncertainty on one side – and with the irksome but well established procedures of meetings and written resolutions on the other – the advice of most company lawyers would have to be that a single-member company should choose certainty not uncertainty.

So far as can be ascertained, that is also the attitude of the Registrar of Companies, who regards the new section 382B as merely a sweeping-up clause to achieve the recording of decisions (that is its heading) rather than its providing a method of making them.

6.11 Directors' insurance

Insurance for directors is a different subject, but since it illustrates some of the same difficulties of identifying what should be the separate roles and functions of companies, their owners, and directors, it justifies a brief digression.

Until 1989, the general rule (subject to the particular exception explained below) was that companies were not permitted to indemnify their directors against liabilities they might incur for negligence, default, breach of duty or breach of trust in relation to the company.[14] That ban on general indemnification also meant that if the director were to insure himself against his potential liabilities, the company could not refund the costs of that insurance.

The exception to the foregoing general ban was that a company *could* indemnify the director against liabilities incurred 'in defending any proceedings (whether civil or criminal) in which judgment is given

---

[14] But in those pre-1989 days, some parent companies did undertake to indemnify the directors of subsidiary companies for liabilities they might incur in performing their subsidiary company duties; the difficulty being of course that of demonstrating that the funds of the parent's shareholders were not being improperly used if a subsidiary's director were to be paid out. Now that the law has been changed, as indicated in the latter part of paragraph 6.11, it is generally accepted that the ambiguities and uncertainties of parent indemnities for subsidiaries' directors outweigh their advantages.

in his favour or he is acquitted'. Given that the company is allowed to procure that the director be indemnified, the company is obviously free to choose whether the indemnity comes directly out of its own resources, or whether it is covered by an insurance policy that the *company* takes out to cover its risk.

In 1989 the law was changed.[15] Companies can now not only indemnify directors for their costs incurred in what we might describe as being found not guilty, but can *purchase insurance* for any unindemnifiable costs and claims, what is described on the insurance policy as 'any loss arising from any claim . . . made against him (that is, the director) . . . by reason of any wrongful act in the capacity of director'.

The standard directors' indemnity policy is therefore now one under which the company pays the premium which covers *it* for sums which it might have to pay to its director (by way of indemnity for his being found not guilty), and covers *him* for costs and claims which the company could not and still cannot pay, but which he is permitted to insure, and for which *it* is permitted to *pay* that insurance.[16]

Share premium accounts

6.12 *The reliefs available from these requirements in the case of mergers and group reconstructions*

This is a subject on which the law has been peremptory since 1947,

---

[15] The law as amended is now in section 310 CA 1985, the original indemnity provisions being in subsection (3)(b), and the new insurance provisions in subsection (3)(a).

[16] Two things need to be said about these policies. First, the company pays the premium on the 'being found not guilty' section of the policy, and if there is a claim on this, the proceeds go to the company so that it can meet its obligation to indemnify its director. That clearly demonstrates the company's insurable interest, and entitlement to the proceeds. As regards the remainder of the policy, it is the director who has an insurable interest, and the proceeds on any claim go to *him*. All that the company is doing, as it is now allowed to do, is to bear the premiums for the insurance.

That leads to the second point, which is the director's tax position. There seems to be considerable confusion (not least in the minds of the Inland Revenue) over the question of the *benefit in kind* on which the director should be taxable, if the company does bear the costs of both parts of this insurance, although it is hard to see any reason for any confusion. If there is a claim the director would receive from the company, and be taxable on, indemnification payments (being found not guilty); that must follow from the fact that what he receives comes from his employer, not from an insurance policy – and what the company covers in *its* policy is its obligation, not his. In any event the director's taxability is precisely what was decided in *Rendell v Went* [1964] 41 TC 641. But in relation to the other part of the insurance policy, it is the company's cost (its bearing of the premium) in providing a benefit by way of an insurance whose beneficiary is the individual that must be the measure of that individual's taxable benefit. The insurer needs to indicate what part of the total premium should be attributed to insurance for the individual's benefit under section 310(3)(a). There are many who would argue that where a director is made personally liable for some loss or damage for which in equity he was not to blame, then it is a misuse of language to say the company is 'benefiting' him by removing that liability. That is not the way in which the tax law was drafted.

but only clearly understood since 1981 – the circumstances in which it is required that share premium accounts be established. When understanding dawned, it was recognised that there should be circumstances in which it is permissible not to set up such an account or to set it up at less than the full level that might otherwise apply.

We carried this forward from paragraphs 3.26 and 3.29, because it fits more sensibly into the chapter dealing with groups than chapter 3 on incorporation. What we undertook to explain was when and why the concept was written into company law that a premium achieved, whether on shares issued for money or money's worth, must be treated as a non-distributable reserve, as quasi-capital. And we also said we would explain why and how these particular rules have needed to be relaxed so as to permit certain unobjectionable transactions.

Throughout this whole discussion we need to keep in mind what purpose a share premium account is designed to serve: to identify as capital funds acquired by the issue of shares, and therefore as available for fixed investment or for retention in the company (circulating capital is still capital, requiring to be maintained not distributed). In that phraseology two further points need to be made clear. The *funds* we are speaking of drawing in may be money or money's worth, but in either case they will be depicted in financial terms in the company's accounts. Second, funds which the company holds for fixed or circulating purposes – which it therefore cannot distribute to its shareholders – are nevertheless by that same definition available to meet creditors' claims.

All of that is one of the accounting implications of establishing, or not establishing, a share premium account. The other is an indirect effect, in that the presence or absence of a premium affects the quantification[17] of profits as well as the question whether they are distributable. Here our discussions of what can happen, as opposed to what *should* be shown in the accounts, will lead towards the conclusion that peremptory law does not necessarily produce wholly satisfactory accounting.

6.13 Shearer v Bercain

This is a saga which only makes sense if one starts far enough back, if one tells the story through to its end, and then stops.

A premium on the issue of shares was originally seen as merely an accounting function; if the nominal value of shares issued was £100, but the cash received for their issue was £500, then it was necessary to make the balance sheet balance by crediting the difference to a reserve. And there was at one time no prohibition on the distribution of that particular reserve by way of dividend.[18] It was also true, as Walton J

---

[17] We described in paragraph 3.23 the need for different levels of depreciation, and in relevant cases provisions for diminution in value of assets, where these have been revalued on the creation of a premium. That description was in the context of a single company's own accounts, but we will see the same principles applying in the consolidated accounts for an *acquisition*. However, we will also see in paragraph 6.27 that there are other ways of massaging, or flattering, reported profits.

[18] *Drown v Gaumont-British Picture Corporation Ltd* [1937] Ch. 402.

noted in *Shearer v Bercain*[19] in his review of the historical development of the law, that most company lawyers would at that time have thought that a share premium could only arise on a cash payment for shares (and he was tactful enough not to have indicated what he thought accountants might have been thinking about).

The implications were clear. Picture a predator company issuing shares with a nominal value of £100 as consideration for its acquisition of the entire share capital of a target whose position was as follows:

Share capital	£ 50
Retained reserves (distributable)	150
Value of company as going concern	500

The shares in the target would be taken into the predator's balance sheet as an asset with a value attributed to them of £100. There never has been anything to prevent the target from distributing its pre-acquisition profits of £150 to the predator (and that remains true to this day). There was nothing to prevent the predator distributing that same £150 to its own shareholders.[20]

However, as an alternative (without taking £150 of cash out of the target) the predator could have revalued its shareholding in the target from £100 to £500, credited the difference of £400 to reserve, and at the distant time of which we are speaking, paid the whole of that £400 as a dividend to its shareholders out of its own resources.

6.14 *The 1947 Cohen committee*

The Cohen committee on company law reform in 1947 identified that last-mentioned transaction as a distribution of the predator's capital; and it went further by expressing the view that any distribution by a company of premiums obtained on the issue of its shares was undesirable. It was the Companies Act 1947 which enacted this recommendation, and first required that share premiums be put to a non-distributable reserve.

Using the previous paragraph's figures, therefore, the predator was then required to credit £400 to share premium account, as well as crediting the £100 nominal value of the shares issued to share capital account. The Act said nothing about the figure the predator was to enter in its balance sheet as the carrying value of its asset, the shares in the target; but common sense, as well as the need to balance the balance sheet, indicated that this was one and the same as the honest estimate made by the directors of the shares' worth,[21] in the process

---

[19] *Shearer (HM Inspector of Taxes) v Bercain Ltd* [1980] 3 All ER 295, 53 TC 698.

[20] If the predator is entitled to the merger relief which we will explain in paragraph 6.20 below, then in spite of what appear to be binding prohibitions set out in paragraph 6.14, the likelihood is that that predator will not be prevented from distributing to its own shareholders the target's pre-acquisition profits. The explanation for this paradox fits better into paragraph 9.26 than it does here.

[21] Lord Greene in the *Steel Barrel* case [1942] 1 All ER 634, see paragraph 3.24.

of quantifying the premium. There was still no reason why the target should not distribute £150 to the predator, but pre-acquisition reserves were blocked from onward distribution.

In his analysis in *Shearer v Bercain*, Walton J found this block achieved statutorily in wording in what was then paragraph 15(5) of schedule 8 to the then consolidation of companies legislation, the Companies Act 1948. The words concerned have since been eliminated in the course of subsequent amendments and re-consolidations. But the block still exists as a matter of general principle. If the target is worth £500 at the date of acquisition, and in the form in which it then stands; and if £150 is immediately extracted from its coffers; then it is hard to see that this is not a *diminution* in its value which requires its owner to write down the carrying value of its shares from £500 to £350. In colloquial usage one says that the dividend received by the predator out of pre-acquisition profits has to be credited against the carrying value of the target, and is therefore not available to credit to the predator's profit and loss account.[22] That is however a considerable oversimplification – and likely to be totally untrue in those case in which the predator qualifies for *merger relief* (paragraph 6.20). Our analysis of what results from the super-imposition of merger relief on top of the principles set out above is best left for paragraph 9.26.

6.15 *The law that resulted from Cohen*

The last two paragraphs have set out the statutory position following the enactment in 1947 of what became section 56(1) of the Companies Act 1948, and is to all extents and purposes unchanged in section 130(1) of the Companies Act 1985:

> If a company issues shares at a premium, whether for cash or otherwise, a sum equal to the aggregate amount or value of the premiums on those shares shall be transferred to an account called *the share premium account*.

We need to put alongside that what Lord Greene had said five years earlier in the *Steel Barrel* case:[23]

> when fully paid shares are properly issued for a consideration other than cash, the consideration moving from the company [must be at the least equal to the par value of the shares and] must be based on an honest estimate by the directors of the value of the assets acquired;

which, eliding the phrase which we have square-bracketed, seems clearly

---

[22] The formation of Bass-Charrington as a holding company, mentioned in Note 1 on paragraph 6.4, blocked the entire reserves of all the Bass and the Charrington companies which came to be owned by that new holding company; they could pay their distributable reserves to it, but it could not pay them on to shareholders. However that arose because the merger took place before merger relief was introduced. We will see in paragraph 9.26 that, with the assistance of merger relief, the new holding company would have been able to establish itself on a less disadvantageous basis.

[23] See Note 21 on the preceding paragraph and paragraph 3.24.

to envisage the creation of a premium on issues for money's worth as well as on issues of shares for cash. And having juxtaposed these two points, we then need to comment on the remark made in paragraphs 3.26 and 6.12 that it took a long time for many company lawyers and accountants to grasp the implications of what Lord Greene had said, and what the draftsman of the 1947 legislation had built on top of it when he demanded share premium accounts.

6.16 *But could that law really mean what it said?*

There were probably two reasons why it was tempting to believe the law must be interpreted in some other way. The first was the matter over which *Shearer v Bercain* was actually fought. Bercain Ltd was a close company, formed to take over on a share for share basis two other, profitable, close companies which had been owned by the same individual who owned Bercain. Under the *shortfall* rules which were in 1971 intrinsic to the tax legislation dealing with close companies, that individual could have been taxed as if companies he owned had paid their profits out to him as dividends, even if they had not done so. But this rule did not apply if the companies were prevented by law from paying dividends.

By inserting Bercain as a holding company between himself and what became its two subsidiaries, the individual claimed (and Walton J agreed) that he had *blocked* Bercain from paying dividends out of what would otherwise have been the distributable profits of those two companies. It is always hard to believe that it can be as easy as that to frustrate complex tax avoidance legislation which has kept people in thrall for more than 40 years; and that it could continue to be frustrated every year from then on merely by the insertion of another holding company between the individual and Bercain, and then between the individual and that new company, and so on year after year.

But it seemed equally hard to believe that the 1947 legislation could have the effects it manifestly did when the shape of any already existing group of companies was altered, for instance by the insertion of an intermediate holding company. That would immediately lead to a blocking of all of the reserves of companies lower down, despite there having been no change in the top holding company, or in its body of shareholders. The phrase 'pre-acquisition profits' seemed unlikely to have been intended to carry such significance.

Mr Justice Walton's judgment in *Shearer v Bercain* was a most unwelcome surprise to a considerable number of people. Regulations had to be introduced to absolve companies who had, prior to the decision, indulged in transactions which that decision had shown to be unlawful. And then a Companies Act of 1981 brought in the reliefs which are now in sections 131 and 132 of the Companies Act 1985.

6.17 *Relief in respect of group reconstructions*

Where wholly owned subsidiaries were moved within a group of companies (acquired by an intermediate holding company for an issue of its shares to what had previously been the immediate holder of the target),[24] the rigours of a share premium account in the acquiring company, and of the blocking of reserves in that company, were obviously neither necessary nor desirable.

Section 132 Companies Act 1985 requires the recipient company to create a share premium account only in a limited set of circumstances, and then to a limited extent.[25] (In these reconstructions it is convenient to use the word recipient in place of predator, and to call its target the s-subsidiary, standing either for sub- or second-. It is also helpful to call the previous owner of the s-subsidiary's shares the transferor.) The best way of understanding the thrust of the relief is, however, to look at a case where a share premium account at some level is obligatory.

Transferor formed a wholly owned subsidiary, recipient, many years ago with a share capital of £1,000; transferor still carries its shares in that company in its own balance sheet at £1,000. Recently transferor acquired the entire £3,000 (nominal) share capital of s-subsidiary at a price of £10,000, satisfied to the extent of £2,000 in cash, and to the extent of the balance by the issue of £500 (nominal) transferor shares. That acquisition is not a transaction for which section 132 provides any relief, and the movements in the various captions in transferor's balance sheet would therefore be as shown in Table 33.

Table 33: Transferor's Balance Sheet

	Before		After
Investments – in group undertakings	1,000	+ 10,000	11,000
Current assets (includes cash at bank)	21,000	– 2,000	19,000
	22,000	+ 8,000	30,000
Capital and reserves – share capital	15,000	+ 500	15,500
– share premium	5,000	+ 7,500	12,500
– reserves	2,000		2,000
	22,000	8,000	30,000

6.18 *Subsequent move of s-subsidiary from transferor to recipient*

What we now suppose is a transaction under which transferor moves its

---

[24] There are complex tax implications (although usually no tax liability) arising from this move; we leave consideration of this to paragraphs 6.51 to 6.56.
[25] We have been discussing predators acquiring shareholdings in target companies, because that has enabled us to illustrate and discuss the theory of pre-acquisition profits, and whether they should be *blocked*. Section 132 however deals also with cases of other non-cash assets moved within a group for an issue of shares – the principles on which the section provides relief from the need to set up a share premium account are exactly similar. The tax implications for non-cash assets other than shareholdings are different, and are dealt with in paragraphs 6.46 to 6.48.

s-subsidiary shares down into recipient, for consideration consisting of the issue by recipient of a further £2,000 shares.

In transferor's own accounts, it seems obvious that its passing of s-subsidiary's shares down to recipient should produce no gain or loss, and that the only change in its balance sheet (underlying the captions which would not themselves change) is that its investment in group companies would be represented by a single £11,000 carrying value for the £3,000 shares in recipient, in place of £1,000 shares in that company at £1,000 and £3,000 in s-subsidiary at £10,000.

The figure at which transferor disposes of its shares in s-subsidiary is not *directly* related to the figure at which recipient brings those shares into its own balance sheet. We know that under the pre-*Bercain* thought processes, few people would have been concerned had recipient brought those shares in s-subsidiary into its balance sheet at £2,000, matching this against its own £2,000 increase in nominal share capital. On a superficial glance, one would say that s-subsidiary's pre-acquisition profits were still blocked from distribution outside the group because (even if they flowed through recipient) transferor would still need to use its receipt of them to write down in its own balance sheet the £11,000 at which it was now carrying its shareholding in recipient (£1,000 original increased by £10,000).

However, the superficiality of that analysis is plain. It is only because we are still thinking that within the £11,000 there is a £10,000 element which particularly relates to the value of the underlying s-subsidiary that we imagine that that £10,000 must be written down. Transferor would not have to write down the carrying value of recipient shares if those shares remained worth £11,000 or more overall. The stripping of the bottom company, s-subsidiary, through recipient into transferor tells us nothing about the value still remaining in recipient attributable to those assets and profit-making capacity it retains. It may well be considerably greater than its £11,000 carrying value. In which case moving s-subsidiary down from transferor to recipient would seem to have unblocked s-subsidiary's pre-acquisition profits.

The statutory reliefs from share premium requirements

6.19 Section 132 Companies Act 1985

This is where section 132 comes into play. Recipient has to create a share premium account to the extent the carrying value of the s-subsidiary shares in the group prior to their shift, that is, the £10,000 at which transferor was carrying them exceeds the nominal value of the shares which recipient issues. Thus the movement in the captions in recipient's balance sheet on its acquisition of the s-subsidiary shares is as shown in Table 34.

The figure required by law is the £8,000 share premium account. The £10,000 carrying value of the asset is simply a balancing figure (but it will also be a figure which can be described as the group cost of the subsidiary). Pre-acquisition profits of s-subsidiary can, after this

Table 34: Recipient's Balance Sheet

	Before		After
Investments – in group undertakings	–	+ 10,000	10,000
Current assets	5,000		5,000
	5,000	10,000	15,000
Capital and reserves – share capital	1,000	+ 2,000	3,000
– share premium[26]	–	+ 8,000	8,000
– reserves	4,000		4,000
	5,000	10,000	15,000

transaction, only be transferred up as far as recipient, because the latter would (in principle) be prevented from distributing them onwards to transferor.[27]

Explaining when and why section 132 requires the creation of a share premium account may, however, make it slightly too easy to lose sight

---

[26] What might seem odd is that the group now has a share premium account of £7,500 on the face of transferor's balance sheet, and a second share premium account of £8,000 on the face of recipient's. Both relate to the same asset, shares in s-subsidiary, acquired on each occasion for more than the nominal value of shares issued. But when one thinks about the asset values shown in the group's various balance sheets, it is clear that the value of s-subsidiary is itself double counted, directly on the face of recipient's, and indirectly (within the £11,000) on transferor's. This all *washes out*, to use the graphic Americanism. One share premium account, and one asset value, disappear when one consolidates s-subsidiary into recipient, and recipient into transferor. (Accounts must always be consolidated *from the bottom up*.)

[27] It is useful to think through the way in which the accounting treatment does in fact block the pre-acquisition profits. What we have envisaged is a a group cost of £10,000 for the s-subsidiary. Its own balance sheet might perhaps show share capital of £3,000 and distributable reserves of £6,000. If the matching net assets were fully valued at the £9,000 at which they stood in that balance sheet, that would mean that the goodwill on acquisition would be £1,000 (paragraph 3.28, and see also further discussion in paragraph 6.28 below). It is obvious that s-subsidiary could distribute £6,000 to recipient, but that the latter could not pass it on to transferor.

But what would the position be some time later, if s-subsidiary had made and retained a further £3,000 of profits? If one says that the value of s-subsidiary was increased by that retention by £3,000, then no writing down of its carrying value would be necessary if it were to pay a dividend to recipient of that £3,000; so that there is no block on the onward distribution of those post-acquisition profits. Further, it is clear that when one looks at a distribution post-acquisition, it is correct to regard the profits being distributed on a last-earned-first-distributed basis. However, as we know from chapter 2, the value of a company which makes and retains £3,000 of profit is increased not by £3,000 but by the present value of the earnings stream that can be earned from the extra assets into which that £3,000 is invested. If the true, economic, answer is that this value increase is greater than £3,000, then recipient would be able to receive more than £3,000 by way of dividends from s-subsidiary before it needed to start writing down the carrying value of its shares in that company; or in other words some part of the pre-acquisition profits would become unblocked by the very process of the company earning post-acquisition profits.

An accountant's answer to this conundrum would tend to be the over-simplification that £3,000 of post-acquisition profits equals £3,000 of value increase only, so that no miraculous unblocking can occur.

of the section's overall relieving purpose. The best simple summary is that shareholdings, and indeed any other non-cash asset, can be moved around at *group cost* without any need for open market valuations at the time of the movements.[28] Only where that group cost exceeds the nominal value of shares issued is a premium called for, and the amount of that premium is then quantified as the difference between the two figures. The directors are not called on to do any honest estimating of the value of the shareholdings or other non-cash assets they receive, for which they issue their own shares.

6.20 Merger relief under section 131 Companies Act 1985

The relief provided by section 131 is quite different from the group reconstruction relief we have been discussing in paragraphs 6.17 to 6.19. The concept here is that if *merger* can be taken to mean the pooling of two companies' assets and liabilities, and the putting into a single operation of their two businesses, and if as a result the combined body of shareholders comprises an aggregation of those who had previously been shareholders in the two separate companies, then there is no logic in requiring a freezing of the pre-acquisition profits of one or both of the predecessor companies.[29]

Merger relief is the statutory exemption from the need to establish a share premium account. One of the obvious differences between this relief and the group reconstruction relief is that we are now once again discussing a predator's (for want of a better word) acquisition of a shareholding in a target company – there is no question of the relief applying to other forms of non-cash assets acquired. Second, this relief is different from, although obviously related to, merger accounting.[30]

---

[28] Not only because the ability to move shareholdings at their original group cost eliminates the need for directors to update their honest estimates, but because generally there should be no requirement to adjudicate the values for stamp duty. But the position is sufficiently complex to demand examination in some depth in paragraph 6.33 and Note 56.

[29] There never was any logic in the blocking of the Bass and Charrington reserves referred to in Note 22 on paragraph 6.14. The companies could have dipped into them (but probably would not have wanted to do so) if they had remained separate companies; logically they should therefore not be prevented from doing so after a merger. This is quantitatively different from the possibility of a predator distributing what can effectively be its own capital (namely the pre-acquisition reserves of a target *bought* with the predator's capital).

[30] Merger accounting rather than acquisition accounting would always be appropriate for companies involved in a group reconstruction under section 132 CA 1985, under which the predator's share premium obligations were relieved or reduced as explained in paragraphs 6.17 to 6.19. At the risk of anticipating some part of the discussion of merger accounting in the ensuing paragraphs, it is worth listing four aspects of the *relationship* between merger accounting and the two Companies Act provisions which can permit the non-establishment of share premiums. First, unless a predator is entitled to, and avails himself of, some such relief, there is simply no room for merger accounting. Second, the way in which we will describe merger accounting (and acquisition accounting) at the beginning of paragraph 6.24 is that each is a *consolidation* process, affecting consolidated accounts rather than the solus accounts

continued

Our examination of merger relief leads naturally into an explanation of merger accounting, and that itself is best achieved by discussing its similarities with and differences from the corollary, acquisition accounting. It is because each of them can only too easily be distorted in actual application that we originally said in paragraph 6.12 that the results achieved in this difficult area, where peremptory law is extended by guidance, are sometimes less than totally satisfactory.

Although it might not seem wholly appropriate for *mergers*, it is convenient to revert to using the term *predator* for the company which becomes the parent by issuing shares to the former shareholders of a *target*, thus acquiring the latter as its subsidiary.

6.21 *Requirements for, and effects of, merger relief*

The previous paragraph was general. We need to be specific about merger relief being exempted from the necessity for a share premium account. Section 131, Companies Act 1985 requires that

- the transaction must not be one which could qualify as a group reconstruction, as outlined in paragraphs 6.17 to 6.19;[31]

- the predator must end up with 90 per cent or more of the equity shares[32] of the target, or if it has different classes of equity, then 90 per cent or more of each. In normal cases this means that the predator must acquire that percentage of the pre-existing equity capital, but the phrase used above, 'end up with', indicates that there could be cases in which the acquired percentage was later increased by cancellation of shares the predator had not acquired;

- there are however two other significances in the phrase 'end up with'. If the predator already held shares in the target, the transaction

---

continued

of predator and target; but that should not blind us to the fact that in bringing the target's assets into the what we are constructing as the predator's consolidated balance sheet, we are substituting them in place of the figure standing in its solus balance sheet as its investment in the target – and the size of that figure is governed by the predator's need, or otherwise, to set up a share premium account. (That is the explanation for the first point.) Third, where group reconstruction relief is taken, the use of merger accounting is straightforward and uncontroversial – the controversy which demands our time and attention relates to companies which qualify for merger relief.

Lastly, it is interesting to make a brief comparison with the position in the United States. One possible form of merger there involves not the acquisition of one company's shares by another (nor the acquisition of the target's undertaking for the predator's shares), but a combining of two companies into one. This commences life with not just all the assets and liabilities, but both antecedent share capitals and retained reserves. Merger accounting is then not a process affecting a consolidated set of financial statements, but is integral to this corporation's solus accounts. However it is ncessary to say that there are stringent conditions to be met before such a merger is possible; the US *control* over the availability of merger accounting is therefore, in this example, tighter than anything we have here in the United Kingdom.

[31] Section 132(8) CA 1985.
[32] Defined in section 744 CA 1985.

on which it is exempted from establishing a share premium is only the *bid* (using that word in a non-technical sense) which lifts its holding from below 90 per cent to something over it.[33] The other point should be too obvious to need mention – we are dealing with an exemption from the need to establish a *share* premium account, that is to say, with an occasion on which the amounts credited in the issuer's accounts need not be the full value of the shares, but instead may be only their nominal value. If some of the target's shares have already been, or are simultaneously being, acquired for cash, the full amount of that cash will obviously be reflected in the predator's accounts; no question of a premium arises. But that does not prevent merger relief being available on any shares issued in the course of the predator's *bid* which lifts its holding from below 90 per cent to a level over that.

Some accounting implications of merger relief in the predator's accounts (solus, not consolidated) are straightforward. Shares issued are credited at their nominal value to the share capital account. If, unusually, the predator brings in the target shares into its solus balance sheet at any figure higher than that the difference is a reserve which is not subject to the particular restrictions applying to a share premium account. But the accounting implication which many people find surprising is a matter we will deal with in paragraphs 9.26 to 9.32: the effects of the *less-than-full-value* attributed to the target's shares on that company's pre-acquisition profits, and on any profit on a sale of it.

6.22 Stamp duty on the acquisition of target's shares

The side issue of stamp duty needs a mention. There is no relief or exemption on the type of merger we have been considering:

- self-evidently what we are envisaging does not proceed from an already existing 90 per cent *group* relationship between the predator and the body of shareholders of the target. We have not envisaged the target as having a single, incorporated, shareholder but if it were so owned, we have not assumed that it and the predator are associated companies,[34] so as to protect the transfer of the target shares from one to the other;

- the exemptions in sections 75 and 77 of the Finance Act 1986, although the headings on those sections do not indicate this, can best be thought of as providing for the *reconstruction* of a single company.

---

[33] When we come to merger *accounting* we will see that SSAP 23 follows a different route in determining whether that accounting method can be used. See paragraph 6.30 and Note 51.

[34] See paragraph 6.33 below for a discussion of the relief for transfers of assets between associated companies.

In the one case its undertaking is moved into a new corporate entity[35] and in the other its shares are acquired by that new entity, but in *both* cases the only shareholders that that new entity has after the transaction are those who were the original company's shareholders before it. There is no room for a predator and its shareholders;[36]

- that leaves only section 76 of the Finance Act 1986,[37] which gives a reduction in the rate of duty from 1 per cent to half of 1 per cent – but which deals only with the predator which acquires a target's undertaking, not its shares. ('Undertaking' has a particular meaning in this context, explained in paragraphs 6.34 and 6.35.)

Stamp duty has been something of a digression – we must move back into the mainstream of our consideration of mergers and acquisitions by looking at merger accounting and acquisition accounting; the accounting profession and the Companies Acts each have something to say about

---

[35] Since the 1986 exemptions from stamp duty do not apply to the acquisitions we have been looking at, analysing what they do cover might be seen as tangential. There is, however, a tangent to that tangent. In paragraph 3.15 we outlined the customary way in which a company is formed, on the shelf in a solicitor's or company formation agent's office; we indicated that it achieves an active status when its subscribers' shares are *transferred* by those subscribers to those who are to be the company's initial owners. This is not wholly compatible with the forms of reconstruction envisaged in sections 75 and 77 FA 1986, since the consideration to be given by the new companies is in each case to consist of nothing other than the *issue* of their own shares to the shareholders of the previous company, and it is difficult to reconcile this with the existence of previously subscribed shares of the new company. If sections 75 or 77 are to be used, one possibility is to have the shareholders of the previous company themselves subscribe pro rata for the subscribers' shares in the new company, and pay for these subscribers' shares. The consideration for the transfer of the undertaking is then the issue of *further* shares (and does not also include the treating of the already issued shares as fully paid as a part of that consideration). A slightly less elegant solution is to have only some of the shareholders of the previous company subscribe for new company shares, but to rewrite the *acquisition* agreement to give those existing shareholders correspondingly fewer shares than they would otherwise have had, so that the proportions are reinstated by the time the acquisition has been completed. A rather more dubious solution than that would be to *forget* the subscribers' shares; not to transfer them to new holders, nor to call up the unpaid amounts. There is an old case, (*Mackley's case – In re Tal Y Drws Slate Company*, [1875] 1 Ch. 247), which appears to constitute authority for the removal from the register of subscribers who have never paid for shares, or taken any part in the company's activities.

[36] We will discuss this in paragraph 6.62 below rather than here, but there is one requirement that is vital for the availability of section 75 exemption – the old company must move its undertaking to the new 'in pursuance of a scheme for the reconstruction of' the old company. The transaction envisaged in section 77, moving shares of the old company into the ownership of the new one is not, as we will see, a reconstruction as that word has been defined.

[37] There is an initial review of the transactions which can be covered by section 76 FA 1986 in paragraphs 6.34 to 6.36 below, and in particular they also contain a discussion of the word 'undertaking' in stamp duty legislation, as used in this and the previous head. Paragraphs 6.59 to 6.61 then comprise an examination in greater depth of all of the questions unearthed about these areas in the intervening discussions.

the circumstances in which each is available,[38] and we must understand what they achieve if used. (We must also appreciate that both operate only in the consolidation of the target's accounts into those of the predator.)

6.23 Acquisition accounting and merger accounting

The concept of a *merger*, as somewhat loosely characterised by those originally designing merger accounting, was the coming together of two operations, two bodies of shareholders, into a single (consolidated) entity. No reason was identified why that entity should not recognise, as profit, and as distributable, all that the separate operations would have recognised; if the operations had continued separately each company would have accounted for its own assets at its own *book* values, and the merger should not change that.

The theories above are thus the antithesis of viewing the predator as making an acquisition; of looking at the predator as deploying resources to acquire an asset which it should regard as becoming part of its *capital* – not as wholly or partly distributable as surplus. Under acquisition theory, unless what is thus acquired is not only brought into the predator's accounts at full value (the *target's* assets transposed into its own, or the consolidated, accounts at what is their fair value at the effective date of acquisition) and unless that full value is matched by share capital and non-distributable premiums in those cases where the acquisition is for shares, then the predator would be in a position to pay its own *capital* out to its shareholders without recognising the diminution in the *value* retained. Creditors, as well as the company and its shareholders, would be disadvantaged.

How we can best lead into the next three paragraphs' comparison of acquisition and merger accounting is by thinking first about the solus accounts of the predator:

- if the predator paid cash to acquire 100 per cent of the shares of a target, the predator's asset (shares in subsidiary) would be brought into its accounts at the price paid. We know this would block the distribution by the predator of the target's pre-acquisition profits;

- if that acquisition we are envisaging had been for shares issued by the predator and if we make the further assumption that a share premium account *was established* exactly the same would apply;

---

[38] The *Statement of Standard Accounting Practice* still in force at the time of writing is SSAP 23, Accounting for acquisitions and mergers, issued in April 1985. As will appear, there have been criticisms of this, and the ASC produced suggestions for its amendment in an *Exposure Draft* No. 48 in February 1990. Following the replacement of ASC by the Accounting Standards Board, the latter has produced further suggestions building on ED 48 in its own *Financial Reporting Exposure Draft* No. 6 of May 1993. The statutory requirements are in schedule 4A to CA 1985, particularly at paragraphs 8 to 11. It is convenient to analyse, compare and contrast these requirements in paragraph 6.30 below, after we have explained the significances of merger accounting.

ACQUISITION ACCOUNTING AND MERGER ACCOUNTING

- but if no share premium account was established, the predator's asset could be shown at an amount equal to the nominal value of its own shares issued.

6.24 *The Consolidation Process*

Each of acquisition accounting and merger accounting is the consolidation process following the formation of a parent–subsidiary group by a transaction which, respectively, must be treated as an acquisition or may be treated as a merger. We do not need a complete, step-by-step, guide to the processes of accounting and consolidation, but it may be useful to point out some salient principles (across the full width of the page where acquisition and merger answers coincide, and separate columns where they differ):

- it is convenient to think primarily in terms of consolidating the balance sheets. One of the figures appearing on each balance sheet is the profit (or loss, but for brevity we can assume that it will be a profit) for the period – and we can think of the consolidation of the profit and loss figures as being merely an analysis of that balance sheet number;

- the consolidation we are thinking about is that at the predator's next accounting date after the transaction. We assume that the target will have changed its *accounting reference date*[39] so that that next date coincides with that of the predator. It makes our explanations much easier if we actually make the more radical assumption that predator and target had always used the same date (so that among other things there is no difficulty over producing the comparative figures for the previous period);[40]

Acquisition accounting

- the target's profits are to be consolidated only for the period from the transaction date to next accounting date;

- that preceding point focuses our minds on the fact that the target's assets are to be brought into the consolidation only at the transaction date;

Merger accounting

- the target's profits for whole of its year to next accounting date are to be consolidated;

- it is, notionally, at the previous balance sheet date that the predator's and the target's assets are to be consolidated;

---

[39] Section 225(1), (3) and (4)(a), CA 1985.
[40] When we come to deal in chapter 12 with the practical aspects of mergers and acquisitions, we will see that there is a convention that 'the accounting date' is defined as being the most recent accounting date of the target before the predator's bid – and it is by reference to accounts to that date that the target's price is fixed. We must therefore use a different phrase, 'next accounting date', to indicate what we mean in the present context.

GROUPS OF COMPANIES

6.25 Bringing the target's assets into the predator's consolidation

• the simplest way of envisaging the process of *consolidation* is to picture the predator's balance sheet, one of the figures on which is an asset *investment in target*. That figure is to be deleted, and in its place are to be substituted the target's own assets and liabilities – stated at amounts which aggregate to the same number as the deleted asset. That statement is true both at the date at which the assets concerned are *brought into* the consolidation (in the words we used at the end of the previous paragraph) and also at the next accounting date;

• in the consolidated accounts, the target's profits can be therefore be thought of as the amount by which the carrying values of the target's assets have altered between being brought in, and next accounting date. Generally, that will be the same profit figure as is shown in the target's solus accounts, but there can be *consolidation adjustments*;[41]

Acquisition accounting

• the predator's asset originally brought in is equal to the aggregate of the nominal value of shares issued plus the share premium established at the transaction date. That quantification of the asset remains the same whether a share premium account is established, or is avoided by means of a claim for merger relief. In that latter case the balance sheet is made to balance by a credit to a merger reserve[41a];

Merger accounting

• the predator's asset originally brought in equals the nominal value of its shares issued for the target's share capital (which is the same figure whether treated as brought in at the transaction date or at the earlier start of the accounting period);

---

[41] An uncontroversial example, because it is required in paragraph 6(2), schedule 4A to CA 1985, is the removal of profits one company may have made on sales to the other, where the goods sold are still in the hands of that other at the period end. There are however many other adjustments which can be argued for in a consolidation.

[41a] The bringing into the consolidated balance sheet prepared under acquisition accounting rules of the *acquisition cost*, (defined in the all-share acquisition we have been envisaging in the text as equivalent to the fair values of the shares issued), is required by paragraph 9(4) of Schedule 4A to CA 1985. The identifiable assets and liabilities in the next head in the text are required to be brought in at fair values by paragraph 9(2), but a considerably more detailed explanation of the proposed accounting requirements is set out in FRED 7, at the time of writing still in exposure draft form. Goodwill is defined in paragraph 9(5) as the difference between these two – the same way we define it in the following head in the text.

It will be immediately obvious that if a share premium account is created on the issue of the shares issued as consideration, this will *balance* the consolidated balance sheet; but that if merger relief is claimed, and therefore there is no such share premium account, the *balancing* will require the creation of a reserve in the consolidated accounts, usually called a *merger reserve*. As noted in footnote 36 on
continued

- the substituted numbers are fair values of the assets and liabilities, tangible and intangible, stated as at the transaction date;

- the substituted numbers are the assets and liabilities taken from the target's balance sheet at the start year in which the merger occurs, but notice that one of these items from the liabilities side of the balance sheet is the target's then accumulated distributable reserves;

6.26 *Balancing the predator's accounts - what the differences are called and what they mean*

Acquisition accounting

- there is likely to be a difference between the *cost* figure in the last head but one, and the aggregate of fair values in the last head. This is the *goodwill* figure to which reference has been made in paragraphs 3.30 and 4.21, and which we will discuss in greater detail in paragraphs 6.28 and 6.29 below. Current accounting thought has been that goodwill should be written off, that it cannot be carried as a balance sheet asset indefinitely.

- at the time of writing, however Financial Reporting Exposure Draft 7 points out that goodwill, as explained above is the difference between a value put on the purchase consideration, which needs to be quantified with some care; and the aggregate revaluation of the assets of the target, which is a figure which can be even more debatable. One particular area, mentioned in

Merger accounting

- again there is likely to be difference between the shares issued in the last head but one, and the share capital (and premium if any) of the target. This is designated a *merger reserve*, and can have either a credit or a debit balance. In contrast to goodwill, there is no requirement that a debit-balance merger reserve be removed from the balance sheet.

---

continued

paragraph 4.21, this is probably the reserve most frequently used for the writing off of goodwill – the procedure we will be looking at in paragraph 6.31 below.

The whole of the foregoing relates to the consolidated accounts. For comment on the position in the solus accounts of the predator, see paragraph 9.25 and footnote 28 thereon.

the next paragraph, is the extent
to which it is legitimate to value
those assets from the perspective of
the predator – to take into account
his intentions to close certain
facilities, for instance, by
allowing provisions to be made for
the costs of doing so. A different
aspect relates to the predator's
recognition of assets of the target
which do not appear in that company's
accounts – *brands*, for instance, or a
pension fund surplus

6.27 *Criticisms possible of each accounting method*

After that brief indication of the differences between the two approaches to what is sometimes called accounting for combinations, it would be useful to indicate that each of these two methods is open to criticism – that there are obvious ways in which each can be used to flatter the results shown by the combined companies:

Acquisition accounting	**Merger accounting**
• if, when the target is acquired, the predator ensures that the target makes a substantial provision (in its accounts up to the date of acquisition) for reorganisation costs, the effect of this does not result in any reduction of profits which are reported by the combination.	• consider an acquisitive predator, whose targets are acquired at the time in their development when their profits are rising strongly, and may well have been acquired towards the end of a two year period showing such earnings growth;
• how it shows up is as an increase in the amount of goodwill (balancing the deflated net assets of the target).	• in addition, there is the probability that a larger, stronger, predator can *buy* disproportionately greater volumes of a smaller, more risky, target's earnings than it could produce itself from equivalent shareholders funds;[42]
• however what this does make possible is for that target in the period *after* that to show higher profits.	

[42] See paragraph 2.20 for the discussion concerning the higher earnings percentage which might normally be expected in the smaller entity. Here we are envisaging the existing shareholders of that smaller entity being prepared to be bought out, for shares in a larger company, on the basis of *their*, not its, percentage. The result is that the larger company buys higher volumes of profit than (the worth of) its shares would themselves generate.

- the apologists for the making of reorganisation provisions say that what they are doing puts, from the predator's point of view, a correct value on the net assets which it had *targeted*, and of the profits which it can and does earn from them. Opponents say this is wholly subjective, and reorganising acquired business should reduce profits in the same way as reorganising existing business.

- the consolidated accounts (including comparative figures for previous years) will show growth in earnings from previous to current years which have nothing to do with current management's skills;

- separating *own* earnings from those *purchased* in this way is not practical.

6.28 Goodwill

We introduced the concept of goodwill in paragraph 3.30, and looked briefly at its possible effects on reserves in paragraph 4.21. But each of those references made clear that we would need to discuss the question whether goodwill was an asset which could be regarded as keeping its value indefinitely, or whether that value had to be regarded as being continuously consumed – and if so what were the principles for reducing its carrying value in the predator's, and/or the consolidated, balance sheets.

The Companies Acts are silent on the subject of goodwill, beyond noticing its existence;[43] they do not give any indication whether it must be written off, and if so when, where and how. After toying with a number of possibilities, the Accounting Standards Committee laid down in 1984[44] that goodwill should be written off, but that this could be achieved either by an immediate write-off against reserves, or by amortising it over a period through profit and loss account. That this choice was held open, in a document purporting to reduce (and preferably to eliminate) alternatives – to specify a standard accounting treatment – indicates the intractability of the subject, and the extent to which various accountants' views differed; no one now claims the option itself is satisfactory.

Goodwill is seen by some people as an asset. They admit it is not only intangible, but that it can only exist in conjunction with the tangible and other intangible assets of a business; it cannot be separated from them so as to be sold or otherwise separately dealt with. If we do try to define

---

[43] Paragraph 9(5), schedule 4A to CA 1985.
[44] SSAP 22. After that standard was issued, the ASC revisited the question, and came up with a proposal (in *Exposure Draft* 47) that goodwill should always be amortised through the profit and loss account. That proposal has been overtaken by events; at the time of writing the Accounting Standards Board has announced that the treatment of goodwill is one of its current projects.

it (albeit without any pretence at precision) the best we could probably do would be to say it is the excess of the value of the business as a going concern over the aggregate of the values of its identifiable assets. That begs more questions than it answers. A business can undoubtedly have a value greater than that of its assets; if one thinks of any professional firm, some part of the excess derives from the skills and attributes of the individual partners, and another part from their relationships with their clients. But those relationships (and the clients) are changing all the time, and every partner becomes one year more senile with each passing year; so might it be truer to say that the goodwill which appears to exist at any point is being continuously consumed away, and if goodwill can be shown to exist a few years later, that is largely *new* goodwill which is being continuously brought into existence?

6.29 *The nature and disposition of goodwill; the debate continues*

If that view of the simultaneous consumption and creation of goodwill is fair, then one thing undoubtedly follows, and a second can be strongly argued:

- the only measurement that can ever be made is wholly subjective, the value in the eye of one prospective purchaser at one specific moment;

- because goodwill is *so* intangible, immeasurable, unaccountable, it is more reasonable to regard it as no more than an accounting difference – not an asset at all.

At the time of writing, the debate remains unresolved between those who would like to write off an asset, and those who can accept that a difference can come to light but do not think that this necessarily means that the business's profits must be reduced by writing it off. There is a second level to this debate; amortisation of goodwill against profits in the profit and loss account has been in the past a less favoured choice than writing off the whole amount against reserves. But there are of course different reserves against which it can be written off, as we saw in paragraph 4.21.

What is more clearly recognised is that neither SSAP 22's choice, nor the room for manoeuvre provided by acquistion accounting and merger accounting, are entirely desirable. At the time of writing, the Accounting Standards Board has published a discussion draft dealing with these aspects of goodwill; and has done so in parallel with FRED 7 which discusses the problems of quantifying goodwill, (as explained in paragraph 6.26 above).

But ASB has dealt prescriptively with two matters referred to in paragraph 4.21, namely that if goodwill is written off against reserves, that action is not the recognition of a loss which needs to (or even may) go through the statement of recognised gains. Second, on a sale of the acquired business, the profit or loss to be put through profit and loss account is the difference between disposal proceeds and original cost, so that any intervening charge-off of goodwill (by amortisation through profit and loss or in a single charge against reserves) must be unscrambled.[45]

6.30 The requirements for merger accounting

Although we have mentioned the existence of Schedule 4A to the Companies Act 1985 as the schedule which sets out the form and content of group (consolidated) accounts, what we have not said in so many words is that it requires that acquisition accounting be the method adopted[46] unless the transaction fits the *requirements* for merger accounting, and that method is chosen.[47] The first of those merger accounting requirements is straightforward: that the predator must hold 90 per cent or more of the target's *relevant* shares, these being defined as those carrying unrestricted rights to participate in distributions and in assets on a liquidation.

The second and third requirements are perhaps rather more surprising, in that they permit that 90 per cent threshold to have been acquired in different ways, and at different times, just provided that there was a final acquisition, lifting the percentage from below 90 to above that level, and the consideration for which was the issue of the predator's shares[48] (or if there was other consideration besides that share issue, its value was not more than 10 per cent of the *nominal*[49] value of the shares). However, there is a fourth and final requirement, namely that the use of merger accounting accords with generally accepted accounting principles.[50]

What SSAP 23 stipulates, in paragraph 11, is that merger accounting may only be used in those circumstances in which the predator's offer was made to all shareholders of the target, that the latters' acceptances lifted the predator from a holding of below 20 per cent to the required level of over 90 per cent.[51] What might have been a nightmare position

---

[45] See paragraph 4.21 and Notes 36 and 37 thereon.
[46] Paragraph 8, schedule 4A to CA 1985.
[47] Paragraph 10, schedule 4A to CA 1985.
[48] A transaction which is generally regarded as an abuse of entitlements to both merger relief and merger accounting is the *vendor placing*. The vendors of the target's shares are given cash rather than predator shares, but this is achieved in a two-step transaction in which they first receive those shares, but are then able to *place* them with an institution. So far as they are concerned, they have not merged, but rather been bought out. So far as the predator is concerned, it has made a cash *acquisition*, paid for out of the proceeds of a placing with an institution of shares which it issues contemporaneously. But the *form* of the transaction makes available both merger relief and merger accounting.
[49] The requirement that other consideration be limited by reference to the shares' nominal value rather than their market value derived from the EC Seventh Company Law Directive. It does not have any logical basis.
[50] Such practice is set out in FRSs and SSAPs, which we have noted do have some legal force, see paragraph 1.25 and Note 18 thereto. It is not therefore wholly surprising to find the Act not just making reference to them but making compliance a condition of the use of this accounting method.
[51] And since this SSAP uses the British concepts which antedated the EC Seventh Company Law Directive referred to in Note 49, we find that if, in the consideration

continued

under the Companies Act turns out not to be possible, a parent claiming to be entitled to use merger accounting after buying out (for shares) sufficient of the minority to lift its holding from, say, 85 per cent to 91 per cent.

6.31 Groups in the tax legislation

This is a forest. If it is difficult to see a wood for the trees, it is far harder to make any sense of a forest. There are just too many definitions of group relationships, of intra-group transactions, and of transactions between group companies and others; many of these must presumably have been designed to enable transactions to be undertaken which are thought generally useful and helpful; for instance capital gains tax-free movement of shares and other assets within a group is allowed,[52] thus making reorganisations possible. But at the same time far too many exceptions have then been made to these general rules, to prevent what the Inland Revenue sees as possible abuses. Still more dangerous than this anti-avoidance legislation are the law's omissions. We will see repeatedly in the paragraphs which follow, and throughout the remainder of this book, that there are transactions carefully exempted from some taxes (for example the transfer of assets freed from a capital gains liability for the transferor, and freed from a stamp duty liability for the transferee), but which are nevertheless thwarted by the legislation's defining them as *distributions* so as to produce an advance corporation tax liability for the transferor, and an income receipt for the transferee.

This cannot be a totally detailed and comprehensive survey. One way in which we will restrict its compass is to indicate the main areas in which the legislation appears to start off down the road of allowing companies in a group to ignore the corporate boundaries separating them from each other (and thus to treat themselves as if they were one larger entity); but then to cut off discussion where these routes are closed off by restrictions superimposed in other legislation. A second way in which we must restrict our length and breadth is to provide references to the statutory material, but not to make any promise that every detail in every provision will be dealt with in our text.[53]

---

continued
  given for the target's shares (any held prior to the final bid as well as those acquired in the course of it) there is an element which is not predator equity shares, that other element must not exceed 10 per cent of the *fair* value of the shares issued.
[52] Provided one is careful enough how one defines 'group', and one remembers stamp duty and value added tax as well as capital gains.
[53] One example of that self-denial can be seen in paragraph 6.44. We mention the main rules defining the capital gains tax group, and explain one of those rules in detail because it is vital for our purposes. But when we address readers' attention to section 170 TCGA 1992, we do not mention that another of the rules requires that only companies *resident* in the UK can be counted into a capital gains group. Similarly, we briefly mentioned the 1986 stamp duty reliefs for reconstructions and so on in paragraph 6.22, and will look in greater detail at section 76 FA 1986 in paragraph 6.34; that follows immediately after our look at the stamp duty relief originally dating from 1930 for transfers between associated companies (in

continued

6.32 VAT group registration – remember also the transfers of going concerns

Registering as a group enables all of the companies in what is chosen to comprise that group to treat their supplies of goods and services, made to others outside the group and received from such others, as having been made by or to the company in the group nominated as its *representative member*. Only it files a VAT return, and that return embodies the others' supplies as well as its own. Any goods or services moving from one group member to another are ignored for all purposes of VAT. The question whether the group is fully taxable or part exempt, and in the latter case the question how its input tax recovery is to be calculated, is determined by looking only at the representative member's figures, own and other.[54]

Customs and Excise are only prepared to allow grouping to commence from the start of a quarterly accounting period of the representative member; the legislation allows them 90 days to consider whether to grant such an application (although they generally take less time than this) and allows them to refuse group treatment where they consider this necessary to safeguard VAT collections.

Notice that the supply of goods and services by one company to another is outside the scope of VAT if supplier and recipient are members of a group. We saw in paragraph 3.31 and will re-examine in paragraphs 11.33 onwards a different way in which some supplies (of goods rather than services) can be taken outside the scope of VAT when they are made in the course of *a transfer of a business as a going concern*, such a transfer being possibly between companies which are associated without having claimed group treatment – but equally it could possibly be a transfer between unrelated parties.[55]

---

continued

paragraph 6.33). Once again, we have directed readers' attention to the legislation, but not specifically drawn their attention to the fact that the 1986 rules apply only to companies incorporated in the UK, whereas there was no geographical limit in 1930. To turn the text into a litany would make it less clear rather than more so.

[54] Section 29 VATA 1983; companies can be grouped if one controls the other, or both are controlled by a third, and for this purpose control is taken to mean being the other's holding company under section 736 CA 1985.

[55] Imagine two companies, one of which makes mainly exempt supplies with a few standard rated ones and the other of which makes entirely standard rated supplies. The first company is able to recover only a small proportion of its input VAT, because the great bulk of its inputs will be *attributed* to exempt outputs, and the VAT on such inputs will be irrecoverable. (That is the technical definition of part-exemption in regulations 29 and 30 in SI 1985/886, the VAT (General) Regulations 1985, which *inter alia* specify the procedure for a part-exempt trader recovering part of his input VAT.) If the two companies are then grouped, the proportions of standard rated outputs to exempt for the two companies taken together will be *better* than for the mainly exempt company looked at alone, so that more of *its* input VAT will be recovered, but correspondingly the other company will lose the ability to recover some proportion of *its* input VAT. Now consider the position if this VAT group wishes to commence a third business, all of the outputs of which will be standard rated. If the company in which that new business is started is

continued

Where transfers of goods or services are not taken out of the scope of tax in one of these ways, one would normally expect that VAT would have to be paid. It is essential to bear in mind both the possibilities, and limitations, of each of these routes throughout the discussions which follow of reconstructions, mergers and acquisitions.

6.33 Stamp duty relief on transfers between associated companies

The basic rule is that no duty is payable on the conveyance of a beneficial interest in any property from one company to another where one owns 90 per cent or more of the other, or a third owns that percentage of each.[56] But that rule is subject to the important qualification that there must be no arrangement under which the companies are to cease to be associated; *nor may the consideration for the transfer be derived from a third party, nor the beneficial interest have been previously transferred by such a third party.*

The necessity for the restriction in the first half of that last sentence is obvious. It is the second (italicised) half, carrying the implication that the transfer concerned is part of a larger series and that outside parties are involved, which calls for some explanation. In the *Escoigne Properties* case[57] Lord Denning gave a graphic description of the *dummy bridge company*. The company which wanted to sell a valuable property hived it down into a 100 per cent *bridge* subsidiary for a small amount of

---

continued

not within the group registration it will be able to recover in full the input tax on its initial investment into buildings, plant and stocks. Immediately thereafter it transfers the business as a going concern to a company within the group registration, which makes the recovery percentage of the group *better* in the same way as explained above – and although on future inputs in the new group company there will be less than a full recovery of input VAT, the initial recovery is already safe in the bank. Not surprisingly, Customs and Excise regarded this as a *loophole*, and closed it in 1987 by enacting section 29A VATA 1985; a part-exempt group can no longer use the mechanism of transferring what had until then been a fully taxable business into the group as a device by which that group can acquire assets in such a way as to produce a full input tax recovery.

[56] Section 42 FA 1930. Section 27(3) FA 1967 overrules (in the jargon, 'disapplies') this relief unless the conveyance is shown not to be connected with any of the arrangements spelled out in that latter section and indicated in the text. Note particularly that these provisions exempt the documents from duty, but that they must still be *stamped* (with what is always referred to as a stamp denoting). The procedure is that the documents are submitted to the Stamp Office Adjudication Section, with a statutory declaration sworn by the parent company's solicitor, or by a director or the secretary, evidencing the entitlement to relief from duty. No one should underestimate the labour involved in preparing such a declaration; for instance, in any group reconstruction involving the movement of assets or shareholdings for consideration left outstanding on open loan account between the transferors and transferees, the Stamp Office insists on details being given of the security and terms of repayment; if the transferee does repay the loan, but also contemporaneously borrows from external sources, the Stamp Office warns that this may infringe section 27(3)(a) FA 1967, and requires that all correspondence between the transferee and its external financier be submitted to the Stamp Office.

[57] *Escoigne Properties Ltd v IRC* [1958] AC 549.

share capital and a large amount of debt. It sold the share capital of the *bridge* subsidiary to the company which wanted the property, and paid a negligible amount of stamp duty on that sale. The purchaser company extracted the property from the *bridge* company, either paying cash which the *bridge* used to repay the original owner, or extracting it for an undertaking that it (the extractor) would pay off that original owner. Before the *bridge* was dynamited, the original owner's hive-down was an exempt transfer; so also was the purchaser's extraction. Anyone foolish enough to try the trick today would pay two lots of duty, because the hive-down and extraction are the two transactions specifically described in that second, italicised, half of the sentence we have been looking at.

Lord Denning is always well worth reading, but his opinion in this 1958 case might be described as prescient. He evinced considerable distaste for what he analysed (although not quite in those words) as a preordained series of transactions containing a step which had no business purpose other than the avoidance of tax. And he went on to quote 'the office of all of the judges is always to make such construction as shall suppress the mischief and advance the remedy'.[58]

6.34 Stamp duty reduction on a predator company's acquisition of the undertaking of a target – section 76 of the Finance Act 1986

The first thing to be stressed is that we are not dealing here with the case of a predator acquiring the shares of a target (from a body of shareholders not related to that predator); there is no stamp duty exemption or reduction on that transaction, a fact which we noted in paragraph 6.22.

The heading of this paragraph refers to a predator's acquisition of a target's undertaking (or part thereof – but we assume for simplicity in all our examples that the whole of the transferor's undertaking is moved, so that that company does itself become valueless in two of the four transactions). The consideration for this acquisition must be the issue by the predator of its own shares either to the shareholders of the target, or to the target itself, although it is permissible to include a cash element not exceeding 10 per cent of the nominal value[59] of the shares. It is also specifically provided that the predator's assumption of the target's liabilities to creditors neither is to be regarded as offending against these requirements about consideration, nor may it reduce the *gross* on which duty is charged (that is to say, the assumption of the liabilities cannot be *netted off* against the consideration for the assets).

---

[58] The quotation comes from *Heydons Case* (1584) 3 Co. Rep. 7a 7b, the date in that citation being some indication of the depth of Lord Denning's learning. But he did accept that he was not allowed, at that time, to discern from reading Hansard what was the perceived mischief or any limitations on the intended remedy.

[59] In Note 49 on paragraph 6.30 we pointed out that the restriction of the cash element to 10 per cent or less of the *nominal* value of the predator's shares had reached UK company law through the EC Seventh Directive on Company Law, and that it had no logical validity. Here we find it seeping into UK stamp duty law – once again an area *harmonised* by the EC, and once again lacking logic.

The legislation[60] provides that the applicable rate of duty is half of 1 per cent, rather than the 1 per cent which applies to most other *conveyances or transfers on sale*.

What we are focusing on in this paragraph is a stamp duty reduction, available for certain mergers and reconstructions. When thinking in merger terms we have been using the words predator and target; if we recognise that we also need to think about reconstructions, it would be easier to use the reconstruction terminology of a recipient company and a transferor. But in either case the stamp duty reduction is only available if what is transferred is *the whole or part of an undertaking*. If one were to say the transferor's 'business'[61] one would convey part of the sense of the word – it could be a trade, but does not need to be because the ownership of investments, or of real property, with a view to deriving income from them is also a business. A company which does no more than hold shares in its own subsidiaries has an undertaking, and the transfer of one of those subsidiaries would be a transfer of a part of that undertaking.[62]

6.35 *Further analysis of section 76 of the Finance Act 1986*

But the most graphic picture of a company and its *undertaking* is to liken the first to a hen and the second to everything she shelters under her wings, whether that be eggs (her own trade or trades), or newly hatched chickens (subsidiaries). The point we must always have clearly in view is that there is a difference between acquiring ownership of the hen (shares in the target) who brings with her indirect ownership of everything she continues to shelter, and acquiring from her the direct ownership of her undertaking – the latter course leaves her to squawk away on her own.

In the light of that it is clear that the acquisitions of undertakings in section 76 fall into four categories. In the first two, we assume that the recipient is an already existing company with shareholders and an undertaking of its own before the transaction; in the last two that the recipient is a newly formed company into which the transferor's undertaking is to be shifted (perhaps because there is some

---

[60] Section 76 FA 1986.
[61] Undertaking is equated to business in *Baytrust Holdings Ltd v CIR* [1971] 3 All ER 76; however the judgment in that case makes it clear that equating undertaking to *assets* is not a safe procedure, not only because a company can own assets which are not connected with its business but because it is self-evident that a transfer of an asset is not necessarily the same as a transfer of part of an undertaking. 'No doubt the business of a greengrocer is to sell fruit, but the pound of apples you buy from him can hardly be described as a transfer of a part of the greengrocer's undertaking.'
[62] The Stamp Office take the view that the recipient must not only receive an undertaking, and carry it on, but it must be the same as an undertaking the transferor was carrying on. If the transferor owned a factory building which it let to a fellow subsidiary (which occupied and used it), that let building would be a part of the transferor's undertaking. But if the transferor had not only owned but occupied the factory until the transfer, and thereafter it continued in occupation paying a rent to the recipient, that recipient's *undertaking* would not be the same as any that the transferor had previously carried on.

legal questionmark over the transferor's own suitability to continue as the vehicle through which its shareholders carry on their business; we give an example in paragraph 6.64):

(1) a merger in which the recipient comes to own both undertakings, and is itself owned partly by its own former shareholders, and partly by the transferor company (the latter still being owned by its former shareholders);

(2) a merger in which the recipient owns both undertakings, and is itself owned directly by all the former owners of both companies (the transferor, and its shares, having lost all value);

(3) a hive-down in which the recipient becomes a wholly owned subsidiary of the transferor, a subsidiary into which the transferor has hived down its trade and assets;

(4) a reconstruction in which the recipient is a new corporate shell which comes to own the transferor's undertaking, and to be owned by its former shareholders (as in (2) the transferor is valueless).

6.36 Other taxes – implications for other taxes of transactions within section 76

That tabulation makes it obvious that in the third case stamp duty could be completely avoided if the recipient were a subsidiary before, rather than as a result of, the transaction. However we will assume that these four possibilities are each equally realistic in the form described,[63] and will move on to taxes other than stamp duty, leaving our tabulation of the four transactions hanging on the wall as the background framework against which we can examine and discuss the implications of these and other similar movements for those other taxes.

We will thus examine, in due course, the protections available to the transferor which has, in all four cases, made a capital gains tax disposal of its undertaking. We will also examine the capital gains tax protections available to the transferor's shareholders who, in the second and fourth cases, have (technically) disposed of the transferor's shares and acquired in their place those of the recipient.

And there are problems arising from the fact that the transferor company has in all four cases *distributed* its undertaking – not admittedly

---

[63] In each of Items (2) and (4) the transferor can be seen to be giving away the whole of its assets – it receives nothing itself by way of consideration for the transfer of its undertaking, (although its *shareholders* receive shares in the recipient company). When we come to analyse what transactions are within the powers of a company, and within the authority of its directors, we will see that it is highly unlikely that a company could give all its assets away – unless the transaction were sanctioned by the court as part of a 'scheme of reconstruction' under (for instance) section 425 CA 1985. See chapter 9, in particular paragraphs 9.13 and onward. However for the purposes of the analyses in this chapter we will assume that these transactions are possible; we will assume that stamp duty and tax law have not been written to define the tax effects of unlawful transactions.

to its shareholders, but in a way which they have dictated or sanctioned, and which therefore has potential advance corporation tax implications for the transferor, and can also reflect through into the quality of the recipient's *receipt*. We need to spend time, and to think hard, about distributions. The slight digression in the next two paragraphs onto connected parties will lead us straight back into those distributions.

But there is a much wider implication of our taking our examination of mergers and reconstructions out of the stamp duty arena into those of capital gains and distributions. We need not, and indeed should not, continue to think of the subject matter of the transfers being limited solely to undertakings. Any asset can be distributed, and unless the consideration received by the distributor comes into a calculation of his *income*, the disposal of any asset is within capital gains tax. Among the assets whose distribution and/or disposal we must particularly consider are shareholdings not just in subsidiaries but in associated companies and portfolio investments.

6.37 Connected parties

This chapter is principally about groups. What we are now discussing sometimes involves companies in a parent/subsidiary relationship, but sometimes does not – the transactions we started looking at in the last two paragraphs involved bodies of shareholders entering into contracts with the companies whose shares they own, and procuring that those companies should make disposals and acquisitions. Before travelling too far down that road, we need to understand the extent to which the terms of any such arrangements may be reviewed, or different consideration figures substituted, for tax purposes.

It is logical to start with capital gains tax. For purposes of this tax (except where this provision is specifically overridden by some other)[64] transactions between *connected* parties are treated as being bargains otherwise than at arm's length,[65] and accordingly the price put on the transaction by the parties can be disregarded, and an open market price substituted.[66]

---

[64] It is overridden, for instance, by the requirement in section 171(1) TCGA 1992 that where an asset is disposed of by one company in a capital gains tax group, and acquired by another, it is to be deemed to move at such a figure that the disponor makes no gain and no loss.

Each company in a capital gains tax group will be connected with each other, as will become clear as we proceed. The opening words of section 17(1) TCGA 1992 which would otherwise require the substitution of an open market value are 'subject to the provisions of this act'. The intra-group transfer provision, as indicated, operates without any restriction or qualification on its applicability, and therefore overrides the market value provision.

[65] Section 18(2) TCGA 1992 contains the primary direction that the transaction is to be treated as otherwise than at arm's length. It applies where there is an asset acquired by one person and the person making the disposal is connected with him.

[66] There are two points. The first relates to the meaning of the phrase 'market value'; is it ever possible for connected parties to claim that the price they have negotiated

continued

Two companies are connected if they are under common control, and a company is connected with an individual (or group of individuals who themselves are connected) if he or they control it.[67] The definition of the word 'control' is that originally drafted into the close company legislation;[68] it includes cases where a person or group of persons:

- exercise, are able to exercise, or are entitled to acquire direct or indirect control over the company's affairs;

- without prejudice to the foregoing, if he or they hold or are entitled to acquire the greater part of the company's share capital, or voting power, or share capital which would entitle him or them to the greater part of the company's income if it were distributed, or rights which would give them the greater part of the company's assets on a winding up.

---

continued

must be left undisturbed because it was actually negotiated at arm's length? This is not a question that has ever come before the courts, but the commonly held view is that the courts would have a considerable degree of discretion what attitude to take on any particular facts that did come before them; therefore if the parties did genuinely negotiate, and if they were properly and separately advised (as necessary) the courts would not be inclined to displace a value they had agreed. Support for those principles is said to be visible in the judge's approach in *Clark v Follett* [1973] 48 TC 677.

The second point is a matter of technical interpretation. It is section 17(1) TCGA 1992 that requires the substitution of market value where the parties are shown not to have been at arm's length. Section 18(2) would tell us that the parties were not at arm's length (and thus lead directly to the substitution referred to) – if section 18(2) applied; the problem is that no part of section 18 seems to apply in those cases where capital gains rules decree that there is an acquisition but it is not matched by any corresponding disposal. When one company issues shares to another, the second makes an acquisition (except in the special case explained in the last few words of paragraph 6.55 and Note 102); the issuing company does not however *dispose* of the shares it issues. It is however the general view that this requirement to substitute a market value operates wherever the parties are connected – that is to say, the connected party legislation outlined in Note 67 leads directly into section 17, without the necessity to use section 18(1) and (2) as links in the chain. This is because of the opening words of section 18(2), 'without prejudice to the generality of s.17(1)'.

[67] Section 286(5) and (6) TCGA 1992. These are complex subsections, which justify being set out verbatim, in case the summary in the text might mislead:

'(5) A company is connected with another company
(a) if the same person has control of both, or if a person has control of one and persons connected with him, or he and persons connected with him, have control of the other, or
(b) if a group of two or more persons has control of each company, and the groups either consist of the same persons or could be regarded as consisting of the same persons by treating (in one or more cases) a member of either group as replaced by a person with whom he is connected.
(6) A company is connected with another person
if that person has control of it, or
if that person and persons connected with him together have control of it.'

[68] Section 416 TA 1988.

6.38 Connected parties' definitions – some illustrations

It can be seen that ICI is not connected with the body of people who own its shares (because those shareholders are not themselves connected with each other in sufficient numbers for one to be able to find a connected body of shareholders who control ICI). But ICI is connected with each and every one of its own subsidiaries, and they are all connected with each other (because the body of ICI's shareholders control ICI directly, and every subsidiary indirectly, there being no need for the shareholders themselves to be connected for this purpose). Additionally, ICI and Zeneca are connected, because there is, and undoubtedly will be for a considerable future period, a sufficient commonality of shareholders for it to be straightforward to find a common control consisting of a few hundred thousand individuals and institutions who remain on both companies' registers, and are entitled to over half of those companies' votes, income and assets.

That substitution of market value in place of any other transaction value is the general rule in the *capital gains* legislation; but there is a quite different area in relation to *distributions* in which these same principles of common control create difficulties. This is the appropriate point at which to explain.

6.39 Distributions – some of the concepts

This explanation starts by looking from a different angle at the merger-by-acquisition-of-undertaking, the transaction in which the company we are now calling the transferor is to transfer its business and assets to a recipient company under a tripartite agreement. The shareholders of transferor agree to procure that transferor makes that transfer, and recipient agrees to issue new shares to those who are at present the shareholders of transferor. That is the merger transaction we originally looked at in paragraph 6.34, and when we tabulated other possible forms in paragraph 6.35, it became item (2).

Transferor's transfer of its assets to recipient, because it is procured by transferor's shareholders, fits into the phrase:

> Any other distribution out of the assets of (transferor) ... in respect of shares in (transferor) ...[69]

These words are one of the primary definitions of a distribution. The resulting advance corporation tax liability for transferor would normally be so onerous as to be a complete bar preventing many asset transfers, and particularly mergers of this kind. Accordingly, a relieving provision was introduced, reading as follows:

---

[69] That definition of a distribution is in section 209(2)(b) TA 1988, and the relieving provision in subsection (6) of that same section. Note that the latter has been quoted in an extremely abbreviated form, and that there are a number of further requirements, not relevant to this particular illustration, which need to be watched.

No transfer of assets ... between one company and another shall constitute ... a distribution by virtue of subsection 2(b) ... above if they are companies ... which ... neither at the time of the transfer, nor as a result of it, are under common control ... .[70]

There are other provisions which extend the meaning of the word distribution, and there are further relieving provisions which then exempt certain of the transactions which would otherwise have been caught. We will come back to this subject in paragraphs 6.50 to 6.53 below; and in paragraph 6.63 we will see that there are some reorganisations which inevitably include distributions not fitting into any of the reliefs. In those cases, the only available course if advance corporation tax is to be avoided, is to liquidate the distributing company. A distribution in liquidation is outside the scope of ACT.[71]

6.40 *Common control of distributor and recipient of distribution*

What we had started looking at in the previous paragraph was an enlarged (merged) recipient becoming owned by an enlarged body of shareholders comprising its own original shareholders and the body of people who continue additionally to be shareholders of transferor.[72] What we have to ask is whether the second category, the *new* holders of recipient's shares, who are also the holders of transferor's shares, are in control – or whether control still rests with the first category, recipient's original holders? If the answer is that it is the new shareholders who have come into recipient who are in control of that company, then we are again looking at transferor's asset transfer as a distribution. Transferor has made a transfer out of its assets (by transferring them all, its undertaking) to recipient, and resulting from the transfer (in particular from the consideration given by recipient to transferor's shareholders), the shareholders of transferor have come to control recipient as well as transferor. If, on the other hand, the answer is that it is the original shareholders of recipient who still control it despite their dilution by an influx of new shareholders, then there is no advance corporation tax cost in the merger.

---

[70] Section 209(6) TA 1988. The 'control' referred to here is identical to the connected parties' control that we were looking at in paragraph 6.37 except that it is to be found in the Income and Corporation Taxes legislation rather than the Taxation of Chargeable Gains legislation. Common control in the former is derived through section 839 TA 1988 in terms which are identical to the relevant parts of section 286 TCGA 1992, and both sections are tied back to the same section 416 TA 1988 (close company, definition of what constitutes control of a company).

[71] Section 209(1) TA 1988. We will look at this matter of distributions in liquidation in paragraph 11.18 and Note 33.

[72] After the transferor has made the transfer of its undertaking it, as a company, is valueless and so obviously are the shares in it still held by its shareholders. But they do still own those shares, and by virtue of them they still control a company which continues to exist – and which has made a distribution. One cannot pretend that the transferor has vanished into thin air as a consequence of the asset transfer.

Some years ago a proposed merger of Carliol Investment Trust and Tyneside Investment Trust was aborted at the last moment *for tax reasons*. It was popularly suspected at the time that those reasons were the final words in the above quotation from the supposed relieving provision. The two trusts had a substantial number of shareholders in common; and the provisions of section 416 of the Income and Corporation Taxes Act 1988, defining control, are so intractable that the two companies were unable to demonstrate that a merged vehicle would not have been under common control with the transferor company. It seemed to the author then, and still seems, an irrational reason for preventing the merger, for which there were good commercial reasons.

6.41 *Common control of distributor and recipient (continued)*

The fourth of the types of transaction we envisaged in paragraph 6.35 was a reconstruction in which the recipient was a new shell company, which received the transferor's undertaking and issued its own shares to those who had been the shareholders of the transferor. That asset transfer is a distribution by transferor, and since distributor and recipient are under common control as a result of the transaction which includes recipient's issue of its shares to transferor's shareholders. The *saving* provision cannot help, and the best available course seems to be the liquidation of the old company, as indicated at the end of paragraph 6.39 and further discussed below in paragraph 6.63.

6.42 **The capital gains tax group**

There are three ways in which the capital gains tax grouping rules are of assistance:

- assets, including shareholdings, and trades, can be moved from company to company in such a group without tax effect;[73]

- a gain made by one company in a group can be *rolled over* against the cost of what is somewhat misleadingly referred to as a replacement asset acquired by any other group member;[74]

---

[73] Section 171(1) TCGA 1992.

[74] Section 175(1) TCGA 1992 stipulates that for *replacement of business assets by members of a group* all the trades carried on by members of the group are to be treated as a single trade. Although deeming this to be so, goes some way towards entitling a second member reinvesting in an asset to roll over the gain made by a different member on disposal of another asset, it does not strictly go far enough. This was the High Court's conclusion in *Campbell Connelly & Co. Ltd v Barnett*, [1992] BTC 164. Knox J. said that the Revenue's *interpretation* in Statement of Practice 8/81, could not seriously be argued to be the meaning of the statutory phraseology, which was not appropriate to entitle the reinvesting company to roll-over relief.

Following that decision the Financial Secretary to the Treasury announced on 15 September 1992 that the Revenue's interpretation seemed sensible to him, and that

continued

- although not strictly part of *grouping* we have seen that there are cases in which an individual disposing of assets to a company for the issue by it of its shares can *roll* his gain into the cost of the shares he receives;[75]

- there are broadly parallel possibilities for companies disposing of assets to subsidiaries for the latters' shares, but these are even more diverse.[76]

But, in addition to the complexities and inflexibilities inherent in the legislation just referred to, there are other ways in which the rules are unhelpful (actively or passively), either because the Inland Revenue has never been persuaded that any change is necessary, or because it is considered necessary that taxpayers should be denied the opportunities that such changes would provide:

- a capital loss made by one company in a group cannot be made use of (surrendered to) another company which has made a capital gain. It is necessary for assets to be passed around the group in such a way that the company finally selling them, making a loss on one and a gain on the other, is the same company – able to set off its own loss against its own gain[76a];

- and in 1993 the Revenue prevented companies using, after joining a group, losses they had sustained before joining.[77]

---

continued

if the High Court's decision were upheld on appeal then *steps would be taken to ensure that the Revenue's practice was continued*, (that is to say the law would be altered so as to line up with the Revenue's interpretation). The Court of Appeal has at the time of writing affirmed Knox J.'s decision in resounding terms, [1994] BTC 12, although this particular facet of his reasoning was not mentioned by the Court of Appeal as necessary to the decision it reached. Presumably the law will be altered in due course, and it must be hoped that the alteration will be made effective from 15 September 1992 if not earlier.

[75] Incorporation under the provisions of section 162 TCGA 1992, see paragraph 3.29.

[76] These arrangements can be available in various sets of circumstances, some of them being referred to in the final heading in paragraph 5.38 above. The way in which various of the arrangements operate can be quite different. In some cases, a sale of the shares will trigger the gain which had been postponed on the original transfer of the asset. In others, it is the sale by the recipient company of the asset which triggers the gain; that second possiblility could give rise to an indefinite postponement of the tax liability, and extremely complex legislation has been brought in, designed to prevent this result in those cases in which the Inland Revenue had not intended to allow such postponement.

[76a] See paragraphs 11.4 onwards for commentary on the 'group assets company'.

[77] Section 177A, and schedule 7A to TCGA 1992. The explanation given here of the ban on use of *pre-entry losses* is over-simplified to the point of being misleading. For instance, a proportion of a loss realised *after* a company joins a group is also to be disallowed, if it enters the group owning an asset already pregnant with loss.

6.43 Group transfer price is retrospectively replaced by an open market price (on a deemed sale and repurchase by transferee) if that transferee ceases within six years to be a member of transferor's group

One aspect of the 'complexities and inflexibilities' referred to in the middle of the last paragraph is that relief earlier given for the transfer of an asset between what were at the time group companies, can be withdrawn if the recipient company leaves the group within six years after having received the asset.[78] The asset concerned is treated as sold and repurchased by the recipient company immediately after that company received it in the intra-group transfer. We will see, when we work through illustrations of mergers acquisitions and disposals in paragraphs 11.4, 11.11 and 12.23 some of the practical problems. At this stage there are three points that need to be made:

- whenever a company leaves a group it is necessary to consider whether any assets have been transferred into it in the previous six years — and this does not mean merely whether there have been any such transfers made in contemplation of the company's departure;

- if a gain is triggered it will be *timed* at the transfer date, not the date of the company's leaving the group. This may be in an earlier year, making its elimination by the realisation of a loss on some other asset impossible;

- thirdly, proceeds of disposal are deemed rather than actual. The legislation permitting a gain to be *rolled over* against reinvestment in a *replacement* asset in another group company proceeds on the fiction that *proceeds* must be reinvested. The Inland Revenue interpret this fiction to mean that, since deemed proceeds cannot be reinvested, there is no possibility of rolling over, and thus deferring, the gain.

6.44 Definition of the capital gains tax group

However what the section 178/179 provisions do necessitate is a clear definition of a group, so that one can determine whether a company has or has not *left* it. That definition is in section 170 of the Taxation of Chargeable Gains Act 1992, and its general shape is well known; at each tier of the group below its *principal company*, ownership is required of 75 per cent or more of any company in the immediately lower tier, but in addition the principal company must be entitled to more than 50 per cent of the profits, and assets for distribution in a liquidation, of every company in its group. (If there were to be a group in which each tier was owned exactly 75 per cent by a company in the tier above, only

---

[78] Sections 178 and 179 TCGA 1992 (often still referred to as section 278, which was its number in the Income and Corporation Taxes Act 1970). The second of the TCGA sections is different from the first only in being designed to operate in the pay and file environment.

the first three tiers would be in a capital gains tax group, since the fourth tier would be only 42.2 percent *owned*.)

The rules are more complex and extensive than that, and reference must be made to the Act (and to the standard books). But one principle does need spelling out. A company can at any time only be a member of one group, and that group is defined by reference to its ultimate parent. If B owns C, the group is the B Group, and its members are B and C. If A then acquires B, the group becomes the A Group, its members are A, B and C, but there is a rule[79] that says that (although the B Group ceases to exist and can have no continuing members) neither of B nor C needs to be treated as having *left the B Group* on its enlargement and metamorphosis into the A Group. However, if A then sells B, both B and C leave the A Group, and so also does A, since it is not possible for A in its solitary state to continue being regarded as a group.[80] If in the alternative A and B remain together, and B sells C, then it is only C that leaves the A Group, and that group continues in existence with a population of A and B.

General principles are, however, not enough. It is the 'complexities and inflexibilities' earlier referred to that we have to accept as central to our dealings with capital gains in groups of companies. We must therefore work our way through the circumstances which give rise to the various problems, and the ways in which these can be handled. (In our discussions of all of this we can leave indexation out of account.)

6.45 *The asset pregnant with gain; value, and transfer price*

If we envisage an asset whose original cost was £20, and which has a market price today of £100, it is easy to see that a company whose corporation tax rate is 25 per cent would end up with £80 of cash if it were to sell the asset and pay the resulting tax. However, although the net disposal proceeds of the asset may only be £80, no one could possibly argue that its *value* was anything other than £100. If the asset could be transferred on a tax-free basis into the envelope of a company, and its present owner could then sell not the asset but the company's shares, his gain would depend on what was treated as his acquisition value for those shares. We look at two possibilities in this paragraph[81], and a third in paragraphs 6.46 and 6.47:

---

[79] Section 170(10) TCGA 1992.
[80] Needless to say, a rule such as this invites taxpayers to take avoiding action. If, before selling B (with C underneath it), A were to buy another subsidiary D off the shelf, then there would still be an A group (A and D) surviving the departure of B; accordingly A would not have left the A group.
[81] It is obviously necessary that we identify in what companies, and by reference to what transactions and deemed transactions the capital gains liabilities arise – and that we see why there is a double charge in the first example, as compared to an apparently unrelieved loss in the second.

However, it is even more important that we have very clearly in mind at all times where the real values lie, and the real profits are being made. For instance, if we

continued

- a subsidiary or fellow subsidiary is formed with capital subscribed in cash of £20, and uses that cash to buy the asset, (a transaction which does not give the asset's original owner an accounting profit or a capital gain). The sale of what we might refer to as the *bridge* company's shares produces both a profit and a capital gain. However the bridge company itself acquired its asset for £20, (in actuality and under the rules for capital gains groups), and is for capital gains tax purposes deemed under the rule in paragraph 6.43 to have sold it for £100, thus incurring a liability for capital gains tax of £20. The purchaser of that bridge company would therefore be unlikely to pay more than £80 to buy it, and the amount of the accounting profit and capital gain arising in the transferor would seem to be £60;

- the subsidiary or fellow subsidiary is capitalised with £100 in cash. Its purchase of the asset for this figure gives the asset's transferor an accounting profit, but not a capital gain because the £100 disposal price in that transferor's hands and the £100 acquisition price in the *bridge* company are both replaced by a deemed £20 price for capital gains tax purposes.[82] However, unless we find any rule saying that the subscriber of £100 cash for the company's shares is to be treated as having acquired them for £20 rather than £100, (and when we do come to look we will discover that there is no such rule), then the sale of those shares for that same £100 would not give its shareholder a capital gain. However, the rule in paragraph 6.43 once again creates a liability in the subsidiary at the time it is sold;[83] this in turn again means that a purchaser of that subsidiary is unlikely to pay more than £80 for it, and that therefore the owner of the shares in that subsidiary is likely to sustain a capital *loss* of £20 on his sale of those shares.

6.46 Movement of the asset for shares – capital gains effects

The third possibility is based on moving the asset into a recipient company which issues shares as consideration to the transferor. This transaction naturally takes the form explained in this paragraph, but it

---

continued

assumed that the company which originally owned the asset was insolvent in the first example, then it would be *ultra vires* for its directors to sell the asset to any company other than a wholly owned subsidiary for a price less than its full market value, because this would allow the realisation of the difference in a company which the transferor's creditors would have greater difficult in pursuing. The transaction could not be made valid by ratification by the shareholders of the transferor company, or even of the group, under the rule in *Aveling Barford v Perion and others*, [1989] BCLC 626. This case is a salutary warning to those who may fail to consider with sufficient care the interests of creditors of each separate company concerned, when working out how some restructuring can be handled, planning for instance that a profit should arise in one company rather than another. We will examine further implications of *Aveling Barford* in paragraph 9.13 below.

[82] Section 171(1) TCGA 1992.

[83] The company being sold, not the vendor of its shares, is by virtue of that sale deemed to have sold and immediately repurchased the asset at the date of the company's departure from the transferor's group, sections 178/179 TCGA 1992.

is possible to develop and expand it into another two forms that we will look at in paragraphs 6.53 and 6.55 below.

In the natural, straightforward, transaction the asset is passed down by the transferor to a recipient company already formed as that transferor's subsidiary, which issues further shares as consideration for the asset. This transaction fits into the Companies Act relief from the need for a share premium (being a group reconstruction as described in paragraphs 6.17 to 6.19 above). The normal accounting procedure would be to pass the asset down at cost, or at the nominal value of the shares issued if that were higher. However, if the asset were to be accounted for at some higher figure, the reserve created in the transferor company would not be a share premium account. This transaction would have been one within paragraph 6.35, at item (3), if we had still been looking only at transfers of *undertakings*; we have since said that we wanted to widen our horizons to bring in those assets which are neither *undertakings* in their own right, nor parts of an undertaking. However, *we now need to exclude shareholdings*. We know from the discussion in paragraphs 6.34 and 6.35 that a shareholding in a subsidiary is likely to be a part of its parent's undertaking – the reason for excluding it from discussion here is simply that there are different rules for shareholdings moved into a company for the issue of its shares, and we will look at those rules in paragraphs 6.55 and 6.56.

For capital gains tax purposes this asset-other-than-shares is treated as being disposed of by the transferor, and acquired by the recipient, at its original cost of £20. The rule requiring original cost for intra-group transfers overrides the rule that would have required an open market value for transactions between connected parties.[84]

6.47 *The issue of shares – meaning of the phrase in this context*

The recipient company issues shares as consideration. We left two points unclear at earlier stages which we must now try to clarify; we described the word 'issues' in paragraph 3.16 as a non-technical usage, but noted in Note 9 that although the courts had given the word different meanings in different contexts, there was a recent case which gave strong guidance. Then, in paragraph 6.36 we said that the logical way of avoiding stamp duty on the transfer of an asset in circumstances like this was to ensure that the recipient was already a 90 per cent (or more) subsidiary of the transferor.

We are therefore assuming here that the recipient has already been incorporated, and that there are already two subscribers' shares, one held by the transferor and one by its nominee.[85] Under the Companies

---

[84] See Note 64 on paragraph 6.37.
[85] The relief from stamp duty we are relying on is section 42 FA 1930, the intra-group transfer of assets provision. (It seems obvious that this must be the most straightforward course – to transfer the asset to a company which is already a subsidiary; it is inconceivable that tax legislation would necessitate or encourage a

continued

Act 1985, section 2(5)(c), each subscriber has *taken* a share without any allotment by the directors, and without the latter having any mechanism for calling up amounts unpaid on those shares. But on the company's registration the subscribers must be entered in the company's register of members (section 22(1)), and it is clear that any sum then remaining to be paid on their shares is a debt due to the company (section 14(2)).

The transaction now contemplated comprises the recipient's directors allotting a further 18 shares to the transferor, and declaring that the non-cash consideration received from the transferor is to be treated as both making those 18 shares fully paid, and as meeting the outstanding debt on the two subscribers' shares.

If, against those facts, we reconsider the phrase 'issues shares', we can deduce that it is used in tax legislation to indicate something going beyond the process of alloting shares. An allotment tends to be conditional, the most usual condition being that of acceptance by the allotee.[86] We are thus steered towards the conclusion arrived at in the *National Westminster Bank* case[87] that for an *issue* nothing short of the shareholders' being entered in the share register will suffice – allotment and allotment letters (renounceable or otherwise) are insufficient, as is the existence of a binding contract entitling the shareholder to demand to be entered on the register, and requiring him to pay for the shares.

6.48 *Capital gains tax implications of the issue of shares*

In the example we are considering, we have undoubtedly seen an issue of shares, and it is the recipient company which was the issuer. Its issue does not constitute a disposal by it for capital gains tax purposes, and we therefore we have no call to identify any disposal proceeds received for a disposal.

What we do need to look for is a capital gains tax acquisition cost of the 20 shares in the transferor's hands. Here we are back into the open market rules explained in paragraph 6.37; transferor and recipient are connected parties.

The asset whose open market value we seek is *the company which issued the shares* concerned. One does not try to arrive at a value for

---

continued

    transfer into a company at the time owned by some other party – with a subsequent need to buy in those shares.)

    However, we do know that there are stamp duty exemptions or reductions in sections 75, 76 or 77 FA 1986; the last of those sections deals with the acquisition of the target's shares, and the first two with the acquisition of its *undertaking*, so that none of them are relevant in the example we are now considering. We mention them only to remind ourselves that to fit into the requirements in each of sections 75 and 77, that the only consideration for the transfer must be the issue of shares, and that the total shareholding after the issue must be proportionate to that of the former company, it is necessary to use a rather different strategy for the company formation and share issue. See paragraph 6.22, and particularly Note 35 thereon.

[86] Section 288(5) TCGA 1992 bears this out; what it says is 'shares ... comprised in any letter of allotment ... shall be treated as issued unless the right to the shares ... remains provisional until accepted and there has been no acceptance'.

[87] See paragraph 3.16, and in particular Note 9 thereon.

the shares, as distinct from the company, which might take into account some different marketplace in which buyers and sellers might be dealing in shares rather than companies. That is clear from *Zevo Finance*;[88] the last few lines of the quotation in paragraph 3.23 confirm that it is the underlying value of the company, not the particular sentiment that the market might have for its shares, that fixes their acquisition cost to the transferor. That conclusion is also borne out by the more recent *Stanton v Drayton* case.[89]

But there is a different question. Does one say that the company is *worth* £100, which is the value of its asset or should one deduct from that its contingent liability for £20 of capital gains, and say that the company's value is £80? The liability is contingent, in that it would only crystallise if the company were sold by the transferor within six years, or if the company sold the asset. And since it is a contingent liability it is by definition one which can only crystallise at an indeterminate future time; there must be a question whether some discounting is called for to recognise the timing element. All these questions are clearly metaphysical – the Inland Revenue's practice is to accept that the shares issued by the recipient can be taken as having an acquisition cost in the transferor's hands equal to the value of the asset it transfers in the opposite direction.

But that may not be the real problem. There is a much more fundamental question which we need to look at in the next paragraph.

6.49 *The acquisition cost of the tranches of shares issued*

The recipient's shares were *issued*, using that word in the sense we have identified, in two tranches. Two subscriber's shares were issued for £2 left outstanding. The further 18 shares were issued for non-cash consideration. For the shareholders' capital gains tax acquisition, the vital point seems to be to identify precisely what that consideration was, because there are two possibilities:

- if the asset transfer agreement simply says that the consideration is the recipient's issue of 20 shares, that would seem to imply that an undivided 9/10ths interest in the asset was the consideration for the further 18 shares, but that a 1/10th undivided interest was consideration given to obtain the recipient's agreement that the debt outstanding on the two subscriber shares had been fully discharged. The first part of that rationalisation clearly gives the transferor a *cost* of £90 (9/10ths of the asset value) for the 18 shares. But the second part leaves the *cost* of the subscribers' shares at £2; the reasoning is as follows. An undivided 1/10th interest in the asset is worth £10, but if only £2 of that is passed to the company *commercially* then

---

[88] *Craddock (HM Inspector of Taxes) v Zevo Finance Co. Ltd.* See paragraph 3.22 and Note 26.
[89] *Stanton (HM Inspector of Taxes) v Drayton Commercial Investment Co. Ltd.* See paragraph 3.25 and Note 29.

the remaining £8 must have been simply *given* to the company; that £8 cannot be attributed to the shares' cost.[90]

- what it seems the asset transfer agreement should recognise is that the subscribers' shares have already been *issued*, and consideration has been given for them in the sense that the transferor has, and has acknowledged, a debt due to the recipient. Although that debt needs to be satisfied, no part of the asset transfer can be properly described as *consideration* for a transaction which is already history. The asset's transfer (except to the extent of £2[91] which is not not consideration for the subscribers' shares, but is the satisfaction of the debt owed for them) is consideration for the second issue, the issue of 18 shares.

On the second assumption, the transferor has, first, a holding of two shares costing £2; then a subsequent acquisition of 18 shares *costing* £98; and the two holdings merge, under section 104(1) of the Taxation of Chargeable Gains Act 1992, into a single holding of 20 shares with an overall cost of £100.

Distributions

6.50 *Why the transfer of the asset to the subsidiary, either for cash earlier put into that subsidiary, or for the issue of the subsidiary's shares, is not a distribution*

Paragraphs 6.45 to 6.49 have been focusing on the capital gains tax position, in the case of the first of those paragraphs on the sale of the asset from parent to subsidiary, and in the later two on its being passed down to the subsidiary for shares. In none of these instances is

---

[90] When we looked at a gift to a company, in paragraph 3.44, we said 'his gift does not alter the number of shares he owns, nor their rights, only the value of the company which is the subject matter of those rights'. See also Note 58 on that paragraph, in which we quoted the Inland Revenue's views on capital contributions (a specific form of gift to a company) that 'it is difficult to see how they could be treated as money expended on shares. The contributions do not affect the rights attaching to the shares and – although there may be an indirect effect – are not, therefore, directly reflected in their value'. This phraseology directly echoes section 38(1)(b) TCGA 1992, which allows the deduction for capital gains of 'enhancement expenditure' (as opposed to acquisition costs deductible under the previous subsection). Enhancement is defined as 'expenditure ... incurred on the asset ... for the purpose of enhancing the value of the asset' but it is also necessary to show that 'the expenditure (is) reflected in the state or nature of the asset at the time of its disposal'. The two subscribers' shares have not been enhanced from nil paid to fully paid – they were acquired on the footing that they would be fully paid as soon as they came into existence on the incorporation of the company. There is nothing in the state or nature of these shares themselves that shows that they have been enhanced by a further £8 on the transfer of the asset.

[91] The whole of this paragraph is written on the basis that the subscribers' shares were subscribed at par. It is of course possible for such shares to be subscribed at a premium; the provisions of section 106 CA 1985 are indicative of this, although they deal only with public companies. Notice however that it would be the company's memorandum which needed to spell out the terms of issue of the subscribers' shares.

a distribution in point, but we do need to understand why. When we first gave a definition of a distribution, we failed to quote to the end of the relevant subsection:

> Subject to subsections (5) and (6) below, any other distribution out of the assets of the company (whether in cash or otherwise) in respect of shares in the company, except so much of the distribution, if any, as represents repayment of capital on the shares or is, when it is made, equal in amount or value to any new consideration received by the company for the distribution.[92]

The second of our transferor's sales generated proceeds of £100, and the transfer of the asset for shares generated a receipt of shares newly issued and valued at £100, so those seem to be taken out by the last line and a half of the subsection. But what about the first of the sales which involved the transferor shedding an asset worth £100 for a price of £20? The true answer is as follows (this true answer differs from one that is often put forward, but about which the author has considerable misgivings; we will look at this matter and those misgivings in some detail in the next two paragraphs).

If one analyses the true meaning of the words 'in respect of shares in the company' they can only mean either that the holders of those shares are themselves receiving a distribution, or that they have been able to direct the payment of such a distribution to some other party. Here we have a situation in which the shareholders of the transferor company hold shares in it before the transaction which reflect its ownership of the asset; after the transaction they still own exactly the same shares which now reflect the company's indirect ownership of the asset. There simply has not been anything *distributed*, using that word either in its ordinary English meaning or as a term of art, in respect of those shares. That, and not the full value consideration, is the real reason why neither a sale of the asset for £20 cash, nor for £100 cash, nor for the issue of £100-worth of shares, is a 'distribution ... in respect of' the shares owned by the transferor's shareholders.

6.51 *A different definition of distribution, and the different route by which it can be avoided – why none of this is relevant to the transactions in paragraphs 6.45 to 6.49*

The answer mentioned in the previous paragraph as one about which the author has misgivings is as follows. There is a degree of truth in it, but it becomes a dubious answer when distorted in an attempt to fit it onto the question in that previous paragraph.

There is a second provision in section 209 of the Income and Corporation Taxes Act 1988 which defines as a distribution a slightly different (but sometimes overlapping) transaction. Section 209(4) looks at the position in which a *member* of a company receives a *benefit* of a greater value than the value of the consideration that member gives,

---

[92] Section 209(2)(b) TA 1988, was quoted in abbreviated form in paragraph 6.39.

arising out of a *transfer*. The transfer can be of assets (which can include cash), or liabilities, and it can be from or to the member. In the case we are considering, the subsection would be in point if one had made the undervalue transfer in the opposite direction, from subsidiary to parent.

Section 209(4) is perhaps unsurprisingly followed by section 209(5),[93] which *removes* from the scope of distributions any benefit such as section 209(4) has identified, if *the company and the member* (in our case now respectively the subsidiary/transferor and the parent/recipient) are in a 51 per cent group relationship. They are of course, so there has potentially been a section 209(4) distribution, but one that is in fact exempted by section 209(5).

6.52 *The relief given by section 209(5) achieves what it is meant to achieve, but cannot be taken as exempting more transactions than it was ever drafted to cover*

So far, we have seen that section 209(4) and (5) are irrelevant to the transaction we were actually looking at; but manifestly produce a sensible answer in a different transaction. Why the misgivings?

It is the final provision of section 209(5) which seems to give rise to the misunderstandings. What it says, clearly and straightforwardly, is that if there is a distribution under section 209(4), which is exempted 'from charge under section 209(4)' by section 209(5), it shall not then be caught and charged under section 209(2)(b). That last is the provision quoted in paragraph 6.50, about 'any other distribution out of the assets of the company ... in respect of shares in the company'. The asset moving at an undervalue from subsidiary to parent would still be chargeable under section 209(2)(b). It stands to reason that we need an extension to the section 209(5) exemption, and that is what we have; a clear statement that anything exempted under section 209(5) is not to be caught by section 209(2)(b).

But it is the clarity of the provision which worries the author:

- it does *not* say that if there is a transaction which falls within section 209(2)(b), but not within section 209(4), nevertheless section 209(5) would exempt it; the words 'out of the assets of the company' in section 209(2)(b) are given an extended meaning by section 254(9),

---

[93] Section 209(4) and (5) need to be quoted in full:

'(4) Where on a transfer of assets or liabilities by a company to its members or to a company by its members, the amount or value of the benefit received by a member (taken according to its market value) exceeds the amount or value (so taken) of any new consideration given by him, the company shall, subject to subsections (5) and (6) below, be treated as making a distribution to him of an amount equal to the difference.

'(5) Subsection (4) above shall not apply where the company and the member receiving the benefit are both resident in the UK and either the former is a subsidiary of the latter or both are subsidiaries of third company also so resident; and any amount which would apart from this subsection be a distribution shall not constitute a distribution by virtue of subsection (2)(b) above.'

and therefore it is not hard to think of transactions which would come within the purview of section 209(2)(b) without being within section 209(4). But the Revenue are known to read this exemption into the words;

- second, there has always been a degree of uncertainty whether any transfer of assets at an undervalue from subsidiary to parent might be within section 209(2)(a), which refers to 'dividends' without defining that word – even in cases where the transfer concerned was not described by the distributor as a dividend, and what one might call the Companies Act dividend procedures were not followed. Once again, the Revenue are known to take the view that this is not the case; and to say therefore that section 209(5) gives all the needed protection.

What we are relying on here is not the words of the statute, but Revenue practice which is hard to square with those words.[94] The author must live with those misgivings.

6.53 The holding company with subsidiaries which are respectively transferor and recipient of the asset

We next come to one of the variations on the transaction we have been working through in paragraphs 6.46 to 6.49, a variation promised as long ago as the first of those paragraphs.

Suppose that we started with a holding company which owned the transferor company which owned the asset, and the holding company also owned the recipient company. The holding company procures that the transferor company transfers the asset to the recipient, and the recipient makes its balance sheet balance by issuing shares to the holding company. (The transferor, of course, shows a loss on the transfer equal to the asset's previous carrying value in its accounts.) For capital gains tax purposes, the transferor's disposal of the asset and the recipient's

---

[94] A Revenue Press Release of 10 September 1971 said, 'where an amount is not treated as a distribution by virtue of (what was then) the proviso to s.233(3) TA 1970, it will not be treated as a distribution under any of the other provisions of s.233.' At that time, the proviso to section 233(3) stopped short without a reference to section 233(2)(b). When the undertaking in that press release was made statutory a year later, the *only* reference was to subsection (2)(b), and not to any other provisions.

On a different aspect, there has never been any specific, public, clarification from the Inland Revenue of their views on what might be described as the *primacy of charge* position between section 209(4) and section 209(2)(b), as illustrated in the text. In both of these cases what we have, and have had since 1972, is statutory wording which does not give the taxpayer the protections which the Inland Revenue are willing to give him in practice. The words in the Act are not ambiguous, so there is no possibility of going to Hansard to see what Ministers intended to enact when they put the 1972 amendments onto the Statute Book. We have the same vulnerability as that explained in Note 74 to paragraph 6.42, where the courts in the *Campbell Connolly* case rejected the (concessionary) reading of the law by the Inland Revenue as being incompatible with the actual words in the Act.

acquisition of it are treated as taking place at original cost.[95] That is straightforward.

Less straightforward is the position of the holding company. It continues to own the same shares in the transferor company, but they have become less valuable because that company has shed one of its assets. The holding company owns more shares than it previously did in the recipient company,[96] and one is forced to the conclusion that the extra shares acquired have a *cost* equal to the value of the asset in consideration for which the recipient issued them; there is nothing in the connected party legislation or elsewhere that says that the holding company's acquisition should be treated as being for zero merely because it procured that the recipient received the asset for which those shares were issued, rather than provided the asset itself.

However, logic would seem to be defied if the holding company were really to be allowed to add to its acquisition costs of its shares in the recipient a figure which it has pulled out of the air, without a corresponding adjustment to the acquisition cost of its shares in transferor. The answer is that there is anti-avoidance legislation[97] which

---

[95] Section 171(1) TCGA 1992.

[96] The position in which the holding company has shares in one subsidiary which have become less valuable or valueless, and has a matching increase in the number and value of shares in another subsidiary, sounds like the situation at which section 136 TCGA 1992 was aimed; if that position occurs as a result of a reconstruction or amalgamation involving the movement of the transferor's undertaking, the holding company (just like a body of individual shareholders) would be treated as not having disposed of the original shares, but the *new holding* would be taken to be the same asset, with the same acquisition cost apportioned as necessary between any separate elements in that new holding. (We will look at section 136 in paragraphs 6.70 and 6.71 below.) But what we are envisaging here is the mere movement of an asset between the subsidiaries – section 136 is not in point.

[97] What section 32(2) TCGA 1992 says is that if the 'actual consideration' given by the recipient is less than the asset's cost, then that is to be treated as producing a material reduction (for the purposes of section 30(1)(a) TCGA 1992) in the value of the shares owned by the holding company in the transferor. When and if the holding company disposes of those shares, it must under section 30(5) TCGA 1992 add to its actual disposal proceeds a sum that appears to the Inland Revenue to be just and reasonable. The effect is thus to increase the capital gain on the holding company's eventual disposal of the transferor, or to restrict its loss.

The theory which underlies this provision is that there is no need to adjust a potential gain which holdings might make on selling transferor, if there were at the time reflected in transferor's value its ownership of an asset which had cost it £20, or alternatively if there was reflected its ownership of £20 of consideration paid in cash. But the theory goes on to say that the gain *would* need adjusting if the asset had been replaced by a mere £1 in cash. Because this was the theory the draftsman had in mind, he referred to the 'actual consideration' needing to be at least as great as the cost of the asset if the consequences of a material reduction were to be avoided. Unfortunately, the draftsman appears to have assumed that 'consideration' always passes from the recipient to the transferor (and would thus be reflected in the value of the transferor's shares); any lawyer could have told him that when the recipient in the example we are examining issues shares not to the transferor but to the holding company that is perfectly good, and adequate, consideration – and it is difficult to see what it is if not actual. The legislation is almost certainly defective.

increases the holding company's capital gain, or restricts its capital loss, if and when it eventually disposes of its shares in the transferor company; its capital gain or loss on the further shares issued to it by the recipient is unaffected by these provisions.

6.54 Why the asset-transfer from one subsidiary of the holding company to another is not a distribution

The transfer is not a distribution, for a reason different from any protection we have so far looked at. We assume here that each of the holding company's subsidiaries is wholly owned, because any other assumption would make the transaction indefensible against the minority shareholders' objections. But we do in fact only need to have 90 per cent ownership to come within the relevant provisions explained below.

We know that the distribution is *in respect of* the transferor's own shares – which are held by the holding company. In a 90 per cent group, there is legislation to extend the distribution so that although it is still a distribution made by the transferor, it can be regarded as being in respect of any other company's shares, those of the holding company for instance, or those of the recipient.[98] The distribution we are thinking about is of course one within the scope of section 209(2)(b) of the Income and Corporation Taxes Act 1988, in respect of the transferor's shares, and we have at this stage identified that by virtue of the extended deeming provisions for 90 per cent groups, it can be treated as a distribution made by the transferor in respect of the holding company's shares or the recipient's shares.

What section 254(4) of the Income and Corporation Taxes Act 1988 then says is:

> Nothing in (the deeming provisions referred to) shall require a company to be treated as making a distribution to any other company which is in the same group.

That does not seem to take us where we want to be, but the Inland Revenue interpret[99] it as if it did; their interpretation is that it means that not only shall nothing in the deeming provisions make this particular transfer into a distribution, but nor shall section 209(2)(b) of the Income and Corporation Taxes Act 1988 itself make it a distribution.

---

[98] Section 254(2) and (3) ICTA 1988.
[99] See the comments made in Note 74 on paragraph 6.42 concerning the Inland Revenue's interpretations. In this instance it appears to hinge on the meaning of the word 'or'. Section 254(2) says that in a 90 per cent group the phrase 'in respect of shares shall mean in respect of shares in that company or any other company in the group'. Thus the asset-transfer by transferor is, and appears to remain, a distribution in respect of its own shares (within section 209(2)(b)), but can also now be regarded as a distribution in respect of the holding company's shares, or of the recipient's shares (under section 254(2) and (3)). Then section 254(4) says that those *extensions* of section 209(2)(b) shall not be treated as requiring anything to be treated as a distribution if it is received by a group member. What it does not say is that a distribution by the transferor which is within section 209(2)(b) in

continued

6.55 The transfer of a shareholding from one group company to another, for the issue of shares by the recipient

There is one more variation on these movements of undertakings and of assets; the last of those promised in paragraph 6.46. This is the movement of shareholdings into other group companies (which can thereafter be identified as being in this regard intermediate holding companies); although some transactions do not necessitate the existence of a capital gains tax group, others do, and it is therefore convenient to assume 100 per cent ownership throughout.

The position is nevertheless far more complicated than might be assumed by those who innocently imagine that everything within a capital gains tax group is exempt and that no movements of any kind have any tax significance. We start with the information in paragraphs 6.17 to 6.19, and proceed to re-analyse it from a capital gains point of view:

- Transferor company starts the exercise with a shareholding in recipient company, of which transferor's acquisition cost some years ago was £1,000;
- Transferor then acquires a second subsidiary (s-subsidiary) from an unrelated party for a total price of £10,000 (partly satisfied in cash and partly by the issue of transferor's shares). We know that it is the contract between transferor and the third party which fixes transferor's acquisition cost at £10,000;[100]
- Then recipient acquires s-subsidiary from transferor,[101] recipient issuing (more of) its own shares to transferor as consideration for its acquisition of the s-subsidiary shares.

---

continued
respect of the *transferor's shares*, is (because the section extends that to regard it also as being in respect of the *holding company's shares*), is *ipso facto* taken out of section 209(2)(b) so far as the transferor's shares are concerned. That would be the effect if one were able to postulate some all-powerful being who decides that transferor's distribution is in respect of holding company's shares *and is therefore not* in respect of transferor's shares. In that event it would follow that section 209(2)(b) would be overridden, and the Inland Revenue's interpretation would hang together. The author does question whether a strict constructionist could read those words and concepts into the statute.

It is worth pointing out that the escape route from distributions through section 209(4) and (5) is not in point. If the recipient were a *member* of the transferor, then we would be looking at a transfer of an asset by a company to a member, in circumstances where the transferor company failed to receive full value for the transfer. It would further be true that company and member were subsidiaries of the holding company. Therefore the transfer would not be a distribution by reason of section 209(5). But none of the provisions we have been looking at in section 254 say anything about companies which are not *members* of other companies being treated as if they were by virtue of being in the same 90 per cent group.

[100] *Stanton v Drayton Commercial Investment Co. Ltd*, see paragraph 3.25, and Note 29 thereon.

[101] This is not a distribution of s-subsidiary's shares out of the assets of transferor in respect of (transferor's) shares, for the first of the two reasons explained at the end of paragraph 6.50. That first reason was that what transferor receives as consideration for his transfer, in the form of further shares of recipient, is full value; there has

We *must* start by thinking about transferor's position (and only thereafter come to that of recipient). Transferor originally held s-subsidiary shares, and as a result of an offer from recipient has come to hold instead further recipient shares. This is a description of the classic share for share exchange,[102] under which transferor is treated for capital gains tax purposes as not having disposed of its original (s-subsidiary) holding, but its *new holding* of recipient shares is to be treated as the same asset as those original s-subsidiary shares, acquired at the same date and cost as they were acquired.

Capital gains tax (again)

6.56 *The recipient's capital gains position resulting from the transfer to it of the shareholding*

We can next turn to recipient's position. It might be thought that it was acquiring the s-subsidiary shares as an intra-group transfer from transferor, and therefore that recipient would inherit transferor's acquisition cost of £10,000.[103] If this were to be the position, it would be mandatory, since the particular provision concerned does not allow for any other result.

---

continued

been no decrease in the value of transferor's assets, and therefore no distribution out of them. (The second reason was that, even if there appeared to be insufficient consideration, the *indirect* ownership of s-subsidiary through recipient is worth no less than the direct ownership of it; that is valid, but perhaps superfluous here.)

[102] Section 135(3) TCGA 1992 applies section 127 of that Act. Note two points: first, this section does not require for its operation that recipient acquire 100 per cent of s-subsidiary, but for present purposes we are assuming that all the ownership links are 100 per cent, including the percentages acquired in bids and offers, as explained at the start of paragraph 6.53. The second point is that section 135(3) only operates *subject to sections 137 and 138*. What is relevant here is that this share for share (often referred to as paper for paper) treatment is excluded unless 'the exchange, reconstruction or amalgamation in question is effected for *bona fide* commercial reasons and does not form part of a scheme or arrangements of which the main purpose or one of the main purposes is avoidance of liability to capital gains tax or corporation tax'. There is a clearance procedure under which either of recipient or s-subsidiary can apply to the Inland Revenue for their agreement in advance of doing the transaction that they accept it as *bona fide*, and as not having tax avoidance purposes. This clearance procedure, and the implications of obtaining clearance, will be examined in chapter 11 below at paragraph 11.27, but before that we will see in paragraph 6.57 what happens if a clearance previously given is withdrawn, the effects being the same as would occur if clearance were withheld in the first instance. At this point the only comment we will make is to say that it is sometimes seen as odd that the application for clearance can be made by the predator (recipient) or the target (s-subsidiary), but not by the person or persons to whom the predator will be issuing shares and who are the beneficiaries of the paper for paper relief, in our case the transferor. The Inland Revenue's answer is quite logical, that the information they need in order to consider whether the transaction is commercial can be better obtained from the companies involved than from any one or more of the ultimate shareholders, and that it is from the predator that they require the undertaking that we will explain in paragraph 6.57 and Note 106 thereon.

[103] Section 171(1) TCGA 1992.

But it is not so, and the reason why it is not is that to fit into the intra-group transfer provisions necessitates that there be a group company *disposing* of the asset transferred as well as one making the matching acquisition.[104] In this instance, we saw in the last paragraph that transferor does *not* make any capital gains tax disposal of s-subsidiary shares for the reasons explained.

The implication of that last point is that recipient's acquisition cost is *not* determined under any intra-group rules, but under normal principles; this is a transaction between connected parties, and an open market price must be substituted, if the parties have put any other price on the transaction concerned.[105]

If we make the assumption, for illustration purposes, that by the time of the movement of s-subsidiary below recipient, the shares in s-subsidiary had increased in value from their original acquisition cost of £10,000 to an open market value of £12,000, then the capital gains tax acquisition cost of s-subsidiary (now held by recipient) has become £12,000, whereas before the transaction that acquisition cost (in transferor) was £10,000.

6.57 The up-rating of the recipient's capital gains base cost

For the recipient, an up-rating from £10,000 to £12,000 of the capital gains tax acquisition cost of s-subsidiary's shares would *appear* to present a tax saving opportunity, if it were intended that these shares were to be sold.

But appearances are deceptive. One of the conditions that the Inland Revenue will put on their clearance of the transaction itself as *bona fide* commercial is that recipient must state that he has no intention of selling s-subsidiary within six years.[106] If recipient does sell within that time, despite the assurance he gave, the Inland Revenue simply withdraw

---

[104] This has always been the Inland Revenue's interpretation of what is now section 171(1) TCGA 1992, and was accepted as correct by most taxpayers. However, after the Court of Appeal had decided in *Westcott v Woolcombers Ltd* [1987] STC 600 that the law had to be interpreted in a different way, the Revenue arranged for their original interpretation to be validated by an amendment of the law from March 1988; this is to be found in the new sub-section 171(3). In the context of disposals in paragraphs 11.19 and 11.20 we will discuss what effects an earlier 'woolcomber' transaction may have if there is a later disposal of the target by the company which has the 'up-rated' acquisition cost for that target.

[105] Section 17(1) TCGA 1992 (transferor and recipient being 'connected' under section 286(5)). The way in which these provisions *mesh* directly with each other was explained in Note 65 on paragraph 6.37.

[106] The Inland Revenue has published, or agreed to the publication of, various statements concerning information required, and their procedures, for considering section 138 TCGA clearance applications. Key among this is an exchange of correspondence, namely the Institute of Chartered Accountants in England and Wales' letter of November 1986, and Inland Revenue reply February 1987. However it is not on this published material, only on his experience, that the author relies when stating that in the transaction outlined the clearance application would need to contain an undertaking on behalf of the recipient that it had no present intention of selling the shares in s-subsidiary.

CAPITAL GAINS TAX

their agreement that the original transaction could be treated on a paper-for-paper basis so far as concerned transferor. That withdrawal can be seen as a reversal of the previous acquisition cost structure:

- recipient acquires the s-subsidiary shares in a transaction in which transferor *does* make a disposal of them, and therefore transferor is deemed to dispose of those shares for their original acquisition value of £10,000, and recipient inherits that same acquisition value;

- transferor does, however, acquire further shares issued by recipient. Since these are *not* acquired as a share exchange, (paper for paper), their acquisition value has to be determined under normal principles. Whether one argues this through the *Zevo Finance* and *Stanton v Drayton* lines or whether one says that section 17 Taxation of Chargeable Gains Act requires an open market value, one gets to the same answer;[107] the acquisition cost in transferor's hands of the further recipient shares can only be an amount equal to the consideration receivable by recipient for which it is making the issue of the further shares. That is to say, transferor has in this scenario an acquistion cost for the recipient shares equal to the market value of s-subsidiary, £12,000.

6.58 Can paper for paper be excluded?

For completeness, we should consider the question whether the taxpayer can himself shut out the paper-for-paper treatment in transferor, and the open market value acquisition in recipient (without forcing the Inland Revenue's hand by a subsequent sale of s-subsidiary)?

The answer seems to be that he can, if the transactions are slightly altered:

- recipient issues its shares to transferor by way of a rights issue; the acquisition value of these shares in the hands of transferor is therefore the cash paid for them;

- recipient uses the cash so received to purchase from transferor the s-subsidiary shares. This is an intra-group transfer within section 171, so that recipient inherits as acquisition cost of s-subsidiary not the present market value of those shares, but transferor's original acquisition cost.

---

[107] *Stanton (HM Inspector of Taxes) v Drayton Commercial Investment Co. Ltd*, see paragraph 3.25 and Note 29 thereon. *Craddock (HM Inspector of Taxes) v Zevo Finance Co. Ltd*, see paragraph 3.22 and Note 26 thereon. For the explanation of the application of the open market price in dealings between connected parties see paragraph 6.37, and in particular Note 65 thereon.

The capital gains tax acquisition values are thus exactly reversed:

	Paragraphs 55 to 56	Paragraph 58
Acquisition cost in transferor's hands of newly issued holding of recipient's shares	Historic cost of s-subsid.	Today's open market value of s-subsid.*
Acquisition cost in recipient's hands of s-subsid.'s shares	Today's open market value of s-subsid.	Historic cost of s-subsid.

The asterisked item is an indirect derivation. If recipient makes its rights issue to raise a sum of cash equal to the present open market value of s-subsid., then that is clearly the *cost* in transferor's hands of the shares thus issued.

The accounting position depends on two unrelated factors. If we assume that the present market value of s-subsidiary is greater than its historic cost, and if we also assume that the nominal value of the shares issued by recipient in paragraph 6.56 was less than that historic cost, then no profit or surplus would arise in the transferor's accounts in paragraphs 6.55 to 6.56; but such a surplus would arise in this paragraph 6.58, being a gain (probably characterised as unrealised) equal to the excess of transferor's new investment in recipient compared to what had been its investment in s-subsidiary.

6.59 Reculer pour mieux sauter

We started our discussions of the tax implications of group reconstructions, acquisitions, mergers, and so forth in paragraph 6.31. Twenty-eight paragraphs later we have not only failed to reach a conclusion, but seem to have failed even to tease out any clear pattern. What we will do is to go back to the tabulation of some types of merger and reconstruction we left hanging on the wall in paragraph 6.35, first to see what we have learned of the transactions; second, to see what we are still missing; and third, to see whether a pattern is becoming any more evident.

6.60 (1) A merger in which the recipient comes to own both companies' undertakings, and is itself owned partly by its own former shareholders, and partly by the transferor company (the latter still being owned by its former shareholders);

the only movement that occurred was that of the transferor's undertaking, passed down by it to the recipient, which issued shares as consideration. We know (paragraph 6.50) that the transferor made no distribution, since it received full consideration. But the transferor disposed of a whole collection of assets (among them the goodwill of its business), and we have not so far identified any provision which would exempt from capital gains tax any assets which might be within its scope, and can disclose here the horrid truth: there is no exemption.

The transferor company, receiving the recipient's shares as consideration for the disposal of its assets and undertaking, is chargeable to capital gains on the difference between its acquisition costs of those assets, and the agreed price receivable.[108] So far as stamp duty is concerned, we had originally tabulated these transactions to see whether we could gain an overall picture of the tax position for the possibilities open under section 76 of the Finance Act 1986, namely the transfers of undertakings costing only half of 1 per cent duty rather than the normal 1 per cent; we do not need to make any further comment on that.

6.60 (2) A merger in which enlarged bodies of shareholders pool their undertakings into a single company - and hive-downs;

the transferor's undertaking was moved into the recipient company, the transferor itself thus becoming valueless, and the recipient issuing its shares direct to those persons who had been shareholders in the transferor. We saw (paragraphs 6.39 to 6.40) that the movement of that undertaking would have been a distribution if the newly issued shares in recipient outnumbered that company's existing shares, so as to give the former transferor shareholders control of it. We have not yet made any comments on the capital gains tax position. We will come to this in paragraph 6.70, but that analysis can only follow our examination of the words 'reconstruction or amalgamation' – in paragraphs 6.62 and onward.[109] (Perhaps it is worth mentioning, as a preview of paragraph 6.70, that the transferor company has disposed of its assets and undertaking, but that is not the only point which has a capital gains significance; the shareholders of transferor have seen those shares become valueless, and have received shares in the recipient company without paying for them.) Stamp duty calls for no further comment, as in item (1) above.

6.61 (3) A hive-down (our preferred word in place of 'reconstruction') in which the recipient becomes a wholly owned subsidiary of the transferor, a subsidiary into which the transferor has hived down its trade and assets;

what we suggested in paragraph 6.36 was that this would be straightforward if the recipient were already a subsidiary of the transferor, which would be the natural consequence of transferor's acquisition of recipient off any shelf. Between parent and 100 per cent subsidiary, capital gains tax is avoided on the asset transfer and stamp duty would be reduced from half of 1 per cent to zero. In the transferor's hands the recipient shares have an open market acquisition cost (paragraphs

---

[108] *Stanton v Drayton*, see paragraph 3.25 and Note 28 thereon.
[109] Our comment on Items (2) and (4) in Note 63 on paragraph 6.36 was that it is highly unlikely that a company could give all its assets away, without requiring equivalent consideration, unless the transaction were part of a scheme of reconstruction under, for instance, section 425 CA 1985.

6.47 to 6.49). The only other point with a tax significance is that there would be no distribution since the transferor receives full consideration.

6.61 (4) Reconstructions to move an undertaking into a new (undamaged) corporate entity;

the transferor's undertaking has been moved *sideways* into a sister company which comes to be owned by the same shareholders as owned the transferor. We said (paragraph 6.41) that we could at that point see no escape from this transfer constituting a distribution. Nothing we have actually explained since would alter that, but there *is* a route past the difficulty. If the transferor were put into liquidation prior to the transaction, and the liquidator was in a position to act on instructions to transfer its undertaking to the recipient for consideration in the form of shares issued by recipient direct to the transferor's shareholders, then the distribution charge would be avoided. A distribution in respect of share capital in a winding up is not a distribution.[110] There is another implication which we have not previously mentioned. If the undertaking transferred was (or included) a *trade*, it is a requirement[111] that there be a degree of continuity between its assessments and those of the recipient company as the successor to the trade. The specific areas for which this is mandatory are the claiming of capital allowances and claims for losses. The fact that this is mandatory, not optional, derives from the provision having been originally introduced as anti-avoidance legislation, in 1954.

Once again, as in item (2) above, we have not yet commented on the capital gains tax position – and will do so in paragraph 6.70 once we have discussed the implications of reconstructions and amalgamations in the intervening paragraphs. In relation to stamp duty, we tabulated this as being one of the possible *acquisitions* on which section 76 of the Finance Act 1986 reduces the rate of duty from one per cent to half of 1 per cent. But a glance back to paragraph 6.22 would show that this transaction may *also* be within section 75, on which the rate of duty is zero – whether it is depends yet again on that word 'reconstruction' – to which we must now turn.

6.62 A scheme of reconstruction or amalgamation

Those words are defined, twice, in capital gains legislation[112] as meaning 'a scheme for the reconstruction of any company or companies or for

---

[110] Section 209(1) TA 1988.
[111] Section 343 TA 1988. For those who enjoy such things, this section can be quoted as one of the best examples of legislation originally introduced for anti-avoidance purposes which remains on the statute book indefinitely, although the underlying provisions (whose avoidance it was designed to counteract) have disappeared half a lifetime ago. We will discuss the significance of this loss carry forward for a predator acquiring a company into which such a trade has been transferred (hived down) in paragraph 12.23.
[112] Sections 136(2) and 139(9) TCGA 1992.

the amalgamation of any two or more companies'. Exactly that same, longer, formulation appears in the Companies Acts.[113] No reference is made to reconstructions or amalgamations in that part of the Insolvency Act which allows transactions similar in almost every respect to those envisaged in the Companies Act, a silence which we will be able to explain below. In the stamp duty legislation, the transaction's being 'in pursuance of a scheme for the reconstruction of the ... company' is a condition for the exemption from duty in section 75 of the Finance Act 1986.[114]

Faced with the circularity of the capital gains definition, and the absence of any other statutory guidance, most textbooks make an immediate dash for the decided cases giving guidance on the meaning of reconstruction and amalgamation. There is a considerable body of case law,[115] which can be roughly grouped into two parts. The older cases provide general descriptions of what the concepts involve; the more recent cases have mainly related to the meaning of the words in section 55 of the Finance Act 1927 (which might be described as a predecessor of, although in terms substantially different from, the legislation now in sections 75 to 77 of the Finance Act 1986). We will draw on this case law as we proceed – but where we will find it is much more fruitful to start is not with the meanings of reconstruction and amalgamation, but rather with the concept of a *scheme* for the one or the other.

6.63 *Arrangements and reconstructions*

The general heading of Part XIII of the Companies Act 1985 is 'Arrangements and Reconstructions', and that part starts with section 425, itself headed 'Power of company to compromise with creditors and members'.

Let us illustrate what this is all about by picturing a company with five shareholders, each of whom is also a debenture holder. The debentures were raised to finance the purchase of the company's premises. Although the company is still in occupation, the premises are considerably larger than it now needs for the reduced scale of its current operations, and there is no prospect of the company being able to sell these premises for

---

[113] Section 427(2)(a) CA 1985.
[114] Section 75 FA 1986 was briefly explained in paragraph 6.22, and referred to again at the end of paragraph 6.61; it permits, so long as this is done 'in pursuance of a scheme for the reconstruction of a company', that that company transfer its undertaking to a new company which gives no consideration to the old company, but only issues its shares to the shareholders of that old company; all of them must become shareholders, and the proportions in which they hold those shares must be identical. Sections 76 and 77 FA 1986 (which we have looked at in paragraphs 6.59 to 6.61, and 6.22 respectively) allow changes in company structures which have some similarities, but which do *not* have to pass the test of being *reconstructions or amalgamations*.
[115] The principal cases in the first group are mentioned in paragraph 6.66 below, and those in the second group in paragraph 6.69 (in each case the citations being footnoted).

more than half what it had originally borrowed to purchase them. The company finds itself crippled, therefore, partly by the interest it must still pay on the debentures, and partly by the deficit on its profit and loss account resulting from its writing down of the balance-sheet value of its asset, together with the annual losses which the ongoing interest charges are causing.

What the company would like to do is to obtain its debenture holders' agreement that they would waive half of the indebtedness. Four out of the five debenture holders are willing, but the fifth refuses. The willing four make it clear that they are not going to go ahead unless the fifth comes into line with them, voluntarily or otherwise, but he is still obdurate.

This is precisely the type of transaction for which section 425 provides a possible way forward. The company formulates its proposal for a compromise with the debenture holders under which they will waive half of the debt. The company (or any debenture holder) applies to the court to summon a meeting of the debenture holders. If, at that meeting, the proposal is approved by a three fourths majority, and if thereafter it is sanctioned by the court, it becomes binding also on the fifth, hitherto objecting, debenture holder.

6.64 Devising a more radical scheme

But the company recognises that that is not enough. It has a deficit on its profit and loss account; it needs to eliminate it, but only *realised profits* can be credited to the profit and loss account.[116] There was at one time some doubt whether the waiver of part of the amounts owed under debentures did produce a profit which is *realised*; but accountants' views are now that it is a realised profit,[117] but this does not go beyond eliminating that part of the deficit arising from the diminution in the value of the property. That still leaves as a continuing deficit on profit and loss account the part resulting from the interest charges.

What the company wants to do is to *reconstruct* its activities into a new company, to transfer its undertaking to it, including that new company's assuming the liabilities under the debentures at half their previous level, and the new company issuing its shares to the shareholders of the old; in short, a reconstruction under section 75. The new company will commence with share capital matched against net assets, but without a profit and loss balance, credit or debit. This is where section 427 of the Companies Act comes in. Rather than simply having a proposed compromise with the debenture holders, the company now has in addition 'a scheme for the reconstruction of (any) company (or companies, or the amalgamation of any two or more companies)'. The

---

[116] Schedule 4, paragraph 12(a), CA 1985. See also the discussion in chapter 4, paragraphs 4.7 and 4.9 to 4.11, about the meaning of the word 'realised' in the Companies Acts, and in accounting terminology.
[117] The Accounting Standards Board's *Statement of Principles*, chapter 4, paragraph 62 (at the time of writing still in discussion draft form).

compromise can be shown to the court to have been 'proposed ... in connection with' the scheme, and this demonstration meets all of the requirements of section 427(2)(a). Accordingly, the court can sanction not only the compromise, but also the scheme – providing in particular for the transfer of the old company's undertaking to the new (subsection (3)(a)), and for the new company's issue of shares and reduced amounts of debentures (subsection (3)(b)).

A scheme sanctioned by the court could make different provision for the dissenter, or it could (as we have envisaged) merely make the whole transaction binding on him. Without the court's powers to achieve that, shareholders and debenture holders could only do what they were allowed to do by the company's Articles, and the debenture deed, and these would also show what claims a shareholder or debenture holder might have if forced to accept a reconstruction. It is probable that no majority of debenture holders could bind a dissenter to a compromise which halved his asset's value and his income from it.

6.65 *Schemes without the courts' sanction*

A *scheme* in the context of the preceding illustration is therefore something which the company, its directors, a majority of shareholders and of debenture holders would wish to have sanctioned by the court.

But if all five debenture holders, and shareholders, were in full agreement from the start, they would evolve exactly the same scheme, and would not take it to the court. They would have no need to incur delay and expense; but more importantly, the court would say it had no jurisdiction to order the parties to undertake a course of action which they were fully empowered and able to undertake, and on which they were already unanimously agreed. The court *can* sanction a compromise, or can sanction both the compromise and the scheme with which it it is connected, but it *may* not be necessary to have the court's sanction in either case. (It is true that we have made life easier than it ever is in practice by assuming that the company has no creditors other than the debenture holders. In reality, the creditors of the old company would be affected by its reconstruction into the new, and it would be their interests the court was anxious to safeguard in sanctioning a scheme.)

Modern Articles might be thought unlikely to give shareholders with less than 25 per cent of the votes the right to block a scheme; if the Articles do not give them this power, it might be unlikely that the courts would give them a block; what seems to follow from those propositions is that the minority shareholders could not prevent a scheme from being forced through, but they could ask for compensation (in a claim of unfair prejudice – what in colloquial usage is referred to as an oppressed minority).[118] However, all of that must be speculation, every case must be looked at on its own merits, and the decision whether to apply to the courts or to go ahead without them must be taken on the facts.

---

[118] Section 459 CA 1985.

The conclusion we are fast coming to is that the *scheme* we have been trying to identify is no more than the reconstruction or amalgamation put into the form of resolutions which can be considered by the company's members. There may be some occasions on which there will be an advantage to be gained from the members' approval being followed and supplemented by the court's sanction; but that second step is far from being a necessity.

6.66 *The definitions of reconstructions and amalgamations*

Having established the context in which we need to consider whether we have a scheme, we can turn to the second question which is whether what is proposed is or is not a reconstruction or amalgamation.

> A reconstruction implies the formation of a new company to take over the assets of an existing company, with or without some difference between the constitutions of new and old companies.

That comes from the *Western Counties and South Wales Telephone Co.* case;[119] but the word 'assets' should be replaced by 'undertaking' as a result of the *Baytrust Holdings Ltd* case.[120] And although the point has become almost academic in the light of the Stamp Office's being now concerned only with a very limited form of reconstruction, that office takes the view that an undertaking must be carried on in the same way before and after any reconstruction (see Note 62 on paragraph 6.34); there seems to be no indication that the other departments of the Inland Revenue are as restrictive as the Stamp Office. At the end of the reconstruction there should be no change in the real ownership, per the *Lever Bros Ltd* case.[121]

On the other hand, in contrast to reconstruction:

> An amalgamation involves ... a different idea. There you must have the rolling, somehow or other, of two concerns into one. You must weld two things together and arrive at an amalgam – a blending of two undertakings. It does not necessarily follow that the whole of the two undertakings should pass – substantially they must pass – nor need all the corporators be parties, although substantially all must be parties.

That comes from the *South Africa Supply Co.* case.[122] What the *Walker's Settlement* case[123] added to it was the insight that the acquisition by one company of all the shares of another is not (unless the companies whose shares are acquired are all to be wound up) an amalgamation. When two undertakings ended up in the same corporate entity in item (1) in paragraph 6.59, and again in item (2) in paragraph 6.60, the description we used was merger, but we could as well have called them amalgamations.

---

[119] *Hooper v Western Counties and South Wales Telephone Co.* [1892] 68 LT 78.
[120] *Baytrust Holdings Ltd v CIR* [1971] 3 All ER 76. See also paragraph 6.34 and Note 61 thereon.
[121] *Lever Bros Ltd v IRC* [1938] 2 All ER 808.
[122] *Re South African Supply and Cold Storage Co. Ltd* [1904] 2 Ch. 268.
[123] *Re Walker's Settlement* [1935] Ch. 567.

6.67 Interpretation of stamp duty legislation and other tax statutes

There is a qualitative difference between the drafting of stamp duty legislation and that of capital gains tax (and for that matter income tax and corporation tax). It is broadly true of all these taxes that there is no equity in a taxing statute, and that clear words are needed to bring the taxpayer within the charge to tax. This concept has been restated many times in decided cases, one of the formulations which can reasonably be quoted (because it is self-explanatory even when quoted out of context) is:

> It is well established that one is bound, in construing Revenue Acts, to give a fair and reasonable construction to their language without leaning to one side or the other, that no tax can be imposed on a subject by an Act of Parliament without words in it clearly showing an intention to lay the burden upon him, that the words of the statute must be adhered to, and that the so-called equitable constructions of them are not permissible.[124]

Where the difference becomes plain, however, is in the fact that stamp duty legislation tends to focus on narrowly defined transactions (in the present instance no more than the scheme for reconstruction), while we will see that the capital gains tax perspective is wider, based on:

• looking first to see that there is a reconstruction or amalgamation, the implication being that if there is such a reconstruction and so on, the existence of a scheme can, more or less, be taken for granted as explained below;

• looking secondly at the relevant disposals and acquisitions to see what part they play in the scheme, or in the *arrangements* which surround it;

• and looking thirdly and crucially, at the question whether the scheme and any arrangements were carried out for *bona fide* commercial reasons, or were tax-motivated.

6.68 Playing down the importance of the scheme

What one might describe as the capital gains tax down-playing of the scheme may not be explicit in, for instance, the opening words of section 139(1) of the Taxation of Chargeable Gains Act 1992:

> where any scheme of reconstruction or amalgamation involves the transfer of the whole or part of a company's business . . .

but when one comes to section 139(5) it begins to become clearer that it is not so much the scheme, but the whole of its surrounding circumstances that one is required to examine:

> This section does not apply unless the reconstruction or amalgamation is effected for *bona fide* commercial reasons, and does not form part of a

---

[124] Lord Atkinson in *Ormond Investment Co v Betts* [1928] AC 143.

scheme or arrangements of which the main purpose, or one of the main purposes, is avoidance of liability to corporation tax, capital gains tax or income tax.

The first thing to notice is that the word separating 'scheme' from 'arrangements' is 'or'. The reconstruction can be part of a scheme; alternatively it can be part of arrangements. That makes sense only if one recognises that the draftsman is using 'scheme' in a rather special way. Here is an expansion of his phraseology, with square-bracketed comments and explanations:

> This section does not apply unless the reconstruction or amalgamation [which only makes sense in the light of subsection (1) already quoted and the definition in subsection (9) if it is read as shorthand for the scheme of reconstruction or amalgamation] is effected for *bona fide* commercial reasons, and does not form part of a [the draftsman's use of 'part' implies that he is looking for some wider] scheme [which he must now be using in its ordinary sense; it cannot be a reference back to the scheme in its technical sense, first because that would make nonsense of the words 'part of', and second because the reconstruction or amalgamation may as an alternative to being part of his wider scheme be part of some wider] arrangements of which the main purpose ...

It can be said that what we are doing is precisely what we are not allowed to do – reading into a taxing statute words which it does not contain. An historian would also say that the words we are looking at were first introduced into the law by section 41 of the Finance Act 1977, and that the draftsman was most unlikely to have had that in mind at that time. What was in draftsmens' minds is always obscure; but the author stands by his exposition, if for no reason other than its being abundantly clear that the Inland Revenue's specialist department handling clearance applications under this, and related, provisions does in fact look at the *scheme*, and the surrounding *arrangements*, in just this way.

6.69 Further definitions

It is clear that reconstruction, as described above, could not include the division of a company into two, each carrying on a part of what had been its previous undertaking, and each separately owned. Indeed, in the stamp duty context, the *Brooklands Selangor Ltd* case[125] decided specifically that such a division was not a reconstruction. But in the context of capital gains tax, the Inland Revenue have issued a statement of practice expressing the *concessionary view* that such a division would constitute a reconstruction.[126] We will see in chapter 11

---

[125] *Brooklands Selangor Ltd v IRC* [1970] 2 All ER 76.
[126] *Statement of Practice* 5/85, the second paragraph of which reads, in part: '... the division of a company's undertaking into two or more companies owned by different sets of shareholders (separate family groups for example) would not rank as a reconstruction. In practice, however, for capital gains tax ... identity of shareholdings in the old and new companies is not insisted upon in the case of a division carried out for *bona fide* commercial reasons.'

at paragraph 11.18, that it is possible to use this statement to avoid the capital gains tax liabilities which would otherwise arise from the division of a company into two or more entities. In particular, it does enable the division of a company as a prelude to some further step, for instance the sale of one of the resulting companies. However, the main reason why this statement of practice seems today to have a somewhat reduced benefit, and why it seems preferable to consider whether use can be made of the demerger legislation which we will examine in chapter 14, is that the real problem was never capital gains tax, but rather distributions. The statement of practice did not directly affect the latter, whilst those who introduced the demerger rules insisted that they were specifically designed to alleviate the distribution problem. We will see in chapter 14 that if a demerger can be achieved, the distribution which would otherwise have occurred is exempted by the legislation – but there are two major problems. The first is that the rules are excessively complex and restrictive; and the second is that if one uses the demerger route it is specifically provided that the two companies which result may not be sold, or otherwise change owners. But the conclusion we will come to in paragraph 11.18, and from a different direction in paragraph 14.7, is that there are two methods of dividing or demerging companies, each of them having its own difficulties and restrictions; each of them made unavailable by the Inland Revenue (by the withholding of clearances) if they believe that what is being done is objectionable; but each needing to be considered as possible solutions to a very specific problem.

If we revert to stamp duty, many of the more recent cases, as we noted in paragraph 6.62, were fought only to define the boundaries that should be drawn around *the scheme*, to discover whether in its narrow stamp duty definition it fitted within the original 1927 legislation, before the relevance of that definition was so substantially narrowed by the sections 75, 76 and 77 of the Finance Act 1986. For instance, if the transferee company was to issue its shares to the transferor,[127] would the scheme be disqualified if there were plans that that transferor would sell, or otherwise dispose of, the shares to another party? and to what extent was the pre-ordination or informality of those plans relevant? In the *Crane Fruehauf* case[128] the issuer of the shares had imposed on the company receiving them an obligation that another party should have a call option over them – which was held to disqualify the scheme. In the *Swithland Estates* case,[129] a less formal arrangement for the purchase of the shares was accepted.

---

[127] It was an alternative available under section 55 that consideration for the transfer of the undertaking could take the form of the transferee's issue of shares to the transferor rather than to its shareholders. This is not possible under section 75 of the Finance Act 1986, although it does form item (3) in our tabulation of the possibilities under section 76.

[128] *Crane Fruehauf Ltd v IRC* [1975] 1 All ER 429.

[129] *Swithland Investments Ltd v IRC* [1990] STC 448. The judgment in this case very ably and clearly summarises the conclusions of the earlier cases, and makes it scarcely necessary to look further afield.

6.70 Capital gains tax on reconstructions and amalgamations

After that general examination of the meanings of the words 'scheme', 'reconstruction' and 'amalgamation', we can now go back to the capital gains tax position in what we had described respectively as the merger and reconstruction possible at items (2) and (4) in paragraphs 6.35 and 6.60 to 6.61, the legislation in which we originally identified these transactions being stamp duty law in section 76 of the Finance Act 1986.

There are two separate capital gains tax transactions in each case, and there are parallel provisions which can give relief, if the requirements for relief are met. It is therefore sensible to mention first those common requirements for relief.

There must be a reconstruction or amalgamation as defined in paragraph 6.66, that is to say, the movement of an *undertaking* from one company to another (or more than one undertaking may move from more than one company) and this is extended to include movements of part of an undertaking. The meaning of undertaking, in paragraph 6.34 and 6.35, can be a trade or business, but it can also include shareholdings in subsidiaries, so that by implication the shares of a single subsidiary can be part of the undertaking of a parent company. No other asset, unless it is integral to a trade or business, is an undertaking.

The reconstruction or amalgamation must be carried out for *bona fide* commercial reasons.[130] When we come, in chapter 11 at paragraph 11.25 and Note 45 thereon, to try to summarise the principles, we will see that the only real conclusion possible is that this is all a matter of judgment based on the facts of each individual case; there is no logical, consistent, precedent-bank against which it is possible to measure every potential transaction which may be proposed. But there are two aspects which can perhaps be mentioned. The test is aimed at identifying and disallowing the negative, rather than at requiring reconstructors to prove the positive. (The negative answer will tend to be that you cannot have relief on your proposed transaction because in the course of it X is allowed to do Y, thus avoiding tax on a gain of Z; it is unlikely in the extreme that the Inland Revenue would make any value judgment whether amalgamating the undertakings of A Ltd and B Ltd was being done for *bona fide* reasons.) Second, one can only form a view whether tax is being avoided if one can determine the *proper* tax, in the absence of a reconstruction. This is the elephant test – almost impossible to define, but everyone would recognise it if they saw it.

---

[130] The full wording of this requirement in relation relief from tax on the movement of the undertaking was set out in the second of the quotations in paragraph 6.68. The parallel wording for relief on the other part of the transaction, the change in the shareholding in the hands of the reconstructed company's owners, requires that there must not be any avoidance of capital gains tax or corporation tax, but says nothing about income tax.

CAPITAL GAINS TAX ON RECONSTRUCTIONS AND AMALGAMATIONS

6.71 *The transfer of the undertaking, and the shareholding changes, in the course of a reconstruction or amalgamation*

The transferor company makes a disposal of its undertaking to a recipient company which is not, either before or as a result of the transaction, a member of any capital gains tax group with that transferor. It is probable, although not invariably the case, that the transferor and recipient will be connected companies,[131] so that the disposal proceeds that the transferor would be required to bring into his capital gains tax computation (were there no relief available to override this requirement) would be the market value of the undertaking.

The relief that is available does override the market value requirement. Section 139 of the Taxation of Capital Gains Act 1992 provides that the transferor shall be deemed to dispose of the undertaking (or part), including each of the chargeable assets that are comprised in it, for such a figure that it makes neither gain nor loss; and the recipient acquires the assets at that same figure.

But we actually need to think a good deal harder about this transfer value. What is said above is true (the connected party rules would have called for open market value for capital gains tax, but this is overriden by the *no-gain-no-loss* figure allowed in section 139); but it does not go nearly far enough. The actual transfer value used in the transferor's books is zero, that is to say the zero consideration paid by the recipient to the transferor. The transfer value used in the recipient's books is likely to be the same as the carrying values (at which the transferor had carried the assets in his own books), but that is acceptable for company law and accounting only if it is a fair value of the assets for which shares are being issued credited as fully paid.[132] If we go back to the transferor's position, it has *distributed* the whole of its assets, leaving itself with share capital on the left hand side of its balance sheet, and *nothing* on the right. Is that lawful, in the light that section 263 of the Companies Act 1985 only permits distribution of profits available for the purpose, and specifically forbids 'paying off paid up share capital'?

---

[131] Paragraphs 6.37 and 6.38.

[132] See paragraph 3.24 for the rule in the *Steel Barrel* case that the directors of any company must make an honest estimate of the value of the assets they receive before issuing shares for them. In the case of a public company the directors' own estimate would have needed to be supported by an independent valuation, were it not for the fact that the transfers we are considering would be within the exemption in section 103(5) CA 1985.

If the transferor had been carrying on a trade (not every undertaking is a trade, but a trade would undoubtedly be an undertaking) section 139 does not apply to its trading stock; the rule applying to it would be that if the recipient took it as trading stock into its trade, and the recipient 'gave valuable consideration', then that consideration fixes the transferor's cessation profit and loss account disposal, and the recipient's opening stock (see paragraph 3.40 and Note 53 thereon). The reason why the quoted phraseology does fit the cases we are considering is the well known fact that consideration is still valuable, and given by a recipient in a way which validates a contract, even if it passes from the recipient to some other party, not to the transferor.

The answer is that the court can undoubtedly sanction it if the company applies for approval for a *scheme*, but the path is so well trodden that few accountants or lawyers would insist that it was impossible without the court's sanction.[133]

6.72 The changes in shareholdings associated with the reconstruction or amalgamation

The other capital gains tax event concerns the shareholders of the transferor company. In each of items (2) and (4), those shareholders continue to own shares in the transferor, but since the latter has transferred all or part of its undertaking, those shares have become worthless or worth less. Contemporaneously, the same shareholders have received shares in the recipient company without, in any direct way, having given any consideration for them.

In this case the relief is provided by section 136 of the Taxation of Chargeable Gains Act 1992. The shareholders are treated as not making any disposal of their *original shares*, nor as making an acquisition of the *new holding*.[134] But the acquisition cost of the original holding is re-attributed to the new holding in an equitable manner. If the transferor company has transferred everything it owned, and has thus become valueless, this will simply mean that the shareholders are treated as having acquired their recipient company shares not at the date of the transaction but at the date they originally acquired their transferor shares, and at the price they paid for those transferor shares. If the transferor company is not valueless, an apportionment of the original cost will be necessary.

---

[133] There is an interesting sidelight on this concept of a company ending with a balance sheet which has share capital, and nothing else, following a transfer of its undertaking. This is precisely the position of the transferor in any merger of two banks. What is different in that case is that bank mergers can only be achieved by Private Act of Parliament, because there is no other effective way of providing that the obligations of the transferor (not only indebtedness to depositors, but all the bank's contractual and guarantee obligations) are validly shifted from its shoulders to those of the recipient bank. Such Acts of Parliament spell out that that is the shape of the transferor's balance sheet, and spell out also that after the transfer *anyone* (shareholder, former creditor, or any member of the public) can petition for the transferor bank to be wound up. As a corporate entity, its life is not worth the paper its original registration certificate is printed on, and it not only cannot be allowed to restart any activity, it does in effect have to be wound up.

[134] The explanation has been phrased solely in terms of shareholders and their shares in the transferor and the recipient; the legislation does allow for the original holding and/or the new holding to comprise or include debentures. There is also a different point. In the definition of an amalgamation quoted in paragraph 6.66 from the *South African Supply Co.* case, it was said 'nor need all the corporators be parties, although substantially all must be parties'. That seems to envisage that when company 1 owned by P, Q & R has transferred into it the undertaking of company 2 owned by S, T & U, those who remain as shareholders in the amalgamated company 1 might only be P, Q, R, S & T, while U stayed out of the arrangement, perhaps continuing to own the rump of company 2. That may be within the definition of an amalgamation, but it would not allow S, T & U to benefit from section 136. That section requires that the new holdings (in companies 1 and 2 after the amalgamation) be 'in proportion to (or as nearly as may be in proportion to) their holdings' in company 2 before it.

CHAPTER 7

CONSORTIA

The meaning of consortium

7.1 Its purpose and how it is managed

It would be the jointly owned company which would probably be most noticeable to a layman, and the term he would be likely to use to describe it would be a 'joint venture'.

What is of greater interest to us is the ownership, and the owners, of that joint company – how they co-operate in establishing it and running it, and what they are able to get out of the venture. Once again, the layman might assume that the only thing that could ever draw the owners into such a venture would be profit. He would be right, but not necessarily in the right way; he would probably be thinking of each owners' participation in the profits earned by their jointly owned vehicle. But they might see the advantages at which they wished to aim rather differently – it is perfectly possible to demonstrate that the owners could derive benefits without their jointly owned company actually generating profits. Let us look at an example.

7.2 Leasing as a sales-aid

One of our joint venturers is a manufacturer of capital equipment, some of whose customers wish by means of finance leases only to have the use of, not to acquire the ownership of, that equipment. Its co-venturer is a financial institution which is prepared to contribute to the venture the funds those customers need in order to obtain the use of assets in this way. The extra sales to the venture are the prime motivation for the manufacturer, and the opportunity for extra lending is that of the financier. Each can also derive ancillary benefits, as we can demonstrate using the figures in Table 35.

Table 35: Corporation Tax of Jointly Owned Leasing Company

	1994	1995	1996	1997	1998	1999	Total
Rentals		2600	2600	2600	2600	2600	13000
Rebate of rentals						(2450)	(2450)
Capital allowances	(2500)	(1875)	(1406)	(1055)	(791)	127	(7500)
Interest		(1055)	(858)	(637)	(389)	(111)	(3050)
	(2500)	(330)	336	908	1420	166	nil
Tax	(825)	(109)	111	300	469	54	nil

Table 35 shows the corporation tax computation of the jointly owned leasing company, and we need to run through it, line by line, in order to be able to explain the basis on which its two owners have set it up:

- on the last day of its 1994 accounting period the leasing company purchases from the manufacturer an item costing £10,000. We assume for this purpose that this is not the first of the leasing company's transactions – that it has been operating at least throughout the year 1994, and therefore that continuity of trading qualifies it for a full writing down allowance in its computation for that year. In each subsequent year it obtains allowances on the reducing balance. These are the first five figures on the third line;

- the equipment is leased to a customer from 1 January 1995, quarterly rentals of £650 in advance being receivable through a five year primary term ending on 31 December 1999. These rentals are shown on the first line;

- on 31 December 1999 the lessee requests the leasing company to take the equipment back and sell it. The sale proceeds of this sale are £2,500, which explains the clawback of capital allowances suffered by the leasing company in that year, when those proceeds are received for an asset whose *written down value* after the previous five allowances is £2,373. The clawback is £127, the sixth figure on the third line.

7.3 The lease terms

- it is a term of the lease that on any such sale, 98 per cent of the proceeds of sale (98 per cent of £2,500 is £2,450) will be paid to the lessee as a rebate of rentals. The leasing company, and its owners, regard its business as being that of a financier providing what is in effect five year finance. It sets its rentals at a high enough level to break even though it retains only a marginal figure of sales proceeds. Another way of saying the same thing is that it does not want to take risks over the asset's residual value and it is accordingly willing to pass substantially all of those proceeds to the lessee. This rebate is an expense in 1999 so far as the leasing company is concerned, shown on the second line;

- the mirror image of the leasing company's unwillingness to take any significant risk over the residual value of the asset at the end of the primary term is that the lessee *is* willing to take that risk; it only commits itself to quarterly rentals as high as £650 on the basis that it will be entitled to a rebate of them at the end of the primary term, giving it substantially the whole of what it hopes and expects will turn out to be a substantial amount of proceeds;

- it is entirely possible that when the leasing company does sell the equipment off the lease, its purchaser will be the manufacturer of the equipment; that manufacturer has an interest in ensuring that there is no flooding of the market with cheap second hand equipment which could depress the market for new items. It may or may not be the case that there is some understanding between the leasing company and the manufacturer, dating from the inception of the lease, how the repurchase price will be arrived at when the manufacturer does eventually repurchase. If there is any such understanding, its terms will of course be of interest to the lessee, when he considers whether a rental of £650 per quarter is or is not economic; but that is not to say that the lessee will always know either that there is an understanding, or what its basis may be.

All of the foregoing are terms which one would typically meet in practice in a leasing transaction, and in particular in one arranged by a financier and a manufacturer working together to boost the turnover and profits of each of them.

7.4 *Further assumptions; the absence of profit and of equity*

There are however two other assumptions underlying the figures in Table 35, neither of which can be said to be quite so realistic. First, that the finance needed by the jointly owned leasing company in order to purchase the asset (and continue to carry it through the lease term) has been wholly borrowed by that leasing company from its financier-shareholder. The leasing company's cashflow for the first year of the lease is shown in Table 36.

Table 36: Leasing Company's Cashflow

	Beginning of period	Rental	After receipt of rental	Interest accruing	End of period
1st quarter	10,000	650	9,350	281	9,631
2nd quarter	9,631	650	8,981	270	9,251
3rd quarter	9,251	650	8,601	258	8,859
4th quarter	8,859	650	8,209	246	8,455
		2,600		1,055	

If the figures in Table 36 were extended to the end of the fifth year, it would be seen that the borrowings had been fully repaid. The interest built into that cashflow is 3 per cent per quarter, which compounds to 12.55 per cent per annum. Our assumption is that it is the financier's entitlement to that rate of interest on his loan to the leasing company which the financier regards as an acceptable reward for his participation in the venture; he does not want the leasing company to pay a slightly smaller rate of interest, which would leave the leasing company showing a profit which it could then distribute between the shareholders, financier and the manufacturer.

Correspondingly, the manufacturer regards his ability to sell the equipment to the leasing company at a price of £10,000 (and possibly to buy it back again at £2,500) as an equally acceptable reward – once again, if the asset had been sold in at a slightly lower price that would have put the leasing company in a position to make a distributable profit; but it is neither shareholders' wish to do this. The second assumption flows from the foregoing. We have not seen the leasing company making any use of its own equity for this transaction, but only using borrowings. In fact, if we were to assume that the percentage interests of the manufacturer and the financier in the leasing company were 30 per cent and 70 per cent respectively, we would have to say that we had not seen that leasing company making use, in carrying on its business, of what we will later introduce as an assumption, £450 and £1,050 paid up share capital put in by its two shareholders.

7.5 The tax advantages of leasing

Everyone knows there is some advantage, but few can explain it.

The tax computation set out in Table 35 is designed to show precisely how that tax benefit arises, and how big it is. Its size can be identified more clearly if we look at a leasing company which is breaking even rather than one which is generating profits; which is part of the reason for that element in our assumptions. The leasing company obtains the benefits of tax reliefs for his capital expenditure and his interest payments, on lines 3 and 4 of the table, earlier than he has to bring into account his income stream in the form of rentals (less rebates) on lines 1 and 2 of the table. The acceleration of capital allowances arises partly because a 25 per cent reducing balance calculation based on a cost of £10,000 is itself *faster* than would be a straightline calculation designed to write down that cost to an expected proceeds of disposal of £2,500 over a five-year period; the other part of its acceleration derives from the fact that the first writing down allowance is available for 1994, the year in which the expenditure is incurred, without any need for the asset to have been in use throughout that year.

There is also, although almost every commentator overlooks this fact, a noticeable *front-ending* of tax reliefs for interest paid. Obviously, the leasing company uses the rentals as he actually receives them to pay the interest due to the financier, and as to the excess of rentals over interest to reduce the principal of the loan. That explains why the interest costs decline through the lease term.

The combined result of these two factors is that the leasing company generates tax losses of £2,500 and £330 in 1994 and 1995 in the computations set out in Table 35; in later years the leasing company's taxable profits come in aggregate to the same figure. But there is an advantage in the *mismatch* – and the ability of the leasing company's shareholders to obtain that benefit for themselves is the second of the ways in which they, as a consortium, have an advantage from this operation, by comparison with companies operating entirely separately. (The first of their advantages was simply the rewards each derived from the pricing of this business, as mentioned in the previous paragraph.)

7.6 Group relief by way of a consortium claim

Let us assume in Table 37 that each of the manufacturer and the financier has a 30 September year-end. Their jointly owned company can *surrender* to them, against their profits to 30 September 1994, three quarters of its 1994 loss (the overlap of the accounting periods).

Table 37: Leasing Company's Surrender of Losses to its Shareholders

	loss to surrender	70% shareholder	30% shareholder
12 months loss to 31 Dec 1994	(2,500)		
proportion to 30 Sep 1994	(1,875)		
claim at 30 Sep 1994 split between shareholders		(1,313)	(562)
tax saving on 1 July 1995		(433)	(186)
12 months loss to 31 Dec 1995	(330)		
proportion to 30 Sep 1995	(248)		
add proportion of 1994 loss 1 Oct 1994 to 31 Dec 1994	(625)		
	(873)		
claim at 30 Sep 1995 split between shareholders		(611)	(262)
tax saving on 1 July 1996		(202)	(86)
proportion of 1995 loss 1 Oct 1995 to 31 Dec 1995	(82)		
claim at 30 Sep 1996 split between shareholders		(57)	(25)
tax saving on 1 July 1997		(19)	(8)

If one looks at that table through the eyes of the 70 per cent shareholder, he has achieved actual reductions in his tax bills of £433, £202 and £19, the aggregate of which is £564. But correspondingly, the jointly owned leasing company, without losses to carry forward from 1994 and 1995, will actually have to find cash with which to meet the tax liabilities shown up by its computations for 1996 to 1999; the 70 per cent shareholder's proportion of these liabilities is of course

£564. If he makes payments to the jointly owned company, on the dates that company is due to make its tax payments concerned, and equal to 70 per cent of each of those payments (and the 30 per cent shareholder does the equivalent), then the jointly owned company can be *kept whole*.[1] Overall, what each shareholder has saved in tax has *preceded* what it has to pay out to obtain that saving – although the aggregate savings and payments have been equal. It is that *mismatch* of cashflows that makes leasing advantageous to the leasing company, or perhaps more accurately to the consortium or group which owns that leasing company.

7.7 The shareholders' agreement

However that does bring us back to the management of the jointly owned company's operations. The agreement which the Inspector of Taxes requires to see, between its shareholders and the jointly owned company, covering the surrendering and claiming of the losses must obviously have an ancillary agreement relating to the payments which are to be made for that group relief, and their timing.

But that would only be a very small part of what the shareholders would need to have agreed. The factor which is the key to everything else is pricing. We assumed that the manufacturer and financier were content with a structure which gave the former £10,000 per item of equipment, and the latter an interest rate of 12.55 per cent per annum on its lending; those translated into the lessee being required to pay quarterly rentals of £650 over five years, and being allowed a 98 per cent rebate out of the asset's sale proceeds.

All of the parties, manufacturer, financier and jointly owned company, need to know what each would be suggesting if manufacturing costs increased or decreased, or if interest rates moved. They also need to

---

[1] A payment made by the claimant of group losses to the company surrendering them is referred to as a 'payment for group relief', and its special significance is that it is itself ignored for all tax purposes; it is neither income of the recipient nor expense for the payer, and nor is it within the scope of VAT. The legislation governing the surrendering, and the claiming, of group relief is in sections 402 to 413 ICTA 1988, the particular provision dealing with payments for group relief being section 402(6). Notice that 'claiming' group relief is a formal process, necessitating an agreement between the companies concerned which in the case of a consortium is defined as being *all* of the shareholder members as well as the company they jointly own (section 412(1)(b) and (2)); also necessary is that the claimant company's claim is submitted within the necessary time limits (section 412(1)(c)). Reference has already been made in paragraphs 5.38 to 5.42 to the fact that group relief ceases to be available once the necessary 'linkage' of beneficial ownership is broken; and we saw in those paragraphs that the breaking of the link can be treated as having happened in three particular circumstances. First, there are widely drawn provisions in schedule 18 to ICTA 1988 which can prevent relief being available if a company's share and loan capital structure is designed so that its 'real' owners are not those who own its ordinary shares. Second, when a company is changing hands the drafting of section 410 allows the Inland Revenue to fix a date earlier than either contract or completion as being the time the link was in fact broken. Third, the link is treated as not existing at any time while there are 'options' which, if exercised, would result in its actually being broken.

know what they should do if it became clear that the lessees would be willing to pay rentals of more than £650, or if it became clear that that figure was too high and needed to be reduced. Tax has a special fascination for leasing companies, and both it and its shareholders would want to know what each expected to do if the rate of corporation tax were increased in 1996, so that the leasing company would no longer be able to fund its increased tax liabilities unless the shareholders increased their *payments for group relief* (or unless the leasing company could successfully increase the rentals charged to the lessee).

7.8 Extending the shareholders' agreement to cover items which are difficult or impossible to forecast

In an interrelated area, the parties need to have an idea of the volume of business they are aiming at – even if it were not the case that this company's activities could to some extent *crowd out* alternative business which either the financier or manufacturer could otherwise be handling, it is always necessary to have aims in view.

Similarly interrelated is the question what should be done if something goes wrong? the most obvious question might be what happens if a lessee defaults? Does the financier bear the bad debt, or does the manufacturer share in it? If one were to say that the financier should bear the whole risk (it being a financial risk) then it would be difficult for this to be done in a way which would not disturb the equilibrium of the jointly owned company. Far more straightforward would be arrangements to take the jointly owned company out of all further involvement.

Thus the financier would take over from the jointly owned company the latter's right to proceed against the lessee for rents unpaid, and to repossess the asset from the lessee. Correspondingly the financier would release the jointly owned company from the amount of the indebtedness outstanding from the latter;[2] and would undertake to sell the repossessed asset to the manufacturer for the agreed £2,500 figure.

If this default took place late on in the lease term, the financier could actually benefit, and the lessee lose; this would be the position if what the lessee failed to pay by way of rentals was less than what it failed to receive by way of rebate of rentals. But whether or not this was the case, and whether or not it was equitable that the financier did shoulder the whole of the risk, it does seem anomalous that the manufacturer would seem actually to benefit; it would in all cases recover a less worn and torn item of equipment earlier than would otherwise have been the case. All of these aspects are ones which lead one to question whether running a jointly owned company on a no-profit-no-loss basis is sensible, given that if something goes awry, that company's business seems likely to have to be taken apart.

---

[2] If the financier forgives debt owed to it by a company which is its 70 per cent owned subsidiary, it may have difficulty in establishing its right to a corporation tax deduction for these 'losses'. Despite the apparent inequity, there are decided cases (for example *Odhams Press Ltd v Cook* [1940] 3 All ER 15) in which such a 'subsidy' to a subsidiary has been held to be non-deductible.

7.9 The autonomous, jointly-owned, company

Some of these problems could be eliminated if the shareholders were to agree that their jointly owned company should stand on its own two feet; that it should be set up so that it could make its own profits, and if there were *financial* losses such as that envisaged in the previous paragraph these should be that company's own responsibility – first to reduce as far as possible both the risks of any losses, and the levels of any that did occur, but second to bear those losses out of profits generated on its remaining operations.

In Table 38 we reproduce the company's projected tax computation showing the revised arrangements.

Table 38: Corporation Tax of Leasing Company which is Autonomous and Profitable

	1994	1995	1996	1997	1998	1999	Total
Rentals		2600	2600	2600	2600	2600	13000
Rebate of rentals						(2450)	(2450)
Capital allowances	(2425)	(1819)	(1364)	(1023)	(767)	198	(7200)
Interest		(793)	(664)	(508)	(314)	(71)	(2350)
Pre-tax profit	(2425)	(12)	572	1069	1519	277	1000
Tax	(800)	(4)	189	353	501	91	330
Post-tax profit							670

Table 38 shows three main differences from the tax computation in Table 35 but it fails to make explicit the fourth difference:

- the company is now aiming to make a profit, cumulatively through the years, of £1,000 on its own account, and therefore recognises that that will be taxable in its own hands. In the tax computations the early years' losses and later years' profits will be as above, but in the company's accounts depreciation will not be charged on the same pattern as capital allowances above; the company will show profits in each year;

- that planned £1,000 of profit comes to the extent of £300 from the equipment manufacturer, who has charged the company only £9,700 in place of £10,000. The capital allowances the company obtains on equipment costing £9,700 and sold for £2,500 have dropped to £7,200;

- the balance of the £1,000 of profit comes from the financier, whose interest receipts from the company have been reduced from £3,050 to £2,350.

THE AUTONOMOUS, JOINTLY-OWNED, COMPANY

7.10 *The financing of the autonomous company, in part, with equity*

The fourth change in the company's position, not so easily visible in the figures in the previous paragraph, is that we now assume that it is financed to the extent of £1,500 with equity (£450 from the equipment manufacturer and £1,050 from the financier). The company therefore needs to borrow only £8,200 in order to acquire equipment costing £9,700 – and that borrowing is immediately reduced to £7,550 by the receipt of the first quarter's rental. The cashflow thereafter is shown in Table 39.

7.11 *The autonomous company needs to earn a reward on its equity*

The tax payments that the jointly owned company needed to make in respect of 1996, 1997 and £262 out of the 1998 payment have been met out of receipts from the shareholders.[3] The final line of the 1999 cashflow shows the whole balance of tax payments due from the jointly owned company as if it had been paid by that company on 31 December of that year, which is of course not quite accurate; it is however a method of avoiding the cashflow extending without end which it would do if one kept cash beyond the end of 1999, earned interest on it in 2000, and thus created a tax liability to be met in 2001, for which cash would need to be retained beyond the end of 2000, and so on.

The cashflow itself, and the summary at the end of it, make clear two further aspects of the operation. First, a leasing company's normal manner of pricing a projected transaction recognises not only that it needs to pay interest on the borrowings which provide part of the asset's cost, but that it needs also to provide its shareholders with a reward on the equity put in by them alongside those borrowings. Second, that reward on the equity, and the underlying equity itself, can both be *taken out* of the lease as the lease borrowings decrease – because the only purpose of the equity is to support those borrowings. The usual rate at which equity and reward are taken out is in proportion to the falling level of borrowings (each figure in the final column of the cash flow is proportionate to the figure in the immediately preceding column).

We do need to make clear that the £1,500 of equity is still retained in the company, supporting borrowings in other leases. The £670 of reward has however been paid out by the company to its shareholders as dividend – this being the jointly owned company's pre-tax profit of £1,000 less the £330 of tax paid on that figure.[4]

---

[3] The receipts from shareholders, 'payments for group relief', were equal to the tax value of the 1994 and 1995 losses surrendered to them, namely £804 in aggregate. These receipts came in as to £189 to meet the 1996 liability, £353 for the 1997 liability, and £262 towards that for 1998; that left the jointly owned company bearing its own tax of £239 for 1998 and £71 for 1999, £330 in total.

[4] A jointly owned company can pay dividends to each of the 70 per cent and 30 per cent members of the consortium which owns it, without the formalities of accounting for advance corporation tax on payment, if a joint election is made under section 247(1)(b) TA 1988. The rules parallel to those explained in paragraph 5.26 for 'group dividends' paid by a subsidiary to its parent.

CONSORTIA

Table 39: Cashflow of the Autonomous Leasing Company showing its Borrowings and Interest, but also its Equity and the Reward it takes on it.

		Start of quarter	Rental rec'd	Tax	After rental	Int'est 1.028%	Equity & rew'd	End of quarter
1995	Qr 1	(8,200)	650		(7,550)	(209)	(193)	(7,952)
	Qr 2	(7,952)	650		(7,302)	(202)	(187)	(7,691)
	Qr 3	(7,691)	650		(7,041)	(195)	(180)	(7,416)
	Qr 4	(7,416)	650		(6,766)	(187)	(173)	(7,126)
						(793)	(733)	
1996	Qr 1	(7,126)	650		(6,476)	(179)	(166)	(6,821)
	Qr 2	(6,821)	650		(6,171)	(171)	(158)	(6,500)
	Qr 3	(6,500)	650		(5,850)	(162)	(150)	(6,162)
	Qr 4	(6,162)	650		(5,512)	(152)	(141)	(5,805)
						(664)	(615)	
1997	Qr 1	(5,805)	650		(5,155)	(143)	(131)	(5,429)
	Qr 2	(5,429)	650		(4,779)	(133)	(122)	(5,034)
	Qr 3	(5,034)	650		(4,384)	(122)	(112)	(4,618)
	Qr 4	(4,618)	650		(3,968)	(110)	(101)	(4,179)
						(508)	(466)	
1998	Qr 1	(4,179)	650		(3,529)	(98)	(89)	(3,716)
	Qr 2	(3,716)	650		(3,066)	(86)	(78)	(3,230)
	Qr 3	(3,230)	650		(2,580)	(72)	(65)	(2,717)
	Qr 4	(2,717)	650		(2,067)	(58)	(52)	(2,177)
						(314)	(284)	
1999	Qr 1	(2,177)	650		(1,527)	(42)	(39)	(1,608)
	Qr 2	(1,608)	650		(958)	(27)	(24)	(1,009)
	Qr 3	(1,009)	650		(359)	(10)	(9)	(378)
	Qr 4	(378)	650		272	8		280
	Qr 4	280	50	(330)	nil			
						(71)	(72)	
						(2,350)	(2,170)	

The cash receipts, rentals plus net retained on asset sale, totalled		13,050
Cash payments of tax were		(330)
		(12,720)
That net cash available went to		
repay initial borrowing	8,200	
plus interest thereon	2,350	
to redistribute into other leases		
the equity original in this one	1,500	
and to pay out a reward on equity	670	12,720

Leasing companies need fairly sophisticated computer programmes to do these calculations, and the reason why it is so difficult to obtain any sensible information from them, or to negotiate in any ordinary sense of the word, is that almost none of their staff understand the arithmetic involved. But let us leave all of that to one side, and use the insights we have gained to think generally about jointly owned companies in general.

7.12 *Management of the jointly owned company*

It is not totally impossible for the shareholders themselves to manage their jointly owned company, but it is always going to be difficult. We considered in paragraph 7.7 a number of matters which would need to be dealt with by the shareholders, if they were to act as joint managers of its operations:

- the structure of their pricing of transactions to the jointly owned company, to enable it to operate as we were then envisaging on a break-even basis, but at the same time giving each of them the appropriate reward from their dealings with it;

- the way in which they would handle the necessary adjustments if any of those pricing, or other, assumptions turned out otherwise than expected – if manufacturing costs changed, if interest rates changed, and if lessees were found to be willing to pay more, or could not be persuaded to pay as much;

- the way in which extraneous factors could be dealt with – changes in tax rates, or the joint company's inability to obtain rentals from a customer who went into liquidation.

All of these matters *can* be dealt with between the shareholders; they could either discuss and agree every matter, on every occasion that agreement was needed – or they could have a detailed agreement indicating how each matter should be handled. But merely recapitulating those particular points, and indicating how they could be dealt with, indicates how complex and time consuming it is likely to be for shareholders to operate their company in this way.

The alternative, what we have been moving towards in paragraphs 7.9 onwards, is to allow the jointly owned company to operate on a more autonomous footing; to accept that it must have its day to day management standing separate from its shareholders, although working within their strategic aims. The latter may retain an overall control in the areas of policy and finance, but the company's own directors can take the necessary decisions in the immediate running of the company and its business.

7.13 One example; the summit meeting

We looked in some detail in paragraphs 5.36 and onward at the *Sainsbury* case.[5] It will be recalled that Sainsbury and a Belgian company (GB) established Homebase Ltd as a jointly owned company, intending that their percentage holdings would eventually be 70 : 30. But Sainsbury started with 75 per cent, and an option to *put* 5 per cent to GB, while GB had the right to *call* for 5 per cent from Sainsbury.

What we were considering in chapter 5 was what that meant for the beneficial ownership of Homebase. But it is some of the information (which came into the public domain as a result of this litigation) about the way in which the shareholders operated their company which is interesting here, the sidelights thrown on this in the evidence given to the Special Commissioner of Income Tax, in the tribunal at which the facts were established prior to the case reaching the courts. He was told how the two shareholders came to their eventual decision that neither would exercise its option to change the shareholding percentage from 75:25 to what had originally been intended, namely 70:30.

Mr Hoyer Millar was the chairman of Homebase, and was also a director of Sainsbury. Clearly in the first of those capacities he would have been in constant touch with the other directors of Homebase, and closely involved in their collective management of the company. Clearly also there must have been meetings at shareholder level, probably more formal in nature at which senior executives of each of Sainsbury and GB were appointed to represent those shareholders in transacting Homebase's formal company business, such as the appointment of its directors, their remuneration, the approval of accounts for the past year and agreement of overall plans for the next. But the meetings about which Mr Hoyer Miller told the Special Commissioner were *summits*, involving only Sir John Sainsbury (the chairman of that company) and himself on one side, and Baron Vaxelaire and M. Dopchie (president and vice-president) on GB's side. Once or twice a year these four discussed, quite informally, their relationships as shareholders in the light of the progress made by their jointly owned company, and their views on future co-operation on its activities. It is always useful in conducting business operations to know what is in your colleagues' minds, but the evidence shows clearly that something beyond this level of informality was essential for the proper running of the business, and was equally desirable if it was necessary to identify when particular decisions were made. Relationships between shareholders (and with directors) need especial care in consortiums.

---

[5] *J Sainsbury plc v O'Connor* [1991] BTC 181.

CHAPTER 8

DIRECTORS – THE COMPANY'S PUBLIC FACE

The duties of directors

8.1 *Relationships with shareholders, creditors, employees and the public generally*

There are many excellent books which set out the powers and responsibilities of directors. It is probably the case that the majority are addressed primarily at directors of public, listed, companies rather than the generally smaller, and generally private, companies which are the main subject of this book. That is of no particular concern, however, since we are not seeking to compete with the books referred to, nor to write a parallel compendium for those who have, on occasion, been famously disparaged as small company directors.

What we will do in this chapter is look briefly at:

- the directors' authority. As we saw in the last chapter (in the particular instance of a company owned by a consortium) it is in practice necessary that shareholders authorise the company's directors to manage it on their behalf;

- in the light of that delegation by the shareholders, we must also examine some aspects of the relationships between directors and shareholders; to see the extent of the latters' ability to control the former – whether there are universal rules or some general usage, and we should enquire whether the answers we come to are a satisfactory way of running companies;

- to look also at the duties and responsibilities directors owe to the company itself; but there are also its employees, its creditors, and (of vital importance in the context of this book) all those other parties with whom the company makes any contracts or does business.

That last aspect will lead us straight into the next chapter, entitled *Maintenance of Capital*, in which we must examine the extent of the company's powers; the extent of and limits on those of its directors; certain matters (for instance a company's giving financial assistance for the purchase of its own shares) which are unlawful; and where these all leave those other parties who may have been involved in these transactions with the company. These two chapters are inevitably intertwined.

8.2 The company's constitution

The Memorandum which the subscribers register with the Companies Registrar in the process of incorporating their company is a statement by them, for the benefit of those who may have dealings with their company, showing who are its subscribers and what is to be its capital; but for present purposes the more important statement is what are to be its objects, and who are its directors.

> ... as a general rule, a company incorporated under the Companies Acts holds out its directors as having ostensible authority to do on its behalf anything which its memorandum of association, expressly or by implication, gives the company the capacity to do.[1]

Most of the questions raised by that statement are matters we will look at in the next chapter, for instance what is the company's *capacity*? What happens if the directors exceed their actual authority, although still within their *ostensible* authority? And what is the position if they abuse their authority?

But we will start by concentrating on the processes under which the directors are given their authority, and through which they are controlled. It is usual[2] for a company being incorporated also to register its Articles of Association, which can be described as the contract between the company and its members regulating their entitlement to take part in the conduct of the company's business, and their relationship with each other as shareholders in it. Those who become its members at any later date automatically become parties to that same contract with the company and with existing and future members. There are certain matters which it is highly desirable should be dealt with in every company's Articles; and it can be argued that it is also desirable that these should generally be dealt with in the same way by different companies.

This is what lies behind Table A, a set of model articles for a company (public or private) limited by shares, prescribed by statutory instrument.[3]

---

[1] Slade LJ in *Rolled Steel Products Ltd v British Steel Corporation and Others* [1985] 3 All ER 52, at 83. But we will see in paragraph 9.5 that third parties dealing with the company and its directors, have, since the events considered by Slade L.J., been entitled to make certain assumptions about the capacity of the company and the authority of its directors.

[2] A company limited by shares (as distinct from a company limited by guarantee or an unlimited company) is not compelled to register Articles of Association when it is incorporated, section 7(1) CA 1985. If it does not do so, the provisions of Table A (as explained in the text) are taken to be the Articles by which the company and its shareholders are governed, section 8(2) CA 1985.

[3] The regulations in which the current Table A is prescribed are in S.I. 1985 No 805. Companies incorporated before that statutory instrument came into force on 1 July 1985 would, to the extent Table A was relevant to them as explained in the text, be governed by the predecessor form of it in effect at the date of incorporation, the most recent before 1985 being the 1948 version. (There were a few minor modifications made at various points between 1948 and 1985, which makes it a bit more complicated than it would otherwise be to identify precisely what a particular company's rules are). The 1948 Table A was incorporated in the text of that Act, and its existence was generally preserved when the remainder of that legislation was repealed in 1985.

It is however necessary to remember that there was one major restructuring of companies legislation in 1980. Prior to that a company registered with the Registrar

continued

If a company does not register its own Articles, then Table A constitutes its Articles; even if it does register Articles, Table A is still applicable so far as the registered Articles do not exclude or alter specific regulations in it, and so far as those Articles do not contain specific rules which are inconsistent with Table A.[4] We will make the general assumption that Table A does apply except where we explain that most companies find it appropriate to make different provisions.

8.3 Shareholders' ultimate control

Table A envisages that shareholders have ultimate control, but that they will delegate to directors of the company not only the management of the company's business, but also a significant part of the mechanics of their own control. Thus shareholders exercise their control at general meetings, either annual or extraordinary (r.36),[5] which the directors normally call (r.37), normally chair (r.42), are entitled to attend and address even if they are not members of the company (r.44), and at which those directors have some control over the way in which decisions are taken, by show of hands or by poll (r.46 and 47). Meetings are not permitted without all shareholders being given advance notice of both the meeting itself, and of the business to be transacted at it (r.38). A quorum of members must be present at any meeting (r.40); such a quorum can be made up of individuals appointed as proxies for members, and as representatives for corporate members, as well as members themselves, but it is clear that the primary shareholders' control mechanism is envisaged as a meeting at which there will be discussions and voting. It is very much as an afterthought, a second best way of doing things, that companies legislation has recognised the possibility

---

continued
  simply as a company, and whether it was public or private, its name always ended with the word *Limited*.
  It could decide (and declare in its Articles, but without the Registrar's involvement) that it was putting restrictions on the transfer of its shares, and forbidding any invitation to the public to subscribe for shares or debentures – or it could decide not to do either of these. In terms of the 1948 Table A, this meant operating, or ceasing to operate, Part II of the Table in addition to those provisions of Part I which the company wished should apply.
  It was only from 1980 onwards that companies needed to *register* as private, or as plc's, and to re-register if they wished to change from one to the other. It is in its Memorandum that a plc must state that it is public, (Clause 2 of Table F in SI 1985 No 805, and section 43(2)(a) CA 1985. And it is section 81 CA 1985, itself supplemented by the prospectus requirements of the Financial Services Act 1986 which are still in the process of being brought into effect, which now apply the share allotment and transfer restrictions.
  It will have been obvious that a number of the provisions we have seen in earlier discussions, (for instance the different rules for valuation by private and public companies of assets received when shares are alloted for a non-cash consideration in paragraph 3.26 and Note 33), could only operate if the company's status as private or public were fixed by something firmer than its self-announced choice.
[4] Section 8(2) CA 1985.
[5] The numbers of the regulations in Table A will be referred to in this form.

of shareholders of a private company reaching decisions by agreeing to, or disagreeing with, written resolutions put to shareholders who do not need to consider them in the same place and at the same time.[6]

No one can suggest that control exercised in this way could be an easy way of making the day to day, reactive and pro-active, decisions that are involved in the management of a company and of its business.

8.4 *The four main areas in which shareholders exert their control*

But the shareholders can and must exercise an effective ultimate control over those to whom they do delegate those functions of management of the company, including the administration of their own controls.

It is the directors of the company to whom the shareholders do this delegating. There is one vital fact which stands out in the previous paragraph, but which we did not spell out in quite these words; the shareholders act as a body, without any mechanisms through which they can exercise their own *controls* by delegation to one of their number or to a committee. Those whom they are controlling, however, are directors, who, because their powers and duties relate primarily to *management*, can generally be expected to comprise a small enough number to be able operate effectively as a committee, and are able to split duties, and delegate authority, between themselves (r.72).

It is against that background that we must look at the shareholders' effectiveness; we can do so by reminding ourselves that there are four areas in which directors are answerable to shareholders (and others beside the shareholders), although we will examine principally the first, second and fourth:

- directors may be appointed by the shareholders or by the directors themselves. Table A provides for directors to retire and submit themselves for re-election on a three-year basis, (r.73 and 74). In private companies the rotation provisions are frequently omitted, and appointments of new directors made by the board rather than the shareholders. The next two paragraphs look at the complex subject of removal of directors;

- shareholders fix the directors' remuneration (r.82), but we will see in paragraph 8.7 below that this statement does not mean quite what it might appear to mean.

- companies legislation requires directors to report annually to shareholders on specified aspects of their stewardship;

---

[6] The procedures relating to written resolutions have already been referred to briefly in paragraphs 3.13 and 6.9 (including Note 11 to the latter paragraph). What we noted there was the legislators' apparent wish to ensure that anyone who would have a right either to vote on a particular matter at a meeting, or to make observations on that matter before the shareholders voted on it, should have notice of any proposal that the matter should be considered by the written resolution procedures; and that his rights to object should also be preserved. The requirements are in sections 381A to 381C CA 1985.

- directors have authority to manage the business of the company, and to exercise all of its powers (r.70). But they have certain duties spelled out in law to the company, to the shareholders and to others; the law also prevents some actions, for example allowing a company 'financially to assist' purchase of its shares.[7]

8.5 Appointment and removal of directors

We do not need to summarise all of the detail in Table A, and in the Companies Acts, but simply to indicate in broad brush strokes what is the overall pattern:

- although Table A envisages directors retiring on a regular basis (all of them at the company's first annual general meeting and one third at each subsequent AGM (r.73 and 74)), it is clear that those retirements are to be a reality only if the director concerned does not want to be reappointed or is actually voted down by the meeting. He is otherwise deemed to be reappointed (r.75);

- if a vacancy occurs, either as a result of the previous head; through death, resignation or disqualification;[8] or simply because there are fewer directors than the company had fixed as its full complement in its Articles or otherwise; then the other directors can fill that vacancy (r.79). But Table A requires that shareholders can only put a name forward with the prior agreement of the directors, and subject to strict prior-notice requirements for the meeting at which the nomination is to be put forward;

- one could perhaps read into that previous head an implication that Table A's draftsman recognised that harmony was essential for the effective operation of a board. But the draftsman made no provision for directors wishing to remove from the board one of their number who was failing to perform.[9] That is a right reserved to the shareholders, subject once again to strict requirements as to notice before the meeting at which this is to be proposed, and to the director's statutory right to *represent* his side of the case to all the company's members;[10]

---

[7] Sections 151 to 158 CA 1985. See paragraphs 9.19 to 9.24.
[8] This book is not a treatise on directors' disqualifications, but the possible causes can conveniently be thought of in four groups: disqualification by the court for the misconduct which makes an individual *unfit*, as set out in the Company Directors Disqualification Act 1986; second, mental illness (r.81(c)), or bankruptcy (which is covered both by section 11 of the CDDA 1986 already referred to, and r.81(b) of Table A); third, reaching the age of 70 so far as concerns directors of public companies, or private companies which are subsidiaries of public companies, section 293 CA 1985; and last, absenting himself without the other directors' agreement from board meetings for six months (r.81(e)). (There is a fifth possibility which is seldom met with today, which is the failure by a director to acquire, or retain, directors' qualification shares in the company of which he has been appointed a director, section 291(3) CA 1985.)
[9] Except in the case of absence without leave mentioned as the fourth reason for removal in Note 8.
[10] Sections 303 and 304 CA 1985.

- but although neither the Act nor Table A gives a board powers to remove one of their number, provision for this is made in the Articles of a substantial number of companies. Whether such a director is removed by the other directors or the shareholders, the court's decision in the *Ebrahimi* case[11] may be relevant. Mr Ebrahimi had a substantial shareholding in a small private company 'formed on the basis of a personal relationship'. When his co-directors and co-shareholders voted him off the board, the House of Lords accepted his petition that the company should be wound up, that being the only course that was fair to himself and to those others.

8.6 Preventing directors' removal, and requiring it

A different aspect of the appointment of directors can be briefly mentioned here. Yet again it has to be said that it is not an essential element in this book's coverage – if it were, it could justify examination in greater detail.

It is often the wish of the original shareholders in family (and for that matter other) companies that a director or directors should be able to hold office for as long as he might wish, without being forced out as a result for instance of a family quarrel which might have little to do with the particular director's conduct of the company's business. There are four strands to this. The director concerned can be given a service contract for a substantial period (that is to say, for more than five years, even for life), but only if that contract does not breach section 319 Companies Act 1985. What that section requires is that such a service contract be approved by a resolution of the company passed at a general meeting. The second point is, however, that such a resolution can at any time be reversed by the company, because its powers under section 303, to dismiss a director by resolution[12] at a

---

[11] *Ebrahimi v Westbourne Galleries* [1973] AC 360. The company, Westbourne Galleries Ltd had originally been a partnership; on incorporation

> 'the parties are now co-members in a company, who have accepted, in law, new obligations. A company, however small, however domestic, is a company not a partnership or even a quasi-partnership . . .'

However the House of Lords went on to explain that the conceptions of probity, good faith and mutual confidence which were at the heart of partnership law were paralleled in companies legislation to the extent that section 222(f) of the Companies Act 1948 (now replaced by section 459 and onward CA 1985) provided redress for oppressed minority shareholders, and in particular that the court could order a company to be would up if it came to the view that this was the 'just and equitable' solution. In the Westbourne Galleries case, Mr Ebrahimi was able to

> 'point to, and prove, some special underlying obligation of his fellow members in good faith, or confidence, that so long as the business continues he shall be entitled to management participation . . .'

(both quotations come from Lord Wilberforce at page 380).

[12] Section 303 stipulates that the resolution to remove a director needs only to be an ordinary resolution; it is not possible for the company to exclude this method of removing a director, by requiring in its Articles or in an agreement with the director

continued

general meeting are not, and cannot be, circumscribed. But although the company's *powers* are preserved, the director can make it difficult for the other members to use them. Section 303 allows the removal of a director but does not remove his right to claim compensation – if he has a long and lucrative contract it may be beyond the company's resources to remove him. And it is legitimate for the company to give his shares specially weighted voting rights so that when he and his co-shareholders vote on the matter of his removal, his votes will outweigh those against him – so-called *Bushell v Faith* shares.[13]

What seems at first to be a mirror-image problem arises in the case of the company which wishes to allow employees to acquire shares, perhaps under one of the tax-driven share incentive or option schemes; but wishes also to ensure that its share register is not over-burdened with former employees whose continuing presence on the register dilutes not only the current employees' control of their company, but also the speed at which the efforts of those current employees could generate growth in the value of their shares if they were the only shareholders. How possible it is to operate a system which requires those retiring (or leaving voluntarily or otherwise) to sell shares is something we will have to examine in chapter 10, when we come to look at share schemes.

8.7 Shareholders' control over directors' remuneration

Next, but still in the context of the control which shareholders may be able to exercise over directors, and the rights of those directors themselves, we need to devote some time to looking at the framework within which directors are entitled to be paid.

What most of the textbooks have to say is that directors have no statutory right to remuneration. Therefore, it is said, if they are to be remunerated their entitlement must be voted by the company, which means in turn that it must be the Articles which set out how the company is to decide the directors' remuneration, that is to say, what rights the shareholders have to approve or disapprove. Thus, in Table A, r.82 requires the shareholders to vote directors' remuneration by ordinary resolution, and r.83 allows the directors to be paid

> ... expenses properly incurred by them in connection with their attendance at meetings ... or otherwise in connection with the discharge of their duties.

---

continued
    that only a special or extraordinary resolution would be effective. However, notice that the word used above is 'exclude'; it is possible for the company to make provision for removing a director by special or extraordinary resolution as an alternative to the section 303 route using an ordinary resolution; if it does then use this alternative route, the director would have no statutory rights to make representations, because these only arise under the section 303 route.

[13] The device of giving a director shares carrying weighted votes which enable him to outvote other shareholders trying to remove him was approved by the House of Lords in *Bushell v Faith* [1970] AC 1099.

However, each of those three sentences refer to directors' *remuneration*; we need to be absolutely clear in out minds what that word means in the context in which it is used in companies legislation, because it emphatically does not mean everything that directors are paid. The principles are as follows (and we need not apologise that this makes matters sound simpler than they ever are in practice, so long as readers accept this as an explanation of concepts, not a formulation which resolves every practical problem).

Directors need to be seen as having two distinct roles, and the ways in which it may be appropriate to reward each role reflects the distinctions:

- a director can be an employee (the general usage would be an *executive*) of his company, with a service contract from it under which he is entitled to a salary (and perhaps a bonus or commission) like any other executive. The emphasis in such a service contract is likely to be that his duties are the management of the company's business (to which he is to devote all his energies), rather than the more difficult to define duty of *directing* the company itself. If the company has share option or incentive arrangements[14] these would be an appendage to his service contract;

- but what the Companies Acts refer to as directors' remuneration is not the pay provided under that service contract. What the Acts are concerned with is any remuneration the directors may receive for their services *as directors*, separate from the above.[15]

---

[14] Share incentive and share option schemes are the subject of chapter 10. One of the features common to all of the tax approved schemes is that they apply only to those who work *full time* (as defined in chapter 10), which is consistent with a director's role under his service contract, but would not otherwise be easy to apply.

[15] One small illustration might help to make clear the Companies Acts' approach. Section 312 says that it is not lawful for a company to make a payment to a director 'by way of compensation for loss of office', without particulars being disclosed to the members and the proposal being approved by the company. That phraseology, and particularly the requirement that it is the *proposal* which the company must approve, can only be read as making it mandatory that the company obtain *prior* approval from its shareholders before any payment is actually made. Why then do we read in the papers almost every day that it has come to light in the accounts of such and such a company that it made a payment of £x to Mr Y, when he left the board in a blaze of publicity a year or more earlier? Why did the company not seek prior approval? One possible reason is that the company claimed that the payment was a *superannuation gratuity*, this being one of the ways in which a company can pay a pension to a director for past services – but that does imply that the company does have not only the ability to pay such gratuities, but some policy under which their amounts can be determined. The fact that the recipient has some type of right to a *pension* payment would tend to make it fully taxable in his hands as income, a result which he might not entirely welcome. The almost invariable alternative, therefore, is that the company makes the payment as compensation not for his loss of the office of director, but as compensation for its breaching his service contract as an employee. Section 316(3) CA 1985 is particularly illuminating here, in that it spells out that the payments referred to in section 312 (which as quoted above calls for prior shareholder approval) 'do not include any *bona fide* payment by way of damages for breach of contract . . .'. In other words, the company does not need to go to its shareholders in advance, if the payment it contemplates can be regarded as compensation under the *employee-type* service contract, and not compensation for the loss of office as a director.

We said in paragraph 8.4 above that the shareholders have the right to fix the remuneration of the directors – but that that statement did not mean quite what it appeared. The powers that the shareholders have relate only to *remuneration* in the second head above; shareholders have no control, under the Companies Act, over the pay that directors grant themselves under their service contracts, for the services they perform as employees or executives. What we described as an appendage to the service contracts, namely share option and incentive schemes which extend to the companies' directors, are submitted by listed companies to their shareholders for approval only because the *Yellow Book* (Stock Exchange – admission of securities to listing) requires this, not because Table A or the legislation suggests that it is necessary.

8.8 *Disclosure of directors' emoluments and other benefits*

The words in the heading of this paragraph are taken from schedule 6 to the Companies Act 1985. Part I of that schedule requires the disclosure in a company's accounts of directors' emoluments (partly in the form of aggregate figures for all directors, but partly split between individuals), as briefly indicated below.[16] Part II of the schedule requires disclosure of loans made by the company to its directors, a subject which is not within the compass of this book.[17]

'Emoluments' are defined in schedule 6 to embrace what we have identified in the previous paragraph as:

- directors' remuneration;

- directors' earnings under their service contracts, described in the legislation as 'otherwise in connection with the management of the affairs of the company or any of its subsidiary undertakings'.[18]

The first of those categories needs to be separated into the remuneration received by directors for services as a director of the company itself, and that for services as a director of subsidiaries.[19] The second heading

---

[16] 'Small companies' as defined in section 247 CA 1985 are exempted from the requirement to disclose in the accounts they file with the Registrar of Companies the details of directors' emoluments (that exemption being in paragraph 3(3) of schedule 8); but that is a *filing* exemption, which does not mean that the company is exempted from disclosure in its accounts prepared for its shareholders.

[17] The making of loans to directors is generally prohibited by section 330(2)(a) CA 1985, but there are exceptions to that general rule (for instance the full stringencies are slightly less for private companies than for public companies). In this book we have only touched this subject tangentially, in paragraph 5.22, in relation to the tax effects of loans by *close companies* to their participators. It is important that we recall the timing, as well as the existence, of a tax liability on these loans, this being one of the matters explained in paragraph 5.22.

[18] Paragraph 1(2)(b)(ii) of schedule 6 CA 1985.

[19] In this connection the word 'subsidiary' is not limited to the normal definition of subsidiary in section 736 CA 1985, but where the individual is a director of another company by virtue of a right of appointment held by his own company, that other is to be regarded as a subsidiary of his own. This position frequently occurs, for example, where a merchant bank holds a share stake in a client company, and has the right to appoint one of its own directors to the board.

aggregates service contract earnings from the company and any subsidiaries. The emoluments figure must also include the *expenses and benefits* which we will come to in the next paragraph, to the extent that these are to be treated as taxable in the directors' hands. Emoluments also include the company's contributions to pension schemes for the directors.[20] But what has to be split (between services of directors of the company, services of directors of subsidiaries, and service contract earnings) is the aggregate emoluments of all of the directors.

The second level of the disclosure is that the total emoluments figure (not split between services as a director, under a service contract, and so on) must be disclosed for the chairman; and the total emoluments figures for each other director must be grouped into bands, so that the number of directors in each £5,000 band is disclosed.

Third, disclosure is required of amounts paid to directors as compensation for loss of office.[21] Although schedule 6 to the Companies Act 1985 does call for certain further disclosures, the foregoing gives a general flavour of its requirements.

8.9 Directors' tax

As if the draftsmen of companies legislation had not made life confusing enough, it is essential that we also say something about tax, because the thought processes, and terminology, used by the Inland Revenue authorities are sufficiently different from that employed in companies legislation to ensure complete confusion.

We introduced in paragraph 8.7 three concepts (remuneration as a director, earnings under a service contract, and expenses of attending board meetings). How these fit into the tax legislation is as follows:

---

[20] Where a company contributes to an individual scheme for a director, its contribution can be identified and will need to be disclosed. However, if a director is a member of a general scheme, and the company's contribution is fixed by the scheme's actuary as (say) 12 per cent of total salary roll, the legislation recognises that it would be inappropriate to regard a particular director's share of that aggregate as being 12 per cent of his own salary – and accordingly no amount need be counted into his emoluments (paragraph 13(3)(c) of schedule 6). There is a different implication of the inclusion in directors' emoluments disclosed in the accounts of the contributions to pension schemes. It has always been Inland Revenue practice to require from companies an analysis of the total figure disclosed, splitting this between the individual directors, so that these figures can be compared with those on which those individuals have paid tax. Since a company's contributions into an approved scheme are not taxable as income of the employee (section 596(1) TA 1988), it is clearly necessary to exclude those contributions in analysing the individual directors' taxable income. It is also necessary to allow those individuals a deduction where they themselves have made contributions into a pension scheme (section 592(7) TA 1988). All of this should be obvious, but it has been the author's experience that the Inland Revenue staff concerned have frequently needed to have it explained.

[21] The phrase 'compensation for loss of office' is used loosely here. We saw in Note 15 on paragraph 8.7 that payments are usually made in the form of compensation for the breach of a service contract (for services as an executive of the company) rather than compensation for the loss of the office of director. The disclosure needed under schedule 6 would embrace amounts paid for both types of compensation.

(a) 'emoluments'[22] is the word used in the Taxes Act which we must think of as including three categories of pay received by a director or employee

(a)(i) pay which accrues on a day-to-day basis, its level usually being stated as a sum per annum, and the most common source as we have seen being the *service contract*; but it is worth pointing out that such a contract does not necessarily involve the director's having a right to continuing *employment* and emoluments for (say) three years despite the fact the the company might want to terminate his services sooner (by the ordinary resolution we considered in paragraph 8.5). A service contract may just as often give its holder, and the company, rights and obligations similar to those of any senior employee, say, three months notice on either side;

(a)(ii) *directors' fees* differ from the pay mentioned above in that fees do not accrue from day to day. Occasionally they are paid on a per-meeting-attended basis, but more usually per annum. In that second case, unless a director serves throughout the full year, he would have no right to a proportion of the year's fee;

(a)(iii) 'bonuses' is not a word which appears anywhere in either tax or companies legislation, but it is convenient to apply it to that part of a director's earnings which is not quantified as remuneration at £x per annum, but is the additional remuneration paid after the accounts have been drawn up by way of a distribution of profits in a company whose shareholders and directors are the same people.

We are trying to think about tax concepts here, but it will be clear from what we said earlier about companies legislation, that the shareholders will have approved a scale of payments for (a)(ii) above, and will need to approve the payments to be made under (a)(iii). Because tax legislation needs to fix not only the amount of income assessable, but also the relevant date for its assessment the timing of the shareholders' approval (or as we will see below in Note 31, earlier directors' agreement) may be of considerable relevance. This applies

---

[22] Tax legislation (section 131(1) TA 1988), like the Companies Act disclosure provisions, uses the archaism 'emoluments'. In the Taxes Act this is defined as *including* (that is to say, the list is illustrative rather than complete) all salaries, fees, wages, perquisites and profits whatsoever. That does not include the expenses and benefits on which the director is taxed – which we will come to later in paragraph 8.9. Nor does it include the company's contributions to the director's pension scheme, which we noted in Note 20 on paragraph 8.8 are counted into emoluments for the Companies Act disclosures, but are excluded by the tax legislation. It is thought that a perquisite is a right to remuneration in non-monetary form, for instance the huntsman's right to the skins of the horses he has slaughtered to feed to his hounds. A profit, in this connection, is probably the right to derive a monetary reward from the employment but not from the employer, for instance the cook's ability to extract payment from the footmen she allows to eat in her servants' hall.

not only for tax liabilities, but also under the National Insurance legislation.

(b) 'expenses properly incurred by them in connection with their attendance at meetings' was the phrase we quoted out of r.83, but the shorthand the Inland Revenue use is 'travelling from home to office';

(c) 'expenses ... (properly incurred) otherwise in connection with the discharge of their duties' was also a quotation from r.83. Here, the very much narrower phrase derived from tax legislation[23] is usually abbreviated to 'expenses wholly, exclusively and necessarily incurred';

(d) 'round sum allowances' paid to reimburse a director for expenses which he is expected by the company to incur in the course of his duties, but for which he is not required to submit detailed accounts to the company. One example of expenditure sometimes dealt with in this way is taxi-fares, where the company knows that the director's duties necessitate his frequently using taxis on the company's business, and the company can be reasonably sure what reimbursement will be fair to him and it;

(e) *benefits in kind*: that is to say, anything provided by the company in non-monetary form. The tax definition[24] is 'accommodation (other than living accommodation), entertainment, domestic and other services, and other benefits and facilities of whatsoever nature (whether or not similar to any of those mentioned above in this subsection) excluding however ...' There then follows a list of exclusions which (like the living accommodation excluded earlier) are taken out merely because there are separate provisions dealing with the tax liabilities;

(f) *the use of assets which are the company's property*: for instance the company car available for private as well as business use.

What the tax authorities have decreed is that a director is to be subjected to income tax under the Pay as you Earn procedures on everything within

---

[23] Section 198 TA 1988. The section permits the 'deduct(ion) from the emoluments to be assessed (of) expenses incurred and defrayed' in the following defined ways. Expenses are categorised as those of 'travelling in the performance of the duties', for which the requirement is that the director must *necessarily* have incurred the expense and defrayed its cost out of his emoluments; and any other expenses, to which is applied the infamous requirement that they must have been 'wholly, exclusively and necessarily incurred in the performance of the duties', and once again defrayed out of the director's emoluments. It is not a purpose of this book to comment on the narrowness of what we describe as infamous words, nor on the fact that the self-employed (and for that matter companies themselves) have to pass rather less stringent requirements for the deductibility of expenses incurred in carrying on the businesses from which they earn their profits (see paragraph 5.4 and Note 11 thereon). What is vital is that we do not overlook the significance of the words 'incur' and 'defray'; these are explained towards the end of paragraph 8.9.

[24] Section 154(2) TA 1988.

any of the three branches of head (a), and in heads (b) and (d), that is to say, on earnings under the service contract, fees, bonuses, expenses of travel from home to board meetings, and round sum allowances.[25] All of the other items, ((c), (e) and (f)), are not *pay* (meaning that PAYE does not have to be deducted by a company when it refunds to a director the sum he had spent on a rail ticket to Glasgow on the company's business), but the amounts must be included on his tax return as part of the director's income within Schedule E. That is the effect of the sections 153 to 168 of the Taxes Act 1988, the provisions dealing with expenses and benefits for directors and those earning £8,500 or more per annum.

But treating the items referred to in those two sentences as income is only a first instance device. At the second instance, the director can make his claim for a *deduction* under the provision referred to in head (c) and Note 23, if he can show that he had 'incurred wholly, exclusively and necessarily in the performance of (his) duties' expense which he had 'defrayed' out of his 'emoluments'.

- it can only exceptionally be the case that a claim can reduce income in any of the divisions of head (a), because not many employees can show that although their employer did not meet their expenses it was *necessary* for them to spend their own salaries in the proper performance of their duties;

---

[25] The legal basis for the Inland Revenue's classification of these items as being within the scope of PAYE is the statutory instrument, the PAYE Regulations (SI 1993/744 made under the authority of section 203(2) TA 1988). However, staff in the Inland Revenue's offices dealing with these matters are more familiar with the Revenue's own interpretation of these rules, to be found in the *Employers' Guide* (Booklet P7 (1992)). This defines heads (a), (b) and (d) as being 'pay that must be included on the deductions working sheet', that is to say, must be subjected to PAYE. The booklet goes on to explain that there are two classes of pay for tax purposes, namely one which is to be subjected to PAYE as indicated above, and one which is not but is to be included on the company's year-end return of expenses and benefits in kind. That might lead one to assume that those two classes are mutually exclusive, but the Revenue demand that round sum allowances are included in *both* classes. This should not be confused with a quite different matter dealt with elsewhere in the booklet, namely that if the employer obtains a 'dispensation' (section 166 TA 1988) the effect is that the general rule no longer applies to the items dispensed, so that those expenses reimbursed to, or paid for, a director need not be counted as part of his income, for PAYE or for year-end returns. Obviously if they are no longer to be regarded as part of income, the director does not need to make any section 198 claim in respect of them. The Department of Social Security has also had fun in phrasing its instructions to those trying to deduct national insurance contributions from directors' remuneration: 'If you pay a round sum allowance whether or not an expense is actually incurred then the whole amount should be included in gross pay. If any specific and distinct business expense is subsequently identified then only any profit element is included in gross pay.' The author admits to having read those two sentences about ten times before being able to identify any interpretation which did not make them self-contradictory. But even if it is possible to reconcile them, there remains a second question, can they actually be applied to the facts of any business situation?

- in the case of head (b), the Revenue maintain steadfastly that travel from home to work cannot be deductible;[26]

- head (f), the value to be placed on the director's entitlement to use assets which remain the property of his company, needs to be thought of rather differently. What the legislation does is to quantify an *annual value* to be treated as the taxable value of the director's benefit (that is to say, his private use of the asset)[27] and the only legitimate deduction from that will be any sum which he *pays* the company for the use of its asset;

- head (e) is broadly similar, in that the cost to the company of the benefit which the company provides (in any form other than giving its director the use of the company's assets) is the measure of the director's taxable income, and subject to what is said below this can only be reduced by anything he himself pays.[28]

That would seem to leave (c) and (d), 'expenses ... incurred ... (in) the discharge of his duties', and 'round sum allowances', as being the reimbursements to him which are, first, to be treated as the director's income but for which he is thereafter allowed to claim under section 198 that he incurred equivalent expense 'wholly, exclusively and necessarily ...' and defrayed it out of his income. However, the sharp-eyed reader will have realised that if the company provides the director with an airline ticket for a business trip, or settles his hotel bill, it simply is not true that *he* incurred expense, nor that he defrayed it out of his income.

---

[26] Since the employer has to pay tax under PAYE on amounts refunded to a director for travel from home to board meetings, his *income* is the equivalent gross. This is what section 164 TA 1988 spells out. What is required by the tax authorities appears to be prevented by the Department of Trade, since section 311(1) CA 1985 says in terms that it is unlawful for a company to pay 'remuneration' free of tax, and goes on in the immediately following subsection to say that any provision by which a company purports to do so shall have effect 'as if it provided for payment, as a gross sum subject to income tax, of the net sum which it actually provides'. If a company is to comply with this, its resolution approving the provision of a rail ticket costing £100 for a director must presumably authorise the payment to him of remuneration of £167.

[27] Section 154 TA 1988 is the general section charging benefits in kind; it is supplemented by section 156 which defines what is to be taken as the *cash equivalent* of those benefits. In the case of assets which remain the property of the employer, but are made available to the employee, the annual value is arrived at under the formulae set out in section 156(5) and (6), and the theory on which these are based is that the whole of the employee's use of the asset is private use on which he should be taxed. The position for cars is obviously different, in that the Revenue accept that there is likely to be business use as well as private, and all they attempt to tax is the value of the 'availability for private use'. Cars are excluded from sections 154 and 156, and the taxable value (the scale rates) arrived at under section 157 and schedule 6 to TA 1988.

[28] This is subject to a mitigating factor; where the company's cost relates to other matters besides the benefit, it is only on a *proper proportion* that the director is taxable. The hotel director, living next door to his hotel, who has his garden maintained by the hotel's groundsman should not be taxed on the whole of the latter's wages, section 156(2) TA 1988.

DIRECTORS' TAX

The company spent the money, and the provision which deems the company's cost to be the director's income is head (e), benefits in kind. That sharp-eyed reader will also have seen that head (e) does not appear to provide for the director claiming a deduction against his *benefit* and that the only claim for for a deduction (under section 198 per Note 23) is a deduction from emoluments. The Inland Revenue have accordingly found it necessary to bend what we have portrayed as the strict statutory rule – so that a director (or employee) can make a section 198 claim even though the individual has not incurred expense and defrayed it out of his income.[29]

If we recapitulate these tax provisions, a director will be taxable on:

	Directors' remuneration in the second head in paragraph 8.7 to the extent this is not otherwise included in the headings below.
plus (a)	service contract pay, fees, bonuses
plus (b)	travel from home, grossed up for PAYE
plus (c), (d), (e)	expenses, round sum allowances and benefits in kind, to the extent that the director is unable to substantiate a claim for a section 198 deduction, and to the extent he has not reimbursed the company for the cost of the benefits in kind
plus (f)	the annual value of the private use of the company assets to the extent the director has not reimbursed that annual value to the company
less	his own pension contributions

The definition of income for National Insurance contribution purposes is not identical, and in particular the time at which that income is regarded as needing to be recognised for National Insurance proceeds on quite different principles from those applying for income tax.[30]

---

[29] Section 156(8) TA 1988.

[30] As one might expect, the rules for directors' national insurance are not identical to those for income tax. We have mentioned in Note 25 that the question whether round sum allowances are or are not to be counted into income is handled slightly differently; benefits in kind are generally not treated as income under national insurance rules, and the director's pension contributions are not deductible. There are also differences in the rules about when income is to be treated as arising (Note 31 below sets out the income tax rules); the national insurance rules are based on an assumption that it is always possible to identify a date when remuneration is voted to directors, or if earlier a date when they took *advances* against such yet-to-be-voted remuneration. Finally, the rules for directors (introduced in 1983, see the factcard NI 274, and the booklet NI 35) require that national insurance contributions be computed on a *cumulative* basis; that is to say, once cumulative pay from 6 April onwards in a fiscal year has reached the threshold, *all* subsequent pay is subject to NIC (up to the upper limit for the director's own contributions, and without upper limit for the company's contributions). This cumulative basis aims to ensure that a director remunerated equally through the year suffers no greater burden than one whose regular income is lower but who receives a substantial bonus at a particular point in the year.

Those income tax *timing* rules, for determining when particular components of income are now to be taxed, were changed in 1989 onto what is referred to as 'the receipts basis', which broadly results in taxation when the sums concerned are received by the director, or are placed at his disposal so that he could draw them down if he wished to do so.[31]

8.10 Directors' responsibility to the company, and to others

Directors have a fiduciary responsibility to the company, that is to say, they must act in good faith in what they believe to be the company's best interests; they must not have any conflict of interest with the company (which means that any transaction between a company and a director, except his own service contract, should be approved by a resolution of the company, unless the Articles allow for such dealings – Table A at r.85(a) does allow such dealings provided they are disclosed to the other directors); and directors must not derive personal profits from their position as directors.

Specifically, section 309 Companies Act 1985 makes one of the director's fiduciary duties which he owes to the company that of having regard to the interests of the company's employees; note, though, that his duty, as is always the case, is owed to the company not to the individuals themselves.

Directors have what is referred to as a duty of skill and care, that is to say a duty, once again to the company, to attend to its business diligently; to exercise the level of skill which they might be expected to possess (this probably being a different standard for the part-time family

---

[31] Sections 202A, 202B and 203A were written into TA 1988 by the Finance Act 1989 (and the latter also included certain transitional provisions in sections 39 to 41 to cover the change-over). An explanation of the Inland Revenue's view how these rules operate to fix the time when PAYE is to be calculated and deducted from directors' remuneration is set out in their press release of 28 July 1989. Payment is to be regarded as being made on the earliest of the following occasions:

(a) when payment is actually made;
(b) when the director is entitled to be paid;
(c) when earnings of the director are credited in the company's accounts or records (even if they cannot immediately be drawn);
(d) if the amount of the director's earnings for a particular period is determined before the end of the period, when the period ends;
(e) if the amount is determined after the period ends, when the earnings are determined;

the last two of those rules relate in the main to those components of PAYE remuneration which are not paid at predetermined rates, that is to say, what we have characterised as bonuses. It is the Revenue's interpretation of the decision in *Re Duomatic* [1969] 1 All ER 161, that if directors are also controlling shareholders, the directors' meeting at which they decide on the figures to be put into what will at that stage be draft accounts is the relevant date, not the later time at which in their capacity as shareholders, they approve the accounts in their audited form, as presented to the company's annual meeting.

member, as opposed to the full-time manager whose remuneration under his service contract may carry some implication about the skills he holds himself out as having); but those two are not inconsistent with the director's being entitled to rely at least to some extent on others for expert opinions, and for delegated tasks.

The Companies Act 1985, Part X, (sections 311 to 347), imposes on directors what the act refers to as 'fair dealing'. We have noted in paragraph 5.22 and Note 42 thereon that the Act generally prevents directors from borrowing money from their companies (although paragraph 8.8 and Note 17 pointed out that this does not prevent the Companies Acts from requiring disclosure of loans which have been made). We need not take up time and space here looking at a miscellany of other requirements in this part of the act, and in other legislation such as the Company Securities (Insider Dealing) Act 1985.

> It is a misapprehension to suppose that the directors of a company owe a duty to the company's creditors to keep the capital of the company intact. The company's creditors are entitled to assume that the company will not in any way [that is to say, without leave of the court] repay any paid-up share capital to shareholders . . . They are entitled to assume that the directors will conduct its affairs in such a manner that no such unauthorised repayment will take place.[32]

However, despite the directors having duties only to the company, not for instance directly to its employees as such, nor to its creditors, it is a fact that the directors doing something the effect of which is to make the company insolvent is a fraud on the creditors. Which leads us straight into chapter 9.

---

[32] Buckley LJ, in *Re Horsley & Weight Ltd* [1982] 3 All ER 1045 at 1055.

CHAPTER 9

MAINTENANCE OF CAPITAL

9.1 Payments out of capital

We ended the last chapter with Lord Justice Buckley's reminder that companies may not repay their capital to their shareholders – except, as he said, by means of a duly authorised reduction of capital. That is of course the law.

In this chapter we will examine three matters. The first is the depletion of a company's assets by way of gifts or transfers at an undervalue. In what circumstances are such transactions merely a breach of the the directors' duties – and where are they beyond the powers of the company? There are a number of recent leading cases on precisely this question, and it is unlikely that the last word has yet been spoken.

The second matter we will look at is one narrow area in which companies can be regarded as breaching the prohibition on repaying capital, namely their giving financial assistance for the purchase of their own shares. Again, we will look at the law's requirements, and the somewhat surprising way in which these are interpreted.

The third subject is rather different. A company is obviously not repaying capital if the distributions it makes come out of what it is permitted to characterise as *distributable profits*. We know instinctively what that phrase should mean, but instinct is not always a reliable guide to what the law does actually say, and mean. It is essential to understand what the rules really are.

9.2 *Capacity and constitution*

What a company can and cannot do, what the courts refer to as its *capacity*, is defined primarily by the company's own constitution. The law under which it operates sets only the outer perimeter fence outside which neither it nor any other company is allowed to venture; one needs to look to the company's memorandum to see what capacity it has for operating within the area, or some part of the area, inside that perimeter. And it is of course generally the directors who have, as the company's agents, to take the actions and undertake the transactions, in which the company is the principal. It must be acting within its capacity, and they must be within their authority.

For a book on company acquisitions, mergers and reorganisations, the leading case must now be *Aveling Barford Ltd v Perion Ltd and Others*,[1]

---

[1] Reported only at [1989] BCLC 626.

but that is not the best place to begin. The better case from which to start is *Rolled Steel Products Ltd v British Steel Corporation and Others*,[2] and in particular Lord Justice Slade's statement already quoted in paragraph 8.2, echoing as it does those two key words 'capacity' and 'authority':

> ... as a general rule, a company incorporated under the Companies Acts holds out its directors as having ostensible authority to do on its behalf anything which its memorandum of association, expressly or by implication, gives the company the capacity to do.

When a company exceeds the capacity given to it by the memorandum it is acting *ultra vires* – words which we will use scrupulously in that sense only. The phrase is sometimes loosely used in relation to directors failing to act properly within their authority – but this imprecision certainly does not help to clarify the difficult concepts we are looking at.

9.3 The facts in the Rolled Steel Products case

It has to be said that *Rolled Steel Products* was an extremely complex case; wherever *ultra vires* questions arise, the facts and issues are unlikely to be straightforward, but what makes these particular judgments so difficult is the number of parties who had been joined in the action between 1969 when the events occurred and 1981 when the case first reached the High Court. Much of the Court of Appeal judgments relate to questions whether those parties should have been allowed to change their pleadings during the course of the High Court hearing in the light of the way in which the judge had allowed it to develop. We must try to eliminate all this from our explanations, and concentrate only on the essential facts – and the principles which the Court of Appeal explained. Lord Justice Slade's judgment runs to over 35 pages, and those of Browne-Wilkinson and Lawton LLJ to a further four and two respectively; we make no attempt to cross-reference each of the propositions in the paragraphs which follow to the relevant page numbers in the Lord Justice Slade's judgment.

A Mr Shenkman owned 51 per cent of the shares in Rolled Steel Products (Holdings) Ltd ('RSP'), and 100 per cent of the shares in Scottish Steel Sheet Ltd ('SSS'). The remaining 49 per cent of RSP was held by trustees of a settlement established by him for his children. He and his father were the only directors of RSP (the board of SSS was not a relevant matter). The main supplier of SSS was Colvilles Ltd, and in early 1968 the amount owing by SSS to Colvilles had risen to over £800,000. The only significant asset of SSS out of which it could have reduced that debt was an amount of £400,000 owed to it by RSP. Colvilles insisted on Mr Shenkman giving a personal guarantee of the £800,000 owed by SSS. After nearly a year of further negotiations, agreement had been reached

---

[2] [1985] 3 All ER 52, at 83.

that RSP would sell some property, the proceeds of which would be made available to SSS so that it could pay off the indebtedness to Colvilles, but RSP had not found a buyer for the property. The actions taken and documented in January 1969 were (1) a guarantee by RSP of amounts then, and in the future becoming, owed by SSS to Colvilles – the figure at that point having been reduced to £383,000; (2) an agreement that if RSP's property had not been sold within a month for a figure sufficient to pay off both SSS's debt to Colvilles above and RSP's own debt to Colvilles which had grown from a relatively small amount to £401,000, RSP would issue a debenture to Colvilles as security for the aggregate amount.

9.4 *The directors' authority*

The first of the issues which it is convenient to discuss is the effectiveness of these two documents. They were executed on behalf of RSP by its directors. The directors had *ostensible* authority (so long as what they were doing was within RSP's capacity; we have not yet got to that question but in answering the one which is in front of us we need to assume that RSP was within it). But the directors were clearly acting as RSP's agents in executing the documents – was RSP bound as principal by its agents' action? It was clearly advantageous to Colvilles that RSP was bound, and in the courts Colvilles (or rather its successor, BSC) claimed just that.

There could be a situation in which directors took some action which the other party reasonably thought was within their authority (that is after all what *ostensible* means) but which was in fact outside it. *Horsley & Weight Ltd*[3] is an example. Two directors of that company bought a pension at the company's expense for a third, which might sound unexceptionable were it not for the fact that the retiring director was the father of one of the two other directors, and in preparation for his retirement had recently made over his shareholding to the son. It was within the company's capacity to provide pensions for its directors, but the two should not have taken the action they did without the agreement of the remaining three directors. In such circumstances, one of the possibilities is that the unauthorised action of the directors could thereafter be ratified; which is just what did happen in *Horsley & Weight*. The two directors involved were the company's only shareholders, and when they initialled the pension proposal policy and signed the cheque, there could be no argument but that their action as individual directors (which should only have been taken as members of the board) had been ratified by the company's shareholders. It could not then be said that the purchase was an improper expenditure of the company's funds. The evidence in the case did not show that either the motives or actions of the two, as directors or as shareholders, could be impugned in any way. (If there had been any impropriety we will see below that the possibilities of ratification are not so straightforward.)

---

[3] *Re Horsley & Weight Ltd* [1982] 3 All ER 1045.

9.5 *The knowledge of the third party*

There is a very important further aspect which fits naturally into the subject of directors' ostensible authority. Any third party dealing with RSP in 1969 was deemed to know what was in its constitution. If what its directors offered was outside its capacity or their authority, the third party was deemed to know, and dealt at his own risk. But he was entitled to assume that any necessary internal management procedures had been complied with, going back for instance to the Horsley case, that the agreement of the other three directors had been obtained. The principle in that last sentence was known as the rule in *Turquand's case*:

> ... persons contracting with a company and dealing in good faith may assume that acts within its constitution and powers have been properly and duly performed, and are not bound to inquire whether acts of internal management have been regular ... The wheels of business will not go smoothly round unless it may be assumed that that is in order which appears to be in order.[4]

However, since 1969 when the events in RSP took place, not only has section 9 of the European Communities Act 1972 come into force, and been embodied in company law as section 35 of the original Companies Act 1985, but that last section has been substituted by the new sections 35, 35A and 35B enacted by the Companies Act 1989. Excerpts from this legislation show how considerably the foregoing has been widened, to the advantage of any third party dealing with a company, but putting the company at greater risk from directors doing what the shareholders might wish they should not do:

> (1) Section 35A: In favour of a person dealing with a company in good faith, the power of the board of directors to bind the company, or authorise others to do so, shall be deemed to be free of any limitation under the company's constitution ...
>
>> (b) a person shall not be regarded as acting in bad faith by reason only of his knowing that an act is beyond the power of the directors under the company's constitution
>>
>> (c) a person shall be presumed to have acted in good faith unless the contrary is proved ...
>
> (2) Section 35B: A party to a transaction with a company is not bound to enquire as to whether it is permitted by the company's memorandum or as to any limitation on the powers of the board of directors to bind the company or authorise others to do so.

9.6 *The directors' misuse of their authority*

The central question we should go back to in the *RSP* case (under the antecedent law) to see the extent of the change is whether RSP was bound

---

[4] Per Lord Simonds specifically approving the *Turquand* rule in the House of Lords in *Morris v Kanssen* [1946] 1 All ER 586 at 592. *Turquand*'s case was *Royal British Bank v Turquand* (1856) 6 E. & B.327.

by the actions taken by its directors as its agents. In the *Horsley* case in paragraph 9.4 that had not been at the issue; the company's contract with the pension company was unchallenged.[5] What the company's liquidator had tried unavailingly to demonstrate was that the retiring father had, with the connivance of his son and the other purchaser, improperly diverted the company's funds – in a contract which the three of them did not have the power to make (although once made it was binding on the company).

If we revert to the *RSP* case and look from Colvilles' point of view at what RSP and its directors did, we see the following:

- RSP gave a guarantee to Colvilles not just for its own debt of £401,000, but an additional amount of £383,000 (end of paragraph 9.3), and backed that up with an agreement to pay that much cash out of the expected sale proceeds of its own (RSP's) property, secured by a debenture;

- in doing so RSP quite obviously benefitted Mr Shenkman, as Colvilles knew, by reducing his own exposure under the personal guarantee he had earlier given to Colvilles;

- Colvilles were deemed to know that in RSP's Articles it was a requirement that documents such as those referred to in the first head be approved at a board meeting at which a quorum of two was necessary, and that for Mr Shenkman to avoid being disqualified from voting on this matter he would have had to declare the benefit he was himself deriving in the second head above. If the advantage of the *Turquand* rule had been available to Colvilles, they would have claimed that they were entitled to assume that the internal management procedure (the declaration of interest) had been followed – but they could not claim this, because they were on notice that it had not. They were sent a copy of the signed minutes of the RSP board meeting (indeed Colvilles' solicitors had drafted them). They could not claim to be entitled *in good faith* to make the assumptions of regularity which *Turquand* would have allowed.

Colvilles' failure to deal in good faith was the the principle which meant that they obtained no rights under the contract with RSP.

9.7 Shareholders ratification in RSP

This cannot yet be a full answer because we have not finished examining the *RSP* facts and inferences; but we should ask ourselves a hypothetical question. RSP was not bound by its guarantee and agreement with Colvilles because the latter had not acted in good faith in obtaining them. But could the shareholders of RSP have ratified what RSP's directors had done only defectively – if RSP had wanted to be bound, could it have rectified matters?

---

[5] What the pension company was deemed to know about the company's capacity, and what it was entitled to assume under the *Turquand* rule were no part of any argument.

THE FACTS IN THE ROLLED STEEL PRODUCTS CASE

In practice, of course, the answer was no ratification; the fact was that RSP's shareholders did not give their consent. The 49 per cent shareholders were trustees who saw no benefit from the transaction – only that the company in which they owned shares had gratuitously given away £383,000 of its assets. The 51 per cent shareholder had benefitted, they had not. It was hardly likely that the trustees could agree. (We mentioned in paragraph 9.3 that nearly a year elapsed between Colvilles first trying to pressurise SSS and Mr Shenkman to reduce SSS's debt, and the time at which a scheme was eventually agreed. A significant reason for this delay was the fact that the only obvious source from which Colvilles could be satisfied was RSP's assets, and Mr Shenkman's advisers were struggling to find a way in which the trustee shareholders could be compensated; this struggle they finally abandoned.)

Second, and this is the question lying at the heart of the company-capacity point which we will come to next, there is RSP's own position to consider. If it was under financial pressure when it merely owed £401,000 to Colvilles, what would the prognosis be when it found itself owing £784,000? What attitude might the creditors of RSP (other than Colvilles) manifest to the transaction which caused a deterioration in their position by that same amount of £383,000?

Each of these questions leads to the further query whether the directors' action has to be described as breach of duty? And if so, to what extent does this change the legal rights and obligations of RSP, SSS, Colvilles, each of the shareholders of RSP, and RSP's directors? To look at these questions we turn next to what some people might perhaps have expected would have been the aspect of the *RSP* case we would have started on – was the transaction really within the company's capacity in the first place?

9.8 *The company's objects clause*

It is clause 3 in a company's memorandum which sets out its objects, and in RSP's case this started unsurprisingly:

> (A) To carry on business as exporters and importers of, and manufacturers of, and dealers in, and buying and selling agents for, iron, steel, copper, bronze, aluminium . . .

but as these clauses normally do, it continued with further lettered sub-clauses listing further activities which the company was empowered to do, ending with what is a common if not standard clarification:

> It is hereby expressly declared that each sub-clause of this clause shall be construed independently of the other sub-clauses hereof, and none of the objects mentioned in any sub-clause shall be deemed to be merely subsidiary to the objects mentioned in any other sub-clause.

If that could be taken at its face value, then the company could have relied on sub-clause 3(K) to give it the capacity to carry on a business of giving guarantees, and on sub-clause 3(L) as respects its borrowing and issuing of debentures:

> (K) To lend or advance money or give credit to such persons . . . as may

seem expedient, and in particular to customers of and others having dealings with the company and to give guarantees ... for any such persons ...

(L) To borrow ... in such manner as the company shall think fit, and in particular by the issue of debentures ...

Each of the actions agreed with Colvilles in January 1969 (guaranteeing SSS's debt, and securing a total debt of RSP to Colvilles) would have been specifically lined up with the separate objects defined in those sub-clauses. Therefore it could not have been said that anything agreed with Colvilles as above was outside the capacity of the company.

But all that depends on our being able to take at face value the declaration that each sub-clause contains separate objects, not merely powers that are ancillary to an object or objects stated in some other sub-clause.

9.9 Separate and ancillary objects

The principles of correct interpretation of the objects clause require us, however, to take account of the instruction to regard each sub-clause as separate only *as far as this is possible*.[6] Specifically it is not possible to say that borrowing is a separate object, because the courts have held otherwise; 'borrowing is not an end in itself and must be for some purpose of the company',[7] that is to say, it must be ancillary to some other object. Similarly in the RSP memorandum, sub-clause 3(K) as carefully explained by Lord Justice Slade can also only be seen as conferring no more than ancillary powers – the giving of those guarantees was not to be an activity of unrestricted scope; they were to be given only for 'such persons ... as may be expedient', and those last four words could only mean as might be expedient for the furtherance of (some other object or) objects of the company.

Remember that in the previous paragraph and this one we have been looking purely at the question whether the January 1969 actions were within the capacity of RSP (ignoring for this purpose the fact that those actions had not in fact bound RSP because of the absence of good faith on the part of Colvilles in its dealing with the directors). At this juncture we have concluded that each action was *capable* of being within that capacity, each being within a power ancillary to RSP's object or objects.

But have we reached that conclusion without giving enough weight to words that we have used about both of the powers above? Borrowing, we said, must be for some purpose of the company, and the giving of a guarantee for the furtherance of the objects. If we do give due weight to those words should we conclude that because the real purpose of each action was the benefit of one of RSP's shareholders, the actions were accordingly outside RSP's capacity?

That line of reasoning is not valid. Lord Justice Slade pointed out

---

[6] *Cotman v Brougham* [1918] AC 514.
[7] Per Harman LJ in *Re Introductions Ltd* [1969] 1 All ER 887 at 889.

that the courts had long ago rejected it. It would lead to intolerable situations; a bank for instance considering lending money to a company which had power to borrow and appeared to be doing so for a proper purpose would nevertheless need in every case to investigate in depth precisely what the company was proposing to do, and did in fact do, with the money.[8]

9.10 *What is in the mind of the directors*

There are of course two sides to that last point; where there is a transaction which appears[9] to be within the company's capacity, and appears also to be being properly handled within the directors' ostensible authority, then a third party dealing with the company concerned need not concern itself with the possibility that the transaction might be shifted outside the company's capacity by the fact that the company might be doing something that is not apparent, or that the directors might have ulterior purposes in mind:

- the first of those two sides is clear in the much quoted statement of Buckley J (also made during the *David Payne* case to which we referred in Note 8) that 'A corporation cannot do anything except for the purposes of its business, borrowing or anything else; everything else is beyond its power, and is *ultra vires*. So that the words for the purposes of the company's business are a mere expression of that which would be involved if there were no such words'. The first of those quoted sentences looks at first to be wholly circular, taking one nowhere. But the judge was doing what we have promised religiously not to do, namely use the words *ultra vires* to refer to the directors' authority rather than the company's capacity.

- the second is the important statement by Lord Justice Slade in *RSP* (important that is in relation to the subject matter of this book):[10] 'If a particular act ... is of a category which on a true construction of the company's memorandum is *capable* of being performed as reasonably incidental to the attainment or pursuit of its objects, it will not be rendered *ultra vires* the company merely

---

[8] A corporation every time it wants to borrow cannot be called on by the lender to expose all its affairs, so that the lender can say: 'Before I lend you anything I must investigate how you carry on your business, and I must know why you want the money, and how you apply it, and when you do have it I must see you apply it in the right way.' It is perfectly impossible to work out such a principle – per Buckley J in Re David Payne & Co. Ltd, Young v David Payne & Co. Ltd [1904] 2 Ch. 604 at 613. (But it has to be said that most loan agreements do require the borower to spell out precisely what he intends to do with the borrowed funds, and to covenant that he will actually do what he says he will.)
[9] It is of course arguable that as a result of sections 35, 35A and 35B CA 1985 a third party dealing with a company no longer needs to have *any* concerns over the company's capacity; the author would not go quite as far as that. Therefore there is still a certain relevance in that party's being confident that neither the company's doing something which was not apparent, nor the directors' having ulterior purposes in mind, will affect his own dealings with the company.
[10] The emphasis in this quotation is his.

because in a particular instance its directors, in performing the act in its name, are in truth doing so for purposes other than those set out in its memorandum ... the state of mind or knowledge of the persons managing the company's affairs or the person dealing with it is irrelevant in considering questions of corporate capacity.'

The reason why this last point is significant is the one question which we have not yet addressed but which we will see is the most difficult of all; does the money have to be returned to the company, or can the third party keep it?

9.11 *Binding transactions, those which are void or voidable and those which are capable of rectification*

The pension company had done a transaction with Horsley & Weight Ltd which was within the company's capacity, and within the ostensible authority of the directors with whom the pension company was dealing (because under the *Turquand* rule the pension company was entitled to assume that they had been properly authorised by their board). That transaction between the pension company and Horsley & Weight was unquestionably valid and binding. There had been a question whether Horsley & Weight itself had a claim against the beneficiary of the pension, or against him and the two directors who had bought him his pension, but the purchasers' motives were not impugned, and all doubt was removed by the fact that the company's shareholders ratified the purchase; those shareholders were absolutely entitled to deny their company any ability to sue.

In the *RSP* case Colvilles attempted a transaction with RSP which we have again seen to be within RSP's capacity (half-way through paragraph 9.9, before we considered and rejected the possibility that we needed to taint the company's purposes by considering the directors' ulterior motives). The reason why Colvilles acquired no rights against RSP (the transaction was void) was that Colvilles had notice of the fact that RSP's directors were not acting within their authority, and therefore Colvilles were not acting in good faith.

If the facts had been other, if Mr Shenkman had declared his interest and Colvilles had therefore been dealing in good faith, RSP would have been bound by the guarantee and agreement.[11]

Going back to the actual facts in *RSP*, we still have outstanding the hypothetical question in paragraph 9.7, whether the RSP shareholders could have ratified the transaction and bound that company to the

---

[11] Unless RSP could have demonstrated that its directors were not acting within their ostensible authority – the reference is to Lord Justice Slade's statement quoted in paragraph 9.2 above, that a company holds out its directors as having ostensible authority to do on its behalf anything which its Memorandum gives the company capacity to do. Had they been outside their authority, and had the third party been on notice that they were not doing what they were for the company's purposes, then under the ordinary principles of agency (nothing to do with the company's capacity or the directors' authority), the third party could not have held the company to the transaction.

guarantee of, and agreement with, Colvilles (the latter would presumably have been only too willing to accept). We said that the answer in practice was that it was inconceivable that this could happen. But the theoretical answer is more complex, and to look at it we need two more cases.

9.12 The facts in the Ridge Securities and Halt Garage cases

These two cases[12] matter only because of their facts; that is to say, the facts found illustrate how the law is to be applied. In *Ridge*, there were excessive payments described as 'interest' made by the company to its parent, but which because the company had no distributable reserves were held to be gifts of capital to that parent, and thus *ultra vires*. In *Halt Garage*, the excessive payments, again out of capital because of the lack of distributable reserves, were described as director's fees payable to a shareholder, but it was held that her services were worth at most one third of what had been paid; the excess was *ultra vires* as an unauthorised return of capital.

There is a general principle that the shareholders of a company can ratify actions purportedly done in its name in circumstances in which those actions have been challenged.[13] But it is clear that the principle cannot apply in cases where the actions themselves are beyond the company's capacity; it was a fact in each of *Ridge* and *Halt Garage* that the excessive payments were returns of capital and therefore *ultra vires*.

When one finds a company which has made payments to a third party, to its parent in *Ridge Securities* and to its director in *Halt Garage*, and those payments are outside its capacity, the third parties have to return those funds. This principle was explained in *RSP* as being derived from the *Belmont* case;[14] a company is the beneficial owner of its funds, not a trustee for them.

> But in consequence of the fiduciary character of their duties the directors of a limited company are treated as if they were trustees of those funds of the company which are in their hands or under their control, and if they misapply them they commit a breach of trust ... so if ... in breach of their fiduciary duties (they) misapply the funds of their company so that they come into the hands of some stranger to the trust who receives them with knowledge (actual or constructive) of the breach, he cannot conscientiously retain those funds against the company ... he becomes a constructive trustee for the company of the misapplied funds.

In both the *Ridge Securities* and *Halt Garage* cases the recipient had to return the funds to the companies.

---

[12] *Ridge Securities Ltd v IRC* [1964] 1 All ER 275, and *Re Halt Garage (1964) Ltd* [1982] 3 All ER 1016.
[13] The principle was spelled out by Lord Davey in *Salomon v A Salomon & Co. Ltd* [1897] AC 22 at 57, and was reviewed (with the existence of its limitations being indicated) in each of *Halt Garage (1964) Ltd*, Note 12 above at 1037, and *Horsley & Weight*, Note 3 above at 1055, as well as in RSP.
[14] *Belmont Finance Corp. v Williams Furniture Ltd (No. 2)* [1980] All ER 393 at 405 per Buckley LJ.

9.13 Aveling Barford v Perion

This brings us to the case already described as now being the leading case[15] in this area – at least so far as concerns the matters dealt with in this book.

Aveling Barford was, in March 1987 owned by a Liberian corporation which was in turn controlled by a Singaporean businessman, Dr Lee. Perion was also owned by Dr Lee. Aveling Barford had made considerable losses, so that in its 31 March 1987 balance sheet its shareholders' funds was as shown in Table 40.

Table 40: Capitalisation of Aveling Barford

Share capital	500,000
Profit and loss account (deficit)	(17,600,000)
	(17,100,000)
Loan from Liberian parent company, subordinated to the other creditors of the company	22,800,000
Equalling the company's net assets	5,700,000

The fact that the parent had subordinated[16] its loan was what prevented the company from being massively insolvent (and allowed its auditors to report that it was a going concern). But the loan was still a loan – subordination is not the same as a waiver by the lender; it could not be suggested that the company had distributable reserves.

Aveling Barford owned a mansion with substantial grounds known as Arnoldfield (which had in happier days been used as a sports and social centre for employees). It agreed to sell this to Perion, conditional on planning permission being granted for housing development; perhaps the word 'agreed' needs qualification, since although Perion's board approved the purchase in October 1986 at a figure of £350,000, the contract eventually produced to Aveling Barford's auditors in July of the following year was dated 10 January 1987 and showed the basic consideration as £350,000 but contained a further provision that if Perion should re-sell within one year for more than £800,000 then Aveling Barford should be paid a further £400,000.[17]

---

[15] *Aveling Barford Ltd v Perion Ltd & Others* [1989] BCLC 626.
[16] The principles of subordination of debt were outlined in paragraph 1.8.
[17] The report of the case makes it clear that there was some doubt whether this agreement was made in January 1987, or whether it was a retrospective rewriting of history in the summer of that year at a time when it had become clear that Perion would be re-selling for more than £800,000. If there had been no binding contract on 10 January, then the earliest date at which it could have been argued that Aveling Barford and Perion were legally bound was the date of completion on 3 February 1987.

9.14 Aveling Barford v Perion (continued)

Before the Perion board meeting in October 1986, Aveling Barford had had a valuation of Arnoldfield from Strutt & Parker at £650,000. The same solicitor, Mr Chapman, acted for both Aveling Barford and Perion, and through him Perion could be taken to have knowledge of this valuation. Therefore, if the property was worth £650,000, Perion was in a position to sell it the next day and make an immediate profit at the expense of Aveling Barford of £300,000. As the matter appeared to stand at the date of the Perion board meeting, it would only have been if the property were resold for more than £150,000 over Strutt & Parker's valuation that the further proceeds would have become payable to Aveling Barford – and even then, Perion would still have been making a profit out of Aveling Barford.

Aveling Barford's directors had a fiduciary duty to obtain the best price they could for Arnoldfield; and selling to Perion at a figure which would seem to enable that company to make an immediate profit at Aveling Barford's expense seemed inconsistent with that duty. Perion and those acting for it were aware that the Aveling Barford directors' proposed action was likely to be in breach of their duties. The likely full extent of that breach may perhaps only have become clear in the months after October 1986,[18] because Perion received a valuation of the property from Humberts for mortgage purposes in November 1986 of £1,150,000; and did in fact resell it in August 1987 for over £1,500,000.

It will come as no surprise to those who have followed the court's thought processes as they have emerged in this chapter so far that Mr Justice Hoffmann expressed his views succinctly:

> On any view, therefore, the sale was a breach of fiduciary duty by Dr Lee. Perion, through Dr Lee and Mr Chapman, knew all the facts which made it a breach of duty and was therefore accountable as a constructive trustee

which, as we saw in paragraph 9.12, meant that Perion must return the profit it made.

9.15 Perion's argument in defence

However, Perion's lawyers advanced a further argument that Aveling Barford's sale to Perion was binding on the former, and that the latter was entitled to retain its profit, an argument which had two parts:

- Aveling Barford's sale to Perion was within its capacity. It may have been at an undervalue but it was a sale, and not a sham; what was done was precisely what the documents showed. Aveling Barford's directors may not have been authorised to make such a sale. But their state of mind and knowledge are irrelevant in considering the company's capacity.[19] An action within the company's capacity, even

---

[18] The possible rewriting of history referred to in Note 17 above could perhaps have been explained, but not justified, by the events which actually unfolded.
[19] See the *dictum* of Lord Justice Slade quoted in the second head in paragraph 9.10.

if taken by directors without proper authorisation can still be ratified by the shareholders. This one had been so ratified, in that Dr Lee had approved it informally at the time it was done, and Aveling Barford's shareholders had given formal approval to its accounts containing details (in an identifiable form) of the sale;

- to strike down the transaction on the basis of the Aveling Barford directors' lack of authority, or state of mind and knowledge, as Mr Justice Hoffmann suggested in the part of his judgment quoted at the end of paragraph 9.14, would be reintroduce into what should be purely a question of corporate capacity all the motive tests which Lord Justice Slade had forthrightly declared to be irrelevant.

It is abundantly clear that the judge's view was that it was not open to the Aveling Barford shareholders to ratify the sale. In looking at his reasons, we can finally answer the question which we first posed (in relation to a possible *RSP* ratification) in paragraph 9.7, and still left open at the end of paragraph 9.11; could the RSP shareholders have ratified their company's guarantee and agreement?

9.16 Mr Justice Hoffmann's limits on ratification

We know that ratification is a general principle, but that there are specific circumstances which make it unavailable. One of those is the case of the company whose action was outside its capacity. In both *Ridge Securities* and *Halt Garage* the payments were held to be returns of capital to shareholders and thus unlawful and by definition outside each company's capacity. In *RSP*, Lord Justice Slade did not have to decide whether the actions could have been ratified, but did say that if they had constituted 'a fraud on the creditors' it would not have been possible for shareholders to ratify them. He did not define that phrase, but earlier in his judgment he had referred to the fact that at the High Court hearing there had been evidence, disputed between the parties, that RSP's granting of the debenture to Colvilles would have caused it to become insolvent.

However, Mr Justice Hoffmann rationalised his refusal to accept that Aveling Barford's transaction was capable of ratification on more forthright grounds. He said:

> It was a sale at a gross undervalue for the purpose of enabling a profit to be realised by an entity controlled and put forward by (Aveling Barford's) sole beneficial shareholder. This was as much a dressed-up distribution as the payment of excessive interest in *Ridge* or the excessive remuneration in *Halt Garage*. The company had at the time no distributable reserves and the sale was therefore *ultra vires* ...

that is to say, it was an unauthorised return of capital. He went on:

> The rule that capital may not be returned to shareholders is a rule for the protection of creditors and the evasion of that rule falls within what I think Slade LJ had in mind when he spoke of a fraud on creditors ... I do not think the phrase was intended to have such a narrow meaning,

those last two words being in reference to the argument put to him that creditors were defrauded only when the company was insolvent, which technically *Aveling Barford* was not.

9.17 Mr Justice Hoffmann's limits on ratification (continued)

That was not killing two birds with one stone, but using two stones to kill the same bird twice. In the first place the sale at an undervalue was a return of capital, therefore unlawful and could not be ratified; in the second place it was a fraud on the creditors which could not be ratified. One could properly describe the possibility of ratification as a dead duck, and when one thinks about it, what killed it was simply the *fact* that the sale at an undervalue could be equated to a return of capital, as had been the payment of excessive interest and excessive director's remuneration in *Ridge* and *Halt Garage* respectively.

The following point was not discussed in Lord Justice Slade's review of the earlier cases, nor in Mr Justice Hoffmann's judgment. In the *Horsley & Weight* case, the leading judgment was delivered by Buckley, L.J., who was in no doubt that the company's shareholders were entitled to, and had, ratified the action of the two directors who had purchased a pension for a third director, himself a former shareholder. Each of Cumming-Bruce and Templeman, LL.JJ., in delivering concurring judgments made the point however that, (although it was not relevant to the case in front of them, and the point itself was therefore *obiter*), the shareholders could not have ratified an action which constituted *misfeasance* by the directors. In elaborating on this word, Templeman L.J. explained that if when they paid away the company's funds the directors were aware that they were pushing it into insolvency, that payment *would have been both a misfeasance and a fraud on the creditors*. However, even if technical insolvency had not been a relevant point, there could still have been *gross negligence amounting to misfeasance* on the part of the directors if the company's problems of cashflow and profitability were such that the directors' payment *threatened the continued existence of the company*.

A breach of fiduciary duty by the directors can be ratified, provided the acts concerned are not also *ultra vires* the company, or a fraud on the creditors. So what precisely is misfeasance? and how is it distinguished from the other phrases mentioned? The author's view is that all are in reality the same, or if there are differences, they are only of degree:

- Threatening the continued existence of the company appears to envisage that the company is not insolvent prior to the act concerned by the director, but is pushed over the boundary into insolvency by it;

- Return of capital again refers to a company which is technically solvent but has no reserves, or insufficient reserves, in order to make the payment;

- Fraud on creditors envisages that the company is insolvent at the time of the unlawful act; although we have seen Mr Justice Hoffmann saying that Lord Justice Slade had used the phrase as also applying to a (technically) solvent company making a return of capital, as in the previous head.

Thus in all cases, the key factor at which one is really looking is insolvency, taking insolvency in the first and third cases as being measured in terms of a negative aggregate of share capital and distributable reserves, and in the second case merely negative distributable reserves resulting from the transaction.

If we were to carry this reasoning into *Aveling Barford*, and if it had been found as fact that the company's continued existence was threatened by the sale at undervalue, then the possibility of ratification could have been killed using this third stone (in place of either of the earlier two.)

9.18 *Making the adjustments*

It will not have escaped the reader's notice that in each of the *Ridge, Halt Garage* and *Aveling Barford* cases the reason why the transactions were regarded as unauthorised returns of capital was that the companies *had at the time no distributable reserves*.

It is quite easy to see the theory, although not necessarily so easy to follow through the practice, of the adjustments needed in the first two cases. Suppose that there were a company which at the start of the period we will consider *did* have £5,000 of distributable reserves; suppose that it had also to be regarded as paying excessive remuneration to a shareholder of £1,000 per month. Clearly the first five months payments are not unlawful – they merely have to be treated as dividends (which can be ratified by the shareholders) rather than remuneration. This will have repercussions in the PAYE and ACT calculations, but the basic end result in the profit and loss account will not be totally different.

After the fifth month, the company must presumably debit the amounts unlawfully distributed to an asset account, showing the amount recoverable from a shareholder in her constructive trustee capacity.

If we then pile even a small amount of Pelion on Ossa, by assuming that the company sells an asset to a shareholder for its book value which is lower than open market value, it would seem that there would be no immediate book-keeping entry; the transaction is unlawful and void, the recipient is obliged to return the asset, and logically the company's books would show that it had continued to own it (and to carry it at the same book value) throughout. That would change as soon as the recipient shareholder sold the asset at a profit. Since she would be dealing with the asset as constructive trustee, and would be obliged to return her profit on its sale to the company, the company could legitimately reflect the sale, and the *realised profit*, in its own accounts. The whole of this would be subject to the need for some provision (perhaps 100 per cent) against the possibility that the company might not be able to recover the whole sum for which the shareholder was liable. The re-emergence of a balance of distributable profits in the profit and loss account would presumably enable the company to recommence paying excessive remuneration. Writing up the books for transactions different from those the company really undertook is never a straightforward matter.

Financial assistance for the purchase of a company's shares

9.19 *Set against the background theory of capital maintenance*

We can now turn to the second aspect of companies acting *ultra vires* by returning capital to shareholders. We can start by recalling the rudimentary theory we introduced in chapter 6, at paragraph 6.3:

- a company can distribute its profits, but must preserve its capital intact (short of liquidation or a properly authorised reduction of capital, neither of these being aspects which we want to pursue here);

- therefore the ways in which (aside from liquidation or capital reduction) shareholders can realise their investment in the company are:

  – sale of shares to an incoming shareholder,
  – sale of shares for cash to a predator company acquiring the target in which our shareholders held shares,
  – exchange of shares into shares to be issued by the predator referred to in the previous head;

Those two sales and the exchange do not need to be thought of as different, and mutually exclusive, transactions – they are just convenient examples of a whole range of possibilities which merge into each other. Why they are convenient for our purposes is that we can further develop our rudimentary theory from them:

- if the purchaser described as an 'incoming shareholder' is able, in any direct or indirect way, to make use of the company's own assets in order to provide his purchase consideration, then that would seem to be a way in which the shareholder who is exiting might be enabled to deplete the company's capital, indirectly. But one's definitions need to be very clear. If the exiting shareholder were to take a substantial dividend out of the company's distributable profits prior to sale, so that the incoming shareholder were able to buy his shares at a lower price than would otherwise apply (but the company needed to borrow significant sums in order to continue its operations), would that be objectionable?

- in the case of the predator's acquisitions (for cash or shares) the question we need to look at in this second section of this chapter is whether those acquisitions are assisted in any way by or through the target.

This gives us a framework for examining the prohibition on the giving of financial assistance. But it will lead to a wider question about the predator's ability to extract other profits from the target – rules strangely at odds with those on financial assistance.

9.20 Financial assistance under sections 151 to 158 Companies Act 1985

These are widely drawn sections, as we will see, and in the first subsection of the first of them the operative words are 'it is not lawful'. A transaction in breach of the requirements is void, and the company and its directors are subject to criminal sanctions.

Although this might seem to be approaching the subject backwards, there are good reasons for explaining the exceptions to the rules before examining what those rules are actually aimed at. First, there is no reason why a company should not pay a dividend out of distributable profits – to the exiting shareholder if his name is still on the register, or to the incoming shareholder once he is registered.[20] The limiting figure is distributable profits, so the question whether the company may not have available cash, and may have to borrow to pay, is not itself a bar. Where a company is to be sold out of a group, and therefore the distributable profits can before it leaves be extracted to its parent as a *group* dividend without any tax cost,[21] this will save capital gains tax for that parent, and reduce the price and stamp duty for the purchaser.

A company is permitted to give assistance to its employees for their acquisition of shares through share option and incentive schemes, or to trustees of employee trusts for their acquisition of shares.[22]

---

[20] If the incoming shareholder is a company, it may be prevented from distributing onwards to its own shareholders such a dividend out of pre-acquisition profits. See paragraph 6.14. Or, on the other hand, as we will see in paragraph 9.26 below, there may be no such block on the predator's distribution.

[21] *Group* dividends under section 247 TA 1988 were the subject of paragraph 5.26, but the essential point for present purposes is that transferring distributable profits from a subsidiary to its parent in this way has no effects for tax purposes. The only result is to transfer value out of the subsidiary's shares, directly into the parent's cash balances. Where a parent artificially deflates the value of a subsidiary to save capital gains tax on its sale there are general anti-avoidance provisions which might be thought to have been designed to cancel the benefit sought to be obtained. (See paragraph 11.16 and Notes 27 to 29 thereon for a brief commentary on *depreciatory transactions* and value shifting generally). But the Inland Revenue has never believed that the payment to a vendor shareholder of a dividend out of the profits his target had earned during his period of ownership, is the kind of *value shifting* which they should attempt to penalise. It is in fact specifically exempted under section 31(1) TCGA 1992 from the anti-avoidance provisions – except to the extent that the dividend comes out of realised profits which have not been arrived at on normal commercial accounting principles, but have been *manufactured* for the purpose of reducing the capital gains tax concerned. To counter these contrived dividends there are specifically directed anti-avoidance provisions in section 31 and the next three sections.

However, there is a postscript to the subject of pre-disposal dividends. While the Inland Revenue are not worried about the payment of a dividend from subsidiary to parent under the *group* arrangements in section 247 TA 1988, (that is to say where the payer does not account for ACT, and the recipient does not treat the receipt as franked income), they are not happy that these pre-disposal dividends can be paid as *ACT dividends*. See paragraph 11.16 and particularly Note 30 thereon for further comment on this question of the form in which pre-disposal dividends can be paid without the Revenue raising objections.

[22] The definition of the schemes and trusts is in section 743 CA 1985, which is written in wide terms, not limited to those which are approved under the various tax frameworks referred to in chapter 10 below.

There is also a broadly drafted exemption for assistance given by a company in good faith and in its own interests in circumstances where the acquisition of the shares was not the main purpose for which the assistance was given. However, proof of motives is difficult enough in the case of individuals and significantly more so for companies. All that can sensibly be said is that the exemption is there, but in view of its imprecise terms, it cannot often be said with any degree of certainty that a transaction comes within it. It would be advisable either to find some other way of achieving the acquisition or to use the *whitewash* procedure.

The whitewash procedure, which is set out in sections 155 to 158 enables a private company, not a public one, to give financial assistance so long as it has net assets and does not reduce these by giving the assistance, or if there is such a reduction it comes out of distributable profits. These requirements are complex, and there are even more complexities over timing; we need to return to whitewash procedures below, in paragraph 9.24.

9.21 Definition of financial assistance in section 152(1)(a)

Although the exemptions listed in the previous paragraph do set the scene, blocking out certain relatively clear areas, one cannot pretend that they give a clear indication what actions do constitute the giving of unlawful assistance:

- gifts by the company to the person acquiring its shares, but it can equally be the person selling, or anyone else;

- that needs to be widened immediately in that the company's subsidiaries are equally prevented from giving assistance;

- second it needs to be widened in recognition that indirect assistance is caught, for instance assistance given through a third party;

- third there are other transactions beside the relatively unusual-sounding making of gifts, which are to be treated in a similar light; one such is the company's putting *spending power* at the disposal of the assisted party,
   - the company giving a guarantee for his borrowings;
   - the company providing security for his borrowings;
   - the company releasing or waiving a debt which he may owe to it;

each of these is again then widened to encompass indirect transactions, and those by subsidiaries, as well as the direct;

- the lending of money by the company to the share-acquirer is also a way in which spending power can be put into his hands. What can quite easily be recognised as indirect lending is caught, where the original loan is made by another party, and its rights to the repayment of the sum concerned are assigned to, or novated into the name of, the company. But these indirect *loans* can still be within the section's mischief in cases where they are scarcely recognisable as loans, and they *assist* the acquirer only by reference to some further action or inaction. For instance, if before its sale the company transfers an asset to the vendor, and the purchase price is left outstanding, that is within the extended definition of a loan. It is the vendor who enjoys that assistance.

It is possible to evolve more complex suggestions, such as that if the company were subsequently to waive the loan this would be reflected in a reduction in the price of its shares. Alternatively, inaction by the company, in failing to demand immediate payment, should also be regarded as assistance, in that the purchaser would logically again be assisted by a lower target share price, reflecting the company's reduced profitability without either use of the asset, or use of the price for which it sold it.

Spinning out ever more complex definitions of who is assisted, and how, does not have any great merit; what is relevant is that financial assistance has been very widely defined, and that it does not necessarily need to be quantifiable.

9.22 *Definition of financial assistance (continued)*

There is a sweep-up clause to the definition, starting predictably 'any other financial assistance given by the company . . .' but then breaking into two branches:

- '. . . the net assets of which are materially reduced'. It is not at all difficult to see that if before its disposal the target sells an asset at an undervalue to the vendor, or buys an asset at an overvalue from the vendor, its net assets will be reduced – and the purchaser assisted because the price he must find is correspondingly reduced. Throughout the interpretation of these sections, market values must be used in arriving at the figure to be attributed to net assets, balance-sheet carrying values not being conclusive. Where there is to be any significant pre-sale reorganisation, the directors would be well advised to consider taking professional advice on valuations.

- '. . . or which has no net assets'. Following as it does the phraseology in the immediately preceding head, it is tempting to read this as envisaging an asset transfer which increases the net liabilities of the target. But it is to be interpreted more widely than that, to catch for instance a transaction in which the target purchased an asset from the purchaser, even at a full value. The assistance can be seen as the target's provision of *liquidity* to the purchaser, particularly if the asset concerned were one which the purchaser would otherwise have found difficult to sell.

The giving of financial assistance of any of the kinds explained above and in the previous paragraph is prohibited if given 'before or at the same time as the acquisition takes place, and for the purposes of the acquisition'. But that again is supplemented by further provisions aimed at assistance given after the acquisition has occurred. What is envisaged is that a 'liability has been incurred' by the acquirer or some other person, and that the company's direct or indirect assistance has the effect of 'reducing or discharging the liability'. Each of those phrases is given a special meaning for these purposes. Incurring a liability includes an alteration in a person's financial position, and reducing or discharging a liability includes restoring his position, in whole or in part. Thus if the purchaser pays cash for his shares, the alteration in his financial position is an obvious reduction in liquidity. If the company subsequently lends him money for the purpose of restoring his liquidity that loan would be caught. But the same might not be true of a loan made for some other purpose.

9.23 Practical implications

Probably the area which sees the greatest number of problems arising under the financial assistance provisions is the management buy-out, where it frequently happens that the managers wish to use the company's assets as security for their borrowings.

But as is the case with all anti-avoidance legislation, whether in the tax field or any other, there will always be unobjectionable transactions caught by the provisions. A company cannot be allowed to undertake transactions which are unlawful and therefore void, and its directors cannot be allowed to risk criminal sanctions for taking their company into them. There is therefore no alternative but to measure up each proposed transaction against the legislation's precise wording; and if it offends, to attempt to find some other way of achieving the desired result, or in appropriate circumstances to use the whitewash procedure.

However, the complexities of measuring up a transaction against the legislation, and the uncertainties that remain, can be illustrated in Table 41.

Table 41: Balance sheets of parent and subsidiary before recapitalisation

Parent				Subsidiary			
Share cap.	100	Own assets	200	Share cap.	50	Own assets	30
Bank loan	200	Inv. in sub.	50	Profit & loss (debit)	(75)		
		Subordinated loan to sub.	50	Parent Subordinated loan	50		
				Creditors	5		
	300		300		30		30

The parent's owner suggests that he subscribe £55 of additional share capital in that company, and it in turn subscribes the same amount of additional capital into the subsidiary. The subsidiary would use the £55 of cash thus received first to pay off its outside creditors, and thereafter to pay off the subordinated loan. The prime objective is to leave the subsidiary with a positive level of shareholders' funds and net assets. The secondary objective is to permit the parent to reduce its bank borrowing from £200 to £150 – regarded as better aligned with its increased share capital of £155.

If one stands far enough back from the transactions:

- the subsidiary's assistance to its parent, in passing the £50 back to the latter by way of repayment of the subordinated loan was not *for the purpose of* the parent's acquisition of shares in the subsidiary;

- it is also arguable that the parent's financial position *vis-à-vis* the subsidiary has not been *restored*, in fact quite the reverse. But against that, the concept of restoring the assisted party's financial position to what it was before the acquisition took place[23] has been widely interpreted, and if £50 out of £55 used for an acquisition is immediately passed back to the acquirer, it seems equally arguable that this does constitute restoration.

If the subsidiary had had net assets prior to the acquisition, it could have been argued that none of the heads in the definition of financial assistance in section 152(1)(a) of the Companies Act 1985 was in point. But the subsidiary clearly did not have net assets. The transaction is arguably unlawful because of that absence of net assets. Despite both companies, and the creditors of both, all having stood to benefit, there are considerable doubts whether the transaction can be allowed to take place – the general purposive exemption may protect it, or it may not. The question whether the parent's position has been wholly or partly restored can similarly be argued either way. This really is exceptionally problematical legislation.

9.24 *The whitewash procedure under sections 155 to 158*

These sections are complex, and it would be inappropriate for us to try to cover every detail in this book; for instance some of what is said below to be required can be ignored in the case of wholly owned subsidiaries, or where a company's resolutions are passed unanimously by all shareholders entitled to vote. Subject to that proviso, the principal requirements for a company to escape the prohibitions are as follows:

- the company must have net assets, and the giving of the assistance must not reduce those net assets – or if it does, it must come out of the company's distributable profits;

- the company's shareholders must authorise the giving of the assistance by special resolution;

- the company's directors must make a statutory declaration that it is their opinion that the company, after giving the assistance, will be able to meet those of its debts which are due, and that this situation will continue to apply for debts becoming due throughout the year following. That declaration must be made unanimously, and since it

---

[23] Section 152(3)(b) CA 1985.

is to be made on a single form (and on the same day as or within one week after the special resolution in the previous head) it necessitates the availability of all of the directors at the critical time. It is also a requirement that they have the auditors' confirmation that, having enquired into the state of affairs of the company, those auditors do not regard the directors' declaration as unreasonable. It is also advisable that the auditors be asked to give a second certificate that the company has net assets, and that the amount of them is not reduced to a material extent by the proposed transaction.[24]

Timing is of the essence, since a special resolution normally requires three weeks' notice of the meeting at which it is to be proposed; the passing of the resolution and the date of the directors' statutory declaration and the auditors' report must all be carefully co-ordinated; and the assistance itself cannot be given earlier than four weeks, nor later than eight weeks, after the date of the resolution (the four-week period coinciding with the time allowed for objections to be lodged with the court by any shareholder opposed to the giving of the assistance).

9.25 The predator's distributable profits after the acquisition

We can now turn to a rather different area; but one in which we can develop further those *rudimentary principles* that a company may distribute its profits but must preserve its capital intact. Rudimentary was the word we used in re-introducing the principle at the beginning of paragraph 9.19 – and we will see as we proceed that the results it produces are odd, to say the least.

What we need is an illustration, showing the figures for a predator company, which has provided an exit for our target's original shareholders by acquiring their shares principally for an issue of its own (that is, the predator's) shares. One of the assumptions we will make is that the predator was able to claim merger relief[25] on the share issue component of its acquisition. However we will also assume that the predator has accounted for its acquisition using *acquisition accounting* rather than *merger accounting*.[26] And the third assumption we will make is that both predator and target are the same companies, with the same balance sheet numbers, as we started looking at in paragraph 6.13. We will need to add some further information to illustrate points we have looked at in the intervening paragraphs – and we will make one small

---

[24] Section 152(1)(a)(iv) CA 1985.
[25] Relief from the necessity to set up a share premium account on the issue of shares by a predator which takes its holding of a target's shares to 90 per cent or more, this relief being available under section 131 CA 1985; see paragraphs 6.20 and 6.21.
[26] In explaining in paragraphs 6.23 to 6.27 the thought processes behind these two systems of accounting, used in the predator's *consolidated* accounts, and how and why they differed, we made it clear that although the Companies Act merger relief is quite commonly claimable, merger accounting is seldom available and even less commonly used.

change to the assumptions, namely that the acquisition was made to the extent of 15 per cent for cash, and only for the remaining 85 per cent by a share for share exchange.

Table 42 maintains two parallel sets of figures, and explanations, dealing respectively with the predator's solus and consolidated accounts.

Table 42: The Predator's Solus and Consolidated Accounts

	Solus	Consolidated
15% of target shares acquired for a cash sum[27] of	70	70
85% of target shares acquired for issue of predator shares having a nominal value	85	85
Although merger relief is claimed and therefore no share premium is created, acquisition accounting requires that the shares issued be recognised at full value, the credit usually being put to a *merger reserve*	nil	340[28]
	155	495
Those totals mirror predator's assets Investment in subsidiary	155	
Net assets of subsidiary as revalued at acquisition date		325
Goodwill arising on acquisition		170
	155	495

[27] The cash offer has been assumed to be at a small discount to the offer made in terms of shares; 15 per cent of the target was acquired for £70 rather than the figure of £75 which would have been strictly proportionate to the value offered in shares.

[28] The merger reserve created in acquisition accounting is of course a consolidated accounts figure — acquisition accounting is wholly a consolidation process; see the explanation in paragraph 6.25, and Note 41a thereon.

It is possible for the predator to establish a reserve account in its solus accounts with a balance equivalent to what it would have credited to share premium account had it not claimed merger relief. If it were to do so, its shares in the target would of course be correspondingly carried at full value on the other side of the balance sheet. This would be unusual, and section 133(1) CA 1985 specifically indicates that a predator is not expected to bring its asset in at full value in this way. It is worth mentioning that it was discussed as a possibility in the appendix to SSAP 23. If the predator receives a distribution out of the preacquisition profits of its target in a case in which that target's shares are carried at full value, then it would be required to use the dividend received to write down the value of those shares. In the discussion in the appendix to SSAP 23, the question was raised whether it was then legitimate to regard an equivalent part of the predator's merger reserve as having become distributable rather than non-distributable, so that the predator could pay the dividend onwards. At that time (April 1985) the ASC said *no firm ruling on this is yet available*, but in the years since then the accounting profession has concluded that there can be no bar to such distributability. FRED 7 makes no reference to this matter.

THE PREDATOR'S DISTRIBUTABLE PROFITS AFTER THE ACQUISITION

9.26 *The target's pre-acquisition profits*

At the date of its acquisition the target's balance sheet in paragraph 6.13 showed share capital of £50, and distributable reserves of £150. Its net assets would therefore have been carried at a matching £200. We have noted that for the predator's consolidation purposes these assets have been revalued to £325,[29] and in addition that consolidation includes a further *asset*, goodwill on consolidation £170, making up the total price paid by the predator of £495.

Whether a company can or cannot distribute a particular sum is a question which has to be determined from that company's own, solus, accounts; amounts shown in consolidations are irrelevant. The carrying value in the predator's balance sheet of the target's shares is £155, as shown in the left hand column in Table 42. If immediately after acquisition the target were to pay a dividend of £150 to the predator, the only two questions the predator needs to ask in considering its own entitlement to distribute that dividend on to its own shareholders are:

- is my receipt a realised profit? If the predator has received a dividend in cash, the answer seems self-evidently to be yes;[30]

- is there a need for a provision to be made against the carrying value of the asset to recognise a permanent diminution[31] in its value? If the target with £150 of cash still inside it was considered by he predator to be *worth* £495, then the stripping out of a dividend of £150 might be expected to reduce its value by that sum, or perhaps a little bit more; but it is hard to see how a provision could be thought necessary to reduce the predator's carrying value below the £155 level.

What we must recognise is that merger relief is the entitlement of the predator to credit shares issued for the acquisition at nominal value rather than at a figure including their *premium* element. Its (more or less) inescapable corollary is that the carrying value of the investment in the target can be less by an equal amount than it would have been but for the relief. Indeed that is the purpose of the relief. And the implication of that is that distribution of an equal amount of pre-acquisition profits is *not* blocked.

---

[29] It would be possible, but probably unusual, for this revaluation to be reflected in the accounts of the target. If its assets were to be so revalued, the credit in the target's accounts would go to a revaluation (non-distributable) reserve, which would have no bearing on the matters we are discussing in this paragraph.

[30] See paragraphs 4.9 to 4.11 for a discussion of the meaning of 'realised' in this context.

[31] A permanent diminution in the value of an asset is the phraseology used in the Companies Acts, paragraph 19(2) of schedule 4, CA 1985. The Accounting Standards Board tends to speak of the asset suffering an 'impairment', which perhaps recognises that it is its 'value to the business' that one needs to focus on, rather than any pure concept of what its value might be.

9.27 The 1947 Cohen Committee

When we originally looked, in paragraphs 6.13 and 6.14, at the acquisition by this predator of this target we said that the 1947 Cohen Committee had identified the procedures then open to the predator as making possible a distribution to shareholders of premiums obtained by it on the issue of its shares; or to put it another way, the distribution by the predator of its capital to its shareholders.

Let us re-examine that theory against the facts now in front of us. The easiest way of making clear what is happening is to show, in Table 43, the transaction in two columns, respectively nominal values of shares, and the underlying *worth* of those shares (that is to say, reflecting not only the companies' fully revalued net assets but also their goodwill – taking this to be the excess over asset values of the shares'

Table 43: Predator's Solus figures compared with 'fair value' figures

	Nominal	Worth
Number of predator shares in issue before acquisition	255	
Worth of predator (aggregate of its fully revalued assets and its goodwill) equates to £5 per share		£1,275
Deduct cash paid away by predator to target's shareholders who opt for cash		70
		1,205
Add shares issued to target's shareholders who opt for shares	85	
Add target's assets brought into predator's group (aggregate of fully revalued net assets and goodwill) equates to £70 plus 85 shares at £5 per share		495
	340	1,700
Transfer of cash from target to predator on payment of group dividend has no effect on group's assets		–
But it does reflect into a distributable reserve in predator's accounts	150	
Distribution of that reserve from predator to its shareholders does reduce group's assets	150	150
	340	1,550
Proportion of that worth owned by original holders 255/340 × 1,550	1,162,50	
Add capital distributed to them as explained in next paragraph	112,50	
Their original 'capital'	1,275,00	

values). The illustration is clearer still if we make the assumption that the predator has no distributable reserves at the date of its acquisition of the target.[32]

9.28 Applying Cohen's thinking to the predator's payment

Of the £150 distributed, £37.50 goes to the former shareholders of the target by reference to their new holdings in the predator. One can argue that they would have been entitled to have distributed to them 85 per cent of £150, that is £127.50 − if the distribution had been made prior to the change in ownership of the target, since that would have been their entitlement by reference to their shareholdings in that company. This argument would therefore say that what they had actually received was less than their full income entitlement, and that it was not therefore a distribution of capital. But this is an argument in equity only, having no legal force.

What seems to be closer to the legal theory can be seen in relation to the original shareholders of the predator. That company has, by spending £70 out of its non-distributable cash resources, and by issuing £85 shares at a premium (which it is relieved from showing) of £340, acquired a company worth £495. How can any part of that acquisition be anything other than capital? And if it is, how can the predator's original shareholders have distributed to them £112.50 out of the predator's assets?

But that again is not the correct legal question. What is correct in law is the two part question set out in paragraph 9.26; has the predator *realised* a profit when it received the dividend from the target, and must the predator provide for a diminution in value of its investment into the target. The answers have already been set out in that same paragraph 9.26.

Much as logicians may recoil from this analysis, it is true that merger relief does directly allow the distribution of at least some element of a company's capital to its shareholders; that if the Cohen theory was designed to stop the distribution of the *capital* that a predator could acquire in the form of pre-acquisition profits of a target, merger relief blows that theory clean out of the ground.

9.29 What happens if the former predator contemplates selling the target?

We can now turn to a different, wider, subject, although we will see that the target's pre-acquisition profits do have some relevance. This wider matter is a proposed sale of the target, in the form in which it currently stands, for £700. The purchaser is willing to allow the

---

[32] After we have developed the figures on the basis of that last assumption that the predator has no distributable reserves, it will be apparent from them that making a different assumption would not alter the conclusions; it is merely easier to identify those conclusions if we exclude predator reserves.

vendor to take a dividend out of the target before the sale, as outlined in paragraph 9.20.

Let us assume for the purposes of this present discussion that the target has not yet distributed its £150 of pre-acquisition profits; and let us also assume that in two years since it was acquired by the predator, the target has earned and retained a further £110 of post-tax profits.[33]

In considering the profit that the company we will now have to start calling the 'ex-predator' can report, we need to be aware what its consolidated accounts should show. But again, in considering what it can distribute, it would be to its solus accounts, and those alone, that one would look. The preceding two paragraphs showed those two *accounts* inclining to quite different answers regarding pre-acquisition profits. But that is nothing to the divergence we will see in relation to profits on the disposal of this subsidiary out of the group.

9.30 *Profit in the consolidated accounts on the sale of the target*

If we start with the consolidated accounts, the position is as shown in Table 44.

Table 44: Ex-Predator's Consolidated Accounts

Acquisition cost of target's assets, including its goodwill (which obviously equals the figure of cash plus the value of shares given for the target) (Note that within these assets are some mirroring the distributable reserves of £150 at acquisition)		£495
Add further tangible assets held within target which mirror its post-acquisition retentions		110
Subtotal, being the group's assets which at this stage are within the target's *corporate shell*		605
Deduct assets which it would clearly be sensible (from a capital gains tax and stamp duty point of view) to transfer by way of *group* dividend to the ex-predator[34]		260
		345
The agreed purchase price before the stripping of that dividend was	700	
Deduct reduction in that price reflecting the retention within the ex-predator of assets received by way of group dividend	260	440
Profit to be recognised in consolidated accounts on sale		95

---

[33] This is the post-tax retention. The group will of course have recognised pre-tax profits, and tax, but this does not alter the point here, which could be spelled out by saying that it is the existence of the assets retained within the target which has really been recognised.

[34] See paragraph 9.20 and Note 21 thereon regarding the payment of a group dividend before sale in order to reduce capital gains tax and stamp duty. The figures in this

continued

That could be described as a step-by-step analysis. A rather more basic explanation would say just three things. First, the group dividend is a mechanical exercise which has no effect on that profit. Second, the group since acquisition has already recognised the target's post-acquisition retentions of £110, and transferring the mirror image assets (if that were to be what happened) to the purchaser for £110 would produce no profit. Therefore, it is the balance of the purchase consideration, £590, that one needs to compare with the original acquisition cost of the target, £495. This produces a profit on sale of £95.

9.31 Profit in the consolidation (continued)

But the figures in Table 44 have taken a short-cut, without explaining the steps omitted. The acquisition of the target's assets, including its goodwill, was originally achieved for the figure of £495. When the predator acquired it in paragraph 9.25, we saw that the figures it brought into its consolidation were:

Share capital	(credit)		£ 85
Merger reserve	(credit)		340
Reduction in cash – (paid out)	(credit)		70
Assets of target as revalued	(debit)	325	
Goodwill arising on consolidation	(debit)	170	

At the time of writing the Accounting Standards Board has not come to a final conclusion how goodwill should be *dealt with* but there has been a commonly (not universally) adopted policy of writing this item off against reserves and the merger reserve is certainly one of those used for this purpose. Let us assume that the predator did in fact write off goodwill against reserves.

That action of writing off goodwill (£170) can be seen as a reduction in the carrrying cost, within the consolidation, of the group's investment in the target from the aggregate of the two debit items above (£495) to the amount of the target's assets (£325).

If that goodwill had been written off through profit and loss account, then on a sale of the target it would be logical and correct to bring back through profit and loss account not the £95 we arrived at in the previous paragraph, but £265 profit on the sale of the target. But we know that goodwill almost never is written off through profit and loss account – in most cases, including this one, the write-off is made direct to reserves.

---

continued

particular example do bring out quite clearly the fact that the target, in its new ownership after the sale, is likely to need recapitalisation by shares or loans to replace the cash stripped out (if that stripping is not done by means of, for example, a bank overdraft which the target can keep in existence indefinitely). Therefore, the pre-sale dividend does have the effect of leaving the new owner with a company which has no distributable reserves, but has increased borrowings or capital in place of those reserves.

To show a correct profit on the disposal it is therefore necessary[35] as a first step to reverse that write-off; to bring back into the carrying value of the asset the goodwill which was attributable at the time of its acquisition. Only thus can one compare like with like, acquisition cost of the target with its disposal proceeds, in deciding what is the profit the group should recognise on its sale.

The *merger reserve* commenced with a balance of £340. When goodwill of £170 was immediately written off, its balance was reduced to £170. But when we reverse the write-off of that goodwill, we restore the balance in the reserve to £340.

9.32 *Profit in the predator's solus accounts*

When we turn to the ex-predator's solus accounts, the position, as shown in Table 45, appears to be capricious.

Table 45: Ex-Predator's Solus Accounts

	Profit & Loss	Balance Sheet
Figure carried in ex-predator's accounts as amount of investment in subsidiary (taking merger relief into account per paragraph 9.25)		£155
Dividend received out of preacquisition profits might, had the above figure represented a full value for the investment, have needed to be deducted from that carrying value as representing a permanent diminution in the asset's value; but that does not apply where as here the carrying value is so much less than full value. Therefore the dividend would be credited to profit & loss	£150	
Dividend received out of post-acquisition profits, credited to profit & loss	110	
Adjusted sale figure for target (£700 minus £260) after taking into account the above dividends payable by target to ex-predator for tax reasons		440
		285
Difference between sale price and carrying value of target appears to be within the definition of realised profit and is therefore also credited to profit & loss	285	
	545	

---

[35] This procedure is required by the ASB's Urgent Issues Task Force Abstract No. 3. ASB does not spell this out, but it is obvious that the merger reserve continues to stand in the consolidated accounts at £340 after the target has been sold (assuming of course that consolidated accounts still need to be prepared).

When one seeks to analyse why the solus accounts of the ex-predator show realised and distributable profits of £545, whereas the consolidated accounts showed earnings over a two-year period of £110 and a profit on the disposal of £95, it is immediately apparent that the difference is the figure mentioned at the end of the previous paragraph of £340. In the consolidation it is retained in a capital reserve. In the solus accounts, it is shown in the profit and loss account as distributable.

That last statement can be rephrased; had merger relief not been claimed the solus accounts would have shown £340 in a share premium account. The effect of the claim for that relief is that there is no requirement in law for the retention of that sum, following the sale of the target, so that it becomes distributable. (It is not the merger reserve which has turned into distributable profit; it is a larger profit that has been realised because the asset sold had previously been carried at less than its full cost, because there was *no* merger reserve in the solus accounts.) The question which must follow from that is whether a company which did distribute such a balance would be retaining its capital intact and whether it would be distributing only its realised profits.

9.33 Is that distributable profit in the predator's solus accounts?

Answers produced by blind logic often seem surprising. Merger relief under section 131 Companies Act 1985 is a relief from the necessity to credit an amount to a capital reserve; a relief from a necessity to treat that sum as part of the company's capital, which would accordingly require to be held intact.

The granting of the relief does not of course make that *non-capital* sum immediately distributable. The most rational way to view the relief's effect *while the predator and target remain merged* is that the amount is held in suspense; its ultimate destination cannot be decided. That suspended status is precisely what Table 42 shows – the solus accounts reflect the relief granted by way of a deduction from the asset value. The investment in the target would in any other circumstances be carried at £495, but the effect of the relief is to reduce that to £155.

When the asset is sold, the period of suspense is brought to an end. The Companies Acts are an imperfect, incomplete, guide to accounting principles and procedures, but they contain nothing to indicate that the amount is not to be recognised as a profit, a realised profit.[36]

---

[36] The Companies Acts say nothing at all about the principles for arriving at the profits on disposals of group companies in these circumstances. All that they do contain is the requirement in paragraph 29(3)(a)(i) of schedule 5 to CA 1985, that there must be a disclosure of the profit on disposal of shares in respect of which merger relief had been claimed in the year, or in the previous two years. But although its heading implies that the schedule's objective is requiring a parent company to disclose information about its related organisations, what the paragraph concerned does actually call for is not the parent's figures. The disclosure required is the figure included in the consolidated profit and loss account. What the parent may be treating as distributable is no part of the disclosure.

9.34 *Further quirks of parent companies' distributable profits*

The Companies Acts' imperfections and incompleteness in relation to distributable profits are not limited to the particular aspect we have been looking at. Imagine a group in which the parent owns two subsidiaries, A and B, and A in turn owns a sub-subsidiary C. C's value has increased during the period in which the group has owned it, and A now sells it to B for full value paid in cash. Thus A makes a profit (but not a capital gain), and there seems to be no reason why it cannot be credited to profit and loss account as a realised profit. If A pays its profit as a dividend to the parent, there is no reason why the parent could not distribute it onward to its own shareholders.

If circumstances had been different, if A had merely revalued C without disposing of it; or had disposed of it to a group company which appeared less able to pay in cash a consideration amount initially left outstanding on inter-company account; then one would say that A's profit was not realised and accordingly not distributable. But the directors in considering distributability do not have to consider what might have been – only what the law has to say about what did actually happen.

In dealing with the criteria for the recognition of profits, paragraph 29 of chapter 4 of the Accounting Standards Board's *Statement of Principles* (still in discussion draft form, but nevertheless having persuasive force) starts off by saying:

> A transaction, by definition, always involves an obvious change in the composition of the assets and liabilities of the entity. Hence arm's length transactions provide conclusive evidence that a change in assets or liabilities has occurred ... and always call for recognition. However transactions not at arm's length can give rise to recognition problems due to lack of independence.

The final sentence in that same paragraph is perhaps significant in the somewhat extreme situation pictured above:

> This often results in a need for additional disclosure about the transaction and, in the extreme, may result in the need to modify its recognition so as to represent faithfully the substance of the transaction.

The ASB strongly suggests that disclosure is called for, but does not appear to believe it can override the Companies Acts in declaring non-distributable a profit which those Acts clearly envisage as distributable. A company's accounts are the responsibility of its directors,[37] and the decision is theirs.

---

[37] Section 226(1) CA 1985, in relation to the solus accounts we are considering here.

Chapter 10

SHARE OPTION AND INCENTIVE SCHEMES

10.1 Identifying the benefit

There are three schemes which are said to be tax privileged

- the profit-sharing scheme,   dating from 1978
- the savings related share option scheme,   dating from 1980
- the executive share option scheme,   dating from 1984

The *profit-sharing scheme* involves a trust, the trustees of which make appropriations to individual employees of shares in the employing company. The trustees need shares to be able to make these appropriations, and they can obtain them either by subscription or by purchase. Each of these necessitates the company providing funds to the trustees, and although in the former case the cash circulates back into the company there is in both cases a *cost* in the company's profit and loss account. Although the trustees appropriate shares to individual employees, those employees undertake (contractually) to allow the trustees to continue to hold those shares for two years (*the retention period*); and until *the release date* (a further three years after the retention period ends) the individual will incur decreasing levels of tax liability should he sell the shares. The method of operation of a profit-sharing scheme is explained in greater depth in paragraph 10.14 below.

One form of *employee share trust* is an integral part of the profit-sharing scheme referred to above, and as such enjoys part of its tax privileges. There are other, stand-alone, purposes for which employee share trusts can be used, and one particular form of the trust does carry a tax-approved label. We will see, however, that its requirements are so stringent, and the tax-disadvantages of failing to qualify so small, that many trusts are set up in a different form purposely to gain the flexibility that the company, and its employees, both need. We comment on some of the uses to which employee share trusts can be put in paragraphs 10.11 to 10.13 below.

The *savings related share option scheme* permits employees to save (out of after-tax income) over either a five- or a seven-year period to acquire shares in the company, the *exercise price* which they pay at the end of the stipulated period being 80 per cent of the value of the shares at the time the options were granted. Savings contracts which qualify for these purposes are offered by the National Savings movement, and by various banks and building societies. As well as the mechanism through which participants *save* the money needed to acquire their shares (rather than needing to sell part of their holdings to finance the acquisition of the remainder) there are two other basic differences between this savings related share option scheme, and the executive scheme to which we will come in the next paragraph:

- the savings related scheme must be open to all full time employees;

- the discount (of 20 per cent) to market value at the time of the grant of the options does represent a *real* benefit, entirely outside the scope of any taxes. We will see below that the executive scheme, although held out to be tax-privileged, does not in fact free its participants from tax in the long run.

The rules, and tax regimes, within which each of these schemes operate are immensely complex and detailed[1] (and this applies to almost the same extent for arrangements which do not seek to fit within the requirements of the tax privileged schemes). A substantial book would be needed to do justice to them, and this is not it. Instead, what we will aim for is:

- an explanation of the operations of each of the tax-privileged schemes, which will therefore point up what may be seen by employees and their employers as unduly restrictive requirements;

- an indication of what the tax privileges actually amount to, so that those contemplating establishing a scheme can make an informed choice whether to aim for those privileges, or to evolve some arrangement which is aimed more precisely at what the company wishes to achieve – where loss of tax advantages might be outweighed by efficiency gains.

---

[1] The basic legislation designed to tax employees on the *benefit* derived from their exercise of share options is in section 135 TA 1988, and that relating to the *benefit* of the appropriation to them of incentive shares is now (in a form that is very much changed from that in which it was originally enacted in 1972) in sections 77 to 80 FA 1988. The tax-privileged schemes are taken outside that legislation (that is to say, they carry exemptions for their participants from the assessments on benefits of options or incentives) by section 185 TA 1988 so far as concerns the two forms of share option schemes, and by section 186 as regards the incentives in the so-called profit-sharing scheme. Each of these last two sections has to be read with schedules 9 and 10 to the TA 1988, which contain a mass of detailed rules and interpretations. If a company wishes to establish any of the three tax-privileged schemes, it is essential that its Rules (and for a profit sharing scheme also its Trust Deed) be approved by the Inland Revenue; and to assist with this process the Revenue has published model Rules, a Deed, and associated documentation. The analysis in this book cannot be taken as a substitute for the degree of detailed study of the legislation that is necessary to design and operate any share scheme.

But where this book may assist those wishing to pursue these questions is in indicating some of the tax aspects of the schemes other than those dealing with the *benefits in kind* on which employees may or may not be taxable; in indicating the perceptions of employees and other shareholders; and finally in trying to show how companies should seek to measure their *costs* against the *benefits* they are seeking, namely the effective motivation of employees.

10.2 The Executive Share Option Scheme

There is therefore a strong case for our starting by asking some very simple questions, and making sure that we understand what the answers are. We can best do this in relation to the tax-privileged scheme that we have not so far mentioned, the *executive share option scheme*. The questions we will be asking, as will soon become apparent, need to look at the scheme from the points of view of all of those parties who have an interest, not only those awarded options or incentives, but those running the company, and the company's other shareholders. The authorities (tax and regulatory) are also interested.

We need some illustrative data so as to be able to demonstrate what happens, but it does not particularly matter if the figures we use are rather larger than would normally be the case for a listed company (that is to say if our illustrative employee is given options over a larger percentage of the shares than would apply in reality). We assume the company has 100,000 shares in issue, and their current price on the stock market is £5. Mr X, the company's managing director, is granted an option over 5,000 shares, the exercise date being either the fourth, fifth or sixth anniversary of the date of grant. The process of *grant* of an option is normally done in the form of a contract (the director offers to enter into the option, and the company accepts), so that he needs to give consideration in order to make the contract binding. However, generally grantees pay only a nominal sum on grant, and we will ignore this. The amount the grantee commits himself to pay if he should exercise his option is normally equal to the share price at the time of grant, that is to say 5,000 shares at £5 per share.

On the fourth anniversary of the grant, the share price has risen to £8, and the managing director borrows £25,000 from his bank in order to exercise[2] his option.

---

[2] The exercise must not be within three years of grant, nor within three years of the previous grant of an option, nor more than ten years after grant, if it is to be an exempt exercise, section 185(5) TA 1988. The Inland Revenue has published model rules for an executive share option scheme, which prevent any exercise of any options in the first three years after they have been granted (except where the optionholder dies, a matter we deal with in paragraph 10.10 and Note 18 below). But this is a good illustration how carefully the rules need to be designed. If there is a takeover of the company (by an unlisted company) in that three-year period, such a rule would prevent the employees from exercising their options before the takeover became effective; and they could not simply wait for the end of the three years and then exercise, because the shares they would acquire at that point would not 'qualify', and such an exercise would therefore breach another of the mandatory rules. If such a takeover is not to act as a fairly major demotivation of those who have their options effectively confiscated, it is advisable to make another exception (in addition to death) to the ban on exercise in the first three years. It necessitates some complicated definition of circumstances, and some careful thought about timing of the exercise – and it will of course mean that the exercise is taxable; but that is preferable to confiscation.

10.3 Identifying the benefit, how great is it, and at whose expense is it provided?

The capitalisation of the company immediately before the exercise of this option was 100,000 shares valued by the market at £8 each. The subscription of £25,000 of cash into the company on the exercise of the options can be regarded as increasing that capitalisation by £25,000, to £825,000. Thus the proportions of this increased capitalisation owned by the existing shareholders, and by the new shareholder, can be seen in Table 46.

Table 46: Analysis of Issuer's Capitalisation

100,000 shares now worth £7.86 per share		£785,700
5,000 shares	7.86	39,300
		825,000

Table 46 shows that the option holder has *gained* £14,300 by exercising his option, in that he paid out only £25,000 in order to acquire shares worth £39,300. That sentence makes it clear that if we say the individual had options over 5,000 shares at £5, or options worth £39,300, we must not imagine that that means the company has given him £25,000 or £39,300. Nor is it true in any normal sense of the words, as we will see below, that the company has given him a gain of £14,300.

But that £14,300 is exactly the same sum that the other shareholders *lost* through the dilution of their holdings, which dropped in value from £800,000 to £785,700. Obviously, the pricing mechanisms of the stock market do not really work as straightforwardly as that — dilution does exist, but is unlikely to be pound for pound the same as the option holder's *gain*. But the principle is clear for all to see; it is not the company which incurs, or suffers, any cost through its grant of an option to its managing director — if there is any suffering, it is that of the diluted other shareholders. We need to come back to this point below, since all listed companies are likely to be owned to a significant extent by institutional shareholders, whose views on dilution of their holdings are clear and firm.

10.4 Identifying the benefit — what are the tax liabilities, and what is the after-tax cash (or asset) left available?

Until 1984 the option holder's *gain* of £14,300 was treated as taxable income from his employment at the time at which he exercised his option.[3] With effect from 1984, as we will see below, further legislation has the effect of exempting (that is to say, taking out of what is now section 135 of the Taxes Act 1988) gains made on the exercise of options under approved schemes, provided the terms of those schemes are strictly observed. We will assume that the exercise of this option did fit within the conditions of an approved executive share option scheme, and that therefore there is no charge to tax on the £14,300 gain on exercise, so that it will not be regarded as taxable income under section 135.

However, the managing director does remain liable to capital gains tax if he disposes of the shares he has acquired under his option. In order to acquire them, we assumed that he had to borrow from his bank, and it is a not unreasonable further assumption that he might wish to sell, immediately, enough shares to enable him to repay that borrowing – this is shown in Table 47.

The illustration shows that he has the cash he will need in a few months to pay his capital gains tax, and is also still holding 1,280 shares, which have a current value of £10,050. If he were to sell them, there would be a capital gains liability amounting to £1,450, and the net cash he would be able to put in his pocket would be £8,600.

Table 47: Optionholder's Realisation of Shares after Exercise

Sale proceeds of 3,720 shares at £7.857 per share		£29,250
Cost for capital gains tax purposes is what he paid, 3,720 shares at £5 each	£18,600	
Capital gain[4]	10,650	
Capital gains tax thereon at 40%		4,250
Net cash available to repay bank		25,000

[3] The tax charge at the time of exercise of the option was legislated in 1966, in what has since become section 135 TA 1988. This was done to reverse a ruling of the House of Lords which had held (*Abbott v Philbin* [1961] AC 352) that a proper analysis of the facts did not support the view that an option holder derived *income* from his employment when he exercised an option.

[4] Our assumptions would lead to there being no indexation allowance. The rules are in section 145 TCGA 1992, although its drafting is so confusing that one could be excused for failing to appreciate this. The section provides that the amount paid on grant of the option, and the amount paid on exercise, shall be treated as separate items of expenditure, each incurred on the date it was actually incurred. (That makes obvious sense, because it would be stretching the words of the legislation in section 38(1)(a) and (1)(b) further than would be justifiable if one tried to treat the first amount as *acquisition* expenditure and the second as *enhancement* expenditure on the same asset.) However, what section 145 does which is so confusing is to refer to the amount the optionholder pays on exercise as 'the cost of acquiring what was sold as a result of the exercise of the option'. The first four words are obviously appropriate, but the remainder of the phrase leaps across from the optionholder's perspective to that of the grantor – and uses the word 'sell' which does not make very good sense where the grantor is a company which binds itself to 'issue' its shares to the option holder rather than to sell them. Once one has deduced that, it becomes clear that the £5 per share paid on exercise of the option is not re-timed to any earlier point, but is treated as paid when the option was exercised.

The reader will immediately spot that £8,600 is equal to the after-tax equivalent of the income of £14,300 which the individual would have been taxed on had his gain on the exercise not been exempted under his approved executive share option scheme. (If this had been a taxable exercise on which he had been liable to income tax on the exercise, the acquisition cost of his shares for capital gains tax would then have been treated as having been increased to £39,300, and he could have sold the shares for that amount without a capital gains tax liability; after he had used £25,000 to repay the bank, and £5,700 to pay his income tax, £8,600 would have been the sum left in his pocket.)

10.5 Identifying the benefit – perceptions of the public, and of the option holder

That seems to show that the tax burden on the exercise of an approved option is no less than would apply if the option were not granted under an approved scheme, or if an option granted under an approved scheme were exercised in a way which failed to qualify for that scheme's tax exemption.[5] But it is not quite as simple as that, because the whole of the income tax bill of £5,700 would in the second and third cases have to be paid immediately, whereas the individual exercising his option in a tax-exempt manner could limit his immediate capital gains tax bill to £4,250, and hold on to the shares whose disposal would cost the remaining £1,450 of capital gains tax. Secondly, although the marginal rates of income tax and capital gains tax may be the same, there is an annual exemption from capital gains, and there are other capital gains exemptions, on death, for instance, and on reinvestment into unlisted companies.

It was in 1966 that the law (now largely reversed) was enacted[6] making the gain on the exercise of an option taxable as income in the year in which that option was exercised. If we follow through the logic, it would not be totally unreasonable to say that the legislators of the day regarded the option holder as enjoying a similar position to that of the employee of a bookmaker, permitted by his employer to back horses after they had won. The gains the bookmaker's employee would enjoy would have been derived from his employment, and they would crystallise when he was enabled to place his winning bets.

There is however a completely different view of what is equitable and logical. This can be demonstrated if we consider a (different) bookmaker's employee who places his bets normally, before the horses leave the starting stalls; we would accept that any sums that employee was clever enough to win would not have been derived from his employment; if there were anything at all to be taxed as *earnings* it would only be any stake money which the bookmaker might have

---

[5] One example of an exercise which would fail to meet the requirements of a scheme is its taking place within three years after an earlier exercise of another option.
[6] Now in section 135 TA 1988, but the exemption which largely reverses this for approved schemes is in section 185 TA 1988.

provided for this employee. In the case of the share options we have been considering, there has been no such equivalent gift of stake money by the company; our managing director contracted to pay the full value (at the time of grant) of the shares, when and if he exercised his options. The options became worth exercising because the shares increased in value – a matter for which the company could not claim credit (any more than the second bookmaker could claim credit for his employee's skill in picking winners).

10.6 The rise in the share price is the real benefit

Those are the two opposing arguments whether there should or should not be a tax liability on the exercise of share options – (and the same applies for each of the other incentives we have mentioned, and will look at further). Many would argue that if the employee gains anything at the time of exercise of his option, it is not analogous to earnings – in part because it costs the employer nothing. The first bookmaker intentionally incurred costs, which we likened to employees' remuneration; but the second bookmaker and the company merely conducted their businesses less successfully than they might have done, by offering odds which did not deter bets they would rather not have taken, and by offering shares for subscription at prices they could have bettered if they had not committed themselves too early. But to a greater extent the option is different from remuneration because it is unrelated to work the employee does *for* the employer, (which is already fully remunerated). Even those who have reservations over either of these lines of argument may be inclined to agree that the extent of the tax exemptions for approved share option schemes is not excessive.

But by far the most important implication that we should have drawn out of the example we have been looking at, is a realisation which only dawns on most option holders quite late in the operation. The money is not made out of tax exemptions, but out of rises in share prices. An employer who holds out the offer of a tax privileged scheme may find some employees motivated by those tax privileges – in the short term; but if the scheme is to succeed in its objective in the medium to long term, it needs to do so, in those employees' eyes, by giving them share value increases, not tax breaks.[6a]

[6a] If the beneficiaries of a share option scheme include directors as well as employees, it can be strongly argued that shareholders and others using the financial information produced by the company would not be properly informed if the *disclosures* made by the company related only to their remuneration in other forms, without mention of the benefits they obtained, or might derive, from share options. The Cadbury Committee (Report on the Financial Aspects of Corporate Governance, December 1992) took the line that full details of options should be disclosed, and so has the ASB, in an Urgent Issues Task Force exposure draft of May 1994. In the US, the Financial Accounting Standards Board has gone further, in an exposure draft of June 1993, by suggesting that it would be proper for companies to recognise in their financial statements a cost of their granting, and of the employees' exercising, options. Needless to say the question how options are to be valued, at grant, and through the period they subsist, is a contentious issue.

continued

This brings us to the first of the early aberrations. In a group, it is not difficult to establish one or more companies whose share values can be made to increase at a faster rate, (and with a greater degree of certainty), than those of the parent company of that group. If one thinks through the ways in which the holders of shares in a subsidiary could be allowed to turn their shares into cash, (for instance by exchanging them for equivalent values of shares in the parent, and then selling the latter), it is clear that options granted over shares in such a special purpose company would have the effect of diluting the interests of the shareholders of the parent in a disproportionate manner. Not only did the tax authorities take strong objection to such devices when the existence of some examples came to light in the late 1960s, but so also did other regulatory authorities. One of the general conditions now required for tax privileged schemes is that the shares should either be those of the holding company, or in those few cases in which a subsidiary's shares are permissible, the company should not be one whose profits, and therefore value, are controlled by the parent.

10.7 Design features

Mention of the *authorities'* objections to schemes based on artificial subsidiaries brings us back to a consideration of the five sets of people who have an interest in the design of option and incentive schemes. We listed them in the first paragraph of this chapter as:

- the employees granted options and incentives;

- the *employer* who is interested in motivating those in the first head;

- other shareholders (interested in motivation, but at the same time not anxious to see their own holdings diluted too far);

---

continued

The legal requirements in the Companies Act 1985 for disclosure in the accounts are less stringent. The general requirement in paragraph 40 of Schedule 4 is disclosure of the number of shares under option, the period during which those options subsist, and the exercise prices. That obviously covers employees' options as well as directors'. This is not an appropriate place to attempt to analyse the Schedule 6 requirements, beyond pointing out that they are all governed by the second requirement in paragraph 11(1), that disclosure is to be made when *sums are paid*, which is hardly adequate to deal with options without some guidance when payment is to be treated as having been made, and how the sum is to be calculated. There is a requirement in Schedule 7, paragraph 2B, for disclosure of directors' options, but it suffers from the twin defects that it requires only aggregates for all directors, and that it requires numbers of shares for which options have been granted and exercised, without any indication of the prices.

Full information is to be made available in the company's register of directors' interests, required to be kept under section 325 Companies Act 1985; this is open for members' inspection during the annual meeting, and can also be inspected by members and others in normal business hours. But availability to the public of a vast quantity of detailed, and in many cases irrelevant, information can only form an effective disclosure if there is some agency through which the parts of it that are *relevant* can be made *readily* accessible.

- the tax authorities;

- other regulatory authorities, whose responsibilities could include such diverse matters as the efficient operation of the capital markets, wage policies and international competition policies.

Not all of the interests of all of these will be identical all of the time, and the design of any scheme will therefore always represent a compromise. Among the other shareholders in the third head are the groupings of institutional investors.[7] Their views can be summarised as being that they are enthusiastic about arrangements which enable and encourage employees to acquire shares for medium to long term investment, but less so about arrangements which provide shares to employees only so that they can sell them immediately – what is seen as giving employees cash remuneration in a way that is thought to be a tax-efficient manner (despite the fact already demonstrated that this is not tax-efficient[8]). Second, they are concerned about dilution of their investments, and insist that the percentage of capital made available under any *scheme* approved by the shareholders[9] should not be more than 10 per cent, and out of those options thus authorised to be granted, the numbers actually granted in any three-year period under the scheme concerned should not be more than 3 per cent. Third, they have reservations about employees being granted immediate replacement options as soon as those granted earlier have been exercised.

And lastly, they believe strongly that options should only be granted on the footing that their exercise is conditional on the meeting of some objective performance targets, appropriately designed to ensure that the employees are properly motivated by the award of options.

10.8 *Design features (continued)*

Exactly how performance targets are defined in order to achieve the greatest degree of motivation is outside the scope of this book. But there are two particular aspects which we should mention. It is theoretically possible to fix the targets which are to apply throughout the life of a particular scheme, and to write them into its rules. But all experience has proved that targets will always need to be adjusted. What is normally

---

[7] There are two bodies which represent the interests of institutional investors (the Association of British Insurers, and the National Association of Pension Funds), each of these bodies acting through its Investment Protection Committee.

[8] But it does have national insurance advantages.

[9] Each *scheme* requires to be approved by the Inland Revenue, this involving their accepting that its rules meet all the requirements. Part of the framework of those rules will be the number of the company's shares that the directors are to be authorised to issue, because it will only be the in the light of the shareholders' approval of this that the board committee running the scheme will be able to grant options over the same number of shares. Generally, the number of shares authorised is sufficient to keep the scheme going for about ten years, this being a convenient compromise between too frequent a need to go back to shareholders and the Revenue for approval, and too long a period which might mean that the rules became increasingly out of date and inappropriate (and eventually had to be replaced and re-approved).

done, therefore, is to set out general parameters in the description of the scheme before seeking shareholder approval: to write the rules to say merely that the directors can grant options conditionally, and then to decide on the appropriate conditions for each tranche of options to be granted – and to clear these conditions with the Inland Revenue prior to grant of that tranche. Repeated clearance is necessary in this way because the Revenue cannot give a blanket approval without being able to see that all of the features of the scheme are 'necessary or reasonably incidental'[10] to its overall objectives.

The hands of both the Inland Revenue and other regulatory authorities are visible in the next feature we need to mention. The executive share option scheme we have so far looked at very briefly can be made available to some employees only, rather than being open to all. If it does have a *cost* in terms of a dilution suffered by other shareholders in the values of their holdings, this is likely to be relatively modest; this is partly because the numbers of shares issued should be kept within limits by the IPC's restrictions, and partly because the optionholders do (almost invariably as we will see) pay into the company on exercise the value of their shares at the time of grant. But we can widen our thoughts to encompass design features of the other two approved schemes, not merely the executive share purchase scheme.

In the case of the profit-sharing scheme, it is usual for employees to be given shares free so that the dilution suffered by other shareholders will be much larger. What the authorities have said is that such schemes can only be operated if membership is open to *all* employees.[11] (Other shareholders should not be asked to accept that dilution to finance only a lucky few; but if the entire workforce stands to benefit, it is less unreasonable for shareholders to accept dilution.) Similarly, the savings related option scheme gives participants the right to obtain shares at a 20 per cent discount below their open market price, and membership must be open to all.

10.9 *Design features otherwise known as general conditions*

We are still discussing the three tax-privileged schemes (the profit-sharing scheme, the savings related share option scheme and the executive share option scheme). We have yet to get into the separate details of the first, but there is one collection of details that it is convenient to dispose of here, since it applies to all three. The tax legislation refers to this collection as the 'general conditions',[12] making the granting of tax approval dependent on a scheme complying with

---

[10] Paragraph 2(1) schedule 9 to TA 1988.

[11] Paragraph 2(3) schedule 9 to TA 1988 says that there must be no features which could 'discourage' any employee from participating. It is not permitted that a scheme be open only to the employees of one company in a group and not to others if the effect of this is to confine membership to directors and senior employees. Paragraph 2(3) applies not only to profit sharing schemes but also to the savings related option mentioned briefly in paragraph 10.1.

[12] The general conditions are in Part II of schedule 9 to TA 1988.

them. It is much more sensible to see them as a part of the design of the scheme, intended to motivate employees; not to think of them as rules imposed which make that objective more difficult.

Only full-time employees can participate in any of the tax-privileged schemes, and those who are already substantial shareholders are debarred.[13] The shares appropriated to employees, or over which they are granted options, must be ordinary shares.[14] We have already noticed that the shares must not be those of a subsidiary; but should instead be those of a company which is either not part of any group, or if it is should be the principal company of that group; but there is an exception – shares in a subsidiary company can be used in a scheme, provided that its parent is listed, and is not a close company.

The shares must not be subject to any restrictions. There were many incentive schemes developed in the 1960s which took advantage of the legislation as it then existed. Shares could be issued in a restricted form, such that employees were only taxable on the value of the shares taking into account those restrictions;[15] for instance £1 shares issued only 1p paid, which did not qualify for dividends or votes until fully paid, and could not be sold until fully paid, would only have a negligible value. As the law stood until 1972, *the removal of the clogs* on the shares' value, which would obviously put a substantial increase in value into the employees' hands, was not an event which gave rise to a tax liability for those employees. The change in the tax rules in 1972 created a liability on such *growth in value* (treating the gain as part of their income from employment). But as an alternative, if there had by then been no charge on a growth in value, it created equivalent tax liabilities on the seventh anniversary of any issue of shares to any employee – even if that did not coincide with any increase in the value in his hands, or with any availability of cash with which to meet the liability. The tax rules were relaxed in 1978 to make possible the approval of the profit sharing schemes we have so far only briefly mentioned. They were further relaxed in 1988, providing that only in those circumstances in which some positive action was taken to increase the value of shares at a time after they had first been appropriated to an employee would there be any tax charge in his hands on a growth in value.

---

[13] A shareholding is substantial (strictly 'a material interest' if we were to use the phrase which the tax legislation employs in this sense here, but uses to mean quite different things in other contexts in other parts of the legislation) at 10 per cent so far as the executive share option is concerned, and 25 per cent for the other two schemes.

[14] The definition of ordinary share for this purpose is in section 832(1) TA 1988, which describes as ordinary all the issued share capital of the company (by whatever name called) of the company, other than capital the holders of which have a right to a dividend at a fixed rate but have no other right to share in the profits of the company. That makes it clear that it is possible that there will be different classes of shares, each of which is referred to as ordinary by the tax authorities. The general conditions require that if there is more than one class of ordinary share, those used in the scheme should not be a class of which the majority is held by employees.

[15] The issue of restricted shares can be described, with hindsight, as the second of the early aberrations; as undesirable in the authorities' view as the use of shares in special purpose subsidiaries which we have already looked at in paragraph 10.6.

But it is nevertheless still an essential part of the general conditions that shares used for any of the tax-approved schemes may not be subject to any restrictions.[16]

10.10 *Tempus fugit*

The particular feature of the design of any scheme which the Inland Revenue does not directly control, but which it is essential that we understand and are able to deal with, is time. Each type of scheme involves there being a period of years between the original appropriation of shares, or the grant of the options, and the time at which the shares concerned become available to the employee, in the sense that he can freely turn them into cash if he wishes. During that period, share prices can change – or to put that point more specifically, they can move down when the scheme's promoters hoped that they would move up, or they can move up more rapidly than was expected. Second, the passage of time will mean that some employees will retire or die (or both) and others will leave (either with or without the mutual consent that is referred to on these occasions).

On the death of an optionholder, his personal representatives[17] have 12 months in which to exercise options he held at the date of his death,[18] and they can also take shares which the trustees of a profit-sharing plan were holding (not yet released) for him; as we will see in paragraph 10.15. In the case of other departures, the employee leaving or retiring, there is a certain amount of room for an option scheme to be designed to achieve what its promoters believe to be the right answer. If they want to be as restrictive as possible, they are entitled to say that those who retire have six months within which to exercise their options, failing which they lapse, and all other leavers' options lapse as soon as they leave. This could very easily force those retiring to exercise options either within three years of grant, or within three years of the previous exercise of an option – either of these making the exercise into a taxable event. Therefore, if the scheme's promoters wish to be as generous as possible to retirers and leavers, they can allow (say) 42 months after the date of departure (or can do this for retirers, but not for other leavers) – thus

---

[16] The only restrictions that are permitted are those under which a participant in a profit sharing scheme binds himself in contract to the trustees of that scheme that he will not dispose of his shares during the first two years after they have been appropriated to him (the retention period).

[17] 'Personal representatives' is a phrase used in tax law to embrace either executors granted probate under the deceased's will, or those granted letters of administration in a case where the deceased died intestate.

[18] The exercise of the options by the personal representatives (assuming this is allowed by the rules, and is done within 12 months of death) is exempt even if it is within three years of grant or three years of the previous exercise of an option, paragraph 27(3) of schedule 9 to TA 1988 overrides section 185(5) TA 1988. Similarly, shares can be taken out of a profit sharing scheme tax free by personal representatives of a deceased employee, because both the release date and the end of the retention period are brought forward (to date of death), section 18.6(4) and paragraph 2(c) of Schedule 10 to TA 1988.

giving the optionholders concerned enough time to exercise without the necessity for creating a tax liability by doing so. It is possible for the company to be given discretion whether to extend a six-month period to 42 months in particular cases, but note that this is not the same as saying that the company can have discretion to declare that a particular leaver's options have lapsed.

This is one indication of the degree of care that is necessary in thinking out, in advance of establishing a share option scheme, exactly how it is to operate – and exactly how generous or otherwise it will be seen to be by those it should be motivating.

10.11 Share trusts

There is another aspect of employee shareholdings which we can appropriately think about in the general context of the design of employee share schemes. It is often suggested that if employees are to be given shares, not only is it necessary that they have some method of disposing of them when they cease to be employed (if not before), but it is highly desirable that they should be required to dispose of their holdings on leaving employment. If they do not, it is said, the efforts that their successors put into increasing the values of shares go largely into the pockets of predecessors rather than for the benefit of those who are still bearing the heat and burden of the day.

The availability of an exit route presents no problems in the listed company whose shares are extensively traded – and it is also true in that case that the extent to which current employees would perceive themselves as working for their predecessors is unlikely to demotivate anyone. But in the smaller listed company and particularly in the company which does not have a listing and is unlikely to gain one in the foreseeable future, both problems can be acute.

The first, an exit route for those who want to sell shares, can be reasonably easily achieved by means of an *employee share trust*;[19] but the company, and the trustees it appoints to run the trust, must have a clear idea what it is going to cost to run this arrangement. For instance, if the trustees are to buy shares back from leavers at a price which matches the expectations that the latter have formed during the periods over which their holdings have been built up, and those trustees are then to re-appropriate the shares (free) to current employees, this is

---

[19] What is referred to is an employee *share* trust. There are trusts for employees which provide benefits for them in cash terms, for instance through the trustees having an entitlement to receive some percentage each year of the company's pre-tax profits, and an obligation to pay this out to employees selected at the trustees' discretion. There are trusts which provide benefits to employees in non-cash forms. And there are trusts which do one or other of the foregoing coupled with an activity of acquiring shares, appropriating them to employees, and/or making available the shares required to meet employees' exercises of options over shares. What we are discussing is the *share* operations of such mixed purpose trusts, or the operations of trusts established specifically to carry out such share transactions.

bound to be an expensive operation. On the other hand, if what were envisaged were an option scheme, in which the trustees' purchases of shares from one generation of shareholders in any particular period were the subject of options simultaneously granted in that same period to another generation, then the trustees' only costs would be those of holding the shares for the period between the granting and exercise of options.[20]

10.12 *The requirement for sales of shareholdings by those leaving employment*

The second possibility we canvassed in the previous paragraph was the idea that employees leaving the company's service should be required to sell their shareholdings. This is obviously not something the substantial listed company would normally wish to do. But very different considerations may apply in the small unlisted company, perhaps formerly a family enterprise, but which has been turned through a management buy-out (followed by a strong policy of encouragement of employee shareholdings) into what might be described as a workers' co-operative.[21] And there are listed companies at the smaller end of the spectrum which are very similar. It is tempting to suggest that the company's best interests lie in its being owned and controlled by those who are, at any time, fully engaged in its endeavours – that it is fair neither to them nor to their predecessors that the latter should be participating in its successes (or vulnerable to its failures) which are ascribable solely to the current work-force. Even if it were argued to be humane (and not totally illogical) that ex-employees should be allowed to stay on the share register, this argument ceases to hold, after those ex-employees' deaths, for their sisters and their cousins and their aunts.

It is not possible to put a *sell-requirement* only on *scheme shares* because that would breach the rule that scheme shares cannot carry restrictions; but if every ordinary share were subject to the same condition (that if it were held by an individual employed by the company, he must sell within a stipulated period of ceasing to be employed), that would not be a restriction as the legislation defines that word. However, it is obvious that the only place in which it would be possible to put such a condition upon the holding of shares would be in the Articles. And it is equally obvious that the trustees of the employee share trust would be the only realistic purchaser of last resort, (if not the only purchaser). They would not only need to have access to substantial funds with which to make the purchases that might be necessary from any substantial holders, but would also need to be able to see how their re-appropriation of those shares to other employees would best serve

---

[20] Assuming of course that every option ever granted is actually exercised. Where an option lapses, the trustees may only be able to re-grant a new option at a lower price – and the financial implications will be less attractive.

[21] Using the words 'workers' co-operative' in their colloquial sense, not as the term of art defined in section 187(10) TA 1988.

the company's objectives (as well as those employees', and the others', needs).

The practical problems do not need to be spelled out in any greater detail. The author has seen this done successfully only once, by a small listed company in New York, where the trustees were able to hold a sufficient pool of shares to be able to support the market price of what was a narrowly traded share. At the same time the trustees were able to take substantial numbers of shares off former senior employees in retirement (an extremely tax-efficient process under US rules) and to re-appropriate them to current employees, who were similarly comforted that their retirements would be looked after in due course. The company's senior employees (at any particular period) regarded themselves as the collective owners of the company, and were entirely happy to see a substantial proportion of its profits paid into the trust each year in order to support the trustees' operations – rather than being paid out as dividends. But at the same time, the fact that the company paid only that low level of dividends to its shareholders did not particularly matter; those senior employees' holdings, together with the trustees' holding, made the company bid-proof.

10.13 *The ESOT, Employee share ownership trust approved under the Finance Act 1989*

To return to UK share trusts, the Government announced in 1988 their intention to formalise in legislation a particular form of employee trust, to be known as the Employee Share Ownership Trust (ESOT):

- the company's contributions to the trustees for the purpose of running the trust would be deductible for corporation tax. Such deductibility was already available under general principles for most employer contributions to trusts not approved under this regime; the advantage, if there is one, is that the availability of the deduction is spelled out for what had in the case of unapproved trusts been areas of some doubt, namely where the employer contributes sums to an ESOT to enable it to repay amounts the trustees had borrowed, to pay interest on those borrowings, and to make cash payments to the employees within the terms of the trust objectives;[22]

- the ESOT could hold shares for seven years before appropriating them to employees which is longer than would be normal, for instance, in the trust which forms part of the profit-sharing scheme (paragraph 10.1 above and 10.14 below and in particular Note 29 on the latter);

---

[22] The timing of the company's deduction is essentially the same as we will see spelled in the next paragraph for a company's contribution to an approved profit sharing scheme, that is to say, the company deducts in the year it makes the payment, so long as the trustees have spent the funds concerned within nine months after the end of that year – but for an ESOT as opposed to the approved profit sharing plan, there is a wider range of matters on which the trustees are allowed to spend the funds.

- what an ESOT can do with the shares it acquires is *either* transfer them direct to employees; *or* transfer them to the trustees of the trust associated with an approved profit-sharing scheme of the type we will look at in the next paragraph. It is necessary to think quite clearly about the tax effects of each of these possibilities, both as regards the recipients, and the ESOT – since where one might have expected to find some tax reliefs in the legislation what one does in fact find is silence;

- if an ESOT transfers shares direct to an employee, that is *not* a transfer which is exempted from tax in the employee's hands (as we will see in the next paragraph, this would be the case were the transfer made by an approved profit-sharing scheme). The difference between the value of the shares, and the amount (if any) the employee pays, is taxed as earnings from his employment. For both his capital gains tax purposes, and that of the ESOT trustees, the latter's disposal and his acquisition are treated as open market value;[23]

- if the ESOT transfers shares to the trustees of a profit-sharing trust, that will enable those trustees subsequently to transfer them on to an employee with the tax privileges we will see in the next paragraph. But so far as the trustees of the ESOT are concerned they have a capital gains tax disposal, although there seems to be nothing to prevent the two sets of trustees agreeing a transfer value such that the ESOT will have no liability (we will see that the profit-sharing trust *can* itself be exempt from capital gains tax on certain conditions);

- the ESOT is liable to tax on dividends received on shares not yet disposed of, at the basic rate plus the additional 10 per cent rate;

- the one clear tax advantage that the ESOT does have[24] is that it should be able to acquire shares at a competitive price from existing shareholders, since it is provided that those shareholders can roll over their capital gains on their disposals, reducing the capital gains tax acquisition cost of some replacement asset.

But the almost insuperable practical problem with ESOTs is that it is a requirement that they should make shares available to all employees on equal terms. This is clearly an impossibility if what the trustees are trying to do is to meet the obligations of a share option scheme by providing the shares which are needed by those employees exercising options – the exercise prices of options granted at different times, but exercised at the same point, are bound not to be *equal*. Even where the purposes of the trust do not include the handling of options, merely the appropriation of shares to employees on some basis or other,[25] the requirement that every

---

[23] Section 17(1)(b) TCGA, because he receives the shares in consideration of his services in his employment.

[24] Now in sections 227 to 229 TCGA 1992.

[25] In all cases other than the appropriation *approved* within the profit-sharing scheme rules, there will of course be a tax liability in the employees' hands in respect of any shares are appropriated by any trust (ESOT or unapproved) at a price lower than the full market value of the shares.

THE APPROVED PROFIT-SHARING SCHEME

full-time employee must be entitled to participate on an equal footing (even if the numbers of shares made available may depend on salary and years of service) is not likely to be consistent with the trust's objects.

10.14 The approved profit-sharing scheme

We introduced this scheme at the beginning of paragraph 10.1 above. What we have been saying about all three forms of schemes is that their tax privileges are almost certainly less important than their other aspects; but in the case of the approved profit-sharing scheme it really is necessary to start from its tax implications in order to make sense of the regulations and the procedures:

- trustees make appropriations of shares to employees, and the employees are exempted[26] from a charge to tax on deemed *income* despite the fact that the shares are appropriated free (the employee pays nothing for the shares, then or later);

- from the date of appropriation onwards, the dividends on the shares are the employee's, and if the shares are still held in the trustees' names, they must pass those dividends on (similarly, the shares' voting rights will be exercisable by the legal owner, the trustees, but they must cast those votes as instructed by the employee);

- for capital gains tax purposes the employee is regarded as having acquired his shares at the date they are appropriated to him and at their full market value at that date.[27]

The employing company meets the costs of the scheme, in that it has to pay to the trustees what the latter need to purchase or subscribe for the shares which they are to appropriate to employees; this is in both cases an expense in the company's profit and loss account, even if in the case of a subscription of shares the cash recirculates into the company. The company's tax deduction for its expenditure is given in the year in which it makes the payments, provided that the trustees have spent the money within nine months of the end of that year in acquiring shares for appropriation.[28]

The trustees' tax position is that dividends received on shares prior to their appropriation are the trustees' income, and if those shares are held, unappropriated, for more than 18 months, an extra 10 per cent tax must

---

[26] Section 186(2) TA 1988.
[27] Market value acquisition cost follows from the fact that the employee receives his shares 'in consideration for or recognition of his services in his employment' in section 17(1)(b) TCGA 1992. (This is a quite different treatment from the one, which we saw in Note 4 on paragraph 10.4, has been made statutory for option holders.)
[28] Section 85 TA 1988. Note that the tax legislation does not require the trustees to have appropriated the shares within the time limit, only acquired them.

be paid on those dividends.[29] The sums the trustees receive from the company are not regarded as their income, but as received on capital account. Similarly, their acquisitions and disposals (by appropriation) of shares are capital gains transactions. We have seen above that the trustees' disposal values (the individuals' acquisitions) are deemed to be open market value, but the trustees are exempt from capital gains provided appropriation takes place within 18 months after acquisition.[30]

10.15 *The approved profit-sharing scheme – release date and retention period*

The next point to make clear is the relevance of the years following appropriation:

- *the release date* is the fifth anniversary of the trustees' appropriation of shares to the employee. On the happening of certain events (to which we will come below) before that fifth anniversary, whether it is the employee who demands these actions or whether they occur for other reasons, what can best be described as a tax penalty becomes payable. The general thrust is that the penalty will be suffered by the employee, but we will see that the Inland Revenue collect it (or a sum which is intended to equal or exceed it) from either the trustees or the company. Second, it is most important to understand that the release date is only brought forward by one of the events which one might possibly expect might accelerate it, that is to say, it is accelerated by the employee's death[31] but is not brought forward by retirement, disability or redundancy, although there are some reliefs for each of these as we will see in paragraph 10.17. This leads to the third relevant point, namely that we need to understand that although the dividends and votes on the shares belong to the employee from appropriation, the shares remain registered in the names of the trustees until released – and we must appreciate under what disabilities that legal ownership places the employee;

- *the retention period* is a period of two years from appropriation. During this period the employee must bind himself by contract with the trustees that he will not require them to transfer the shares to him, or otherwise dispose of them. The penalty for a breach of this contract is rather more draconian, namely the loss by the scheme of its approved status – but it has to be said that such breaches are more or less unthinkable. The retention period is shortened by the employee's death, retirement, or his cessation of employment through disability or redundancy.

---

[29] This tax rule, and that in Note 30 below, both encourage appropriation within 18 months, but if the share price is rising, seem to encourage it as late as possible in that period. This is a tax rule that encourages appropriation within 18 months after the trustees' acquisition. In the case of listed companies, the Investment Protection Committees require immediate appropriation.
[30] Section 238(2)(d) TCGA 1992.
[31] Section 186(4) TA 1988.

THE APPROVED PROFIT-SHARING SCHEME

10.16 *The approved profit-sharing scheme – events before the release date which result in a tax penalty*

Against that background, and bearing in mind that the legal title (the entry in the company's share register) is in the trustees' names, we can look at the events which trigger the tax penalty referred to in the first head in the previous paragraph:

(1) the trustees selling the shares, or receiving a capital sum for them for instance on a takeover for cash consideration (but the trustees are allowed to receive shares in a predator company on a takeover of a target on a share for share basis, and can treat the new shares received for all purposes of the scheme as if they were the original shares appropriated);

(2) the employee selling his interest in the shares to the trustees (so that they become beneficial owners as well as legal owners);

(3) the employee directing the trustees to transfer the legal ownership of the shares into his own name (he is of course contractually prevented from doing this during the retention period, but only discouraged by the tax penalty thereafter).

The first part of item (1) above clearly envisages that the employee may instruct the trustees (after the end of the retention period but before the release date) to sell the shares; however, the trustees *must* be prevented by the rules of the scheme from disposing of the shares by way of anything other than a sale for full value. Taking that provision into account alongside the fact that all that the trustees 'own' is the legal title, it seems likely that the employee would have difficulty in borrowing against the shares. The normal way of giving security would be for the legal owner of the shares to deposit the certificate with a signed blank transfer; there would be no further action necessary by that legal owner to effect an actual re-registration into the lender's name, and nothing the legal owner could do to prevent this. It therefore seems that such a deposit by the trustees would in the circumstances constitute a *disposal* which was not for full value and would thus breach the rule mentioned above, and would thus be impossible for the trustees to contemplate.

10.17 *The approved profit-sharing scheme – the penalties*

If an employee does any of the things set out in heads (1) to (3) in the previous paragraph before the release date, the tax penalty exacted is in effect the retrospective withdrawal of the exemption he originally enjoyed – that is to say, an assessment is then made as referred to in the first head in paragraph 10.14 on the value of the shares appropriated to him as if this value had been earnings from his employment. That sentence has been carefully worded. It is the shares' original value (what the legislation refers to as their 'locked-in value')[32] which is assessed, not the value at the date of the offending transaction. It does not matter whether the individual is still employed, or retired (or even dead) at the time of the transaction, the assessment is still made as if he were an employee.

In the cases numbered (1) and (2) in paragraph 10.16, the trustees have in their own hands the cash resulting from the disposal of the employee's shares. They retain and pass to the employing company a sum equal to the shares' locked-in value, passing only any excess to the employee. The employing company applies PAYE to the sum it receives, and passes only the balance to the employee.

In the case at (3) in paragraph 10.16, the trustees will not have any cash in their hands, but they may hand the shares over to the employee *only* if he passes to them a sum equal to the basic rate of tax applied to the locked-in value; the trustees account for that sum to the Inland Revenue as if it had been PAYE, and it is then up to the employee to agree what is his actual liability, and obtain a repayment or pay any further tax as appropriate.

But there is one important qualification to the above. In the final year (out of the five up to the release date), only three-quarters of the locked-in value is taxed, rather than the whole. If the employee has reached retirement age, has left service through disability or has been made redundant, then at whatever point after the end of the retention period but before the release date the event takes place, only half of the locked-in value is taxed.

If at the end of that the reader is left with the impression that the approved profit-sharing scheme has been designed for the convenience of the Inland Revenue rather than the motivation of employees, the author would not gainsay such a view.

10.18 Are tax privileges worthwhile?

We have examined how an executive share option scheme needs to be operated in order to gain approval, and what that approval means. We have only looked more briefly at the savings related share option scheme, but its general purposes and benefits can be seen by comparing it with what we have seen of the executive scheme. We have also seen how an approved profit-sharing scheme operates, and what its

---

[32] Sections 186(4) and 187(2) TA 1988. There is what may be regarded as a small qualification to this statement, in that there can *also* be assessments raised in circumstances that the trustees receive *capital receipts* in respect of the employees' shares. One form of capital receipt might be a capital distribution by the company, but perhaps a more common one in practice is the payment from a company to a shareholder who fails to take up a rights issue, where the company sells his rights on his behalf. In this case, the capital receipt is assessed, section 186(3) TA 1988, subject to a *de minimis* exemption referred to as the appropriate allowance, section 186(12) TA 1988.

tax privileges mean for its participants. And finally we have looked at the basic purposes that may be served by a share trust, and seen that although there is a particular form of trust which is held out as enjoying particular tax advantages, there are very real disadvantages in setting up a trust in this form.

The author's strong advice to any company considering any scheme of any of these types is that the company should, first, work out what it wants to do – what it believes in its particular circumstances will best fit the bill of motivating employees, and spreading share ownership. Only thereafter should the company examine whether this can be done (perhaps with some modification) through one of the tax-privileged schemes, and if it can, whether the changes which are necessary are made worthwhile by the tax savings that can be achieved.

Going for tax privileges at any cost is far from the obvious answer to every company's needs.

CHAPTER 11

DISPOSALS

11.1 Introduction

Predators are not always unwelcome; nor are they invariably excessively predatory. Targets and those disposing of them (disponors) are described as defensive, but that is also a matter of degree.

However, it makes sense in this and the next chapter to deal with disposals and acquisitions on the footing that the parties are talking, but only warily – that each is looking for the other's weak points, and actively seeking his own advantage. Those assumptions will enable us to examine the rules of war.

Or perhaps we should describe them as rules of the game. What we call them is actually less important than the fact that there are generally recognised procedures, evolved over the years for reasons of general business efficiency. It is particularly important that each of the parties knows not only what it can expect from the other, but what it can expect from its own professional advisers and from those on the other side. That does not mean that no one should ever step outside the conventions. But it does mean that doing so will be disruptive, and therefore inefficient and costly, unless the person who takes this course himself understands where he is crossing the lines, how that will affect each of the others, and the extent to which it will necessitate his trying to redirect their efforts so that all continue to work towards the same objective.

Let us go back to the thought that a disposal is a defensive exercise. The target, and particularly its management, needs to be defended against those criticisms that the sale process will bring to the surface. Most obvious are those the predator will use in an attempt to talk down his purchase price; potentially more damaging are the effects on the target's and the disponor's managements, and those companies' standing in the eyes of their suppliers, bankers, customers and others. It is essential that a disponor plans this operation carefully, that it puts together a selling team who know what they are aiming for, and the time-scale within which they aim to achieve it; that this team and their professional advisers are thoroughly familiar with the target's affairs so that the predator's demands, questions and challenges can be anticipated.

11.2 *The common features of disposals and acquisitions*

It is in that context that it is sensible to start by thinking, from the disponor's and target's points of view, about the disposal of assets, trades and companies before considering (in the next chapter) what the

INTRODUCTION

predator[1] should have in his mind in deciding how and at what price he might buy. Each must understand and anticipate what the other can be expected to think and do; but it is with the disponor's prime objectives that we need to start.

Intending disponors are generally affected by a number of broadly similar factors. We have mentioned the most significant contextual ones in the last paragraph. From here on we will concentrate on organisational and procedural matters. But in doing so we will see that disponors will frequently wish to handle their disposals in a particular manner; if we understand what are the critical factors, and what advantage the disponor may derive from fitting his disposal into some recognisable pattern, a structure having features common to many disposals, then we can begin to see whether there are also advantages in this for the predator – or if there are likely to be disadvantages, then where the trade-off between the parties may lie.

The whole of what we have said so far could be read as saying:

- disponors and targets must do what this chapter tells them, and should read the next one only to find out what they can expect to have done to them;
- and vice versa;

but it really is not as easy as that to draw dividing lines, and compartmentalise this material. Everyone needs to know, and be able to act on, the principles in both chapters. Additionally, although most of what we will be looking at will be sales of shares in companies, we do also need to think about sales of businesses together with the assets of those businesses, and sales of separate assets.[2] The disponor, whether of assets and business, or of shares, may be a company, or may be an individual or individuals. As indicated, it really is not practical to try to deal with each possibility in watertight sections. What we will aim to do is cover the principal business/asset disposals before the share disposals; without being overly concerned that companies' and individuals' disposals will often not need differentiation; when they do, we can probably contrast and compare rather than segregate.

11.3 *Setting the scene*

There are two points which it is essential that everyone involved in disposals or acquisitions should consider at the outset:

---

[1] The author needs to spell out one convention. The word 'predator' may already be stretched when used to mean the purchaser of a company, because we already know that such purchasers are not always unwelcome or predatory. But in this and the next chapter we will stretch the meaning of predator even further; a predator need not always be a corporate entity, and his target need not always be a holding of shares in a company.

[2] It is perfectly true that shares are themselves a form of asset, but it will reduce confusion if we stick rigidly to the convention of only referring to shares as shares, and using the word assets to refer to assets other than shares.

- Value Added Tax, as it applies to whatever *supply* (of goods, because the disposals we are discussing will seldom involve the supply of services) is being made by the disponor to the predator. One possibility is of course that what is being supplied is shares in a company, which should be exempt under Group 5 Item 6 of schedule 6 to VATA 1983. Much more complex is the position where a trade and assets are being transferred, because this will either, if the disponor is registered for VAT, be a supply of goods on which VAT needs to be charged; or, if the disponor is engaged in a business in which he has not been required to register because his VATable supplies are insuffient, it will be a supply which he is entitled to treat as exempt despite the fact that its subject matter would not seem to suggest this;[3] or it will be a supply which is outside the scope of VAT, because it fits the criteria for a *transfer of a going concern*. We will need to look at transfers of going concerns in some depth in paragraphs 11.32 to 11.35 below;

- Employment protection, particularly in relation to the Transfer of Undertakings (Protection of Employment) Regulations. This exceedingly complex question will be the subject of paragraphs 11.36 to 11.41.

There is one final piece of scene-setting called for. Some parts of this chapter attempt to explain, for businesses organised in a *normal* way, the effects of their owners' decision to dispose of them, and the effects on the owners themselves. Other parts address a slightly more complex question, the extent to which some change to the business can improve the disponor's position. But there is a third area in which it is perhaps even more difficult to be confident one can identify the correct guiding principles, that of the business which has always been *organised* (if that is the right word) to deal with one type of disposal, but which now faces another. One example of this is the subject of the next paragraph.

11.4 Group asset companies

The basic thought process is that there can be a degree of flexibility achieved in a group by holding in one specific company those assets on which a disposal may give rise to capital gains or losses, rather than having these assets dispersed around the group companies. If a capital loss does occur, the *only* method by which tax relief can be obtained is by ensuring that a capital gain arises in the same company, either in the same year or as soon afterwards as is feasible. If a company in a group makes a capital gain, it is possible for:

- a trading loss sustained in the same period or any of the next three by that company to be set against it;

---

[3] See head (2) of paragraph 11.32, and Note 69 thereon.

- a trading loss sustained in the same period by another group company to be surrendered to the first under the group relief procedures;[4]
- rollover relief can be claimed, that is to say the gain can be treated as a reduction of the acquisition cost of another asset acquired by that or another group company;[5]

but none of these can be regarded as an efficient method of reducing tax liabilities if there are, at the same time, capital losses sterilised and incapable of use in some other group company. Bear in mind also that group relief is a system of utilising losses against profits only within the same period – there are no carry forward or carry back provisions.

At this stage one can say that flexibility seems likely to be improved by holding assets in a group assets company.

For the group which does not at present have a group assets company, and is contemplating establishing one – but at the same time is also contemplating the possible sale of one or more subsidiaries in addition to certain assets which might have been moved out of those subsidiaries into the group assets company – the question is whether the sales of subsidiaries might be made more expensive in terms of capital gains tax as a result:

- one possible case is where one or other of the disposal of the subsidiary, and disposal of the separate asset, produces a loss which cannot be relieved. One reason for the non-availability of relief may be that the loss arises in an inappropriate company, (this itself possibly being *inappropriate* as a result of the uncertainties over roll-over relief in groups, stemming from the *Campbell Connelly* case referred to in Note 5 above and explained more fully in Note 74 on paragraph 6.42). A second possible reason for the non-availability of relief may be the anti-avoidance legislation concerning depreciatory transactions and value shifting;[5a]
- another case in which there may be an additional tax cost from taking an asset out of a subsidiary before selling both asset and subsidiary can best be seen as an effect of the tiering and cascading of capital gains tax which we considered briefly in paragraphs 5.29

---

[4] See paragraphs 5.23 and 5.24 for an explanation of group relief.

[5] But as explained in Note 74 on paragraph 6.42, there are at the time of writing problems over the reinvestment being made in a different company from that which realises the gain on the *old* asset. The Revenue's earlier *interpretation* of section 175 TCGA 1992 in a Statement of Practice 8/81, (all the companies in a group to be treated for this purpose as one), has been shown to be wrong by the High Court and the Court of Appeal in the *Campbell Connelly* case, [1994] BTC 12. The Financial Secretary to the Treasury has promised a change in the law, which at the time of writing is still awaited.

[5a] The anti-avoidance provisions in the capital gains tax legislation which can disallow losses caused by *depreciatory transactions*, or can increase the size of certain gains, are outlined in paragraph 11.16 and Notes 27 to 29 thereon. That paragraph gives only a brief indication of the effects of this extremely complex legislation, a full explanation being outside the scope of this book.

to 5.31. Consider a subsidiary whose value is estimated to be £1,500, but whose shares in the hands of its parent have a capital gains tax acquisition value of £700. Inside that subsidiary is an asset whose market value is £1,000, but whose capital gains tax acquisition value (not on an intra-group transfer) is £400. If the subsidiary is sold as it stands, the gain on that sale would be £800. If the asset were taken out of the subsidiary into another group company at its full value of £1,000, the value of the subsidiary would still be £1,500 and the gain on its sale would be the same £800, but in addition the other group company would have a gain of £600 on selling for £1,000 the asset whose acquisition value of £400 it inherited on an intra-group transfer. Logic suggests that if the asset were transferred out of the subsidiary not at full value but at £400, then the value of the subsidiary thus stripped would fall from £1,500 to £900, and the gain on its side would be reduced to £200, so that the aggregate gains on subsidiary and asset would be the same £800 that would have arisen on the sale of the subsidiary with the asset still inside it. But we will see as we proceed, particularly in paragraphs 11.7 to 11.9, that although logic may be a good starting point, lateral thinking is a much more effective tool in finding the optimum tax solution – and that even lateral thinking must take account of Companies Act, and accounting, principles.

Before we leave the desirability of the creation of a group assets company, we should note that one advantage of doing so has recently been removed. It used to be possible, by judicious choice of due dates for payment, and dates of passing of cheques, to obtain a tax deduction in a rent-paying company in an earlier year than that in which one suffered tax in the corresponding rent-receiving company; the new sections 33A and 33B written into the Taxes Act 1988 by the Finance (No. 2) Act 1992 put a stop to that.

11.5 *Group asset companies (continued)*

Next, we need to face the obvious question for the group which has an assets company, but has not already got all of its assets in that company; if there are good reasons for ensuring that capital losses and capital gains should be made in the same company, is it impractical to transfer assets out of whichever company they may be located in, into the chosen company, before selling them out of the group?

There are three parts to the answer. It is an obvious way to avoid the disadavantages of section 179 of the Taxation of Chargeable Gains Act 1992. We mentioned that section in paragraph 6.43. Its scheme is to counteract what has always been called the envelope trick. If there is an asset whose capital gains tax acquisition cost was £500, but whose current value is £5,000, then the company which currently owns it could transfer it to a subsidiary in consideration for the issue by that subsidiary of shares.[6] It is now the subsidiary which owns the asset and has inherited the £500 acquisition value. What its parent owns is shares in a subsidiary with an acquisition cost of £5,000.[7] Were the parent then to sell its *envelope* with the asset inside it for £5,000, it would make no capital gain; but section 179 counteracts this, in the event that the parent sells the subsidiary within six years after the asset transfer into that subsidiary, by deeming that the *subsidiary* sold and re-acquired the asset at the date at which it was *transferred* into that subsidiary. A moment's thought shows that such a liability represents the worst of all possible worlds. It can easily crystallise a gain deemed to have been made a number of years before the triggering event (sale of subsidiary) so that interest as well as tax is payable. It crystallises in the subsidiary which means that the prospective owners of that company will want to be indemnified.[8] If the disponor group does have capital losses which could have been set against a gain, the least likely of all possible companies in which those losses would be located is this subsidiary. And the final reason why we described the section 179 liability as the worst of all worlds is that because the gain is only *deemed* and not real, there are no proceeds and therefore no possibility of a reinvestment of proceeds to claim rollover relief.

This is a set of circumstances which strongly suggests that the offending asset might be better stripped back out of the subsidiary before the latter's sale; and sold separately to the predator out of the most appropriate company in the disponor group.

11.6 *Stamp duty*

We looked in paragraph 6.33 at the *Escoigne Properties* case.[9] What Lord Denning there described as the dummy bridge company started as a subsidiary in the disponor group so as to be able to acquire the property for £100 of share capital and a very large amount of debt; stamp duty was not payable on that asset transfer because it was within the 90 per cent group exemption.[10] When the bridge company was sold for £100 to the predator group, the only consideration figure of

---

[6] But the section is widely drafted. It still operates even if the transferee company pays full value, in cash, so that whichever group company owns the transferee's shares sees no alteration in its share value at all. The critical factor is that the asset shift into that transferee company took place on a *group basis* under section 171 TCGA 1992, which is of course mandatory regardless what price is actually paid.

[7] Because there is no capital gains tax rule which displaces, here, the principles in *Zevo Finance* and *Stanton v Drayton*, see paragraphs 3.22 and 3.25, in fact they are reinforced by the connected party provisions in section 17 TCGA 1992.

[8] There is a second point about indemnification. Since it is the subsidiary (the target) which will need funds to pay the tax, there are arguments that it, rather than its new owner (the predator) should be indemnified. There are generally thought to be greater difficulties and dangers in indemnifying a target than in indemnifying the purchaser, because the target's receipt is less obviously of a capital nature than is a receipt by a predator.

[9] [1958] AC 549.

[10] Section 42 FA 1930.

which the value was taken into account for stamping was that £100. The next step, the extraction of the property into the predator group, was again covered by the 90 per cent group exemption – despite its being the transaction which enabled the predator group to pay full value to the bridge, and enabled it in turn to repay its indebtedness to the disponor.

The group exemption provisions were amended by section 27(3) of the Finance Act 1967 to prevent this abuse, but the amendment has the effect of doubling up the stamp duty. Under subsection (c) duty is payable when the property is transferred into the bridge, because of the *arrangement*[11] that the disponor and the bridge should cease to be associated companies; and under subsection (a) when the property is extracted into the predator group, because the consideration paid by the predator, although going in the first instance to the bridge would indirectly be received by the disponor which would never have been the predator's associate.

The moral is obvious. There is no harm in the disponor selling a property from one of its group companies, separately and directly, into the predator group. There is no harm in the disponor moving the property from one company in his group to another, in order that that second can sell it into the predator group *just so long as this movement takes place, and the consideration for it is settled, before any sale is agreed from the second company to the predator.* The reason for this proviso is that once the sale onwards has been agreed, the Stamp Office will argue that the consideration being paid by the second company in the disponor group to the first is to be provided, indirectly, by the predator.[12]

However one needs to think very hard before inserting the property into a company which is to be sold to the predator. In principle this will create a problem under section 179. Second, one would expect that it could easily double the stamp duty, since the transaction would appear to be in danger of costing stamp duty on the transfer *into* the target company under section 27(3)(c) mentioned above, namely a charge because there are *arrangements* for the target to leave the

---

[11] Stamp duty exemption on intra-group transfers is claimed by a statutory declaration made by a director or secretary of the transferee, or its solicitor. This individual must say, on oath, that 'it is intended that the relationship between the companies shall be maintained' and that the transfer document was not executed in pursuance of or in connection with an *arrangement* as described in section 27(3) FA 1967. However the Stamp Office appear to work to a rule of thumb, outlined at the end of this paragraph 11.6, to determine whether there are any such arrangements in existence. This stamp duty procedure is thus rather different from the corporation tax decision process for establishing whether there are offensive *arrangements* for a company to leave a group, as set out in the Statement of Practice, and Extra Statutory Concession, referred to in paragraph 5.40 and Note 71 thereon (in relation *inter alia* to group relief).

[12] The statutory declaration referred to in the previous footnote calls for a statement that the purchaser, here the second company in the disponor's group, 'shall continue to be the beneficial owner of the assets'. If this statement cannot be made, the Stamp Office demand to see copies of correspondence, agreements, company minutes and so on relating to the future disposal of the property.

disponor's group, while there will also be a second charge on the whole worth of the target when its shares are sold by the disponor. However, it seems that the Stamp Office adopt a simple rule of thumb on this. Until the Heads of Agreement[13] has been signed, there are no such arrangements, and the transfer into the target is covered by the group exemption; as soon as the Heads has been signed (regardless of the fact that it may not in any legal sense mean that there are any enforceable arrangements as we will see in the next chapter) the group exemption ceases to protect transfers of assets into the target.

11.7 *Unbundling a company before sale*

We said at the beginning of paragraph 11.5 that there were three parts to the answer whether it was practical always to sell assets out of a group *through* a group assets company, rather than arranging for those assets to be held throughout their ownership in such a company. We have looked at section 179, and at stamp duty. The third aspect is the transfer values to be used, from other group companies into that capital gains company, for accounting and company law purposes.

The best approach to this is oblique; so oblique that it is hard to see that anybody is approaching anything. What we will do is start by thinking about a related, and equally difficult subject, namely *unbundling*. Here, the first difficulty is providing a generalisation which is an adequate definition of unbundling,[14] and this may itself lead to any explanation we can give being incomplete. That then leads on to the thought that opportunities may often be missed, simply because people's thinking is not attuned to watch for those opportunities and to produce solutions which may benefit disponor and predator. Another difficulty is what this book is all about – solutions if they are available will invariably cut across tax, company law, and accounting; in microcosm, unbundling as we will see in the next two paragraphs provides a good example why we must be comfortable crossing and recrossing these frontiers, switching language and therefore thought patterns as we do so. All of that leads towards our explaining unbundling by means of a particular example, in the hopes that the general principles can be discerned. Consider the balance sheet of a company which is about to be sold, as shown in Table 48.

The outside right hand column shows that the company has a value which exceeds the separate values of its assets by £800 – and it should therefore be worth £2,000 to a purchaser. For reasons that will become apparent in the next two paragraphs, what we are aiming to do is to sell the property out of this company into another disponor-group company better able to shelter the gain, then to sell both the property, and the target company illustrated above, separately, to the predator.

---

[13] The Heads of Agreement, and its place in the normal disposal and acquisition negotiation and documentation, is the subject of paragraphs 12.2 and 12.3 below.
[14] Three-year-old children define everything pragmatically, by describing what it does, rather than what it is. Buttons are to keep you warm. Unbundling is to get the best post-tax price for what you have to sell.

Table 48: Balance Sheet of Target

					Value
Share capital	100	Property at cost	400		1,000
Profit & loss	500	Net current assets	200		200
	600		600		
				Goodwill	800
					2,000

11.8 Working through the thought processes of unbundling

The potential purchaser with whom discussions are in progress says that if he is asked to take on the property, which he can see is pregnant with a gain of £600 (liability thereon say £200) then he is only prepared to pay £1,800. That argument would look irrefutable if the property had been transferred from another disponor company in the last six years, so that the liability crystallises automatically inside the target company on sale under section 179 of the Taxation of Chargeable Gains Act 1992. It may be a less compelling argument if the sale of the asset and the crystallisation of the gain are at the predator's discretion.

However, the compelling answer, if the disponor could manage it, would be to offer separately the company at a price of £1,000, and the property (if the predator wants it, but otherwise it can be sold in the market) for a further £1,000. That implies that it is the disponor who is willing to crystallise in his own hands the capital gain of £600 on selling the property. But the disponor would say that if he had a choice between a capital gain of £1,900 on selling the company unaltered, and capital gains of £900 on the company and £600 on the property, then stripping must be preferable.

Those figures need some scrutiny; if the capital gain on the sale of the company is to be reduced from £1,900 to £900 by the strip, that can mean one of three things. We need to consider each of them in turn.

First, the company might have transferred the property, for nil consideration, to an associate company. That associate inherits the capital gains tax cost, and makes a gain of £600 when it sells the property (whether to the predator or to someone else). The company, stripped as above, is then sold to the predator for £1,000, and since the acquisition cost of its shares in the hands of the parent which makes this sale was £100, that parent's gain is £900.

But the first of those transactions is not actually possible for two reasons. First, it will usually be *ultra vires* the company and beyond the scope of the directors' authority to give away a valuable asset, and it may be a fraud on the company's creditors; all of which we saw in paragraph 9.13 onwards when we were looking at the *Aveling Barford* case. And second, reduction of the company's net assets (by the transfer into the vendor's group) is financial assistance for the purchase of its shares, paragraph 9.21. Because the first transaction is unlawful, the second is void in consequence – that is the sale of the stripped company to the predator for £1,000.

11.9 Working through the thought processes of unbundling (continued)

The second possibility is that the company sells the property for full value to its associate, realising an accounting profit of £600, but not making a capital gain; once again the capital gains rules for transactions in a group have the result that the associate inherits the £400 base cost, and again it is the associate which makes the capital gain on the disposal outside the group.[15] The company had distributable profits of £500 before this sale, and these have been increased by the transaction to £1,100. It has also £1,000 in cash (assuming that its associate has paid for the property) and it declares a dividend of that amount to its parent. Those transactions solve the illegalities that were involved in the different proposals in the previous paragraph, in particular because as we have seen in paragraph 9.20 the payment of a lawful dividend is absolutely excluded from constituting financial assistance. We will see in the second and third points in paragraph 11.16 that one does have to consider the effect of such a dividend on the immediately following sale of the payer under the capital gains tax rules; the conclusion reached in that discussion is that there should not be problems. But it does look as if there will possibly be some time constraints; the intra-group transfer of the property must be completed before the outside purchaser of that property comes on the scene, if the stamp duty exemption is to be obtained, paragraph 11.6. And it is necessary that the company can say that its sale proceeds are *realised* (paragraph 4.10) if it is to be able to declare a dividend out of them.

Therefore one might consider the third of the possible transactions. Section 276 of the Companies Act 1985 deserves to be better known than it is. If we revalue the property in the company's balance sheet from cost of £400 to its market value of £1,000 the increase of £600 would be credited to a revaluation reserve, which would be non-distributable. But what section 276 says is that if the property is itself to be distributed as a dividend *in specie*,[16] then that otherwise non-distributable reserve is treated as distributable for that purpose. Stripping the property out of the company by way of a dividend to its parent is by far the most elegant way of side-stepping the problems which might otherwise arise over financial assistance, and shedding assets at an undervalue. It is exempt from stamp duty under a provision which does not require that the recipient make any statutory declaration that he intends to

---

[15] That associate will have a tax liability to provide, and it does not on the face of it have any profits out of which to make the provision if it has bought and sold for £1,000.

[16] The payment of such a dividend does require that the company has already existing distributable profits at least equal to the carrying value of the property that is being paid away as a dividend.

retain the property.[17] Although the recipient will take the property into his balance sheet at a carrying value of £1,000 and will therefore not report a profit on its sale out of the group, he will have credited £1,000 to profit and loss when receiving the dividend and that same recipient will also recognise a second £900 of profit when it sells for £1,000 shares in its subsidiary which it has been carrying at £100. Its capital gains tax position is that it has gains reduced by the unbundling to £600 on the property and £900 on the shares, that being not the full reduction that could be obtained. Selling the right things in the right way does work wonders.

11.10 Trade and asset transfers – cessations and clawbacks of reliefs for the disponor

The decision-making in this area is more complex than is sometimes appreciated. What we need to do is to identify:

- first, what are the effects for the disponor of disposing of a trade and assets;

- next, we will look briefly (in the next paragraph) at the possibility of rearranging the transaction in the opposite way – whether the trade can be *hived down* into a company, and that company be sold. Hive-downs are a significant subject, and the greater part of our examination will fit better into chapter 12, at paragraphs 12.23 and onward, so the aspects we point up here need to be seen as fitting into a wider context, and as affecting the predator just as much as the disponor;

- thereafter, on the basis that the hive-down was a possibility, but one that was inappropriate for our particular case, we need to go back to the subject of trade and asset disposals, in order to look at some of the flexibilities, as well as vulnerabilities, that they are unlikely to provide in the real-life situation.

First, therefore, what are the effects for the disponor of his disposal, (otherwise than inside a company), of a trade and assets? The answer is different for individual disponors and for companies:

Individual disponors

- the principles have been set out in paragraph 3.34 so far as concerns the individual's income tax (see also Note 43 on that paragraph as regards loss carry forward);

Company disponors

- is what is transferred the whole of the company's trade? (as opposed to a part, or one trade out of a number) because a complete

---

[17] A dividend *in specie* is exempt from stamp duty as a voluntary disposition (*Wigan Coal & Iron Co. Ltd v IRC* [1945] 1 All ER 392) and is now within item L in the Stamp Duty (Exempt Instruments) Regulations 1987, SI 1987 No. 516.

cessation of trade will bring about the end of an accounting period, see paragraph 5.6 and Note 17 thereon;

- does the transfer constitute a distribution? The answer should of course be that it does not, if full consideration is given, but the question does need to be asked. If there is a danger that the transfer could be a distribution, and the transferee is a company, is it taken out by one of the relieving provisions? The one most likely to assist would be section 209(6) TA 1988, see paragraph 6.39;

- what assets (not forgetting goodwill) included in the transfer will give rise to a capital gains tax liability? can any such gains be rolled over by reinvestment of the proceeds?

- if stock in trade and work in progress are transferred, what is the price at which they are treated as disposed of and acquired by the disponor and predator respectively? Paragraph 3.40 and Note 54 dealt with an individual's transfer to a company, but the principles are the same for a company's transfer;

- so far as capital allowance assets are concerned, the elections available for transferor and transferee to use a transfer value in line with written down value (see paragraph 3.40 and Note 52) are only available for transfers between connected parties. Use of open market value is unavoidable;

- the stamp duty principles have been set out in paragraphs 3.37 and 3.38, and apply to a company's transfer of a business and assets just as they do for such a transfer by an individual.

Remember that all of the foregoing are written on the basis that the trade and assets are not inside a company at the time of disposal. Second, that VAT needs consideration (paragraphs 11.32 and onward), and so also may employment protection (paragraphs 11.36 and onward).

11.11 *Hive-downs, viewed as an alternative to the sale of a trade and assets*

It may be helpful as a matter of procedure, and as a matter of packaging something more readily saleable, for an individual to incorporate his business before selling it, this being a transaction which it is certainly possible to see as one kind of a hive-down. But this does not have any significant effect on his own position on the two-part disposal (to the company and of it), as compared with a simple disposal of the business.[18]

---

[18] The statement in the text is that the individual's disposal of the company into which he has incorporated his trade 'does not have any significant effect' on his own position; that masks the technical position that what he is actually disposing of for capital gains tax purposes is shares, and the acquisition cost of those shares is equal to the market value of the assets transferred into the company, reduced by the gain which he himself would have made on that transfer to the company had he not been allowed to *roll it over* against the cost of the shares under section 162

continued

However, the area in which hive-downs are really of significance is in the corporate area – the transfer of trades and assets into new companies prior to the sale of those companies. What we are thinking about is the extent to which this can change the position of the transferor company, as compared to its position if it were to transfer the trade and assets direct to the predator as envisaged in the last paragraph:

- whereas it would have been the disponor of the trade and assets which would have been liable to corporation tax on capital gains on those disposals, it will be the hive-down company which suffers the charge, under section 179, if the assets leave the disponor's group wrapped into the *envelope company*;

- the disponor does of course dispose of shares in the hive-down company. A corporate disponor's acquisition cost for capital gains tax purposes of those shares would be the market value of the assets transferred into the company, so there would not be a double charge to tax – the only charge would be inside the hive-down company under section 179 as mentioned in the previous head. If one assumes that the value of the assets, and therefore the value of the shares in the hive-down company, is (say) £1,000 but that the gain in the hive-down company is £600 and the tax on that is £200, then logic would suggest that the predator would only pay £800 for the hive-down company. This would give the disponor a capital *loss* for tax purposes – but it must be stressed that these are illustrative and theoretical figures only. We will come back to this point in paragraph 11.17 below;

- capital allowance assets move into the hive-down company from the transferor at written down values in the manner explained in paragraph 11.14 below, this being mandatory under section 343 TA 1988;

- Losses can be carried forward from the transferor to the hive-down company, again under section 343;

---

continued

TCGA 1992. It would be essential for the individual to incorporate his business by that *normal* method in section 162 (see paragraph 3.35), rather than the alternative method based on gifts of business assets (paragraph 3.41), because the latter has the effect of enlarging his capital gain when he sells his shares in the company to the predator. (When one analyses the question whether it alters his overall liabilty to sell shares rather than other assets, the answer is that it should not do so – and this is true not only in relation to his transfer into the company of capital gains assets which are pregnant with gain, but also current assets such as stock in trade and debtors, both of which are also reflected in the consideration for which he sells the shares.)

He needs to be aware that he will be doubling up stamp duty on transferring assets to a company, before selling that company at a price which reflects the values of those same assets.

There is one other tax point: he can transfer (for the purposes of his and its tax computations) capital allowance assets to his company on incorporation at tax written down values rather than open market values (see paragraph 3.40 and Note 52 thereon).

TRADE AND ASSET TRANSFERS – THE VALUES USED

- for the reasons explained at the end of paragraph 11.6, one would want to make sure that any asset transfers (from transferor company to hive-down company) were carried out before there was an agreement to dispose of the hive-down company – because otherwise it would seem that stamp duty would no longer be eliminated under the group exemption.

11.12 Trade and asset transfers – the values used, and the possibilities of carry forward of losses and other reliefs

In the previous paragraph the point was made that the values put on stock in trade and work in progress, and on capital allowance assets, transferred from one company to another as part of the transfer of a trade will be, respectively:

- the consideration given for the stock in trade and work in progress;[19]

- the net proceeds to the person in question of the sale of the machinery or plant;[20]

this being simply a part of the general assumption made by the draftsman that parties at arm's length would negotiate their sale and purchase price in such a way that each element within it could be regarded as being an open market price.

What is often suggested is that those parties are in a position to, and frequently do, *bend* the prices put on individual assets so as to obtain an advantage; usually but not always this is seen as an advantage for one not automatically coupled with an equal disadvantage for the other. One case in which there might be a perceived advantage for both is where goodwill was overvalued at the expense of other net assets; the disponor might be able to roll over his gain on goodwill whereas profits on other assets would be likely to incur full tax liabilities. What the predator might see as his advantage is not a tax matter, but the ability (as we saw in paragraph 6.27 above in relation to acquisition accounting when one company acquires the share capital of another) to report larger profits in the period after the acquisition than would otherwise have been the case. But when one thinks that through, the predator's larger reported profits would in this instance cost larger amounts of tax; this is the difference between this trade and asset acquisition which must be directly dealt with in the accounts of a predator company, and the accounting presentation on which we were commenting in paragraph 6.27, which was effective principally for the consolidation rather than the solus accounts of predator or target.

---

[19] Section 100(1)(a) and section 101(1)(a) TA 1988.
[20] Section 24(6) CAA 1990 as regards machinery or plant, and there are corresponding provisions for other categories of asset.

11.13 Trade and asset transfers – the values used (continued)

Since every case is different, and it is only possible in this book to deal in generalities, there are only three points that call for a mention:

- the Inland Revenue does undoubtedly believe that it has the power to reallocate an overall price between the different elements within it;[21]

- if the taxpayer gets it wrong, there is no possibility of his thereafter being able to claim that the allocation should have been different from that set out in the documentation;[22]

- any dispute between taxpayers and Revenue in this area would be purely a matter of fact, not law, so it is not surprising that there is a dearth of reported cases reaching the courts. Whether the Revenue takes cases in front of the Commissioners every day is not information to which the public is privy, but an intelligent guess would be that the Revenue would have difficulty in obtaining the level of background information that valuers appearing for the Revenue would need in order to be persuasive witnesses. None of that can be taken, however, to indicate that Inspectors of Taxes are ineffectual negotiators when they wish to attack a taxpayer on a subject such as the allocation of a sale price. The procedure of standing the taxpayer in front of a bullet-pocked wall, and indicating that his life will not be worth a fig unless he agrees, tends to be quite productive.

---

[21] The case usually quoted is *EV Booth (Holdings) Ltd v Buckwell* [1980] 53 TC 425, although that was a *capital gains tax* case in which the documents incorporated an apportionment of the sale proceeds which the taxpayer sought, unsuccessfully, to set aside for tax purposes. The case which is directly relevant to the question whether either Revenue or taxpayer can require a change to the transfer price of trading stock is *Jacgilden (Weston Hall) Ltd v Castle* [1969] 3 All ER 1110. The authorities reviewed in the course of the *EV Booth* capital gains tax case included *Moore v RJ Mackenzie & Sons Ltd* [1972] 48 TC 196, a case in which value to be attributed to stock in trade transferred at discontinuance was at issue. Megarry J set out how he thought the Inland Revenue could approach such a reallocation of proceeds, but ended this part of his judgment 'let me make it clear, I am not for one moment saying that such an argument would succeed, nor, for that matter, that it would fail ... however, neither before me nor, so far as I can perceive, before the Special Commissioners was there a trace of such a contention either in establishing the necessary foundation of fact, or in the process of argument'.

[22] The capital gains tax authority here is the *Booth* case referred to in Note 21. However the most elegant exposition of the principles is that of Lord Greene in *Henriksen v Grafton Hotel Ltd* [1942] 24 TC 453 at 460: 'An attempt was made to rescue this argument from shipwreck by saying ... [what was actually argued in front of Lord Greene is not important] ... This argument has a familiar ring. The answer to it is that this was not the contract which the parties chose to make. It frequently happens in income tax cases that the same result in a business sense can be secured by two different legal transactions, one of which may attract tax and the other not. This is no justification for saying that a taxpayer who has adopted the method which attracts tax is to be treated as though he had chosen the method which does not, or vice versa.'

11.14 Trade and asset transfers – the carry forward of losses, and so on

That brings us to the last of the implications for the disponor's and predator's (or target's) taxation flowing from a sale of a trade and assets. What losses or other reliefs can be carried forward?

The short answer for an individual's losses is that there is no carry forward available. But that should perhaps be qualified by the mention of two provisions – even though they seem unlikely to be of assistance in the circumstances we are envisaging of a disponor selling a trade and assets to a predator. We have explained that for the individual disponor, section 386 of the Taxes Act 1988 (Note 43 to paragraph 3.34) permits him to treat income subsequently derived from a company into which he has incorporated his trade as if it had been income from the trade itself – thus giving him the ability to carry forward losses at the date of incorporation against that subsequent income. However those conditions – that the consideration for his sale of his business must be solely or mainly shares in the predator, and he must retain all of those shares throughout any year in which he is to be entitled to claim relief – seem to make this relief unlikely to be relevant for the general run of cases we are considering.

If the disponor is a company, we have mentioned section 343 of the Taxes Act 1988 in paragraph 11.11. Headed 'Company reconstructions without a change of ownership', it started life as an anti-avoidance provision, and applies on a mandatory basis whenever the necessary conditions are present.[23] Those conditions are that a trade is transferred from one company to another, and that at some point within two years after the transaction the ownership of the transferee is (to the extent of 75 per cent) the same as that of the transferor at a time within the year before the transfer. This therefore allows the normal hive-down which takes place a few days before the sale of the company. Section 343 creates a mandatory continuity of capital allowance treatment between the companies, and there is also an availability of loss carry forward. Provided that what is transferred is an activity rather than merely an asset (or collection of assets), the section can operate by treating this as the transfer of part of the trade of the transferor, and/or treating it as becoming part of the trade of the transferee, but we will see when we come to look at the whole of this from the predator's point of view in paragraphs 12.20 and onward that this can give rise to difficulties in identifying just what losses do carry across to the hive-down company.[24]

---

[23] There is another anti-avoidance provision at section 395(1) TA 1988 relating to the reconstruction of a leasing company, but it is too specialised in scope to be appropriate to be dealt with in this book.

[24] Hiving down a trade and assets is a procedure very often adopted by liquidators, but it is not confined to liquidations. We will continue in paragraph 12.20 and onward the discussion of the advantages and disadvantages of hive-downs; in particular we will consider there the problems that a liquidator's hive-down may create for the *predator*, such as the problems he may have in quantifying losses and tax written down values of

continued

But those are the only circumstances in which losses can be carried forward on a trade and assets transfer; the conditions seem unlikely to be met; but even if they are it is clear that these provisions fail to make any provision for capital gains tax losses, or for reliefs to be shifted into the hive-down company for advance corporation tax or for franked investment income. All of these remain in the transferor company, and die if its activities come to an end.

11.15 Pre-disposal dividends

Where a subsidiary is to be sold out of a group, and the original cost of its shares was less than the amount now expected as those shares' disposal proceeds, one should always consider whether it is practicable to reduce the capital gains tax liability by deflating those sale proceeds (the assumption is pound for pound) by taking a dividend out of the subsidiary.

This was a procedure we introduced in paragraph 5.30, and it is worth repeating here one of the comments made in that paragraph. It is extremely unlikely that it will be possible to remove by dividend the whole of the company's increase in value. In the balance sheet (Table 48) in paragraph 11.7, the maximum dividend that appeared to be possible was £500 (which seems likely to have required a bank borrowing if it were to be paid in cash); we can see, on the other hand that the company has over its life retained £500 of realised profits, but has also increased its value by building up goodwill of £800, and has an unrealised profit on its property of £600 (although we did in the end turn that last £600 into a realised profit, and distributed the property in which it is reflected).

Second, the disponor must be responsive to the predator's attitude concerning the suggestion that a pre-disposal dividend be taken out of the target company. When we first started thinking about predators owning companies which had pre-acquisition distributable reserves, we indicated in paragraph 6.14 that the general result of the Cohen Committee reforms of Company Law in the late 1940s was that such profits could be distributed by the target to the predator, but that the latter was prevented from distributing them to its own shareholders. But when we re-analysed this in paragraph 9.26, we saw that *in cases where the predator had claimed merger relief*[25] *on his acquisition* there was probably no bar to his distributing such profits to his own shareholders. In the example we have been looking at, the dividends we have envisaged have reduced the target company's distributable reserves from £500 to

---

continued
assets to be carried forward, the first of these being particularly complex in the light of the two sets of provisions about loss-restriction where the transferor is insolvent, and where there has been a change in the way in which the trade is conducted.

[25] Merger relief is an exemption from the need to create a share premium account, section 131 CA 1985, see paragraph 6.20.

£100; *prima facie*, it looks as if the predator will need to recapitalise the target, either by re-inserting into it the property, or a replacement property (at a minimum acquiring such a property in a group asset company elsewhere in the group). And the predator may think new equity or even loans are less flexible and attractive than having a balance on profit and loss account.

11.16 *Pre-disposal dividends (continued)*

Three other things need to be said about pre-disposal dividends.

First, *the distribution of a company's assets by way of dividend lawfully made* is altogether outside the prohibitions looked at in paragraphs 9.19 to 9.24 on the giving of financial assistance by a company for the purchase of its own shares.[26]

Second, there are two pieces of capital gains tax anti-avoidance legislation which cannot be ignored, although they are seldom in point. If a pre-disposal dividend were large enough to create a capital gains tax loss, that loss would not be effective. That is the result of the *depreciatory transactions* legislation,[27] in existence since the start of capital gains tax, but which in the author's experience has seldom proved of any particular difficulty or danger in practice. The other provision[28] would have the effect of deeming the disponor to have sold the target company not for what it actually realised on the sale, but for that amount increased by 'such amount as appears to the Inspector ... to be just and reasonable having regard to the scheme or arrangements and the tax-free benefit in question', the reference to arrangements, and to the tax-free benefit being to '... arrangements (which) have been made ... whereby (a) the value of the asset (target company) has been materially reduced, and (b) a tax-free benefit has been conferred on' specified persons which would include the target's parent and any associated companies. However, that legislation is specifically overridden by a provision which says that any *normal* dividend[29] paid by the target to a company which is in the same

---

[26] Section 153(3)(a) CA 1985.
[27] Section 176 TCGA 1992.
[28] The quotations come from section 30(5) and section 30(1) TCGA 1992, and the overriding exemption from them is in section 31(1) of the same act. The latter section refers to the company paying and receiving the dividend as needing to be 'associated', but defines this (section 33(9)) as meaning members of a capital gains tax group (see paragraph 6.44).
[29] That explanation requires us to give some indication what is a *normal* dividend, and what might be abnormal. This takes us back to the point made in paragraph 11.15 that it is unlikely that a company would normally be able to pay a large enough dividend to remove the whole of its parent's capital gains tax liability – simply because the company would be unlikely to have sufficient distributable profits to achieve this. But there was a scheme whose only purpose was artificially to inflate the distributable profits of the target (without at the same time increasing its assets) this being done in order to enable its assets and therefore its value to be deflated by the payment of a larger dividend than would otherwise have been possible. This is the type of dividend which the value shifting legislation will stike at, characterised in the text as *abnormal*. (See section 31 TCGA 1992, originally enacted by section 136 FA 1989.)

capital gains tax group as itself is not to be treated for these purposes as materially reducing the target's value.

Finally, these pre-disposal dividends are within the legislation which we will have to examine in paragraphs 11.21 and onward below dealing with *transactions in securities*. It is, as we will see, highly desirable to obtain *advance clearance* for them from the Revenue. Experience indicates that this will only be given for dividends paid under group elections, and that franked dividends will be refused.[30]

11.17 Pre-disposal reorganisations of companies – the possibility of splitting a company

Assume that a company (oldco) is owned by three individuals, and that it carries on two trades. Its owners want to sell one of those trades and to retain the other.

One possibility would be that the company simply sold that trade and its assets. An alternative would be that the company incorporated the trade into a subsidiary company (newco); we have already looked briefly in paragraph 11.11 above at the process of hiving down a trade into a subsidiary. In each case, however, it is oldco which is selling a business or selling shares. It will be oldco which will

- either pays corporation tax on capital gains on the gain which it makes on the sale of the business; or

---

[30] A *group* dividend is one on which the payer does not account for ACT (paragraph 5.26), and which would therefore in the hands of the recipient company (in this case the disponor) cost ACT if that recipient wished to distribute it on to its own shareholders. The opposite is a franked dividend, on which the ACT is the payer's (target's) responsibility, and which the disponor could pay on to its own shareholders without further cost.

If we look for the rationale for the Revenue's refusal to accept that the target may pay a franked dividend, it is hard to see this at the target's own level. The target would presumably only want to adopt the franked route if it had sufficient profits which had suffered mainstream corporation tax in the previous six years to enable the ACT to be recovered – or if it itself had franked income so that no ACT needed actually to be accounted for. In either of these cases, it would seem both irrational and somewhat penal for the Revenue to say to the target you may not take those advantages in your current ownership – you may avail yourself only after the change of ownership; and yes, we realise that that may mean you probably will not be able to take advantage at all, because by then you will have paid away your distributable profits.

But if we look at the matter in a more superficial way, what the Revenue might be thinking is as follows. There is at the moment £500 of retained profit in a company. We want to take capital gains tax on a gain which reflects that retention if the individual owner(s) of the company sell their shares. That being our aim, it does not matter to us whether the £500 is in the target or the parent of the target – in either case it underlies the same individually held (principal company) shares with the same base cost. But if we let that £500 reach the principal company in the form of franked income, we are inviting the shareholders to take it out of the corporate sector in a form which will avoid capital gains tax. The intellectual rigour of that argument is not great; the author believes it produces capricious and somewhat penal results. But it is difficult to see how the Revenue can be persuaded of the irrationality of their ways.

- will receive proceeds for the sale of the shares which will (according to our illustrative figures in paragraph 11.11) give it no liability for tax, but the predator will have reduced the amount of those proceeds to reflect newco's section 179 liability.

What can then be made available in cash terms to the shareholders from oldco would become available only in the form of a dividend. Clearly oldco would pay ACT on that dividend, the cost of which would be greater in the second head than in the first, simply because there is no set-off against mainstream tax in the second. Exactly how great would be the overall tax cost of oldco's tax, and of the shareholders' higher rate tax on the dividend, is something which would need to be estimated with some care.

But what can be said with little doubt is that paying tax in the company and then a second time in the shareholders' hands is likely to result in greater liabilities than would arise for the individual shareholders had they been the direct owners of newco, and had they themselves been selling their shares in it.[31]

We have seen various straightforward ways in which newco could be established as the recipient of the trade which oldco wishes to sell, and could be so established in the direct ownership of the three individuals who own oldco. When we were looking at the possibilities of reconstructions which fitted within the stamp duty and capital gains legislation (in paragraph 6.61) Item (4) would have achieved this objective. What we then noted, however, was that this reorganisation had the considerable defect of running into a distribution charge, in that the transfer sideways of one of oldco's trades into newco (for which the only consideration was newco's issue of shares to the individual shareholders of oldco) was a distribution by oldco.

11.18 *The possibility of splitting a company (continued)*

Recapitulating the facts we are envisaging, we have oldco which has two trades, and is owned by three individuals. Newco is formed, and one of the trades is transferred into it, the consideration it gives being the issue

---

[31] It is not necessary to demonstrate this in figures. One part of the explanation is that the company's tax, whether at 25 per cent or 33 per cent, is not wholly imputed on to the shareholder, so that his total 40 per cent tax burden lies on top of some amount of *sticking* tax in the company. The second part of the explanation is obvious when one thinks about cash, gains and indexation; if an individual's proceeds of sale are £100, reduced by acquisition cost to a gain of £70, and that is reduced in turn by indexation to a taxable amount of £50, then the individual will have £80 of spending money. If the £100 proceeds were received by oldco and reduced by 25 per cent tax on the same taxable gain, the company would have £87½ in hand. However without the need for detailed calculation it is obvious that the effects of ACT and the shareholder's higher rate tax would leave the latter with less than £80 of spending money in these circumstances. A third part of the explanation is that when one considers the workings of such capital gains tax reliefs as retirement relief, or rollover relief for reinvestment into unlisted companies, it is clear that they would directly increase the cash in a shareholder's hands if it was he who was selling newco shares; it is painfully obvious that these reliefs would be unavailable if it was oldco which was selling.

direct to the three individuals of its own shares. (We know that there are Companies Act problems over oldco giving assets away, but put those on one side for the moment.)

The tax implications of this transaction that we have identified at earlier stages are that oldco's transfer of its trade is a distribution, and it costs stamp duty at 50p per £100. However, the three individuals are protected from capital gains tax disadvantages when their shares in oldco decline sharply in value, and they receive shares in newco without paying for them; this fits into the paper-for-paper provisions[32] in section 136 Taxation of Chargeable Gains Act 1992. And oldco is regarded for capital gains tax purposes as transferring the trade to newco on a no-gain-no-loss basis under section 139 of the same Act.

These capital gains tax effects were recognised, and their impact was widened in the Revenue's *Statement of Practice* No. 5 of 1985; what it allowed (as we noted briefly in paragraph 6.69) was that the separation of the trades into oldco and newco could be a *division* of what had been a single company, so that oldco came to be owned thereafter by (say) P and Q, R's shares being cancelled; and newco issued its shares only to R, not to P or Q. The statement of practice still allowed the section 136 and 139 capital gains tax benefits for the shareholders and of the companies. Although, as we noted in paragraph 6.69, a division is not a *reorganisation* for stamp duty purposes, the widened transaction still fitted into section 76 of the Finance Act 1986, and qualified for the half-rate charge to stamp duty.

That left the distribution problem, but the accepted method of solving this was liquidation. What one needed to do was to set up two companies, each to be owned direct by the shareholders of oldco. Then oldco was put into liquidation, with an instruction from its shareholders to the liquidator that rather than distribute its assets to them, he should distribute one trade and its assets to each of the new companies in consideration for those new companies issuing their own shares direct to the individual shareholders. The fact that oldco's distribution was made in the course of its liquidation was sufficient to take it outside the distribution legislation.

We will see when we come to demergers in chapter 14, that the procedures explained in this paragraph appear to form a back door route to demerging oldco – and a route which does not contain any of the safeguards which the Inland Revenue felt it necessary to write into the demerger legislation. This back door is still open, but only a crack;[33] anyone who wants to use it will inevitably have to apply for

---

[32] See further commentary in paragraph 11.26 below.
[33] The Inland Revenue did attempt to shut and bolt this door completely in the late 1980s, and how they did this is a fascinating insight into the practical workings of legislation which operates entirely on discretionary clearances.

The relevant legislation was not changed then, and has not changed since; the words at the end of section 209(1) TA 1988 still say 'but references in the Corporation Tax Acts to distributions of a company shall not apply to distributions made in respect of share capital in a winding up'. What seems to have happened is that in the late 1980s the Inland Revenue believed they could reinterpret these words, and claimed that in
continued

the clearances we will be looking at in paragraphs 11.25 and 11.27 below, for transactions in securities, and for paper-for-paper capital gains tax treatment, and they will find that the Revenue use those clearance applications as a method of preventing transactions of which they disapprove – and disapproval can be expected for any transaction which could not get through the demergers front door; there are at least two very good reasons (in the Revenue's view) why this transaction could not fit through the front door. However, our examination of this area fits better into chapter 14, at paragraph 14.7 than it would into this chapter.

Where that seeming unlikelihood that they will get the clearances they need leaves our three shareholders who wish to sell one of the two trades out of their existing company (oldco) is with a choice:

- they can carry out a reorganisation along the lines permitted by SP 5/85, so that it will be they rather than oldco which is the disponor, and what they will be selling will be newco rather than a trade and assets. But oldco will have incurred a distribution charge on the movement of the trade and assets;[34]

---

continued

the case of the type of reorganisation described in the text, this phraseology was appropriate only to protect distributions made on the final winding up and striking off of a company; therefore a distribution by the liquidator on instructions from the shareholders was not covered. This meant that oldco's distribution of its two trades to the two newcos was still a distribution on which ACT had to be paid.

Interestingly however, broadly similar phraseology appeared until 1992 in section 278 TA 1970 (the predecessor of section 179 TCGA 1992). The charge on the envelope company leaving a group with an asset transferred into it within the previous six years was not to apply if the reason for its leaving the group was 'its being wound up or dissolved or another member of the group being wound up or dissolved'. The Revenue once again began to claim in the late 1980s that that meant finally wound up, not simply put into liquidation. But in 1991 they announced that they had been advised that this interpretation was not legally supportable. (This is the usual coded language indicating that the Revenue have lost a case in front of the Special Commissioners.) They therefore changed the statutory wording, so that section 179 now says that the section 'does not apply to cases where a company ceases to be a member of a group in consequence of another member of the group ceasing to exist'. (This was one of those changes of wording which was deemed always to have had effect, section 25(1) F(No2)A 1992).

The wording of section 209(1) could not be altered in a similar way (because its other repercussions would have been too great) so that the Revenue has had to re-open this door, at least to the extent indicated in the text.

[34] What we have been discussing has been oldco's transfer, in liquidation, to each of two newcos of a trade, and those newcos' issue of shares to the shareholders of oldco. In those circumstances, oldco and the newcos are never members of the same group, and there is no question of any of these companies *leaving a group*. But if one assumed that oldco owned all the shares in two trading subsidiaries, and that it was its shareholdings in them that it transferred, respectively, to each newco then the distribution charge would be the same, and so would all the capital gains tax and stamp duty implications except that one would *also* have to consider the application of section 179 TCGA 1992 on each of the trading subsidiaries leaving the oldco group when they became subsidiaries of the two newcos. The question would be whether they had had assets inserted into them on a tax-free transfer within the previous six years.

- alternatively, the sale of the trade and assets can be made by oldco itself, not its shareholders – although what is sold may be a company into which the trade and assets have been hived-down.

The route chosen will primarily reflect the individual disponors' estimates of their own tax liabilities on the two bases, the different tax liabilities on each basis for the company they continue to own, and the extent to which those individuals have tax reliefs available which would not be capable of use except by picking one route and not the other.

11.19 The effects of previous reorganisations

In paragraph 6.56 and Note 104 thereon we examined what is often referred to as the *Woolcombers* reorganisation. If A owns B and C, it is possible for C to be moved down to become a subsidiary of B, the consideration being the issue of further shares by B to A.

Starting the analysis of this process with the assets which A ceases to own, and comes to own in the course of this transaction, we see that A originally owned shares in C and came as a result of B's takeover of C to own new shares in B. This, provided that the transaction was carried out for *bona fide* commercial reasons (and we will come back to this in the next paragraph) is the classic description of the paper-for-paper exchange fitting within section 135 of the Taxation of Chargeable Gains Act 1992, and thus permitting A to be treated as not having disposed of his C shares, but as having acquired the new B shares at the same date and price as his original C shares. But the relevant fact which is included in that explanation is that A is deemed to have made no disposal of his C shares; when we move to the analysis of B's position, it has acquired the shares in C, and has acquired them from A which is a member of the same capital gains tax group as B, but B's acquisition is *not* matched by any corresponding disposal by A. This means that the normal rules for intra-group transfers of assets are inapplicable, since section 171 demands both an acquisition and a disposal.

What we saw in paragraph 6.56 was that B's acquisition value for C's shares was their open market value, because there was in this instance no rule which overrode or displaced the open market requirement for transactions between connected parties. This transaction can therefore be regarded as a method of providing a tax-free uplift in the acquisition value of the C shareholding – the group held these shares originally at A's cost, and now holds them at B's open market value. What happens if B sells C? Does B incur a lower capital gains tax liability as a result of its up-rated acquisition value?

11.20 The effects of previous reorganisations (continued)

If the Revenue come to the conclusion that the sole or main reason for the reorganisation was to reduce the tax payable on a prospective sale of C, then their answer is quite clear (and effective to prevent what they see as tax avoidance, but without adding a penalty in doing so). What they say is that the original purpose of the reorganisation was, despite A's claim to the contrary, the avoidance of tax, and by saying this they displace the claim that it was done for *bona fide* commercial purposes; that denies A its paper-for-paper relief, and means that A did dispose of its shares in C, the consideration being shares in B. In these different circumstances, this does constitute a disposal by A, and therefore what applies to it is the intra-group rule which says that A makes no gain on its disposal; but the two other points which follow from that are, first, that B inherits from A the acquisition price that A had for the shares in C, and that it is the holding of B shares which A comes to own which are acquired at open market value. In other words, instead of having A holding B at an original price, and B holding C at an uplifted price, the original and the uplifted prices are reversed. When B now comes to sell C to the predator, the full amount of capital gains tax becomes payable as if the original reorganisation had not taken place.

The Revenue's indication is that they will adopt this procedure of retrospectively withdrawing agreement to the paper-for-paper claim if within six years after it there is a sale of the company whose acquisition cost has been uplifted.

11.21 Transactions in securities

The phrase 'transactions in securities' is part of the heading of the group of anti-avoidance sections originally enacted in the Finance Act 1960 under the title 'Cancellation of *tax advantages* from certain transactions in securities'.[35]

A tax advantage was explained by Lord Wilberforce as follows:

> The paragraph, as I understand it, presupposes a situation in which
> - an assessment to tax, or increased tax, either is made or may possibly be made
>
> - that the taxpayer is in a position to resist the assessment by saying that the way in which he received that which it is sought to tax prevents him from being taxed on it, and
>
> - that the Crown is in a position to reply that if he had received what it is sought to tax in another way he would have had to bear tax.
>
> In other words, there must be a contrast as regards the 'receipts' between the actual case where these accrue in a non-taxable way, with a possible accruer in a taxable way, and unless this contrast exists the existence of a tax advantage is not entablished.[36]

A large part of the underlying tax structure which made dividend stripping possible has long since been swept away. But these extraordinarily widely drafted provisions remain on the statute book, giving the Inland Revenue the power to counteract transactions which they

---

[35] The original sections were sections 28 and onward FA 1960. They are now sections 703 and onward TA 1988.
[36] *CIR v Parker* [1065] 43 TC 396 at 441. The typographical layout is not Lord Wilberforce's.

regard as objectionable – to assess the taxpayer on the basis of other transactions which were not those he carried out.[37]

11.22 *Transactions in securities (continued)*

We will need to examine

- what kinds of transactions are within the compass of the definitions in the legislation;

- what types of tax liability which may be argued for by the Revenue are to be compared with what tax liabilities the taxpayer might otherwise have incurred; it is absolutely clear that it does not help an individual for him to show that he is subject to capital gains tax on his receipt, because that tax is outside the required comparisons in the section;[38]

- there are also questions which follow on from the transactions the Revenue might argue for, such as the question when the resulting tax liability would arise; but these questions are less important for present purposes, because if a transaction is caught by the legislation it is generally the case that either it will not be proceeded with, or that it will be restructured so as to present a *normal* liability which the Revenue can assess without resort to this legislation.

It is often questioned whether the UK needs to have general anti-avoidance provisions in its tax legislation; rather than having a procession of ever more complex piecemeal provisions enacted by the Inland Revenue when they perceive an abuse, aimed specifically at that abuse, but too often failing to prevent some variation designed to outflank the prohibition. In the area of transactions in securities, the answer is that we have had general anti-avoidance legislation on the statute book since 1960.

But despite the uncompromising width of the powers given to the Inland Revenue, we will also see as we proceed that there are transactions to which they will not raise any objection; and there is a clearly defined and efficient mechanism for taxpayers to apply for clearance before undertaking transactions which are technically within these provisions but which the taxpayers believe to be acceptable.

11.23 *Paragraph D companies*

The most widely drawn, and most relevant today, of the five 'circumstances' envisaged in the legislation is the fourth, referred to as D:

---

[37] Parliament, when it enacted the 1960 legislation, had travelled a long way from the concepts expounded 18 years earlier by Lord Greene; see the quotation from the *Grafton Hotel* case in Note 22 on paragraph 11.13.

[38] Although there are some who hold the opposite view, it is also widely thought that corporation tax on capital gains is also outside the sections' comparisons. Section 709(1) TA 1988 speaks of 'profits or gains', which is a phrase which specifically excludes capital gains – see section 833(1) TA 1988.

TRANSACTIONS IN SECURITIES

- the companies to which it applies are referred to as D companies – and are all companies which are either under the control of not more than five people, or whose shares are not listed;[39]
- there must be 'consideration' received by a person in such a way that he does not pay tax on it as income;
- the 'consideration' referred to must be of the kind defined in section 703.C(l), in language which is obscure to start with, but is then (as is the case with almost every word in these provisions) redefined in wider terms;
- the consideration must be received 'in connection with the distribution of (the company's) profits' – again a phrase redefined in such a way as to include almost anything.

The most sensible way to try to understand what is at issue is to look at what is probably the most infamous of the cases[40] that the Inland Revenue have taken, and won, on this legislation. The Cleary sisters, between them, owned two profitable companies; they sold one to the other, receiving as sale proceeds an amount which the purchasing company could otherwise have paid to then as a dividend. The Revenue claimed that either:

- the purchaser's payment to the sisters of the purchase price was a 'transfer of assets' (under the rule which the sections' draftsman has happily misappropriated from Humpty Dumpty, that 'a word means just what I want it to mean, neither more nor less', it becomes legitimate to read 'transfer' in place of distribution, and 'assets' in place of profits), so that the section applied without further ado;
- or what constituted the distribution of profits was the purchaser's application of assets (which 'represented' profits, apparently in the sense that both existed, and that they appeared on opposite sides of the balance sheet)[41] in discharge of its liabilities, and that it was in this connection that the sisters received non-taxable money.

11.24 *The distribution of profits*

It is important to notice the other side of the comparison. If the sisters had not done the transaction they did, what they could have done in

---

[39] Section 704.D(2) TA 1988.
[40] *CIR v Cleary* [1967] 44 TC 399; until recently the infamy seemed to lie at the door of one particular member of the House of Lords who decided this case against the taxpayer, but who seven years earlier had been Attorney General and in that capacity had assured Parliament in the debates on the legislation they were considering that the Revenue would not use it against the specific transaction that the Cleary sisters later undertook. Following *Pepper v Hart* [1993] 1 All ER 42, we now know that all of the other members of the House of Lords could have read Hansard, and taken note of the assurances given by the Attorney General, when they were considering the Cleary case. Their decisions as well as his can be regarded as one of the great inequities of British justice.
[41] Building societies seem to suffer from the same confusion in implying that they have reserves which they can lend.

order to get the same cash into their hands would have been to cause the purchasing company to pay a dividend. In circumstances where the company has no distributable profits, the sections' impact may be less.[42] What seems to have been objectionable from the Inland Revenue's perspective in the *Cleary* case was that the sisters had extracted cash from the companies without changing anything else; they owned both companies before, and they continued to own them afterwards (although one of them they owned indirectly). It is that question whether anything has changed which is central to the Revenue's perception, and we can illustrate it further by looking at the *Wiggins* case.[43]

Wiggins was a picture-frame restoring company which found in 1965 that a picture-frame it had bought some years earlier for £50 contained an old master worth substantially over £100,000. The plan then hatched involved the major part of Wiggins' business being transferred into an associate company, leaving Wiggins with only a few items of stock including the picture-frame concerned. Then the individual who wanted the old master bought the share capital of Wiggins and liquidated it, giving the liquidator instructions to transfer the picture-frame and its contents to him. The Revenue assessed the vendor of Wiggins' share capital on his receipt. He pointed out that at the time he sold Wiggins, its purchaser could not have paid him the consideration in any other way than as capital. However, the judge took the view that, given the fact that this had all been planned as a tax reduction exercise, he was not restricted to looking at the purchaser of those shares as the only possible source of the payment – if Wiggins had sold the picture, it could have paid a dividend, and that would have been the income receipt he was entitled to compare with the actual capital receipt. The proceeds of sale 'represented' the value of Wiggins' stock in trade and were taxable.[44]

11.25 *The exemptions and procedure for applying for clearance*

It is clear that *Wiggins* is the exception to the rule. The normal vendor who sells the share capital of a company, and as it is usually expressed 'walks away, taking no more interest in the company', will not face a section 703 assessment on his proceeds. How Wiggins fell foul of this was that it transferred significantly the whole of its trade to its associate, and the original owners were able to continue their frame restoring activities as if nothing had happened.

---

[42] If the company itself, voluntarily, removes its distributable profits, for instance by using them to pay up a bonus issue of shares, that will not help it resist an assessment. But it is an interesting question whether the interposition of a holding company which does not claim merger relief – exactly the transaction which was considered in *Shearer v Bercain* [1980] 3 All ER 295, paragraph 6.13 – would be caught by the words 'or apart from anything done by the company in question would have been available for distribution'.

[43] *CIR v Wiggins* [1979] 2 All ER 245.

[44] In the provision's drafting, proceeds of sale which represent stock in trade are fully taxable, but those that represent other assets are to be split between the part deemed to equate to repayment of the capital originally subscribed, which is not taxable, and the balance which is taxable.

Transactions are taken outside the mischief of the sections if they are:

- carried out either for *bona fide* commercial reasons or in the ordinary course of making or managing investments; *and*

- none of them had as their main object, or one of their main objects, the obtaining of a tax advantage.

That is a dual test, both halves of which have to be met. It would be possible to spend a considerable amount of time analysing the cases in which the courts have examined and pronounced upon the commerciality of taxpayers' actions[45] but it is almost certainly more useful not to attempt an all embracing synthesis of legal principles and rules (which we can be certain would elude us) but merely to remind ourselves of some generalities:

- the owner of a company who sells his shares for cash and leaves the purchaser to run it, and to take any future dividends from it has nothing to fear from section 703;

- but in almost any other circumstances, one would need to recommend that clearance be applied for.[46] First, it being impermissible to take into account in deciding whether one has obtained a tax advantage the capital gains tax that will be paid, but only the income tax that will not, there are more circumstances within the ambit of these sections than common sense might suggest;

- second, it is easy to assume that the sections only operate when a company is distributing profits (albeit in some unusual way). The *Wiggins* case shows that the relevant principles of interpretation allow that the vendor of Wiggins' share capital can be assessed as if he had received a distribution of profits, at a time when Wiggins had not made the profits concerned and when they obviously did not show up on its balance sheet. When those profits were later realised, the fact that another party was assessable on them was of no assistance to reduce or eliminate what was clearly double taxation;

- third, it has to be stressed that if clearance is given it will only be valid if all of the facts have been disclosed (for instance the transfer of Wiggins' trade to an associate as well as the company's later sale, even though the latter took place some years after the transfer of the trade);

---

[45] Such an analysis would take us into the line of cases of which *Furniss v Dawson* [1984] 1 All ER 530 is perhaps the most famous, with Lord Brightman's dictum in the House of Lords that, when dealing with a composite transaction, it is possible to ignore steps inserted which have no commercial purpose other than tax avoidance, even though those steps have commercial effects. One can expend considerable energies in trying to reconcile the lines taken by different judges in the different cases, without coming to any really clear conclusion other than that it is really all a matter of judgment based on the particular facts of each case.

[46] The clearance procedure is in section 707 TA 1988.

- and commercial reasons are always better explained by those who have been running the company, than by those who seek merely to give them advice on tax.

11.26 Share exchanges (paper-for-paper transactions) including earn-outs

Section 135 of the Taxation of Chargeable Gains Act 1992 provides that a shareholder's receipt of shares or debentures issued by a predator company, in exchange[47] for his shares or debentures in its target, is not to be treated for capital gains tax as a disposal of his holding of the target's securities, but he is to be treated as if the new holding he comes to own in the predator had been acquired at the same date, and same cost, as his previous holding in the target. Although this is a procedure we have already seen used for reorganisation of groups of companies, its most frequent application in the context of the disposals and acquisitions we are dealing with in these chapters is likely to arise from a general offer[48] made by the predator for the target's shares (or one class of them), made initially on the condition that the predator obtains control; but it is possible for the predator to release that condition at a later stage. The offer may of course include a cash alternative as well as the paper, in which case the relief applies only for those taking paper. Where the paper which a shareholder receives is a debenture or loan note[49] the

---

[47] Section 135 is a complex provision, and it is necessary to comply precisely with its requirements to obtain this relief. It is not the purpose of this book to spell out these requirements *in extenso*, and the reader is referred to the Act, or to the standard books. This is particularly important in the light of the fact, mentioned in the third head in paragraph 11.27, that *clearance* given by the Revenue under the procedures explained in that paragraph does not guarantee that the taxpayer has complied with the provisions of section 135 – only that the Revenue accept that the transaction is *bona fide commercial*.

[48] The phrase 'general offer' is not defined. However a 'takeover offer' as defined in section 428 CA 1985 would clearly be a general offer:

'an offer to acquire all the shares, or all the shares of any class or classes, in a company (other than shares which at the date of the offer are already held by the offeror), being an offer on terms which are the same in relation to all the shares to which the offer relates or, where those shares include shares of different classes, in relation to all the shares of each class'.

However, it is clear from the drafting of section 135 TCGA 1992 that a general offer is intended to embrace a wider range of transactions than section 428; for instance section 135 allows, in terms, that the offeror can *except* target shares already held by the offeror's subsidiary, while section 428 as quoted above allows only an exception of those directly held. What should perhaps be said is that general offers are like elephants, difficult to define but easy to recognise when you meet them.

[49] The legislation refers to these as 'qualifying corporate bonds', and defines them in section 117 TCGA 1992. That definition makes it possible to devise interest-bearing (non-equity) securities which however do not fit within the definition, and are colloquially referred to as 'non-qualifying corporate bonds'. Such securities are not exempted from capital gains tax, and are treated under the paper-for-paper relief as if they were shares – that is to say, *the clock does not stop* at the time of the exchange, and indexation continues to be available until they are disposed of.

SHARE EXCHANGES INCLUDING EARN-OUTS

capital gains tax which he would have paid had he sold his original shares at that point is calculated, but this does not become payable until the debenture or loan note is sold or redeemed. This procedure is generally referred to as 'stopping the clock', one of its features being that indexation ceases to be available from the time of the exchange.

It is possible for the predator not only to issue shares or debentures to the target's shareholders at the point of takeover, but also:

- *either* to undertake to issue further shares or debentures at a later point, for instance when the target's results for a period subsequent to takeover have been determined, or conditionally upon the target obtaining a listing;[50]

- *or* at the time of takeover to create for the target's shareholders a loan note, whose terms are fixed at that time and which is then issued, but of which the amount is only to be determined by reference to some later event.[51]

The additional shares, debentures or loan note are often referred to as an earn-out; the Revenue fully accept that earn-outs are a common feature of the commercial world. They are the diametric opposite of the concept explained at the beginning of paragraph 11.25, of the vendor walking away, taking no more interest in his former company. But the Revenue do not regard it as appropriate, on that account, to argue that

---

[50] The technical point here is that if the predator issues securities at the time of the takeover, and gives an undertaking that it will later issue further securities, the undertaking is not itself the issue of a security, and would not strictly bring the later issue within the requirements for the paper-for-paper relief to be available. The Revenue have said, in extra statutory concession D27, that they will nevertheless accept the undertaking as being a security. See Note 51 below for some comments on the accounting treatment of such an undertaking in the balance sheet of the party giving it.

There are other ways than relying on ESC D27 in which the parties can bring themselves within the share-for-share exchange provisions (at the time of the predator's original issue to the target's shareholders) although the amount of the deferred consideration cannot then be ascertained. Those target shareholders can for instance retain some shares which are made the subject matter of a deferred (and conditional) sale agreement for a consideration which reflects the achievement of the profit targets. Alternatively, the shareholders can be issued a loan note the terms of which include conversion rights based on the profit achievement (this last possibility, involving as it does a loan note whose *amount* is fixed, but whose *conversion terms* are not, would seem to produce an even stranger balance sheet treatment under the explanation given in Note 51).

[51] Notice that in this case, unlike that in the previous head, the predator has issued a security. It is therefore necessary that this be shown on the face of the predator's balance sheet, and the views of the Accounting Standards Board on this matter are set out in paragraphs 84 to 86 of the Exposure Draft *Fair Values in Acquisition Accounting*, (FRED 7). This indicates that where the predator has an obligation to pay cash (or an obligation under a debt security whether issued or to be issued) this has to be treated as an obligation to transfer economic benefits (to the previous owner of the target), and therefore it must be shown as a liability on the predator's balance sheet. If it is not possible to measure its amount precisely, then the best estimate must be used, and this must be refined and improved as time passes. However, if the predator is liable only to issue shares, this obligation does not constitute a liability to transfer economic benefits, and need not be shown on his balance sheet – until, of course, the shares are issued.

earn-outs should fail the *bona fide commercial* test – at least those earn-outs which appear to be commercially driven, rather than tax avoidance planning, will be accepted. However the fact that this is an area in which firm guidelines are scarce, and judgment is all, has vital implications for the clearance procedures. It is to these that we must now turn.[52]

11.27 *Clearance for paper-for-paper transactions*

Parallel to the clearance mechanisms already examined for transactions in securities, there are arrangements for clearance in advance[53] to be obtained for the paper-for-paper treatment for holders of target company securities. These arrangements reflect the fact that once again the relief is only available on a basis very similar to that indicated in paragraph 11.25 above, namely that the exchange of securities is to be effected for *bona fide* commercial reasons, and that the avoidance of capital gains tax or corporation tax is not its main purpose or one of them.

A number of points need to be spelled out about applications for such clearances:

- it is unnecessary to apply in respect of any holding of less than 5 per cent in the target, because clearance is automatic for such small holders;

- when clearance is applied for, it is the target or the predator which is entitled to apply (the shareholders of the target are not allowed to do so despite its being they who are affected by the clearance given). The logic behind this requirement is that it is the companies, not the shareholders, who are likely to be properly placed to explain the commercial factors which led to the proposed takeover and to give information about all shareholders not merely their own positions;

- clearance, if given, relates to the Revenue's acceptance that the proposal is commercially, not tax, driven. The Revenue do not, by giving clearance, guarantee that the proposed transaction fits all the conditions in section 135 of the Taxation of Chargeable Gains Act 1992. It is up to the taxpayers to ensure that this is the case – but the Revenue insist that like all questions of fact it can only be the subject of their final agreement after the takeover has taken place;

- thus the granting of clearance will not itself clarify the following point. If the predator's issue of shares or debentures meets the

---

[52] In an exchange of correspondence between the Institute of Chartered Accountants in England and Wales (letter of November 1986) and the Inland Revenue (response of February 1987), the latter indicated that if the deferred element of consideration had the effect of putting cash into the hands of the target's former owners while allowing the capital gains tax charge to be deferred, they would regard this as an abuse, and would withhold clearance. The phrase they used to describe the loan note element of some schemes they had seen was 'a post dated cheque'. Subsequently they have relaxed this stance to indicate that they would not normally object to a loan note having a life of over six months – but would be inclined to ask what was the commercial justification for any security having a shorter life than that.

[53] Section 138 TCGA 1992.

requirements of section 135, the target's shareholders would enjoy the full *roll-over* treatment explained at the beginning of the previous paragraph; but if the predator's issue is debentures which fit into the definition of *qualifying corporate bonds* (Note 49 on the previous paragraph), and their issue still meets those same requirements, then the transaction is lifted out of section 135's full roll-over and dropped instead into the more limited *hold-over* (the *clock-stopping* procedure) under section 116 of the Taxation of Chargeable Gains Act 1992 referred to at a later point in the previous paragraph.

• those last two items put a heavy onus on the predator. It will be one of the points which he includes in his offer to the target's shareholders that he is able to indicate their tax treatment, and although this may not be a guarantee, the predator takes ultimate responsibility for ensuring the fairness and accuracy of every statement he makes in his offer.

11.28 The loss of beneficial ownership

In paragraph 11.6 we noted that if property is to be moved within the target group before being sold out of that group to the predator (or a company in the predator's group), it is essential that the internal movement take place before the external sale has been agreed.

The same principles apply, of course, to the other kinds of internal rearrangements we have been comtemplating before a target company is sold. In brief, it is essential that they be achieved before the parent company of that target loses the beneficial interest in its shares – a concept which we have already explored at length in paragraphs 5.32 onwards, but particularly in paragraphs 5.40 and 5.41. Perhaps it is worth repeating that:

• it ceases to be possible to pay a dividend under group arrangements once the payer has ceased to be beneficially owned by the recipient, since this terminates the group election under section 248(4) of the Taxes Act 1988;

• not only does the breaking of the beneficial ownership make it no longer possible to transfer assets or shareholdings out of a target using group capital gains tax freedom from charge, but it will also trigger off the section 179 charge on the target if at that time it contains any asset transferred into it within the previous six years on a group basis;

• although the principles are the same for stamp duty (in order to preserve the entitlement to transfer assets within a group without duty), the way in which they are applied in practice is slightly different, as we saw in paragraph 11.6 above;

But those are only some of the effects of the loss of beneficial ownership. We have, as indicated, looked at this at some length in chapter 5; although it is clearly important not to lose sight of it here, we can discuss the practical side of this matter more appropriately in the next chapter when we come to deal with the Heads of Agreement on which the predator will want to obtain the signature of the target's vendors.

11.29 Directors' compensation for loss of office

When a private company changes hands, one would normally expect the incoming shareholders to want to appoint their own board of directors. It is therefore a normal part of the agreement for the sale of of the company's shares that the directors' resignations will be handed over at completion along with the share transfers and other documentation.[54]

If the resigning directors are also shareholders, they might be in a position to suggest that the terms of the predator's acquisition should provide them the third and/or fourth as well as the first two of the following:

- predisposal dividend;
- sale proceeds for their shares;
- compensation for loss of office;
- special pension contributions.

This book does not seek to deal with the whole subject of personal tax; it is clear that an individual benefiting from a contribution paid into a pension scheme by his employer would not normally pay tax on such a benefit – he would be taxed at a later stage on the pension that resulted. Although he would be taxable on his compensation receipt, the regime under which this is assessed means that the tax burden on the receipt may be less than would apply under capital gains tax to additional proceeds for the sale of shares. There is thus some incentive, in some cases, for the resigning director to seek some part of his disposal proceeds in one of other of the third and fourth forms. If the choice lies between the first two heads, there are reliefs from capital gains tax (either in a permanent form, such as retirement relief, or temporary, such as rollover relief into shares in an unlisted company), but leaving those aside it is likely that the tax burden on the individual would be the same whether the company distributed £1, the predisposal dividend being 80p, and the ACT 20p,[55] or on the other hand the company retained that £1 so that its shares changed hands for that much more than would otherwise have been the case.

---

[54] Although almost the whole of the next chapter describes the progress towards completion, and the documentation of that progress, it is not within the compass of this book to attempt a full inventory of the documentation and actions which are involved in a normal completion.

[55] The statement in the text is true as it stands, because it is related solely to the individual's tax liability. Had one been addressing the company's liability, then the question whether the ACT was recoverable against past mainstream liabilities, or would be recoverable against future mainstream liabilities, would also need to be taken into account – and in this case, the question of *past* or *future* should logically affect the purchase price of the target.

What is relevant for the purposes of this book, however, is the legitimacy of any of these proposals, and their tax effects not principally on the recipient, but on the *target* and *predator*.

11.30 Directors' compensation for loss of office (continued)

We know that it is a general principle underlying all offers made in a listed company context that similar terms must be offered to all of the target's shareholders, that giving Mr X more per share than Mr Y (on the footing that the former's holding has a greater strategic value than the latter) is not permissible. Even outside the listed company context we have seen in Note 48 on paragraph 11.26 what are the Companies Act concepts of 'takeover offers' and what appear to implications of the undefined 'general offer' in the tax legislation.

But section 314 of the Companies Act 1985 goes further than any of these in the specific area it addresses. It requires a director to disclose to the shareholders any payment proposed to be made to him by way of compensation for loss of office, or to obtain his agreement to resign, when such a payment is proposed in connection with a bid for the company (including a bid for a controlling interest or any lesser level of shareholding). The director is required to make every effort to ensure that this disclosure is included in the offer document. And the proposal must be approved[56] at a meeting of the shareholders whose shares are the subject of the bid. The director and bidder are each subject to a fine if disclosure is not made – and any payment the director does receive is to be regarded as held by him on trust for the shareholders generally unless they have approved its being made to him.

Those requirements apply to payments which we can broadly describe as compensation for loss of office. If the company had previously established a pension scheme for the director, and if a review of its funding at the date of his retirement disclosed that some additional contributuion could be made into it, then one could argue that that special contribution did not need to be looked at as a part of the compensation package. However, such a contribution clearly needs to be disclosed[57] in the company's accounts. The question is therefore merely whether it should be approved as well? The argument against is that if it is a '*bona fide* payment by way of . . . pension' it would be exempted,[58] but the author's view is that a director could be well advised to go for approval as well as disclosure. Notice that it is irrelevant whether the cost of any of these items is borne by the target rather than directly by the predator.

---

[56] Section 315(1)(b) CA 1985.
[57] Paragraphs 1(4)(c) and 13(3)(c) of schedule 6 to CA 1985.
[58] Section 316(3) CA 1985. It is an indication how unsatisfactory are the procedures for amending and updating Acts of Parliament that those parts of the Companies Acts dealing with approval of directors' remuneration refer only to *payment* of directors' pensions. The concept that those pensions might come from funded schemes to which the company had made *contributions* (and that therefore the level of contributions might be of interest to shareholders and others), appears only in the accounts disclosure provisions in schedule 6 to CA 1985.

11.31 The tax position on directors' compensation for loss of office

The fact that there may be some advantage for the individual receiving either compensation for loss of office, or the benefit of a special pension contribution, should not blind one to the fact that the overall cost will undoubtedly be greater if the paying company is unable to deduct the expense in arriving at its own corporation taxable profits.

It is worth recalling the point mentioned in paragraph 5.4, that if an expense is related not to the carrying on of a company's trade but to its closure, it will in principle be non-deductible.[59]

The more relevant questions are however likely to arise in continuing companies than in those whose businesses cease. The decided cases clearly demonstrate that the courts have been prepared to look at the matter as purely one of fact – was the payment compensation for loss of office or was it something entirely else? The word 'compensation' means just that, what a court would be likely to award as damages if the injured party took his case to court.[60] When made to the directors in the context of a change in the ownership of a company it is much less likely that any ex-gratia payment could be said to have been made wholly and exclusively for the purposes of the trade – an expense incurred in

---

[59] The leading case on this point is *Godden v A Wilsons Stores (Holdings) Ltd* [1962] 40 TC 161, which related to compensation paid to the manager of a rubber estate when his employing company sold that estate and ceased trading. However there is a fine line between that and the case of *O'Keeffe v Southport Printers Ltd* [1984] 58 TC 88, in which a company negotiated with its trades unions an agreed date of 10 February 1978 for its cessation of trade and declaring its workforce redundant. The Commissioners found as a fact that the redundancy payments resulting from this were paid 'for the purpose of achieving the orderly conduct of the company's business up to its cessation' and were deductible. This finding of fact was not disturbed by the courts.

Since that date redundancy payments, whether statutory or in excess of the statutory requirements, have been made deductible under section 90 TA 1988. Deductibility of such payments for the paying company is of course different from the question of their taxability in the hands of the recipient. Section 579(1) TA 1988 exempts statutory redundancy payments from being taxed as income under schedule E, but section 580(3) requires that they 'be taken into account' in considering whether an assessment is appropriate under the *compensation* regime in section 148 TA 1988. The significance is that a statutory redundancy payment could never, itself, exceed the £30,000 threshold in that section, but it is necessary to aggregate all payments to see whether the total exceeds £30,000. Where a company pays more than is statutorily required (what is referred to as a non-statutory scheme), the Revenue generally accept that that payment is taxable if at all under section 148 – but they have reserved the right to look at the basis of any such scheme in order to ensure that what is being paid is what it purports to be (see SP 1/94, issued following the House of Lords comments in *Mairs v Haughey* [1993] BTC 339).

[60] Until 1981, a definition for tax purposes of 'compensation for loss of office' was spelled out in paragraph 13 of schedule 8 to the Taxes Act 1970, because at that time different rules applied to the taxation of compensation receipts and *ex gratia* receipts. The harmonisation of those rules in the Finance Act 1981 enabled the definition referred to to be repealed, but that does not mean that the interpretation of the phrase has altered. The approach in paragraph 8 of schedule 6 to CA 1985 is to define the offices and other positions for the loss of which a director might be compensated, rather than to attempt to identify what part of any payment should properly be called compensation, and what must be recognised as being a payment for something else.

carrying on the trade with a view to the generation of profits from that trade in the future.[61] Certainly it is true that in none of the reported cases was it suggested by the payer that it was as an ex-gratia payment that his expense should be deducted.

When the courts examined the facts in the two leading cases decided in the 1930s, they concluded in the first[62] that the *compensation* was non-deductible, being a distribution of profits, where the recipients were the company's only shareholders, and the sum paid was equal to the balance on profit and loss account. In the second[63] the payments were held non-deductible, having been paid not in the interests of the company but those of its purchaser; in that second case the payments seem to have been agreed as part of the resolution of a family row, in which those shareholders who wished to sell (and the purchaser) needed to persuade the remainder to sell. A similar factual conclusion was reached in two more recently reported cases[64] and interestingly in a third in which the directors paid off were not even shareholders of the target.[65]

11.32 Asset disposals and VAT

This is one of the subjects we undertook, in paragraph 11.3, to deal with; the other is protection of employment. The complexity of each of them justifies their being put into separate groups of paragraphs, but in each case their correct place in the sequence of events should be at the forefront rather than an afterthought.

If the disponor of *assets* is registered for VAT, then there is a likelihood that he will be making a disposal in the course of his business activities, and that therefore VAT must be charged on top of the price at which the assets are being sold. This applies whether one is talking about the kind of assets which are normally sold in the course of that business (for example, stock in trade), assets which are seldom sold (for example, machinery and plant), or those assets which are not normally thought of as transferable within or outside the scope of the business activities (for example, the goodwill of the business itself, which we described in paragraph 6.28 as not having an existence separate from the business and its assets, in the sense that it could not be disposed of or otherwise dealt with separately).

The general rule is that on a sale of *goods*[66] VAT must be charged by the disponor to the predator. There are a couple of minor qualifications

---

[61] See paragraph 5.4, and Note 11 thereon.
[62] *Overy v Ashford Dunn & Co. Ltd* [1933] 17 TC 497.
[63] *Bassett Enterprise Ltd v Petty* [1938] 21 TC 730.
[64] *George Peters & Co. Ltd v Smith* [1963] 41 TC 264, and *George J Smith & Co. Ltd v Furlong* [1968] 45 TC 384.
[65] *CIR v Patrick Thomson Ltd (in liquidation)* [1956] 37 TC 145.
[66] Each of the three items listed as examples in the text would be treated for this purpose as *goods*. In particular, Customs and Excise have made it clear in Press Notice No. 790 of 10 December 1982 that even though goodwill may be no more tangible than the excess of the consideration over the values of the other assets transferred, it is nevertheless *goods* and liable to VAT.

that must be made to that statement but the most important exception relates to the position where the goods concerned are the assets of a *business* which is transferred as a *going concern*; a matter we will move onto the next paragraph:

(1) the assignment of a debt (or, in context, the transfer of a portfolio of trade debtors) is a transaction which is exempt – the consideration for it is exempt income. What that might be thought to mean is that the disponor would potentially become part-exempt, and would be unable to deduct some part of the input tax he might have incurred attributable to the transfer (VAT on solicitors' fees, for example). But debt assignment is one of those items which in the case of a non-financial company gives rise to exempt income without that income affecting the question whether the recipient is part-exempt, and if so what loss of input tax deduction he might suffer;[67]

(2) there could be a business which was so largely exempt that it had not registered for VAT, because its taxable supplies were non-existent or below the registration threshold. The sale of its assets might be expected to put it over that threshold in the month of the sale[68] and thus require registration but this is subject to the statutory relief allowing an exempt business not to count the proceeds of disposal of its *capital assets*;[69]

(3) but by far the most significant qualification is that the business' transfer of its assets *may* come within the VAT provisions dealing with transfers of going concerns.

11.33 Transfer of a going concern

The requirements, which make a transfer that of a going concern, (TOGC), need to be put into context without further ado:

- there is no choice. If a transfer is regarded by Customs as within the definition of a TOGC, VAT must not be charged, but if it is not within that definition VAT must be added to the transfer price of the assets (and if it is not added, the prices will be treated as VAT inclusive). A disponor who is in doubt will wish to charge VAT, and account for it to Customs to avoid the possibility of a penalty; but the predator is then likely to demand that the disponor repay VAT charged if Customs take the view that the transaction was after

---

[67] Regulation 33(1)(e) of the VAT (General) Regulations 1985, (SI 1985 No. 886) allows what is actually exempt income to be treated as if it were taxable for this purpose, except in the cases of what we have described as the *financial* companies listed in regulation 33(2).

[68] At the time of writing, £45,000 of taxable supplies expected in the ensuing 30 days would require that a business register.

[69] Paragraph 1(5) of schedule 1 to VATA 1983; the *capital assets* concerned would be plant and machinery, office machinery including computers and office furniture, cars; and a capital sum derived from the assignment of a lease under which the landlord had been charging VAT.

all a TOGC, and therefore the predator had no right to an input deduction. The disponor then faces the problem of trying to persuade Customs to refund output tax he need not have paid;

- if the transaction is a TOGC, the disponor makes no supply at all (neither taxable nor exempt), but a corollary is that attributable input tax is fully deductible.[70]

In order for a transfer to qualify as a transfer outside the scope of VAT (which is how a TOGC is categorised), it must be a transfer of a *business* (or part of a business) together with the assets[71] of that business. What is transferred must have been carried on as a going concern by the disponor, and in the hands of the predator must not only be capable of separate operation, but must also in fact be carried on as *the same kind of business* whether separately or integrated into the predator's own business. If the disponor is a taxable person, the predator must either already be registered, or become registered immediately on the transfer.[72]

Where the assets include a building for which the disponor has made an election to waive exemption, the predator must make the same election. Thus if a landlord has made the election for a particular building in order to reclaim the input tax on a refurbishment of it, he is prevented from thereafter transferring it in a TOGC to an associated

---

[70] This sounds wrong, but is not. The explanation is that input tax is non-deductible if it is *exempt input tax*. Exempt input tax is that attributable to the making of exempt supplies, and it comes in two shapes. If a business makes *only* exempt supplies, then it is clear that all of its input tax must be attributable to those exempt supplies, and must all be non-deductible. If it makes a mixture of taxable and exempt supplies, input tax is first identified to one or the other – and to the extent that it is not feasible to split it in any other way it is split pro rata. But the input VAT on the solicitors' fees for a TOGC cannot be identified with any exempt supply, and nor can it be split pro rata between exempt and taxable because it relates to neither. There is thus no provision within VAT legislation requiring or authorising any disallowance of any such input VAT.

[71] Guidance from Customs and Excise speaks of the assets as *including* stock in trade, machinery, goodwill, premises and fixtures and fittings. It is indicated that not only must 'the business or part of the business be a going concern at the time of the transfer', but that 'the assets ... must be intended for use by the new owner in carrying on the same kind of business'. Reading all of that together, it seems clear that Customs would not necessarily expect either cash or debtors to be transferred (and in fact the way that VAT relief for bad debts is dealt with also indicates that Customs do not imagine that debtors would be transferred when a business changes hands). But apart from that, there seems to be an indication that all other *business* assets would go across. Assets not required for business purposes would appear not to be envisaged as being covered by the relief.

[72] These requirements are in the VAT (Special Provisions) Order 1992, SI 1992 No. 3129. That order was made to provide for the continuity between disponor and predator which is envisaged in section 33 VATA 1983; it is a part of that continuity, for instance, that the predator's entitlement or requirement to be registered should be determined by reference to the turnover of the disponor.

Another part of the continuity relates to preservation of records, in that the order envisages that the disponor's records will be handed over to, and preserved by, the predator. However, if the parties wish the records to be retained by the disponor, and Customs accepts that this should not result in any greater likelihood of their being lost or destroyed, then this can be agreed.

company with a view to that associate selling it on an exempt basis. Because it is a requirement that the associate must also have elected to waive exemption, it in turn will either have to sell it on a taxable basis, or if there is to be a TOGC to the predator, then the predator will also have to waive exemption.

11.34 *Sales of let buildings as TOGCs*

Customs and Excise accept that the letting of a single building can constitute a business, or part of a business. Therefore, if we picture a disponor group of companies which has adopted the *group asset company*[73] procedure, it is possible for that *asset-company* to sell[74] a building to a similar company in the predator's group. This is parallel to, but not the same transaction as that in which:

- either a target company is sold out of the disponor group into the predator group, that target being the tenant of the building;

- or a company in the target group sells a business to a company in the predator group, together with the assets of that business. Those assets do not include the ownership of the building but only an occupational tenancy held by the trader in the disponor group from its asset-company, and replaced for the predator's trader by a similar tenancy from the predator's asset-compamy.

We are addressing the VAT implications, on the basis that we are specifically focusing on a building, owned by an asset-company, and let by it to another company which occupies it for the purposes of its business. The first question we need to answer is whether, if the two companies are *grouped* for VAT purposes, the description in that previous sentence is can be correct for VAT purposes? Or whether *grouping* makes the two companies into a single VAT entity, so that what we have to say we are looking at is not a let building at all, but a building whose ownership and occupation are both within that single entity. Anyone other than a tax professional would think it not only astounding but also infinitely depressing that when VAT has been in operation for over 20 years, there can still be uncertainty over the answer to such a fundamental question, but that is the position at the time of writing. However, the better view (and certainly the safer one) is that the asset-company and the trader-tenant should *not* be put into the same VAT group.

What we are still trying to focus on in this paragraph is only the sale of the building from asset-company to asset-company. In the first head, the tenancy survives that change of ownership. In the second, there is at approximately (not necessarily exactly) the same time both a change of ownership and an assignment of the tenancy.

---

[73] See paragraph 11.4.
[74] The word in the text is 'sell', but it is also possible to obtain TOGC treatment for a let building in cases in which its *owner* transfers his interest by assignment of his leasehold, or where he grants a lease out of his own leasehold interest (where he has a 99 year lease for instance, out of which he grants the predator a 98 year lease).

11.35 Sales of let buildings as TOGCs (continued)

Let us assume, in order to see what would be the implications, that the sale of the building from the one asset-company to the other were not a TOGC, and would accordingly be a standard rated transaction.

The three cases in which it is to be expected that VAT would be chargeable (in the absence of TOGC treatment) are:

- sale of freehold or assignment of lease for a building for which disponor has elected to waive exemption. This is almost certainly the important head – if the disponor asset-company incurred input VAT on the purchase of the building, on its construction, or on a major refurbishment, it would have ensured that exemption was waived in order to be able to recover that input tax;

- sale of freehold within three years of practical completion of building completed after 1 April 1989;

- first sale of freehold after 1 April 1989 of a building completed before that date, but not fully occupied before that date.

Looking at that list from the viewpoint of the predator's asset-company, it seems there would normally be a cashflow advantage if the substitution of TOGC treatment (in place of a standard rate charge) meant that VAT did not need to be charged on his purchase price; second, the fact that he would need only to finance the VAT-exclusive price could mean that he was prepared to pay more than he might otherwise have done for the building concerned; third, it should not be overlooked that if VAT is charged on this purchase, the purchaser finds himself liable to stamp duty on the VAT-inclusive price rather than the price without a VAT element. The list also makes it seem likely that there will equally be an advantage for the disponor's asset-company in achieving TOGC treatment for the building's sale, in that in all three cases it is probable that that asset-company will have incurred construction or refurbishment expenditure on the building for which he will have claimed an input deduction.[75]

If the asset-company were (probably unusually) letting the building on an *exempt* basis, treating its sale as a TOGC does provide the input tax deduction (Note 70 on paragraph 11.33) if nothing else.

---

[75] If he had been the occupier of the building, and had been using it in the course of a fully taxable business, then that input tax deduction would have been given by reference to that trade; but were he later (after using it in a standard rated trade) to dispose of the building on an exempt basis, the provisions of the capital goods scheme are precisely aimed at recapturing that input tax deduction. The capital goods scheme is in Part VA of the VAT (General) Regulations 1985 (SI 1985 No. 886). Oversimplifying at the risk of inaccuracy, what it says is that if an input tax deduction had been given for expenditure on a building on the assumption that the *outputs* that building generated would be wholly VATable (the sales of goods produced in the building), and that assumption was then falsified by the building generating an exempt *output* (the sale on an exempt basis of the building itself), then the earlier input tax deduction can be *adjusted*.

11.36 The Transfer of Undertakings (Protection of Employment) Regulations 1981

These regulations,[76] generally referred to as the TUPE regulations, were aimed at implementing in UK law the provisions of the EU Acquired Rights Directive of 1977. Community law, including Directives, is purposive and teleological, that is to say it is to be applied by first identifying the end result at which its draftsman had been aiming, and then interpreting its provisions in such a way that they achieve those objectives in the particular facts and circumstances of the case in hand; this is of course a very different approach from the older methods of interpreting English statutes (although less different from the civil law system in Scotland). But, as we will see below, the greatest difficulties and uncertainties flow, in this case, from two main areas in which the purposes of the Directive itself are unclear – and in one of these two, it is the British Government itself which seems to be the party most determined to argue for an interpretation different from that put on the Directive by a very large proportion of the commentators.

If an employer transfers a business as a going concern, and the transferee takes on what had been the transferor's employees, then:

- those employees are not to be regarded as having been dismissed or made redundant by the transferor; and

- if they were subsequently to be dismissed or made redundant by the second employer, their claims for compensation should be based on their having continuity of employment through the change – service with both of the employers would be counted;

- any claim for compensation thus lies against the second employer (but that second employer does not inherit from his predecessor any obligations relating to the employees' pension rights or schemes).

There are all sorts of qualifications and elaborations which we will need to make, but that is the basic intention of the Directive.

11.37 *It is not possible to opt out of the TUPE regulations where the necessary conditions are present*

A number of points flow direct from the explanation in the last paragraph. First, the regulations have no relevance where a company changes hands – in those circumstances there is no transfer of employment, since the company as employer is the same legal entity before and after its change of ownership. But if there is a change of employer, and if the other necessary conditions are fulfilled, then the regulations apply; it is not possible for the two employers, or either of them and the employees, to agree that a different legal position should be regarded as applicable.

What is perhaps even more significant is that the TUPE regulations

---

[76] SI 1981 No. 1794.

were designed to write into UK law the requirements of the Acquired Rights Directive; which must be taken to mean that those requirements need to be made *effective*. Thus, the Commission took the UK Government to the European Court of Justice (Case C-382/92, 8 June 1994, treated by the press as being related to the Brighton dustmen), alleging that there were two major provisions in the Directive which albeit mirrored in the TUPE Regulations, were nevertheless not *incorporated into UK Law*, because they did not adequately protect the employees that Community law said should be protected. The first point is that the Article 6 of the Directive requires that *representatives of employees* be informed and consulted. The UK's Regulation 10 envisages information of and consultation with trades union representatives by employers who recognise such trades unions, but provide no mechanism for employees whose union is not recognised or who are not members of any union, either in terms of their having a right to information, or to appoint a representative who would have appropriate rights. The European Court ruled that this was unacceptable. It ruled at the same time that the UK's Regulation 11 was equally unacceptable; what it purports to do is to impose sanctions against employers who fail to inform and consult, the amount of those sanctions to be paid to the employees who have suffered. However, the court took the view that the effect given to this in the UK is insufficient of a deterrent to employers, in that there is a ceiling imposed on the aggregate of this sanction and the *protective awards* payable to employees who are not consulted over redundancies.

11.38 The economic entity which must be transferred

The first of the necessary qualifications and elaborations of the basic principle is an attempt at a definition of what it is that must be transferred if the regulations are to be applicable.

It must be 'an economic entity which is capable of operating as a going concern, and which retains its identity'.[77] If we focus first on the question what is meant by an economic entity which retains its identity, the historic approach in English law had been to stress that a mere transfer of the assets is insufficient, because it is necessary also to transfer the trade, using that last word to mean that not only must the contracts with suppliers and customers continue, but the business activities must also remain unchanged. For instance, in *Melon v Hector Powe*,[78] the transfer was held by the House of Lords to be a mere transfer of assets, because

---

[77] The quotation does not come from either the Acquired Rights Directive or from the TUPE regulations, but from Guidance on the interpretation of the latter issued by the Office of Public Service and Science (Mr William Waldegrave, Chancellor of the Duchy of Lancaster) on 11 March 1993. This guidance is non-statutory, and as indicated it needs to be read with the explanations and elaborations that the text spells out. It is useful in making clear the Government's views, expounded by Mr Waldegrave, on the question of contracting out of Governmental and local governmental service, to which we will come in paragraph 11.41 below.
[78] [1981] 1 All ER 313.

the transferee operated the factory as a different business, supplying different customers, despite the fact that the transferor had guaranteed to take a substantial part of his production for a short period after the transfer to help him over the start-up period of his new business, and that the employees after the sale carried on working in the same factory on the same machines, in many cases doing the same sort of work, on no less favourable terms under new contracts with the purchaser.

The European Court of Justice tells us[79] that it is simply a question of fact whether there has been a transfer of an undertaking or business, and that a Court or Tribunal should determine this by reference to all of the facts; and that those facts should particularly include what was the type of undertaking, whether all the assets had been transferred, in particular the premises, whether the majority of employees had been transferred, the degree of similarity of activities before and after the transfer, and the extent of any break in those activities at the time of the transfer. There seems to be a clear implication that whereas the previous English law strained to say that there had not been a transfer, the thrust of the European law is to accept that there has – unless the parties are able to produce compelling evidence to the contrary.

11.39 Must the economic entity be a commercial venture?

The second aspect is that UK law developed from income tax and corporation tax concepts (in particular the question whether a loss could be carried forward on a transfer of a trade) to recognise as an undertaking capable of being transferred 'any trade or business but ... not (including) any undertaking which is not in the nature of a commercial venture'. That wording was included in Regulation 2 of the original 1981 regulations. It was proved to be unduly restrictive by a 1992 European Court of Justice decision,[80] which decided that employees of charitable bodies involved in drug rehabilitation activities, subsidised by a local authority, were covered by the Acquired Rights Directive. There was no need for the entity to be established as a commercial venture. It has been necessary to correct the UK legal position to bring it into line with what it should have been from the start.[81]

11.40 Dismissals and redundancies because of the transfer

The third point is one of particular practical difficulty. The theory of the Directive may be clear, but how it operates in actual circumstances is much less so. The theory is that if there is a transfer, then all

---

[79] *Spijkers v Gebroeders Benedick Abattoir* [1986] 2 CMLR 296. This is however just the first leading case in a developing area. For instance, the court decided on 14 April 1994, in the *Schmidt* case, (C-392/92 [1994] IRLR 302) that the Directive applied where cleaning services provided by a single employee were contracted out; in that instance there was no transfer of assets, only a transfer of the employment of the individual, from the previous employer to the successor.

[80] *Dr Sophie Redmond Stickting v Bartol* [1992] IRLR 366.

[81] In the Trade Union Reform and Employment Rights Act 1993.

employees have continuity and protection. It hardly needs stating that any employee dismissed after the transfer would claim compensation from the transferee employer. But those dismissed because of the transfer are also entitled to claim from that transferee (and the transferor is absolved) because that is what Regulation 8(1) says. It is the words 'because of' which give rise to the difficulty, or rather to the two difficulties. The first of these is that the UK regulations only apply[82] to those employed immediately before the transfer, so that if someone has been dismissed days or even hours before, his dismissal would lay the transferor open to a claim, not the transferee. However, that provision of the regulations was shown to be contrary to the intentions of the Acquired Rights Directive.[83] Therefore, in a case[84] in which a company in receivership dismissed its workforce an hour before the transfer, and the transferee then immediately started recruiting them on lower rates of pay, the House of Lords decided that the UK regulations must be read purposively, so as to apply to any employee who was employed immediately before the transfer 'or would have been so employed had he not been unfairly dismissed because of the transfer'.[85]

---

[82] Regulation 5(3) says that the continuity and protection in Regulation 5(1) only apply to a person so employed immediately before the transfer. These words have been held, in *Secretary of State for Employment v Spence* [1986] IRLR 248 to mean exactly what they say; that the word 'immediately' could not be given any wider interpretation.

[83] In *P Bork International A/S (in liquidation) v Foreningen AF Arbedsjsledere I Danmark* [1989] IRLR 41, the European Court of Justice treated employees dismissed before but because of a transfer, and subsequently re-employed by the transferee, as having been employed at the time of the transfer.

[84] *Litster v Forth Dry Dock & Engineering Co. Ltd* [1989] ICR 341.

[85] There is a further uncertainty; in *UK Security Services (Midland) Ltd v Gibbons and others* EAT 104/90, a company was put up for sale by tender. An hour before the tenders were opened, two employees were dismissed. They said the TUPE regulations applied, and claimed against the successor employer. He, of course, pointed out that he did not even know of the existence of the former employees; if there had been an unfair dismissal of them it was the former employer's dismissal, and their claim lay against him under the normal provisions of section 57(3) of the Employment Protection (Consolidation) Act 1978.

The basis of the employees' claim was that Regulation 8(1) of TUPE shifts the employment contracts to the successor where the 'reason or the principal reason for the dismissal' is the transfer of the business. The tribunal found as a fact that this was the case, and the appeals tribunal said that this was justified. The shift arises through the operation of those extra words which the House of Lords says, as mentioned in the text, should be read into the regulations: '... or would have been so employed had he not been unfairly dismissed *because of the transfer*' (*emphasis added*).

However, the Employment Appeals Tribunal went on to comment on what the position would have been had it not been able to determine on the facts that the employees were still employed immediately before the transfer because they had been unfairly dismissed *because of the transfer*. What the EAT said was that the dismissals were unfair because there had been no consultation; the unfairness shifted their employment contracts to the successor. The implication is that the italicised words in the previous two sentences are superfluous. If there is a dismissal which the predecessor claims to have been for an economic, technical or organisational reason (the next matter discussed in the text), and even though the dismissal would have been fair in that context but it is actually unfair for a different reason, then the employees are to be regarded as still employed immediately before the transfer, and their employment contracts shift to the successor employer. This clearly goes further than *Litster*.

However, all of those indications that the regulations apply, that continuity and protection are provided, and that it is the transferee employer who is at risk, are overridden if the dismissal was for a reason which is for 'an economic, technical or organisational reason entailing changes in the workforce of ... the transferor ... before ... a relevant transfer'.[86] Such dismissals may be unfair under the general law, but are altogether outside the scope of the TUPE regulations. The problem is of course distinguishing the economic, technical and organisational reasons from any others; more or less the only unequivocal guidance we have on the interpretation of the words is that a change in the workforce is a change in its numbers, not just in its terms and conditions.

11.41 The contracting out of governmental and local government services

The major unresolved question is whether the TUPE regulations apply. The view of the Government is that they do not, the reason for this being that there cannot be a transfer of an economic entity capable of operating as a going concern, and which retains its identity, when what is happening is that there is no change in the Government's (or local government's) statutory responsibility to supply the service concerned, and all that is happening is that that organisation is buying in, from an outsider rather than an insider, the services needed to fulfil its statutory duty.[86a]

If that view turns out to be wrong, then any organisation which takes on responsibility for a contracted out service will relieve the Government (or local government) of its obligations for redundancy and later dismissals;[87] and those obligations seem likely to crystallise

---

[86] Regulation 8(2) of the TUPE Regulations.

[86a] Regulation 3 of the UK regulations provides that they apply to the *transfer from one person to another of an undertaking situated immediately before the transfer in the United Kingdom or a part of one which is so situated.* If that phraseology were taken to mean that the transferor must have been the *owner* of the undertaking up to the time of transfer, and the transferee must then acquire ownership, there would obviously be difficulty; without doing some violence to the English language, it would be difficult to say that such a regulation could apply to the non-profit making enterprise such as the charitable body involved in drug rehabilitation, (paragraph 11.39 and Note 80 thereon). It would be an additional reason for saying that the TUPE regulations could not apply to local authorities. But in what has come to be thought of as the Brighton dustmen's case, (European Court of Justice Case C-382/92, 8 June 1994), the UK as respondent made it clear to the Court that it did not argue for such an *ownership* interpretation; on the contrary, following the House of Lords in *Litster*, (paragraph 11.40 and Note 84), the UK Government fully accepted that the interpretation of the UK regulations must coincide with that of the Acquired Rights Directive.

[87] Separately from the guidance referred to in Note 77 on paragraph 11.38 above, the Department of the Environment has made it clear that 'it would regard as anti-competitive any attempt to structure contracting out arrangements to make the Regulations apply'. The background appears to be that, as has been indicated earlier, the regulations are considered by Government not to be relevant generally to

continued

CONTRACTING OUT OF GOVERNMENT SERVICES

should the contractor lose its contract at a later date. In circumstances where a second (replacement) contractor will almost certainly have been hired precisely because it will undertake to do things differently from the first, and will not simply accept a transfer to it of the first contractor's economic entity, as a going concern, this would put an excessively heavy penalty on the first contractor.

What it is possible to say on this point is that a European Court of Justice case[88] decided that where the contracted out service was that of providing an in-house canteen (there was an express agreement that the canteen staff would be transferred), it was possible for that to constitute a transfer covered by the Acquired Rights Directive, although the canteen service was to be provided to the organisation for a fee, and the organisation's own obligations to provide meals for its other staff using the canteen was not altered. However, the ECJ sent the matter back to the national court for determination under the appropriate criteria. This opens up, but certainly goes nowhere towards resolving, the fundamental question. Is the economic entity the same entity where:

- it produces its meals for a charge to each individual eating;

- or it produces its meals for a fee paid to it by the employer;

- or it produces its meals as an integral part of the employer's organisation, its management and workforce paid by, and directed by, the employer organisation itself?

In paragraph 11.38 we said the previous UK law had strained to say there was no transfer. Community law appears to incline in favour.

---

continued
  contracting out, but there are exceptional cases in which they would apply. In those cases, the Department (or local government) would be saved the costs of redundancy – and it could be that the contractor would be given an assurance that his contract would be continued without his being compelled to incur any substantial redundancy or dismissal costs. Such a procedure could be said by the relevant Department to meet its formal obligations to contract out services, without its making any real changes. If that is a fair analysis, then it is clear that those who have taken on the mission of achieving changes that are *real* (the Department of the Environment numbers itself among these) would be unsatisfied.

[88] *Rask and Christensen v ISS Kantioneservice A/S* November 12 1992, ECJ.

CHAPTER 12

ACQUISITIONS

12.1 Introduction

An acquisitions chapter can be more focused than one which attempts to deal with disposals.

We spent the last chapter discussing two separate matters, despite our heading being no more than 'disposals'; how a company should dispose of a trade and assets (or of shares in a subsidiary) was the first of those two – but the second was how the disponor company should seek to pass the maximum value to its own shareholders. (We did of course also make passing references to disposals by individuals of trades and assets, or shares in their own companies – where the two parts of the process become merged into a single operation, but it was still an operation which had a purpose beyond the actual disposal itself.)

The subject matter of this chapter can however be merely the operational process of making acquisitions. With the exception of one particular aspect, we will not deal in any great depth with the preliminary stages before the start of the process, in which the company's management decide on their expansionary strategy, and their shareholders authorise them to issue shares as consideration for the acquisition (or to place shares,[1] or borrow, to provide cash consideration). Nor will we devote much time to the later processes of integration of the acquired target into the predator's group – or in the alternative the reorganisation/dismemberment of that target, leading to the predator's disposal of significant parts of what he has only recently acquired. We are mainly concerned with targets which are not listed companies – and the predators we will be dealing with, those making the acquisitions, will also mainly be unlisted.

The preliminary matter mentioned above, whose impact on these acquisitions must always be at the forefront of our minds, is the Financial Services Act 1986.

---

[1] Placings can include the so-called *vendor placing*, in which the predator issues shares to the former shareholders of the target, but they are then enabled to place those shares with institutions; the target's former shareholders thus effectively get cash consideration. The benefit to the predator is that he is allowed to claim merger relief (section 131 CA 1985) and to bring his investment in the target into his own balance sheet at a figure less than its full value – which would not have been possible if the purchase of the target had been for cash, and the placing had been a separate exercise. We described this transaction in paragraph 6.30 and Note 4b as being generally regarded as an abuse of the requirements for merger relief (and merger accounting if it is also relevant).

12.2 The Financial Services Act 1986

What we need is a general overview, and one which is related specifically to the acquisitions of privately held companies.

There are two main prohibitions in the Act, each with a series of exceptions; unless the transactions we have in view can be fitted within one of these exceptions they can only be carried out by (or with a substantial degree of assistance from) an authorised person. We are all familiar with the legends printed at the foot of lawyers' and accountants' letters: 'Regulated by the Law Society in the conduct of investment business, and Authorised by the Institute of Chartered Accountants in England and Wales to carry on investment business.' That phraseology does not spell out that there are different levels of regulation and authorisation. Not every firm will be entitled to deal with transactions of the size we are likely to be looking at. If an acquisition cannot be fitted within one of the exemptions, (and assuming that it is over the threshold size the predator's lawyers and accountants can handle), it will need to be *promoted* by an organisation with the necessary authorisation. In paragraph 12.28 below we outline the part that a merchant bank can play in a listed company acquisition; they will unquestionably be sufficiently authorised but there are others who will be able to deal with most private company acquisitions – the corporate finance departments of the large accounting firms, for example.

12.3 *The Financial Services Act 1986 – investment business*

However, let us revert to the Act's prohibitions and the exceptions from them. The first prohibition is that no one may engage in *investment business* unless authorised[2] (and as explained above the word authorised has always to be understood to mean 'authorised to carry on that type and level' of business). Investment business[3] includes buying and selling investments, arranging deals for investments, and managing investments; and investments[4] include shares, debentures, bonds, loan stock and other instruments creating indebtedness. Just about the only types of acquisition that do not come within the Act's purview, therefore, are those of trades and assets, and (probably) an acquisition of an interest in an entity which has no share capital or equivalent, such as a partnership.

There is one significant, and relevant, exception from the prohibition on carrying on investment business. The definition of investment business excludes the acquisition or disposal of shares in a target company if the following two conditions[5] are met:

---

[2] Section 3 FSA 1986. The section refers not just to persons obtaining authorisation under Chapter III of the Act, but to there being specified organisations exempted from the need for authorisation, such as the Stock Exchange and overseas investment exchanges, money brokers on the Bank of England list, and the Society of Lloyd's.

[3] Part II of schedule 1 to FSA 1986 sets out the full definition.

[4] Part I of schedule 1 to FSA 1986 sets out the full definition.

[5] Paragraph 21 of schedule 1 to FSA 1986. That paragraph incorporates the definition of 'connected individuals' referred to in the text, a definition which is not quite the same as that used in the capital gains tax legislation which we looked at in paragraph 6.37.

- the shares concerned carry 75 per cent or more of the voting rights in the target company, or would when added to target shares already held by the predator give that predator 75 per cent or more of the votes; and

- each of the parties, that is to say, the predator and disponor, is either:

 a company; or
 a single individual; or
 a group of connected individuals; the directors and/or managers of the target constitute such a group, and it includes also the immediate family of each of them. Where that target is to be acquired by individuals rather than a predator company, the individuals who are to be its directors and/or managers are similarly connected, and again the group extends to include the immediate family of each. In addition to that a partnership is a group of connected individuals, if it is the disponor of, or intended to become the owner of, the target.

12.4 *The Financial Services Act 1986 – investment advertisements*

The second prohibition in the Act is on the issuing of 'investment advertisements', a phrase whose meaning is far from self-evident.

It is defined[6] as any advertisement (which in context means any document, letter or circular, and could include spoken, telephoned and broadcast words as well as written, although the spoken and telephoned word is more likely to be prevented by the restrictions on 'unsolicited calls'), inviting those to whom it is addressed to enter into an 'investment agreement'. The latter is itself defined[7] as an agreement the making or performance of which by either party constitutes the carrying on of investment business.

There are a number of exemptions from this prohibition:

- investment advertisements can be issued to those who are sufficiently expert to understand any risks involved;[8]

- investment advertisements can be issued for the purpose of the take-over (whether for cash or on a paper-for-paper basis, or with a choice) of a private company whose shares have not been listed or

---

[6] Section 57(2) FSA 1986.
[7] Section 44(9) FSA 1986. This provision must rank as one of the best examples ever of how to assemble a statute. Subsection (9) is tacked onto the end of a section entitled 'Appointed representatives' in the part of the Act which exempts them, along with the other organisations mentioned in Note 2 above, from the provisions of the Act. It is true that their principals need to control appointed representatives' activities for other parties including their advice on, and promotion of, investment agreement, but that is an odd pretext for putting into that section, in that part of the Act, a definition which is relevant for all of the *real* purposes of the Act.
[8] Section 57(3)(c) FSA 1986 authorises the Secretary of State to specify the circumstances in which this requirement is met, and his specification is in Article 9 of SI 1988 No. 316.

quoted, in the UK or elsewhere, in the previous ten years. There are further voluminous and detailed requirements which must be met,[9] of which we will only mention one, namely that the take-over must be unanimously recommended by the directors of the target. The author has to say that the conditions for this exemption to apply are so difficult that, in practice, it is easier to have an authorised person promote the take-over;

- the third exemption for the issuance of investment advertisements closely parallels that for the acquisition (or disposal) of the shares of the target company in the circumstances set out in paragraph 12.3 above. That is to say, the exemption in that paragraph permits the transaction itself, by excluding it from the definition of investment *business*. What we are considering in this paragraph is in effect the exclusion from the investment *advertisement* restrictions of the paperwork necessary to achieve the acquisition of the shareholding in that target company.[10] It has only been thought necessary for it to deal with acquisitions, and disposals are not covered, in the light that it is more likely to be the predator than the disponor who will be *advertising*.

12.5 Heads of agreement

Assuming that the parties have determined whether, and if so, how, the Financial Services Act is relevant to the deal they have in view, we can step into the process at the stage at which the *Heads* is under discussion, marking the end of the first stage of the prospective predator's preliminary negotiations with the intending disponor. We described the parties in paragraph 11.1 as talking, but only warily, each looking for the other's weak points and actively seeking his own advantage.

There are three things which can normally be said about the Heads. First, the signed document may or may not be, in legal terms, *an agreement*; but it certainly should not be an agreement by the vendor that he will sell, or by the predator that he will buy, the target – in those cases in which the Heads does have some degree of legal force, it should not be in that area that it binds the parties. Sometimes, although we will see that this is probably exceptional (and undesirable), the Heads may be no more than a statement by each party that they are in discussions and hope that these will lead somewhere.

The reasons which we have already noted,[11] and will continue to see in evidence as we proceed, can be described merely as technical ones why it is seldom in the interests of any of the parties that the disponor's

---

[9] Article 4 of, and the schedule to, SI 1988 No. 716. It would be inappropriate to precis these requirements in the text, and those readers intending to rely on this exemption must study the terms of the Statutory Instrument with care.
[10] Article 5 of SI 1988 No. 716.
[11] See paragraph 11.28.

ownership of the target be broken at as early a stage as this.[12] Thus, the parties will try to ensure not only that beneficial ownership of the target remains with the disponor, looking at this is a question of law; but also ensuring that the Inland Revenue are not able to say that 'arrangements have come into existence' for the target to leave the group of companies of which it may be a member, using those words in the sense that they are given in *Statement of Practice* No. 3 of 1993 (see paragraph 5.40 and Note 71 thereon). If the Heads does contain an indication that the predator is willing to buy, his willingness will be expressed to be conditional, one principal condition being his not discovering during the next stages of the acquisition process some fact about the target which would radically alter his willingness to make the acquisition, or to make it at the price originally envisaged.

12.6 Heads of agreement (continued)

But the fundamental, as opposed to technical, reason why the Heads should not commit the predator to buy, or the disponor to sell, is that this would prevent either of them from negotiating any change in the terms, would prevent the predator from taking warranties and indemnities, and would make pointless any investigations he would otherwise have carried out.

There are however three clauses in the Heads which are normally made legally binding, namely:

- *confidentiality* – predator and disponor will normally want to agree that the fact that they are in discussions should be kept confidential, at least until it becomes considerably more certain that a deal will result. The target's business would be damaged, and so would the disponor's ability to sell it elsewhere, if it became known that discussions had been started with a particular purchaser but later terminated for reasons which could never be disclosed. And the disponor and target will also want to make sure that if the predator does eventually break off the discussions, any information he has obtained in the course of them (and of the investigations he and his accountants and lawyers have carried out) is not passed on to anyone else;

- *exclusivity* – the predator will want an undertaking that while the disponor is engaged in the discussions which are the subject of the Heads, that disponor will not actively, at the same time, be attempting to sell to another potential predator;

- *costs* – in some cases one party is made responsible for the other's costs in the event that the deal does not proceed.

---

[12] But the way in which the Stamp Office interpret, and give effect to, signatures on the *Heads* appears to have little to do with the legal position; see paragraph 11.6 and Note 11. It is very important that any internal reorganisations of properties and shareholdings in the target's group which are dependent on stamp duty exemptions should take place before the Heads is signed.

Each of those points makes it immediately obvious that the Heads must attempt to define some later make-or-break stage of the discussions. If the parties are reasonably confident that they will be able to complete a deal, the fact that negotiations have been in progress can then be announced – usually in terms that the target's acquisition by the predator is under discussion but is still subject to contract. If on the other hand they have come to the view that nothing will come of their talks, both of their undertakings to maintain confidentiality remain, but the disponor can be released from his agreement that he would not look for another purchaser.

12.7 The purchase contract

The drafting of a purchase contract is the next stage of the process once the Heads has been agreed. But that word 'drafting' can have a special meaning – the contract's terms are themselves in this sense best seen as part of the acquisition process.

Probably the best way for us to examine the acquisition process and the legal and tax constraints which can affect its shape, is to hang our examination onto the drafting process. It is therefore sensible to make the assumption that the first responsibility for the drafting lies with the lawyers of the predator. It is because we will be looking at it from their point of view that we have used the phrase 'purchase contract' in the heading of this paragraph. What the document is actually likely to show on its front sheet, below its date, is:

[Name of disponor or vendors]

and

[Name of predator]

and

[Names of warrantors and/or guarantors]

SHARE SALE AGREEMENT

relating to

[Name of target company]

There will be occasions on which none of this happens in this way. The contract may have been written by the disponor before discussions started with any prospective predator; because it may be the disponor's judgment that he will only be able to sell the target, or will achieve a better price for it, if he shuts potential purchasers out of most of the examinations and all of the negotiations we will be looking at in the next few paragraphs. Liquidators are one class of disponors who do generally adopt this course.

12.8 The purchase contract (continued)

It is the purchase contract, not the Heads, that will generally constitute the binding contract committing the vendor to sell and the purchaser to buy, and resulting in the vendor losing beneficial ownership of the target and the purchaser acquiring that ownership.[13]

Even that statement must however be made in qualified form; there are two not infrequently met reasons why the parties may be unable to reach a binding contract, only one which is conditional. The first is that those parties may recognise their need for Inland Revenue clearances;[14] and recognise that if clearance is not given, either the transaction will have to be abandoned, or at the minimum renegotiated in a different form. The second reason why only a conditional contract may be possible is the necessity for the purchaser to obtain shareholder approval. In one of its most common forms, this would necessitate the agreement's spelling out that it was conditional on:

- the purchaser sending its shareholders (within a stated time) a circular in the form required by the Stock Exchange notifying them of the proposals, and calling a meeting at which they can vote on them;

- the shareholders giving the necessary approval, again within a stated time;

- if the purchaser's listing (quotation) was suspended on the announcement, its shares being readmitted to the list after the shareholders' approval is given.

---

[13] See paragraphs 5.36 and 5.37 for the Court of Appeal comments in the *Sainsbury* case ([1991] BTC 181) that if beneficial ownership was lost by one party, it must in any normal commercial circumstances pass simultaneously to the other. This effectively overturned an earlier decision of the same court in the *Wood Preservation* case (paragraph 5.35, [1968] 45 TC 112) to the effect that it was possible for the vendor to lose beneficial ownership without its being simultaneously acquired by the purchaser – that it could go into suspense for a time. In *Sainsbury*, the court said that this could only occur in exceptional circumstances – not in the normal case of a sale and purchase of a company. (Thus *Wood Preservation* was not wrong, it was just so much of an exception to every rule that it could not be relied on as any kind of precedent.)

[14] We looked in paragraph 11.25 and Notes 45 and 46 thereon at the clearance that can be requested from the Inland Revenue that they accept that no party has obtained a 'tax advantage' from a 'transaction in securities', that advantage requiring that he be assessed in such a way as to counteract it. Although the provisions are so widely drafted that a very large proportion of company sales might technically be within their scope, we saw in that part of chapter 11 that the Revenue are willing to give clearance when it is demonstrated to them that the transaction was carried out for *bona fide* commercial reasons, and that tax avoidance was not its main, or one of its main, objects. Then in paragraph 11.27 we saw the parallel clearance obtainable by a predator or a target for the vendors being offered a share exchange, once again dependant upon the Inland Revenue's acceptance that the totality of the transaction was being done for *bona fide* commercial reasons and was not tax-motivated.

If the purchase consideration is payable in cash, but is to be provided from the proceeds of a placing of shares by the purchaser, there may be double conditions (it is wrong to describe them as cross-conditions). The predator will give himself an added degree of protection by making the purchase agreement conditional on his placing being successfully arranged, and the parties with whom the new shares are to be placed will make their subscription conditional on the purchase agreement being completed.

12.9 Date of completion

The last word in the last paragraph was 'completed', and although we have only just started our consideration of the terms of the contract, it is useful to think ahead to completion. This is of course the process in which each of the contracting parties does what is necessary to effect the transfer of legal ownership of the target's shares, and/or any other assets being sold and purchased; the settlement of the consideration contracted to be paid for them; the granting of whatever security and giving of whatever guarantees are called for by either side; and the stepping aside of the target's previous management in those cases in which it is a part of the contract that the predator will replace the previous management with his own.

It is the target as it stands at the time of completion that the predator acquires. What its assets and earning power had been thought to be at some earlier date may no longer be a fair guide to what the predator should pay, or the disponor should ask. One possibility for the predator is to try to fix the purchase price only at the time of completion; he arrives at a provisional price at a previous accounting date of the target, and converts that into a formula based on the accounts prepared as at that date. It might for instance be 110 per cent of net assets, substituting an independent valuation on an agreed basis in place of the balance sheet carrying values of property and other fixed assets. Accounts prepared to the completion date could then be similarly adjusted, so that the 110 per cent formula would produce the required price.

The alternative, and the procedure we will follow through in the next few paragraphs, is acceptance by both predator and disponor that they will work on the target's accounts for the period ended before completion, adjusting the consideration to reflect only some changes in the figures between accounts and completion. This may sound unsatisfactory and unworkable, but it is usually less costly and disruptive than preparing completion accounts, and safe enough and fair for all parties.

12.10 The Warranted Accounts

Following through that assumption, therefore (that the purchase is to be agreed on the basis of the target's most recent accounts, completed and audited, to a date some time before completion), the first necessity is to identify the accounts and the accounts date (the Warranted Accounts and the Accounting Date).[15]

If that Accounting Date was (say) six months prior to the time when the main negotiations occur, then one would expect that audited, statutory, accounts would be available to the negotiators, and that these would be a key tool in those negotiations. For instance, when we looked at the balance sheet in paragraph 11.7 (of the company before unbundling) we identified that its property had a capital gains tax acquisition cost of £400, and a current market value of £1,000; these figures being important in relation to identifying not only what the predator would realise from a disposal of the asset after he had made the acquisition, but also what would be the prospective tax liability flowing from that realisation. When the predator looks at the target's accounts, he can ask the vendors: 'if the fixed assets were realised for the figures at which they are carried in the accounts, would a tax liability arise?' That question does not demand that the vendors express a view on the market values of the assets — a matter on which the predator must form his own views, and take his own ultimate responsibility. But it does give the predator the comfort of knowledge which only the target itself could otherwise be expected to have access to:

- whether assets have been revalued in such a way that their capital gains tax acquisition values are significantly lower than what might have been assumed to have been their *bases* for tax;

- whether gains on the disposal of some earlier assets have been *rolled over* by deduction from the capital gains tax acquisition costs of the assets currently held, so that on a disposal of those assets owned at present a liability would arise reflecting two generations of gains.

12.11 *The Warranted Accounts (continued)*

That question, whether a sale of the fixed assets for their balance-sheet carrying values would give rise to a tax liability, would of course also require an answer in relation to the target's capital allowances — was the tax written down value of plant and machinery in *the pool* less than the depreciated value at which the assets concerned were carried in the balance sheet? — and all the equivalent questions for industrial buildings, and for any other category of capital allowance assets.

The accountants charged by the predator with the task of investigating the target's figures and business may well ask the foregoing in the form of questions. The predator itself, and its lawyers, may take a more stringent and formal line; if they demand a warranty from the vendors in the form of an outright statement made by those vendors in the contract that 'the sale by the target of its fixed assets at their balance sheet carrying values would not give rise to a tax liability', the vendors can respond to that demand by either:

---

[15] It is a drafting convention that words or phrases defined in a legal agreement as carrying a specific meaning are indicated in the text of the agreement by capital letters.

- signing the contract in the belief[16] that the statement is true. If it subsequently transpires that it was not true, that will constitute a breach of warranty;

- declining to sign the contract with that warranty included as one of its terms. There are warranties asked for on occasion which it would not be appropriate for the vendor to give; and unless one side or the other backs down, one has a 'deal-breaker' position. But this hardly seems likely to be the case in relation to the warranty that we are considering because there is a third course open to the vendor;

- disclosing the extent to which the statement is untrue.

We will see below that it can usually be arranged that disclosure allows the vendor to escape liability for *breach* of a warranty, but that it emphatically does not enable him to escape any effects which disclosure itself may bring (the most obvious of these being a demand by the predator for an adjustment of the price). One of the objectives of the requests for warranties, particularly in the tax field, is to force full disclosure of the target's actual and prospective liabilities.

However, before we rush on to the effects of disclosures, we need to be quite clear what a warranty is and does.

12.12 *The implications of warranties*

Those without a legal training sometimes bracket the words warranties and indemnities as if they meant much the same, and had much the same effects. It is vital to understand how different they are, and the differences in the ways in which they work.

A warranty is (here) a statement made by the vendor, and admitted by him to be essential to the basis on which the predator contracts to purchase the target. If, between that contract and the date of completion (assuming that exchange of contracts is not followed immediately by completion, which does often happen) it turns out that a warranty is untrue, that *breach* entitles the predator to *rescind* the contract (to declare unilaterally that he declines to proceed to completion), without incurring any liability by doing so. This would be the ultimate sanction, in that the contract will normally spell out that only a material breach of warranty, or some material event or circumstance which renders a warranty untrue, misleading or incomplete, would be expected to be

---

[16] The vendors' lawyers will attempt to write into the contract that the vendor only gives warranties, or at least some warranties, 'to the best of his knowledge and belief', this being done in an attempt to absolve the vendor from liability if he did believe, after proper enquiry, that white was white – even though subsequent events showed that it had been black all the time. This is always, however, a hotly contested area, and vendors' lawyers tend therefore to concentrate on putting this qualification on certain specific warranties only, rather than all; they try to identify those where the vendor could not know what the real position would turn out to be, in the fullness of time. On which of these bases would a builder give a warranty that none of the houses he had sold in the past ten years would be found to have latent defects in their construction?

taken by the predator as a pretext for rescission. The predator's more usual course before completion would be to call on the vendor to *remedy* the breach. Many remedies take the form of payments of cash by the vendor – if for instance he has warranted that the target's pension scheme is fully funded, and it turns out to have a deficit, then a payment by the vendor (or the target) to the trustees is clearly the appropriate form of remedy. A breach of the potential-tax-liability warranty we have been considering is less clearly remediable by injecting cash into the target – it might be more appropriate to agree a price reduction for the target to recognise the over-hanging tax charge. A breach of a warranty coming to light after completion gives the predator grounds for seeking damages.

A predator should not ask for, and a vendor should decline to give (should he be asked) warranties about information in the public domain. The predator can find for himself information about the target's market place, for instance, without the vendor warranting that it is one of only two cutlery manufacturers in Sheffield, whereas 30 years ago there were a hundred. The reason is obvious; the predator could not claim to have relied on information from the vendor when making the purchase, if it was readily available from other sources – or at best he could only claim that the degree of the vendor's contributory negligence was so small as to be properly ignored.

12.13 *The implications of warranties (continued)*

What might be called the *original warranties* will in part have been given as at the Accounting Date, and in part at the contract date. The potential-tax-liability warranty could only have any straightforward application as at the Accounting Date since it needs to be made by reference to the carrying values of fixed assets in the Warranted Accounts drawn up to that date. The fully-funded-pension-scheme warranty could logically be made as at the date of the contract, since the employer will have been required to make periodic contributions into the scheme after the Accounting Date as well as before, and the level of each of those contributions will have been set by the actuary to achieve, and maintain, what he had considered an adequate level of funding.

However, most contracts require that the vendors' warranties 'be deemed repeated at Completion'; the implication is that changed circumstances may have rendered untrue at completion what had been true at the Accounting Date or the date of contract. If breaches of these repeated warranties come to light subsequently, it will self-evidently be too late for rescission or remedy, and the predator's relief will be by way of an action for damages.

But we made the point at the end of paragraph 12.8 that there is no breach of a warranty if the vendor discloses that what the predator has invited him to say is not in fact true. Thus, the vendor might disclose that although, at the Accounting Date, a realisation of all other fixed assets at their balance sheet carrying values would produce no tax liability, that was not true of the target's office accommodation in a development area, where a disposal of the *relevant interest* would give rise to a claw-back of capital allowances of £x. As regards the repetition of such a warranty at completion, the vendor needs to be very clear what it is he is being asked to say. If it is no more than that 'it was true when I originally told you, and is still true now, that if I had sold the assets as at the Accounting Date, such and such would have been the result', then there is little problem in repetition. But if repetition is phrased in terms of a notional sale of assets *at completion*, that requires a hypothetical balance sheet from which notional carrying values, based on notional depreciation policy, can be derived.

12.14 *Disclosures against warranties, and the disclosure letter*

Let us have a recap of the rules:

- predator asks vendor to warrant the truth of some statement on the basis that predator will thereafter be able to say, should the statement prove untrue, that he (the predator) had relied on it when contracting to buy the target, and that the vendor knew that he (the predator) was relying on it for this purpose, so that the breach entitles the predator to be compensated (if the time for rescission is past);

- vendor says that he cannot give the warranty requested because the statement is not true (or is untrue to an extent described). He therefore says that his *disclosure* means that the predator cannot claim to have been relying on the warranty when he entered into the contract – and therefore there is no possibility that the predator can claim to have suffered damage by reason of any action or negligence by the vendor;

- predator demands an indemnity (which is the next subject we will come to).

What that makes obvious, if it has not been obvious before now, is that the whole process of disclosure of information by the vendor to the predator (and the predator's agents, his lawyers and accountants, for instance) needs to be tightly controlled. What the predator needs is:

- to be able to identify those whites that he did not have any means of knowing were actually black;

- but where he had in entering into the contract relied on the supposition that they were white;

- and the vendor had contributed to the predator's error and made no effort to disabuse him thereafter.

The second and third are the points that encourage the predator to demand warranties on every conceivable subject. And it is because of the first that the predator tries to insist that nothing has been *disclosed* in a satisfactory manner unless it has been included in the formal *disclosure letter* which usually forms one of the schedules to the contract.

12.15 *Indemnities contrasted with warranties*

The legal characteristics of an indemnity are essential to an understanding of the part that the giving of indemnities plays in the acquisition process.

It is in the capacity of a *covenantor* that the vendor (or someone standing behind him to assure the predator that the vendor's obligations will be met) gives his indemnity. His covenant (promise) is simply that he will pay the predator such an amount of money as is necessary to *restore the predator's financial position*, should some specified subsequent event show that the predator had acquired a target whose assets were less than they had been represented to be, or (generally more pertinent) whose liabilities were greater than had been claimed. The covenantor's promise is effectively unilateral, although the deed is likely also to contain undertakings by the predator concerning the conduct of the claim – a matter we will hold over for discussion in paragraph 12.32 below. The predator does not need to show that there has been a breach of a contract, and that he is entitled to damages. All that he needs is to demonstrate that a liability (defined in the deed) has crystallised, and that of itself necessitates the covenantor making the payment.

Another distinction between the rights that a predator may have to recover damages for breach of a warranty, and to recover under an indemnity, is that the general law limits actions under an *agreement* to a six-year period whereas a claim under a *deed* has twice as long a period before it becomes barred. The effective periods within which claims must be notified and quantified under each are, however, normally agreed between the parties (in the contract and the deed respectively) at numbers of years rather less than the outside limits allowed by law. By way of contrast, when it comes to limiting the total liability under warranties and indemnities, it is usual for the limits to apply to the aggregate of claims under both the warranties and the indemnities. Such limits may specify minimum sizes for any individual claims; stipulate that no claim will actually be paid unless the aggregate of the individual items comprising it is over a minimum amount; and provide that the maximum payable can never exceed (for instance) the original consideration.

The liabilities most commonly covered by indemnities are those for tax, but indemnities may cover any potential liability or any other matter which would have the effect of reducing the target's net assets. Indemnities may be in quite general terms, or when an indemnity is agreed upon following a specific disclosure, it may be drafted in considerable detail. If we go back to tax indemnities, these are normally set out in a self-contained deed of indemnity, frequently referred to as the tax deed, or the tax covenant. But to understand what it involves, and the concepts upon which it is based, one first needs to think rather clearly about target companies and the taxes they might become liable to pay. And that leads us to consider the wider subject of how targets' profits may be dealt with; this whole series of paragraphs has been covered by the principal heading on paragraph 12.10, 'The Warranted Accounts'. We need to think what the predator is looking to receive from the target and from the vendors, out of those accounts, and subsequently.

12.16 Profits and pricing

There is no right answer, and no wrong; what follows is merely one way in which acquisitions can be handled, and frequently are. Its merits are perhaps its simplicity, a certain logic, and the fact that it is widely accepted.

The vendors sell, and the predator purchases, on the basis of the Warranted Accounts, drawn up to an Accounting Date which we have assumed to be approximately six months before the date of the contract, perhaps therefore more than six months before completion.

The target's beneficial owners up to the contract date (or the date it becomes unconditional) are the vendor shareholders, and they remain its legal owners up to completion. The subject matter of the sale is shares in the target company, but we can see the principles involved if we contrast this position with what we would recognise as *right* had that subject matter been tenanted land. We would say in that case that the vendor was selling a capital asset, land, but that the income that the land produced should continue to flow into the vendors' hands until completion, and from then the purchaser should become entitled to those rents. But we know that shareholders do not normally receive, and certainly have no absolute right to, each period's *profit attributable*.

After the vendors identify what they want to take out in the form of pre-disposal dividends,[17] they can demand a price for their company which reflects not only the balance of those profits it has earned up to the Accounting Date, but also those it can be expected to earn (assuming continuation of business on a normal basis) through to the date of completion.[18]

12.17 Identifying tax liabilities for indemnification

The principle in the last paragraph could loosely be described as the predator acquiring the company *cum-profits*, in that any ordinary profit earned from normal trading since the Accounting Date remains in the target and goes to the predator; so also do all the earlier profits, to the extent they have been retained at the Accounting Date, and are reflected in the target's assets at that date. In all of these cases the actual and prospective profits are, so far as the target's own accounts are concerned, calculated from *its* base costs for stock in trade and work in progress; while in the larger perspective, the extent of the predator's benefit from these target activities depends on the price the predator paid, which may have first been based on the Warranted Accounts, but which the parties mentally adjusted to accommodate these further profits, and the assets representing them, retained within the target at completion.

---

[17] See paragraph 11.15.
[18] It would in the alternative be possible to draw up accounts to completion, and to adjust a price fixed at the earlier Accounting Date to reflect the profits earned in the intervening period (post-tax profits presumably, although that is arguable) but we are demonstrating that there is no inescapable need for such precision.

If this is the basis of the purchase, it is logical and equitable that the target should expect to bear the tax on these profits – that the vendors should not be expected to shoulder this tax. Thus the documentation will say, or fail to say, a number of things:

- there will be a warranty that tax liabilities for periods up to the Accounting Date have been provided in the Warranted Accounts, this being necessary for the predator's evaluation of the assets and liabilities of the target at that date;

- there may be a warranty or other provision in the contract, particularly if some time has elapsed since the Accounting Date, about ordinary profits since that date. But if there is such a provision, it usually takes the form of a warranty that the latest management accounts show the trading position since the Accounting Date, that there is nothing untoward about this. But one would not expect any undertaking that the vendor would make good any tax liabilities on these profits in the type of deal we are envisaging in these paragraphs;

- the deed of indemnity will say that the vendors will indemnify the purchaser for *all* tax liabilities which crystallise after the date of the deed *except* for two classes (we are dealing in this paragraph only with liabilities on ordinary trading profits). The first exception is that the vendors will not give an indemnity for liabilities which have been provided for in the Warranted Accounts; and the second is that they will not give an indemnity for tax on profits earned subsequent to the Accounting Date (before or after completion), so far as these arise on the ordinary trading profits we have been discussing. The second, as we will see, is contrary to the deed's general thrust.

12.18 *Identifying tax liabilities for indemnification (continued)*

Besides its straightforward liabilities on trading profits, a target can be expected to have three other types of tax liability, and if we explain how they can appropriately be dealt with in the documentation, we will at the same time see how the predator tries to ensure that he knows what liabilities he is taking on with the target. In all cases, he will have to assume that any of these transactions occurring before the Accounting Date will be shown in the Warranted Accounts, and that in his investigations of those accounts he will be able to see whether adequate tax provisions have been made.

(1) Tax liabilities which arise out of specific actions taken by the target, rather than the day-to-day accrual of trading profits. The sale of a fixed asset for a capital gain is an example, so is a sale of a capital allowance asset giving rise to a claw-back of allowances, and a third is the payment of a dividend on which an ACT liability arises. The predator will demand that the vendors warrant that no such transaction has occurred since the Accounting Date up to the date of completion. If the vendors disclose any occurrence, the predator will wish to ensure that the target has resources to meet the tax. This is not

a type of liability which will be excluded from the deed of indemnity, but the predator will regard his ability to call on the covenantors for payment as a fall-back which he would hope not to have to use.

(2) Tax liabilities which arise out of a combination of actions, one of which may have been taken by the vendors/target before completion or may have been completion itself, but the second of which is either completion (again) or some other action taken by the predator thereafter. The classic example here is the intra-group transfer of an asset into the target in the six years before completion, for which completion triggers off a section 179 liability[19] (although if the intra-group transfer had been between two target companies which are sold together, it would be the predator's later sale of one or other of them which would trigger off the charge). The predator's difficulty is often that of bringing the original transfer to light. He will demand warranties, and if these are erroneously given he will have grounds for seeking damages. But his right to be indemnified by the covenantors may be a simpler route.

12.19 Identifying tax liabilities for indemnification (continued)

(3) The third of the potential tax exposures of the target is the easiest to overlook, but at the same time can frequently be by far the largest and most difficult to deal with. The target might, as an example, have been paying round sum expense allowances to staff without accounting for PAYE.[20] It is abundantly clear that the tax liability arises because *employees* have income on which tax should be paid, but the Revenue's statutory entitlement is to demand that the *employer* should pay over the tax to them. We could put a broad description on this whole area of target tax exposure by describing it as tax for which the company is liable to account, as opposed to tax for which in the days before pay and file it was liable to be assessed.

The predator will obviously demand warranties from the vendor that the target has complied with not only its PAYE obligations, but all other requirements that it collect the Revenue's, and Customs', taxes on their behalf and account for these to the authorities. He will ask for information about the most recent PAYE, and VAT, audits performed on the target's operations – and would be well advised to recognise that a single company may well have more than one *PAYE scheme* so that an audit of one only of these should perhaps not be regarded as giving total comfort.

What must be very much less satisfactory for the predator in these circumstances is to have to rely on the vendor's warranty that the

---

[19] See paragraph 11.5 for an explanation of this provision designed to prevent the envelope trick.
[20] The principles under which the Inland Revenue determine what is *pay* for PAYE were briefly explained (in relation to directors) in paragraph 8.9, particularly in subparagraph (d) and Note 25 thereon.

Warranted Accounts contain full provision for all of the target's tax liabilities up to the Accounting Date. There might have been no allowances paid before then, so the warranty was correct. If there had been earlier allowances, one has to assume that the target's wages staff thought they were operating within the law, that they believed the expenses had been properly incurred. Thus the 'best of the knowledge and belief' of the vendors justified their warranty. An Inland Revenue challenge made, and accepted by the predator, after completion might not be an entirely satisfactory base from which the predator could seek damages from the vendors for breach of warranties.

The predator would say that an unqualified warranty would be quite adequate, but would also admit that an indemnity was better. In practice they are not alternatives, but both are used.

12.20 *Devising the formula which defines the liabilities to be indemnified*

What we have seen in the last three paragraphs is:

- the general rule is that all tax liabilities which crystallise after the date of the contract are to be indemnified;

- but there are certain exceptions. First, any liability which has been provided in the Warranted Accounts is excluded – that is straightforward;

- next we saw at the end of paragraph 12.17 that liabilities on ordinary trading profits earned after the Accounting Date are to be excluded (at least on the basis of our assumptions about the deal that has been struck);

- but for the specific *actions* in the first subparagraph in 12.18 the indemnity does need to cover liabilities arising from actions after the Accounting Date – in this case the cut-off date is completion;

- under the second subparagraph in 12.18 what needs to be indemnified is any liability flowing from a *two-part transaction* of which the first part takes place at any time before completion (whether before or after the Accounting Date), or where completion is itself the first part;

- then in paragraph 12.19 what we must seek to do is identify all those liabilities which relate to periods or events before completion and which the target has not itself *got under control*. The informality of language recognises that it is simply not possible to adopt the concepts of provisions in Warranted Accounts. Eleven months into an accounting period the tax authorities assume that the profits a company has earned are zero in the context that its tax liability on these ordinary activities can correctly be shown in its books at zero; one month later a tax liability crystallises, and the statutory accounts drawn to that date must needs reflect it. But when one thinks of the month-by-month build up, and payment off,

- of PAYE collection and liability
- of NIC collection and liability
- of ACT, and income tax withheld from annual payments
- of VAT collection from customers, payment to suppliers, and payment of the net difference to Customs & Excise,

the extent of the covenantor's liability under the indemnity he is asked to give is rather more difficult to define.

12.21 *Devising the formula which defines the liabilities to be indemnified (continued)*

If what one needed to do, in order to draft a deed of indemnity, was to quantify the covenantor's liability then the drafting would be difficult indeed. Defining each category of liability, including the start- and end-point of each, would be equally complex.

Fortunately the draftsman's task is slightly easier. First, he needs only to provide for liabilities, or in the phrase customarily used in deeds 'claims for taxation'. He can assume that the authorities will not *claim* anything which has already been paid over to them (or if they do, the target will have the demand cancelled). Next he will limit the claims to be indemnified by saying that it is only taxation that results from an *event* before completion, including the event of completion itself. This gives him the appropriate cut-off, provided he makes the definition of *event* wide enough to cover the sale of the capital asset giving rise to a capital gain, the payment of a dividend giving rise to ACT, the neglect of a PAYE requirement to withhold tax from a round sum allowance to an employee, and the first part of the two-part transaction which gives rise to the section 179 liability – just to give some examples.

Then he can start to narrow his ambit to exclude the specific matters against which it is agreed that the covenantor will not indemnify him. In the illustration we have been looking at, this means the tax liabilities on ordinary trading profits after the Accounting Date; but another normal example is usually described as the predator's voluntary act outside the normal scope of its business. If the purchaser acquires the two target companies referred to in the parenthesis in (2) in paragraph 12.18, one of those companies having earlier transferred an asset intra-group to the other, then the predator's sale of one or other company will trigger off a section 179 liability; why should the covenantor meet this, when it was the predator's choice to trigger the liability?

The complexities of the drafting must not, however, obscure the purposes of this whole exercise. The predator needs to investigate – to identify – the target's exposures; warranties can help in the identification process, but predators and vendors can miss things, and suing for damages under breached warranties is uncertain. The indemnities are the second string to the predator's bow.

12.22 The predator's objective – including the special case of the predator which is a company owned by a management buy-out team

In the main sections of this chapter so far we have looked at the *Heads of Agreement* and the *Purchase Contract*, and have spent quite a lot of time explaining how the warranties and indemnities fit into the latter, and also fit with the target's *Warranted Accounts* which we have assumed play an important role in the predator's decision whether he wants to buy, and if so at what price (and with what covenants and guarantees). But this has been a lawyer's look – from a lawyer's perspective – at an acquisition process seen as principally driven by drafting; investigation and negotiation have been grossly underemphasised.

We must recognise where the centre of gravity really lies: in the hands of the predator. It is only as a part of the predator's team that the lawyer does his enquiring, drafting and negotiating, and similarly that the accountant does his investigating.

It is the predator, as leader of the team, who needs to have very clearly in his sights at all times:

- precisely what he is negotiating to acquire. This may of course be an established company; or merely a trade to be taken out of such a company, perhaps with some assets from another; or it may be a newly formed company into which the trade and assets concerned have been *hived down*[21] by the vendors. We will look in the next paragraph at some of the advantages and disadvantages of hive-downs;

- precisely what he is prepared to allow the vendor to do to the target before sale. At its simplest, this may be the stripping out of a pre-disposal dividend (see paragraph 11.15). At a more complex level, it may be that some unbundling of the company is involved (as in the illustration in paragraphs 11.7 to 11.9);

- precisely what he is prepared to pay. This question will lead us directly into what we describe in paragraph 12.29 below as the continuous evaluation process which the predator should be engaged in as the acquisition process unfolds, and as more information comes into his hands;

But there are two other particular aspects. We need to explore in rather more depth what are the implications for the predator of acquiring a company into which a trade and assets have been hived down, and we will look at the technicalities, and at the strategy, in paragraphs 12.23 to 12.27.

The other point is rather different. If it is a management buy-out team which is behind the predator, everything else that we have, and will, notice in this chapter is still relevant, but there are some additional points that drive this particular class of predators:

---

[21] As will become apparent in paragraph 12.23, we are using the word 'hive-down' in an extended sense.

- if, as will generally be the case, the buy-out team is supported initially by a bank supplying a part of the finance for the buy-out, it is likely that this will be some mixture of straightforward loan, *mezzanine*, and equity. From that buy-out team's point of view, the cost of their acquisition therefore has to be seen as a mixture of the immediate price of the target, and the price of repaying/buying out the bank at a point in the medium term future. It is not sensible to produce one line answers to problems all of which differ, but it is quite probable that a part of the answer may be the company's purchase of its own shares from the bank (and in particular such a purchase out of the proceeds of a new issue), all of this being a subject we look at in some detail in chapter 13;

- it will also generally be the case that the management buy-out team, and perhaps other managers and staff, will have borrowed money to subscribe for the shares in their predator company (which will thereafter become the owner of the target, the latter being a trading company while the predator is not). The problems of ensuring that the interest payable on such loans is deductible against the income of the individual borrowers is not insuperable, but it does need care. The main sections in the tax legislation are 360(1) and 361(3) of the Taxes Act 1988;

- third, it will almost inevitably be found, when arrangements are fully analysed, that the target provided or continues to provide financial assistance to the predator for the purchase of the target's shares. This does not prevent the transaction, but it does necessitate a *whitewash* by the target's directors and shareholders in the manner indicated in paragraph 9.24. The special point here is that the target's viability is of equal interest to the financiers as to members of the buy-out team.

12.23 Hive-downs

It will be recalled from paragraphs 11.10 and 11.11 that the normal meaning of *hive-down* is a transfer of a trade and assets from a parent to its subsidiary, which may be done for shares or for cash. The tax consequences will be somewhat different if the parent is in liquidation at the time of this transfer. There is another transaction referred to in paragraph 11.18 which would not normally be thought of as a hive-down, namely the transfer of a trade and assets into a company owned by the same shareholders as own the transferor — the trade and assets in this case moving across on a tax-free basis under section 139 TCGA 1992. We will look at these as three separate possibilities:

- live parent to subsidiary;
- parent in liquidation to subsidiary;
- company to parallel company in same ownership.

In all three cases the carry forward of losses from transferor to transferee, and the continuity of capital allowance treatment between them should be available regardless of the later change of ownership of the company into which the trade has been hived down.[22] This is subject to two qualifications; first, there is a restriction on the amount of losses that can be carried forward in a case in which the transferor's losses have rendered it insolvent,[23] because there would otherwise be a possible doubling up of losses, first as trading losses in the transferee company, and second as a loss on the shareholders' investment in the transferor or as a loss in the form of bad debts incurred by those, including associated companies, who may have supplied the transferor. The second restriction occurs if there is a major change in the nature or conduct of the trade, comparing the positions of the transferor's trade in which the losses have been incurred with the trade the transferee carries on thereafter.[24] This second restriction is not something that can necessarily be determined and quantified at the time of the transferee's change of ownership; it depends how the new owner of that transferee develops its activities thereafter, and is in that sense a matter of the predator's own choice. No predator could possibly expect a disponor to warrant that losses available at the time of hive-down would be capable of being set off thereafter.

In all three cases, stock in trade and work in progress will move across from transferor to transferee at the price agreed between the parties, and put through their accounts, whether this is an open market value or not.[25]

---

[22] Section 343 TA 1988 deals with losses and capital allowances – see paragraphs 11.11 and 11.14, and has the effect of carrying them forward from one corporate entity to its successor. After such a carry forward there can be a *subsequent* restriction on the amounts usable, if there is a change in the ownership of the successor entity, and certain other changes which we will look at in Note 24 below. But there are of course other tax reliefs which are incapable of the leap from one corporate entity to another. One, for instance, is the advance corporation tax. If the predecessor had paid ACT on a dividend, its successor can never claim the benefit of that payment against a later years's corporation tax liability.

[23] Section 343(4) TA 1988.

[24] Section 768 TA 1988. This provision deals, in the hive-down context, with a change in the nature or conduct of the trade, comparing the way in which the loss-making trade was carried on in the hands of the previous company, with the way it is subsequently carried on by the transferee company. The provision is simply designed to restrict the level of the losses transferred by section 343 which can be utilised against profits generated after the change. The fact that the ultimate ownership of the transferor before the hive-down, and of the the hive-down company after it, are different is an essential part of the provision's applicability, but the actual hive-down itself has no relevance – the company actually trading before and after the change in the conduct and so on of the trade, and the change in its ownership, can be the same corporate entity or different.

Thus, where a target company is sold in a straightforward way by a disponor to a predator, the section might be relevant. The likelihood of this is perhaps less in such a case, where predators generally buy companies with a view to continuing and increasing their activities; as compared to the position in the liquidation of a company, where predators may buy 'shells' (to use the word loosely) in the hope that they can be built into something rather different from what the company in liquidation may have achieved.

The provision also applies where an earlier trade had shrunk to little or nothing, but in the predator's hands it is built up again to a significant size.

[25] Sections 100(1)(a) and 101(1)(a) TA 1988.

But the capital gains tax position will be different for the three different cases:

- where the trade and assets are transferred by a company not in liquidation to its subsidiary, this is an intra-group transfer giving the parent no gain or loss, but creating a section 179 liability if the parent then sells its subsidiary;

- where the parent is in liquidation, its transfer of assets to its subsidiary is treated for its capital gains tax purposes as being made at open market value.[26] The sale of the subsidiary is not 'leaving a group' and section 179 does not apply.[27]

- the third case is that of the companies which are owned by the same shareholders, but are not part of a capital gains tax group. (We know that the transfer of assets from one to the other is not protected from being a distribution, see paragraphs 11.17 and 11.18 and Note 33 on the latter.) However, provided that the transaction is accepted by

---

[26] Although, as explained in Note 27 below, the sense in which a parent in liquidation *owns* its subsidiary is a rather special sense of that word, it is unquestionably true, for reasons explained in that Note, that this transfer could not be covered by the intra-group transfer (capital gains tax free) provision in section 171 TCGA 1992. It is equally clear that parent and subsidiary are not at arm's length, and that section 17(1)(a) TCGA 1992 therefore applies to substitute market value for any other figure which the liquidator may put on the transfer.

[27] When a company goes into liquidation it ceases to be the beneficial owner of its assets, but they remain legally vested in it. The company's directors cease to be able to deal with those assets, and it is the liquidator who will thereafter sell them or otherwise deal on the company's behalf with them. But the liquidator's standing, and that of the directors, is not the relevant point. The assets' beneficial ownership goes into suspense on liquidation (*Ayerst v C & K (Construction) Ltd* [1975] 2 All ER 537); if the liquidator forms a subsidiary company, the ownership of its shares will similarly be in suspense. The company's disposal of any asset, including its disposal of the shares in the subsidiary referred to in the previous sentence, is made by it (by the liquidator acting in right of the company) for the benefit of the company's creditors and contributories – and in that sense can be regarded as similar to a dealing with trust property. But each such disposal is a disposal by the company for capital gains tax purposes, on which the company is potentially chargeable to tax.

Prior to the company's (the liquidator's) disposal of its assets as above, and despite the fact stated above that the beneficial ownership of those assets has become suspended, they are not regarded as having ceased to belong to the company for capital gains tax purposes; that is to say, the passing of the resolution to wind up changes the nature of the company's ownership of its assets, but does not constitute a disposal by it and an acquisition by the liquidator of all of its assets (if for no other reason than that there cannot be a disposal without any transfer).

If we moved out of the hive-down context to consider the position where the company being liquidated owned a subsidiary before it went into liquidation, the passing of the resolution to liquidate would not break the group relationship (section 170(11) TCGA 1992). When at a later stage the company disposed of that subsidiary, that would be a capital gains tax disposal, and the breaking of the group. It is therefore possible that section 179 *might* be applicable at that stage – but only for assets transferred between parent and subsidiary on an intra-group basis, which by definition must mean transfers before the parent went into liquidation, not after. No part of these last three sentences is relevant to the hive-down transaction for a company whose liquidation has commenced prior to the time of that hive-down.

the Inland Revenue as being carried out for *bona fide* commercial reasons, and not for tax avoidance, then a trade or undertaking, together with its assets, moves for capital gains tax into the transferee at the transferor's base cost.[28] When the transferee's shareholders sell their shares in that company, that does not constitute any leaving of a group; it is true in that sense that this transaction does seem to allow the vendor to put his asset into an envelope, and sell the envelope, without section 179 biting.[29]

Thus the predator may be buying a hive-down company with assets inside it having an original (vendor group) cost in heads 1 and 3, or having an open market cost in head 2. And the predator will be running into an automatic and unavoidable section 179 liability in head 1, but not in the other cases. It is obviously important, as we pointed out in the last paragraph, that the predator knows precisely what he is buying.

12.24 Hive-downs, identifying what the predator is acquiring

The last paragraph highlighted the fact that stock in trade and work in progress should move from transferor to transferee at whatever price is agreed between them; that the acquisition price of capital allowance assets for the transferee will be the 'written down value' in the transferor's computations; but that the acquisition price of capital gains assets will depend on which of the three possible hive-down methods has been used – and so also will the question whether the transferee company arrives in the predator's hands with a section 179 liability triggered off by its change of ownership.

That is all very interesting and theoretical. Of much greater interest to the predator is the commercial reality. He is acquiring a company whose books and accounts show no history of the activities which it has so recently acquired. It may be described by the vendor (particularly if he is a liquidator) as a 'clean company', meaning that as a corporate entity it has no over-hanging legal exposures – that it cannot for instance be sued or prosecuted for some transaction which the transferee may have been involved in before it (or perhaps its parent) went into liquidation. However, even that cleanliness is less sparkling than it once may have been. We have examined in paragraphs 11.36 to 11.41, for instance, the Transfer of Undertakings (Protection of Employment) Regulations, whose effect can be to saddle the hive-down company with considerable liabilities for redundancy for employees, based not just on service with it but on prior service with the predecessor company.

---

[28] Section 139 TCGA 1992.
[29] But although the tax legislation encourages us to think that this is an unproblematical transaction (the transfer of a company's assets into a *parallel* company, which gives no consideration to the transferor, only issues its shares to the shareholders of that transferor), we have seen in paragraphs 9.13 and 11.8 that it is most unlikely to be legitimate under normal Companies Act principles. In paragraph 14.5 below we conclude that it is likely only to be possible if done under a scheme approved by the court under either section 425 CA 1985 or section 110 Insolvency Act 1986.

What the predator needs is information – if he is to make a rational decision whether to buy, and if so at what price. One piece of information he needs relates to the TUPE regulations, as indicated; but there is much more.

12.25 *Hive-downs, identifying what the predator is acquiring (continued)*

This book does not pretend to be a treatise on how to make acquisitions, particularly not a treatise which guarantees the reader that he will not get his fingers burned in the process. Our objective throughout has been to look at the legal and accounting framework within which the businessman does his damnedest. But when we were looking in paragraphs 12.10 to 12.14 at the framework of warranties asked for by the predator and his lawyer from the disponor and its lawyer, we saw the way in which these warranties fitted with, supplemented, and above all attempted to give an enforceable character to, the target-information which the disponor was giving in support of his asking price.

What the predator should still be looking for is target-information. The form in which he must now seek it will be somewhat different; what happened in the past does still have some relevance as an indication of what might continue to happen in the future – but the normal warning contained in that phraseology has three further aspects to it. First, if what is being hived down into a target company is less than the whole activities of the transferor, or is cobbled together from the activities of more than one company in the transferor group, how easy is it to obtain a reliable guide to what would have been the separate results of these activities if they had each been accounted for as a discrete entity?

Second, how certain can one be that the business has not melted away in the sale process? For instance, there may be some degree of loyalty from the purchasers of ink on paper towards the printing company which sells them the service of putting the first on the second. But the one thing those purchasers will always insist on is that their printer must be able to deliver faultless work to a deadline. The very fact that the printing business is hived down and sold can be enough to fracture customers' confidence – and there is little doubt in the printing trade at present that there are more printers looking for business than there are customers looking to have their needs fulfilled.

12.26 *Hive-downs; verification, and the business's records*

It is however in the third area that there should be more scope for the predator to investigate what he is buying; there should be a possibility that he can give some degree of enforceability to his acquisition by means of warranties (or even indemnities, although these must be less likely); and he must recognise that getting things wrong will be a total disaster.

An illustration will bring out the point. The business of a package holiday company succeeds or fails dependent on its ability to charter economically the flights which its customers want, and to hire economically the hotel accommodation they require. In the case of flights, that ideally means the company being able to fill entire aircraft, but as a second best it necessitates the company knowing some considerable time in advance the numbers flying out, and returning, who will have to have space found for them on other operators' charters. What could be disastrous for a predator would be to acquire a target business whose commitments were inadequately recorded.

Holidaymakers pay a deposit of 10 per cent when they book, probably in the early months of the year. They pay the remaining 90 per cent a matter of a few weeks before departure. If it is only when they offer (or are asked for) that balance of the price that the operator can see precisely what dates of outward and return flights had been promised to each of them; if his bookings of aircraft are then found to have been incorrect; but if he knows that being scrupulous in honouring his commitments is the only way in which he can continue to sell holidays in a highly competitive marketplace; then his having acquired a target company in reliance on records of its commitments which later proved to be inadequate can correctly be called a disaster. (He must of course also expect some melting away of holidaymakers who, after paying the initial deposit to the previous business, hear that it is in trouble and are willing to abandon that deposit for the certainty that rebooking elsewhere appears to offer.)

12.27 *Hive-downs; verification, and the business's records (continued)*

The predator's requirements are no different from what he needs in any other case:

- details of the assets he is buying – in the example we have been looking at the asset is intangible, simply the benefit of holidaymakers' custom and contracts;

- details of the commitments he is taking on. Our illustration graphically brought out how vital is the need for accurate information in the package holiday business, but in other businesses the need may be just as great.

If a predator is acquiring an established company, he may equate earning power over the years immediately preceding the acquisition, with the ownership of, and ability to operate, the assets with which those profits were earned; and equate it also with what he may realistically assume to be the business's continuing future commitments for goods or services to be supplied to customers. But we should never lose sight of the fact that the only reason anyone ever investigates the target company's past on behalf of a predator is to form a view of what the future holds for that target in the ownership of the predator concerned.

That future is dependent on:

- the existence of the profit-making machinery, whatever is its form in the case that is being considered;

- the target's title to that machinery;

- the fact that profit-making machinery consists, as it necessarily should, of two interlocking parts, namely the ability to deliver, and the availability of purchasers for the product;
- those purchasers' contracts for what the business has said it can and will deliver being of a kind, a volume, and at a schedule of future dates, which the business can meet;
- the cleanliness of the company he is being offered.

Each of those is reasonably easy to identify, but not necessarily so simple to quantify and to verify – and must, if the vendor will give access, be investigated for the predator. If the vendor can be pressurised into giving it, each could be the subject of a warranty. If neither access nor warranties are available, the predator must understand how little he has to rely on in relation to the deal being offered. There are other less tangible factors, such as management availability and quality, where 'investigation' can only be less scientifically carried out, and warranties are clearly not appropriate.

Success in acquisitions means analysis of what is on offer, not just in the sense of examining the target, but examining how it can best be examined; not just contracting to purchase it, but ensuring that that purchase can be properly effected and enforced. Examination is the subject that we must look at next.

12.28 Due diligence

The phrase 'due diligence' originally referred to the investigations carried out by a merchant bank to decide whether it could promote an offer on behalf of a predator which wished to become the bank's client for this purpose – an offer to be made for some other listed (target) company. The bank's investigations were aimed at satisfying itself, first, that what the prospective client told the bank about itself was true; second, that what the predator wanted the bank to promote was a sensible bid – well judged, and within the predator's capability; and third, that that bid had a better than even chance of success. What merchant banks deprecate most is associating themselves with fraudsters or with failure.

That description of due diligence remains true for acquisitions of listed companies. In particular, the *investigation* that is possible for the bank under the third head will not include its having access to the books of a listed target, or being able to quiz its management. No shareholder or potential shareholder can be given access by a listed company to information not available to other shareholders. Therefore the bank and its team of accountants and lawyers will have to content themselves with analysing information in the public domain.[30]

---

[30] Merchant banks' value is that they are rather better than most others at organising the teams that do this investigating; that because of this, they add a degree of credibility and authority to what they put into the offer document which results from their investigations; and that they have skills in obtaining information which, although

continued

It is with unlisted, generally private, companies that we are principally concerned in this book. In this chapter's acquisitions, therefore, the phrase 'due diligence' is used with a rather different meaning, namely the combination of the investigation described above with a further one which the predator (and his team) are allowed by the vendors to carry out into the records and circumstances of the target.

That word 'allowed' does need to be stressed. No one can force the vendors to permit a potential purchaser to crawl all over a target. As we have seen, liquidators almost invariably sell their hived-down businesses on a take-it-or-leave-it basis, with little if any opportunity for the purchaser to discover what he is buying until he has paid his money and walked away with his prize. Other vendors tend to assume that they will only achieve a sale, and certainly will only achieve a sale at an acceptable price, if they are entirely open with the prospective predator. His demands for information (that is to say, for information which is to be warranted by the vendor) tend to be based at least in part on a belief that breaches of warranty have a value in themselves as grounds for actions for damages;[31] but we have already disparaged that as purely the lawyer's perspective.

12.29 Due diligence (continued)

The predator's perspective should be subtly different from that of his lawyers and accountants. Information gained in the course of all of their investigations[32] needs to be *put together*, and *put to use*, by the predator or under his close supervision, and it should have three main uses:

- identifying whether there is anything *wrong* with the target which would necessitate the predator calling off the deal. If this is to be done, both costs and faces will be saved if it is done rapidly rather than later;

- identifying grounds for reductions in consideration. Even if the actual amounts are not quantified on each occasion, what is needed

---

continued
it may technically be public, tends not to be easily accessible – the identity of the target's major shareholders and their likely response to an offer being examples. And of course merchant banks are entitled under the rules of the Stock Exchange and the Take-over Code to act as promoters, as well as having the appropriate authorisation under the Financial Services Act.

[31] If warranties are appropriate and have been given – but see paragraph 12.12. The predator and his merchant bank (whose investigations are limited to information in the public domain) can expect no warranties for the reason explained in that paragraph.

[32] The accountants' investigation can loosely be thought of as an *audit*, although there are in fact significant differences in aim and method. The lawyers' investigation tends to be in the form of questions and answers – the pre-contract enquiries will for instance elicit answers to such questions as whether the target has a pension scheme, if so, whether it is a defined benefit scheme, if so, whether it is fully funded, and so on. Apart from providing a key to the points which need further investigation and verification, all this gives a further guide to the contract drafting, and the structure of the deal.

is immediate raising of warning flags, not a boxful of flags tabled at the point the contract is due to be signed;

- and assuming the deal does finally proceed to completion, there is a real benefit obtainable from ensuring that the target does have the information about its affairs which is necessary for its sensible integration into the predator group. To give one straightforward example, harmonising terms of employment of the target's employees with those already employed in the predator group may not be easy, but one can be certain it would be even more difficult if there were any doubt over what were the employment terms, and length of service, of the target's employees.

Each of those heads indicated a *use* to which the predator could, and should, put the information he obtains. And there is a fourth use: at the time the parties signed the Heads, the vendors had a fairly firm idea what it was they wanted to sell, and what pre-disposal reorganisations they envisaged carrying out before doing so. Similarly, the predator also had a fair idea what he was trying to acquire, and the extent to which the vendor's proposals meshed with his requirements. But the investigations will almost certainly bring to light alterations that the predator will want to make. It may be, for instance, that he decides that he does not want to take on some particular subsidiary of the target, and that it needs to be transferred elsewhere in the vendor's group so as not to be included in the sale. Immediate flag-waving is even more important here than it is in relation to price adjustments.

Completion

12.30 *The last chance for altering or aborting the acquisition*

That last point, that the predator may well change his views on what he does and does not want as he becomes more familiar with what is on offer, has immensely important human dimensions which have to be slotted into the process of making the acquisition.

An example might best illustrate what could be involved, an illustration which moves us forward to the final stage in the process, namely completion. This can follow on immediately after contract, or it can be separated from it by an interval which is sufficiently long for the vendors to organise what needs to be done, to obtain any consents on the receipt of which the contract had been made conditional, and sufficiently short to satisfy the predator's wish to get his hands on the target, and to get on with the earning of profits in its business. When we mentioned completion briefly at the start of paragraph 12.9, we described it as the process under which legal ownership of the target (and of any other assets) was moved from the vendor to the predator – beneficial ownership having moved already on signature of the contract, or on a conditional contract becoming unconditional. And we said that if this were a part of the plan, if it were spelled out in the contract that this was part of the deal, at an appropriate point in the series of directors' and shareholders' meetings which completion involves, the target's existing directors would table their resignations, and the predator's replacements would be appointed in their stead. But let us suppose that this was not a part of the original plan; let us assume that the predator wanted to retain the existing management, had discussed this with them, and had agreed with them what would be the form of their service contracts. That last aspect is likely to have been drafted into the purchase contract, the precise terms of these service contracts (whether or not generous and long-lasting) being set out in the form of agreed drafts initialled by the parties, with a requirement that they be signed up at completion.

What we now imagine is the predator's change of mind. On the basis of what he discovers in the course of his investigation, he wants to sign up one of the two directors, but not the other. They are brothers, perhaps, each a substantial shareholder but there are further substantial holdings of shares spread around the family, and some of those family members have loyalties lying one way and some the other. That really does put the whole transaction back to the negotiation stage, and bring back to mind the problems of compensation for directors which we were considering in paragraphs 11.29 to 11.31.

12.31 *Completion – also the start of a different era for vendors, target and predator*

Legal title to the target passes to the predator at completion, and the purchase consideration is paid over; but that is not the end of the parties' contractual relationships, in fact there are a number of new rights and obligations which come into existence at completion. It is advisable to be aware of the main points that the parties would expect to write into the contract:

- the vendors and warrantors undertake to dissociate themselves from the target, not to represent themselves as any longer the owners of, or in any way involved in the management of, the target. This provision is commercially essential, but at the same time the extent and form of the publicity may need to be agreed, and handled jointly with care by the parties in a case in which the business's goodwill is based significantly on continuity of management, and continuity of its relationships with customers;

- the vendors may be expected to undertake not to compete with the target – including in particular not to solicit business from the target's customers, or otherwise to interfere with its business. The legal principles are clear but their application is not always easy. The general rule is:

  All interference with individual liberty of action in trading, and all restraints of trade of themselves, if there is nothing more, are contrary to public policy, and therefore void.[33]

---

[33] Per Lord Macnaghten in *Nordenfelt v Maxim Nordenfelt Guns and Ammunition Co. Ltd* [1894] AC 535 at 565.

But the words 'if there is nothing more' are cover for a number of different types of exception. The one most relevant is that a vendor who has built up a business and wishes to sell it is undoubtedly allowed to undertake not to compete; public policy allows (indeed encourages) him to give the purchaser an undertaking without which that purchaser's position would be *insecure*,[34] and therefore without which the vendor would not be able to realise the value of what he had built up.[35] But the correct procedure is to analyse what are the legitimate interests of (in this case) the predator which he wishes to protect, and to see whether the restraints that he seeks to impose are excessive – by reference to public policy, and also in reference to the freedom of individuals to earn their living. The balancing act was well illustrated in 1984 in the case of a solicitor prevented after retiring from partnership from working for clients of his former firm, which was held to be legitimate protection by it of its interests and in line with public policy that young solicitors should be enabled to join such firms in the knowledge that the firms' client-base and goodwill could not be cut away. The individual who had left the firm had an entitlement to earn his living, but the restrictions imposed on this were not unreasonable;[36]

- the vendor and the warrantors must expect continuing obligations to observe confidentiality about the business of the target, and probably also about the basis of its disposal to the predator;

- the vendor and warrantors need to decide whether they can agree to the predator having an unfettered right to assign to another party (for instance on the predator's onward disposal of the target or some part of its activities) the rights which the predator has against the vendor and warrantors – those rights for instance outlined in this paragraph, but also the general rights for breaches of warranty and so on. One of the more complex areas in which the ongoing interest and involvement of the vendor/warrantors, and the interests and involvements of the predator and target, may not be entirely in line is examined in the next paragraph. Complicating this further by making it possible that the vendor will need to deal not with the predator, but

---

[34] The word 'insecure' comes from the *Herbert Morris* case cited in Note 35. It chimes particularly happily with the rationale for the decision in the much more recent tax case of *Kirby v Thorn EMI plc* [1987] STC 621. A subsidiary of Thorn sold three of its subsidiaries to General Electric, and the purchaser, as well as paying Thorn's subsidiary for the companies, paid Thorn itself £316,000 for a covenant by Thorn that no company in its group would thereafter compete. The Court of Appeal decided that this was subject to corporation tax on capital gains in Thorn's hands as a sum derived from Thorn's *goodwill*, that is to say, its ability, if it had wanted, to acquire or establish subsidiaries in the same trades, to attract back the customers of the companies sold to General Electric.

[35] *Herbert Morris Ltd v Saxelby* [1916] 1 AC 688 at 713 to 714.

[36] *Bridge v Deacons* [1984] 1 AC 705, an appeal to the Privy Council from the Court of Appeal of Hong Kong. The Privy Council was not persuaded by the retired solicitor's own argument that his former firm was so much the largest firm in Hong Kong that preventing him from working for its former clients was effectively preventing him from working. But these cases are always matters of degree.

some assignee of the predator, (not identified at the time vendor and predator contract), adds further doubt to an already doubtful area.

12.32 Conduct of claims

This matter can best be illustrated in relation to *claims for taxation* made under the tax indemnity by the predator against the vendor (probably the claim will be made direct against the covenantors, and if they are different from the vendors they will have a right of recovery against the latter; but for present purposes it is simpler to discuss the problem as if it was the vendor who was in the front line). The general principles of the indemnity were explained in paragraph 12.15, and the way in which the indemnity is likely to be drafted in paragraph 12.21. What we did not go on to look at in that second paragraph was the extent to which it is reasonable for the predator to allow the vendor, if he is to be asked to pay tax demands, to be able to step into the predator's shoes to contest those liabilities with the Inland Revenue or with Customs and Excise.

The assessments will of course be raised against the target, so what we are really discussing is the possibility of the vendor standing behind that target, making the decisions, pulling the appropriate strings, and bearing the costs incurred in the dispute. Described like that, the procedure sounds as if it should be uncontroversial between predator and vendor. But life is seldom simple. The target and predator are likely to be concerned about their continuing good relationship with the tax authorities – the vendor's concern is only with the disputed liability, and if relationships are sacrificed for an immediate gain, aggressively won, that is what the vendor was seeking. Second, corporation tax and capital gains tax disputes can be taken to the Special or General Commissioners without any publicity, but a case appealed from there to the High Court immediately opens the target's business and business methods to public scrutiny.[37]

The *conduct of claims* clauses (in the deed of indemnity and for warranties in the purchase agreement) need careful consideration by the parties – against the background of any expected claims that may emerge, and in the light also of the parties' views on publicity and other aspects of disputations. What may be a minimum safeguard for each of the parties is agreement that no claim will be disputed without confirmation from a barrister agreed between them that they stand a more than even chance of success.

---

[37] There is an added difficulty if one tries to permit appeals to the Commissioners, but to prevent the case being taken on from there to the High Court. If a taxpayer wins at Commissioner level, and it is the Revenue who appeal to the High Court, the taxpayer is not allowed to go to the High Court for a consent order, that is to say an order in the Revenue's favour which will stop them from arguing their case in the High Court, in public. If the Commissioners as a judicial body concluded that the taxpayer is right, the High Court will not, without hearing argument, agree that the taxpayer was wrong; 'the law is a matter for decision by the Court after considering the case, and not for agreement between John Doe and Richard Roe, with the Court blindly giving its authority to whatever they have agreed', per Megarry J in *Slaney v Kean* [1969] 45 TC 415, at 416.

CHAPTER 13

COMPANY PURCHASES OF OWN SHARES

13.1 Introduction – Part 1: the law in 1980

The Companies Act 1980 enacted for the first time what had previously been a matter of case law,[1] that a company may not purchase its own shares. That legislation still exists, as section 143(1) of the Companies Act 1985.

But even at the time of its enactment, the principle was subject to a number of exceptions. These are not the subject which is our prime concern in this chapter, but it is useful to list them, to be able to see that that statement that a company cannot acquire its own shares had only ever been true in a limited sense:

- when a company reduces its capital, having obtained the consent of the court to do so, it is correct to say that it is the company which does the reduction – meaning that the company first acquires the shares and then cancels them. Neither it, nor the court, can make shares disappear while in the ownership of some other person;

- there are various other circumstances besides a pure capital reduction in which a court can order that a company acquire shares and cancel them, for instance the shares of a minority dissenting from a company's resolution to turn itself back from a public company to a private company, and the shares of a similar minority objecting to a change of the company's objects, also shares of a member who has suffered unfairly prejudicial conduct;[2]

- where a company's Articles provide for this, it can forfeit shares (including accepting shares surrendered to it in lieu of forfeiture) for non-payment of amounts due on those shares;

- and the 1980 Act also introduced a principle which seemed to be a breach of what was at that time thought to be the common law, that a company could not be a member of itself.[3] The 1980 provision[4] allowed a company to accept a transfer to itself of its own shares provided that it did not pay anything for them.

---

[1] *Trevor v Whitworth* [1887] 12 AC 409.
[2] Sections 54, 5 and 461, respectively, CA 1985.
[3] Although it had been clear prior to 1980 that shares in a company could be held by a nominee for it (*Kirby v Wilkins* [1929] 2 Ch. 444). The current provisions about nominees holding shares for the issuing companies are in sections 144 and onward CA 1985.
[4] Now section 143(3) CA 1985.

13.2 Introduction – Part 2: The Companies Act 1981 and the Finance Act 1982

The historic background is set out in the previous paragraph. The foreground, as it presently exists, consists of two elements, company law and tax, and it is these two that we will be concentrating on in this chapter. The first was added by the Companies Act 1981, brought into force on 15 June 1982; the provisions are now to be found in sections 159 to 181 of the Companies Act 1985. Those sections cover redemption as well as purchase – the essential difference between the two being that a redeemable share is acquired by the issuing company from the holder at a time, and at a price, stipulated in the terms on which it was issued; purchases take place if, when, and at prices, determined by the members, by special resolution. It is with the latter that we are principally concerned.

It will be recalled that the definition (for the purposes of tax) of a 'distribution' includes:

> any other distribution (that is other than a dividend) out of the assets of the company (whether in cash or otherwise) in respect of shares in the company, except so much of the distribution, if any, as represents repayment of capital on the shares . . .[5]

that being a succinct description of £300 of cash, if a company were to purchase for £400 shares whose nominal value was £100.[6]

The tax provisions originally enacted in 1982, and now in sections 219 to 229 of the Taxes Act 1988, lay down the conditions in which that £300 is exempted from the distributions legislation, that is to say, the company does not have to account for ACT when paying it, and the recipient is not taxed on it as income. But as soon as £300 is made *not-income*, it is clear that that moves the full £400 rather than only £100 within the purview of capital gains tax, as proceeds of the former shareholder's disposal of the share.[7] The Inland Revenue's view

---

[5] Section 209(2)(b) TA 1988.
[6] Some commentators question whether, when a company *purchases* shares from a shareholder and only cancels them after that purchase, it is safe to assume that the £100 can be described as a *repayment* of capital. However, section 209 has to be read with the provisions of sections 254(6) and (7) which appear only to make any sense at all if it can be assumed that the amounts originally paid up on shares are regarded as *repaid* when those shares are purchased. The author's experience has been that the Inland Revenue have never questioned the interpretation suggested above. There is a quite different matter over which corporate lawyers sometimes express uncertainty – it stems from the phraseology 'purchase' of own shares. This suggests that the shares, which were assets of the shareholders, become assets of the company: and if they are then cancelled, the company has a capital gains loss. This seems to the author wholly misguided, in that a share, as a bundle of rights against a company could not possibly be an asset in the company's hands. Its 'purchase' is more like the removal of a liability than the acquisition of assets.
[7] Section 37(1) TCGA 1992 allows the deduction from the total proceeds of disposal (£400), of any part of those proceeds taxed as income (£300) in the hands of the recipient, thus leaving only £100 to be treated as the capital gains tax receipt – but only if the £300 is a distribution, and therefore income of that recipient.

is that where the vendor of shares is a company, its receipt (the full £400) is *always* within corporation tax on capital gains, regardless whether the purchaser is treated as having made a distribution or not.[8] This view (which is not universally agreed, although not yet legally challenged) flows from a company's not including in taxable income a distribution from another company, and having no basis for excluding it from its gains.

We will examine first the company law provisions, and then come back to the tax position for a more detailed examination not just of these concepts, but of the detailed rules which allow purchase to be exempted from the distributions legislation.

13.3 The capital redemption reserve

The key to understanding what a company's purchase of its own shares actually involves, and means, is to visualise what such transactions would do to the company's balance sheet. We will start by ignoring the question whether some of the following transactions may not be possible (strictly that they may be possible only if further requirements are met), because looking at their implications brings out with startling clarity why the authorities have written into the law many of the restrictions they have. Looking at those extra requirements and procedures can be our subsequent task.

In each of the tables which follow, we will show:

- in the left hand column the company's balance sheet before the transaction;

- in a second memorandum column (not in our tables having any effect on the balance sheet numbers) the nominal value of the shares being bought and the price being paid. Nominal value will always be less than price paid – but that nominal value will always be a fully-paid figure. Part-paid shares cannot be bought by the company;[9]

- in the third column, the required alterations to balance sheet figures for share capital and distributable profits;

- and in the right hand column, the balance sheet which results from the transaction.

But there are two procedural points which it is essential to mention at this stage; first, share purchases must always be paid for in cash on completion – it is not possible to purchase shares on credit.[10]

---

[8] *Statement of Practice* SP 4/89. This is the position for a company's purchase of shares held by a vendor which is a company. If the transaction were not purchase but redemption, the Revenue's view (indicated in a letter published in *Tax Practitioner* December 1991) is that the receipt in the hands of the company falls into section 122 TCGA 1992 rather than section 37, and accordingly has to be taxed in a way which seems to the author a curious perversion of the facts; but this is too specialised a point to spend time on it in this book.
[9] Section 159(3) applied by section 162(2) CA 1985
[10] Section 159(3) applied by section 162(2) CA 1985, again.

Second, the transfers which are shown to the capital redemption reserve are statutory requirements. The purpose of that account is *to maintain the company's capital*, meaning by that that the company is put in such a position that its net assets are not reduced by the transaction itself (nor by any further distribution which would be legitimate after it) below the figure at which its nominal share capital stood before the transaction.[11] Perhaps the best way of starting to think about the capital redemption reserve is to say that it is analogous to a share premium account, although we will see that this is not wholly accurate.

13.4 *Illustrative balance sheet for the simple transaction*

In each of the examples in Tables 49 to 53, 100 shares out of 500 are to be purchased, the consideration for these 100 shares being £400.

Table 49: The Simple Transaction

		Memo		
Fixed assets	600			600
Current assets – other	750			750
– cash	500	(400)	(400)	100
Liabilities	(350)			(350)
	1,500			1,100
Share capital	500	(100)	(100)	400
Capital redemption res.	–		100	100
subtotal	500			500
Distributable profits	1,000		(400)	600
	1,500			1,100

The shares purchased by the company are cancelled after that acquisition. Therefore, after it the company only has 400 shares in issue. But the company's *capital* has to be *maintained* (at the subtotal line) at the level of £500, that being the purpose behind the requirement that £100 be transferred into the capital redemption reserve.[12] And it is because the entries in the 'fixed capital' section of the balance sheet are simply *in-and-out*, that the way in which this purchase is usually described can be seen to be true, namely that it is a purchase 'wholly out of distributable profits'.

---

[11] There are transactions in which this is not true, as we will see below; for present purposes (our first three examples) it is an adequate working rule.
[12] Section 170(1) CA 1985.

THE CAPITAL REDEMPTION RESERVE

But of course we know that that last description is a company law, and accounting, description. If this were a transaction which was a distribution for tax purposes, that distribution would be £300 – the balance of £100 being a repayment of capital.

In a purchase of shares 'wholly out of distributable profits', some part of the reason for *maintaining capital* at £500 is that this leaves the creditors with the same *cover* that they had before the transaction. Even if the company were to distribute the whole remaining balance of distributable reserves, £600, it would still have £850 of total assets to cover £350 of liabilities. Before the purchase, if it had distributed the whole £1,000 of its then distributable profits, its total assets remaining, and its liabilities, would have been those same figures.

13.5 *Purchase partly out of proceeds of a new issue*

That provides the key to understanding what happens if the purchase is made *partly out of the proceeds of a new issue* (which we will illustrate in Table 50 as being of 20 shares, issued as consideration for a non-cash asset valued at £80).

Table 50: Purchase Partly out of Proceeds of a New Issue

		Memo			
Fixed assets	600				600
Current assets – other	750		80		830
– cash	500	(400)		(400)	100
Liabilities	(350)				(350)
	1,500				1,180
Share capital	500	(100)	20	(100)	420
Share premium account	–		60		60
Capital redemption res.	–			20	20
subtotal	500				500
Distributable profits	1,000			(320)	680
	1,500				1,180

The figure which must be credited to capital redemption reserve in this case is the excess of the nominal value of the shares purchased, £100, over the total proceeds of the new issue, £80, that is to say, £20.[13] Capital is maintained at the same level of £500, so that the creditors have their same cover.

---

[13] Section 170(2) CA 1985.

Once again the company law and accounting description of the transaction can be seen to be accurately reflected in the distributable profits line – the purchase, £400, having been met to the extent of £80 out of the proceeds of the new issue, only requires to be *paid for* out of distributable profits to the extent of the balance of £320.

13.6 Purchase partly out of capital

A similar picture emerges from what is described as a purchase partly out of capital, as shown in Table 51.

Table 51: Purchase Partly out of Capital

		Memo		
Fixed assets	600			600
Current assets – other	750			750
– cash	500	(400)	(400)	100
Liabilities	(350)			(350)
	1,500			1,100
Share capital	500	(100)	(100)	400
Share premium	660	–	–	660
Capital redemption res.	–		40	40
subtotal	1,160			1,100
Distributable profits	340		(340)	–
	1,500			1,100

Starting from the bottom, we see that it is necessary to use distributable profits,[14] and that it is only as permitted exceptions (extending the possibilities after distributable profits have been exhausted) that the company can use other sources. We will come in paragraphs 13.8 and 13.9 to the procedures the company must go through, and the requirements which need to be fulfilled, before it can use anything beyond distributable profits.

However at this stage we will assume that it has proved possible, so that we can see its balance sheet implications. What company law refers to as 'the payment out of capital' is the excess of the purchase consideration, £400, over the distributable profits utilised, £340, that is to say, £60. To the extent that the nominal value of the shares being purchased, £100, exceeds this payment out of capital, the excess of £40 must be credited to capital redemption reserve.[15] What this shows, at

---

[14] Sections 160(1) applied by section 162(2) CA 1985.
[15] Section 171(4) CA 1985.

the subtotal line for 'fixed capital', is a reduction from £1,160 before the purchase to £1,100 after it, which makes sense of the description quoted above of a purchase paid for partly out of capital. That is the extent to which the company has *reduced its capital* rather than maintained it, and in doing so has reduced the cover enjoyed by its creditors.

13.7 Purchase out of capital which exceeds the nominal amount of the shares purchased

The balance sheet implications are rather different in Table 52. What we show is a purchase *wholly out of capital*, but it is not that that is the significant feature – rather that the capital payment exceeds the shares' nominal value.

Table 52: Purchase out of Capital Exceeding Shares' Nominal Value

		Memo		
Fixed assets	600			600
Current assets – other	750			750
– cash	500	(400)	(400)	100
Liabilities	(350)			(350)
	1,500			1,100
Share capital	500	(100)	(100)	400
Share premium	760		(60)	700
Revaluation reserve	240		(240)	–
Capital redemption res.			–	
	1,500			1,100
Distributable profits	–			–
	1,500			1,100

As indicated, in this case the payment out of capital is the full £400 because there are no distributable profits available out of which any part of it could be *paid*. That *payment out of capital*, £400, therefore exceeds the nominal value of the shares being purchased, £100, and the excess is permitted to be charged against *capital*,[16] without there being any question of any transfer into capital redemption reserve. What the Act spells out, in fact, is that the £300 excess can be debited against 'capital redemption reserve, share premium account, or fully paid share capital ... or ... revaluation reserve', without giving any indication as to the order in which these are to be used. But whatever accounts

---

[16] Section 171(5) CA 1985. Provided of course that the transaction is itself possible, as to which see paragraphs 13.8 and 13.9 below.

are debited, the effect is very clear at the *fixed capital* subtotal (and the grand total of shareholders' funds), namely that the company has reduced its capital by £400, this being the amount of its *capital payment*.

13.8 Procedures for purchase of shares out of capital

Perhaps the best way to lead into this subject is to consider what would happen if, immediately before starting the process of share purchase, the company concerned arranged for the interposition of a holding company between itself and its shareholders, (as in *Shearer v Bercain*),[17] that holding company not claiming merger relief.[18]

We assume that the company itself is the one we were looking at in Table 49, with £1,000 of distributable profits – and that its total value can be taken to be £2,000. We also assume that the new holding company is formed with a share capital of £500, of which 100 shares are subsequently to be repurchased for the £400 we have previously been using. And we recall that if there is to be such a purchase, it has to be paid for in cash immediately, which means that the holding company needs to acquire £400 of cash. Let us therefore consider its opening balance sheet, as shown in Table 53, shown for the purposes of this discussion on the basis that it has not claimed merger relief.

Table 53: Opening Balance Sheet of Holding Company

Investment in subsidiary	2,000
Current assets – cash	400
Borrowings	(400)
	2,000
Share capital	500
Share premium account	1,500
	2,000

The first thing to say is that although that holding company has a subsidiary with £500 of cash in its bank account, the borrowings shown in Table 53, if the holding company had borrowed from, or with the assistance of guarantees or security from, its subsidiary, would be in breach of the rules about financial assistance.[19] But if the borrowing had been successfully achieved without such breach, then we do seem

---

[17] [1980] 3 All ER 295, see paragraph 6.13.
[18] Section 131 CA 1985.
[19] Which is not to say that such a borrowing is necessarily impossible – just that it would need to be *whitewashed* under the procedures we looked at briefly in paragraph 9.24 (section 155 CA 1985) allowing a private company to give financial assistance provided it has been able to meet these requirements.

on the face of things to have arranged matters in such a way that the holding company can purchase shares out of its share premium account, while the subsidiary's distributable profits are preserved.[20] But that is a highly dubious conclusion, in the light of the points we need to bring out in the next paragraph.

13.9 *Procedures for purchase of shares out of capital (continued)*

For all purchases of shares by a company, not just those out of capital, it is necessary that:

- the company's Articles contain power for it to purchase its own shares;

- the purchase concerned is authorised by the company by special resolution;[21]

- the contract covering the specific shares being purchased must be available for inspection at the company's office for 15 days up to the date of the meeting at which the special resolution is to be proposed.[22]

Where capital is to be used for, or towards, the purchase, it is a requirement that before the members of the company (in this instance the holding company) can consider the proposal, the company's directors must have considered a set of accounts drawn up for the purpose, and on the basis of that consideration made a statutory declaration that the company should be able to meet its debts not only in the immediate aftermath of the purchase, but in the course of its carrying on its operations in the year thereafter.[23] There are then tightly drawn time limits within which the shareholders' special resolution must be passed to approve the purchase, and thereafter a timetable in which it is required that all of this must be publicly advertised and time allowed for creditors to object, before the actual payment can be made.

But this perhaps obscures the question why we are doing it in the first place? The holding company's borrowing is going to need to be serviced and repaid sooner or later. The most straightforward source from which

---

[20] Preserved, that is to say, in the solus balance sheet of the subsidiary, and not (or not yet) distributed to the holding company by way of dividend. In the circumstances we have envisaged, it would not be possible for there to be any onward distribution out of the holding company, because without merger relief that is prevented, see paragraphs 6.13 and 6.14, and also 9.27 and 9.28.

But the exercise has a point if the subsidiary is in one of those lines of business in which its own capital adequacy is paramount, (banking, insurance, and agency companies in the Lloyds market), since it is obviously advantageous that it should not need to dissipate its available reserves.

[21] Section 164(2) CA 1985, but this has been subject, since 1990, to the possibility for a private company of adopting the alternative written resolution procedures under sections 381A and onward of the Act.

[22] Section 164(6) CA 1985.

[23] Section 173(3) CA 1985.

this could be done would be a dividend from its subsidiary.[24] Paying a dividend was what we were originally trying to avoid; perhaps all that we have avoided is the immediate payment – we have gained a delay so long as the lender does not demand repayment.

If it is true that there is a *bona fide* commercial reason for interposing the holding company,[25] and if there is agreement between all the shareholders that the remainder wish to stay, while the one who is to go is content with what he is being offered, it would be much simpler for the holding company to make an offer for the company's shares on a basis which allowed the stayers to accept a share exchange, whilst the leaver took a cash alternative.[26]

13.10 Stamp duty

In the suggested takeover for shares and cash at the end of the previous paragraph, it is clear that with one or more shareholders taking cash, the share capital issued by the predator will not mirror what had been that of the target. That mirroring, under section 77(3)(e), (f), (g) and (h) of Finance Act 1986, would be a requirement if stamp duty were to be avoided on the takeover. Without it, duty will be payable on all of the transfer documents by which the target shareholders (all of them) transfer their target shares to the predator.

But what we have been discussing in the main in this chapter has been company purchases of own shares – not takeovers of the kind in the last paragraph. The stamp duty position on purchases of own shares is odd, to say the least. When the legislation was first introduced, the authorities had intended to bring in a specific exemption from stamp duty, but there were doubts whether section 52 of the Companies Act 1981 did achieve this. What companies relied on was a written answer by the Chancellor of the Exchequer given on 30 April 1984 to a Parliamentary question. This stated that stamp duty was not payable because nothing was *transferred* to the company which was purchasing its own shares; another statement about which there was room for doubt.

However, section 66 of the Finance Act 1986 (fulfilling a Community obligation) has changed all of that. Duty is now payable. The form 169 which has now to be filed with the Registrar of Companies by any

---

[24] A lawful dividend never constitutes financial assistance for the purchase of a company's shares, section 145(3)(a) CA 1985.
[25] If the interposition of the holding company does *not* have a *bona fide* commercial purpose, then the existing shareholders of the company will be subject to capital gains tax when they exchange their shares in the company for those in the holding company, see section 137(1) TCGA 1992, and commentary in paragraphs 11.26 and 11.27.
[26] The new holding company would need to borrow in order to finance the cash element in its takeover offer (and the borrowing would need to be medium term at least, unless it were able to obtain the cash by stripping an immediate dividend from its target). That borrowing could only be made from the target if the financial assistance *whitewash* procedures were possible, as referred to in Note 19 on paragraph 13.8. One would also strongly recommend that any holding company proposing this transaction should obtain clearance for it under section 703 TA 1988, as explained in paragraph 11.25.

company purchasing its own shares must be stamped *ad valorem* (that is to say, by reference to the total amount paid to the shareholders) at the rate of 50p per £100. The form 169 is treated as if it were a document transferring shares to the company on a sale.

Schemes and arrangements

13.11 *The purchase by a party other than the company itself*

At the end of paragraph 13.9 we were considering the possibility that, instead of a company purchasing its own shares, a holding company might be inserted over the top of the company, on a basis enabling one shareholder to take cash while the remainder took shares. This would need to be accepted by the Inland Revenue as being done for *bona fide* commercial purposes if:

- the remaining shareholders are to gain *paper-for-paper* relief under section 135 of the Taxation of Chargeable Gains Act 1992, as outlined in paragraphs 11.26 and 11.27;

- the shareholder who is bought out is not to be challenged under the transactions in securities provisions explained in paragraphs 11.21 to 11.25.

13.12 *Schemes and arrangements outlawed by the tax legislation*

But tax, as well as company law and procedures, is a main subject of this chapter. Let us turn to a straightforward purchase by a company of its own shares, in which it is equally essential that this purchase should be accepted[26a] by the Inland Revenue as not constituting a *scheme* if the shareholder is to obtain the capital gains tax treatment indicated in paragraph 13.2 rather than the payment being treated as a distribution by the company. There are two separate types of scheme which are outlawed:

- one of the general conditions which we will come to is that the shareholder being bought out must end up with a substantially reduced holding (or no holding at all) in the company. That condition is then widened to say that one must take into account not only the individual's own holdings, but must aggregate with them the holdings of his associates.[27] But once one becomes familiar with the workings of the minds of those who draft anti-avoidance legislation, one expects to (and does) find that if there is a scheme under which, after the first shareholder has sufficiently reduced his holding, an associate is enabled to acquire a holding which would have prevented the

---

[26a] The clearance procedures are in section 225 TA 1988.
[27] The definition of associate is in section 227, and the definition of connected persons (which is necessary to follow through the ramifications of associate status) is in section 228.

principal's disposal from qualifying, then that scheme is unacceptable. Further, even where no arrangements can be proved, if an associate does in fact acquire such a holding within 12 months, the draftsman deems there to have been a scheme, and disqualifies the original purchase;

• the second, and more important, form of outlawed scheme is one whose main purpose, or one of whose main purposes is the avoidance of tax. This is complex, and needs a detailed examination.

13.13 *Benefiting a trade without there being a scheme*

Section 219(1)(a) Taxes Act 1988 is difficult. Part of the difficulty is understanding what it means; we will see that despite the narrowness of its phraseology the Inland Revenue do in fact interpret it in a fairly reasonable way. But the underlying difficulty is trying to identify what may have been in the mind of the draftsman. The section exempts a payment by an 'unquoted, trading'[28] company, to a 'UK resident' shareholder (for the purchase[29] of his shares) from being a distribution provided that:

• the purchase is made wholly or mainly for the purpose of benefiting the company's (or a subsidiary's) trade; and

• the purchase does not form part of a scheme the main purpose or one of the main purposes of which is to enable the shareholder to participate in the profits of the company without receiving a dividend; and

• nor does the purchase form part of a scheme whose main purpose (or one of the main purposes of which) is the avoidance of tax.

The *tax* which is not to be avoided is income tax and corporation tax, capital gains tax being excluded.[30] One might think that there was a considerable, if not complete, overlap between the second and third heads, because it is hard to see why (or how) anyone could scheme to participate in profits without receiving dividends, were it not for tax reasons. But there is a distinction, and one which the author finds a most enlightening insight into the minds of those who draft tax anti-avoidance legislation.

---

[28] The company's being *unquoted* is the first of the requirements if a purchase is to gain non-distribution status, and the company's being a *trading* company or the holding company of a trading group is another. A third is the next matter mentioned in the text, namely that the shareholder must be resident and ordinarily resident in the UK in the fiscal year in which the purchase takes place (section 220(1) to (3) TA 1988).

[29] The section refers to redemption and repayment as well as purchase. Neither of these is directly relevant to the subject matter of this chapter. Their indirect relevance is said (by the commentators referred to in Note 6 on paragraph 13.2) to be that if *repayment* is different from *purchase*, this must be an indication that a purchase does not include any element of repayment of the capital paid up on the shares. However, that seems to the author hardly to be a conclusive argument, and in any event it seems quite clear that the Revenue's view is that purchase does include such an element.

[30] Section 832(3) TA 1988.

The third head is put into the legislation as a warning flag, to tell those who are tempted to avoid tax but are easily scared off, that they would do better to avoid the temptation rather than the tax. It is the second head which the Revenue would use for enforcement purposes, if it ever became necessary. The reason for this is that they would have no difficulty whatever in demonstrating the existence of the scheme referred to in that second head – it consists of the passing of the resolution by the other shareholders for the purchase of this individual's shares.[31] When one analyses the meaning of the word 'purpose' in that second head, it can be seen that it actually means no more than 'effect'. In the third head, the word 'purpose' quite clearly means 'motive'; the Inland Revenue, and the courts, are only too well aware of the problems of proving what are taxpayers' motives.[32]

Thus it seems that every purchase will derive from a scheme; the question is whether it 'results in' the shareholder 'participating in profits'. Common sense suggests that in the normal case the shareholder will be bought out at a value which reflects his own and the other shareholders' views on the earning power of the company in the future. Only to a small extent will will that value be based on the company's retained earnings for the past, which is the only meaning that could be ascribed to the *profits* in which he might participate. But those who interpret statutes (particularly Companies Acts and tax legislation) do not use common sense as a guide; shares are normally purchased out of distributable profits, so how could it be argued, they would ask, that the vendor was not participating in profits?

13.14 Benefiting a trade without there being a scheme (continued)

Therefore, if that second head in section 219(1)(a) were to be strictly construed, there would not seem to be any possibility that *any* share purchase could avoid disqualification.

In fact, we know that the Inland Revenue do not use any such approach – they do not disqualify a purchase provided it fits their views on the correct interpretation of the first head, the one which requires that the purchase be 'made wholly or mainly for the purpose of benefiting a trade'. They quoted the following as examples in a consultative document published in September 1981 when the legislation was under consideration:

---

[31] And possibly his and their passing of a resolution to alter the company's Articles to enable it to purchase its own shares.
[32] The clearest example of the difficulty of identifying a taxpayer's motives can be seen in *Mallalieu v Drummond* [1983] 2 All ER 1095. Lord Brightman's dictum imputed to Miss Mallalieu motives which she did not know she had – a process which would seem to enable the thought-police to exercise a degree of control which might surprise many UK citizens:

> 'I reject the notion that the object of a taxpayer is inevitably linked to the particular conscious motive in mind at the moment of expenditure. Of course the motive of which the taxpayer is conscious is of vital significance, but it is not inevitably the only object which the commissioners are entitled to find to exist.'

- the buying out of a dissident or apathetic shareholder;
- when a family shareholder retires or dies with no children to succeed him;
- payment of capital transfer tax on the death of a shareholder.

They were rather more specific in August 1982, in *Statement of Practice* No. 2 of 1982:

> The test indicates that the sole or main purpose of the transaction is to be to benefit a trade of a relevant company and not, for example, to benefit the vending shareholder (although he usually will also benefit) nor some wider commercial purpose to which he may put the payment he receives nor any business purpose of a relevant company if it is not a trade . . .
>
> If the problem being resolved by the transaction is a disagreement over the management of the company, the main purpose may nonetheless be to benefit a trade if, as will usually be the case with a trading company, the disagreement has or can reasonably be expected to have an adverse effect on the running of the trade . . .
>
> More generally . . . since it will normally be unsatisfactory to retain an unwilling shareholder it is expected that the condition will be shown to be satisfied where, after taking into account the interests of any associates, the vending shareholder is genuinely giving up his entire interest of all kinds in the company. The case of a boardroom disagreement has already been mentioned; other examples where this might happen are:
>
> (a) an outside shareholder has provided equity finance (whether or not with the expectation of . . . sale to the company); he is now withdrawing his investment;
> (b) the proprietor of a company is retiring to make way for new management;
> (c) a shareholder has died leaving shares in his estate and his personal representatives or the beneficiaries do not wish to keep them.[33]

In each of those cases, it will be a total withdrawal that is relevant, not just a substantial reduction. But the latter is one of the matters we need to look at in the next paragraph.

13.15 Other requirements of the tax legislation

The shareholder whose shares are being purchased must have held them for five years before that purchase.[34] The rules here do allow him to

---

[33] The reference to personal representatives (a phrase which embraces executors of those who die leaving wills, and those granted letters of administration to administer an intestate estate) selling shares comes from the *Statement of Practice*. There is also a statutory reference to the sale of shares by personal representatives being a valid basis for exemption from the distribution treatment for tax purposes, where that sale was the only practicable way of meeting an inheritance tax liability. This is however a narrower exemption than it might appear, because the main provision in section 219(1)(b) not only requires that the whole, or substantially the whole, of the purchase price be used for that tax liability, but it is qualified by section 219(2) which makes it a condition that the inheritance tax could not without *hardship* have been paid from any other source.
[34] Section 220(5) to (9) TA 1988.

count in the time for which he had held *original* shares, where what he is selling are shares received on a takeover under paper-for-paper exchange arrangements. The rules also allow, if he has acquired shares at different times, that he can regard those that are being purchased as the ones he had acquired earliest; and if he had not only made acquisitions over a period of time, but also made disposals before the purchase we are looking at, those disposals can be regarded as being of his most recently acquired shares.

Notice that the five-year period is itself an all or nothing test – any share purchased by the company after four years and 11 months fails totally. But if, of the parcel of shares being purchased, half had been held for five years and a month, and the remainder for four years and 11 months, it is only the latter half which fail.

The last point which we need to make is that the legislation requires, if non-distribution treatment is to be obtained, that the vendor reduce his holding *substantially*.[35] We have already seen that this is largely an irrelevance so far as concerns the types of shareholders whose *out-purchase* is envisaged in the *Statement of Practice* as being for the benefit of the company's trade – those listed in the second half of the previous paragraph, whom the Revenue envisages needing to cease to be shareholders altogether if the transaction is really to benefit the trade. When one comes to examine how the statutory reduction can be consistent with that, it seems:

- the inheritance tax purchase referred to in Note 34 need not be a purchase of the entire holding;

- there may be *disagreement* cases in which the company simply cannot afford to buy out the whole of the disaffected shareholder's holding, and his total removal has to be envisaged as being done in two or more[36] purchases. Presumably it can be regarded as a benefit to the trade through the period between those steps if, with only half as many shares, the individual can only be half as disagreeable.

---

[35] Section 221 TA 1988. The measure of substantiality is that the shareholder's percentage (of the reduced capital) after the transaction must less than three-quarters of what his percentage was before. Thus if he had 40 shares out of the 100 issued by the company, and 15 shares were purchased, he would have 25/85ths of the company thereafter, which is 29.4 per cent – less than three-quarters of his previous 40 per cent. Because the whole of this legislation was written by draftsmen obsessed with avoidance, the test based on numbers of shares is backed by a further test based on profit-distributions, in case (by using shares with special rights) the vendor was able to maintain his dividends at a level showing no substantial reduction. These two tests are further supplemented by a requirement that, after the purchase, the vendor-shareholder must not be 'connected with' the company (section 223(1) TA 1988).

[36] There is of course a difference between making two separate purchases of separate tranches of a shareholder's holding, and a purchase of the whole which is to be paid for by instalments. That instalment transaction is unlawful under section 159(3) CA 1985, applied by section 162(2), which requires that a purchase must be paid for, in full and in cash, at completion. We noticed in paragraph 13.3 this requirement of section 159(3) applied by section 162(2) CA 1985.

CHAPTER 14

DEMERGERS

14.1 Introduction

The concept of a demerger is quite simple. If P, Q, R and S are the shareholders of a company which carries on two distinct trades, they should be able to separate those trades, one into each of two companies; and it ought to be possible, if the parties want this, for one company to be owned by P and Q, the other being owned by R and S (rather than both companies being owned directly by all four of them).

Reconstructing a company in this way does give rise to Companies Act problems which we will look at; but it is sensible to identify what are the tax liabilities that might be expected to arise. The legislation introduced in the Finance Act 1980 (now in sections 213 to 218 of the Taxes Act 1988) purported to remove these liabilities and make the process a straightforward one. Many practitioners have reservations about its success in achieving this.

If we call our existing (two-trade) company A, and the new company to which one of those trades is to be transferred B, then the form of the tax liabilities that would arise, in the absence of the possible reliefs we will come to in the paragraphs which follow, would depend on whether B is formed as a subsidiary of A and at a later point ceases to be a member of *A's group*, or whether it is formed as a parallel company owned by the same shareholders as own A (or some of them). This is shown in Table 54.

14.2 *Re-examination of those potential tax liabilities*

In that table of tax exposures (Table 54) the first point worthy of note is that the Inland Revenue did provide an exemption from stamp duty in the original 1980 legislation. This was abolished in 1986, and the charge is now at the normal rates.[1]

---

[1] The original exemption was in paragraph 12 of Schedule 18 to FA 1980, and it contained not only an exemption from stamp duty on *a document executed solely for the purpose of effecting an exempt distribution* but also an exemption from capital duty on the share capital of new companies formed for the purposes of a demerger. Capital duty has since been abolished, and we need not worry any more about it. What section 73(4) FA 1986 did was to substitute a charge at 50p per £100 in place of the stamp duty exemption, but this amendment only operated for the period from March 1986 to the date of *big bang* on 27 October 1986, and then disappeared. The result is that there is now no exemption; it is necessary to analyse each of the documents concerned under the ordinary rules. Thus, in paragraph 14.3 below,

continued

INTRODUCTION

Table 54: Tax Exposures

	Parent/subsidiary	Parallel company
Distribution by A, and income for A's shareholders or for B	A's transferring B to the shareholders of A, (or some of them)	A's transferring a trade and assets to B, (on the instructions of A's shareholders, some or all of whom may become shareholders of B)
Capital gains	No gain or loss on transfer of trade and assets from A to B, but s.179 liability when B leaves A's group A disposes of shares in B Shares in A lose value, this being associated with receipt by shareholders of shares in B, which appear to be a capital distribution	A's transfer of trade and assets to B Shares in A lose value in the hands of shareholders and they receive shares in B without giving consideration
Stamp duty	Transfer of shares in B from A to shareholders	A's transfer of trade and assets to B

The second point to note is that the distribution charge, and the form of the capital gains tax charges, in the right hand column are something we have met before, most recently at paragraphs 11.17 and 11.18, when we were considering the possibility of transferring a trade and assets into a parallel company as a prelude to selling it. What we said at that point was that the capital gains tax problems should be capable of solution, using section 136 Taxation of Chargeable Gains Act 1992 to apportion the original acquisition costs of the A shares between those A shares retained and B shares acquired, and using section 139 to exempt the trade/asset transfer from A to B. We noted the existence of the Revenue's Statement of Practice (to which we will return in paragraph 14.7 below)

---

continued
- the first head envisages a company transferring a trade and assets to a subsidiary, which could be exempt under section 41 FA 1930 were it not for the fact that transferor and transferee are to cease to be associated, section 27(3)(c) FA 1967, and therefore needs to be stamped at 1 per cent. The second transaction in that first head is the payment of a dividend *in specie*, which is exempt, see paragraph 11.9, Note 17.
- in the second head, the demerger distribution is the movement of one of the company's trades into the parallel company, a transfer which could be expected to be stamped at 50p percent under section 76 FA 1986, (it cannot be exempt under section 75, because the division of a company is not a *reconstruction*.
- in the third head, the preliminary trade transfer to a subsidiary follows the same rules as in the first, and then the demerger distribution of the subsidiary's shares to the parallel company would be charged at 50p percent whether one relied on those shares being a part of an undertaking (see paragraph 6.34), or merely regarded them as marketable securities.

which appeared to hold out that solution to the capital gains tax charge. That use of sections 136 and 139 is very much a part of the demerger legislation – supplemented as appropriate by further exemptions to cover the other parts of the transaction. But we said in paragraph 11.18 that what seemed to be a theoretical solution to the distribution problem was in practice not available in the circumstances we were looking at in that paragraph. Despite the fact that the demerger legislation *could potentially* remove the distribution liability, we will see as we proceed that its operation is very restricted; it could not exempt the transaction outlined.

Thus we knew in paragraphs 11.17 and 11.18 what were the tax exposures in that right hand column, and we had seen how it had been possible at one point to avoid them; that is not, however, the route the demerger legislation takes. The approach in these sections is, as we will see, to establish a large number of conditions which must be met or complied with; and behind that minefield, the structure of the provisions is to identify those distributions[2] which are acceptable, (that is to say are made by a company in the course of a demerger which is itself acceptable and where the distribution additionally meets a number of other tests), and define them as *exempt distributions*. Section 213(2) then removes the distributor's ACT liability and stops the receipt from being income in the hands of the recipient. Section 192 follows this up, in cases where this would not otherwise be so, by preventing the exempt distribution from being a capital distribution, extending what we could call section 136 treatment to shareholders of A and B to whom it would not otherwise apply (because their holdings in the new company would not be proportionate to those in the old), and also removing any section 179 charge on a company leaving a group.

14.3 The three possible forms of demerger

The legislation envisages three ways in which distributions could be made, which (conditional on all the other requirements) could be exempt distributions:

- the distribution as a dividend *in specie* by a trading company of its shareholding in another trading company which had up to that point been its 75 per cent subsidiary;[3]

- the distribution by a company of a trade and assets to a parallel company which gives no consideration to the distributor but instead issues shares direct to the shareholders of that distributor;[4]

---

[2] The Inland Revenue's view, spelled out in SP 13/80, is that a transaction must be a 'distribution' within the tax definition before it can be reclassified under these provisions as an exempt distribution. This is of some significance, because what would in the ordinary English sense of the word be described as a distribution would not be within the tax sense of the word if the distributing company was in liquidation.
[3] Section 213(3)(a) TA 1988.
[4] Section 213(3)(b)(i) TA 1988.

THE THREE POSSIBLE FORMS OF DEMERGER

- the distribution by a company of shares in a trading subsidiary to a parallel company which gives no consideration to the distributor but but instead issues shares direct to the shareholders of that distributor.[5]

Each of the demergers set out above is in its simplest form. One can double-up any of these cases, distributing shareholdings in two separate trading subsidiaries, for instance. On the basis that what the Inland Revenue want to see after the transaction is a trading activity in at least two companies[6] (not themselves forming a group), they do not insist that the distributor itself has to be one of those two, or that it remains a trading company, or even remains in existence. It could be stripped bare by the preparatory hiving-down into the two separate trading subsidiaries of its activities, and following that distribution to holders of the shares in both companies could be dissolved without being wound up.

There is a whole raft of what we might describe as detailed administrative conditions, which it is convenient to relegate to a footnote.[7]

There are other conditions which are more fundamental, to which we need to give some consideration:

- first, there is the point about trading. The entire demerger legislation is based on there being two trades, one separated into a new company, and the other either left in the company where it was before, or also placed into a different new company. Separating a trade from an activity which is not a trade, an investment activity for instance, will not pass the tests. And 'trading', so far as the Revenue are concerned, does not include trading in shares and securities, in land, or in commodities/futures;

- second, the purpose of the demerger must be 'to benefit a trade' (the legislation does not require that both trades will benefit, but

---

[5] Section 213(3)(b)(ii) TA 1988.
[6] There are further levels of complexity possible if the distributing company is a member of a group. One obvious possibility is that the distribution of one of its trading subsidiaries leaves it not as a trading company itself, but as the holding company of another (retained) subsidiary which is a trading company. But it is also possible for the distribution to leave the distributor as a *subsidiary* of a trading company, although the distributor does not itself carry on a trade.
[7] Every company (distributor, recipient and subject matter) must be UK resident, section 213(4) TA 1988. Where shares are transferred they must constitute the entirety of the holding of the distributor, and where a trade is transferred, the distributor must not retain an interest in it, section 213(8)(a) and (b), but each of these requirements does actually allow for some modest 'retention' by the distributor. The concept of retention of an interest in the transferred trade has to be distinguished from the principles under which a trade is to be identified; if the distributor carried on a wholesale and retail business selling fruit and vegetables, he could *demerge* the retail end, or the retail end of the fruit business. The fact that neither had been a separate trade of his is no bar – what fits it within the requirements is that it is capable of being carried on as a separate trade by the recipient, SP 13/80. Where the recipient, whether of a trade or of shares, is a company (that is to say, in the second and third forms of distribution) that the company's only activity after that must be the operation of the trade, or the holding of the shares, so received, 213(8)(c).

obviously their new owners would hope that that would be the position). We have examined the Revenue's interpretation of this phrase in paragraphs 13.12 and 13.13; that interpretation was mainly published two years after the original enactment of the legislation we are now looking at, but we can assume that that interval had allowed the Revenue to refine and crystallise their views. There is every indication that they intend the test to be the same in the two contexts. And it is equally clear that the demerger legislation contains the same strictures about the absence of a tax avoidance motive on the part of those involved as was the subject of our comments in paragraph 13.12 – those comments apply here as strongly as they did there.

14.4 *The third fundamental*

The separation of two trades is the first of the fundamental requirements; the benefiting of a trade and the absence of a tax avoidance motive the second.

The third is that the whole purpose of the legislation, in the Revenue's view, is to separate the ownership of the different companies which emerge, 'between the shareholders of the company which existed beforehand'. We opened this chapter with P, Q, R and S owning A which carried on two trades, and moved to a position in which P and Q remained the owners of A, divested of one of its trades, while R and S owned B which had acquired that trade. There would be no reason why A should not remain in the ownership of all four shareholders (perhaps in different proportions), and B come to be owned by any or all of the same individuals – again in any proportions. The author has dealt with one demerger in which the ownership of the two companies was a mirror image, but where those owners believed that management of the distinct trades by different generations, and the introduction of an executive share option scheme in one of the companies but not the other, constituted the *benefit* which justified the changes.

That explanation makes it abundantly clear that the Revenue do not regard as appropriate uses of the legislation:

- demerging trades into two companies each directly held by the shareholders in order to sell one of those companies;[8]

- demerging trades into two companies each directly held by the shareholders as a preliminary to liquidation of one of the trading companies – so that the shareholders could get the cash into their

---

[8] The bar against the sale of the demerged company is in section 213(11) TA 1988, which prevents the distribution from being exempted if there is a sale after the distribution. The interpretation which the Revenue put on that word 'after' in SP 13/80 was 'at any time after'. This is the transaction which we discussed in paragraph 11.18 and Note 34 thereon; we said there that it was not possible, but held over the explanation of what prevented it for this paragraph.

own hands direct, rather than its needing to go to the company which continued to own the continuing trade;[9]

- demerging trades into two companies each directly held by the individual shareholders as a preliminary to some other device by which the shareholders could turn one company into cash. The legislation provides that the exemption given on a demerger will be withdrawn if within five years after it the shareholders receive a 'chargeable payment' connected with it.[10] This is defined extremely widely, but the simplest example would be a transaction which allowed the shareholders to get cash by selling one company to the other (a re-merger); the Revenue have not forgotten the Cleary sisters.[11]

14.5 Practical possibilities

What we have seen in the last four paragraphs has been a possible transaction, the splitting of a trading activity (out of a company or group) into two companies directly owned by the shareholders. The transaction itself is a narrow one, but the tax legislation which purports to make it possible is narrowed even further by its concentration on tax avoidance. When we come to look at the question whether these tax structures can actually be made to work in practice, the answers are disheartening.

Let us start with the second and third of the three forms listed at the start of paragraph 14.3. Each involved the *original* company passing all, or a significant part, of its assets to a parallel company – receiving no consideration itself for doing so, but the parallel companies were to issue shares to the shareholders of the original company. The second of our forms of demerger involved the transfer of a trade and assets in this way, and the third involved the transfer of shares in a trading subsidiary.

We know that under company law it is improper from several angles for a company to give its assets away; our most recent rehearsal of the legal principles which generally prevent it was at the end of paragraph 11.8 above, but the fuller examination of these problems was in paragraph 9.13 onwards where we were examining the *Aveling Barford* case. One possible way of avoiding the difficulties would be a scheme involving the liquidation of the original company, perhaps a scheme in the formal sense of that word under section 110 of the Insolvency Act 1986. But that is not possible, because any 'distribution' which the original company made in liquidation would not be a distribution within

---

[9] Section 213(11) TA 1988. The legislation also prevents the recipient company of the demerged trade from issuing redeemable shares, which could again be used for this same abhorrent process of getting cash into the shareholders' hands, section 213(8)(d) TA 1988.
[10] Section 214 TA 1988.
[11] *CIR v Cleary* [1967] 44 TC 399. See paragraph 11.23, and Note 40 thereon.

the tax sense of that word, and therefore could not be made into an 'exempt' distribution by the demerger provisions (see Note 2 above).

The transfer of a company's assets to the parallel company therefore appears possible only under a scheme (again in the formal sense) under section 425 of the Companies Act 1985. If this is to be made to operate in a way which fits within the tax legislation, the court must be persuaded not only that the distributing company should be allowed to remain in existence (that it be not dissolved), but also that the distribution be accomplished in a form which complies with the tax requirements.

14.6 *Practical possibilities (continued)*

The author admits that he has never managed to achieve a demerger using either of the parallel company methods.

That therefore leaves the first of our forms of demerger, by dividend. The original company (which we earlier called A) hives down a trade and assets into a newly formed subsidiary B. That is uncontroversial from a company law point of view, is exempt from the distribution legislation, and protected from capital gains by the intra-group transfer provisions. A then declares a dividend, to be satisfied by the distribution *in specie* of its shareholding in B.[12] The declaration of that dividend causes B to leave A's group, but B is exempted from a charge under section 179 of the Taxation of Chargeable Gains Act 1992.[13] The dividend is itself exempted from being an ACT-type distribution by the demerger provisions, and is also exempted from being regarded as a capital distribution by A for capital gains tax purposes.[14] The dividend is a disposal by A for purposes of corporation tax on chargeable gains of its shares in B; there is no exemption for this, but if we are talking about a disposal of shares issued by B on a hive-down which immediately precedes their disposal, there will have been no growth in their value in A's ownership, so there will be no gain.

Finally, the shareholders see a fall in the value of their A shares when that company disposes of a considerable part of its assets and earning power (not by hiving it down, because that of itself does not alter the shareholder values, but by the payment away of the hive-down company); and they acquire shares in B, without having paid anything for them, and they do this in a distribution which is not income in their hands. What one would hope is that those shareholders would:

• not be regarded as having made any disposal of their A shares;

---

[12] See paragraph 11.9 and Notes 16 and 17 thereon for the explanation of dividends *in specie*. Note in particular that the paying company does need distributable profits equal to the carrying value in its accounts of the asset it is to distribute – but in the case of a newly formed hive-down company one would expect the parent to be carrying its investment in that company at no more than had been the carrying value of the assets transferred down to it (section 132 CA 1985). Note also that there is no stamp duty on the share transfers that effect this change in the subsidiary's ownership (for the reasons explained in Note 17 on paragraph 11.9).
[13] Section 192(3) TCGA 1992.
[14] Section 192(2)(a) TCGA 1992.

- but be able to reallocate what had been the original cost of those A shares between the two holdings which they continue to own as a result of the demerger, shares in A, and in B.

Happily, the legislation envisages that this should happen,[15] and seems to envisage that it should happen on a wider footing than section 136 TCGA 1992 normally does. Thus all of P, Q, R and S originally owned A shares. Section 136 applies if all of them retain A shares with lower values, and all become owners of B shares. What we want to achieve is P and Q retaining A shares with value flowing out of them into shares in B, but at the same time value flowing into them from the A shares previously held by Q and R; those last two are to have any value removed from their A shares, somehow or other. The words of the Act do not allow for this, but the Revenue have never shown any qualms over being able to achieve it. This legislation does make it possible to achieve a particular type of transaction which was not possible before its enactment. The time, effort and care that has to be taken to make sure that one does not fall foul of any of the anti-avoidance provisions are likely to increase the transactional costs quite noticeably – in particular, the author is unrepentant in his view that despite the apparent multiple-choices offered by the legislation, there is really only one way in which the transaction can be put together.

But there is another side to this coin; the legislation has been specifically designed to ensure that a demerger within its protections shall be a demerger and no more. It is not possible to use these provisions to achieve one step in any larger exercise. It will be obvious that anyone contemplating a demerger transaction *must* take advantage of the provision allowing for advance clearance to be obtained from the Inland Revenue, section 215 of the Taxes Act 1988. And it will be equally obvious that what is done after the demerger must not put in jeopardy the reliefs granted; there must be no question of the receipt of a chargeable payment in paragraph 14.4, or of the sale or liquidation of the company.

14.7 The back door to demergers

In paragraph 11.18 and again in paragraph 14.2 we promised to come back to the subject of the Revenue's *Statement of Practice 5/85*. This, it will be remembered envisaged a situation in which oldco was owned by (say) three individuals, P, Q and R. Oldco was carrying on two trades, and what was desired was to split it into two companies, one carrying on each trade, and one owned by P and Q, while the other was owned by R. This was envisaged as happening by oldco transferring one trade to each of two newcos, and those newcos issuing their shares respectively to P and Q, and to R.

---

[15] Section 192(2)(b) TCGA 1992.

DEMERGERS

For capital gains tax purposes, the *Statement of Practice* provides what we might describe as the extended protections of sections 136 and 139 of the Taxation of Chargeable Gains Tax Act 1992, as outlined in paragraph 14.6 that is to say, P and Q receive their new shares in their newco in exchange for their shares in oldco under paper-for-paper treatment (and likewise R gets his newco shares for his oldco ones), and oldco transfers its undertaking to the newcos on a no-gain-no-loss basis. If the form of oldco's *undertaking* were shares in two trading subsidiaries rather than two trades directly carried on, those two trading subsidiaries could be transferred to the newcos, with the same capital gains tax treatment as outlined above – but note that this does *not* include any protection against the subsidiaries being charged under section 179 Taxation of Chargeable Gains Act 1992 if they leave the oldco group with assets received on intra-group transfers within the previous six years.

What we pointed out in paragraph 11.18 was that the *Statement of Practice* thus failed to provide all the protections that the demerger legislation does provide; specifically it fails to prevent the section 179 charge – but far more disastrously, it fails also to prevent oldco's distribution of its two trades to the newcos from being 'distributions out of the assets of the company in respect of shares ...' within section 209(2)(b) of the Taxes Act 1988. That distribution charge can be avoided by putting oldco into liquidation, usually doing so as part of a scheme under section 110 of the Insolvency Act 1986.

If this works, it therefore achieves all the same tax exemptions as the demerger provisions. But it is clear that it does so without the need for all of the conditions we have looked at earlier in this chapter. The detailed administrative conditions in Note 7, for instance, are not a requirement; but neither are what we identified as the fundamental conditions at the end of paragraph 14.3 and in paragraph 14.4. It is not possible, for instance, for the Inland Revenue to withdraw clearance if one of the shareholding groups sells its *division*, or receives a *chargeable payment*. It is equally clear that if a *front-door* clearance application were to be made for a transaction which fits this profile, that front-door application would be refused. One immediately obvious reason for this is that the distribution made by oldco in its liquidation is not one which is a distribution in the tax sense – and it cannot therefore be *exempted* under the demerger provisions. We made this point in Note 2 above.

It is abundantly clear that the Inland Revenue tries to ensure that demergers are not allowed to happen through this back door which would, if restructured so as to fit the front door, fail one of the conditions the legislation requires. We have mentioned, as an example, the intention that one of the companies should be sold. This would bar the front-door route to a demerger; if the Revenue are aware that it is envisaged that it would follow an SP 5/85 division, they will decline to give clearance for that division when such clearance is applied for under the transactions in securities, and paper-for-paper provisions. However, this illustrates the great danger of legislation by clearance application. There will be inevitable occasions when the Inland Revenue allow a transaction through the net because they are not told everything which they would regard as relevant for a *demerger* clearance; the taxpayer is after all applying under entirely different provisions, and the available guidance on what he needs to disclose would not require such an unburdening of his soul. On the other hand, there will be perfectly unobjectionable transactions into which the Inland Revenue read ulterior motives which were never in anyone's mind.

INDEX

Abbreviated accounts, 1.n.15
Accountants' investigation, 12.n.32
Accounting policies note to the accounts, 1.26
Accounting Standards, 1.25
Accounting Standards Board, 1.n.18, 4.2
   Statement of Principles, 4.2
Accounts (see also financial statements; *accounts* Companies Act word for balance sheet and profit and loss account, *financial statements* is ASB word for all four statements)
   abbreviated, 1.n.15, 8.n.16
   summary financial statements 1.n.15
   statutory, 1.n.15, 5.7
   warranted accounts, 12.10 directors' responsibility for accounts, 1.23, 8.4
Accruals concept, 2.n.8
Acquisition accounting, 6.23–
Advance corporation tax (ACT), 1.34, 1.35, 1.n.26, 5.8–, 12.20 non availability of carry forward to successor on transfer of a trade, 11.14
Agent and principal
   relationship distinguished from that of parents & subsidiaries, 6.n.12
   third party dealing with directors as agents for company, when he knows that those directors are not acting for company's purposes, 9.n.11
Allotment of shares, 3.16
Alternative accounting rules including current costing, 2.4, 2.6
Amalgamation, reconstruction or (Scheme of, under s.425 CA 1985), 6.n.63, 6.62–
Arrangements for a company to leave a group, or to cease to be owned or controlled by its existing owners, 5.38, 5.40–, 11.n.13
   stamp duty significance of *Heads of Agreement*, 12.5
Articles of Association, 1.10, 3.14, 8.2, 13.9
   Table A as substitute, and as rule where Articles are silent, 8.2, 8.n.3
   possible requirement for employee shareholders to sell on leaving co, 10.11, 10.12

Asset values, 2.1, 2.n.2
   assets acquired for the issue of shares, 3.20, 3.27, 3.39–
   the directors' honest estimate of value, 3.24, 3.26
   assets of an unincorporated business acquired, compared with shares acquired when an incorporated business is acquired, 3.30
   assets acquired on incorporation of company by gift from shareholder, 3.44
   value to the business, 4.19
Associated companies, stamp duty exemption, 5.32
Auditors'
   appointment, 1.25, 6.8
   consent to written resolutions, 3.13, 6.9
   qualified opinion, 1.27
   report whether accounts show true and fair view, 1.23, 1.27
   role, 1.24–
   accountants' investigation of target on behalf of predator distinguished from an audit, 12.n.32

Bad and doubtful debts, 5.4, 7.n.2
Balance sheet approach to accounting, 4.2, 4.16, 4.18
Banks, and the Banking Acts 1979 and 1987, 1.2, 13.n.20
Beneficial ownership, 5.32–, 5.37, 11.28, 12.5
   passes in normal case to purchaser simultaneously with leaving vendor, 5.34, 5.37, 12.8, 12.n.13
   effects of loss of beneficial ownership, 5.38, 11.28
   not broken for general purposes by *Heads of Agreement*, 12.5
   company in liquidation, beneficial ownership goes into suspense – special rules which follow, 12.n.27
Benefiting a company's trade
   company purchase of own shares, 13.13–
   demergers, 14.3
Blocking of pre–acquisition profits, or otherwise, 6.14, 6.16, 9.26–, 9.34
Bona fide commercial reasons, not forming part of a scheme or arrangements of which the main

421

INDEX

purpose . . is the avoidance of tax, 6.70, 11.25, 11.27, 13.12, 14.6
Brands, (and other intangibles), 2.2
Buildings – values, 2.2–
Bushell v Faith shares, 8.n.13

Called up share capital, 4.1
  stated in Memorandum, 8.2
Capacity – see Company's capacity
Capital contributions, 3.n.58
Capital expenditure, 5.4, 5.n.13
Capital gains tax
  share exchange (paper for paper) when shareholder receives predator shares in exchange for target shares is not a CGT disposal/acquisition if *cleared* by Revenue, 11.27
  beneficial ownership, 5.33
  acquisition costs
    shares issued in satisfaction of debt, 3.17, 3.n.16, 3.n.17
    shares acquired under profit sharing scheme, 10.14
    shares acquired under approved option scheme, 10.n.4
  losses – limited uses to reduce other liabilities, 11.4
    non–availability for carry forward to another co on transfer of trade, 11.14
  losses on loans to unlisted trading companies, 3.17, 3.n.13
  losses on shares in unlisted trading companies which can be treated as income losses rather than capital gains losses, 3.n.13
  disposal of a company's undertaking, 6.36
  non–disposal by shareholder of his holding when it becomes valueless – and he receives a new holding in a predator company, 6.36, 13.11, 14.2, 14.6, 14.7
  groups, 6.42, 6.44
    leaving the group, 6.43, 6.44, 14.6, 14.7
  roll–over relief in groups, 6.42, 6.n.74, 11.4, 11.n.5, 12.10
  non–availability within CGT regime of any arrangements similar to *group relief*, 6.42
  non–availability of relief for *pre–entry losses*, 6.42
  depreciatory transactions, 11.n.5a, 11.16, 11.n.27–29
  sale of asset pregnant with gain, 11.8
  envelope trick (company leaving the group owning an asset received within six years on intra–group transfer, that asset being pregnant with gain), 6.43, 6.45, 11.5
  possibility of undoing transfer into group assets company, 11.5
  s.179 charge removed in demerger, 14.2
  need for indemnities on sale, 12.18
  s.179 charge removed for two companies leaving group at same time, 12.21
  the *dummy bridge* company is directly caught, 11.6
  shareholding moved within group for consideration consisting of issue of shares by recipient (Woolcombers case), 6.55, 11.19–
  step–up in value of shareholding in hands of recipient of those shares, 6.56
  effect of subsidiary's disposal of the stepped–up shares within six years, 6.57, 11.19
  exclusion of possibility of a claim for paper–for–paper relief which would involve Woolcombers pattern of acquisition costs, 6.58
  trustees of profit sharing scheme conditional exemption, 10.14
Capital maintenance, 4.14–, 9.1, 9.33, 9.34
  capital redemption reserve in purchase of own shares, 13.3–
  in context of alternative accounting rules designed to compensate for inflation, 4.15
  fixed and circulating capital, 4.12–
  capitalisation of profit, 4.n.21
  return of capital, 9.12, 9.17
Capital redemption reserve, 13.3–
Carrying value, 2.2, 2.3, 3.27
Cashflows, 4.3
Central mind and management of companies, 6.n.10
Change in the nature or conduct of a trade, 12.n.24
Chargeable payment in demerger, 14.4
Claims for taxation, 12.21
Clearances, Inland Revenue
  share exchanges, paper–for–paper, 11.27
  transactions in securities, 11.25
  demergers, 14.6
  company purchase of own shares, 13.12.n.26a
  share options and incentives, 10.n.1
Close companies, 5.n.43, 10.9
Company's capacity, 8.2, 9.2–, 9.8
  ultra vires – acts which are outside that capacity, 9.2
  knowledge of third parties concerning the company's capacity, 9.5
  acts which are within the company's

422

INDEX

capacity, but of which the *real purpose* is an ulterior one, 9.9
state of mind or knowledge of directors or those dealing with them is irrelevant to questions of corporate capacity, 9.10
Compensation for loss of office – see Directors, compensation for loss of office
Completion, 5.n.57, 12.9, 12.30
  warranties deemed repeated at completion, 12.13
  as point at which income starts to belong to purchaser – concept, 12.16
  non-competition clauses and restraint of trade, 12.31
Conditional contracts, 5.n.57, 5.n.61, 5.n.65
Conduct of claims, 12.32
Confidentiality, 12.6
Connected parties, 3.29
  for capital gains tax, 6.37
  for distribution purposes (under common control), 6.39
  for the exception from Financial Services Act 1986 of acquisition of 75 percent of unlisted company from group of connected persons, 12.3, 12.n.5
Consortium
  the companies which jointly own another, 7.1
  members of the consortium financing and operating their jointly owned company, 7.4, 7.7–
  equity, and reward for equity in the jointly owned company, 7.10–
  shareholders' agreement in the jointly owned company, 7.12–
  the jointly owned company distinguished from the consortium which owns it, 7.1
  relief, 5.39, 7.5–
Constructive trustee – third party knowing company acting beyond capacity/breach by directors of duties, 9.12, 9.14
Contract (in the text referred to as the purchase contract but the vendor would call it the sale contract), 12.7
  legally binding, 12.8
  conditional on Revenue clearances, 12.8
  conditional on shareholder approval, 12.8
  rescission, 12.12
  profits (and tax thereon) of accounting period which brackets completion date, 12.16
  investigations by prospective purchaser, supplementing any disclosure he can force by enquiries and demands for warranties, 12.26–, 12.28–
Contracting out
  employees contracted out of state earnings related pension scheme, 1.n.23,
  of government and local government services, 11.41
Control
  Companies Act concept, 6.5
  substance rather than form in s.416(2) TA 1988, 5.33
  capital gains tax (imports s.416 TA 1988 concepts), 6.37
  distribution legislation (imports s.416 TA 1988 concepts), 6.39
  controlled subsidiaries, in the context of share option and incentive schemes, 10.6
Conversion of debt into equity, 3.17–
  limitation on CGT cost of equity if reorganisation provisions apply, 3.17
  creditor connected with co, 3.18
Corporate tax compared with tax on earnings for the unincorporated business, possibility of retentions, 3.8
Cross options, 5.36, 6.n.7, 7.13
Current cost accounts one form of alternative accounting, 2.4, 2.6
Current purchasing power accounts, 2.n.5
Creative accounting, 1.23

Debt into equity, conversion, 3.17
Deductible expense for tax in arriving at profits of trade, 5.3
  employee share trusts, 10.13
  profit sharing scheme, 10.14
Deduction of tax at source from interest, 1.n.24, 12.20
Deferred tax, 3.n.53, 5.3, 5.n.14, 5.18–
Deficit on liquidation, 1.20–
Demergers, 14.1
  separation of two trades into separate companies, 14.3
  benefiting a trade, 13.14, 14.3
  the ban on a subsequent sale or liquidation of one of the demerged companies, 14.4
  the ban on other devices by which the shareholders could obtain cash (a *chargeable payment*) from their ownership of one of the companies, 14.4
Department of Trade, 1.2
Depreciatory transaction – see Capital gains tax, depreciatory transactions
Directors'
  appointment, 1.10, 6.8, 8.1, 8.4–
  to fill casual vacancy, 8.5

INDEX

removal by shareholders, 8.5, 8.6
   by Board under Articles but not under Table A, 8.5
authority (including their ostensible authority), 8.1, 9.2–, 9.4–
knowledge of third party concerning directors' authority, 9.5
compensation for loss of office, 1.n.21, 8.n.15, 8.n.21, 11.29–
the individual's tax, and that of the company, on compensation for loss of office, 11.31
disqualification, 8.n.8
duty of skill and care, 8.10
fraud on creditors, 9.16, 9.17
misfeasance, 9.17
trustee of funds of company; if they misapply funds so another receives them with knowledge, he is constructive trustee, 9.12, 9.14, 9.18
indemnification *for being found not guilty*, 6.11
insurance, 6.11
loans to directors, 5.22, 8.8, 8.n.17 (note for loans to company see under shareholders)
remuneration, 1.10, 8.1, 8.4, 8.7–
   Companies Act meaning, 8.7
   Companies Act disclosure, 8.8
   Tax meaning, (incl. timing of receipts), 8.9, 11.31
   Nat Ins. meaning(incl.timing of receipts), 8.n.30
pensions, and disclosure of cost of provision, 8.n.20, 8.n.22
remuneration free of tax, 8.n.26
responsibility for accounts of company, 1.23, 8.4
responsibility for deciding what is, or is not, a realised profit on an intra group disposal, and whether the facts must be disclosed, 9.34
duties to, and responsibility to, company are fiduciary, 8.1, 8.10, 9.12, 9.14
responsibility to employees, creditors, only indirect through company, 8.10
service contracts (in the context of directors' security of tenure), 8.6, 8.n.15
service contracts (as a method of remunerating the director for duties as an executive of company), 8.7, 8.8, 12.30
service contract with predator and/or continued contract with target, 12.30
Disclosure letter, 12.14
Dismissal of staff on liquidation, 1.17

Disposals
   the selling team, 11.1
Disqualification – see Directors, disqualification
Distributable profits, 3.5–, 9.25–
on subsequent sale of target company acquired with benefit of merger relief, 9.29–
comparison of profits on sale of target in solus accounts, and in consolidation, 9.32
distributability of profit on intra-group transfer of a subsidiary company, 9.34
distributability of revaluation reserve when asset on which it was created is paid as a dividend in specie, 11.9
Distribution of surpluses, or of assets, forbidden for guarantee companies, 1.1
Distributions in an ordinary English, and a tax, sense, 3.5–, 5.8
high cost of distributions where ACT is unrelieved, 3.6
desirability or otherwise, 3.7
disposal by a company of its undertaking, 6.36
asset or undertaking received by a company which issues shares to shareholders of transferor of asset, as a result of which companies come under common control, 6.40
in respect of shares in the company, where asset still remains owned, albeit indirectly, by distributor, 6.50
member receives a *benefit* of greater value than consideration given by that member (s.209(4) TA 1988), 6.51
relief from charge on member's benefit, where asset moves from subsidiary to parent, 6.52
asset moves at parent's instance from one subsidiary to another, 6.54
exemption from the charge of company purchase of own shares, 13.2, 13.12–
exemption in demergers, 14.2, 14.n.2
but not in *demerger through back door*, 14.7
Dividends, 1.10, 1.32, 1.33, 3.5–, 5.8
advantage of dividend which costs no more tax but can be lent back to company, 3.10
in specie, 11.9, 11.n.16, 11.n.17, 14.3, 14.6
stamp duty exemption, 11.n.17
need for distributable profits at least equal to asset's carrying value, 11.n.16

424

INDEX

Dividend cover, 2.11
Dividend policy – listed and unlisted companies compared, 2.19
Division of a company, 11.17– (see also demergers *through the back door*)
is not a reconstruction, 6.69
Double tax relief, 5.n.32
Due diligence, 12.28–

Earnings – comparative cost to company, 1.32
Earn-outs, 11.26
Employee share trusts, in particular the cost to the co, 10.1, 10.11
  timing of tax deductibility for company, 10.n.22
  as a possible purchaser of shares acquired under options or profit sharing, 10.11, 10.12
  exemption from financial assistance rules, 9.20
  ESOTs approved under FA 1989, 10.13
Employment protection (TUPE regulations), 3.32, 11.3, 11.36–
Envelope trick, 6.43, 6.45, 11.5
ESOTs – see Employee share trusts
Exclusivity, 12.6

Fair Trading – Office of, 1.2
Financial adaptability, 4.3
Financial assistance – existing shareholders deplete capital of company even if it is the incoming shareholder who is assisted, 9.19
  breadth of the definition, 9.21–
  the *sweep up* definition, 9.22
  problems of identification illustrated, 9.23, 11.8
  whitewash procedure, 9.24
  the need for *net assets*, 9.24
  statutory declaration of solvency, 9.24
  lawful dividend is exempted from being financial assistance, 9.20, 9.29, 11.9
  pre-disposal reorganisations need to check financial assistance implications, 9.22, 11.8
  management buy–outs, extra degree of care (and probably whitewash) needed, 12.22
  interposed holding company with a need to borrow cash from its subsidiary, 13.8
Financial Services Act 1986, & financial services companies, 1.2, 12.2–
  investment business, 12.3
  investment advertisements, 12.4
  take–over unanimously recommended by target's directors – exemption

from ban on issue of investment advertisements, 12.4
  investment agreement, 12.4
Financial statements
  primary, 4.2, 4.20
  elements, 4.n.7
  generally accepted accounting principles, 4.n.14
  measurement, 4.8, 4.19
  realisation of profit, 4.9–
  recognised gains, statement of, not to include goodwill write–offs, 6.29
  recognition; accounting process of recognising items for financial statements, 4.4, 4.6, 4.20
Financing company in part with loans from shareholders, provided by them out of post-tax income, 3.10
  the effect on a subsequent sale, 3.11
Floating charges, 1.13, 1.n.7
Forfeiture of shares, 6.n.35, 13.1
Fraud, 1.25
Fraud on creditors, 9.16, 9.17
Fundamental accounting concepts, 1.27, 2.n.8, 4.n.12, 4.17

Gearing ratio, 2.33
Generally accepted accounting principles, 2.22, 4.7, 6.30, 6.n.50
Going concern – fundamental accounting concept, 1.n.9, 2.3
Goodwill, 2.2, 2.21, 4.21, 6.26, 6.28
  on acquisition of business and assets, differentiated from share acquisition, 3.28, 3.30
  the dangling debit, 4.n.36
  separable; the meaning of the concept, and the extent to which it has been discredited, 4.n.38, 6.29
  write–off of goodwill is not to go through the statement of recognised gains, 6.29
  write–off to be unscrambled if business is later resold, 6.29, 9.31
  the choice between writing off against a reserve, and amortising through profits, 6.28, 6.29
  the use of merger reserve for writing off goodwill, 4.n.36, 6.n.41a, 9.32, 9.33
Group assets companies, 11.4–
  transfer values of assets into that company for tax and company law, 11.7
  possibility of undoing into a group assets company an intra-group transfer that would be caught by s.179, 11.5
Group income, 5.26
  election, 5.8, 5.39, 7.n.4

INDEX

Group of companies
  the concept of ownership, 6.4
  the concept of 'control', 6.5
  group accounts, 6.5
  tax concepts, introduced, 6.31
  group asset companies, 11.4
Group reconstruction relief, 6.17
Group relief, 5.23–, 5.39
  arrangements for a company to leave a group, 5.36–, 5.40, 7.n.1
  payments for group relief, 7.n.1, 7.6
Guarantee companies, 1.1
Guarantees, 1.6, 9.3, 9.8
  lease guarantees, 1.9

Heads of agreement, 11.6, 12.5
  not a legal obligation to purchase or any such obligation conditional, 12.5
  fundamental reasons why *heads* must not contain legally binding obligations to buy, 12.6
  confidentiality and exclusivity, 12.6
Historical costs, 2.2, 2.4
Hive–downs, 11.11–, 12.23
  mechanics and pricing of the transfers into the hivedown company; timing of the *arrangement* for sale of co, 11.12–, 11.n.21
  need for analysis of exactly what purchaser is buying, 12.24–
  carry forward of losses, etc under s.343 on mandatory basis, 11.14, 12.23
  but restriction of loss carry forward if parent insolvent, or if change in nature or scale of trade, 12.23
  from parent in liquidation, 12.23
Holding company and subsidiary companies, 6.5
  holding company interposed as in Shearer v Bercain, 6.16
  prior to holding company purchasing its own shares, 13.8
  or alternatively to achieve same result by holding company buying out one shareholder for cash, 13.9, 13.n.26
Holding gains, 2.n.4

Impairment, asset suffering an, 9.n.31
  word *impairment* compared with *diminution in value*, 9.26
Imputation of corporate tax to shareholders on dividends, 1.34
Income tax, deduction at source, 5.21, 5.n.41
Income tax treatment of loss on shares subscribed for, 3.17
Incorporation, 3.1
  the irreversible step, 3.1
  procedure, 3.14
  shelf company procedures, 3.15
  the sole trader's business, 3.32–
  the alternative method of incorporating the sole trader's business, 3.41–
  alternative method can result in company not needing to carry its assets at full values, 3.42
  hold–over for the individual of gains on assets transfered to company in alternative method of incorporation, 3.41
  the doubling up of capital gains exposure when assets are given to a company in alternative method, 3.44
  cessation of the sole trader's business, 3.34
  plant & machinery, and other capital allowance assets, election for transfer at tax wdv, 3.38
  stock & work in progress, the value for transfer, 3.38
  note: above three headings also set out position for individual hiving trade down into company prior to sale of that company to a predator. Compare this with position if he sells trade and assets to predator without prior incorporation, 11.10, 11.11, 11.n.18
  continuity of pension scheme, 3.32
  transfer deemed to be of net assets for capital gains tax, 3.35
  hold–over of individual's capital gain, 3.36
  conveyance of gross assets for stamp duty purposes, 3.35, 3.37
  possibility of saving stamp duty, 3.38
  comparison of tax liability and retentions with those of unincorporated business, 3.8–
  full capitalisation (shares and share premium account) of company incorporated in standard way, 3.39
Indemnity, deed of indemnity associated with share purchase contract (share sale contract), 12.15, 12.21
  claim under indemnity distinguished from claim for damages for breach of warranty, 12.15
  period for which claim remains valid, 12.15
  identifying tax liabilities for indemnification, 12.17–
  conduct of claims, 12.32
Indemnity by company for director *found not guilty*, 6.11
Informal decision procedure, 3.13, 6.10
Insolvent, 1.5, 1.14, 9.16–
Insolvent liquidation, 1.16, 3.2

INDEX

Insurance companies, and the Insurance Companies Acts, 1.2, 13.n.20
Insurance for directors, 6.11
Interest
  comparative cost to company, 1.32–
  tax relief for members of management buy-out team on personal borrowings, 12.22
Internal controls, 1.24
Investment advertisements, 12.4
Investment agreement, 12.4
Investment business, 12.3
Investment protection committees, 10.n.7, 10.n.29, 10.7, 10.8
Issue of shares
  for cash, 3.16–
  for non-cash consideration, 3.16, 3.20, 3.35
  the need for a valuation of assets acquired by a public company for issue of shares, 3.26
  at a discount, 3.n.10, 3.23
  for work to be done, 3.28–
  by existing subsidiary, for acquisition of asset from its parent, 6.49

Knowledge and belief, best of, basis on which warranties given to purchaser, 12.n.16
Knowledge, state of mind and knowledge of directors – see Company's, capacity, knowledge etc irrelevant

Last–in–first–out basis of stock valuation, 2.6
Lease guarantees, 1.9, 1.17, 1.n.10
Lease termination on events of default, 1.17
Leaving a group – see under Arrangements for a company to leave a group
  see also under Capital gains tax, leaving a group
  see also Group Relief, arrangements for a company to leave a group
Legal ownership, 5.32, 10.16
  shares in profit sharing scheme before release by trustees of scheme, 10.14, 10.15
Liabilities falling due measure of solvency, for *whitewash* and other purposes, 1.5, 9.24, 13.9
Licensed Insolvency Practitioner, 1.16
Limited liability, 1.4–, 1.20, 3.2
Limited by guarantee, 1.1
Liquidation, 1.16–, 5.34
  deficit, 1.20–
  distributions in liquidation treatment for tax, 6.n.71, 11.18, 11.n.33, 14.7
  special rules for ownership of company's assets, and for their disposal, 12.n.27
  does not cause a subsidiary to leave its (liquidated) parent's group, 12.n.26
  repossession of leased assets on liquidation, 1.18
Liquidity, 1.15
Listed companies, the Yellow Book and the Stock Exchange, 1.2, 12.8, 12.28
Loans by company
  to participators, 5.22
  to directors, 5.22, 8.8 Note: see under shareholders for loans to company
Loss carry forward on transfer of a trade into a company
  by individual, 3.34, 3.n.43
  by predecessor company, 11.11, 11.14, 12.20

Maintainable profits, 2.8, 2.21
Management buy–out, 12.22
  recognising the MBO team's need at a later stage to buy out their financier, 12.22
  tax relief for interest on MBO team's borrowings, 12.22
  financial assistance, 12.22
Matching, part of fundamental accounting concept of accruals, 4.17, 4.n.27
Memorandum of Association, 1.10, 3.14, 9.8–
  capital, 8.2
  company's capacity, 9.2, 9.8–, 9.16
    entitlement of third party to assume co. acting within capacity, 9.5
    real purposes not within company's capacity, 9.9, 9.n.9
  objects clause, 8.2, 9.8–
  objects – separate and ancillary, 9.9
Merger accounting, 6.n.20, 6.n.30, 6.23–
  requirements (in Company law as expanded by SSAP 23), 6.30, 6.n.50
Merger relief, 6.n.20, 6.20–
  more or less certainly permits distribution of pre–acquisition profits, 9.26, 9.28
  effect on distributable profits of sale of target, 9.29–
  comparison of profits on sale of target, in solus and consolidation, 9.32
  can be regarded as an amount held in suspense while the target is still owned, but its disposition on the sale of the target can produce a distribution of capital, 9.33
  vendor placing – as a device used by predator to qualify for merger relief, 6.30, 6.n.48, 12.n.1

427

INDEX

Merger reserve (in acquisition accounting), 4.n.36, 6.25, 6.n.41a, 9.n.28, 9.32
  remains in consolidation even after target is sold, 9.32
  but in solus accounts merger reserve unlikely to exist, and its *mirror image* is released on target sale, 9.32
  reversal of the write–off of goodwill if the target is subsequently sold, 6.29, 9.31
Merger reserve (in merger accounting), 6.26
Misfeasance, 9.17
Motive of avoiding tax, 11.25, 13.13, 13.n.32

Non–competition clauses, 12.31
Non–deductible expense, 5.3
Non–qualifying corporate bonds, 11.n.49
Not–for–profit–companies, 1.1

Objects clause, 9.8–,
  change in objects can be oppression of those objecting entitling them to relief, 13.1 Note: see also Memorandum of Association
Off–balance sheet transactions
  the possibilities of avoiding consolidating a subsidiary, 6.6
  the possibility of not showing a subsidiary's contingent liability either in its own accounts or in the consolidation, 6.6
  the possibility of disguising ownership and/or control of a 'subsidiary', 6.7
Office of Fair Trading, 1.2
Open–market price, 6.n.66, 11.12, 11.13, 11.n.21, 11.n.22
Operating capacity (concept of current costing), 2.21, 2.n.7, 4.15
Oppression of minorities, 8.5, 8.n.11, 13.1
Options
  gain on exercise, 3.29
  effect on beneficial ownership, 5.36, 5.42
  cross options, 6.n.7, 7.13 Note: see also Share option schemes, & Savings-related share option schemes
Ordinary creditors, 1.19
  rank pari passu, 1.n.13

Paper–for–paper share exchanges, 6.55, 6.n.102, 11.26–
  clearance procedures, 11.27
Parent undertaking and subsidiary undertakings (and within the first the sub–group which are parent companies), 6.5
Participators, loans to, 5.22
Pay and file, 5.6
PAYE regulations, 8.n.25, 12.21
  PAYE liabilities, 12.20
Pension schemes, 1.n.22, 3.32, 8.8, 8.n.20, 11.29, 11.30, 11.n.58, 12.12
Permanent diminution in value of assets, 9.26, 9.n.31
Personal guarantees, 1.6
Plant & machinery, and other capital allowance assets, election for transfer at tax written down value into newly incorporated company, 3.40
  but the non–availability of such elections when capital allowance assets are transferred between companies which are neither connected parties nor within s.343 TA 1988, 11.10
Pre–acquisition profits, 3.28, 6.13, 6.14, 6.16, 6.n.27, 9.26– (these references are to distribution to predator; for distribution to vendor see pre–disposal dividend)
  dividend received by predator which has claimed merger relief, 9.26, 9.28
Pre–disposal dividend, 5.29–, 11.15–, 12.16
  on group income basis, 5.30, 9.n.21, 11.n.30
  does not offend against financial assistance rules, 9.20, 9.n.21, 9.29, 11.16, 11.n.30
  capital gains tax anti avoidance legislation is generally irrelevant, 11.16
  as a transaction in securities, 11.16
Pre–disposal reorganisations
  need to check financial assistance implications, 9.22, 11.8
  need to get timing right (stamp duty & intra group dividends), 11.9
  effect on sale of earlier reorganisation dealt with on *Woolcombers* basis q.v., 11.19
Predator's right to assign benefit of contract, or of indemnities (including effect of that on conduct of claims), 12.31
Pre–emption, 3.16
Pre–entry losses – see under Capital gains tax, non-availability of relief for pre–entry losses
Preferred creditors, 1.18
Pregnant with gain – see Capital gains tax, sale of asset pregnant with gain
Preliminary enquiries, 12.n.32

428

INDEX

Principal & agent; relationship
  distinguished from that of parents and subsidiaries, 6.n.12
  relationship of directors to company, 9.n.11
Private companies, 1.3, 8.n.3, 13.1
Profit sharing scheme (a form of share incentive scheme), 10.1, 10.14
  rules and trust deed, 10.n.1
  exemption from tax of benefit to employee on appropriation, 10.14
  capital gains tax acquisition cost, 10.14
  legal and *beneficial* ownership of shares until release; dividends and votes, 10.14, 10.15
  dilution of other holders' interests, 10.8
  exemption from financial assistance rules, 9.20
  motivation of employees depends on growth in share price not on tax privileges, 10.6
  general conditions for approval, 10.9
  clearances, 10.n.1
  deductibility of cost to co and timing of deduction, 10.14
  rules and trust deed, 10.n.1
  release date and retention period, 10.15
  tax penalties on *locked in value* on events before release date, 10.16–
  employees' possible exit route by selling shares to employee share trust, 10.11, 10.12
Profits
  definition in terms of accounting requirements, 4.6–, 4.9–
  effect on distributable profits of sale of target, 9.29–
  realised profits, 2.22, 5.4, 9.33, 9.34
  on sale of business, on the purchase of which goodwill had been written off, 6.29
Promoters of acquisitions or reorganisations, authorised under Financial Services Act, 12.2, 12.28
Provisions
  for losses, 5.4
  for bad and doubtful debts, 5.4
Prudence – fundamental accounting concept, 1.27, 1.29, 2.n.8, 4.6
Public companies, 1.3
  minimum share capital for start of business, 3.14
  turning back into private companies, 13.1
Purchase of own shares, 13.1
  power in Articles, 13.9
  special resolution, 13.2, 13.9
  paid for in cash at completion (no deferred purchase), 13.3
  exemption from the tax legislation on distributions, 13.2, 13.12–

procedures for purchase whether out of capital or out of profits or proceeds of new issue, 13.9
stamp duty, 13.10
period of ownership before purchase, 13.15
substantial reduction of holding, 13.15 13.n.35
definition of *schemes* the Revenue can refuse, and their interpretation of rules, 13.13–
shares purchased must be fully paid, 13.3
benefiting a trade meaning, 13.14
to meet inheritance tax liability, 13.n.33

Qualified opinion by auditors, 1.27
Qualifying corporate bonds, 11.n.49

Realisable value of assets, 2.2
Realisation basis of accounting, 1.n.9
Realised profits, 2.22, 5.4
  on sale of business, on the purchase of which goodwill had been written off, 6.29
  directors' responsibility for deciding what is a realised profit, 9.34
Recognised gains, statement of, not to include goodwill write–offs, 6.29
Recognition; accounting process of recognising items for financial statements, 4.4, 4.6, 4.20
Reconstruction or amalgamation (Scheme of, under s.425 CA 1985, 6.n.63, 6.62–
  does not for stamp duty include a division of a company, 6.69
  for capital gains tax purposes, a division of a company is by concession regarded as reconstruction, 6.69
Redemption of shares, 13.2, 13.n.8
Redundancy payments on liquidation, 1.17
Registrar of Companies, 1.2
Repossession of leased assets on liquidation, 1.18
Reserve
  merger reserve (in acquisition accounting), 4.n.36, 6.25, 6.n.41a, 9.n.28
  reversal of the write–off of goodwill if the target is subsequently sold, 6.29, 9.31
  merger reserve (in merger accounting), 6.26
Residence of companies for tax, 6.n.10
Restraint of trade, 12.31
Retained earnings, 2.9
Return of capital, 9.12, 9.17

INDEX

Revaluation
  policy, 2.4–
  as an assistance to those outside the company rather than to management, 2.5
  of assets, its effect on reported profits, 2.n.3,
  used at one time to create distributable profits, 6.13
  to realisable value (break-up value), 2.3, 2.5
  to value to the business (current cost), 2.3, 2.4
  contingent tax liability not visible to predator – need for disclosure and warranty, 12.10–
Revenue clearances
  share exchanges, paper–for–paper, 11.27, 12.8
  transactions in securities, 11.25, 12.8
  demergers – incl those *through back door*, 14.6, 14.7
  company purchase of own shares, 13.12, 13.n.26a
  share options and incentives, 10.n.1
Risk, 2.33

Savings related share option scheme, 10.1, 10.n.11
Scheme of reconstruction or amalgamation under s.425 CA 1985, 6.n.63, 6.62–
  the *scheme* is an essential part of the stamp duty implications, 6.68
  for capital gains tax the scheme may be only a part of some wider arrangements, and it is their implications which are equally important, 6.68
  does not for stamp duty purposes include a division of a company, 6.69
  for capital gains tax a division of a company is by concession treated as a reconstruction, 6.69
Scrip dividends, 5.8
Secured creditors, 1.18
Security over assets, 1.6
Separable; the meaning of the concept, and the extent to which it has been discredited, 4.n.38, 6.29
Separation of business from its owner by incorporation, 1.21, 3.12
Shareholders
  Articles; contract between shareholders, 8.2
  agreement, 7.12–
  ultimate control, 8.3, 8.4
  delegation of management to directors, 8.3

meetings and voting; *mechanics* delegated to directors, 8.3
ratification of acts purportedly done by company which have been challenged, 9.12, 9.n.13, 9.15–
funds, 2.34, 4.1, 9.13
loans from shareholders, 1.7, 3.10
subordinated loans from shareholders, 1.8, 9.13
  co. made solvent, but not given distributable reserves, 9.13
  advantages of drawing a dividend which costs no more tax but can be lent back, 3.10
  advantage on sale of co, 3.11
Share exchanges (paper for paper), 6.55–, 6.72, 11.26–,
  earnouts, 11.26
  general offer, definition, 11.n.48
  the special case, and its extended forms, in which the shares issued are consideration for issuing company's receipt of a trade, rather than takeover of a target, 6.71, 13.11, 14.2, 14.6, 14.7
  clearance procedures, 11.27
Share incentive schemes (carry no tax privileges except in special case of *profit sharing* scheme q.v., but earlier tax penalties have largely been removed), 10.1,
  absence of restrictions on shares issued (the removal of which could otherwise create a growth in value – *removal of clogs*), 10.9
  growth in value charge, 10.9
  exemption from financial assistance, 9.20
Share issues
  for cash, 3.16
  called up share capital and unpaid calls, 4.1
  for non-cash, 3.20
Share option schemes (executive share option schemes; see also savings related options, share incentives & profit sharing), 10.1–
  rules, incl life of scheme in terms of no of shares authorised under it, 10.n.1, 10.7, 10.8
  grant of options, 10.2
  gain on exercise exempted in approved scheme, 10.4
  general conditions for approval, 10.9
  capital gains tax acquisition cost, 10.n.4
  exercise, and exercise price, 10.1, 10.2
  exemption from financial assistance rules, 9.20
  dilution of other holders' interests – institutional investors' *protection committees*, 10.3, 10.7, 10.8

INDEX

motivation of employees depends on rises in the share price – not on tax privileges, 10.6
performance targets, 10.8
death, retirement or termination of employment, 10.10
clearances, 10.n.1
employees' possible exit route by selling shares to employee share trust, 10.11, 10.12
Share premium account, 3.26, 3.39–, 6.12, 6.15
relaxation of the requirement to establish a premium, 3.26, 3.31, 6.16–
use for purchase of own shares, 13.7
Share sale agreement or contract } See *Contract*
Share purchase agreement or contract
Share values, 2.1
nominal value of shares is relevant for comparison with other consideration for availability of merger accounting, 6.30, 6.n.49
nominal value also relevant for stamp duty relief under s.76 FA 1986, 6.34, 6.n.59
Shearer v Bercain, 6.13
Shelf companies, 3.15
Single–member companies, 3.13, 3.15
subsidiaries in a group as examples of single member companies, 6.8
role of shareholder of single member subsidiary company, 6.8
role of director of single member subsidiary company, 6.8
'written resolutions' as a possible way of handling decision–taking, 6.9
'informal decisions' as a different method of validation, 6.10
Solvency, 1.8, 1.15
Spargo's case, 3.21
Splitting of a company, 11.17–, 11.n.33
Stamp duty
on straightforward incorporation of sole trader's business, 3.37
avoidance on oral contract for transfer of assets to company and its share issue for cash, 3.21, 3.38
conveyance of gross assets for stamp duty purposes, 3.35, 3.37
land & buildings; legal ownership left with sole trader, who contracts with company that he will convey legal title to a third party when company sells its beneficial interest, 3.38

on gifts; abolition of the voluntary dispositions head of charge, 3.42
on dividends *in specie*, 11.n.17
associated companies exemption (s.42), 5.32, 6.33, 14.n.1
associated status ceases on signature of *Heads*, 11.6
statutory declaration for the claiming of associated companies exemption, 11.n.11, 11.n.12
on acquisition of target shares, 6.22
on acquisition of target undertaking, 6.22, 6.33, 6.34, 14.n.1
drafting of legislation, and its interpretation, 6.67
dummy bridge company, 6.33, 11.6
undertaking, 6.34
on company purchase of own shares, 13.10
on demergers, 14.n.1
on reconstruction taking form of transfer of trade to new company which issues shares to shareholders of original company (s.75 FA 1986), 6.22
on reconstruction taking form of interposition of holding company with mirror image capital structure between company and shareholders, 6.22, 13.10
State Earnings Related Pension, 1.n.23, 3.n.2
Statutory accounts, 1.n.15
Steel Barrel case, 3.24
Step–up in value – see Capital gains tax, step–up in value of shareholding
Stock dividends, 5.8
Stock exchange, 1.2
Stock profits, 2.n.4
Stock & work in progress, the value for transfer into newly incorporated company, 3.38, 11.12, 11.n.21
moving to a hivedown co., 12.23
Subordinated loans, 1.8, 1.n.13, 3.n.12
are still loans; not waived in a manner which would turn amount into realised profit, 9.13
Subscribers to Memorandum, 3.14
Subsidiary and holding companies, 6.5
Subsidiary undertakings and parents, 6.5
Summary financial statements, 1.n.15

Table A, 8.2, 8.n.3 (see also Articles of Association)
Takeover Panel, 1.2
Take–over unanimously recommended by directors of target – exemption from ban on issue of investment advertisement, 12.4

INDEX

Tax
- advance corporation tax, 5.8–
- irrecoverable ACT, 5.13, 5.15
- unrelieved ACT, 3.6
- tax charge, 5.2
- deduction of income tax at source, 5.21
- in two tiers, 3.3–, 5.29–
- provision, 5.2
- debtor or recoverable, 5.2, 5.10–
- effective rate; *special circumstances* which affect liability to tax, 5.3, 5.n.4
- liabilities in groups; the need to maintain integrity of each company in group, 5.5, 5.25
- of directors, 8.9
- tax privileges are not what motivates employees in share option and incentive schemes – it is rises in share prices which do so, 10.6
- tax indemnities in purchase contract, 12.15, 12.17–, 12.21

Threat to continued existence of company, 9.17

TOGC (for VAT purposes; transfer of business as going concern), 3.33, 11.3, 11.32–
- assets transferred in course of registered business, 11.32
- capital assets transferred by unregistered trader, 11.32, 11.n.69
- assignment of portfolio of debtors, 11.32, 11.n.67
- sale of let buildings, 11.34–

Trade & asset transfers
- cessations and clawbacks of relief for individual, 3.34, 3.40
- cessations and clawbacks of relief for the co disponor, 11.10
- value put on stock in trade, 11.12, 11.n.21
- value put on goodwill (which in this instance is not merely a consolidation adjustment), 11.12
- non–availability of carry forward of losses, 11.14
- capital gains tax exemption of transferor who receives no consideration (its shareholders receive shares issued direct by transferee), 6.71, 12.23, 14.2, 14.3, 14.5
- VAT, including transfers fitting into the TOGC rules, 11.32–, 11.n.67, 11.n.69 (see further under TOGC)
- protection of employment under TUPE regulations, 11.36– (see further under TUPE)

Trading wrongfully, 1.5, 3.2

Transactions in securities
- definition, 11.21–

Paragraph D companies, 11.23
- transfer of assets and distribution of profits, 11.23, 11.24
- pre–disposal dividends, 11.16, 11.21–
- bona fide commercial transactions and the absence of tax avoidance motive, 11.25
- clearance procedures, 11.25

TUPE Regulations (Transfer of Undertakings – Protection of Employment), 3.32, 11.3, 11.36–
- not possible for either party to opt out of rules, 11.37
- not possible for UK Government to fail to incorporate all provisions of Directive, effectively, into UK law, 11.37
- economic entity, meaning, 11.38
- whether economic entity must be commercial, 11.39
- dismissals/redundancies *because of* the transfer, the economic/technical/organisational alternative, and those employed *immediately* before, 11.40
- dismissal unfair for another reason – effect on employment immediately before, 11.n.85
- contracting out of governmental and local government services, 11.41
- hive–downs, 12.24

True and fair view, 1.27–

Trusts, employee share, 10.1, 10.11
- exemption from financial assistance rules, 9.20
- ESOTs approved under FA 1989, 10.13

Ultra vires, 9.2
Unbundling, 11.7
Undertaking, 5.n.47, 6.34
Undervalue, 9.14, 9.17
Unexpired costs (pool of), 2.7
Unilateral relief (for foreign taxes), 5.n.32
Unincorporated business
- calculation of tax, and of retentions possible, 3.8
Unpaid calls, 4.1
Unrelieved ACT, 3.6

Value Added Tax
- liabilities, 12.20
- on assignment of debts, 11.32
- TOGC (transfer of business as going concern), 3.33, 6.32, 11.3, 11.32–
- sale of *capital assets* of an unregistered business, 11.3, 11.32, 11.n.69
- sale of let buildings as TOGCs, 11.34–

432

group registration, 6.32
representative member, 6.32
Value of assets to the company (value to the business), 2.1, 2.3, 4.19
  honest estimation by directors of value of assets for which co issues shares, 3.24, 3.26
  valuation by independent expert in such valuation in case of public company, 3.26, 3.n.33
  independent valuation not required for acquisition of shares in target, or target's business, 3.n.33
  implications for subsequent profit calculation of bringing assets into a/cs at value at acquisition, 3.27, 3.37–
Value of company as a company, 2.1
Value to shareholders of their interests in the company, 2.1
  where the company has borrowings as well as equity, 2.25–
Value of an undertaking to do work or perform services, 3.28
Value–shifting, 9.n.21, 11.4, 11.n.5a, 11.n.27–29
Vendor placing – as device to enable predator to obtain merger relief, 6.30, 6.n.48, 12.n.1

Warranties, 12.12
  best of knowledge and belief, 12.n.16
  demanded to force full disclosure, 12.11
  disclosure letter, 12.14
  breach of warranty, 12.11, 12.12
  remedy of breach, 12.12
  repetition of warranty at completion, 12.13
  rescission of contract, 12.12
  warranted accounts, 12.10
  limitation of claims, 12.15
  limitation of claim period, 12.15
Water tank analogy, 3.3–
Whitewash procedure, to allow what would otherwise have been unlawful financial assistance, 9.20, 9.24, 12.22, 13.n.19
  similar procedures when company purchases shares out of capital, 13.9
Wholly owned subsidiary, 6.5
Woolcombers reorganisations, 6.56, 6.n.104
  effect at time of sale of previous reorganisation on this basis, 11.19–
Writing off of expenditure, 1.29, 2.22
Written resolutions procedure, 3.13, 3.15, 6.9, 8.n.6, 13.n.21
Wrongful trading, 1.5, 1.14